# Toyota Culture

# Toyota Culture

## The Heart and Soul of the Toyota Way

Jeffrey K. Liker
Michael Hoseus
and
The Center for Quality
People and Organizations

New York  Chicago  San Francisco  Lisbon
London  Madrid  Mexico City  Milan  New Delhi
San Juan  Seoul  Singapore  Sydney  Toronto

Copyright © 2008 by McGraw-Hill. All rights reserved. Printed in the United States of America. Except as permitted under the United States Copyright Act of 1976, no part of this publication may be reproduced or distributed in any form or by any means, or stored in a database or retrieval system, without the prior written permission of the publisher.

1 2 3 4 5 6 7 8 9 0   FGR/FGR   0 9 8 7
ISBN 978-0-07-149217-1
MHID 0-07-149-217-8

Editorial and production services provided by Print Matters, Inc.

This publication is designed to provide accurate and authoritative information in regard to the subject matter covered. It is sold with the understanding that neither the author nor the publisher is engaged in rendering legal, accounting, or other professional service. If legal advice or other expert assistance is required, the services of a competent professional person should be sought.

*—From a Declaration of Principles jointly adopted by a*
*Committee of the American Bar Association*
*and a Committee of Publishers*

McGraw-Hill books are available at special quantity discounts to use as premiums and sales promotions, or for use in corporate training programs. For more information, please write to the Director of Special Sales, McGraw-Hill, Two Penn Plaza, New York, NY 10121-2298. Or contact your local bookstore.

# Contents

# Part Three. People Supporting Processes                223

# Acknowledgments

We would like to thank Toyota for access to its organizations and its people. This includes Toyota Motor Corporation in Japan, Toyota Motor Sales, Toyota Motor Engineering & Manufacturing North America (TEMA), and Toyota Motor Manufacturing Kentucky (TMMK). We would like to thank (in order of appearance in the book)

## Toyota Motor Manufacturing

Tom Zawacki, General Manager of General Administration TMMK and President, Center for Quality People and Organizations (CQPO)

Hiroyoshi Yoshiki, Former Treasurer, Vice President of Administration and Senior Advisor, TMMK

Gary Convis, Former President, TMMK and Member of the Board of Directors, TMC, current Senior Advisor Toyota

Nate Furuta, Former Vice President TEMA, current CEO and President, Toyota Boshoku

Jeannie Hughes, Assistant Manager Assembly, TMMK

Pete Gritton, Vice President of Human Resources, TEMA. Founding President, CQPO

Steve St. Angelo, President, TMMK, Senior Vice President TEMA

Lisa Richardson, Regional Trainer Stamping, TEMA Team Member Development Center

Eddie Back, Regional Trainer Body Weld, TEMA Team Member Development Center

Anna Marie Eifert, HR Specialist, TMMK

Don Jackson, Senior Vice President, TMMTX

Cheryl Jones, Vice President Manufacturing, TMMK

Charles Luttrell, Assistant General Manager, TMMK

Shelby Shepard, Skilled Trades Team Member, TMMK

Nila Wells and Kim Sweazy, Public Relations Specialists, TMMK

Ashley Ray, HR Specialist, TMMK

Renee Brown, Team Members, Quality Circle Coordinator, TMMK
Ernie Richardson, HR, Medical Manager, TEMA and TMMK
Terri Manning, HR Safety Specialist, TMMK
Nancy Banks, Manager Corporate Communications, TEMA and TMMK
Wil James, President, TABC
Mark Daugherty, HR Manager, TEMA
Craig Grucza, HR General Manager, TMMK
Yoshihisa Nagatani, Executive Coordinator, TMMK
Shunji Endo, Coordinator, TMMK
Ken Kreafle, General Manager Engineering, TEMA

Others at TEMA who helped with access, gather materials, data, photos, etc.
Mary Diggins, Nancy Roy, Doug Rose, Rebecca Lucas, Jacky Ammerman, Parker Shannon, Caren Caton, Rick Hesterberg, Perry Bowling and Sig Huber.

We also thank the many people of Tupelo, Mississippi who shared their special story of winning a Toyota plant.

## Toyota Motor Sales, USA

Sanford Smith, Corporate Manager of Real Estate and Facilities
Jim Lentz, President Toyota Motor Sales, USA
Jim Farley, former Group Vice President and General Manager of Lexus
Mike Morrison, Vice President and Dean of University of Toyota (and author, *The Other Side of the Business Card*)
Joe Kane, Associate Dean, University of Toyota
Will Decker, Associate Dean, University of Toyota
Mamie Warrick, Corporate Manager and Dean of Education, Planning and Business Operations, University of Toyota
Tracey Doi, Group Vice President and Chief Financial Officer
John Kennelly, Vice President, corporate tax and international customs
Rosario Criscuolo, owner of the "Elite of Lexus" award winning Lexus dealership in Ann Arbor, Michigan
Mark Templin, Group Vice President, and General Manager, Lexus
Jack Hollis, Vice President, Scion

Special thanks to Jennifer Brigham of Media Relations who worked tirelessly to organize visits and assist in editing the book.

## Others

David Meier, Co-author of *Toyota Way Fieldbook* and *Toyota Talent,* did some of the early planning and made the introductions that led to this book and made contributions at several key points.

Robert Kucner, author of *A Socio-Technical Study of Lean Manufacturing Deployment in the Remanufacturing Context* (University of Michigan PhD dissertation), contributed case studies and concepts from his dissertation research.

Michael Balle, co-author of *The Gold Mine: A Novel of Lean Turnaround*, read drafts of a number of chapters and offered key insights that led to reorganizing chapters and emphasizing the stories.

Tanya Menon, University of Chicago, who shared her insightful research on Asian versus Western differences in perceptions of leadership.

Gary Bergmiller, author of *Lean Manufacturers Transcendence to Green Manufacturing: Correlating the Diffusion of Lean and Green Manufacturing Systems* (University of South Florida Ph.D. dissertation), who shared his insights into the relationship between lean and green.

We would also like to recognize and thank the Center for Quality People and Organizations (CQPO), the third coauthor of the book. CQPO is a not for profit organization Toyota supports with the mission to share the Toyota Way with education, community, and business organizations by utilizing the experiences of former Toyota leaders. (To learn more about CQPO go to www.cqpo.org)

Special thanks go to the Board of Directors; without their vision and support there would not be a Center.

Pete Gritton, Founding President of CQPO, Vice President of Human Resources, TEMA and TMMK.

Tom Zawacki, Current President of CQPO, General Manager of General Administration TMMK

Dallas Blankenship, Vice President of CQPO and Superintendent, Scott County Schools

Randy Cutright, Treasurer of CQPO and Director of Business and Finance, Scott County Schools

Pamela Trautner, Secretary and Executive Director, Lexington Partnership for Workforce Development

Board Members, Andrea Adams (Kentucky Primary Care Association), Ken Carroll (University of Kentucky), Allen Cawley (Innovation Station), William Crouch (Georgetown College), Craig Grucza (TMMK), Arlie Hall (University of Kentucky), Jeanica Matlock (TMMK), Jim Moak (Georgetown College), Francis O'Hara (Scott County Schools), Barry Papania (Georgetown Community Hospital), Stu Silberman (Fayette County Schools), Jim White (Kentucky Community and Technical College System)

Recognition and thanks go to CQPO contributing authors:

**John Bugbee.** John is a Senior Consultant and Trainer for CQPO who works in the areas of organizational development, human resource management, training curriculum development, and project management. In several capacities he worked for 30 years for universities, government agencies, non-profit foundations, and a number of companies.

**Gene Childress.** Gene Childress is a Senior Consultant and Trainer for CQPO. He is an experienced Human Resources consultant serving a diverse group of clients from both the private and public sector. He currently is working with a program called QUEST, a meeting facilitation and problem-solving program for schools and community groups.

**Roy Jay.** Roy is a Senior Consultant and Trainer for CQPO. He is also president and founder of Roy Jay Development Group. Roy worked at TMMK for 14 years as a Manager of the internal TPS group and Manager of the Plastics Plant. Prior to TMMK, Roy was a senior project engineer for General Motors.

John and Gene developed the first Human Systems model based on early HR work and together with Roy and Mike Hoseus and their Toyota experience developed the Lean Culture class for the University of Kentucky. It is this foundation upon which this book is built.

Other CQPO Contributors include Tracey Richardson, Ellen Bowman, Jean Jeffords and Teresa Elder.

*    *    *

I would like to thank my precious wife Suzy and children, Ben, Leah, and Lindsay for their love, patience and sacrifice of early mornings, evenings, weekends, and vacations with Dad while I worked on "the book". I want to thank Jeff Liker for seeing the need in the field and for appreciating the Human Systems model and material as a foundation on which to build this book and for taking both to a much higher level. I want to thank him for his patience and honest feedback throughout the process. It has been an opportunity for growth and development that I appreciate. Special thanks to John Bugbee for his help in developing, organizing, editing material and his personal encouragement along the way. Personal thanks to Toyota and my Japanese and American mentors throughout my career, giving me the opportunity and development I needed.

—**Michael Hoseus**

My family lived through yet another book about Toyota...and there are more to come. I very much appreciate the love and support and humor of my wife Deb, my daughter Emma, and my son Jesse. I am particularly grateful (in a masochistic sort of way) for the help of my son Jesse. Jesse carefully read through the first seven chapters and gave me critical (and I mean critical) feedback. In the Toyota fashion he focused on the deviations from standard (e.g., "I want to learn how to develop my people so that they identify problems, and so far it has been five pages and you have barely said anything"). I remember rewriting the introduction to chapter 6 at least seven times before Jesse would give me a pass to go on.

Seriously, (other than Mike Hoseus) Jesse made more of a contribution to the book, read it more discerningly, and helped continuously improve it more than anyone. I also appreciate Mike's patience, hard work, and positive attitude when I gave him some of the same critical feedback my son gave to me. He obviously learned his lessons well about accepting feedback from his time at Toyota. It was Mike's inspiration that led to this collaboration and the decision to write this book, so blame him.

—Jeffrey K. Liker

# Foreword

Several years ago a well known corporate leader and several of his senior staff paid a visit to our Georgetown plant. They wanted to learn about the much heralded Toyota Production System (TPS). Part way through the discussion being held with our management team he asked, "Why are so many Japanese still here? You guys have been in operation for awhile now. Our team has taken over many companies in the past and in just a few months we were running it better than the previous owners. Why is it taking you guys so long?"

My first reaction to the question was, finally an outsider that gets it. He knows this TPS thing is more complicated than it looks and is just kidding me. It is not just about low inventories moving through a pull system! But as we talked I realized he was not joking. He really meant, 'why haven't you guys picked it up yet? This isn't rocket science.' Other than being a little insulted (okay more than a little), I was amazed once again. Here was another titan of industry, very successful and yet he couldn't see it either. He was just being honest (or arrogant) enough to voice a thought many of our visitors have probably had over the years.

The Toyota Production System seems to be a simple set of principles about operating activities that are reasonably easy to grasp. It has been observed and studied to death. It has even been implemented in thousands of companies around the world with varying degrees of success. But the general consensus still seems to be that no one does it quite as well as Toyota. Why? What is the magic?

My humble opinion is that most companies miss seeing the "blood flow" of TPS, the human resources philosophies and strategies that make it work at Toyota. How we manage our people is the fluid that connects all the working parts and brings them the oxygen and nutrients to keep them all working as they should. If there is magic to TPS, then this is it: successful implementation of human resource philosophies that create the buy in and engagement of the people necessary to run such a simple but intricate system.

Lest anyone think this is the mad raving and chest thumping of "some HR guy," please understand I am not talking about the HR department—although we do play a unique role as facilitators and keepers of the philosophy. I am talking about the culture that guides our business every day and is owned by the operations people at all levels throughout our organization.

What I learned from the Japanese, who have been working so hard to teach us slow-learning Americans, is what it truly means to respect people and develop them to continuously improve. It requires a level of patience, a long-term view, a focus on process, and the ability to understand where the individual is in his or her development. All these characteristics unfortunately seem alien to our culture. Our Japanese trainers had to patiently teach us and sometimes undo decades of learning; and I for one really appreciate that they never gave up.

My friend, the corporate leader, was correct about how quickly we should have been able to get it. If getting it meant laying out the equipment in a reasonable flow, figuring out how to eliminate two out of ten people, and printing the kanban cards, that should not have taken long. We had the models in Japan to copy if we wanted. The Japanese who taught us, however, were not interested in teaching us to copy. They were trying to teach us to think and act in the Toyota Way. We did not call it that at first, but that was exactly what it was. They realized how important this was to our long-term success and they would patiently teach us for ten years if necessary. When they saw us get impatient with a group leader because his department was falling behind, they would coach us. When they saw us jumping in and implementing a solution before we had thought through what the problem was, that was another coaching opportunity.

Much of what we learned is a rigorous way of thinking about problems and a deliberate way of developing people that frankly was not in our vocabulary when we started. Moving machines takes minutes, but changing the way people think and act takes many years. What we call culture is the way we automatically think and act every day. After years it becomes ingrained in you. For example, solving problems through plan-do-check-act seems more natural to me now than jumping in and firefighting. Being patient with someone struggling to learn, when you yourself were once struggling to learn, now seems like the only way to manage.

This culture has become second nature to those of us who have spent decades with Toyota, but it is a mystery to most outsiders. We frankly are not even all that good at explaining it to others who have not lived it. The book you have in your hands has done as good a job as I have read. Dr. Liker understands our internal culture as well as anyone I know outside the company, and Mike Hoseus is one of us who grew up with the system. Here, you get a glimpse into the "behind the scenes" systems and processes that are not obvious to the casual observer. They are what connect the people to the technical parts of the Toyota Production System that, together form the "Toyota Culture."

A word of caution, however, is to not read this book with the intent to copy the Toyota Culture into your organization. When we started the first wholly-

owned Toyota Plant in America, we could not just copy the policies and procedures from Japan into our plant and our country. As I mentioned, our Japanese
trainers did not want us to copy but to learn, adapt, and improve. We spent years,
through trial and error and intense discussions, identifying the key systems and
principles that could not be left out or changed and transplanted those and then
created new ones to fit the needs of our business and our people. I recommend
you do the same.

**Pete Gritton**
**Vice President of HR**
**Toyota Engineering and Manufacturing of**
   **North America**
**Former Vice President of HR**
**Toyota Motor Manufacturing Kentucky**

# Preface

# From the Toyota Way to Toyota Culture

## THE TOYOTA WAY IS ABOUT CULTURE

*The Toyota Way*, written by the co-author of this book, Jeffrey Liker, summarized the management principles of Toyota in a 4P model: Philosophy, Process, People, and Problem Solving (see Figure P.1). The 4Ps form a pyramid, the foundation of which is a long-term *philosophy* that focuses on adding value to customers and society. Building on that is Toyota's investment in lean processes, which concentrates on shortening lead time by eliminating waste. Eliminating waste is done by people using rigorous problem-solving methods—the top two layers of the pyramid. Toyota's management system is described by fourteen principles within these four levels (see Box).

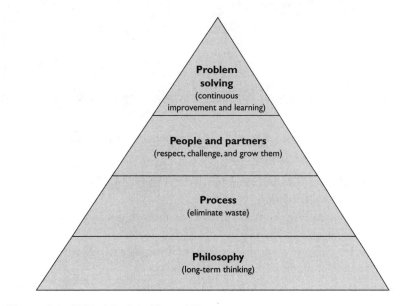

**Figure P.1** 4P Model of the Toyota Way

# Fourteen Principles of the Toyota Way

## Long-Term Philosophy

Principle 1. Base your management decisions on a long-term philosophy, even at the expense of short-term financial goals.

## Lean Processes: The Right Process Will Produce the Right Results

Principle 2. Create a continuous process "flow" to bring problems to the surface.

Principle 3. Use "pull" systems to avoid overproduction.

Principle 4. Level out the workload (*Heijunka*)— like the Tortoise, not the Hare.

Principle 5. Build a culture of stopping to fix problems, to get quality right the first time.

Principle 6. Standardized tasks and processes are the foundation for continuous improvement and employee empowerment.

Principle 7. Use visual controls so no problems are hidden.

Principle 8. Use only reliable, thoroughly tested technology that serves your people and processes.

## Develop and Challenge Your People and Partners through Long-term Relationships

Principle 9. Grow leaders who thoroughly understand the work, live the philosophy and teach it to others.

Principle 10. Develop exceptional people and teams who follow your company's philosophy.

Principle 11. Respect your suppliers by challenging them and helping them improve.

## Problem Solving and Continuous Improvement Drive Organizational Learning

Principle 12. Go and See for Yourself to Thoroughly Understand the Situation. (*Genchi Genbutsu*)

Principle 13. Make decisions slowly by consensus, thoroughly considering all options; implement decisions rapidly.

Principle 14. Become a learning organization through relentless reflection (*hansei*) and continuous improvement (kaizen).

Source: Jeffrey Liker, *The Toyota Way*, New York: McGraw-Hill, 2004.

If we look carefully at the fourteen principles they are all statements of beliefs and values. They are about Toyota's culture:

**Philosophy** is about Toyota's purpose and why they exist.

**Process** is about what Toyota believes leads to operational excellence—constantly eliminating waste.

**People** are what drive the company forward and culture is what teaches the people how to act, think and feel to work together toward a common goal.

**Problem Solving** is the way Toyota people focus their efforts to continually improve.

While *The Toyota Way* was a book about Toyota's Culture, we felt there were missing pieces. There was far more detail to fill in about each of the 4Ps. Thus, we are writing a series of books. *Toyota Talent* (2007) is already available. *Toyota Processes* and *Toyota Problem Solving* are currently being written (both with David Meier).

This book on Toyota Culture delves into far more detail about the human systems of Toyota. It was written with Mike Hoseus and the Center for Quality People and Organization (CQPO). Mike has worked with the Toyota plant in Georgetown, Kentucky for 20 years, most of which has been as a manager and later by supporting Toyota through the not-for-profit CQPO. Mike managed assembly and human resources and most of the employees of CQPO are formerly of Toyota. With this depth of experience we provide examples from the Georgetown plant. We cover how Toyota selects and develops people and gets them committed to the mission of the company. We go into some detail on human resource systems for health and safety, planning to ensure stable employment, and how management policies and goals are deployed through the organization. We will also learn about teamwork, leadership, and communications. We will then address the question of how other companies can learn from Toyota culture.

## TWO MODELS OF THE TOYOTA WAY

Since this book is about Toyota's culture we use Toyota's internal version of the Toyota Way as a model (discussed in Chapter 1). They unveiled *The Toyota Way 2001* (internal training document) and represented it as a house with two pillars—Respect for People and Continuous Improvement. The foundation has five elements—challenge, kaizen, *genchi genbutsu* (go and see), respect, and teamwork. When Liker wrote *The Toyota Way* he read Toyota's internal document and based the 4P model in part on that document so it is no surprise they share a good deal. Toyota's house and author Jeffrey Liker's 4P model are shown side by side in Figure P.2. In Liker's *The Toyota Way* the five foundational elements of Toyota's house were shown along side the 4Ps to illustrate the relationship (as shown in Figure P.2). While each of these models segment the system somewhat differently, they both have a lot in common including:

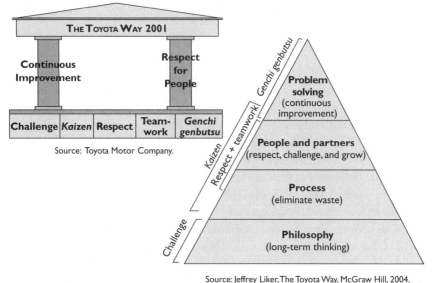

Source: Jeffrey Liker, The Toyota Way, McGraw Hill, 2004.

**Figure P.2** Two Models of the Toyota Way

1. **Total Systems Views**. Both are intended to represent a *system*. By this we mean all the parts are interrelated. Toyota is showing this as a house because any weak link in the house—foundation, pillars, roof—will make the house weak. The 4P model is also intended to be a kind of structure, like a pyramid, with each level (P) acting as a foundation for the next level. If any of the 4 Ps is missing the system will not work. So for example, with a short-term philosophy you will end up only implementing selected tools in selected processes that will have immediate results for specific short-term metrics and not make a large investment in people and thus never create a learning organization that is continuously improving. Without the tools at the process level problems will not be visible, making it less likely people will develop their abilities to think and solve problems.

2. **Lean Tools Support People and Continuous Improvement**. This is very clear in Toyota's model. Toyota placed lean tools like *kanban* and cells as a subset of the foundational element of "kaizen." In fact they are not shown in the house because they are a lower level of detail. If you break down *kaizen* further in Toyota's model you get the sub-elements of: "kaizen mind and innovative thinking," "building lean systems and structure," and "promoting organizational learning." If you look at the relationship between the two models, Toyota's *kaizen* overlaps with three of the 4Ps: Process, People, and Problem Solving. But in both models the point is that

lean processes are there to support people and problem solving (respect for people and continuous improvement).

3. **There is a Process-Orientation Rather Than a Results-Orientation.** *The Toyota Way* distinguishes between these two orientations.[1] Process orientation refers to managers who work to get the process right with an understanding that the right process will lead to the right results. Results orientation refers to a management style that targets specific results; any process that works is equally good. Describing these two as alternatives as if they are opposites is misleading. Toyota's philosophy tends to be influenced by Eastern thinking, where they do not see things as mutually exclusive polar opposites. In fact, they are extremely results focused but they see a harmony between the process and the results. For example, no team members would get high praise for working on an improvement project unless they had clearly delineated the expected results from the project. The results should be measurable and the project should track actual results relative to the target. But they also would not get high praise if they did not follow the right process, which includes *nemawashi*—getting input from others to generate consensus. The project would not simply be judged based on the results, but rather by how much the team members learned by doing the project. Both models provide a set of principles of the right process to do things—think, develop processes, develop people, and solve problems.

4. **Both Models place the Highest Value on People Continuously Improving.** *The Toyota Way 2001* has as its pillars "respect for people" and "continuous improvement." The 4P model has at the highest levels developing people (respect, challenge, and grow) and problem solving (continuous improvement). In both models, the lean tools and processes are subordinate to helping people to identify and solve problems and continuously develop.

The individual parts of the Toyota Way are all interrelated with culture. Even a mechanical task like setting up a *kanban* system—for example, identifying how many parts should be stored in the buffer and thus how many cards to print—has a different meaning in varying cultural contexts. In a results-oriented culture, it is a means to a specific result. There is too much inventory that is creating cost overruns and we want to reduce inventory by 25 percent. So we'll install a *kanban*

---

[1] For more information on process versus results orientations see: T.Y. Choi and J.K. Liker, "Bringing Japanese Continuous Improvement Approaches to U.S. Manufacturing: The Roles of Process Orientation and Communications," *Decision Sciences*, Vol. 26, Number 5, Sept/Oct. 1995.

system because we heard that this tool reduces inventory. We put together a team of lean engineers, and perhaps a few six sigma Black Belts, train them in *kanban*, and they go all over the corporation implementing the system. After one year there is some form of *kanban* in all the plants—at least for the higher dollar volume items—and inventory comes down. All is well. But is it? Will inventory continue to come down? Will it stay down? Do people in the plant really understand *kanban* and how to use it as a tool for continuous improvement? The way the people in the plant think about the system will determine whether this is a short-term tool applicable as a one-shot fix and unsustainable or part of a long-term process of creating a culture of continuous improvement.

In this book we reveal how Toyota selects, develops, and motivates people to become committed to the goal of building high quality products in a safe and fair work environment. Respect for people and continuous improvement go hand in hand. Treating people as permanent members of a community sets the stage for teaching people not only to do their jobs, but to continually improve products and processes. Carefully selected, well trained and challenged people combined with exceptional processes leads to exceptional results. The lean mindset is a result of a broader culture that supports and engages people. Toyota culture is the key ingredient in Toyota's success as the global leader in operational excellence.

# Part One

# What Is Toyota Culture?

*Each person fulfilling his or her duties to the utmost can generate great power when gathered together, and a chain of such power can generate a ring of power.*

—Kiichiro Toyoda, Toyota Motor Company founder

# Chapter 1

# The DNA of Toyota Lies in Its Culture

*Just yesterday I spent a whole day with 30 of our young executives. At least 50 percent of them were from outside Japan. They had broken up into teams to tackle different problems, and they made presentations based on what they had learned about using the Toyota Way to tackle them. When I asked, many of them said they were now able to understand the Toyota Way fully. That's totally wrong. Two or three months isn't a long enough period for anyone to understand the Toyota Way. The managers may have understood what's on the surface, but what lies beneath is far greater. I asked them to explore that. There's no end to the process of learning about the Toyota Way. I don't think I have a complete understanding even today, and I have worked for the company for 43 years.[1]*

—Katsuaki Watanabe, president, Toyota Motor Corporation

## WHY ARE LEAN AND SIX SIGMA PROGRAMS NOT ENOUGH?

Companies throughout the world are trying to find a way to get their employees engaged in improving processes. Some have used six sigma as a program to develop experts in statistical problem solving, while others have concluded they need to "lean out processes" from the bottom up using simpler concepts of pull and flow and invested in lean programs. A more recent trend is using a lean six sigma program, which is seen as the best of both worlds. Lean tools are taught at the working level because they are simpler to understand and lead to quick wins while six sigma black belts lead complex, more involved, several month-long projects to drive the bigger dollar savings. These programs certainly are effective in driving down costs, and many companies tally up the cost savings to impress investors with the large numbers. Unfortunately there is usually something missing in these lean six sigma efforts.

---

[1] "Lessons from Toyota's Long Drive," *Harvard Business Review*, July-August, 2007, pp. 74–83.

Ask someone deeply trained in the Toyota Production System (TPS) to visit those "lean operations" and they are likely to give them low ratings. The TPS expert will not look at the charts and graphs of the six sigma projects or the impressive cost savings. They will go right to the *gemba*—where the work is done—and walk the process. They will look for interruptions in flow—waste. They will observe people doing the work to see if they are following a repeatable standard process. They will also look for evidence of quality problems such as repair bays. If they see material flowing smoothly through the plant from start to finish in a steady cadence and people actively engaged in doing value-added work based on a defined pace (called *takt* time) they will be very impressed. They will be even more impressed if there is evidence of visual management showing at a glance the state of the operation and whether processes are in standard. However, the most impressive thing will be seeing evidence of people on the floor actively engaged in daily problem solving. Unfortunately we rarely see much evidence of any of these things. The charts and graphs look great in the conference-room presentations, but the reality of the shop floor is far from the TPS ideal.

From the time Toyota first started its operation, the leaders believed that the key to success was investment in its people. The Toyota culture has evolved since the company's founding and is the core competence of the company. It is the reason why operations are lean, cars hit the market on time and on budget, chief engineers developing cars deeply understand the customer, company executives anticipate long-term trends and have clear strategies, and every employee (called team members) is vigorously working on achieving the annual plan of the company. The Toyota Way is first and foremost about culture—the way people think and behave is deeply rooted in the company philosophy and its principles. At the core it is about respect for people and continuous improvement, and this has not changed since the company's founding.

Almost every company president talks about culture and asserts that people are their most important resource, but do they believe it? Given the opportunity to go from paying $25 per hour to $1 per hour in a low-wage country, how many company executives would consider reestablishing their companies in unfamiliar, but more economically friendly terrain? After the standard hiring process and an employee training program, the company would be in business in their new locale, but would this be enough to imprint their company's existing culture on the new hires? Would management even know exactly what company culture they were trying to imprint?

When Toyota sets up shop in a new country, they carefully study the local community and determine how best to develop the Toyota culture in that environment. From past experience, they have learned that it requires both time and patience. It took about 15 years at Toyota Motor Manufacturing in Georgetown, Kentucky—the first wholly owned Toyota assembly plant in the U.S (referred to throughout this book as TMMK). Even though Toyota prides itself on being a learning organization and has shortened the time it takes to build its culture elsewhere, it still takes years to develop.

Many companies have become frustrated with *kaizen* events and six sigma projects that yielded great short-term results but had no sustainability. They are searching for something more, and we believe the missing element that creates long-term results is the Toyota culture. And while Toyota's version of its culture varies from country to country or even from community to community, there is an important core set of principles and practices at work that any company can learn from. This book describes and examines the DNA of the Toyota culture.

## WHAT IS CULTURE? (IT'S ALL IN OUR HEADS)

Before we get ahead of ourselves we should pause and reflect on the often invoked word "culture." We frequently hear managers say things like "It's all about culture." "It's a people issue." "The tools are the easy part; the culture change is the hard part." "Lean works in Japanese culture where it was created, but not in our culture." On the positive side, statements like these reflect one's understanding of the importance of culture and its integral role in turning an organization into an effective company. The downside is that different people have different interpretations of the word "culture."

Every year in coauthor Liker's course on work organizations, student teams are asked to conduct interviews in real organizations in order to understand their business objectives and internal organization. One team had conducted interviews at a local company and reported back that they had a problem in writing the required paper, explaining that, "The company we are studying does not have a culture. They are relatively new and have not written down their mission statement and do not have company social events. They give out a turkey on Thanksgiving, but that is about it." Every year students struggle to identify the culture of the organization beyond its most superficial characteristics. Why is this task so hard?

It's hard because we have to decipher what is in people's heads. When confronted with a new culture, anthropologists start by simply observing how people live. They see many artifacts. They watch how people interact. They might witness deferential behavior indicating a status hierarchy and then they begin to piece together a story about the culture. Finally, they listen to the people; their questions become a way to get into their subjects' heads and more deeply understand what this community believes and values.

One useful definition of culture that fits well with what the Toyota Way is about is:

> *…The pattern of basic assumptions that a given group has invented, discovered, or developed in learning to cope with its problems of external*

*adaptation and internal integration, and that have worked well enough to
be considered valid, and, therefore, to be taught to new members as the
correct way to perceive, think, and feel in relation to those problems.²*

From this definition we see that culture goes deep into how all members of
the organization perceive, think and even feel. There are many models that illustrate that culture exists at multiple levels. In *The Toyota Way* (2004) we used an
iceberg to illustrate that what is seen above the surface is only one aspect of
culture. Most of the iceberg is below the water and this is where the deeper aspects
of culture reside. A model by Schein (1984)³ shows three levels of a pyramid
(see Figure 1.1), which are:

1. **Artifacts and Behavior.** Artifacts and behavior are what is seen at the
   surface level. This is what an anthropologist first observes. At this level we
   see objects, the physical layout of the workplace, how people behave, and
   written documents such as policy manuals. These observations are valuable
   but don't tell the whole story. Take for example Toyota's *andon* system,
   which is often associated with stopping to fix quality problems. (The
   andon is the light that goes on when a worker pulls the cord to stop the
   line.) Does Toyota want everything to stop to fix such problems each time
   they occur? To understand the significance of artifacts like the andon
   system, we must dig deeper into the culture and study the shared norms
   and values of people at work.

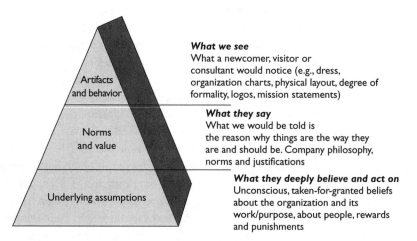

**Figure 1.1** Three Levels of Culture

---

² Schein, Edgar. "Coming to a new awareness of organizational culture," *Sloan Management
   Review*, Winter 1984, Vol. 25, No. 2, pp. 3–16.
³ Ibid.

2. **Norms and Values.** Norms are generally accepted rules of behavior. They are not necessarily written down, but "everyone knows" basic rules of behavior like how to dress, what is appropriate to say, if it is acceptable to be late to a meeting, and if it is okay to interrupt the boss. "Values" are the principles we live by. When asked what a company stands for, one normally describes an understanding of the organization's professed values. Looking more deeply at the andon system, we find it reflects the Toyota value of surfacing problems to continually improve the system. Any worker can pull the cord, which causes a light to turn on and distinctive music to play. The team leader is expected to be on the spot almost immediately to diagnose the severity of the problem, and to hopefully override the system by pulling the cord again before the line actually stops. If the problem is serious enough, the team leader will not pull the cord (and thus not override the team-member pull) and production will stop. If a Toyota leader was asked why they allowed the line to stop, she might make the point that the value the organization places on quality is higher than hitting production numbers.

3. **Underlying Assumptions.** Deep down, what do we assume about the nature of the organization and our role in it? Do we believe that the role of the employee is to do their best to help the organization become successful? Do we assume that management has its own interests that are in conflict with ours causing us to struggle every day to defend ourselves? Do we believe that work is a means to make money to live or is it a means of contributing to society? Often our assumptions run so deep that we cannot imagine anything different, like for example when we use the phrase "It is human nature." Some assumptions are in our subconscious and are difficult to articulate. Some we may not even be aware of. For example, in American society if asked why people desire to advance in their careers and make a lot of money, people are apt to shrug or laugh. "Isn't it obvious?" they might say, "Doesn't everyone want money and success?" When something seems obvious, the cultural analyst senses a deeply held assumption at work. One of the underlying suppositions in the andon system is that people need the support of others to solve daily production problems. If workers are left on their own, they may get through the day but will not really be able to solve problems at the root cause. Another underlying assumption is that the production worker's key role is to identify and call attention to problems even if it leads to stopping production. This requires an environment of trust in which there is no question whether pulling the andon is the right choice; workers must not fear a reprimand and, in fact, may receive praise for identifying a problem.

One story as told to us by Tom Zawacki, General Manager, General Administration, TMMK, illustrates the difficulties outsiders can have deciphering the deeper culture:

> *Former Ford President Red Polling wanted a tour of TMMK and to talk to executives. Mr. Cho agreed and made the arrangements. Mr. Cho was very respectful of Polling and his position and remembered the contributions Ford made in the early development of Toyota. Polling showed up with a large entourage from Ford and went on a special tour set up just for them. They could go wherever they wished and ask any questions. After an hour and a half Mr. Cho asked, "What do you think?" Polling said: "I did not see anything unusual." Mr. Cho asked if he had any suggestions and Polling made a few suggestions. It was clear that Mr. Polling was disappointed by the visit and did not see what he expected. After the visit Mr. Cho called together his team that had arranged the tour and said, "We learned a very valuable lesson today. We have the same equipment and systems as Ford, but what Mr. Polling did not see was our competitive advantage, which is our people. We are successful because we have intelligent, caring, highly successful team members."*

Thousands of people visit Toyota plants every year and make observations at both the artifact and behavioral level. They then have an opportunity to ask some questions. We have been on many such tours at the Georgetown, Kentucky plant with groups and have observed frequently that the Q&A regarding Toyota's approach remains at the artifact and behavioral level. Questions are often:

- What types of monetary rewards do employees get for building quality products?
- How do you measure performance?
- What is the level of absenteeism?
- Do people object to having to work overtime without a lot of notice?
- How does Toyota get people to make so many suggestions every year?

While Toyota's formal reward and punishment system is certainly interesting, it is only part of the story. The questions visitors tend to ask tell us more about the culture of the visitors than about Toyota! We learned that the visitors come from a culture where they believe the primary way to elicit desired behavior is through formal reward and punishment systems. They cannot imagine why anyone would do anything unless it is measured and delivers an immediate cash reward, or at least a tick mark on their performance evaluation report.

At Toyota there are small rewards at the team level and the potential of more significant bonuses shared by everyone if the plant and company perform well.

Delving deeper into the values and assumptions of the Toyota culture, we can see this approach reflects the value placed on teamwork. More broadly, Toyota wants its team members to develop the highest level of accountability and ownership and as such to understand that their fate is tied to that of the company.

If we think of organizational culture in terms of Venn diagrams, it is the shared beliefs, values, and assumptions that tie individuals together at work. The organizational culture in the Venn diagram to the left in Figure 1.2 is weak. The four individuals share very little and Joe in particular is an outsider with little in common with the others in terms of his values and beliefs about work. In the right-hand diagram the organizational culture is much stronger and more cohesive despite the personal differences. Notice that even in the strong culture, each individual has his or her own beliefs, values, and assumptions about work that are not shared across the group; note that the circles do not completely overlap.

If you were to draw a Venn diagram depicting Toyota leaders, you would find a great deal of overlap in beliefs in terms of the company's core values and the right way to manage people. As you move to the level of individual workers, we suspect there would be more variation in values and beliefs but still a strong common thread.

Dating back to founder Sakichi Toyoda, Toyota leaders have taught the Toyota Way to all of their team members. A strong assumption within Toyota's culture is that managers are leaders and leaders are teachers. This is something you cannot easily see simply touring a Toyota plant. The most important job of

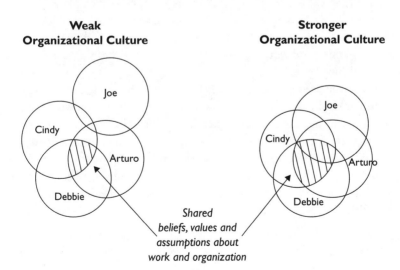

**FIGURE 1.2** Organization Culture Is the Shared Beliefs, Values, and Assumptions between People Working toward a Common Purpose

the manager is to teach young members Toyota's way of defining, analyzing, communicating, and solving problems. All of the authors of this book who worked for Toyota were assigned full-time "trainers" to teach on-the-job, day-by-day, over many years, how to think and act in the Toyota Way. We know of few companies in the world who teach their approach and deeply socialize employees so rigorously and consistently over time.

## PEOPLE ARE THE HEART AND SOUL OF THE TOYOTA WAY

The Toyota Way has been evolving within Toyota since the company's birth as a producer of automatic looms in 1926. Founder, Sakichi Toyoda, based the original Toyoda Automatic Loom Works on deeply held beliefs that concerned both the purpose of the company and how all of their members should be treated. His original reason for creating an easier-to-use wood loom was to help the women in his small farming community who were working their fingers to the bone. Expanding from this founding principle, the purpose of the company has always been twofold: to benefit society as well as their team members who make up the fabric of the company.

The Toyota story starts with Sakichi Toyoda, who grew up in the late 1800s in a remote farming community outside of Nagoya. At that time weaving was a major industry, and the Japanese government wishing to promote the development of small businesses, encouraged the creation of cottage industries, which subsequently spread across Japan. Small shops and mills that employed a handful of people—mostly housewives—was the norm. As the story goes, Sakichi was dissatisfied by the hard work he saw his mother, grandmother, and their friends putting into spinning and weaving, and wanted to find a better way to relieve them of this punishing labor.

This was an age in which inventors had to get their hands dirty. As an example, when Sakichi first developed a power loom, there was no power available to run the loom, so he next turned his attention to the problem of generating power. Steam engines were the most common source of power, so he bought a used steam engine and experimented with running the looms from this source. He figured out how to make this work by trial and error and by getting his hands dirty—an approach that would become part of the foundation of the Toyota Way. As Eiji Toyoda (1987)[4] later wrote:

*The looms didn't budge because the steam kept leaking. Faced with no other choice, they took the engine apart and found that the leaking was caused by*

---

[4] Toyoda, Eiji, *Toyota: Fifty Years in Motion*, Kodansha America; 1st edition, 1987.

*worn piston rods. Although they knew that the problem could be remedied by turning the rods on a lathe, the mill was located in the middle of nowhere; there just weren't any lathes nearby. So they spent the whole night filing the rods down. When they put the steam engine back together again, it worked.*

Throughout his life, Sakichi was a doer, not a manager. He was a great engineer and was later referred to as Japan's "King of Inventors." While Japan sometimes is viewed as a country that copies the technology of others, Sakichi Toyoda was an innovator: he continuously improved his automatic looms and ultimately sold the rights of one to the Platt Brothers in England so he could help his son start up Toyota Motor Company to expand into the growing business of automotive production. He said to his son Kiichiro "Everyone should tackle some great project at least once in his life. I devoted most of my life to inventing new kinds of looms. Now it is your turn. You should make an effort to complete something that will benefit society."

This quote tells us much about Toyota culture. We get a sense of the influence of the Toyoda family as founders and leaders continuing today. We can feel the emotion underlying the company. It is not a business as much as a calling for the greater good and the engine driving it is continuous improvement.

Kiichiro was sent by his father to the prestigious Tokyo Imperial University to study mechanical engineering. He focused on engine technology. He was able to draw on the wealth of knowledge within Toyoda Automatic Loom Works on casting and machining metal parts. Despite his formal engineering education Kiichiro followed in his father's footsteps of learning by doing. Shoichiro Toyoda, son of Kiichiro, described his father as a "genuine engineer" who, "... gave genuine thought to an issue rather than rely on intuition. He always liked to accumulate facts. Before he made the decision to make an automobile engine he made a small engine. The cylinder block was the most difficult thing to cast, so he gained a lot of experience in that area and, based on the confidence he then had, he went ahead."[5]

Kiichiro Toyoda, like his father, was passionate about innovations, big and small. He was quoted as saying, "We are working on making better products by making improvements every day."

Kiichiro Toyoda's cousin, Eiji Toyoda, took over the company when Kiichiro took responsibility for the company's financial hardship in the 1940s and resigned. Eiji Toyoda led Toyota for decades through its most difficult times struggling to survive and through its most prosperous times growing it into a global company. He never wavered from his fundamental belief in what makes the company run,

---

[5] Reingold, Edwin. *Toyota: People, Ideas, and the Challenge of the New.* London: Penguin Books, 1999.

"People are the most important asset of Toyota and the determinant of the rise and fall of Toyota."

The Toyoda family members also seemed to have a knack for identifying talent from outside the family. A series of inspirational leaders have followed in their footsteps each making a unique and profound contribution to the development of Toyota as a company and as a culture. Taiichi Ohno is known for his leadership of the Toyota Production System. Famous chief engineers like Tatsuo Hasegawa who led the design of the first Corolla and Kenya Nakamura who headed up the first Crown program helped lead the creation of Toyota's remarkable product development system. Shotaro Kamiya was one of the inspirational leaders behind Toyota Motor Sale's obsession with "customer first."

Contemporary leaders have continued the tradition of developing an internal culture focused on continuous improvement and respect for people and intensely focusing on making positive contributions to the world at large. We will learn later in this chapter about Fujio Cho and his passion for documenting and spreading the Toyota Way culture globally. His predecessor, Hiroshi Okuda, took every opportunity to emphasize the role of Toyota as a citizen of the world, "We wish to make Toyota not only strong but a universally admired company, winning the trust and respect of the world."

Companies in many industries have been attempting to learn "best practice" approaches from Toyota, and are particularly interested in eliminating waste and developing lean processes that are efficient and reduce cost. Lean processes are part of the story at Toyota, but there is much more involved that allows Toyota to infuse quality into its corporate culture in locations around the world. While there have been many documented successes of duplicating aspects of Toyota, few organizations have approached creating the type of culture that enables Toyota to develop exceptional people relentless in their focus on continuous improvement. The challenges for these companies lie in their culture.

In this chapter we will argue that culture is multi-layered and is rooted in deeply held assumptions. These cultural assumptions differ across countries and can either support or impede a company's ability to learn from Toyota. You will see, for example, that Japanese culture is based on long-term thinking and collectivism where the individual is subordinate to the group, while the opposite is true in Western cultures where short-term thinking and individualism are much more prevalent. This does not mean Toyota culture does not work in Western countries, but that it is somewhat different and has its own set of challenges.

## *The Toyota Way 2001* First Documented the Culture

We are often asked whether any other company outside of Japan can learn from Toyota given its roots run so deep in Japanese culture. Interestingly, Toyota faced these same cultural challenges as they spread their operations throughout the world. For most of its life, the company operated solely in Japan and created no written record of the Toyota Way. It simply was the way things were done throughout the organization; new members gradually became socialized into the culture through on-the-job exposure and training. Quotes from Toyota's founding members along with the company's rich oral tradition of values, beliefs, and stories were used to socialize employees into the Toyota Way, yet there were no operations or procedure manuals documenting its culture. As Toyota grew and began to teach the Toyota Way to its Japanese suppliers and then ultimately to its employees and suppliers around the world, there was an increasing need for a written record of its approach—oral tradition alone would not suffice. It took nearly ten years of writing and rewriting before *The Toyota Way 2001* was released under the watch of then-president Fujio Cho. In the preface, Cho wrote:

> *The rapid growth, diversification and globalization of Toyota in the past decade have increased the scope of our company's manufacturing and marketing presence throughout the world. Today, having invested authority and responsibility in a worldwide network of executives, we are preparing to operate as a truly global company guided by a common corporate culture.*

Many people have learned about lean production as a set of methods for eliminating waste, and the house of the Toyota Production System (TPS) has become very popular. The Toyota Way model actually supersedes TPS and is, in fact, quite different in its emphasis. In TPS the core pillars are *just-in-time* and *jidoka* (intelligent automation)—both technical concepts. The foundation under the pillars emphasizes stability through standardized processes and preventative maintenance. People are at the center of the TPS house but most lean applications implemented outside of Toyota focus specifically on the tools used to take waste out of processes.

Figure 1.3 features the Toyota Way model as presented in the company's internal document. Note that the core pillars of the house focus on people: their continuous improvement and respect for others. Principles of JIT and other lean tools are in the model, but they are buried a layer down in the foundation (and not shown in the house at this level) as sub-methodologies supporting kaizen.

The way this model and document were created is itself telling about Toyota's culture. We get a glimpse into the passion about its unique culture and the role of consensus decision making. The project originally was led by Fujio Cho when he was President of TMMK for the simple purpose of documenting the Toyota Way, particularly to teach American managers. There was agreement that some form of documentation would be valuable as Toyota grew globally, but there was also concern about how to write down something as subtle and implicit as culture and something that was continually evolving. After twenty revisions, intense discussion and debate, and ten years of work, finally Fujio Cho said let's freeze it and call it

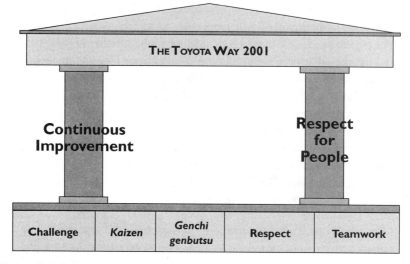

**Figure 1.3** Toyota Way 2001

*The Toyota Way 2001.* He acknowledged that the Toyota Way would continue to change but this would be the 2001 version. Hiroyoshi Yoshiki helped Cho in establishing TMMK and recalls the struggles in writing this document:

> *The creation of the Toyota Way 2001 took ten years. We started working on it in 1991. It was the first effort to explain to American executives Toyota principles. The Japan side could not really help because they never tried to articulate it. We created the first rough draft. Mr. Cho was here and we discussed it with Mr. Cho a lot. When Mr. Cho went back to Japan and became President of the whole company finally the Toyota Way came up. Before that we had 20 revised versions of the Toyota Way. We could not get 100 percent agreement. We finally agreed to call it The Toyota Way 2001 to acknowledge there is not 100 percent agreement on what the Toyota Way is and it is always changing.*

The document is thirteen pages in length. It explains the principles underlying the model in Figure 1.3 and liberally illustrates the thinking with "historical words." It is worth briefly summarizing the high level concepts in Figure 1.3. At the top level are the two pillars, continuous improvement, respect for people and "all Toyota team members, at every level, are expected to use these two values in their daily work and interactions."

Respect for people is a broad commitment. It means respect for all people touched by Toyota including employees, customers, investors, suppliers, dealers, the communities in which Toyota has operations, and society at large. Respect for people has sub-categories of "respect" and "teamwork" shown in the foundation of the house:

**Respect:** We respect others, make every effort to understand each other, take responsibility and do our best to build mutual trust.

**Teamwork:** We stimulate personal and professional growth, share the opportunities of development and maximize individual and team performance.

Continuous Improvement is the second pillar. Toyota leaders believe people who are continuously improving are what have allowed Toyota to grow from a small loom company in a farming community to a global powerhouse. Continuous improvement is defined as, "We are never satisfied with where we are and always improve our business by putting forth our best ideas and efforts."

There are three subcategories under "continuous improvement" that complete the foundation of the Toyota Way house:

**Challenge:** We form a long-term vision, meeting challenges with courage and creativity to realize our dreams.

*Kaizen:* We improve our business operations continuously, always driving for innovation and evolution.

*Genchi Genbutsu:* We practice *Genchi Genbutsu*—believing in going to the source to find the facts to make correct decisions, build consensus, and achieve goals at our best speed.

Below each of the five foundational concepts are further detailed concepts. For example, under kaizen are three subcategories: kaizen mind and innovative thinking, building lean systems and structure, and promoting organizational learning. It is interesting that Toyota has adopted the term lean that was originally coined in *The Machine That Changed the World*, a book that defined Toyota's approach to operational excellence as a new paradigm that is the next evolutionary step beyond mass production.[6] It is also interesting to note that "lean systems and structure" is buried two levels down in Toyota's model and not the focus.

Toyota has come a long way from its roots as a small startup making automatic looms. In the first quarter of 2007 it surpassed General Motors in quarterly sales for the first time in history, selling a total of 2.35 million vehicles worldwide. It is perhaps the most benchmarked company in the world for its famed production system and operational efficiency. With over 290,000 people, 523 subsidiary companies throughout the world, 19 overseas affiliates, and 52

---

[6] The term "lean" was never historically used within Toyota. It was first introduced in *The Machine That Changed the World* as a way to describe the new paradigm of manufacturing that Toyota had developed that led to doing more with less. See Womack, James P., Daniel T. Jones, and Daniel Roos. *The Machine That Changed the World*. New York: Rawson Associates, 1990.

overseas manufacturing companies in 27 countries,[7] Toyota has had to quickly learn how to spread its culture.

The main challenge when expanding its operations around the globe is that the organization absolutely refuses to compromise the Toyota Way philosophy. It is Toyota's belief that without a strong Toyota Way culture in every part of the company globally, it will lose its competitive advantage.

## A DEEPER ANALYSIS OF CULTURE

The question of which world-class Japanese management practices can be exported to other countries has puzzled academics and companies for decades. An earlier book, *Remade in America*,[8] addressed the question of what happens to Japanese management systems when they are exported from Japan to America through Japanese direct investment. The answer: The hybrid culture that evolved in the United States is not an exact replica of that same Japanese company, though the result can still be highly effective.[9] The implication is that exporting a culture is much more difficult than it at first seems.

"Change management" has become a standard consulting package for some companies. It was particularly prevalent in the 1990s as part of packages offered by companies selling information system "solutions" intended to fix business processes. Change management is purchased to sell employees on the new business processes and IT systems they are expected to embrace. There are standard training packages and communication programs developed to pour into the employees a new way of thinking. When we listen to managers talk about changing people and culture it often sounds highly mechanistic. Changing culture in this way has been compared to playing a game of billiards where managers have the cue stick. The billiard ball model seems to reflect much of Western management's approach to effecting change within an organization.[10] Consider that

---

[7] As of June 2006.

[8] Liker, Jeffrey K., W. Mark Fruin, and Paul S. Adler. (eds.), *Remade in America: Transplanting and Transforming Japanese Production Systems*, New York: Oxford University Press, 1999.

[9] Mary Yoko Brannen uses the term "recontextualization" to describe how the same items or concepts take on different meanings when brought into a different culture. Brannen, Mary Yoko, Jeffrey K. Liker and W. Mark Fruin, "Recontextualization and Factory-to-Factory Knowledge Transfer from Japan to the U.S.: The Case of NSK," in *Remade in America: Transplanting and Transforming Japanese Production Systems*, edited by Jeffrey K. Liker, W. Mark Fruin, and Paul S. Adler, New York: Oxford University Press, 1999: pp. 117–154.

[10] The billiard ball concept was shared with us by Mary Yoko Brannen who also introduced us to the concept of recontextualization, which describes how cultural artifacts take on new meanings when applied in different cultural settings.

aspect of the organization you wish to change as a billiard ball and assume you have an approach that will bring about improvement. If you hit the cue ball in the right place in the right way, it will set in motion a predictable process that leads to the desired result.

Any intervention can be thought of in this way. If workers are performing the same job in different ways and one desires a more efficient standardized process, send industrial engineers out to simply "implement standardized work." Hit the standardized work ball in the right place at the right angle. In other words, if we teach the right things—or implement the right tools—we will get the desired result whether it is productivity, quality, or cultural change.

In reality, systems involving people are complex, and information systems or communication alone will not change the overall process. To really effect a change in the process, you must change the people; people's beliefs and values are rooted in their culture.

Even the same tool or method can have a very different meaning in different cultural contexts. For example, one study credited Tokyo Disney's success in part to the intentional manipulations of Western cultural symbols.[11] In one scenario, this was done by making the exotic familiar while at the same time keeping the exotic, exotic. In an attempt to make the exotic familiar, Frontierland was renamed Westernland at Tokyo Disneyland. While the Japanese are familiar with the Old West through television Westerns, the word "frontier" holds no comparable meaning for them. As another example of making the exotic familiar, while Americans might think of the cowboy as the ultimate individualist who rides off into the sunset alone, in Disney Japan, cowboys are displayed participating in group activities (around camp fires for example) that better fit the Japanese collectivist culture. On the other hand, the exotic maintains its allure by reinforcing the differences between Japan and other countries. For example, non-Japanese employees speak only English and do not wear nametags. By understanding how the Japanese think about America, the Disney theme park was redesigned in subtle ways to appeal to their psyche.

Now let's consider what that means for managers who dream of learning from Toyota about how they, too, can dominate the competition. Maybe they hire a consultant and tour a Toyota plant where they see many interesting things. The factory is clean and organized, materials and tools are placed neatly in their places by the operator so that there is minimal wasted motion; the workers seem to know exactly what they need to do and work in a disciplined manner with tightly

---

[11] Brannen, Mary Yoko, "Bwana Mickey: Constructing Cultural Consumption at Tokyo Disneyland," in *Remade in Japan: Consumer Tastes in a Changing Japan*, edited by Joseph Tobin. New Haven, CT: Yale University Press, 1992.

scripted movements. Andon cords hang by every operator which when pulled, signal some sort of out of standard condition, causing someone to come and help or the production line stops.

What actually happens with such managers is that they set up Toyota's tools and methods in their own culture, and they do not work the same way. It is like a body rejecting an incompatible heart transplant. They completely miss the real purpose of the tools. Instead of becoming powerful tools for continuous improvement that team members can use for decades to grow the company, they are taken out of context and become additional management controls used to reprimand employees. That's when lean is viewed as mean. As we will discuss through the course of this book, Toyota was not able to exactly transfer the original culture in Japan to other countries. The Toyota Way was changed to a new blended culture, however Toyota insisted on retaining the essential principles of the Toyota Way that are crucial for a successful outcome. In reality Toyota had to learn what was essential over time through trial and error and kaizen.

Different levels of cultures emerge as we move from nations to locales to the organizations in those regions to departmental groups and to the individuals in those groups. Figure 1.4 illustrates these many levels. A given factory exists within a company's culture as well as within the local and national cultures. The Toyota Way in the Georgetown, Kentucky plant will not be exactly the same as that in the Princeton, Indiana plant. The locales are different, the history is different, the people are different, and the succession of leaders is different.

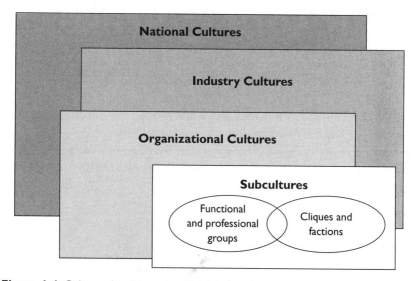

**Figure 1.4** Cultures Are Nested at Multiple Levels

However, they both are located in the United States and have some things in common because of this heritage that differentiate them from the Japanese-born employees at Toyota who helped set up the plants and teach the Toyota Way. As part of Toyota, the team members in both the United States and Japan have a common culture that sets them apart from others in Indiana and Kentucky who work for other companies. We call this Toyota's organizational culture, which is sometimes also referred to as "work culture." There are many differences across individuals in their upbringing, beliefs, and personal values, and Toyota does not need to make everyone think the same way at this level. What is important to Toyota is that there are some core values and beliefs about how work gets done at Toyota that are deeply shared.

It would be a mistake to assume Toyota has perfected developing a uniform culture even within a given operation. There are subcultures that form naturally in a plant. For example, the subculture of plant floor managers is different from that of the human resource managers. Managers have a different subculture compared to production workers. Within production workers, as a group, there is a subculture of union advocates that is different from that which is not disposed toward unionizing.

Toyota works hard to develop a common culture across the company, even between the shop floor and the office. For example, Human Resource (HR) managers would have typically worked in the factory as shop floor managers. HR representatives, many of whom previously worked in production, are assigned to specific areas of the plant and are expected to spend the majority of their time in those areas of the plant to gauge the culture and develop team members. Spending the majority of your time in front of your computer, thereby isolating yourself from the people who perform the firm's value-added work, is alien to the Toyota Way.

Achieving strong alignment among the varying levels of culture is a difficult process that has been one of the main challenges for Toyota as the company has expanded globally. It begins with selecting employees and partners, and then extends to maximizing every opportunity to teach and socialize the team member into the organizational way of thinking. It takes years and is a career-long endeavor. Ultimately the ability to absorb the company's culture lies in people's heads, in how they think, act, and react to different circumstances. From a common American perspective we might think of this negatively as brainwashing. From Toyota's perspective this is building the DNA in all team members.

When Gary Convis was President of Toyota Manufacturing in Kentucky, he was asked how long it takes to teach a manager hired from outside the company to be a Toyota manager. His answer: "about ten years."[12] He explained that

[12] Liker, Jeffrey K., *The Toyota Way: Fourteen Management Principles from the World's Greatest Manufacturer,* New York: McGraw-Hill, 2006, pg 295.

it is relatively easy to learn job knowledge, technical skills, quality and process requirements, etc. and the appropriate things to say, but it is another matter to actually behave the right way at all times. Often when people are under stress, they tend to revert to what they have known in the past such as yelling and micro-managing. Convis believes it takes about ten years for him to trust that while under stress the manager will behave appropriately using this as an opportunity for coaching and teaching. Consistently applying step-by-step problem-solving methods to daily problems supports the proper Toyota culture development. They don't want robots; they want problem solvers who can stabilize the shop floor so further kaizen and innovation can occur within the culture of continuous improvement and respect for people.

# THE CHALLENGES OF TAKING CULTURE ACROSS BOUNDARIES

In this book we use many examples from Toyota in America and particularly from TMMK. Several of the authors from the Center for Quality People and Organizations "cut their teeth" at this plant. They know the struggles Toyota had in developing the culture at that plant. When you look at the results after years of development, it looks easy. As they can attest, it was far from easy. A big part of the challenge is that Toyota's culture evolved in Japan where the culture is quite different from U.S. culture.

To understand how Toyota culture came about in Japan and the challenges of developing it in other countries, we need to understand cross-cultural differences. In this section we discuss these differences and particularly what it means for transferring the Toyota Way to the United Sates.

## Cross-National Culture by the Numbers

A starting point is looking at the numbers. One of the most rigorous quantitative studies of cross-national culture is the work of Geert Hofstede and his team members.[13] They did extensive surveys, interviews, and observations in over seventy different countries. Based on this research, they identified five "primary dimensions" that differentiate national cultures. Figure 1.5 presents data on these five dimensions for the United States, Japan, and an average of the world ratings. We define each of these dimensions and the implications for learning the Toyota Way across countries below:

---

[13] Hofstede, Geert and Gert Jan Hofstede, *Cultures and Organizations: Software of the Mind,* New York: McGraw-Hill, 2004. The scores on the values can be viewed for any country or combination of countries at the Web site www.geert-hofstede.com.

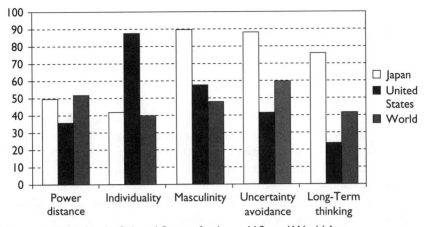

**Figure 1.5** Hofstede Cultural Scores for Japan, U.S., and World Average.

**Power Distance:** This is the extent to which the less powerful members of the society expect and accept that power is distributed unequally. Note that this does not measure how dominant the powerful are in the society but rather the degree to which the people at the bottom of the hierarchy accept this power imbalance. Neither the United States nor Japan stand out markedly on this dimension compared to the world average though the United States is below average, meaning individuals near the bottom of the power hierarchy do not accept inequality. This could make it challenging to spread the standardized work and aggressive targets from the top that are characteristic of Toyota's system.

**Individuality:** On the other side of this continuum is "collectivism." This is the extent to which individuals are integrated into groups. In individualistic societies each individual looks after him or herself. In collectivist society, the individual belongs to highly cohesive groups that protect the individual in return for unquestioning loyalty to the group. The United States is one of only seven countries with individualism as the highest value of all cultural traits and all of these are Western countries. Japan is much more of a collectivist society. The Toyota Way emphasizes teamwork. The team comes before the individual. Statements like "I accomplished this" are strongly discouraged. One of Toyota's challenges has been to build this collectivist orientation in their American organizations.

**Masculinity:** This refers to the degree to which the society is dominated by male values, that have particularly assertive and competitive orientations. Both the United States and Japan are above average on masculinity, but Japan is off the charts on the degree of masculinity. Certainly Toyota grew up with male domination and for most of its years women played decidedly subordinate roles. This has recently changed in Japan with women finally functioning in professional roles as engineers and managers, however, it remains a rare occurrence. The United States is also a bit above average in masculinity. Perhaps the masculine values of Japan have helped influence the strong value of competition within Toyota.

**Uncertainty Avoidance:** This addresses the society's tolerance for uncertainty and ambiguity. Societies strong in this category are uncomfortable with unstructured situations and prefer structure such as strict laws and rules. Japan is near the top of the world on uncertainty avoidance while the United States is considerably below average. Interestingly, even inside Japan the world-beating Toyota is known as a conservative, risk-averse company having been founded in the Aichi prefecture, which is known for its extreme thriftiness. The United States is known for an entrepreneurial spirit associated with people willing to take risks. In light of these contrasts, it is not surprising that the strict structure of standardized work seems natural for Toyota in Japan, while Americans voice strong fears of becoming shackled by rules and standards.

**Long-Term Orientation:** Countries that have a long-term orientation value thrift and perseverance. The foundation of the Toyota Way model is long-term thinking. Patience and perseverance are both highly valued within Toyota. In fact the biggest struggle we have observed in American companies wishing to learn from the Toyota Way is their short-term orientation and need for every action taken in the name of lean to pay for itself very quickly.

## East versus West Means a Different Way of Thinking

Cognitive psychologists have taken another look at East-West differences studying the different ways Eastern and Western people think.[14] These studies have found broad commonalities in ways of thinking between diverse Eastern countries like Japan, Korea, China, and Singapore, compared to modal ways of thinking in the West. Those of us who have been learning about Toyota for many years were struck by how well the East versus West differences help explain how Toyota is different from most Western companies seeking to learn from Toyota.

The story goes way back to Western philosophers like Aristotle and Plato and Eastern religions rooted in Buddhism, Taoism, and Confucianism. Nisbett[15] finds historical differences that seem very compatible with Hofstede's distinction between collectivism and individualism and writes:

> *The Greeks, more than any other ancient peoples and in fact more than most people on the planet today, had a remarkable sense of personal agency—the sense that they were in charge of their own lives and free to act as they chose.*

---

[14] Nisbett, Richard E. *The Geography of Thought: How Asians and Westerners Think Differently...and Why,* New York: Free Press, 2003. This book is an excellent synthesis of many studies comparing how people from Eastern versus Western cultures think.

[15] Ibid,. pp. 2–3.

*One definition of happiness for the Greeks was that it consisted of being able to exercise their powers in pursuit of excellence in a life free from constraints.*

*The Chinese counterpart to this was harmony. Every Chinese was first and foremost a member of a collective, or rather of several collectives—the clan, the village, and especially the family. The individual was not, as for the Greeks, an encapsulated unit who maintained a unique identity across social settings.*

*The Chinese were concerned less with issues of control of others or the environment than with self-control, so as to minimize friction with others in the family and village and to make it easier to obey the requirements of the state, administered by magistrates. The ideal of happiness was not, as for the Greeks, a life allowing the free exercise of distinctive talents, but the satisfactions of a plain country life shared within a harmonious social network.*

In this sense Toyota fits well the underlying assumptions of Asian culture that emphasize harmony, membership in a collective, and at the same time an emphasis on self-control. For example, many companies have picked up on the concept of a kaizen event to drive improvement. A team of people is brought together for five days and analyzes an operation, comes up with ideas for improvement, and implements the improvements. A trained facilitator who is a "lean expert" is driving the group and leading them through the improvement process. On Friday the group reports out to management on the project, and results are often tallied to justify the costs of all the kaizen events. A similar approach is used at Toyota but it is called *jishuken* which means "voluntary self study." In the Toyota approach there also is a trained facilitator but the facilitator is called the *sensei* or teacher. The sensei does not do anything except challenge the group and ask tough questions. The sensei often refuses to answer questions when the group wants to know "the right answer." Individuals in the group are expected to be motivated to improve themselves through this activity and the sensei is a guide and coach for their self-improvement. The results are important as a reflection of the achievements of the group in learning, not as a justification for the cost of the event.

Looking even deeper than the level of how East versus West looks at groups and harmony there are some basic differences in cognition—how the world is looked at. The results of research studies comparing East and West show the following differences in basic cognition:[16]

- Patterns of attention and perception, with easterners attending more to environments and westerners attending more to objects, and easterners being more likely to detect relationships among events than westerners.
- Beliefs about controllability of the environment, with westerners believing in controllability more than easterners.

---

[16] Ibid, p 44.

- Tacit assumptions about stability versus change, with westerners seeing stability where easterners see change.
- Preferred patterns of explanation for events, with westerners focusing on objects and easterners casting a broader net to include the environment.
- Use of formal logic rules, with westerners more inclined to see logical rules to understand events than easterners.

These differences are quite fundamental and help explain some of the ways westerners view lean compared to the intent within Toyota. The general tendency in the West is to view lean as a tool kit that can help control the work environment to achieve specific measurable objectives. We award "black belt" status to experts trained in the tools who go into the work place to get the results…much as a hunter goes into the jungle to bring back the kill. Six sigma is attractive because it suggests a very logical structure. In six sigma classes we have seen the instructor proudly write: $Y = f(X)$. That is, the outcome—Y—is a function of a set of independent variables—X. If you can identify and measure the independent variables you can improve the system. Essentially what is happening is we are objectifying the workplace and seeing simple cause and effect relationships while losing sight of the people and the complex dynamics of the environment.

When Toyota sensei look at improving the workplace they do not see a bunch of independent variables to be manipulated. They see a bunch of people working in a process that is filled with waste. Their goal is for the people to learn to see the waste as they do and learn to use clear and rigorous thinking and teamwork to solve problems thereby attacking the waste. They realize that most ideas for improvement are simply good guesses and need to be verified through experimentation, so they want many experiments to be run by many people working in the process who are constantly monitoring the results of the experiments and learning. The task of the sensei is to develop the people sufficiently to start this process moving and periodically come back to challenge the people to think even more deeply about problems.

## Is the Toyota Way a Direct Reflection of Eastern Thinking?

We are often asked whether the Toyota Way is unique to Toyota or a reflection of Japanese culture. That is akin to asking whether it is about national culture or company culture. The answer is both. Obviously Toyota is a Japanese company and the Toyota Way evolved in Japan. The fundamental differences in the way of thinking between East and West strongly influences the ability of Americans to learn from Toyota.

It is clear that the Toyota Way is more a reflection of Eastern culture than Western culture. Given this, one might ask: What stands out about Toyota? Is Toyota any different than other Japanese companies? If not, why is Toyota so much more successful than most other Japanese companies?

Toyota is a unique blend of Japanese culture, the special conditions of Aichi prefecture where Toyota was founded, the influence of the Toyoda family and the great leaders in Toyota's history, and particular characteristics of the auto industry. Toyota has always been a very independent company. "Self-reliance" is one of the core values of Toyota and they started out in the farming community of Aichi prefecture far from the big city. Toyota has always done it their way. Perhaps the farming mentality led Toyota to want to be financially and technologically independent. The origins as a company founded on innovation by great inventor Sakichi Toyoda may account for the adaptability and creativity throughout Toyota.

Perhaps because of the profound influence of Sakichi Toyoda, who believed in contributing to the group and society, but also was a brilliant individual inventor, Toyota seems to stand out in placing a high value on both group and individual achievements. The Asian view that the tallest nail will be pounded down speaks to the actual fear of being singled out for individual accomplishment in Japan. Toyota does not want the tallest nail to be pounded down. The creation of the Toyota Production System is a great example. Ohno was an unusually aggressive leader by Japanese standards and by Toyota standards. He believed in teamwork but in many ways he was more of a dictator than a team player. Ohno would always give credit to the team, but he was extremely strong willed and single minded in his vision for manufacturing. No one would stand in his way. Many of his actions created disharmony at Toyota and are very counter to the desire for harmony and consensus. He only managed to last in the company because of the personal sponsorship of Eiji Toyoda who saw something special in him. Step by step, Ohno developed the Toyota Production System. He pulled together ideas from many places—experiments with making looms, detailed study of Ford Motor company and Henry Ford's theories, the quality methods of W. Edwards Deming, the training methods of the American military, and many others. Ultimately this became a unique total system that has been adhered to religiously within Toyota. It was the drive of an individual genius, who was a nail who stood out, who created one of the greatest accomplishments of the twentieth century—the Toyota Production System.

There are similar stories in product development and sales. For example, in product development, the main driver of innovation and of achieving aggressive targets is the chief engineer who has a very strong personality and is revered within Toyota culture. The phrase "it is the chief engineer's car" is commonly heard giving tremendous credit to an individual who is presiding over the efforts of thousands of people.[17] Chief engineers are known to have strong and very

---

[17] See discussion of the "Michael Jordan" of chief engineers, Ichiro Susuki, who led the design of the first Lexus in Jeffrey Liker, *The Toyota Way*, New York: McGraw-Hill, 2004.

different personalities, from calm and reflective who fit the Japan way to aggressive and demanding who would seem more at home in the West.

Toyota has also been unusually open to learning from the West and becoming a global company moving beyond their conservative local roots. Sakichi Toyoda admonished, "Open the window, it is a big world out there." Toyota has refused to be shackled by tradition, whether Japanese or otherwise. The company is about constantly challenging assumptions at the detailed level of work motions of the individual worker or at the level of corporate strategy. In the *Toyota Way 2001,* it states, "We continue to search for breakthroughs, refusing to be restrained by precedent or taboo."

Nonetheless, the Toyota Way is very rooted in Eastern culture. The challenge then becomes how can Toyota possibly bring the Toyota Way to Western countries when the basic cultural assumptions are in some cases antithetical to the local culture? The answer to the question is that Toyota has brought key aspects of the culture to the West with remarkable success through a process of experimenting, reflecting, and learning. This book addresses how they have managed to do this.

When considering all of these differences, one might think that it is impossible for Americans to follow the Toyota Way. It would be perfectly understandable if the early Toyota leaders from Japan had become frustrated by these very diverse cultural tendencies and gave up on many aspects of the Toyota Way. They could have simply let the highly individualistic Americans compete for pay and promotion as individuals and reward outstanding individual performers or let Americans do their own individual jobs and give up on cross-training. Why not give up on standardized work and let individuals do the job their own way?

But the early Japanese leaders refused to compromise. The spirit of challenge is also a value of the Toyota Way and the early leaders established the goal that they must transfer the essence of the Toyota Way to America regardless of the culture. Of course the first question was: what is the essence? Even that was not obvious as the Toyota Way was simply the way they did things. Through discussion, debate, and experimentation, and with the help of the Americans, they began to figure what of the culture needed to be transferred. There were modifications, such as small individual rewards, but no wholesale change in the fundamental values.

The approach taken was to begin by selecting Americans, particularly leaders, who best fit the Toyota Way culture. Leaders are intensively interviewed for their "character," and extensive evaluations identify team-oriented employees. Who is this person deep down in their moral fabric? Once people are brought into the cultural values of the Toyota Way, it is drilled into them every day, much like a boot camp experience. The result is that the individuals become Toyota team members and then transfer this culture to the next generation of employees and so on. When the first American plants were founded, the Japanese remained in the background reinforcing the values as "coordinators" or "trainers," though in decreasing numbers year by year.

## THE CHALLENGES OF CHANGING CULTURE AT OTHER COMPANIES: A WARNING

Unfortunately, most companies throughout the world that are adopting lean practices are going about it the wrong way. They often describe what they are doing as "adding tools to the toolkit," or they express a need to "lean out a plant" because costs are too high. Other companies are adopting lean six sigma and believe that combining both as two complementary tool sets yields something more powerful than either one individually. This approach reflects a number of tendencies of Western culture:[18]

- The very short-term orientation in the West that Hofstede quantified.
- A strong Western belief in controllability of the environment, compared to the Eastern view in the need to adapt to the environment which is seen as less predictable or controllable.
- A strong bias in the West toward the use of rules of formal logic to understand and predict the world, compared to the more holistic and intuitive approach in the East.

These tendencies lead Western companies to see Toyota's accomplishments as the result of simple cause and effect relationships between a set of definable and transferable tools and specific performance outcomes like cost reduction or inventory reduction. Figure out the Toyota secret tools and you too can be successful like Toyota. There is nothing wrong with using process improvement tools to get specific results and in fact, this is at the core of kaizen at Toyota. The problem is when there is a failure to understand the broader cultural context that allows this to happen repeatedly and broadly throughout Toyota. The following two contrasting company stories illustrate how the culture at Toyota compared to a Western company has a very strong influence on the meaning of tools associated with lean manufacturing.

### Case One: "I messed up" (On line at Tsutsumi, The Camry Plant in Toyota City, Japan)

This first story is from Mike Hoseus,

*As a new group leader, I was sent to Tsutsumi to spend a month getting an appreciation of working on the line and mastering one process. The team*

---

[18] The second two Western tendencies in this list are based on Nisbett, Richard, *The Geography of Thought*, New York: Free Press, 2003.

*leaders told us no one would be able to complete the whole job by the end of the month, but I was determined to prove them wrong. I was installing liners underneath the wheel well when my air gun slipped, and the driver bit scratched the paint on the inner lip of the wheel well. I gasped and looked around—no one saw me do it—but they had told me to pull the andon (rope) cord if I made or caught any defect. It was my moment of truth. My first reaction was to let it go. No one would probably see the scratch anyway, and no one would know that I made it. But my conscience got the best of me, and I wanted to see if they really meant what they said about admitting mistakes. So I pulled the andon and the team leader came to fix the problem and showed me how to hold the bit with a free finger in order to stabilize it better. But he did not seem angry at me for making the scratch.*

*Then at break we gathered for our afternoon group meeting where the group leader gave out information on safety and quality issues and heard back concerns from the members.*

*They spoke Japanese so I could not understand what they were saying until I heard the words, "Mike-san." Well that got my attention so I listened carefully...more Japanese and then "scratchee scratchee" ... and then more Japanese. So here it was; finally I was going to get called out for messing up and they were going to do it in front of everyone. Then, all of a sudden, the whole group looked at me and clapped and smiled and patted my back and shook my hand as they headed back to the line. I couldn't believe it, after double checking with an interpreter just to make sure, they were applauding me because I made a mistake and I admitted it. I felt like a million bucks, and guess what I did the next time I made a mistake?*

## Case Two: "This is Lean?"

This was reported to one of the authors by an engineer of a company going through the lean transformation process:

*They had told us in training that solving problems was important in lean, and that we should all work together as a team in order to do it. A machine operator called me and told me he had an issue with a safety guard on a piece of equipment. They also told me that it was important that I "go and see." So I left my desk and went down to the work area to meet with the person and look at the equipment and consider the safety issue. I spent some time talking with the operator and understanding the issue when I was paged to see the plant manager. When I got to his windowed office, he and the HR manager were both there and wanted to know what I was doing down there. After explaining the situation, I was hoping for some recognition and support, but instead I got reprimanded. I was told "you can't just talk with every operator about their safety issues. Once they tell you that makes us liable with OSHA, and we can get in a lot of trouble. Just do your job!" I left the room thinking "I thought lean was supposed to be different."*

Case Two is obviously a dramatic example, but unfortunately, from personal experience and reports of organizations going through lean transformation we have countless examples of the organization's culture making it difficult to learn some of the basic methods of the Toyota Production System. Consider the following examples in which coauthor Liker was personally involved:

■ A large mining company wanted lean as part of a broader transformation process and claimed they wanted "Toyota's culture." It took about one year to do the planning and get the buy-in but now they were anxious to get going. We explained that culture change is only possible by doing actual projects at the gemba (where the work is done). We suggested that these projects would have to be started at first in a single mine designated as a model for learning and engage the people directly involved in the mine's operations. The primary purpose of the lean transformation project was to get the people and managers at the mine thinking and acting with a lean mindset. The business metrics would follow. This is the "inch wide and a mile deep" approach. Once this model mine had gained sufficient traction, the learning would be systematically spread throughout the rest of the organization. They were obviously not too happy with focus on one mine rather than blasting lean across the enterprise, but went along with our recommendation. After two months they wanted to know when the results would come in but we suggested it would take a little more time. In the meantime they had contracted another consultant and started to work on other mines as they did not want to wait for our experiment. After six months of work and some notable progress (highest tons delivered in its history, improved uptimes, etc.) the initiative started receiving heavy criticism from the corporate office.

The corporate office was continually asking for detailed PowerPoint presentations and digital photos that could be sent back to headquarters documenting the culture change, and they were not seeing enough reports from consultants. When the corporate managers were invited to the site for a "go and see" they spent less than a day reviewing the various projects while sitting in a conference room and no time at all at the gemba or with the leadership at the mine. The consultants were puzzled as to how you can observe culture change from an air-conditioned conference room with almost no interaction with the site. Shortly thereafter, the consultants were fired and a new consulting group was brought in. This group was excellent at PowerPoint presentations and gave the corporate managers everything they wanted; namely the ability to monitor progress without ever leaving the comforts of their own offices hundreds of miles away. Instead of working with the leadership team on the importance of true problem solving and people development, the new approach focused on rolling out 5S in all areas, effectively transitioning to an "inch deep and a mile wide" approach. The pilot mine continued on its own and used its own money to sponsor Liker's consultant for another six months and continued to grow its new culture and break performance records, but was largely ignored as a model for the rest of the company.

- A large shipbuilding company was acquired by a larger defense contractor that had an active lean six sigma program, and was asked by the new owner to develop a lean program as well. With the guidance of a consulting firm, they conducted value stream mapping and kaizen workshops over a three-year period in the shipyard and ultimately in engineering. Tremendous success stories along with dramatic improvements in cost, quality, and lead time arose from this effort; the program was presented to the parent company as a huge success. As it evolved, the company needed someone to take ownership over the program. In the meantime, a six-sigma master black belt had been hired to lead the quality office. Quietly watching the progress of the lean program, he periodically expressed displeasure that the individual projects were not being properly tracked via rigorous metrics and it was not clear if the projects that would have the largest impact were being selected. At some point the organization decided to move the management of its lean effort, which had been run by the operational groups, to the quality office. Shortly after making this move, the black belt informed the consultants that their contract would not be renewed. The lean projects then became lean six-sigma projects. Those who were most passionate about the lean transformation were moved back to their operational roles. The culture that began to emerge was stopped in its tracks and lean six sigma then became a program focused on picking projects with political import and looking for cost reductions.

It was obvious to us that each of these companies was missing a key aspect of the Toyota culture. They were implementing various tools to get specific results but not building a culture of continuous improvement at the gemba. In fact, they neither understood nor valued the real cultural changes that were beginning to emerge within their own companies. We believe this is the reason so few companies have seriously learned from the Toyota Production System. The results-oriented culture that needs to be changed is the major barrier to culture change.

## CAVEAT: TOYOTA IS MADE UP OF PEOPLE— AND PEOPLE ARE NOT PERFECT

As you read this book you will learn about the elements of Toyota culture and will be presented with many examples of the things Toyota does to ensure that these positive culture elements become the reality of day-to-day activity. In our experience, Toyota is remarkably good at this. Their culture is strong and cohesive, and well aligned. There is a conscious effort by the senior leaders to develop the Toyota culture in accord with the principles of the Toyota Way. They work hard at it. They realize it takes decades and not months. But they are not perfect!

Any of the authors of this book who have been close to Toyota, or worked for years inside the company, can share their horror stories. They can tell you about the people who left because they felt mistreated and the grievances brought to the human resources department—and about specific trainers from Japan who were violating basic principles of the Toyota Way. In Chapter 13 we will tell the story about a sexual harassment case at TMMK that upon investigation led to the realization that HR was not trusted to support the workforce and communication had broken down. This led to a thorough investigation of the root causes of the problem and major overhaul of the management system. The good news is that the problem was seriously and thoughtfully addressed. The bad news is that the problem occurred in the first place. Unfortunately the world is not a neat and controlled environment. There is always variation, and people are generally more variable than machines.

The important thing in Toyota is how they deal with these deviations from the principles. Do senior leaders even recognize deviations or are they so far from the daily work that they only get good news and do not notice what is really going on? Do they stop and take action to address the problems and learn? Our experiences with Toyota have generally been very positive in this regard. Senior leaders in particular truly care. They often seem to want to know the bad news more than the good news, and seek to confront problems.

Toyota has worked hard to create a deliberate, intentional set of policies and leadership practices that have proven effective in creating a very positive culture. The human system is not perfect but, true to their nature, Toyota continually works on improving it. In fact the human system is imperfect and the resulting culture never lives up to the lofty ideals of the true Toyota Way. Throughout this book, we will highlight positive features of Toyota more than their unfortunate slip-ups, although a few such examples and how Toyota addressed them will be included. We don't claim that 100 percent of these errors are addressed; however we strongly support the organization's principles and believe any company who wants to be high performing needs a similar set of tenets that bring together the tools and people in an integrated system.

## SUMMARY: REASONS FOR HOPE?

This book is about Toyota culture and focuses mostly on how a highly successful hybrid version of its culture has been created in the United States. In reality it has been very challenging for Toyota even though Toyota's top leadership is absolutely committed to the Toyota Way and is in it for the long term. On a positive note Toyota has been very successful even with all of the national cultural differences seemingly working against them.

Mostly in this book we are trying to provide a picture of what Toyota culture is and how it operates. The final chapter will address the question about how other companies can learn from Toyota culture.

## KEY POINTS TO CONSIDER FOR YOUR COMPANY

1. The Toyota Way is a unique combination of Japanese culture, the specific culture of the early farming communities of Aichi prefecture, the Toyoda family leadership, influences from American experts, and the specific evolution of the Toyota group.
2. Toyota has been very aggressive at globalizing but has done it organically, growing from within, and working to maintain Toyota culture in all of its operations globally.
3. Toyota has faced challenges in bringing their culture, which has many strong Japanese elements, to other countries with very different national cultures.
4. Western culture in particular poses challenges to the Toyota Way due to strong individualism in the West, short-term thinking, and a different way of thinking about cause and effect.
5. Toyota has learned over time the essential elements of the Toyota Way needed to maintain the strength of the company and refuses to compromise on transferring those elements to other countries.

6. Toyota continues to learn how to teach the Toyota Way in other countries through explicit training (e.g., *Toyota Way 2001*), on-the-job mentoring, and extremely consistent leadership.
7. Toyota's success in bringing the Toyota Way to its local operations throughout the world gives hope to other companies seeking to learn from Toyota that this is possible.
8. The Toyota Way continues to evolve as Toyota grows, faces new circumstances, and globalizes, and Toyota is far from perfect.

# Chapter 2

---

# The Human
# Systems Model

*The companies that survive longest are the ones that work out what they uniquely can give to the world—not just growth or money but their excellence, their respect for others, or their ability to make people happy. Some call those things a soul.*

—Charles Handy, management author/philosopher

## TOYOTA'S TURNAROUND FROM BANKRUPTCY: REFLECTING AND REINFORCING CULTURE

Many companies today are turning to lean in a time of crisis. The rapidly changing global market demands that organizations be responsive in order to keep pace. Only those that respond quickly and skillfully will survive. So how is Toyota relevant in this context? Some say that Toyota had it easy because they have been in a constant growth mode since World War II, while consistently making a profit. They question how Toyota's great and lofty principles would hold up if the company had ever faced near bankruptcy.

But Toyota did indeed go through a business crisis in the late 1940s, not long after Toyota Motor Company was formed and shortly after Japan's involvement in World War II. The Japanese economy was in a depression and people were not buying cars, so Toyota had to extend itself financially to fund the company. The banks said to cut costs by laying off employees or they would shut them down. Kiichiro Toyoda, the founder of the auto company, handled the situation in the Toyota Way.

First, he met with employees and explained Toyota's financial situation, informing them that the company would need to reduce team members employment by about 1,500 in order to stay afloat. Toyoda asked any employees willing to voluntarily step down from their positions to do so, and with this one request got the number needed without any involuntary layoffs. Second, he took personal responsibility for the state of Toyota (even though as the founder and partial owner it was completely beyond his control) and personally resigned from the company. From his point of view, he had failed the company and failed the people; so how could he continue to both lead and draw money away from the company?

In the midst of this crisis, Toyoda held a meeting of senior executives to reflect on the future of the company and make decisions that would profoundly shape the future culture of the company and its employees. Together they agreed to commit to three principles:

1. Toyota would not give up on the business and would continue to work hard to become a prosperous automotive company that actively contributed to the development of the Japanese economy.
2. Labor-management relations would be founded on mutual trust.
3. Labor and management would work together on productivity improvements to create mutual prosperity and to maintain and improve working conditions.

The reaction to this crisis was to begin to formally articulate the Toyota Way culture, which emphasizes mutual trust and respect for all people that come into contact with the company. The actions of Kiichiro Toyoda also strongly reinforced that culture. The founding principles of Toyota Motor Company were based on the view that employment is more than a financial transaction. It is a mutual investment by the company and the employee in a long-term partnership to develop both the company and the employee. Letting go of loyal employees, even when they agree to leave, is painful, and there is no way around that. It represented the failure of Toyota's goal to achieve mutual prosperity. But when the necessity of severing ties became apparent, it had to be done in an open, mutually trust-based way. Toyota is a learning organization, and it learned a deep lesson from this disaster. When Kiichiro Toyoda resigned, his cousin, Eiji Toyoda, took over, and the remaining leaders of the company agreed on two commitments for the future:

1. They would not allow the company to get in a situation where they have to lay off employees again. This promise has led to preventative safeguards, like a large cash reserve (about $30 billion) to ride out rough times in the business.
2. They would be very cautious about expanding full-time employment too quickly to forgo the risk of having large numbers of extra employees when, and if, the business goes down. This has led to both very careful planning of employment levels and the use of "temporary workers" to buffer against economic fluctuations.

Ask someone to define "lean" and you will get a variety of answers; most will focus on a set of methods for "reducing waste." What Toyota leaders realized in their moment of crisis was how much they valued people. Eliminating waste is done *by* people, not *to* people. Lean tools focus on the product value stream in order to eliminate waste in making the product, but they don't attend to one of the most critical value streams within the organization: the people value stream.

# SUPPORTING THE TWO CRITICAL VALUE STREAMS: PRODUCT AND PEOPLE

## The Core of Toyota Culture Is Not Negotiable

Toyota has kept its identity as a company, including its philosophy and principles, remarkably consistent for many years. Its values of trust and continuous improvement permeate its commitment to long-term thinking, developing people, standardization, innovation, and problem solving. It is a learning organization that literally thrives on its people engaging in identifying and solving problems together and achieving results that will benefit everyone.

The Toyota Way culture is the critical ingredient in the company's organizational DNA, and it allows for constructive local adaptation of a global company at the same time that it avoids the potential pitfalls of diluting the Toyota Way. The culture at a Toyota plant in Georgetown, Kentucky is not identical to that of a Cambridge, Ontario, plant, nor is it the same as the culture in Jakarta, Indonesia. Each plant has certain unique cultural elements based on its specific context, as defined by its history, locale, leadership, and people. However, while local culture certainly is a strong influence in the company's widespread global branches, Toyota has developed certain core principles that must be present in every Toyota operation regardless of location.

In this chapter, we summarize the human systems model around which this book has been organized. At the center of the model is the people value stream, which is essential to understanding why the Toyota Way has met with such unprecedented success. We believe that the X-factor in Toyota's ongoing success is the way Toyota develops people to not only do their jobs but to think deeply about problems and become committed to the Toyota value system.

## The Missing People Value Stream

The concept of a value stream has become a common part of the vocabulary of organizations that want to improve. "Value stream mapping" may be the most used lean tool, and it can have a powerful effect on a team's ability to understand how much waste is produced in the total process of converting raw materials to finished goods. In value stream mapping, the product's path is followed from raw material to finished goods, documenting both value-added processes and wasted steps. Value added is defined as when the part is physically being transformed to what the customer wants. Any activity that costs time and money and does not add value is defined as waste. Value stream mapping helps team members understand how the product flows and identify the wastes in the process. For example, is it being moved about from place to place? Is it sitting in inventory? Are there quality problems creating the need for rework?

We can use this methodology on a conceptual level to understand the people value stream. In value stream mapping, there are process boxes in which value is added, and between these process boxes are inventory triangles that represent waste. It is typically found that the greater part of the life of a product is "waste" as it is being moved someplace or sitting in inventory. Imagine if you had the time to map a person's entire career, starting with when they first joined the company. For our purposes, value is added when the person is learning and being challenged. These periods are shown as the process boxes, while every hour spent not learning is represented by inventory triangles—waste. A person's work may be productive, but for our people value stream, if the work does not contribute to learning and development, it will be classified as waste. We would probably expect that most of the careers mapped would exhibit a lot more waste than value-added development. After all, most of us spend a fair amount of time doing routine work, taking breaks, or sitting in ineffective meetings. We suspect this is true at Toyota as well, but we believe a significantly larger portion of time at Toyota brings to its members value-added learning and development. Even on the shop floor, workers who perform routine production tasks spend a great deal of time in training where they are taught the higher-level skills of their jobs. They learn multiple skills such as problem solving and group development and practice these skills regularly. They also learn more about safety and have the opportunity to become team leaders. All of these capabilities lead to the development of an entirely new set of advanced skills.

At Toyota, the term "system" is used quite often, and the product value stream and people value stream are literally intertwined in a system that makes up the DNA of the Toyota Way. Developing people into problem solvers takes waste out of the system and leaves a leaner system in place. Without the waste of inventory a delay or quality problem will immediately shut down the process. This means that problems surface quickly and thus challenge team members to respond to and learn from the obstacles that they encounter on the job. When these two value streams are connected and that DNA is reproduced, it forms the "Toyota culture," which makes it possible not only to implement but also to sustain the Toyota Way (see Figure 2.1).

## Problem Solving Connects the Two Value Streams

The importance of problem solving in the Toyota culture cannot be emphasized enough. It serves the very vital function of connecting the product and people value streams. If the product value stream and the people value stream make up the organizational DNA of the company, problem solving is the code that connects the two.

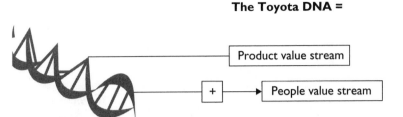

**The Toyota DNA =**

Product value stream

+ → People value stream

**Figure 2.1** The Intertwined Product and People Value Streams

Without a practical and continuous problem-solving process that is used on a daily basis, there will be a gap in any company's lean transformation. Toyota emphasizes that the tools of the Toyota Production System (TPS) are designed to highlight and identify problems within its organization. *Kanban*, continuous flow, and Just in Time all expose problems that one may not see otherwise. The same is true for 5S, Standardized Work, and Andon. The interplay of these systems sets company standards, thus enabling the process of identifying waste-producing, out-of-standard conditions. For example, if we reduce the quantity of parts brought to the production line from one day's worth once per shift to one hour's worth every hour, we will notice problems with those parts much more quickly and there will be immediate pressure to solve the problems, since there is less than one hour of parts available before we shut down. The out-of-standard condition is observed more quickly, and when it is observed, the potential consequences are severe.

The key to success is to have a production system that highlights problems and a human system that produces people who are able and willing to identify and solve them (see Figure 2.2). This requires team-minded people who are not only competent enough and well trained enough to identify and solve a problem, but who also trust their supervising group leader, feel safe in identifying the problem, and are motivated to solve it.

We put mutual trust at the center of Figure 2.2 because it is instrumental in creating an environment that both encourages the identification of problems and motivates people to solve them. Without trust in their employers, employees are reluctant to admit to the existence of problems and learn that it is safest to hide them. Now imagine a company that has not established mutual trust: A team from the front office value stream maps the process and then implements a kanban system here and some standardized work there, and even hangs an andon light connected to a cord to stop the line. What is likely to happen? If inventory is reduced, problems will surface more quickly, but is the worker likely to pull the cord and identify the problem? Is the worker going to try and solve the problem or throw up her hands and say it is management's responsibility? On the other hand, if problems are hidden, the entire system of continuous improvement stops

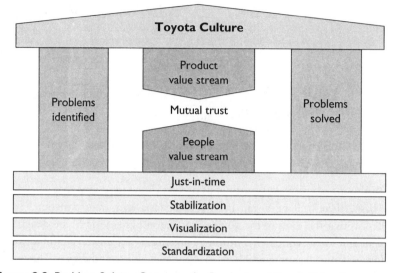

**Figure 2.2** Problem Solving Connects the Product and People Value Streams

functioning and the lean systems lose their value. In the *Toyota Way 2001* document, there is a sub-element called "promoting organizational learning," which includes learning from mistakes:

> *We view errors as opportunities for learning. Rather than blaming individuals, the organization takes corrective actions and distributes knowledge about each experience broadly. Learning is a continuous company-wide process as superiors motivate and train subordinates; as predecessors do the same for successors; and as team members at all levels share knowledge with one another.*

In Chapter 1 we told a story that concluded with Mike Hoseus receiving applause for admitting a serious mistake on the job. This would be a startling ending to the story in most organizations as it would be outside the cultural boundaries of normal behavior to reward someone for "messing up." In fact, if a group in most plants applauded a mistake, it would probably be to poke fun at the team member. Mutual trust is what makes it possible for individual employees to admit problems and take responsibility for solving them.

## THE HUMAN SYSTEMS MODEL

Describing something as complex as the culture of a company is no easy task, and any model will necessarily be a simplified abstraction. There is one story told among Toyota employees that Taiichi Ohno tore up early versions of the house representing TPS because he felt one could not capture the depth of TPS with a static illustration and that it was a waste of time to even try. TPS was a living, evolving process and he would say: "If you write it down you will kill it." Learning was at the *gemba* (the place where the value-added work is done). Despite the echoes of Ohno's admonition, we decided to do our best to represent the human systems model that has allowed Toyota to become so successful, in a way that is applicable to other companies and countries. The model, shown in Figure 2.3, is oversimplified, to be sure, yet as models go, it is reasonably complex and to truly understand what it means takes years of practice.

We could find no better way to represent the human system than as a traditional systems model with inputs, a core transformation process, supporting subsystems, outputs, and a purpose.[1]

The system we are focusing on is the people value stream and its direct supporting systems inside Toyota. Because we are focusing in this book only on the people system, there are certain parts of Toyota that fall outside our prescribed boundaries. For example, we show the production system principles—the technical principles of TPS—as outside the boundary of the human system; they are shown as an input. We also show Toyota's philosophy and values as inputs. They have been established over the decades of the company's lifetime, and they have a major influence on the quality people value stream that we would see in any individual plant or organization within Toyota. The chapters in this book are organized to explain each element of the Human Systems Model in some detail, but first we will provide a broad summary here.

We find it is best to understand the system from the outside in (something management guru Peter Drucker always advised) by asking these questions:

- What is the purpose of the organization?
- What are the key outputs that help achieve the purpose?
- What are the key inputs needed from the environment, and how do we filter these to select only those we want to let enter the system?

## Outside the People Value Stream: Purpose, Outputs, and Inputs

According to the systems model, any given organization should have a very clear understanding of its purpose, and Toyota has a remarkably clear vision that is broadly shared among the leaders of the company. There are a variety of mission statements in the various business divisions within Toyota that change over time, but each one always includes these fundamental elements:

---

[1] Taylor, James C. and David F. Felten, *Performance by Design: Designing Sociotechnical Systems in North America*, Upper Saddle River, NJ.: Prentice Hall, 1993; Pasmore, William A., *Designing Effective Organizations: The Sociotechnical Systems Perspective*, New York: John Wiley and Sons, 1988.

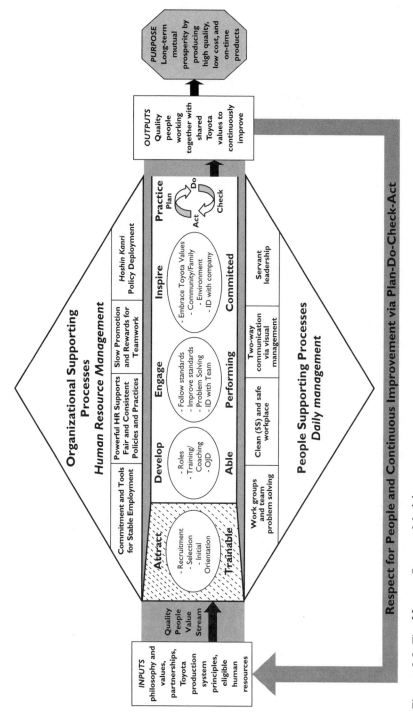

**Figure 2.3** The Human Systems Model

- add value to customers and society,
- contribute to the economic growth of communities and countries in which we do business,
- contribute to the stability and well being of team members, and
- contribute to the overall growth of Toyota.

In a sense, we could argue that every organization has a basic understanding of its purpose—it wants to be successful. And a for-profit company quite simply wants to make a profit, with the understanding that a bigger profit is better. But mere profit accruement is not the end of the story for Toyota. Toyota thinks long term, viewing profits as a means to long-term mutual prosperity for all stakeholders in both the company and the communities in which it does business, but it also knows that profits are the result of competitive advantage. The competitive advantage comes from doing an exceptional job of adding value to society, and to achieve this, the people value stream must produce key outputs: quality people producing high-quality, low-cost, and on-time products.

The inputs to the Toyota Way culture are its:

- philosophy
- values
- partnerships
- production system principles
- job competencies, and
- eligible human resources.

Toyota never leaves it up to the human resource department in a local operation to hire and develop people in isolation. The way people are selected and developed, rather, is very much influenced by the broader culture of the organization. And, as we discussed in Chapter 1, the last thing Toyota wants to leave to chance is its culture, so it has invested heavily in ensuring that its philosophy and shared values shape the way employees are selected and developed so that they learn from and reinforce the company's culture. Partnerships are developed over decades and become an input that influences the employee selection and development process. As a result, employees enter into a broad network of established relationships.

## The Core People Value Stream

In the product value stream, we start with the customer and ask what the customer is willing to pay for. We then follow the flow of material and information and distinguish value-added work from waste.[2] In the people value stream, we

---

[2] Rother, Mike and John Shook, *Learning to See*, Cambridge, MA: Lean Enterprise Institute, 1998.

can still ask what the customer is willing to pay for but then add: What are the employee characteristics we know will result in our giving customers what they are willing to pay for? At a minimum, we need to develop people who are capable of doing the necessary core value-added tasks, whether these are manual tasks, running machinery, or core knowledge work, like engineering tasks. Beyond doing the work, these same people have another role to perform that is just as critical, and that is to improve the process. As a result, we judge value added as those processes that lead to "quality people producing high-quality, low-cost, and on-time products." To accomplish this, we argue that the value-added steps are:

1. **Attracting** people with the right characteristics who are trainable and can contribute to the value-adding processes.
2. **Developing** those people so that they have the capability to do quality work every day.
3. **Engaging** the people so that they go beyond doing the work to improving how the work is done through rigorous problem solving.
4. **Inspiring** the people so that they are committed to the organization and will continue to learn, grow, and do their best for the customer, community, and society.

Think of these as the value-adding steps and then ask yourself: "Over the span of our employees' careers, how often is value being added by our company?" If—from the point of view of the person entering the value stream—there is activity to attract, develop, engage, or inspire them to achieve the goal for the customer, the people value stream is adding value. Everything else is waste from the point of view of this value stream. Of course, other activities are adding value in the product value stream, but the focus now is just on the people value stream. How much value is being added to your people value stream? If you put a limited effort into attracting people, give them limited training when they first enter the organization, do little to engage and inspire them other than put them to work and monitor whether they follow the rules, then the value-added percent is likely to be very low. At Toyota, people do many tasks on a daily basis that simply have to be done. Not all of these tasks develop, engage, or inspire them, but we believe the value-added percent is high compared to other organizations although this has never been measured.

While the analogy of value stream mapping is helpful in and of itself, it should be carried one step further so that you can develop a future state map for your company. First grasp your current situation, then develop a vision of where you want to be, and finally develop a plan to close the gap. Toyota's human systems model can help guide your future-state vision.

## People-Supporting Processes and Daily Management

There are many systems in place to support team members as they are developing
to become committed members of Toyota. One might think that developing team
members is the function of the training department which puts together a schedule of classes, but Toyota's history is rooted in learning by doing what is taught on
the job by highly skilled mentors. It is more of a craft-based system. Intimate daily
contact is the way the apprentice is trained. Similarly throughout Toyota new hires
are immersed in living the Toyota Way daily through involvement in work groups,
in a clean and safe environment, with intense communication, and guided by
leaders who are there to support and teach:

1. **Work Groups and Team Problem Solving**—At Toyota the old adage
   "ALL of us are smarter than any of us" is truly practiced on a daily basis.
   Many companies have taught problem solving and have groups that meet
   periodically to make improvements, but Toyota has integrated this into the
   daily management system. Getting the right people together to solve a
   problem is the way much of the work gets done in engineering, sales,
   finance, and in the factory. People are organized into work teams with
   team leaders and review daily progress, taking problems as opportunities
   for kaizen.

2. **Clean and Safe Workplace**—Leaders must articulate and reinforce their
   commitment to a healthy and secure work environment. This starts with
   a health and safety system that reflects company policy and compliance
   with laws and regulations. The bigger issue is to put in place systems to
   prevent health and safety problems and then respond rapidly to health
   and safety issues and accidents. Like Toyota, your company could implement a variety of formal mechanisms, such as health and safety committees that respond within the same day that a health or safety issue mate-
   rializes. In addition, leaders must promote preventive safety measures,
   safety awareness, and ergonomics awareness that alert team members to
   abnormalities with potential health and safety consequences.

3. **Two-Way Communication and Visual Management**—Toyota leaders
   work continuously to ensure open channels of communication throughout the team by emphasizing the key values of mutual trust and respect,
   sharing the management point of view, and encouraging team members to
   participate in team activities and share their ideas. There are a variety of
   mechanisms we will discuss for formal face-to-face communication, and
   we will also emphasize the principle that all leaders should manage from
   where the work is done, not an isolated office.

4. **Servant Leadership**—Compared to traditional organizations, Toyota's organizational chart stands on its head. Put the core value-added worker at the top and it is a better representation than the top-down structure we are used to seeing in most corporate organization charts. Leaders coach, teach, and support the members of the work force that are doing the value-added work. In other words, they serve the team. They do this by clarifying and reinforcing common goals, specifying and integrating team roles and job tasks, articulating standardized work, providing training for required job competencies, scheduling regular team meetings for supplying timely information, assisting in resolving issues, and ensuring earned recognition.

## The Organizational-Supporting Processes and the Role of HR

Once you have developed your future-state value stream flow, you need to identify the formal systems required to support this flow. Often these are represented on a product value stream map as kaizen bursts, which represent specific supporting process improvements (kaizen) needed. The organizational supporting processes to a large degree fall under the auspices of the human resources (HR) department.

The roles and responsibilities of the HR department are multifaceted, and its function at Toyota goes way beyond hiring people and administering policies related to pay, promotion, and benefits. It seems that in many companies the role of HR is largely to act as people accounting systems. Indeed now there are technical service companies that will allow you to "outsource your HR function" to save money which basically denigrates HR to a computer systems function.

At Toyota, HR does much more than manage databases and it is certainly not a function that can be outsourced. In fact, since people are so integral to its management philosophy, HR is one of the most important and powerful departments in the company. HR managers typically enter the department by way of other job rotations, such as production management and production control, so that they have an understanding of the core value-adding processes. As evidence of its influence within the company, Toyota has intertwined HR with its production management department, and as such, HR is involved in daily concerns of team members on the shop floor. In fact at Toyota no one can be promoted or get a raise without HR approval. They are not simply administering procedures manuals; they are intimately involved with the career paths of all employees, and they must know the people personally and understand in detail their performance and career paths. What's more, HR at Toyota is considered to be every manager's job. The role of HR is to partner with manufacturing while facilitating ownership by manufacturing. Let's consider each of the organizational supporting processes that HR facilitates:

1. **Commitment and Tools for Stable Employment**—Stable employment is the foundation of Toyota's commitment that team members are its most important resource and investing in team member development is a top priority. It is well understood throughout Toyota that, short of an economic catastrophe for the entire company, like that of the late 1940s, employees will not be laid off. This provides a safety net that allows team members to safely participate in continuous improvement, even when the project is focused on eliminating positions to improve productivity. The HR department at Toyota is the company's key aid in providing this job security due to its prowess in stable employment management. It has developed sophisticated methods to predict labor needs and uses temporary work forces (not guaranteed employment security) as a flexible shock absorber against natural economic cycles.

2. **Fair and Consistent HR Policies and Practices**—Obviously HR strives to infuse fairness into all of its policies and actions, but this common company mission statement takes on a different meaning at Toyota. If you were to follow HR representatives at Toyota around and watch what they actually do, you immediately would discern the Toyota difference. While employees stationed within most companies' HR departments might spend the majority of their time in front of a computer screen or answering the phone, at Toyota, HR representatives roam throughout its many departments to keep abreast of the latest company happenings. This is referred to as *genchi genbutsu* within Toyota, which means going to the actual place where the work is done to see and understand company situations firsthand. Disciplinary issues, employee dissatisfaction, kaizen promotion, and employee career progression are just a few of HR's responsibilities. HR representatives must always be visible to team members and aware of what is really going on in the workplace. To ensure fair and consistent HR practices, Toyota employees cannot be promoted or given pay raises without HR approval. If employee pay and promotion is left solely to the discretion of supervisors and managers, which in most companies is the case, then individual differences in understanding of company promotion policies will cause variation in their administration and consequently low employee morale and lack of trust.

3. **Slow Promotion and Rewards for Teamwork**—Becoming a Toyota leader does not happen overnight. It is as much a maturation of the individual as it is a set of management tools and techniques. People mature in their self-confidence and interpersonal sensitivity at different rates but for all people it takes time—years and even decades. Since Toyota views the employer-employee bond as a long-term relationship the company is willing to be patient and allow each person to mature and grow into the level of leadership that fits their capability. In turn they expect the

individual to have patience and take any position as an opportunity to learn and grow. Teamwork is more highly valued than seeking to stand out as an individual genius. The individual who needs to be fast tracked through the company and get lots of individual recognition will not be a good fit in the Toyota environment.

4. *Hoshin-Kanri* (**Policy Deployment**)—Developing people so they learn how to solve problems and continually improve the work is a marvelous asset, but how does this energy and creativity get directed toward a common goal. Much of Toyota's continuous improvement is driven by hoshin-kanri, also referred to as policy deployment, which is a system of setting objectives for improvement, starting at the very top of Toyota and coming to agreements at every level down to the team member. Each employee has a hoshin, which is defined as specific measurable objectives that are reviewed throughout the year. When all team members feel like they are a valued long-term part of a team whose fate is tied to the fate of the company, hoshin-kanri is a powerful mechanism for converting their energy into exceptional levels of performance.

# THE MODEL IS NOT A SILVER BULLET—IT IS WHAT YOU DO EVERY DAY

We would like to say, "Study the model, implement each of the constructs in your organization, and then sit back and watch people get healthy and wealthy." If only it were that simple. The model is not something that can be quickly implemented, like issuing a policy manual or installing a computer system. It is a living process that comes from decades of learning, evolving, and growing.

Unfortunately we observe all too often that smart and insightful people who can solve real-world problems with laser sharp accuracy become clouded in their thinking and judgment when envisioning a new program. The phrase "program of the month" comes from senior management, which dreams up new programs that get superficially implemented at the artifact level and never become part of the deeper culture. What does penetrate deeply into the culture are the provisional mindsets that programs come and go and that the managers who buy into programs with the help of outside consultants are not to be trusted. The operative word here is "dream." The programs are dreams, not reality.

We must reemphasize that Toyota is made up of people, and since people are not perfect, not every action of every person every day supports the human systems model. But the correlation between what Toyota says are its values and what leaders in the company actually do is remarkably high compared to other organizations that we have experienced. The spirit of *genchi genbutsu* is to go and actually see the current reality, without preconceptions. That applies to the culture. Leaders at Toyota must be brutally honest about the reality of the culture and what needs to be improved. Problem solving applies as much to problems of culture as to product quality issues.

This book is about bringing your reality closer to the ideal of your desired future state by:

- Developing your people value stream to increase the value-added time in which people learn and develop job and leadership skills.
- Evolving the people supporting processes so people are coached, taught, and engaged every day in continuous improvement and learning.
- Putting in place the organizational supporting processes to enable development of a healthy culture supporting the development of quality people.
- Integrating the product value stream and people value streams through your lean production principles so you can achieve long-term competitive advantage and mutual prosperity.

## SUMMARY

Toyota is known for its famed "Toyota Production System" and companies all over the world are working to "implement" the system in their organizations. In most cases the results are impressive in spots but are overall disappointing. What they are missing is a strong "human system" which for Toyota is the key ingredient to long-term competitiveness. The technical and social systems work together to create a culture of teams working to solve problems. The tools of the production system are designed to expose problems, while the human systems are designed to attract, develop, engage and inspire people to solve those problems. The "Human Systems Model", while not a silver bullet, is a depiction of how all the factors come together to create Toyota culture.

## KEY POINTS TO CONSIDER
## FOR YOUR COMPANY

1. Toyota's production systems are designed to "expose problems" and are a means to the end, and not the end.
2. Toyota's human systems have a "core value stream" that seeks to add value to every member of the organization.
3. Everyone understands and acts upon the purpose of "mutual long term prosperity."

4. Problem solving is the focus of the organization, with people feeling comfortable to admit they have a problem.
5. People are supported in problem solving and learning by committed and knowledgeable leaders and daily management systems.
6. HR systems are designed and implemented to support both the production and the people value streams.

# Chapter 3

# Toyota Way + Local Environment + Purpose = Success

*A business that makes nothing but money is a poor business.*

—Henry Ford, innovating automaker

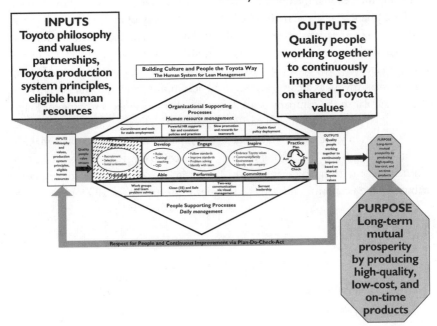

**INPUTS**
Toyota philosophy and values, partnerships, Toyota production system principles, eligible human resources

**OUTPUTS**
Quality people working together to continuously improve based on shared Toyota values

**PURPOSE**
Long-term mutual prosperity by producing high-quality, low-cost, and on-time products

## PURPOSE—WHY ARE WE HERE?

What is the purpose of the corporation? Why do employees come to work? These are very basic questions with very obvious answers. A private corporation exists to make money and the employee comes to work to make money. What binds them together is unbridled self-interest. We can look at basic economic theories, Taylorism, and even Marxism, and they all make the same assumption: the employer-employee relationship is a simple business transaction. Traditional economists, starting with Adam Smith, the author of the seminal economic treatise *The Wealth of Nations*, assumed the mutual advantage of this business relationship for management and the worker. Marxists, on the other hand, would say a capitalist company will always exploit the worker and that manager-worker relationships are thereby inherently fraught with conflict.

Frederick W. Taylor, father of scientific management, believed that the relationship is often characterized by uninformed management mistreating and misusing workers, but he allowed for the possibility that if managers are enlightened by scientific thinking, they can increase productivity and share more profit with the workers, which creates a win-win situation for employer and employee. Regardless of their differences, all three perspectives assume the relationship is solely a matter of economic self-interest for all involved parties.

Toyota leaders maintain a very different perspective from those of the economic forefathers and presuppose that there are reasons other than financial gain that companies exist and employees come to work. Employers and employees alike still have financial goals, certainly, but there are a variety of things that each party desires from the relationship beyond money. Ask Toyota employees at any level in the organization what they hope to get out of their jobs, and you will get many common answers akin to those listed as employee goals in Figure 3.1. Ask Toyota leaders what Toyota as a company wants to accomplish, and you will get answers that are similar to the company goals. What ties them together is striving for long-term mutual prosperity, but each party has goals that go far beyond making money.

It is certainly the case that Toyota as a company, wants and needs to make a profit, but that is not the driving purpose of the company. Rather, Toyota leaders will tell you the company exists to satisfy customers, contribute to society, contribute to the economy, and achieve long-term prosperity for all employees and

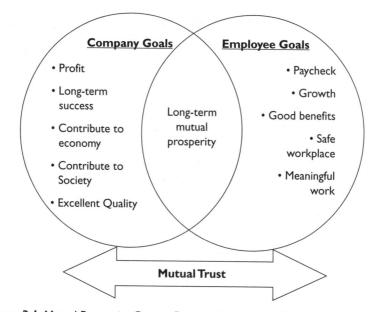

**Figure 3.1** Mutual Prosperity Creates Partnership between Company and Employee

**Figure 3.2** A Partnership between an Organization and its Employees

partners. Employees, too, expect the minimums of a paycheck and benefits, but they also desire the personal growth that comes from a lifetime of working in a positive environment. They want to continue learning, develop new capabilities, and work for a company that is making a positive difference in society. When we add up the interests of each party, the common purpose is long-term prosperity for team members, the company, and society.

Figure 3.2 illustrates the respective roles of the company and its employees in this partnership. Simply put, Toyota's goal is that its employees contribute their best effort to the achievement of the purpose and prosperity of the company and then take their fair share in compensation. In the process the employees achieve growth and satisfaction by participating actively in continuous improvement. Mutual trust is the bond that turns the individual goals of the company and the employees into a partnership.

Kiyoshi (Nate) Furuta was assigned to head up human resources at the start up of NUMMI (New United Motors Manufacturing, Inc.), Toyota's joint venture with General Motors in Fremont, California. Toyota was in the midst of dealing with American labor unions—and in particular, a militant chapter of the local United Auto Workers (UAW)—for the first time. Furuta spent time to personally get to know the new NUMMI employees and listened carefully to understand their needs and desires. Furuta knew instinctively that talks and negotiations between the organization and the union had to start by defining the purpose of the relationship and their respective roles and responsibilities.

In a personal interview with Furuta, he explained:

*We went back and forth many times. We had a preliminary letter of intent. It described some of the essentials, like the production standards and mutual trust (which is the most difficult concept). If unions had to fight, we wanted it to be against management and not mutual trust. The union, management, and workers each have responsibilities. The union must cooperate with management to increase productivity—the most basic concept. In exchange, we said if there was a difficult time, we would suffer first—management, not the employee. In a long, fiscally difficult time, we will cut the salary of management first. Then we pull in previously outsourced jobs, and then think about reducing the workforce. We cannot promise job security. The union then accepted cooperation to improve productivity.*

In this interview, Furuta explained that both parties initially had to agree that increased productivity was necessary in order to achieve mutual prosperity. He also went a step further and promised that management would suffer before its team members because it is management's role and responsibility to provide stable employment. He described how the company and the union arrived at a sense of mutual trust, which served as the necessary foundation that the remainder of the negotiations was built upon. And Furuta kept his promise: Shortly after startup, sales dropped by almost 30 percent. Management did not lay off a single employee, but rather put them to work on making improvements and got a state grant to further train the team members.

We have asked managers from other companies many times whether it is a good investment to keep highly paid people employed painting floors, doing small improvement projects, and training during months when sales are down. The common answer is "it depends on the business case." Toyota's leaders did not calculate the costs and benefits at NUMMI; they simply lived up to their commitment of providing job security for their workers. And what did they get in return?

The first benefit was loyal employees for many years. After several months, Toyota took action (rushing a new Toyota Corolla into the lineup) which raised sales up to their projected levels and eventually far surpassed the initial projections. If Toyota had laid off employees during the downturn, it would have been forced to hire new employees and, in a sense, restart the company to develop the new workers and win their trust. Instead, Toyota already had a highly loyal, well-trained workforce that trusted the company.

The second benefit was that the company's leaders showed by example to Toyota employees throughout the world that Toyota lives up to its commitments and values team members. Layoffs in the Freemont, California branch would have destroyed the trust and member commitment in Toyota's operations throughout the world. When you clearly understand Toyota's long-term focus, the business case seems pretty obvious.

# OUTPUTS—QUALITY PEOPLE WORKING TOGETHER TO CONTINUOUSLY IMPROVE BASED ON SHARED TOYOTA VALUES

If a core belief of the Toyota culture is that "we build people and cars simultaneously, using the Toyota Way," one of the outputs of this process should be "Quality People." How does Toyota define a quality person? If we look back at the way team members are developed, as defined in the Human System Model (Figure 2.3), we get a holistic view of the characteristics that go into Toyota's idea of a quality person. As we see in the people value stream, a quality person is trainable, able to perform in a team, follows and improves upon standards, is inspired by the company culture and objectives, and contributes positively to family and the community. We have worked with many organizations and one thing is certain—there are some high "quality people" working at every company we visit. The differences at Toyota are the pervasiveness of quality people and the strength of their cultural bonds. Toyota puts as much effort into developing quality in people as it does in creating zero defect products. The results are a large majority of quality people who define and sustain the Toyota Way culture.

## Quality People Lead to Quality Results

The human systems model assumes that investments in the quality people value stream pay off in competitive advantage and long-term mutual prosperity. This suggests that building the right culture leads to the necessary business results for success. In a personal interview, former senior vice president for manufacturing, Toyota North America, Gary Convis, said:

> Most people see Toyota's success as using TPS to minimize cost and build quality into the processes. There is some truth to this, but the engine that drives it is Toyota culture. It is so powerful. There are no KPIs (Key Performance Indicators) where you can measure the degree of reinforcement and support for this key part of the cultural existence, but it is there. It is so consistent and so fundamental. It is the lifeblood of what makes us so successful.

There is an element of faith in Toyota's investment in its people. *The Toyota Way*[1] described Toyota's faith in its TPS processes in this way: "The right process will produce the right results." We can extend this belief to the people value stream—investing in developing people the right way will lead to the right results.

---

[1] Liker, Jeffrey, *The Toyota Way*, New York: McGraw-Hill, 2004.

If Toyota had a narrow and short-term view of its goals, it probably wouldn't place as much faith in the value of investing in its people. For example, if the goal was to maximize profits every quarter, Toyota would combat a drop in revenues with reduced costs by eliminating both jobs and training investments. At Toyota, however, the drive for perfection is directed into five outlets: safety, quality, cost, delivery, and morale (SQCDM). From day one, every employee is reminded that if together as a company they can accomplish these goals, they will be taking another step toward fulfilling the purpose of long-term mutual prosperity. This is where the people value stream and the product value stream come together.

The need to achieve targets for all these factors—SQCDM—is central to Toyota culture, and it is tracked daily. Developing a culture that can sustain all five of these KPIs at once is a significant challenge. In fact, early in the launch of a new plant, the primary focus of Toyota's management for at least three years has been safety and quality. Toyota views a new plant like a baby that must be carefully nurtured and grown. For its first three years it is protected from too much pressure by the "mother plant" assigned to help grow it. In these first three or more years, the plant will make only one product and the volume will be relatively low and very steady. There will not be pressure for cost reductions. As the plant matures, challenges to add products, add volume, and decrease cost will be added.

## Launch a New Culture with an Obsession for Quality

Toyota Motor Manufacturing in Georgetown, Kentucky (TMMK) illustrates how when a plant starts up the focus is almost one dimensional on quality. Over time, the focus is broadened out, but at start up it was almost obsessive. Employees and managers alike were intent not only on doing their jobs to standard, but on inspecting every car for any possible defect that could affect the customer. There was a gung-ho attitude and every individual was expected to stop the line for every question even if it meant crippling the plant. Team members were pulling the andon cord for everything. Every spec, every gap was suspect to "eagle-eyed" members. The Japanese trainers patiently taught team members to think beyond minimal customer specifications. For example, if the customer requires a minimum three millimeter gap around the glove box, the inspection standard could be set at two millimeters. That means we pull the andon if it is 2.5 millimeters even though it is technically within specification.

The Japanese trainers through their words and deeds continually demonstrated that quality comes first. There was a time in the first year of building the new Camry when a "possible loose bolt" on a front suspension was identified by a team member. He was doing a tightness check on a machine and discovered a malfunction on the alarm system that monitored proper bolt tightness. The team member did as he was taught and pulled the andon to alert the team leader of the potential problem. The line came to a stop, and the team leader used a tool to check tightness on some of the cars that had passed the equipment prior to detecting the problem. The bolts were all in the proper range of tightness.

By this time the Japanese trainer had come to the problem area, alerted by the andon signal and the stopped line. He coached the team leader and now the group leader in the Toyota problem-solving method, emphasizing that no "suspect cars" ever make it to a customer. The trainer worked with his subordinates to determine the "suspect range." The bolt in question was a critical control item, so it was measured by the team leader using Statistical Process Control (SPC) methods. A sample of five cars was measured for each shift, and the average and range of the results were tracked. The last measurement had been done during the prior shift, but there was still almost two hours worth of cars built afterwards. Meanwhile, the problem was not found until almost an hour into the next shift, so there was almost three hours' worth of suspect cars.

Each vehicle built has a "sequence number," so a list of the 180 cars was printed and a unit of team and group leaders was assembled to find each of the 180 cars listed and measure and confirm the tightness of each bolt. All of the 80 cars that were still on the assembly line were checked and found to be OK. The unit of team and group leaders confirmed the production equipment was in proper functioning order and the line was restarted. Meanwhile, the search for the other 100 cars continued. Some of the cars were being checked in off-line inspection areas for other issues, such as water leaks and paint quality. These cars were all checked and also found to be alright.

By this time, the production control department had discovered the same defect that the team had detected. Unfortunately, about 25 cars had already been shipped to Toyota Motor Sales. Production control was immediately informed, and all outgoing shipping trucks and trains were stopped so that a team of "tightness checkers" could track down the remaining 25 cars. At the end of the day, a grand total of zero defective bolts were found. All of this effort took place because of "possible defects," which led some American managers to question the decision to halt Toyota's shipping fleets for "only 25 cars" when 155 out of the first 180 cars checked out okay. The Japanese made it very clear that it was not an option to think they were alright based on statistical probability; they would not stop until they **knew** that 100 percent were alright.

Many people ask the question, "How did Toyota establish this 'culture of Quality First' in its American plants?" During the first three years of the ramp-up of the Georgetown plant, the entire focus of Japanese management was on safety and quality, but that did not mean that the new American workforce would be able to grasp that right away. There still seemed to be an innate American drive for competition and for "going fast." At the beginning of production launch in 1988, the plant started building literally just one car a day to ensure that its quality was comparable to that of the Camrys being built in Japan. Once that was confirmed, the plant increased production to two a day, and on each subsequent day, if the production quality was confirmed to meet Toyota standards, the number was increased. It took this type of dramatic demonstration and absolute consistency of direction over several years to deeply imprint the Americans with quality consciousness.

## Stopping the Line Is Everyone's Responsibility

One day toward the end of the ramp-up of production for a new model there was a problem with getting the correct gap around the glove box door. Thinking back to the prior example of the customer requirement determined to be a three millimeter gap, with the Toyota standard being set at two millimeters, in this case the actual condition on the car coming out of the process was four millimeters and out of standard. The team member installing the glove box door was informed of the problem, but the problem kept coming out of the process. The team member was observed and was following every step of the standardized work to the letter with one exception—he had noticed the gap was a little off but chose not to pull the andon. Apparently he did not want to slow the line down and thought it was no big deal. Because of this decision, the whole line filled with cars that had glove box doors with gaps larger than two millimeters.

Soon, the final assembly line shut down completely, and it wasn't long before every line in the entire plant came to a complete standstill. All of the group leaders in the assembly plant were called over to the end of the line to see the cars with defective glove boxes parked at the end of the line. This simple little gap had shut down the whole line. At a Toyota production line there is an in-line inspection station where the quality standards are confirmed. When the cars with the problematic glove boxes got there and were found to be out of standard, the inspectors marked it on a ticket in order for it to be repaired. Toyota sets up a small number of off-line repair spots. When these spots become full, the line and the next car that needs repair has no where to go, so the line is stopped.

The Japanese trainers taught all the group leaders an important lesson that day about the importance of quality and the Toyota Production System that is set up to ensure it. That day, there were 500 team members doing their best to maintain high quality and build as many cars as possible. Because one team member failed to use the andon to confirm the quality of his part because he did not want to slow down the line, he ended up stopping the entire line anyway. The stopping of the line alerted everyone in the plant to the issue and all of the right resources were able to come together back at the process in order to work to solve the problem. All the group leaders went back and shared this valuable lesson with their groups. The culture established by Toyota was one where employees felt safe to pull the andon, even if so doing shut down the entire plant, because in fact, if they didn't pull it, the plant would shut down anyway if the problem persisted without attention. The message that everyone got that day was clear, at Toyota, quality was indeed more important than production.

## One Step and Then Another

Once the Toyota leaders at TMMK were able to confirm that there was a total commitment to quality, and it had indeed become part of the culture, they were able to start increasing the expectations to include the other key business indicators. After a full two years the leaders were able to start introducing the concepts of productivity and cost improvements into the picture. If a group was meeting their quality goals, then they were given the goal to do so within a certain limit on downtime of the line. This transition was done with constant coaching from the Japanese to continue to put quality first and to not hesitate to pull the andon and stop the line if quality was in jeopardy. In the meantime, this was always being checked by having the fixed amount of repair parking spaces off-line, so that when they were filled the line would stop anyway. Even this off-line repair area was in a state of constant improvement. When the plant started there were enough spaces to hold 10 cars at a time. As the quality from the team members continued to improve, the Japanese trainers kept challenging the plant to get even better and reduced the number of spaces to eight and then six.

The continuous improvement maturation process finally included all aspects of the production system. Once a group or plant was able to hit its safety, quality, and downtime goals (which took another year in the maturation process), it was given the challenge of reducing the number of processes needed to do so. This reduced the number of team members needed to build a car and resulted in lowering the cost of producing the car. It took almost two years before this process became part of the culture. Half of the battle was teaching team members how to identify and eliminate waste, as well as how to work as a team to do so, while the other half was getting them to trust in the promise that nobody would ever "improve themselves out of a job."

Over the years as TMMK matured, the challenges kept coming. Supplier and material-handling issues were identified by continuously reducing the amount of inventory of parts. In-process stock and buffers were repeatedly reduced, while the number of different types of vehicles and their complexity of build kept on increasing. Toyota team members were being integrated into the Toyota culture of continuous improvement, which includes all the areas represented in the "human systems model."

# THE INPUTS TO THE ORGANIZATION

If we think about the launch of a new plant and how Toyota goes through the process of hiring and creating quality people and teams, it may seem as though that plant is operating in isolation. But while they are developing people from scratch, Toyota has the benefit of a rich history and highly developed culture at the company level that creates many inputs, or influences, on how the particular culture develops in a new plant. If we think in terms of the three levels of culture (Figure 1–2), many company-wide processes immediately get passed on to the new organization at the following levels: basic assumptions of the Toyota Way; norms and values; and artifacts and behavior. We will now focus on three key inputs to the development of Toyota culture in a new location: Toyota philosophy and values; production system principles; and how Toyota even influences eligible people to hire. These inputs shape the experience of team members as they enter the organization and as they live and grow throughout their careers.

## Philosophy and Values

We have discussed some of the history that produced Toyota's philosophy and values, and even more background is provided in *The Toyota Way*.[2] After near bankruptcy in the 1940s, Toyota's commitment to developing a financially self-sufficient, layoff-free environment established a foundation for the culture that we see today. These commitments became the fundamental values of mutual respect and continuous improvement upon which the Toyota Way is built, but there are other values and philosophies that are important to the Toyota culture. For example, beliefs such as "long-term outlook" for supplier and employee relationships, every worker is an inspector, the team member is the expert, and supervisors work for their members are all values or philosophies that make up Toyota culture.

More recently, these philosophies and values were written down, some for the first time, under the leadership of former Toyota President Fujio Cho. He explains in the foreword to *The Toyota Way 2001:*

> We have identified and defined the company's fundamental DNA, which summarizes the unique and outstanding elements of our company culture and success. These are the managerial values and business methods that are known collectively as the Toyota Way. It is essential that our global leadership team embrace the concepts of the Toyota Way as we achieve our business goals in host countries that have a wide variety of customs, traditions and business practices. I urge every Toyota team member all over the world to take professional and

[2] Liker, Jeffrey, *The Toyota Way*, New York: McGraw-Hill, 2004.

*personal responsibility for advancing the understanding and acceptance of the*
*Toyota Way.*

As we will see in Chapter 11, Toyota culture finds its origins in the Toyota leaders who live and teach its philosophy. All Toyota managers must go through intensive training in the Toyota Way values, with both formal classroom training and on-the-job mentoring. These managers then become the teachers and coaches for all employees down to and including team leaders, who serve as key links between management and hourly employees.

If Toyota spends years developing leaders who live its philosophy and gives new plant startups three or more years to establish a basic culture of quality, we have to wonder about companies who think developing a greenfield plant is easy. These companies do not start off with Toyota's strong foundations of rock solid culture and leadership, and are thus at a serious disadvantage. Without that strong foundation, we would expect it would take even longer than three years to establish a basic quality culture.

## Production System Principles

Just as new employees enter their particular branch of Toyota under the tutelage of key leaders who have extensive experience working in the Toyota Way, they also walk into an operation that is set up with a very defined set of operating principles. As previously discussed, the people value stream depends on the product value stream, and vice versa. For this reason, it is important to recognize the TPS tools as an input to the people value stream. TPS is sometimes thought of as a set of techniques, like Just-in-Time, but in reality it represents deeply held beliefs about how to develop operational excellence.

The production-side principles are well known:

1. Just-in-Time—holding as little inventory as possible.
2. Pull System Production—letting demand for orders pull production rather than pushing production at the customer.
3. Profit by Cost Control—letting the market define reasonable selling prices and making a profit by controlling the difference between production costs and selling price.
4. Built-in Quality—catching defects as soon as they are created or seen, then addressing them at that point rather than at the end of the line.
5. Flexible Workforce—maintaining flexibility and motivation in the workforce to enable quick response to changes in market demand. It also involves using techniques such as standardization of process, visual control, cross-training, rotation, and broad job classifications with consistent pay to make shifting of resources possible.

*The Toyota Way Fieldbook*[3] goes into detail about the tools and methods of TPS and emphasizes that TPS is a way of thinking about how to set up an operation and how to continually improve that operation. The production system principles become a way of organizing operations and paint a vision of what the operation should ideally look like.

While "the never-ending pursuit of excellence" makes a good advertising slogan, it really does accurately portray the culture at Toyota. Hiro Yoshiki, former Vice President of General Administration and Senior Advisor of TMMK, explains in a personal interview how this attitude was passed down from Ohno.

*His attitude was to "keep trying to find the problems." His impossible dream was to obtain the manufacturing operation "that God created," where everything runs smooth[ly] and there is no inventory, no safety or quality issues, and no mental stress. To reach a little closer to the dream is to find every improvement opportunity and work on getting to the manufacturing heaven.*

Hajime Ohba is the former director of the Toyota Supplier Support Center, which was originally established to provide free TPS support to American companies. A student of Ohno, Ohba wanted to continue in Ohno's tradition of foregoing satisfaction until Toyota reached manufacturing heaven. One of Ohba's first clients, Summit Polymers, a company that makes various small interior plastic parts for Toyota, continued as one of his star students for over 15 years. After many years of teaching TPS to Summit Polymers, Ohba visited one of its plants in Kalamazoo, Michigan to check up on its progress. The plant's staff members were proud of their many accomplishments, including some recent automation, pull systems, production leveling, and many examples of visual management. Ohba looked at—but did not respond to—all of the plant's big accomplishments. Instead he asked them to look down the aisle at the parts flow racks and tell him what the problem was. After receiving a series of blank looks, he pointed out that the racks were not all level with the aisle line that was painted on the floor as a visual indicator for parts delivery people. Not only did this create an unorganized "visual management" system, but it also caused the parts delivery person extra work, even if the rack was only one foot off the line. This is a fine example of the way Ohba worked to focus his students on the tiniest details in the pursuit of "manufacturing heaven."

As discussed in Chapter 2, TPS was designed to identify and highlight production problems. It makes sense, then, that both Toyota's management principles and its ways of doing business are centered on solving problems via employee

---

[3] Liker, Jeffrey and David Meier, *The Toyota Way Fieldbook*, New York: McGraw-Hill, 2006.

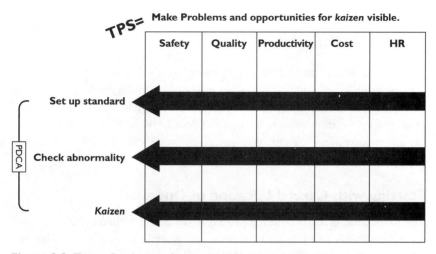

**Figure 3.3** Toyota Production System highlights problems

engagement. If TPS highlights problems, people are needed to solve them. Figure 3.3 illustrates how the "toolkit" of the Toyota Production System leads to establishing visual standards, surfacing problems, and engaging people in solving those problems. This is why continuous improvement—or kaizen—is a core value for Toyota. Without kaizen the tools of TPS would be useless.

In Toyota culture, the way to think about problems and the continual drive for perfection is inclusive of even the smallest details and is never-ending. It becomes a way of thinking and looking at things in a certain way. The following is an example, from a visit by Mike Hoseus to one of Toyota's plants in Japan illustrating that even the smallest of details matters.

> *On a visit to Japan, I was touring through an office at a Toyota plant and the supervisor wanted to show me an example of a suggestion that an administrative assistant had just implemented. He took me to her desk and grabbed a Number Two wooden pencil. He asked me, "What do you do with the pencil after you work your way down and there is only a couple of inches left?" Being quick on my feet and showing my "knowledge of waste elimination," I responded, "I use it all the way down to where I can no longer hold it with my fingers, and then I throw it away." He said, "Exactly. That is what most do." But then he opened the drawer and had the assistant proudly display the collection of pencils that had two of the "no-longer-usable" pencils taped together in order to get the use of another couple of inches of lead. I was impressed. Here was one of the richest companies in the world taping pencils together for another inch of lead. On the way out, my trainer commented, "Think of the power of your organization when you have all members thinking like this."*

# CREATING A POOL OF ELIGIBLE HUMAN RESOURCES

The final input into the Toyota people value stream that we will discuss is the available pool of human resources. What is unique to Toyota is how proactive it is in creating and nurturing this pool. It does not simply build a plant and then wait until prospective employees show up at the door to begin hiring. Rather, Toyota has a very intentional and strategic process to create and maintain this pool of eligible workers.

## Starting with Careful Location of Operation

The foundation of Toyota's hiring process stems from its philosophy that it will grow and prosper as a company from internal growth. Its strategy is to become number one by growing internally rather than "buying" other, external companies. This allows Toyota to start from scratch in a new area (known as a greenfield operation) and create the Toyota culture from the ground up. Many people studying lean manufacturing and Toyota have correctly observed that it is a lot easier to create a culture than to change an existing one. This is certainly true and for this reason Toyota works very hard to take this opportunity to create the right culture from the beginning.

The first step of the process is to select a site on which to build a plant. When Toyota was deciding where to locate its first completely-owned assembly plant in the United States, it had the whole country to choose from. Hiroyoshi Yoshiki was a member of the site selection team, and he explained why they chose Georgetown, Kentucky:

*Why Georgetown? Logistics was a big factor. We wanted to be along the automotive road from Detroit and to be near the many parts suppliers along Interstate 75 and 64, which went right by Georgetown. There were other good candidates, like Tennessee, and we recommended some finalists by considering work force, closeness to Interstate 75, closeness to supply base, and...distance from the traditional auto industry home....And we wanted to start a greenfield. We thought a clean, fresh workforce would be better. We understood the challenge in finding enough qualified candidates in the skilled area, but we took that risk. We started from nothing but thought that it was better to instill basic principles and practices into people who did not have past experience and knowledge.*

*We understood from the NUMMI experience that we could work with a union, but also experienced lots of things we had not known. There were several things we wanted to do at the NUMMI plant that we could not do...because of the union. For example, we did have success with flexibility by being able to reduce job classifications down to three, but we still had bumping issues through seniority. We wanted to have a good workforce with maximum flexibility in training and assignments. If we have to follow seniority, management cannot pick the best person for the job.*

*We also liked central Kentucky. It was a rural area, and the feeling was that this area was not well developed, so people were hungry for better jobs. The Kentucky government was eager to attract Toyota, so incentives played a certain role. We visited and ate at local restaurants, and people came up to us to say they wanted to work for Toyota. Some people attacked state government and asked, "Why give away tax money to a foreign company?" But we found people friendly here with a good work ethic, especially with the area being high in farming. Agriculture is hard work, day and night.*

Toyota had the luxury of a new plant start-up—a greenfield operation; it was able to start from scratch with the workforce. As Yoshiki mentioned, it was more important that Toyota's newest workforce have an open mind to learn the Toyota Way than be skilled at building cars. They chose the Kentucky site because of favorable government incentives, proximity to rail and interstate transportation, and a hardworking "farm ethic," which they felt was consistent with people being open to learning the Toyota Way.

## Developing a Capable Labor Pool

Even the luxury of choosing the community in which to locate a new plant is not enough for Toyota. They are used to influencing the labor pool long before they set out to hire someone. In Japan, Toyota starts the process of preparing young people for entry into its culture by collaborating with the local school system. In what is now called Toyota City, there is a Toyota high school system. In the middle-school years, the students are assessed for their career interests and aptitudes and are given choices and directions that conform to their competencies. There are three general career paths within Toyota:

- a production worker
- a skilled trade's maintenance worker (welding, electric, programming robots, etc.)
- an engineer

Based on these choices, they can take one of three different educational paths. Most of the students who choose to work for Toyota out of the local school will choose the production worker path. At Toyota High School they live in dormitories and learn, work, and play together. Of course, they will continue to learn the core educational classes of reading, writing, and arithmetic, but now they will also be exposed to the Toyota Way, including the technical aspects of building cars, the components of TPS, and the values and interpersonal components of teamwork and Toyota culture.

When Toyota first started the plant in Kentucky, it was not an option to develop its own feeder school system. Instead, the rigorous selection process described in Chapter 4 was used to identify employees from the existing pool who already had the qualities and skills desired. Only about five percent of those who initially were assessed actually passed through Toyota's strict standards. As time went on Toyota wanted a higher yield and decided to creatively collaborate with the community to increase the capabilities of the potential labor pool somewhat like what it does in Japan.

In 1999, local schools asked TMMK to participate in Kentucky's active School to Work programs, a program instituted in many states that helps provide students with high academic grades with necessary workforce skills. Seeing this as an opportunity to work more closely with the schools and perhaps help improve the quality of the workforce, TMMK met with Scott County School System's Superintendent, Dallas Blankenship. Would Scott County schools be open to exploring ways to work with TMMK to bring Quality Circle techniques into the classroom in grades K–12 as teaching tools? Blankenship agreed and had TMMK meet with the district curriculum committee. Neither TMMK nor the schools wanted to create another add-on "program." Instead they wanted to weave the Quality Circle techniques into the fabric of learning in the school system. The Quality Circle process is based on teams selecting problems they want to work on and learning to use structured problem solving methods to solve the problems. Toyota would teach the problem solving methods. The result was a joint proposal to the school board for a three-year pilot program. The board agreed, and an organizational committee with equal membership from Toyota and the school system established the Quest for Useful Employment Skills for Tomorrow (QUEST).

After a year of work, the organizing committee had adapted TMMK's industrial Quality Circle facilitation and problem-solving techniques to a school setting. It also had adopted the following mission statement:

> *To establish a continuous learning environment of mutual respect and trust in school-related communities by teaching problem-solving processes and utilizing teamwork which improves all students' abilities to learn current curriculum and prepare them for real-life choices.*

QUEST was eventually run by a six-person team—four from TMMK and two from the school system—and was partially funded by a federal Goals 2000 Grant. TMMK also donated copiers, computers, and other equipment to the effort, while the schools provided space and other supports. Implementation began with a training session for all administrators and principals within the system, with the goal of having school leadership—board, faculty, and staff—both understand

and model the concept. Two high school teachers then volunteered to adapt the techniques to one of their classes, and the resultant learning teams were so successful that the decision was made to expand. In the summer of 1999, QUEST held its first faculty training session for 23 teachers from every school within the Scott County School System. This was followed by training another 100 teachers in the summer of 2000 and more than 130 in 2001. Mike Hoseus was assigned by Toyota as a representative to support the program and observed the following:

> *We thought we'd train teachers and they'd train students and the students would use this on school problems in the cafeteria and in extra-curricular activities. But we knew, too, that a big light would go on regarding the value of this for all kinds of activities at all levels, especially for basic learning in the core curriculum. And that's what happened; teachers found that these were useful tools for basic teaching. So they incorporated them into social studies, mathematics, science, literature, and so on. The teachers found that the tools worked; students were more engaged and excited and worked harder; learning was quicker; scores went up. We taught them the process, and they are adapting it and sharing their new lesson plans with others.*

Scott County and Toyota concurrently deepened their School to Work program. TMMK now provides tours for high school students and faculty members, sponsors Junior Achievement and school-based enterprises—like a student-run bank and store—and students even manufacture a simple product. QUEST, however, is TMMK's major contribution to local systemic educational improvement.

QUEST techniques were eventually introduced to the entire Scott County School System, from grades K–12, including both gifted and special education students. Administrators use the techniques in staff meetings that concern everything from finances to school bus scheduling. Representatives from 12 school districts outside Scott County have attended TMMK's training sessions and are incorporating QUEST techniques in their systems. QUEST now guides Scott County Adult Education's curriculum. Georgetown College has used QUEST in its marketing classes, and the University of Kentucky is introducing QUEST to teachers and administrators in graduate level education courses. [4]

While the QUEST program was increasing the capability of the overall labor pool, Toyota saw the need to supplement the program with more targeted training to more specific groups. In order to more closely mirror the system that was first implemented in Japan, Toyota had to build a more comprehensive pipeline of students who were "ready, willing, and able" to enter into the same three categories of careers as those in Japan: production, skilled trades, and engineering.

---

[4] Whiting, Basil J., *The Quest Program, Toyota, and School in Scott County Kentucky*, KY: Senior Fellow, The Manufacturing Institute, Brooklyn, New York, 2002.

The QUEST Manufacturing Academy was established in collaboration with the University of Kentucky and the Kentucky Community and Technical College System. This program was designed to work directly with high school students for one year in order to expose them to career opportunities in manufacturing at the same time it gave them hands-on training in the competencies Toyota looks for in its selection process. The program encompasses four counties surrounding the Georgetown plant and starts with middle-school students by giving them a tour of the plant and introducing them to careers in manufacturing.

At the high-school level, students in grades 10–12 apply for the opportunity to participate in the Academy. The Academy is introduced into the classroom via different courses of study at different schools, including an electronics class at a technical school, a pre-engineering program, and a general career class. The teachers are trained in the QUEST methods of teamwork and problem solving, and then they incorporate these into their students' regular curriculum. Meanwhile, the students participate in a series of field trips and activities designed to give them both a more in-depth understanding of careers in manufacturing as well as an opportunity to develop the skills and competencies needed to be successful.

The Academy's curriculum includes over 60 hours of activities including:

- tours and hands-on activities at the University of Kentucky College of Engineering
- tours and hands-on activities at both the Statewide Central and Bluegrass Campuses of the Kentucky Community and Technical College
- tours of the Toyota plant with hands-on activities in the actual new-hire assessment and the new-hire training areas
- forty hours of hands-on workshops held during class, after school, and on Saturdays that teach the specific skills that Toyota and other manufacturers are looking for, such as:
  - teamwork
  - communication and conflict resolution
  - safe work awareness
  - quality awareness standards
  - following standards
  - using standards to facilitate the Plan-Do-Check-Act (PDCA) improvement process
  - visual management (graphic literacy/reading and interpreting data)
  - process diagnostics to facilitate safety, quality and productivity improvements
  - assembly and body shop skills (using tools, performing at line speed pressure, choosing parts from reading a manifest)

At the end of the year, students demonstrate their skills and competencies in a series of tasks to receive certification. Once they are certified, they have the opportunity to:

- go through the hiring process of the temporary agency for Toyota,
- go to a co-op program that allows them to work at Toyota and learn the company's skilled trades at the same time that they attend the technical college and earn their associates degree. Toyota has collaborated with the local technical college such that its campus is located at the Toyota plant and is open for all the community,
- go to a college of engineering and later co-op with Toyota, and
- go to a college for other studies and work for Toyota part-time in the evenings or in the summer.

Toyota runs programs in collaboration with community groups, such as the Adult Education Community, the local Workforce Investment Board, and others, in order to "build the skills" of the adult labor pool in the area. For example, Toyota has a program that allows participating members of the local Latin American community to work for Toyota's temporary agency at the same time that they are earning their GED, learning English, and being trained in the technical, interpersonal, and problem solving skills that Toyota desires in its employees. At the end of the program, if the participants are able to demonstrate their competency in all of these areas, they are hired by the temp agency for full-time work on the production line.

The practicality of these programs helps Toyota keep the pool of qualified applicants as large as possible and reinforces Toyota's long-term planning process, which has identified a large gap in its manpower needs that will peak in 2013, when the first large group of 25-year career retirees starts to leave to company. With its implementation of the QUEST program in 1999, Toyota demonstrated its long-term planning process and its commitment to directly impacting the quality of the potential labor pool in the community.

*The Toyota Way*[5] concluded that Toyota is one of a handful of large multinational corporations that is a true learning organization. If this is true we would expect Toyota to learn from experiences in Georgetown, Kentucky when building new plants. Indeed it began putting that learning to work immediately after selecting a new plant site in the small town of Tupelo, Mississippi (population about 35,000) to begin making the Toyota Highlander in the fall of 2009. The immediate investment of $1.3 billion and employment of 2000 people plus additional employees hired by suppliers that locate in the area will have a huge impact on the region. It is common for large companies locating a plant to make deals

---

[5] Liker, Jeffrey, *The Toyota Way*, New York: McGraw-Hill, 2004.

with the state and local governments for tax abatements and significant funding for training of employees and Mississippi made its share of agreements with Toyota. However, Toyota went beyond sitting back and taking money for training. Toyota partnered with a community organization called the CREATE Foundation to begin having an impact on education in the area within months of selecting the site by committing $50 million. Toyota will distribute $5 million each year for ten years to CREATE. The details of how to spend the money were not worked out immediately, but the bulk of the money will go to K–12 education, building on what Toyota learned in Georgetown, Kentucky.

Tupelo as a community pulled together and fought to get Toyota to select a site in a nearby town. In fact the regional Community Development Foundation is one of the best in the United States and had already started preparing the site for an automotive assembly plant in advance of knowing what auto company might move there. They were determined to find one and as far as they are concerned they landed the biggest prize possible—a Toyota plant. They were selected by Toyota based on *genchi genbutsu*—going and seeing and feeling this is a community that can fit the Toyota culture. Toyota executives visited most of the major factories in the area and talked to workers on the line. They visited community organizations. They made endless visits including a visit from Dr. Shoichiro Toyoda. They asked countless questions. They were concerned about the small size of the potential labor pool, but Tupelo leaders had answers to all their questions. Ultimately they selected Tupelo because the local culture—particularly the teamwork and community mindedness—was a good fit.

The whole community from the time of selection began anxiously awaiting the arrival of their new neighbor and virtually every business was asking: What can we do to prepare for the arrival of Toyota? One community leader lamented: "There are policy changes I wanted for years and could never get passed, but now if you say the word 'Toyota' it is done."

Obviously not every company can locate in an area and command the attention of the entire region. We would not expect a small company to lay out $50 million to help develop the educational system in the area. The point is that Toyota thinks about the culture long in advance of even preparing the plant site. Toyota not only adapts to the local conditions but goes beyond this and proactively works to positively influence the environment.

# SUMMARY: LAYING THE FOUNDATION FOR TOYOTA WAY CULTURE

Toyota's human system operates in a broader environment and must be tightly integrated with the environment. It starts with the business purpose of mutual prosperity and the targets for quality, cost, delivery, safety, and morale. Toyota is focused on "building quality people" that will in turn produce quality products. The drive toward both is pervasive and constant. Inputs to the people value stream include Toyota's philosophy and values, Toyota Production System principles, and the pool of eligible human resources from which to draw. Toyota is intentional and deliberate in its selection of new plant locations and in influencing the "quality" of the potential work force in that location.

The keys to the successful standardization and replication of the Toyota culture time and time again have been Toyota's planning and up-front work. Everything that has been talked about so far in this chapter is part of the planning process of creating a Toyota culture.

Collectively, the inputs we defined in Figure 2.3 are well understood by Toyota as necessary for success, but they are not necessarily incorporated into the processes of most of the companies we work with. Companies that desire to establish a Toyota culture, in regards to purpose, outputs, and input, would want to consider how their companies compare to the key points below.

## KEY POINTS TO CONSIDER FOR YOUR COMPANY

1. The purpose of Toyota is long-term contribution to society, the local community, Toyota team members, and the growth of Toyota. This perspective allows Toyota to make long-term investments in people, product, processes, and technology.
2. The company communicates a clear purpose and clearly delineates the roles of the company and team members in their partnering relationship— long-term prosperity is the goal for all stakeholders.
3. The leadership sends consistent messages to team members that quality is never to be sacrificed and that the company's leaders are willing to make investments in quality people.
4. The leadership integrates into daily operations the organization's core values and management principles.
5. The company carefully filters all inputs into the organization and even makes investments in the local community to improve those inputs.
6. The company has an operating system based on problem identification, waste reduction, and human systems that respect each team member's ability to solve problems.

## PART ONE SUMMARY

Toyota started out as a small and struggling Japanese auto company striving to be something more. It started out with the vision of Sakiichi Toyoda who wanted his son Kiichiro to contribute something great to society. It was a family owned business rooted in the ethics of a small farming community off the beaten track of Tokyo. The frugality of Aichi prefecture is famous in Japan and reflected in Toyota as a passion for eliminating waste. As Toyota grew great leaders contributed their thinking and sweat to building a distinctive company culture that is best characterized as a learning organization. The Toyota Production System is one result of the learning process but beneath the surface of the bells and whistles of TPS is an underlying philosophy now articulated as respect for people and continuous improvement.

We began the book with some cultural theory and described three levels of culture: what we see on the surface, what leaders of the organization profess, and the deeper underlying assumptions that seem so basic, members of the organization may not even be able to clearly articulate. These three levels are used in Figure I.1 to summarize what we have learned so far from our analysis of the roots of the company and the external environment that influences Toyota culture. We will use a similar diagram at the ends of Parts II and IV to summarize the analysis in those sections.

In the early days of Toyota as a company it was not necessary to be very explicit about the Toyota Way. It did not have a name and was just the way things were done in Toyota. Implicit underlying assumptions were taught to junior mem-

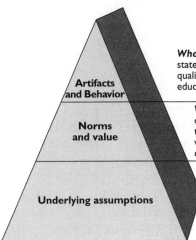

**Artifacts and Behavior**

*What we see:* Toyota Way house, TPS house, mission statement, statement of values, Japanese company, high quality ratings, TPS tools (e.g., *andon, kanban*), community educational programs

**Norms and value**

*What they say they value:* Respect for people, continuous improvement, customer first, contributing to society, challenge, self-reliance, "the right process will produce the right results," investment in community, safe environment, quality, quality, quality!

**Underlying assumptions**

*What they deeply believe and act on:* Corporations have broad obligations to people, partners, and society; satisfying customers is a matter of honor; senior executives are caretakers of a social institution that should exist beyond their lifetimes; companies must adapt to the environment but can also exert control over the environment.

**Figure I.1** Summary Cultural Analysis

bers as the way to think and act through daily lessons. In the high context society of Japan it was not unusual for much to be unsaid and in Toyota it was almost the corporate religion to avoid writing things down. Learning was best done at the gemba—by doing.

As Toyota globalized and has had to incorporate a broad circle of people from many nations and cultures it has become increasingly necessary to bring underlying assumptions into the realm of the explicit. We might say the middle part of the pyramid—what is explicitly stated as values and norms has grown larger. *The Toyota Way 2001* writes down many of those explicit assumptions about what it means to be a part of Toyota.

To more deeply understand what is seldom stated—the true underlying assumptions—it is necessary to delve into Japanese culture. We must understand the high context culture of Japan which is based on relationships and obligation and responsibility. It is not very Japanese-like to think of a company purely as a business based on utilitarian relationships between owners and workers. Toyota owners, executives, and managers view the company as a mini-society which strives for mutual prosperity for all members and partners. We must understand the company as a complex network of relationships as much as a complex network of business transactions. Concepts like trust, honor, and partnership are more potent in this business context than concepts of contracts, cost-benefit calculations, and business strategy. Toyota must function as a successful business to accomplish any of its objectives, but the goal is more than to make a profit. Toyota is a living organism that seeks to keep on living and growing and continuing for the long term.

One interesting aspect of Toyota culture is the dichotomy between humbleness and a remarkable optimism that people can do anything they set out to do energetically. The spirit of challenge is about taking on greater and greater challenges and winning each and every time. Even the environment is not to be taken as a given. If the environment is not providing high enough quality people, Toyota will influence the local community to raise the level of the people. What drives the passion for innovation and improvement is discomfort that the next crisis that threatens the company is right around the corner. Yet, once a target is set, there is such unbridled optimism that the target will be met one might think this is an arrogant company that thinks it has no weaknesses. To counter this time and time again top leaders remind the masses that the greatest danger for Toyota is complacency and arrogance.

In many ways Toyota is filled with paradoxes but resolves the paradoxes to make breakthrough after breakthrough. These breakthroughs in thinking do not happen because of lean or six sigma or the next CEO hired, but through people developed and trained over decades of a career. How Toyota develops people to be thoughtful and committed problem solvers is the subject of the next section.

# Part Two

---

# The Quality People Value Stream

*The power of mind and innovation is infinite. When you see that innovation happen you see another possibility that you could not see earlier. As you look around the corner the world is bigger. That ability to contribute to the company and team members and society grows.*

—Gary Convis, former executive vice president, Toyota Motor Manufacturing North America

Part Two of *Toyota Culture* dives into the core people value stream organized around the four stages of the process: attract, develop, engage and inspire. People with the right qualities must be attracted so that they can be socialized into the Toyota Way, they must be developed to be able to do the jobs they are assigned, they must be engaged to contribute to continuous improvement, and ultimately, they must be inspired to become committed members of the company, community and society.

The International Human Resources Department of Toyota in Japan has developed three key documents whose purpose is to make explicit the significant points and daily activities that comprise Toyota culture: *The Toyota Way 2001, The Toyota Way in Human Resources Management 2002,* and *Human Resources Management Guiding Model, Version 2, (Rev.) April 2005[1]*. Our collective experience at Toyota and these references are the main resources for the chapters in this section of the book.

---

[1] These publications are all internal publications produced by Toyota's International Human Resources Department in Tokyo, Japan and are regularly updated.

The Toyota Production System is famous for its Just-in-Time system of material handling—getting the right amount of the right part at the right place at the right time. The same principle holds true for Toyota's people value stream: deliver the right people, in the right amount, at the right time in line with company needs. As with any process at Toyota, once the standard is set, the Plan-Do-Check-Act cycle is applied: a plan is made, then implemented (Do), follow-up steps are taken in order to monitor effectiveness (Check), and further changes are made as needed to create a new standard. There is never a single, perfect process. Processes are always evolving and improving, particularly as Toyota has been globalizing and learning the ins and outs of other cultures.

# Chapter 4

# Attract Competent and Trainable People

*I am looking for a lot of men who have an infinite capacity to not know what can't be done.*

—Henry Ford, innovating automaker

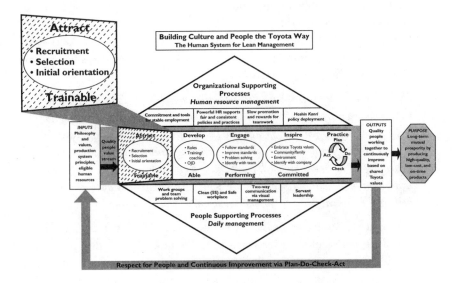

## SELECTING EMPLOYEES FOR LIFE

Why does a company hire people? The answer is obvious: because they have positions to fill. It could be that someone leaves or that sales have increased, or it could be that there is a need for a new type of expertise. A position opens up and you fill it. Often the hiring manager does most of the searching and interviewing and then works in conjunction with the human resource department to address the administrative and legal considerations. While this seems like an obvious course of action, it is not the way things work at Toyota, where the expectation is that people hired will be with the company for life. So every hiring decision is taken very seriously. To balance out hiring and carefully plan for future needs, the human resource department plays a much more critical role. In fact, only HR can approve of a position opening, and even more important it is HR that makes the final hiring choice. Hiring for a specific opening does happen on occasion but since the employee is expected to join the company for life the first job is not all that critical. Who knows how long that job will last? Among engineers, Toyota decides on the number of engineers with different specialties they will need based on a long-term model of growth and replenishment of positions. They may decide they need 50 electrical engineers, 60 mechanical engineers, and 20 chemical engineers in a given year. Then they go out and find the best people from the top universities in Japan who will fit the culture. They will spend a few years learning and doing generic work (like computer-aided-design) before settling into a particular engineering specialty. Toyota did not originally hire the engineers to work on a specific job. They hired based on long-term need and then invested in development of the new engineer, figuring out later what they should work on. The main issue in deciding on numbers is to avoid overstaffing so the jobs of those hired can be protected for the long term.

Pete Gritton who was Vice President of HR at TMMK when we interviewed him, learned this lesson from his mentor, Hiroshike, very early in his first assignment making staffing decisions. Gritton said,

> *Hiroshike told me the first time I was assigned to staffing, "Your job is to protect the job security of 8,000 people, and do not ever compromise that. Toyota has a history of 40 years of job security. Do not screw it up. We expect people to exert extra effort when we need it, but nothing can replace the sense of job security. If we do one thing well, it is planning our staffing so as to protect the reputation of Toyota and respecting the long-term job security of team members. It is a critical point in Toyota. We agonize over every hire."*

With such a strong emphasis on employment stability, each new hire is considered from a company-wide perspective. "Required personnel" is a matter that is widely discussed among all divisions in order to verify the business and manpower need, the anticipated competencies required, the work roles, and the indispensability of the positions. These deliberations, in keeping with business exigencies and company values, also inform the decisions about the use of temporary vs. full-time manpower. In Chapter 12, we will examine the logistical process of "stable employment manpower planning" that uses carefully constructed models to plan the numbers of full-time and temporary personnel to hire.

After deciding to hire, a premium is then placed on the quality of the hire. If firing employees who do not work out as expected is easy, there is not much incentive to select people carefully. Hiring for life means each and every hire is carefully scrutinized and a rigorous review process is needed. Toyota is known for careful planning and attention to detail. Nowhere is this more evident than in the hiring process. As much as Toyota works to design and build quality into its cars, its recruitment, selection, and new hire orientation process is the first quality assurance filter of the people value stream.[2]

---

[2] *Human Resources Management Handbook*, Manpower (1) Hiring, Toyota internal document pp. 5–9.

# HIRING THE RIGHT PERSON, IN THE RIGHT AMOUNT, IN THE RIGHT FORM, AT THE RIGHT TIME

## The Right Person

Imagine yourself as part of the start-up team at a greenfield operation and you are in charge of hiring the workforce. What kind of person would you look for? Would you want someone with experience in the auto industry, or who at least had factory experience? Would you want somebody that is accustomed to working long and hard days with tools and machinery? Consider the following case example:

### Hiring the Right Person Case Study

Candidate: Female, with nine years experience as a hairdresser, specializing in perms and coloring.

How would you vote on hiring this person for assembly work if you were the personnel manager: Yes? No? Maybe? So you decide to bring her in for an interview and in walks a petite woman, in a pink suit, with 3-inch heels and 1-inch nails. What's your decision now?

Jeannie's interviewers consisted of a panel of four people: two production managers, a Japanese coordinator, and a HR specialist. Using the Toyota behavior-based interviewing method, it was revealed that Jeannie grew up on a farm in Southeast Kentucky and was a self-proclaimed tomboy with four older brothers. She worked alongside her brothers doing the farm work, repairing the equipment, and restoring a 1957 Chevy and late model Corvette. Jeannie went to beauty school because she was tired of going to hairdressers and having them make mistakes and do poor-quality work. Her goal was to be able to cut her own hair with good quality, a skill that she possesses and still uses after 30 years.

Jeannie had mechanical aptitudes unusual for a hairdresser and the interview revealed many instances in which she was faced with challenging situations and worked with groups to successfully solve the problems. In the interviewing process it was also revealed that Jeannie had been successful in any business she was in, and the reason she was dressed in pink with heels and polished nails was because her current profession was in the field of beauty: If she dressed like a factory worker she would not be representing her current expertise. She promised the interviewing panel that, if given the opportunity for a new profession in the auto industry, her nails, heels, and clothes would be appropriate to that new career.

Jeannie was hired as a team leader (an hourly leadership position) in assembly in 1988 on the trim line, assembling doors and carrying responsibility for the safety, quality, production, cost, and morale of five team members. She demonstrated in her career the skills and abilities that the selection system looks for. Her teamwork and interpersonal skills facilitated her team's success and she was promoted to group leader over the door line in 1992 (a salaried supervisory position).

Her mechanical and problem-solving skills, as revealed in the selection process, were repeatedly demonstrated in the plant. One example involved damage to the side mirrors on the front doors of the Camry. There were a variety of reasons for the damage that caused the mirrors to be thrown away. This scrap was a cost issue for her team and she was determined not to let it become a cost issue for the customer. She set up a temporary repair area in order to reduce the scrap costs while maintaining Toyota quality. This area allowed Jeannie and her team members to "build high quality" mirrors using the salvageable parts from a few damaged mirrors in order to make one good one.

Jeannie knew that this was only a temporary countermeasure until she could solve the real problems that were causing damage to the mirrors. The biggest problem her team had was scratching the mirrors with the air tool used to attach the mirror to the door. Jeannie's team members were shooting screws into mirrors using an air tool with a Phillips head screwdriver bit, and the bit would slip off and damage the mirrors. She led the team to work together and come up with a better method and then trained each member in the new standardized work method. The amount of scrap got better, but the problem still occurred. Jeannie was then able to facilitate meetings with product development engineers from the Toyota Technical Center and suppliers, and together they eventually had the design of the mirror changed to incorporate a hex-head bolt for attachment instead of the small screw. This made it much harder for the bit to slip off the bolt and eliminated the problem. Not only that, it saved the team members and the company a very valuable couple of seconds per car.

Toyota's unique hiring and selection process sifts and sorts and then yields an employee, such as Jeannie, who is not only capable of doing the job, but who is also committed to the job and company for the long term. A common hiring mistake made in other organizations is that they look to satisfy an immediate need, and may or may not be successful even in this short-term goal. Toyota's approach is to match the competencies (i.e., skills and abilities) the company needs with those of the applicant to successfully meet both the immediate need, and the characteristics needed to grow into new roles and positions. For team members, it builds trust in the company and helps engage them for the long term since they know they will have an opportunity to grow with the company. From the company perspective, this is a key tool in developing effective managers. Jeannie Hughes is now an assistant manager in the assembly plant who is responsible for getting over 2,000 parts to 1,000 team members for 1,000 vehicles every day. Her career with Toyota reached the 20-year mark and counting.

## In The Right Amount: Based on Long Term Employment Needs

In companies where hiring is left up to individual managers to determine needs for their departments, over-hiring is a common mistake. Many times this can be done with the best intentions, but still misses the long-term perspective. A big project comes along or sales pick up and there is a need for more engineers, a larger sales force, or more production workers. Individual departments lobby for headcount to meet the increased demand. That is fine until sales go back down or the big project ends and is not immediately replaced by the next big project. There is generally a time lag before those who were hired are let go as hiring is usually easier than firing. At some point, an executive realizes there is too much "fat" in the system and orders an across the board reduction in force. Toyota prefers to use a principle like *heijunka* or smoothing from the Toyota Production System. Ups and downs in hiring and firing means, in good times, retraining new employees into the culture (which takes years) and, in bad times, firing employees which destroys trust. Both are disruptive and examples of waste in the people value stream.

### *Hiring the Right Amount Case Study*

From Mike Hoseus: When I was an assembly plant manager we were not meeting our goals of safety, quality, productivity, and cost. The group leaders were all telling me that they had no help and all their team leaders were on line. When we checked the data, they were right: the team leaders were doing production work on line an average of over 75 percent when our standard was 50 percent. The standard stated that at least half of the team leaders should be freed of working on a production job so they could roam and answer andon calls. In Toyota terms, we had a problem. The team leader online percentage was 25 percent over standard and we had long-term medical leaves, military leaves, and the usual number of growing vacation days to be covered. I was able to show that this was the trend for the last year and that it was likely to continue for the next year if we did nothing about it. We put together all the facts and went to HR in order to hire more team members to make up for the higher-than-standard number of absences, and to take care of the people. Everyone was tired and we were not meeting our goals.

I had my facts and my current people in mind in making the request for more people. Certainly human resources would agree. They did not. It was a humbling lesson for me in learning the Toyota culture. I was shown that most of our problems in terms of being over standard were due to having too many people on work-related medical leave. Those injuries were my responsibility to control and improve. By simply hiring more people, I was not addressing the root cause and really taking care of my people, even in the short term. Also, if I was given the opportunity to simply hire more people, then when the people on medical leave returned to work, I would be in an "overstaffed" condition and would not be taking care of my people for the long term either. We ended up solving the problem by HR helping to temporarily shift other resources to my department in order for me to have the resources needed to get some of those team leaders off the line and identify the root causes of the medical leaves to stop others from leaving. When the employees who were out returned to work, we were able to reassign those who had helped us for the short term project. I remember thinking this was a good example of how the "Toyota culture" differed from my typical "American management" mindset. This entire topic will be discussed in more detail in Chapter 12, Commitment and Tools for Stable Employment.

## In the Right Form

Another key point in preventing the problem of over hiring is to be able to select the right type of employment status according to the work need. It is important for job security to be able to have some percentage of the workforce as temporary employees (called variable work force). This is not a unique strategy, but what is unique is how Toyota selects and treats this valuable asset. The selection of temporary individuals is similar to the process used to select full-time employees at Toyota, and will be covered in detail later in this chapter.

The unique aspect of being part of the variable workforce at Toyota is that efforts are made to include the person as part of the "team" and the Toyota culture. To be sure, there are pay and benefit differences and legal aspects that properly differentiate the two, but on the floor the same values of mutual respect and trust and continuous improvement hold true. Temporaries go through the same people value stream as full-time members, though the quantity of training they receive may not be as much. They are treated like team members, and even though they are there as a variable component to hedge against economic downturns, managing them involves the goal of never needing to let them go. In fact, the common goal between the company and the temporary employees is that they go through the value stream successfully; that is, being trained, performing up to standard, and committed, and then converting to full time employment at the end of the two-year temporary assignment. Through 2006, at the Georgetown Plant, 100 percent of the temporaries who performed their job with quality were converted to full-time team members at the end of their assignment.

## At The Right Time

Similar to Toyota's Just-in-Time parts delivery system, the hiring system must also deliver on time to the customer (i.e., the production department). This is especially important in the lean Toyota environment. For example, it is critical to maintain the proper balance of the correct number of team leaders off-line, responding to andon calls on a daily basis, in order to realize the overall goal of building the highest quality car, at the lowest possible cost, in the shortest amount of time. As mentioned earlier the standard that has been effective at Toyota is that a maximum of 50 percent of the team leaders are working on the line at any point in time. If there are too many team leaders working on the line, instead of off-line supporting members, it can put a burden on the team members, and negatively affect the uptime percentage of the plant. If there are too many off-line, it can have a negative impact on the cost key performance indicator of labor-hours per unit.

## FUNNEL MODEL OF RECRUITMENT: MANY PROSPECTS LEAD TO FEW HIRES

It can help to think of this process in terms of a funnel. As the funnel in Figure 4.1 illustrates, Toyota wants a large number of potential members at the front end of the funnel in order to yield the right number of matching members at the other end. As discussed earlier, this is particularly important since Toyota is so selective, and thus only a small number of people make it through the selection process successfully. Once Toyota determines how many openings to fill, in what form, and the type of person needed, recruiting can begin. We will begin by looking at how Toyota deals with the recruitment end.

One of the factors that helps to attract a large number of people at the beginning of the process is being the employer of choice in the area. This starts with competitive pay and benefits. As will be discussed in more detail in Chapter 14, Toyota's wage and benefit system ranks near the top of the auto industry, and is

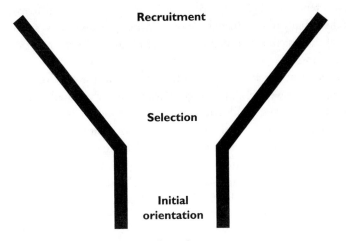

**Figure 4.1** Recruitment to Selection Funnel

typically competitive with similar jobs in the area. This has been the case for the last 20 years. In addition to paying well, the company must be perceived well by employees. Indeed, word of mouth recruiting performed by current Toyota team members continues to help create a steady stream of potential candidates into the recruiting pool. This starts with viewing team members as the most important asset. One Toyota executive stated the sentiment well, "Team members are the only appreciating asset we have. Everything else starts depreciating from the moment we buy it."

We offer a one week Toyota culture workshop, sometimes through University of Kentucky, which takes participants through the human systems model. They have opportunities to reflect on Toyota's approach compared to their own and identify ways they can reduce the gaps. The insights from these workshops provided examples used in various parts of this book. In discussing this issue at one of these workshops, an executive of a large manufacturing company lamented: "That is our problem. We do not see employees as assets. We see them as expendable commodities and, in turn, we do not pay them anything. We are unable to recruit the best, have no system to select the best, and have problems engaging them in the work, and then we wonder why we get the results we are currently getting."

## SELECTION: LONG-TERM MATCH

A primary reason companies are trying to learn from Toyota is that it has a different culture that gets more out of its people. Because the Toyota culture is so distinct, it is not possible to find people who have already worked for another company and demonstrated all the competencies Toyota is seeking. The challenge is to evaluate them in two ways: for their past experience and behaviors that are most consistent with those required to be successful in the Toyota environment, and for their ability to demonstrate those behaviors in work-related situations. The premise of the system is that past and current behaviors are the best predictors of future behaviors.[3]

The Japanese leaders responsible for starting up the new plant wanted to select people who were bright enough to learn, and who could understand and implement the Toyota Production System. Early on in its staffing efforts at TMMK, Toyota used job analysis information to identify specific work behaviors, and job criteria known as dimensions, which are necessary for success in its production environment. Since TMMK was a greenfield start up with no plant to observe locally, the job analysis was done by observing six comparable positions at the NUMMI plant in California; they were: team member (production

---

[3] *TMMK Production Selection Process Overview*, in-house document, pp. 1–13, 1999.

and maintenance), team leader (production and maintenance), and group leader (production and maintenance). In addition, Japanese supervisors and the first American supervisors were interviewed regarding the types of skills and behaviors they were looking for in their workers for these positions. The dimensions were comprised of work behaviors that could be observed and measured in the selection system.[4] These are generic behaviors that apply to all three positions, though the requirements are more stringent for team leader and group leader positions. The dimensions identified were as follows:

1. **Team Orientation**—Uses appropriate interpersonal styles and methods in helping a team reach its goal; maintains group cohesiveness and cooperation and facilitates group process; provides procedural suggestions when appropriate; is aware of needs and potential contributions of others.

2. **Initiative**—Originates action and maintains active attempts to reach a personal or team goal; self-starting rather than passively accepting. Takes action, beyond what is necessary to achieve goals; proactive not reactive; seeks information needed to do job; takes action as opposed to waiting to be told what needs to be done; feels ownership for job; accepts responsibility for work and/or team effectiveness; provides support to team members and will take action to correct a situation collaboratively with team members if required (e.g., absenteeism, quality).

3. **Oral Communication**—Effectively expresses ideas and information in individual or group situations (includes organization, gestures, and nonverbal communications) and has active listening skills.

4. **Problem Identification**—Identifies individual or group issues and problems; secures relevant information (fact-finding/data collection); relates various data from different sources and identifies cause/effect relationships.

5. **Problem Solution**—Develops, alone and with others, alternative courses of action and makes decisions, which demonstrate use of factual information based on logical assumptions, and takes organizational resources into consideration. Solutions should take into consideration the values and culture of the organization.

6. **Practical Learning**—Learns quickly; able to follow directions. Quickly assimilates and applies new job-related information which may vary in complexity; demonstrates reasonable and prudent attention to operating instructions and directions as established through organizational policy or supervisory requests.

---

[4] *Development Dimensions International, Proposal to Toyota Motor Manufacturing for the Development and Implementation of a Selection System for Group Leaders, Team Leaders, and Team Members of the Georgetown Kentucky Plant*, October 10, 1986.

7. **Work Tempo**—Performs a repeated task at a specific tempo without unnecessary expenditures of time or waste of supplies and materials; demonstrates a consistent rate of speed for accomplishing an activity in a specific order.

8. **Adaptability**—Maintains effectiveness in varying environments, tasks, responsibilities, or people situations.

9. **Mechanical Ability**—Able to accomplish basic mechanical tasks.

Obviously it would be hard to find anyone who had all of these characteristics, and much of the training and socialization of new members focuses on developing these abilities. Nonetheless, Toyota wanted as many of these characteristics as possible and needed instruments that could be effective, defensible, and efficient at measuring applicants' ability—that is, their capacity to demonstrate these behaviors in the performance of past work experiences or simulated tasks. In order to be effective, the instruments had to identify and measure performance; to be defensible, the instruments had to be clearly job related (to the job analysis data); and to be efficient, the instruments had to be able to manage a large number of applicants in reasonable timeframes. For example, in the case of TMMK, over 100,000 people applied, and more than 25,000 actually went through the selection process, yielding approximately 3,000 people who were ultimately hired as salaried group leaders (like first-line supervisors), hourly team leaders, and hourly team members. Compared to the process many other companies use the time investment and rigor of Toyota's process might be surprising, particularly since it was used to hire hourly team members who would do one-minute cycle production jobs. As we have discussed Toyota expects far more from the team member than to simply perform the one-minute job to standard.

## Toyota Georgetown Original Recruitment and Selection Process for Hourly Team Members

It is worth going into some detail on the Toyota Georgetown case to illustrate how it recruited and selected team members since it answers the question: How does Toyota actually identify and measure work competencies in applicants? There were seven phases altogether.

### Case Study: Toyota Georgetown Selection Process—1987–1990
**Phase 1: Advertising and Recruitment**
*Applicant indicates interest in employment.*
Toyota worked from a broad pool of applicants who were informed of employment opportunities via public media articles about the new Toyota Plant and the local State Department of Employment Services. At the outset, the pool consisted of more than 142,000 applicants.

## Phase 2: Orientation, Application and Testing

*Applicant attends a realistic job preview.*
The purpose was to provide an orientation to the Toyota plant and its philosophy, and to provide a self-select opportunity for those applicants who may not want this type of job. A video set out a picture of Toyota's operations in Kentucky that was upbeat, focused on the need for employees who wished to be a part of a new wave in auto manufacturing, and who desired to develop high quality cars at competitive prices. It was also authentic in portraying the work pace as constant and challenging.

*Applicant completes an application form.*
The aim of the application form was to collect information on the applicant's previous employment that would yield useful content for preliminary assessment of his/her fit with the job, especially in terms of technical and supervisory experiences and initial indications of achievements and accomplishments. The application form differed from the ordinary "name, rank, and serial number" version of its day, by asking for specific examples of job accomplishments.

*Applicant completes general aptitude test.*
The purpose of the paper and pencil general aptitude test was to screen applicants by reliable and efficiently assessing cognitive, perceptual, and psychomotor skills; the specific test used was the General Aptitude Test Battery (GATB). The test yielded information on the applicant's reasoning and practical learning abilities that (at that time) was found to be a valid predictor of training and job performance.

*Applicant completes a job fit inventory.*
The purpose of the job fit inventory was to assess the extent to which tasks and activities characteristic of the work at Toyota fit the applicant's preferences. Using the results of the job analysis, a two-part questionnaire was constructed; the first part consisted of a number of statements in which the applicant would rate the importance of the statements on a five-point rating scale, the second part consisted of ten statements in which applicants rate their agreement toward each statement on a five-point rating scale. An example of a job fit question was, "I prefer working by myself rather than with a group of people." It measures not only the applicant's ability to match Toyota's criteria, but also his/her desire and motivation to do so. It aimed to weed out applicants who would have no problem performing the job successfully, but who would not be motivated to do so for a long time.

*A screening decision is made.*
Using the information from the selection process to this point, initial decisions were made about those who would continue and those who would not. The overall pass rate for the aptitude test was about 42 percent leaving about 60,000 people. The selection team then reviewed 60,000 applicants and were able to identify 40,000

to be scheduled for the assessment center. Of those 40,000, some had moved, others had found other jobs resulting in 28,000 applicants actually going on to Phase 3.

## Phase 3: Assessment Center Exercises

*Applicant attends two half-day testing sessions.*

The assessment center sessions provided an opportunity for applicants to demonstrate the behaviors associated with the competencies required to work at the Georgetown Plant. Structured exercises allowed the applicant to exhibit competency-related target behaviors: basic team skills and production skills. Trained assessors observed the behaviors in each applicant, and scored them each according to a standard method and set of criteria. The measurement of the competencies is described in more detail in the shadow box later in the chapter.

*Applicant attends basic team skills day one session—three exercises.*

1. The Group Discussion Exercise was used to assess the applicant's ability to work effectively in unstructured group or team situations. The work dimension behaviors that the assessors were looking for were positive group contributors, initiative, and verbal communication. In a one-hour period, three to six applicants met in a leaderless group setting with no assigned roles. Four short case studies of typical problems faced by team members were presented. The applicants were asked to advise on problems involving productivity, fellow team member disputes, worker safety problems, and tardiness and to submit consensus recommendations for each.

2. The Team Problem Solving Exercise was aimed to assess the applicant's ability to collect data relevant to a situation by asking questions, reach a logical conclusion or decision after the data has been collected, present conclusions in a meaningful manner, and defend a decision and prepare counterarguments. The work dimension behaviors that the assessors were looking for were reading, literacy, problem identification, problem solution, and oral communication. In a one-hour period, three to six applicants were asked to engage in tasks involving fact-finding and decision making. Each applicant was given a brief description of the immediate circumstances concerning a production problem. The task was to seek information and make a decision regarding the problem within a limited period. During the fact-finding phase, the applicant might obtain additional information by questioning the resource person. At the conclusion of the fact-finding phase, the applicant made an oral presentation of decisions made. Once the presentation was completed, the resource person might question the applicant to probe his/her quality of reasoning, attempt to clarify thinking, etc.

3. The Manufacturing Exercise was aimed to assess the applicant's ability to make key decisions regarding work efficiency and to work effectively in structured group situations. The work dimensions that the assessors were looking for were meeting membership, initiative, oral communication, problem identification, and problem solution. In a two-hour period four to six applicants were placed in the role of team members of a small firm assembling electronic components onto circuit boards. Roles are self-assigned and applicants must make key team organization decisions regarding planning and allocating resources.

*Applicant attends production skills day two session—one exercise.*
The Project "T" Exercise was designed to assess the applicant's ability to perform quality work at a specific tempo without unnecessary expenditures of time or waste of supplies and materials. The work dimension behaviors that the assessors were looking for were practical learning, work tempo, adaptability, problem identification, problem solution, mechanical ability, job fit/motivation. After being given instructions, a demonstration and a brief discussion period, in a two-hour period the individual applicant repeatedly performed a series of six to nine assembly steps while moving from position to position. At the completion of the exercise, the applicant was asked for a better way to design the assembly task.

*A screening decision is made.*
Using the information on applicants' participation in the selection process to this point, decisions were made as to those who would continue and those who would not. Of the 28,000 who attended the Assessments, 12,000 passed the standard criteria.

## HOW DOES TOYOTA MEASURE A COMPETENCY?

Earlier we listed nine job dimensions for a select set of positions. They reflected the job analysis information of team members, team leaders, and group leaders' positions at Toyota.[5] Take the dimension of initiative as an example. Initiative is defined as "the ability to originate action and maintain active attempts to reach a personal or team goal—being self-starting to do what's necessary." The initiative *dimension behaviors* are:

---

[5] "Job Analysis" is the process of learning about the tasks, duties, responsibilities, and working conditions associated with a job. Thus, job analysis information may be used to determine the important dimensions of behavior for job success." Richard D. Arvey, *Fairness in Selecting Employees,* New York: Addison-Wesley, 1979, p. 114.

1. seeking information needed to do the job,
2. taking action as opposed to waiting to be told what to do,
3. feeling ownership for the job,
4. accepting responsibility for work and/or team effectiveness, and
5. providing support for team members and taking action to correct a situation with a team member if required.

Small group simulation exercises allow applicants to engage in these initiative-related behaviors. One such exercise is a Team Problem Solving Exercise that focuses on a series of customer complaints about product quality. Applicants are asked to share key information with each other on product process flow, relate complaint information to possible production process issues, and come to consensus on solutions.

Trained assessors look for initiative-related behaviors as the applicants participate in the exercise. *Assessing applicant behaviors* involves the following functions:

1. observing applicants' behaviors,
2. recording the instances of behaviors observed,
3. classifying the behaviors recorded using standards, similar to the ones numbered 1–5 in the definition of "initiative" above, and
4. evaluating the types and amounts of behaviors and assigning a score.

The applicants are expected to meet the minimum standards in all of the competency dimensions. They could, however, offset a lower score in one dimension with a higher score in another.

Gene Childress was in charge of implementing and administering the Georgetown Plant Assessment Center from 1987–1989. In that period, more that 25,000 applicants performed the assessment center exercises. Gene remembers it well:

> *What was amazing to me was how well the exercises allowed the applicants to show the abilities Toyota was looking for. Sitting with a group as an assessor, you could see them in action and you had a record. I remember one man who thought that the best way to lead a problem solving group was to stand up and shout at everybody who didn't agree with him; basically, he shut the group down. Another time a woman just started asking the others what they thought about the problem and how to deal with it; everybody participated. It was as clear as could be who was effective and who wasn't. The other thing that surprised me was that the applicants just seemed to forget that I was there and taking notes; they just got right into the task.*

## Phase 4: Final Screening

*Applicant reference and employment history check.*

TMMK also did the usual reference and employment verification. Working with the State of Kentucky Department of Employment Services, Toyota was able to review past work records for work history (with signed permission from the applicant). In addition calls were made to references. The references and work history yielded work dimension information related to initiative, practical learning, and job fit/motivation and focused on past work records involving absenteeism, on-the-job performance, punctuality, initiative on the job, and job stability.

Typically, the checking process required about one hour. This process of checking references went beyond the usual "Did this person work for you, for how long, and in what position?" Toyota's reference check included questions such as "Please describe this person's ability to initiate improvement in your organization." Many times the HR professional helping with the reference check would turn the call over to the person's supervisor, and the real information would be captured. All of the questions were focused on the person's abilities to demonstrate the competencies. Approximately 10,000 people remained in the process at the end of this phase.

*Applicant attends a structured interview.*

The aim of the structured interview was to determine which applicants would be hired for a six-month, on-the-job observation training period. The work dimensions that the interviewers were looking for were oral communication, adaptability, initiative, job fit/motivation, and mechanical ability. Using an interview guide, the interviewers (a team made up of production managers, group leaders and a HR specialist) gathered specific behavioral examples that indicated the applicant's ability and motivation to perform effectively in the targeted position of team member. The interviewers were taught how to ask effective follow-up questions to pin down behaviors. Careful notes were taken and used to assist in the determination of which applicants would enter the final selection pool for the targeted position of production team members.

All interviewers were trained and certified in the structured interview process. They were taught the dimensions/competencies and how to ask questions that allowed the applicant to demonstrate these dimension-related behaviors and competencies in the past. All interviewers were trained how to probe for a "STAR" in the applicant's story as he/she responded to the questions. This way of scoring is known as STAR (Situation or Task, Action and Results). During the interview, each interviewer collects the STAR information, and then rates each dimension/competency on a scale from 1–5. At the end of the interview the team discusses each member's findings, and shares the scores and rationales. The team then comes to consensus on one score for each dimension/

competency. Approximately 8,000 people remained in the pool at the end of this phase.

Structured or behavior-based interviewing is now fairly common and asks the applicant to describe specific examples in their past to demonstrate the identified competencies. Questions include topics such as: "Tell me about a difficult challenge you have faced at work and what you did to solve it?" This question is obviously checking the applicant's competency in problem solving, but may also offer insight to her ability to work in a team and use interpersonal communication. As the applicant answers the question, the interviewers are scoring the answer based on the applicant's ability to give specific examples. Often the tendency is for the applicant to speak in generalities.

It is also desirable to have more than one person in on the interview in order to minimize subjective bias and to facilitate fairness and consistency throughout the process.

Two hypothetical example interview excerpts are contrasted in the box below.

## BEHAVIOR-BASED INTERVIEWING HYPOTHETICAL CASE EXAMPLES

**Applicant:** I am a great problem solver.
**Interviewer:** Can you give me an example?
**Applicant:** My current boss tells me all the time how well I solve problems.
**Interviewer:** Can you give me an example of one you actually solved?
**Applicant:** Well, I was on a problem solving team and we had this problem with a process and the team got together to fix it.
**Interviewer:** What was your role with the team in solving the problem?
**Applicant:** I was a member of the team.
**Interviewer:** What was your role, specifically, in the solving of the problem?
**Applicant:** I went to the meetings.

This interchange would be scored low regarding the competency of problem solving. The interviewer is looking for the applicant to describe the situation (or task), summarize her actions, and describe what the results were in connection with her actions. It is apparent from the applicant's responses above that she personally had no real role in the problem solving activity, or does not have the communication skills to explain her role which is also a weakness.

Compare and contrast the first interchange with the next:
**Interviewer:** Tell me about a difficult challenge you have faced at work and what you did to solve it.

**Applicant:** I love to solve problems.

**Interviewer:** Can you give me an example?

**Applicant:** Sure, my work team was having a problem with getting orders out late to our customers. I volunteered to gather the data from the last month, the following week, and all the specific criteria regarding the late orders. For example, which ones were the most occurring, least occurring, from which shifts and which departments etc.? When I brought the data back to the team, it was clear that 80 percent of the late orders were due to one part from second shift. I volunteered to work nights for a week in order to go to the shift and observe exactly what was happening. What I found out very quickly is that they were not following the procedure that we had set up on the day shift to process the parts as they were finished. They were stacking up the parts until the end of the shift, and sometimes, they did not even get them processed until the end of the next shift. I spent the rest of the week on nights, working with the supervisor to set up a standard method for their shift, and then helped to make sure all the operators were trained on the procedure. We then set up a tracking method to insure that all new operators were also trained before they started the job. As a result, we took care of that entire 80 percent of the late orders due to that part and shift. Our overall results then were better than our company target for late orders.

Obviously this is a dream answer and would almost never happen unless the applicant already worked for an excellent lean company, but it illustrates the ideal type of answer. This applicant was able to give many more specific examples and descriptions of the situation, in addition to details about her actions and how they affected the results. This applicant would score at the very top on the problem solving competency. It is easy to see the effectiveness of behavior-based interviewing from these examples. In a normal application, questionnaire, or interview process, both applicants might well have answered that problem solving is important; that their work experience included working in problem solving teams, and that they were competent at solving problems. By digging deeper, the Toyota interviewers were able to better differentiate potential team members.

## Phase 5: Health Assessment

*Applicant takes a physical examination.*

The purpose of the physical examination was to determine if the applicant's general health would adversely impact on the ability to work effectively on strenuous production jobs. The work dimension the physician was looking for was job fitness. A reliable and valid general medical examination was administered by a competent medical authority. At the end of this phase 6,000 people were identified as viable candidates for employment and were offered the opportunity to come to work for TMMK and enter Phase 6.

### Phase 6: Probation Period
*Applicant is observed on-the-job during the probation period.*
The purpose of the on-the-job observation during the probationary period was to assess the entire set of work dimension behaviors in actual production conditions. During the six-month on-the-job development period, applicant's suitability for long-term employment was determined through systematic observation of job behaviors by team and group leaders.

An overall summary of the process and number of applicants through probation is shown in Figure 4.2. TMMK selected all the original team members, team leaders, and group leaders with this same process. The top hundred were the first group leaders and the next 500 highest scores were the team leaders, and the rest were team members. Other plants such as the newer plant in San Antonio, Texas have kaizened this and are borrowing team leaders for start up from other plants rather than hiring off the street, and later promoting the new hires who do well in start up and score well in the promotion system. This way they launch with experienced team leaders. TMMK found it difficult to launch the plant and develop team leaders from scratch at the same time.

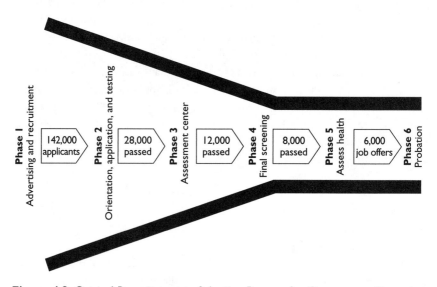

**Figure 4.2** Original Recruitment to Selection Process for Georgetown, Kentucky

**Phase 7: Final Screening Decision for Full Employment**
Based on actual performance in the probation process, decisions were made as to those who would continue and those who would not. In a comment from a Toyota culture workshop, one outside executive was impressed by the rigor of the process and a bit distressed how weak his company's process was in comparison:

> *You know, my company has all kinds of requirements, specifications, and guidelines for bringing raw materials through the door into my plant. It is a long, expensive process with all our suppliers and we take it very seriously. Meanwhile, our current hiring process allows just about anybody in the door, and then we do the narrowing-down process through our turnover and firing.*

## Improved Toyota Georgetown Recruitment and Selection Process

Recruitment and selection was the focus of a major kaizen effort at the Georgetown, Kentucky plant. From the time these processes were developed at NUMMI and TMMK in the mid- to late–1980s, they have been implemented, refined, and improved in a variety of Toyota plant settings, such as Canada, Japan, Alabama, Texas, Mexico, and West Virginia.[6]

The forces driving this continuous improvement were several:

1. The newer plants' implementation and improvement of their predecessors' lessons and efficiencies;
2. The evolution of team members' work and correspondingly updated job analysis information;
3. The innovations in assessment technology involving use of computers;
4. The increasing availability of workplace-focused problem solving training in schools, workforce development programs, and other companies; and
5. The need for greater precision in identifying applicants' skill sets related to Toyota work and culture requirements.

In 2005, Toyota Georgetown redesigned its entire recruitment and selection process to incorporate the collective improvements made throughout the global Toyota system. The new process is pictured in Figure 4.3. Select International is a contract company that supplies Toyota with a temporary workforce. In addition, there is a Central Kentucky Job Center, a one-stop center made up of city and state employment offices. These offices are key partners in contributing support

---

[6] "TMMK Production Selection Process Overview," in-house document, pp. 1–13, 1999.

**Hiring Flowchart—Manufacturing**

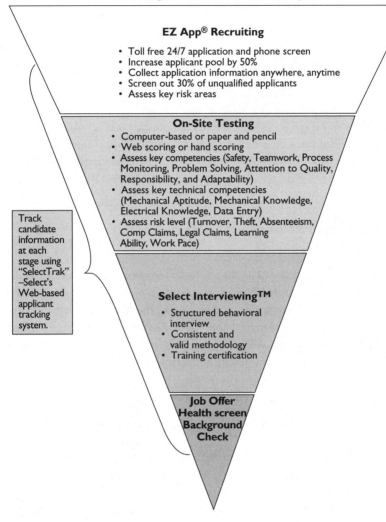

**EZ App® Recruiting**

- Toll free 24/7 application and phone screen
- Increase applicant pool by 50%
- Collect application information anywhere, anytime
- Screen out 30% of unqualified applicants
- Assess key risk areas

**On-Site Testing**

- Computer-based or paper and pencil
- Web scoring or hand scoring
- Assess key competencies (Safety, Teamwork, Process Monitoring, Problem Solving, Attention to Quality, Responsibility, and Adaptability)
- Assess key technical competencies (Mechanical Aptitude, Mechanical Knowledge, Electrical Knowledge, Data Entry)
- Assess risk level (Turnover, Theft, Absenteeism, Comp Claims, Legal Claims, Learning Ability, Work Pace)

Track candidate information at each stage using "SelectTrak" –Select's Web-based applicant tracking system.

**Select Interviewing™**

- Structured behavioral interview
- Consistent and valid methodology
- Training certification

**Job Offer Health screen Background Check**

**Figure 4.3** New TMMK Recruitment and Selection Process starting 2005

in recruiting applicants, scheduling, and administering computerized assessments. A third-party consulting group also worked with Toyota in order to develop the key phases of the process.[7]

---

[7] Select International is a leading provider of selection and development solutions for global 2000 companies. To learn more about the type of selection process described above, please contact Select at 1–800–786–8595 or visit www.selectinternational.com.

The process began with selecting permanent hires, but then temporaries were added and they went through the same screening process. It is described below, starting with the application known as "EZApp®."

**First Phase**—"EZApp®" or "EZ Application." This application is initiated by the candidate via any touch-tone phone or on the Internet, which starts the filtering process based on answering such basic questions as:

- Do you have a legal right to work in the United States?
- Are you willing to work any shift?
- Have you been convicted of a felony within the last 10 years?

These are key questions that are considered "knock out" questions, such as the right to work, and if not answered correctly the system will automatically notify the applicant at the end of the application that they are currently ineligible and not being considered for employment. There are other questions that aren't really knock out questions but cumulatively add up to help screen in candidates who have a higher chance of being successful and a lower chance of turnover. Approximately 20 percent get knocked out at this stage. If the applicant passes this first phase, they go on to phase two. The State of Kentucky Job Center notifies the applicant and schedules their Web-based testing.

**Second Phase**—Web-based testing. The State of Kentucky facilitates and proctors this Web-based testing known as SAM (Select Assessment® for Manufacturing developed by Select International). It is usually administered in groups for efficiency purposes. The reason for proctoring by the state is to confirm the identity of the person actually answering the questions of the assessment. The questions include a range of items: simulations to test cognitive processes, realistic scenarios, values, problem solving, covering a broad range of competencies. An example online simulation is shown in Figure 4.4, in which the candidate is asked to keep all of the gauges on the left out of the red using the mouse, while simultaneously looking at the series of numbers on the right and determining if the series is the same or different. The goal is to keep all of the gauges out of the red zone and do as many comparisons as possible. This highly useful exercise demonstrates the ability to multi-task, and it is not dissimilar from actual job tasks.

**Third Phase**—Production Simulation. In this phase, potential applicants are scheduled for a six-hour day at the plant to simulate a day of work. These are simulated processes done on actual cars in the plant, but off the production line. There are four exercises set up to simulate work in the assembly and body weld areas, since these are where most of the new hires are initially placed. Applicants are given training in plant safety procedures, including the wearing of a bump cap

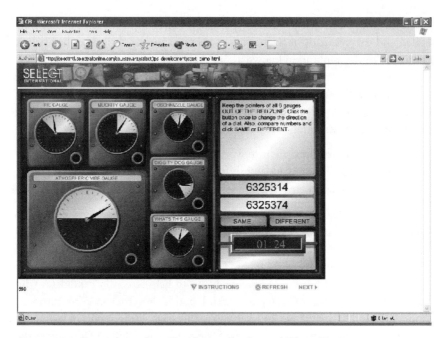

**Figure 4.4** Example on-line Simulation for Second Phase Testing

for head safety, gloves for hand protection, and safety glasses. All of this is done using the same standardized work and documents that are used with actual production team members. In this way, training and orientation into the Toyota culture is already underway, even before actual hiring decisions are made. Applicants spend an hour and a half doing production tasks at each of four work stations that include the following:

1. Reading instructions from a monitor, the applicant shoots bolts with an air tool into a floor panel and inner roof of a car in a designated sequence, while sitting inside the car's shell body (see Figure 4.5). Performance of this task checks the applicant's ability to follow instructions and apply basic tool knowledge, as well as demonstrating accuracy and manual dexterity while maintaining an acceptable work pace.

2. Reading instructions from a monitor inside the car, the applicant pulls a wire harness through the inside of the car body, gets out of the body, walks back to the trunk area and connects the wire harness to a set of colored connections. These tasks monitor the ability to follow standardized work under time constraints. The results of the exercises are tabulated electronically by computer based on the quality and quantity of the applicant's performance. More weight is given to quality than to quantity.

**Figure 4.5** Applicant shooting bolts with air tool in assembly exercise in the Assessment Area

3. Reading instructions, the applicant makes welds with a simulated welding device hanging from an overhead pulley (see Figure 4.6). The monitor instructs them on where to make the weld and they maneuver the welding device and make the weld. There is in fact no spark and no real weld, but the device registers the positioning of the weld gun. They are evaluated on both quality and quantity.

4. Taking colored weight discs (ranging from 3–10 pounds) off designated pegs, the applicant walks them over to another set of pegs to place them · on the one identified by the computer instructions. The pegs range from near the floor to six feet high. This exercise checks both the mental and physical stamina of the applicant. In a number of instances it has caused applicants to call it quits right in the middle of their assessment. This experience indicates the importance Toyota places on an accurate job preview component, so that applicants get a practical idea of what the work will be like, and to see if there is a good match between the job and the person. It assists both the candidate and the company to find the mismatch early, rather than two weeks or two months after both parties have invested precious time and money.

**Figure 4.6** Applicant doing simulated "welding" exercise in the Assessment Area.

**Fourth Phase**—Background/Reference Check, Interview, Drug Screen, Physical, and Job Offer. This phase has remained similar to the original process set up at the start up of the plant.

The hiring process is also set up to be a fair and consistent process that is legally defensible in terms of its reliability and validity. Many times when we are describing the process we are asked how Toyota is able to do all of these checks, assessments, and demonstrations and not get sued. The fact of the matter is that Toyota has gotten sued over its hiring process, but it has never lost a case in court over its hiring process, because they have never varied from their standard process.

Everyone hired at Toyota has gone through the same process and has been able to meet the standard scores necessary to be selected. It doesn't matter "who you know" to get hired at Toyota. A person reviewing the process recently asked the question, "How does word-of-mouth recruiting factor into the hiring process? Does someone get an 'intangible score' if recommended by someone on the inside, such as a family member?" In fact there is no "intangible score," which is how the integrity of the system has been maintained and no cases have been lost.

Ellen Bowman, a recent retiree of the plant, was a specialist in the recruiting and hiring process for close to 20 years. She recalls many people asking her the same question.

*It was as if I had won the lottery, and relatives I didn't even know I had would call asking if I could help get them hired at Toyota. Of course, all I could do was direct them to "the system" to go through it like everyone else and if they got hired, it was because of them and not me. We were trained to give this same answer to everybody—it didn't matter if the Governor of the state called with the same request. I remember when my cousin went through the system and he got hired. I was the hero of the family get-togethers for a whole year. It didn't matter how many times I told them that I had nothing to do with it, they still said, 'Yeah, sure, thanks so much, Ellen.' This went on until another cousin went through the process and did not get hired. Well, I went from hero to goat real quick, and they finally believed that I really had nothing to do with someone getting hired at Toyota.*

## Selecting Toyota Executives

Toyota has had success in growing their own leaders from within, but with the company's rapid growth they have had to hire more senior managers from the outside and develop them as leaders. To find people who at the start have the patience and some of the personal characteristics to learn the Toyota Way requires an intensive recruitment process. Gary Convis, who was President of TMMK during its most rapid growth period, describes what they were looking for to promote from within or hire a leader from outside:

*We look for someone who has ability and personal drive and appreciation for team members' work itself. A person who is humble and can respect the work others can do, and can use their problem solving skills as they slowly go up the ladder can have greater influence. First, I need the right kind of people that I then challenge while running daily operations. TPS leaders have to really understand the right way to manage people and it takes years to develop. I look for the person who manages naturally the Toyota Way when we hire them and when we promote them. We do not promote the smartest guy on the block who can make a great presentation. That may be valuable and fit certain parts of our business. In manufacturing we need the personal touch—respect for individuals—and the ability to motivate and truly partner with people at all levels.*

Steven St. Angelo was hired as executive vice president of TMMK in April of 2005 and in June of 2006 became president when Gary Convis took over all North American manufacturing. It was the first time an American was appointed from outside Toyota to such a high level in a major plant. Toyota leaders felt that those who were eligible for this position within the company were either unavailable or not ready. They chose to look outside and picked someone with demonstrated leadership success in the auto industry. St. Angelo worked for General Motors for 31 years. Even while he was a manager at General Motors he was fascinated by the Toyota Production System and sought out opportunities to study NUMMI: "I would go to NUMMI for six weeks at a time before I was assigned there. I would then implement at least one item I learned back at GM. We started to develop the GM Way from the Toyota Way."

Later he was assigned to NUMMI as a senior advisor where he really got to learn TPS deeply by living it. He was selected by NUMMI because he had the leadership characteristics they were looking for: "They were very cautious about who they would stick in there. They wanted someone humble and who was not going to be on the cover of Ward's Auto World. They wanted someone with the right DNA."

St. Angelo's first interview at NUMMI lasted a full day. During lunch they had him go on the floor for one and a half hours and come back with observations. While on the floor, he wrote four pages of observations. At General Motors, when a plant manager goes to someone else's plant it is not acceptable to criticize anything. So he felt a bit awkward as he started going down his list. He found the NUMMI executives were very interested in what he was finding. St. Angelo asked if it was appropriate to be calling out areas to improve and they asked him to please continue. As St. Angelo explained, "I do not know if I could have done that in GM—openly criticizing plant operations like that. They were not so much interested in what I was finding but more interested in what I looked for and what is important to me and why I was looking for these things."

St. Angelo waited for a call on whether he was accepted and then got another call saying they wanted him to fly out the next day to Japan and meet top executives. While there, he met with approximately 15 top people including Akio Toyoda and Fujio Cho. He flew back to Detroit and waited for a phone call and got another NUMMI call saying they wanted to talk to him one more time. This time it was more of a technical discussion asking more detailed questions. After St. Angelo got the job he asked what they were looking for. He later learned from his Japanese coordinator: "On the first visit to NUMMI we were evaluating your technical capability and genchi genbutsu abilities (to observe directly actual production and see waste). When we invited you to Japan we were trying to understand your character, DNA, and type of soul. Who is Steve St. Angelo? Does he just know the tools or the way of thinking?"

There is no question that NUMMI is strategically important to Toyota and that Steve St. Angelo as a potential vice president was important. Meeting with a Toyoda family member and three of the managing directors of Toyota in Japan so they could assess his "type of soul" illustrates that Toyota takes selection seriously.

### Pay Me Now or Pay Me Later

A common question or response from executives reviewing this interview process is: "How does Toyota afford to take all of this time and effort to hire someone?" Of course, our response is "How do you afford not to?" The overall benefit of hiring someone for the long term who follows the values and works to continually improve the process is, as the commercial says, "priceless" and hard to calculate on a balance sheet. The practical dollar and cents indicator that Toyota uses to reflect how well their hiring process is doing is the turnover or attrition rate. The rate of turnover at TMMK as of 2007 for full-time hires was less than 3 percent per year.

Most companies track this number but don't necessarily use it to drive improvement. One company we worked with decided to and was surprised by what they found. Their turnover rate was 18 percent, with most leaving within the first year. They calculated that the cost of hiring and training someone at their facility was over $5,000. More than 500 employees per year were leaving the company and had to be replaced. The observation made by the team assigned to the project was: "We don't have a screening component to our selection process. We bring in whoever shows up and then the first year on the job acts as the screen. We had no idea how much it was costing us."

This company decided to implement a system similar to the one being used by Toyota. Certainly the systems will cost money to design, implement, and maintain. The team has calculated that if they can improve the attrition rate to just 12 percent they can pay for the new system.

## SUMMARY

In the Toyota Way, the attraction, selection, and orientation of quality team members, from the production line member all the way to the position of president is a critical part of the people value stream and in growing the Toyota culture. As discussed, the Toyota Way values of mutual respect and trust, continuous improvement, and the corresponding core competencies are the common threads tying the processes together in a systematic manner.

## KEY POINTS TO CONSIDER FOR YOUR COMPANY

1. Human resources has the responsibility for a consistent hiring process used company-wide that seeks to obtain the right person, in the right form, in the right amount, at the right time.

2. There is a defensible process for advertising, reviewing, and evaluating applications that is clearly based on job duties, responsibilities, and competencies.
3. The applicant is asked to demonstrate key job competencies through paper and pencil (or Web-based) tests and behavioral work task simulations and questions followed by a probation period on the actual job.
4. There is a clearly articulated orientation curriculum and corresponding schedule of sessions aimed at initially familiarizing new employees with all significant company policies, procedures, work expectations, and programs. The training and socialization process at Toyota starts *during* selection.
5. There is a system to collect data and monitor effectiveness of the overall system and drive improvement activities.

# Chapter 5

# Developing Competent and Able People

*It is not enough to do your best; you must know what to do, and then do your best.*

—W. Edwards Deming, quality guru

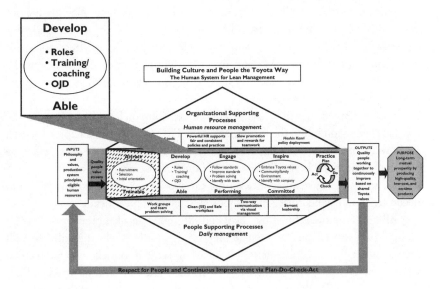

## TOYOTA TRAINS PEOPLE LIKE THEY ARE ALL SURGEONS

Now that Toyota has worked so hard to attract and select the kinds of people who can prosper in the Toyota Way culture, what do they do with them? Of course they could put them into dull, boring jobs with little training and support and hope some of the cream rises, but that would be a wasteful People Value Stream. For decades Toyota has worked diligently to develop a strong and effective culture of people who are continually improving its processes. Toyota is a learning organization and a lot has been gleaned about how to do each and every job. Much has also been learned about how people can effectively work together, communicate, and solve problems. It would be foolish to assume that people coming in the door, even if they have the types of personal qualities Toyota desires, will simply know everything about how to do the job and about how to acclimate to the Toyota culture, so they must be taught both.

You often hear in Toyota the analogy of the operator as a surgeon, which is used to describe the production workers putting together the car as the surgeons of the factory. They are the only ones adding value in the factory so all other supporting staff must add their value by helping them by bringing them tools, parts, information, and whatever other support they need. We might extend the analogy of a surgeon to everyone working for Toyota.

It is well accepted that surgeons need a great deal of professional training to do their jobs. It starts with medical school but that mainly gives them the book knowledge. None of us want a surgeon operating on us with a book in one hand and the scalpel in the other. The surgeon learns the craft of surgery on the job serving under experts and taking increasing responsibility over time. Now we are not arguing that every job on the assembly line has the complexity of heart surgery. But every job has been dissected and improved and documented in standardized work and improved again over and over. The production worker is taught the current best way with the precision of teaching surgery. And this applies to the engineer and the group leader and the HR specialist.

In this chapter, we will focus most of our attention on how Toyota teaches the routine production job to the team member at TMMK. Later in Chapter 17, we'll see how Toyota Motor Sales has dissected each and every job at a Lexus dealership and teaches precisely how to answer the phone, greet customers, repair and wash the car, and perform maintenance on the car. No job is considered too menial to deconstruct and standardize, and all jobs are taught in great detail.

All new employees hired by Toyota go through a detailed orientation process and then are sent to their jobs where they are rigorously taught the skills to fulfill their most basic job requirements. They have to settle into their roles as qualified team members who can do quality work in the right way and on schedule. In a manufacturing role, this means performing each step of the job very precisely according to the standardized work to takt time (i.e., the rate of customer demand). In a supervisory role, it means using considerable judgment in daily tasks, coordinating responsibilities and information with many other people, and performing to the schedule. This all requires developing unquestionable expertise, because jobs at Toyota have been improved over time to demand such high levels of skill. There is no such thing as "unskilled labor" at Toyota. When companies talk about unskilled labor, it simply means that no one has taken time to work out the details of how to do the job at a high level, and they are throwing people into unstable and poorly defined processes.

At the same time as new hires are learning the basic skills of the job, they are being socialized into the Toyota Way of doing things. For example, just being taught to do the job in a highly disciplined way in a well organized environment by a caring team leader tells the new employee something is different. At this company, people care about the company, the customer, and the employee. It is not even enough to meet the quality standards and quantity requirements of the job. There is a Toyota Way of observing, thinking, communicating, and behaving that must become part of the mental makeup of the employee, and this indoctrination starts from the first day on the job. In reality it started in the recruitment process.

# GETTING STARTED: TEAM MEMBER ORIENTATION

The Human Resource department is responsible for the new team member for the five-week orientation period, after which the team member is turned over to the home department. The aim of the orientation program is to begin socializing the new team member to the Toyota production environment and culture. An example schedule is shown in Figure 5.1. It shows only three days allotted to get the basic concept across. All five weeks are mapped out hour by hour in order to use the time of all members efficiently and to continue to send the message to the new hires that they matter and that how they use their time matters. In production, the orientation is also the beginning of the team members' three-month probationary period, so it is important to both them and the company that they get off on the right foot. The schedule is given to each member and team members are expected to give daily feedback to the instructors on how things are going for them. The orientation involves the following components:

## Work Conditioning

The team member participates in systematic exercises designed to strengthen muscles and increase endurance in a state-of-the-art fitness center. Supervised by health and fitness professionals, the regimen focuses on exercise equipment and aerobics that relate to the kind of work, flexibility, and endurance required of production tasks. The physical workouts are complemented by educational presentations that emphasize injury prevention, strength training, low-back care, ergonomics, and nutrition. The fitness center is available for team members' use outside of work hours so this orientation is also used to train them on how to use the equipment and encourages continued workouts after the orientation.

## Human Resource Policies

The team member is trained on the policies and basic production procedures that facilitate a new employee's adaptation to the environment and culture. In addition to learning the mechanics of basic human resource policies, safety procedures, and pay and benefits, emphasis is on expectations of the team member's role in the production process. Top management personally welcomes the new members and explains how each team member is critical to the continuing success of the company's operations. This portion of the program is run by

| TIME | NO O.T. | NO O.T. | NO O.T. |
|---|---|---|---|
| 1st / 2nd | **Monday** | **Wednesday** | **Friday** |
| 5:15–7:15 p.m. | | **CQPO** Intro to Quality Circles | **CQPO** Review/Testing Modules 1–4 |
| 7:15–7:30 p.m. | | **Break** | **Break** |
| 7:30–9.45 p.m. | **GPC TRAINING IN ASSEMBLY** | JIT primary process by Production T/L / OJT 25% primary | OJT 25% primary With Professional Team Member |
| 9:45–10:30 p.m. | | **Lunch** | **Lunch** |
| 10:30p–12:30 a.m. | | JIT secondary process by Production T/L / OJT 25% secondary | OJT 25% secondary With Professional Team Member |
| 12:30–12:45 a.m. | | **Break** | **Break** |
| 12:45–1:05 a.m. | | Travel to Fitness Facility | Travel to Fitness Facility |
| 1:05–2:00 a.m. | | Core/cardio circuit | Work conditioning circuit |

| | Each new hire is to fill out this form daily during 2nd break (5 minutes of company time) and leave it with their GL. Each new hire is to return this traning schedule to hfc staff by Friday. | | |
|---|---|---|---|
| Did you train with a professional team member? | | | Y / N |
| Was the training schedule followed? | | | Y / N |
| Are you experiencing any discomfort performing processes? If yes, did you report it to your TL or GL? Is additional training needed? | | | Y / N  Y / N |
| NEW HIRE COMMENT SECTION | | | |
| DAILY NH SIGNATURE | | | |
| GROUP LEADER/ TEAM LEADER COMMENT SECTION | | | |

Source: April Crosby, Health, Fitness Corporation, 05/2006

**Figure 5.1** Portion of TMMK New Hire Training Schedule

members of HR with help contracted out to the Center for Quality People and Organizations (CQPO).

## Production

HR completes its orientation and then hands the team member over to the home department to get trained on the actual production job. In this period, the team member performs actual production-line tasks, gradually adjusting to production process and quality standards. The Toyota Job Instruction methods used are detailed in *Toyota Talent* (2007)[1] and summarized later in this chapter. The team member learns a few relatively simple production jobs (called "freshman jobs") outside their home department before being assigned permanently to a specific production area. The Orientation Program group leaders and fitness professionals then conduct follow-up reviews to insure that each team member is properly using the ergonomic procedures emphasized earlier in the program.

In the event that a new team member chooses to resign early, there is a personal meeting followed later by an exit interview. The intent here is to grasp the true reasons for their decision and to determine if effective countermeasures can be formulated to increase the retention of new hires in the future.

In the Georgetown plant, the rate of attrition has historically run less than three percent per year for full-time hires (for those who enter the orientation training) and slightly higher for temporaries. We believe this relatively low attrition rate is partly due to the initial thorough orientation that gradually eases the employee into the Toyota culture.

## TRAINING TO DO THE JOB

After orientation, team members are assigned to their home department and trained by the team leader and group leader to do the actual jobs they will be performing as part of the team. When we consider training, we usually think about a group of people sitting in a classroom with a teacher in front using visual aids and presenting, or if we think of on-the-job training, we usually picture someone being sent off to do the job with a little bit of instruction and someone else watching over him until he gets it. Toyota uses different training approaches for different purposes, taking each one very seriously. Consider the different training modes in Figure 5.2. Within Toyota, each is highly developed.

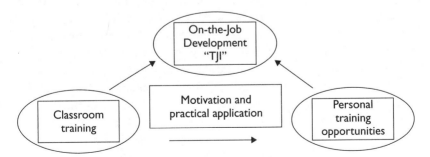

**Figure 5.2** Human Resources Development Modes

---

[1] Liker, Jeffrey, *The Toyota Way*, New York: McGraw-Hill, 2004.

Toyota is not a school and clearly identifies most strongly as a manufacturing company. So, how is it that they value training so highly and think so deeply about it? We would suggest that there were many influences on this aspect of Toyota culture:

1. Origins in a farming community. Farmers knew the future of their business depended on how well they trained the next generation, which usually meant family members that they cared about deeply or those whom they in essence adopted into the family.
2. The high value placed in Japanese culture on education. As a resource-poor, tiny island nation the development of human resources was clearly the most valuable asset in Japan.
3. The high value placed in Japan on honing skills of many kinds. One can go to Japan and look at doll making, or developing a Japanese garden, or preparing sushi, or the precision with which the hotel room is cleaned to appreciate this aspect of Japanese culture.
4. *Monozukuri*—the art of making things—is a term often used within Toyota with reverence to emphasize this is the backbone of the company. In Japan, the value placed on manufacturing skill is reflected in national competitions in welding and quick die changing and other manufacturing skills. Denso, Toyota's largest supplier, has an annual manufacturing Olympics and the winning Olympians are honored with their pictures on a wall of fame.

Toyota places the most emphasis on the On-the-Job Development (OJD) portion of the training modes listed earlier. This is another aspect of Toyota culture: the high value placed on learning by doing. One of the core values of the *Toyota Way 2001* discussed in Chapter 1 is *genchi genbutsu*, which in general refers to going to see the actual problem to understand deeply, but is much broader and reflects the value placed on "getting your hands dirty" and learning by doing. Sakiichi Toyoda invented the first wooden loom by getting his hands dirty. He was taught carpentry by his father and used this skill and his ingenuity to make a semi-automatic wooden loom that was much simpler to use and saved a lot of labor. Kiichiro Toyoda and Eiji Toyoda learned the car business by getting their hands dirty, taking apart American cars and studying the details of craftsmanship. The Toyota Production System was developed by Taiichi Ohno by experimenting and trying things. There is a famous story of the Ohno pond where he tossed out parts of machinery that failed when he was trying to make improvements in the machine shop. It was said there were more machine parts than water. It would be totally alien to the Toyota culture to say "I just got my degree in subject X so I am an expert in it." What have you really done? How did you demonstrate your mastery? What contributions did you make to improve the craft?

In the sections that follow, we will briefly consider various training modes, beginning with the more traditional classroom training and personal training opportunities. We then devote an entire section to the more central approach of on-the-job development.

## Classroom Training

In the days of Taiichi Ohno, classroom training was not highly valued. Anyone caught studying manufacturing in the classroom would be sternly shown to the shop floor where they could really learn something of value. Ohno's idea of classroom training was to hold the class in the factory. His famous Ohno circle, discussed in *The Toyota Way (2004)*[2], was his way of teaching people about TPS. He would paint a circle anyplace on the shop floor and ask them to stand in the circle all day long and observe. Every couple of hours he would come back and ask what they saw. When he was satisfied that they were deeply observing the process and seeing the waste, he would let them go home. He would never tell them what he saw. They never got "the right answer" from the master. Yet he was clearly teaching and most people who stood in the circle describe this as one of the most profound learning experiences they ever experienced. The training was a start in teaching them the meaning of *genchi genbutsu*. They learned that their first, superficial impression of the process told them very little about the real waste in the system. To really understand the problem took far deeper observation than they were used to.

This way of teaching is philosophically similar to the Socratic Method. Socrates would ask questions and not give answers, drawing responses out of the students. The purpose is to make the students think for themselves. Sometimes in Toyota, TPS is referred to as the "Thinking Production System." There are real life lessons every day when inventory runs out, when a quality problem is caught and the line stops, or when someone cannot achieve the takt time and has to pull the andon cord. These disruptions force the work group to think. This is the Toyota Way of teaching, and is also quite natural in Japanese culture.

Now fast forward to Toyota of today; we might expect that classroom training is banned from the company. Yet there are courses galore in plants, in engineering offices, in parts distribution warehouses, and in sales offices. We could interpret this modern trend in different ways. One way is that the company is going down hill and the Toyota Way is getting diluted. Just like their Western counterparts, Toyota employees sit in the classroom mindlessly watching PowerPoint slides flash before their eyes. This is a depressing thought indeed.

---

[2] Liker, Jeffrey, The Toyota Way, New York: McGraw-Hill, 2004.

Alternatively we could interpret this more positively as an adaptation to globalization and a process of learning more effective ways to use classroom training. When Fujio Cho led the writing of *The Toyota Way 2001*, he was taking a position. Yet one of Ohno's best students, Fujio Cho, wrote it down. He did this because the world is changing. It was no longer possible to assign each person to a mentor who grew up with TPS to teach them daily like the master blacksmith taught the apprentice. The company was growing too rapidly and there were not enough sensei to go around. As plants were launched globally, the ratio of teachers to students was getting tiny, so new teaching methods were required.

Toyota is always up for a challenge, and certainly the aggressive growth of Toyota has created a formidable one. How do you teach large numbers of people distributed all over the world with small numbers of instructors and still capture the experience of learning by doing? How can Toyota avoid the trap of watering down the essence of its culture by relegating it to PowerPoint? One good example of finding a balance between mass classroom training and learning by doing is the *Toyota Way 2001* training.

The creators of this training agonized over how to strike an appropriate balance. When the *Toyota Way 2001* was first spread globally every executive and manager and leader in the company was required to go through this training. In the classroom they were taught the basic tenets of the Toyota Way. They learned the words and concepts behind the words and also studied some basic history of Toyota and learned how famous Toyota leaders thought about these concepts. Within Toyota that abstract classroom training would never be enough. The student was exposed to ideas but did not develop any real skills. The training included case studies to solve, and then managers identified real problems from their region. Then they had to go back and work on solving the real problems. In addition each manager then had the responsibility to go back to their areas and train all of their staff in the same class. This accomplished two main benefits. The first is the well known principle that the more a person teaches something the better they learn it. But the main point was that by teaching it to all their subordinates they were involved in the discussions; questions and challenges were brought to them by people highlighting areas needing improvement. At the end of the training sessions the leaders were now accountable, face to face with all of their people to not only follow the Toyota Way themselves but also to be the champion and guardian of it for their entire section. There were mentors available for day-to-day coaching. At the executive level this included executive coordinators in Japan, but by this point there also was a strong cadre of American managers who had deeply learned the Toyota Way through years of mentoring and experience and could now mentor others.

Over the years classroom training has become a more central part of learning at Toyota. Classroom training is efficient. We can get exposed to many concepts in a short period of time. One of the complaints of Americans who were trained by *sensei* in the early days is that they were told what to do but not *why* it should be done that way. It was a process of discovery and arguably they wanted to be spoon fed. Regardless, Americans want to know why. Classroom training can explain the whys. There is a recognition in Toyota that part of learning is developing an understanding of basic concepts. Organizing thought patterns is useful, but within the practical manufacturing-oriented world of Toyota this abstract learning must be converted as quickly as possible into actual skills and action. So every course has some sort of action component. It is recognized that people do not really assimilate the learning and do not develop practical skills by simply listening to an instructor. They have to do something themselves and have some eye-opening experiences. There are a variety of exercises, hands-on simulations, and practical shop floor activities to provide this experience.

One example of this type of progressive learning experience is the group leader pre-promotion training program. This training, with its progressive phases was designed by Anna Marie Eifert, an organizational development specialist with TMMK. Before team leaders are promoted to group leaders, they are given four weeks of training. The training is designed to be delivered in progressive phases with each including a demonstration of competency by the student. The key competencies addressed are leadership/interpersonal skills and problem-solving skills. The training begins with lectures, moves to role plays and simulations, then to on-the-floor practice, and finally to on-the-floor implementation. In each phase, there is confirmation that key learning has taken place and the student is able to demonstrate the competencies. The final phase confirms the students are practicing the skills they learned, and that those skills are leading to improved business results in their area over several months after the training.

An example of one of these progressive phases is problem-solving training. In the problem-solving simulation there is a "mini factory" set up for the participants to build "model Land Cruisers." The group leaders are working to produce the units with the highest quality, with the lowest cost, in the shortest amount of time. They track variables such as the amount of workforce needed, the Work-in-Process inventory (WIP), the quality and delivery. There are seven rounds of production run, with the opportunity for the group leaders to problem solve and make improvements between each round. Since the training is held in the factory they can go and see between rounds to observer similar processes on the shop floor. Later they will go to the floor in groups of three to work on a problem on a real process and develop an A-3 problem-solving report to summarize the problem solving process.

Class instructors have reported that they are literally able to see the "lights come on" as a result of this layered approach. This is much different than the typical check-off-the-box supervisor training. Toyota has found that it takes this commitment of time and repetition to make sure the learning takes place.

Students have reported the same dynamic while adding they never knew how much problem solving depended on their interpersonal skills as well as their technical skills. One team, reporting on their "on the floor problem solving" noted that they had to talk to 17 people to work on solving this one problem. With each of the individuals, they had to practice their new questioning and listening skills in order to get the facts and information they needed to solve the problem. The phases of the training are summarized in Table 5.1.

**Table 5.1** Phases in Group Leader Pre-Promotion Training Program

| Phase | Delivery Method | Demonstration to Confirm Learning of Key Competencies. |
|---|---|---|
| I(A) Classroom— leadership/interpersonal skills | PowerPoint and lecture of Toyota Way values, interpersonal communication and conflict management | Written quizzes |
| II(A) Simulation— leadership/interpersonal skills | Preparing A–3 on a videotaped role play of a conflict situation to practice skills | Observation, assessment, and feedback by peer observers and trainer |
| I(B) Classroom problem solving skills | PowerPoint and lecture | Quiz on key points and graded Case Study exercise |
| II(B) Problem Solving Simulation | Simulated factory using model vehicles, running seven rounds of production, utilizing problem solving process to make improvements | Each round is measured in terms of KPI's and students progress is documented. Students complete A–3 problem solving report to summarize their improvement activity |
| III On-the-floor practice | Groups of three select an actual problem on the floor and work through the steps of problem solving as a team to complete an A-3. | An actual A–3 problem solving report is completed as a result of the activity with a report out to managers. |
| IV On-the-job implementation | NA | At designated intervals after the training, Group Leaders are surveyed by form and person, including observation to confirm practicing of learned skills. Gaps are addressed with coaching and development. |
| V Impact on the key performance and business indicators | NA | At designated intervals, correlation between group leader demonstration of competencies and ability to meet business goals is grasped and gaps are addressed with further coaching and development |

The number of classroom courses has grown considerably at Toyota. An example of the "core training" requirements for each level of the organization at TMMK is shown in Table 5.2. The training that is listed as "core" for each classification is to be completed by that individual while in that position, unless the course is designated as "pre-promotion." Again we emphasize that classroom training at Toyota combines presentation with action by the students. The actual formal presentation by an instructor is kept to a minimum.

**Table 5.2** Example of Classroom Training Matrix for Toyota

| Course Name | Hrs | Manager | GL | Specialist | TL | TM | Staff |
|---|---|---|---|---|---|---|---|
| Coaching | 8 | C | C | E | | | |
| Diversity | 16 | C | C | C | | | E |
| Gaining Agreement | 7 | C | C | C | | | |
| GL Pre Promotion | 160 | | C | | | | |
| How to Speak | 16 | E | E | E | E | E | E |
| PDCA | 8 | C | C | E | E | | E |
| Problem Solving | 16 | C | C | C | C | E | C |
| Problem Solving II | 16 | C | C | C | C | | E |
| Standardized Work-STW | 8 | C | C | C | C | | |
| TPS Principals | 8 | | | E | | E | E |
| Job Instruction | 10 | C | C | E | C | E | E |
| Situational Leadership | 16 | C | C | E | E | | |
| Leading Improvement | 7 | C | C | C | | | |
| Learning from Reflection | 7 | C | C | C | | | |
| Meeting Facilitation | 16 | C | C | C | C | E | E |
| Philosophies of Efficiency | 8 | C | C | C | E | | E |
| A–3 Proposal Writing | 8 | | C | C | E | C | C |
| Quality Circles—Leading | 8 | C | C | C | E | E | E |
| Quality Circles—Managing | 4 | E | E | E | E | E | E |
| Listening and Facilitation | 7 | C | C | C | | | |
| New Hire—Mfg. Training | 64 | | | | | C | |
| Responding to Conflict | 14 | C | C | C | E | E | E |
| STW for Office | 8 | E | E | | | | C |
| Suggestion System | 3 | C | C | E | E | | |
| TL Pre Promotion | 120 | | | C | | | |
| Time Mgt. | 8 | E | E | E | | | E |
| Understanding Change | 7 | C | C | C | | | |
| Worksite Communication | 16 | C | C | E | E | | E |
| Write Right | 16 | E | E | E | E | E | E |

Key: C = Core Class/Required, E= Elective, Hrs = Length of Course, GL = Group Leader, Specialist = Engineers, HR, Accounting etc., TL = Team Leader, TM = Team Member, Staff = Administrative Support

## Personal Training Opportunities

Toyota calls personal training opportunities "self-initiated development," because individual employees must choose to attend them. These personal training opportunities are usually initiated by an individual to address a need or gap that is not presently being addressed with current "company development opportunities." They can be offerings inside or outside the company, and they are important both for content and process reasons. From a process perspective, these opportunities are effective vehicles for employees to cultivate self motivation. They also foster communications and relationships between employees. From a content perspective, they address an identified gap in someone's development.

Examples of internal personal training opportunities would include working on project teams such as a safety committee or a cost improvement task force. These committees are held at different levels of the organization (i.e., section, department, and plant and therefore are available to every level the organization). Another example of an internal personal training opportunity especially for team members is the Quality Circle. Any team member at Toyota can volunteer to go through a paid training course on overtime in order to become a Circle Leader. After eight hours of training, this person can start their own Quality Circle and facilitate a team through the process of solving a problem (approved by the group leader). This is a great opportunity for team members to develop their leadership, communication, and problem solving skills. In fact, one study done at TMMK showed that the majority of team members promoted to team leader had experience in a Quality Circle.

An example of a usually "external" activity that TMMK has made "internal" is known as the "Reach for the Stars" (STARS) program. It is a program offered in collaboration with five area colleges that are organized to deliver classes both on-site at the plant and electronically to interested students. The classes are held after shift and are completely voluntary for team members. The most attended programs are the Bachelors in Engineering or the Bachelors in Organizational Development. Tuition is reimbursed up to 100 percent by the company depending on the grade achieved in the class.

There are numerous examples of individuals who have completed degrees in the STARS program and were able to advance their careers at Toyota as a result. Team members have earned their engineering degrees or other bachelor degrees and have transferred to support areas as specialists. Many people in middle management have earned their bachelors and masters as a way to help develop themselves for executive positions. For example, Cheryl Jones, vice president of manufacturing at TMMK joined TMMK in 1987 as a group leader. She was working as a manager at the local grocery store when Toyota hired her. She utilized the STARS program to earn her Bachelors in Management in 2004 and is currently pursuing her Masters. Hundreds of others have done the same. Many people ask: what is the ROI on this program and how can it be justified? This is an example of Toyota's commitment to the long-term relationship and development of its team members, even if the short-term benefits cannot always be quantified.

An example of an external personal training opportunity may be some specialized training that is offered at other providers. Several managers at Toyota have chosen to attend, with the support of Toyota, the Center for Creative Leadership at University of North Carolina, and its program. Several executives have attended the Wharton School of Business and its executive development programs. From vice president to team member, countless people have utilized this form of development at Toyota.

# ON-THE-JOB DEVELOPMENT (OJD)

We have worked with many companies and discussed with them how they train people. They proudly show their training center and state-of-the-art audiovisual facilities; every detail of the lectern that controls the audio visual has been thought through. In one state of the art facility of a furniture manufacturer they invested in all the bells and whistles and the only place to run the presentation was from behind the lectern in the front of the room and off to the right corner. A huge projection screen took up most of the front of the room. So the instructor sat down at the lectern and ran the show. They clearly had no concept of eye contact between the lecturer and student, and little concept of interaction. It was like going to the movies. When we asked how people actually learned the details of how to do the job they said, "Oh, that's all learned on the job. Our people on the floor are responsible for training new people to do the job." When we went to the floor and asked detailed questions, we discovered something entirely different. On-the-job training essentially meant: "We will get you started and then you are on your own."

On-the-Job Development (OJD) at Toyota is a very different process. Going back to its farming roots, there is a great appreciation within Toyota of what it takes to develop real skills. Go to any successful working family farm and you will find that the parents or grandparents are teachers. They teach those with less experience how to do a multitude of tasks needed to run the farm—preparing the soil, planting, picking, baling hay, repairing equipment, tending animals, basic carpentry, and more. The young person who may one day take over the farm, needs real skill in each of these areas and will benefit from the accumulated knowledge of generations of farmers.

At Toyota, OJD is arguably the most important responsibility of all managers and Toyota has developed a systematic approach. Toyota uses the term "development" because it is broader than what we often think of as training. Training is what you do so the worker can perform the job and meet the numbers. Development is growing the team member so they become increasingly capable at doing the job, at critiquing how to do the job, at improving how the job is done, and eventually at training others.

The process of training a Toyota production worker is summarized in Figure 5.3.[3] Before the team members have even been assigned to the team where they will be working as part of the orientation they will get training in what Toyota calls "fundamental skills." These are taught at a new organizational innovation for Toyota: The Global Production Center. Then they are assigned to a team with a team leader and group leader who introduce them to others and assign them to the first job they will learn. That job has been broken down into tiny work elements that are taught piece by piece using the Toyota Job Instruction (TJI) method. The individual team member continues to be supported full time until she is comfortable doing the job throughout the shift to takt time. We will discuss each of these steps in turn.

## FUNDAMENTAL SKILL TRAINING (GPC)

Prior to going to the line to learn an actual job, the team member participates off-line in job tasks that reflect plant processes performed at a rate that gradually increases to production line standards. The simulation area is known as the Global Production Center (GPC) and is a standardized process worldwide for Toyota to train new members. The first GPC was in Japan, where they put together the

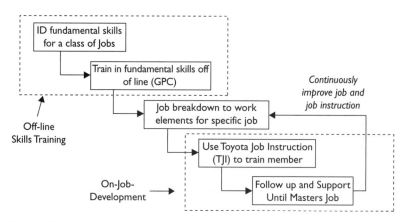

**Figure 5.3** Step-by-Step Progression to Stable Job Performance

---

[3] The methodology and the Global Production Center discussed below are described in great detail in Liker, Jeffrey and David Meier, *Toyota Talent: Developing People the Toyota Way*, New York: McGraw-Hill, 2007.

standards and then began training people from around the world. The next step was to set up three more centers to service the globe. They were located in Thailand, Europe, and the United States. Georgetown, Kentucky, was selected as the location for the U.S. center and it is located just beside TMMK. There are smaller GPCs at the plant-level. TMMK was the first North American model and then each U.S. plant sent potential "trainers" there in order to be trained to go back and set up the equivalent area at their plant. This process of piloting and improving, developing regional centers, and then standardizing globally is characteristic of Toyota.

In the early days of TMMK, group leaders and team leaders learned from Japanese trainers who came to the plant for three-year stays. The group leaders and team leaders were taught how to train team members to do their job using Job Instruction training (described later in the chapter). That has not changed, but now there is standardized pretraining in fundamental skills through GPC prior to learning a specific job. The foundation for training and standardization at each of the GPC centers is the fundamental skills training and it is built around the visual video manual. This manual has text and audio (translated for any language) and video to instruct the new hire with the details of the specific skill to learn at each station. There is a laptop computer and set of headphones at each station for the trainee to review the manual while practicing at the corresponding work station. The visual manual walks the trainee through each step of the skill using video clips and still pictures. Alongside the video is written standardized work on how to perform each step of the fundamental skill. As the video plays, demonstrating the skill, key points relating to safety, quality, and productivity flash up on the screen in text. The manual is paced and stops at each step along the way in order to allow the trainee to practice what she just learned.

It is a student-directed system, with a trainer available to answer any questions. Once the team member understands the skill and practices it, she demonstrates her ability to the trainer. If they reach the standard, they move on to the next station. If they are not able to reach the standard, they review the video manual again and spend more time practicing. With a Web-based system, Toyota can put all of the best practices from around the world on a video-training manual. This means every member across the globe is learning the fundamental skills in the exact same way. If there are any updates or improvements, the rest of the globe will have it in less than 24 hours. Toyota describes the visual manual as follows:[4]

> *While permitting flexibility at the application level within each plant, Toyota sought a "common base" for manufacturing at Toyota plants worldwide. That meant finding the best practices and eliminating individual*

---

[4] http://www.toyotageorgetown.com/gpc.asp

*methods. Since Toyota traditionally taught skills on a person-to-person basis, knowledge was implicit and—because kaizen meant continuous improvement—rarely written down.*

*Drawing upon the vast experience of its experts, Toyota selected and organized the best practices for each skill. Toyota applied digital technology to compile these methods into "visual manuals," keeping text to a minimum, while using photos along with short animation and video clips to facilitate rapid comprehension. Slow-motion videos enable trainees to grasp skills that tend to be demonstrated too rapidly by seasoned human experts. Such skills can be as basic as the knack of rolling a bolt from palm to fingertips. In all, GPC has about 2,000 visual manuals in stock, covering a vast repertoire of automotive assembly processes.*

### From Visual Manuals to Standardized Work

*For efficient and effective skills training, personnel pass through four stages at GPC: (1) Trainees acquire basic knowledge using visual manuals. (2) They practice fundamental skills, such as how to tighten screws so they are not too loose or too tight, tightening actual screws at specially designed work tables. (3) They progress to "element work" training, such as joining a door lock rod and door handle. (4) They learn the basics of standardized work, including how to start and end an operation, the kanban system of just-in-time parts ordering, and how to use the andon system to halt the line if there is a problem.*

### Action Training and Image Training

*The regional GPC "best skill training area" in Georgetown is 8,000 square meters. Here, up to 130 trainees hone their skills on approximately 400 specially developed work tables and pieces of simulation equipment. In practicing "element work," trainees gain the ability to perform each task within a standardized time frame, which is essential to maintaining takt time to keep an assembly line flowing smoothly.*

*The German word takt means rhythm or musical meter and in production it is the amount of time the team member has to complete their job based on customer demand. A rhythmical approach to movement is key to achieving proficiency in these jobs. In car-body painting, for example, precise yet rhythmical body motion not only improves efficiency, it also helps assure complete and consistent paint coverage.*

*Image training is also important, particularly for assembly stages that require operations outside the worker's field of vision such as behind a door panel. To rapidly gain proficiency, the trainee uses visual manuals and off-line or "static" skill practice to develop a mental image of what his or her hands will be doing during "dynamic" assembly on a moving line.*

> *Best practices are selected and refined based on ergonomics. They contribute to worker safety and avoidance of physical strain in addition to enhancing manufacturing efficiency and quality.*

The GPC's trainers are all experienced in production coming from the ranks of group leaders and team leaders who were made available by productivity improvements. It is a rotating assignment that also helps train the workforce as more and more leaders get experience as trainers. Any trainer in the GPC must be certified which takes six months of learning and testing and GPC trainers must be recertified every two years. When the team member passes all of the tasks (10–15 per department), the new hire is ready to report to his or her production supervisor and begin the actual training in their processes using the job instruction method (described later in this chapter).

Lisa Richardson is the Regional Master Trainer for Stamping located at the Toyota North American Production Support Center in Georgetown (North American version of the GPC). She came from TMMK and has spent most of her career in stamping, trained first by the Japanese trainers and then by the American managers. She toured us through the area with obvious pride in the stamping fundamental skills training area and in her opportunity to be spending time training Toyota members in these skills. As good as her original training was with the Japanese trainers in the early 1990s, it was not even near the detailed level it is now with the GPC areas.

> *"In stamping, we focus our fundamental skills training on safety, quality, and productivity," Lisa described. "As a safety example, one of the key fundamental skills for stamping is part handling, which makes up a large part of a stamping team member's job. On a daily basis, a stamping team member picks up and handles parts many times. Since stamped parts are made of steel, the edges of these parts are sharp, like razor blades. It is critical stamping members have the skill to handle these parts safely to prevent lacerations.*

Some stamped parts are large, heavy and awkwardly shaped. As a result, handling these parts incorrectly can result in lacerations. Lisa recalls, "When I was a new hire at Toyota, I was taught it was important to handle parts safely and to wear the proper safety equipment, but was not trained in detail regarding what that meant."

One example of the GPC training is the fundamental skill of part handling. Part handling training is broken down into four fundamental skills:

- center of gravity
- where to hold the panel
- how to hold the panel
- grip force to use

The training begins by teaching team members about the "center of gravity" (COG) and how to locate it on any part. The importance of COG relating to part handling is, by understanding where the COG is located, a team member can make an informed decision about where to safely place their hands to pick up the panel.

The exercise starts with a simple corrugated plastic square that is 3 foot by 3 foot, made up of 9 separate squares (see figure 5.4). Obviously the COG of a square is in the middle of the center square. Then, in the training, the trainer makes various shapes, allowing the trainees to practice discovering the COG on unusually shaped simulated parts.

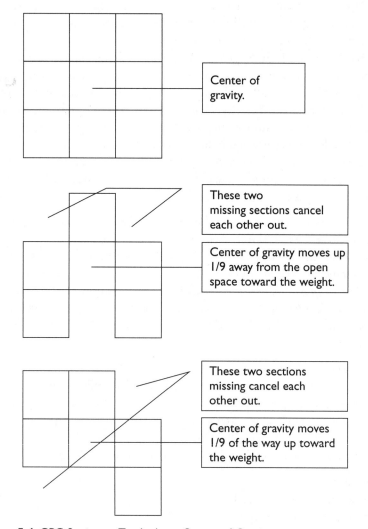

**Figure 5.4** GPC Station to Teach about Center of Gravity

For example, if the upper right hand square is eliminated, the COG will move diagonally 1/9 of the way down toward the lower right-hand corner. The trainees then place an X where they think the COG is now and an answer template is placed down to give the trainee immediate feedback.

Once the team members are able to correctly locate the new COG on these simulated squares, they are permitted to move on to a simulated production part made up of corrugated plastic. One part example is a corrugated plastic cutout of a door inner panel. The panel is approximately three feet by three feet, similar to the training square, but now, the shape is irregular and has holes in different locations, just as a real part would have. The team members take the skill they just learned on the square and transfer it to the practice part. Once they locate the COG on the practice part, they are taught to use this information to decide on where they will actually pick up the part. This will help them in two areas: first with correct position and ergonomic posture and second, where to pick up the panel in a location that is secure, not allowing it to slide through their hands. In addition, the members are taught the proper type of grip to use on the part so they get the maximum surface area of their hands on the panel, ensuring a good grip prior to picking up the part.

When the new members master the practice parts, they then move on to actual steel parts they will be handling in the stamping area. The members practice what they have learned about part handling on the real production part. The final portion of panel-handling training is where the team member is taught to use just the right amount of grip pressure to pick up a part. A dynamometer (grip strength testing device) is used to allow the member to practice what correct grip force feels like. The dynamometer is a gauge that measures, in kilograms per square inch, the amount of grip force a member is using. The members practice squeezing the gauge until they can identify the pressure they are applying. Then they are taught to apply three times the weight of the part pressure for each hand for the part they are picking up. For example, if a part weighs four kilograms, the member needs to apply 12 kilograms of pressure with each hand when they pick this part up. This is important because using a light grip force may allow the panel to slide through their hands, a laceration hazard, and using too heavy a grip force may lead to ergonomic, cumulative trauma injuries.

By utilizing a global curriculum developed from Toyota best practices, and by delivering this training in a systematic, detailed manner by a TMC certified trainer, stamping team members now have the knowledge and skill necessary to safely handle parts in their daily work. Putting all these part handling skills together, TMMK members have been able to improve the safety rate in the stamping area.

The master trainer in TMMK's body weld area is Eddie Back. He described teaching the fundamental skills of welding using actual pieces of production equipment and making actual welds. Most of the welds made on a car are resistance welds so most of the time and practice is spent here. Inspection is also a key skill in the welding area. Members are taught to first use "tactile" inspection to be able to feel a defect that can't even be seen. These defects are "felt" with either the gloved hand or with a stone so team members must be taught how to use the right amount of pressure. If they use too much pressure, the defect will be hidden from them because there will be no sensitivity. If they use too little pressure, it won't be uncovered. In order to teach this skill, a simple kitchen type scale is used with a metal plate. The standard pressure needed to properly detect problems is 1.5 kilograms per square centimeter. This is similar to the pressure used to take wax off a car. Team members are able to practice on these scales and get immediate feedback on the amount of pressure they are applying with their hands or a stone. Once they are able to consistently apply the standard amount of pressure on the scale plate, they move to a practice car door and attempt to find the defects that have been "set up" on a practice door. The door has both bumps and dents that are not visible to the naked eye. The members test their "feel" and then place a magnet over each defect. Then a plastic template is placed over the door with corresponding marks where the defects are. The members get immediate feedback on their accuracy. Once they can find all 30 defects they are able to go to another "test" door to demonstrate their skill and be certified by Eddie.

The body weld area also teaches part fit, with both the gap and the levelness of two body panels coming together (see Figure 5.5). This is a quality area in which Toyota is famous and has basically defined the "level" of quality for an entire industry. Once again, the GPC has a practice area set up for the team members to learn how to detect both the levelness of two parts and the gap between the two. Two practice panels are set up with dials that change both the gap and levelness of the panels, while displaying the amount of each on a dial that is hidden with a hinged cover. The trainer adjusts the parts to different degrees of gap and levelness

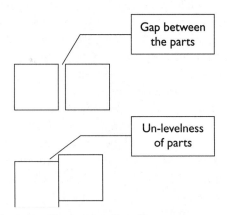

**Figure 5.5** GPC Station to Teach about Part Fit

and the new member has to feel and look and be able to identify the amount of gap and "un-levelness" within 0.3 millimeters—about the size of the height of 3 sheets of paper stacked on each other. The team members are trained to be able to identify this small of a difference using only their touch and vision. No measuring is allowed. By certifying team members have this ability they are setting the team members up for success when they start working on an actual production vehicle and insuring that Toyota quality is going to the customer.

According to the Toyota Web site, the skills of new members have improved and training time has been cut in half. "By providing high-level consistent training to multiple employees simultaneously, Toyota has cut training time in half while raising the level of skill acquisition." Toyota measures how much of the skill the student learns during the time of the training and calls this "instructional efficiency." For example, if two students each take a one hour class but one gets twice the score of the other on a test, that would suggest twice the efficiency in learning from that class. Toyota's studies suggest that GPC multiplies instructional efficiency by a factor of 6 to 10 times (see Figure 5.6).[5]

The GPC has been so successful in training new hires at TMMK that the decision was made to have all of the current team members go through the training as well. All team members in the plant took turns getting off-line for two to three days to go through the training, and as the next step group leaders went through the

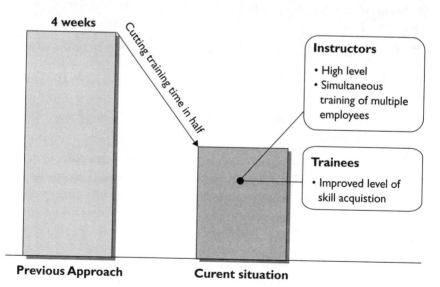

**Figure 5.6** GPC Greatly Improves Instructional Efficiency

[5] http://www.toyotageorgetown.com/gpc.asp

center. Though they had been trained extensively through OJD they found that they had all learned in different ways and were missing some of the fundamental skills.

# STANDARDIZED WORK AND JOB BREAKDOWN

In most companies someone in the newcomer's department is given the assignment to teach him the job—it is up to that individual to figure out what to teach and how. Since there is no standardized work, the student learns the job the way the person doing the teaching happens to do it. They are with the trainer so briefly that they have to improvise and fill in a lot of the details on their own. The result is that everyone does the job his own way, and there is no real organizational learning. Kaizen to the job becomes each individual making his own improvements, but these do not get shared with others and incorporated into the new standard way.

Standardized work is the foundation for creating a repeatable process that reliably produces the desired result. Standardized work is also the foundation for training. You cannot train someone until you know how to do the job. It is also impossible to improve an unstable process that is being done differently by everyone. Any improvement simply becomes just one more way of doing the same job.

To teach a team member how to do a job, the method must be clearly defined. At Toyota, standardized work is the best way we know to do the job today, until a better way is identified and proven. Standardized work includes:

1. Takt time concept—How often should a work product be produced (e.g., one unit per minute)?
2. Standard work sequence—Which steps should be followed and in what order?
3. Standard work-in-process—How much inventory is allowed between steps in the process?

To have truly standardized work, the job and surrounding processes have to be stable. If customer demand is changing every day, the takt time concept does not mean much.[6] If parts, tools, and other materials arrive at different times in different quantities or are in different places all the time, there cannot be a standard work sequence. If machines are breaking down or quality problems are popping up randomly, this will affect the standard work-in-process and the timing and the work sequence. In other words, you need a stable process to have standardized work, and you need standardized work to break down the job for job instruction training.

---

[6] For information on how to level the schedule under conditions of high product variety and variable demand see Liker, Jeffrey and David Meier, *The Toyota Way Fieldbook*, New York: McGraw-Hill, 2005.

Toyota is training people within a stable environment with group leaders and team leaders proficient in how to do the work and how to teach it. The work has already been broken down to the tiniest detail: how to position your body and your hands, where parts should be, what the safety protocols are, and which quality key points need to be attended to. Just-in-time systems have been established. With all this preparation, Toyota uses the job instruction method.

Of course most companies are not Toyota and do not have this degree of stability or level of standardization in their workplace. So what are they to do? The answer is to approach this step by step. We recommend avoiding the tendency to blanket the organization with training before any of the systems are in place to effectively use the training. We would rather see a company be selective about processes or areas and develop some level of stability in that area; this is to develop at least rough standardized work and then begin the training process in just those areas. The learning in those pilot areas can then be used to move to other areas and eventually across the plant. A method for organizing to do this is described in *Toyota Talent*.[7]

## Job Instruction Method

OJD begins with learning the basic job of the team member. Figure 5.7 is a summary of the Toyota Job Instruction (TJI) process. It has evolved within Toyota from an American methodology called Training within Industry (TWI). The basic

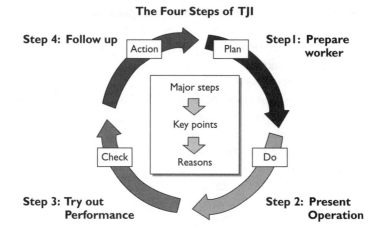

**The Four Steps of TJI**

Step 4: Follow up — Action — Plan — Step1: Prepare worker

Major steps → Key points → Reasons

Check — Do

Step 3: Try out Performance — Step 2: Present Operation

Note: The TJI method originated with the American Training Within Industry (TWI) program.

**Figure 5.7** The Toyota Job Instruction Training Method

---

[7] Liker, Jeffrey and Meier, David, Toyota Talent, 2007.

TJI process is deeply ingrained in the Toyota culture and has not changed in over 50 years. This continuity is the basis for a deep culture.

Toyota Job Instruction is based on two main processes: the training material and the training method. Both are laid out and facilitated in terms of the familiar Plan-Do-Check-Act process taught by W. Edwards Deming. Here is a high-level summary:

1. The Job Instruction Sheet—This is the detailed document (generally a single page per training session) on how to do the job, and is the main training material. It consists of:
   a) Major Steps—A Major Step within an element is an action necessary for advancing the element to its successful completion.
   b) Key Points—Key Points are those operational points on which the success or failure of a particular job depends. They are related to quality, productivity, cost, and safety. They are also those points which make the job performance easier (e.g., perceptions, tricks, experience, techniques, timing, and special knowledge).
   c) Reasons—What happens if the key points are ignored? Why are they done this way? What is the reason?
2. Training Method
   a) prepare trainee
   b) put the trainee at ease
   c) state the job (using Standardized Operation Sheet)
   d) find out what the trainee already knows about the job
   e) get the trainee interested in learning the job
   f) position trainee favorably so he can see you do the job
   g) present operation
3. Demonstrate the Operation Three Times
   i) show and explain one element and its major steps at a time (first time)
   ii) stress each key point (second time)
   iii) explain the reasons for each major step and key point (3rd time)
   iv) instruct clearly, completely, and patiently
   v) try out performance
4. Trainee Performs the Operation Four Times
   i) have trainee do the job silently and correct own errors (first time).
   ii) have trainee explain to you each element and major steps while performing the job again (second time).
   iii) have trainee explain each key point as the job is performed again (third time).
   iv) have trainee explain the reasons (fourth time).

     v) continue performing job until you know the trainee knows it thor-
      oughly.
     vi) follow-up.
5. Leave the Trainee to Work on his Own but not Unattended
6. Designate Whom the Trainee Should Go to for Help
7. Check on Trainee Frequently
8. Encourage Questions
9. Give Any Necessary Extra Coaching and Taper Off the Follow-up

## Follow Up and Support Until Student Masters the Job

Through TJI the student learns first the individual steps of the job and finally can complete the entire job according to the standardized work. At this point his level of knowledge and skill is still rather low and fragile. If he is left to his own devices, he will tend to fall back on ways he personally finds it easy to do the job and forget the reasons for specific key points. Another problem is the ability to consistently meet the takt time. He may have done the job within the takt time for a number of cycles, but if left on his own, he may slip up on some cycles and get behind and then struggle to catch up. To do so he may skip steps, such as quality checks.

    The instructor's responsibility is to stay with the student until they can comfortably perform the job to takt time following the standardized work. This is known as the "stabilization stage." The advantage of having team leaders act as the JI trainers is that they are already there on the floor. If they have a student they just trained, they have to stay particularly close to that person. They can also ask the people in the job ahead of or behind the new trainee to watch out for that person and help out when needed. Since experienced team members rotate and know all the jobs they can easily help coach the new member through the stabilization stage.

    We should note that the same philosophy and basic method applies in all jobs at Toyota, even outside manufacturing. You will see a structure comparable to the group leader–team leader structure in all functions and they are responsible for developing their people in a rigorous and systematic way.

## The Role of the Toyota Team Member—Training for All Temporaries and New Hires

Parallel to new team members going through the GPC and learning their jobs through the TJI method and following their standardized work, they are also learning their role through a structured Manufacturing Training Program. The program combines classroom lectures, interactive simulations, and some on-the-floor training that reinforces where the *gemba* is.

The program is designed for all new temporary workers who come to work for Toyota and all new hires. There are two phases to the program consisting of 40 hours of training in Phase I and 24 hours of training in Phase II. At this point, almost all new people coming into the Georgetown plant come in as temporaries. Temporaries are given two years to complete Phase I. People coming in directly as new hires are given six months to complete Phase I. Phase II is completed over the course of the next three years for both temporaries and new hires.

This program is outlined in Figure 5.8. The modules begin with safety principles, Toyota Way values, Toyota Production System principles, teamwork, communication skills, and problem solving. The training is facilitated by the Center for Quality People and Organizations (CQPO), using trainers who all have direct production experience with Toyota. In order to pass, the team members must attend all sessions, complete all assignments, and demonstrate competencies covered in the classroom material. The team members must pass each stage successfully in order to get a wage increase, and move on to the next phase. For example, in the first phase of Safety, Values, and TPS Principles, the members will have ten hours of training over their first two months. If they attend the classes, pass the exams, and are able to demonstrate understanding of the key concepts, they will get an increase in pay and move on to the next phase. Members are paid overtime wages to attend and if they are unable to pass the tests, they are able to take the classes again (without pay) until they do pass.

Most of the homework and demonstrations focus on problem solving, with the members picking up real problems from the floor and applying the problem-solving process, step by step, with coaching from both the classroom instructors and their team leaders. At the end of the 40 hours of training, the members summarize the entire process using the A-3 problem-solving report, presenting it to the rest of the class.

For the variable workforce this training has a special meaning because it can mean the difference between getting hired or not into a long-term role at Toyota. After successfully completing the first 40 hours of training in two years, the temporary will have the opportunity to become a full-time hire at Toyota. This will happen only if the member also has a good work and attendance record and there is no downturn in the need for members. In fact, almost every temporary employee at TMMK had an opportunity to become full time up through the writing of this book.

Once the temporary member is converted to full-time, the member is then enrolled into the next phase of training, which involves another 24 hours spread over the course of three years. Phase II continues to teach the Toyota competencies, but then goes even further to build on the existing foundation. For example, with standardized work (STW), the first module includes the basics of STW, with the philosophy, importance, and benefits of following it. The problem-solving

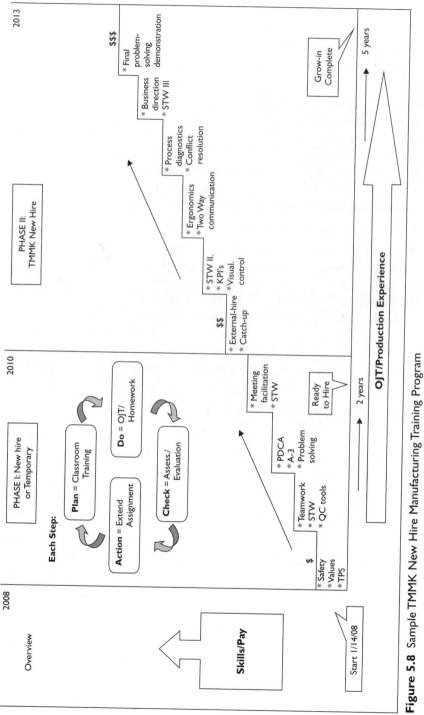

**Figure 5.8** Sample TMMK New Hire Manufacturing Training Program

homework on the floor includes observing standardized work and problem solving for any deviations that are found. In the STW II module, the new hires are taught how to actually construct a standardized work chart for a process on the floor, and in the STW III module, they will be able to teach someone else how to both construct and follow the standardized work. This is so powerful it bears repeating that *all experienced hourly production workers will have the skill to train other production workers how to construct and follow the standardized work.* At the end of this three-year phase, new hires will have had periodic raises to correspond with their passing each phase and will now be at the "full grow-in" rate, making the same hourly rate as all the rest of the production team members.

## Continuous Improvement of Job Training

In many companies, managers do not understand the importance of making the on-the-job development of their subordinates a priority of their daily work. Training is viewed as the responsibility of a training department. At Toyota, every senior person is a teacher for their more junior colleagues, and those doing OJD are explicitly taught how to do such training. In fact, OJD is a class that is offered to all managers and supervisors at Toyota and focuses on how to use a standardized process to customize one's development of a subordinate. The purpose of OJD is to develop team members who "practice the Toyota Way." A supervisor's job is to facilitate the growth of a subordinate by helping her perform "good work." "Good work" is defined as being challenging, motivating and providing a sense of achievement or personal growth.[8]

These three components line up with the Plan-Do-Check-Act (PDCA) process of Toyota. In the **Plan** stage, the supervisor needs to know his subordinates' strengths and weaknesses and know the work that needs to be done and then provide work that "slightly stretches" the skills of the person. In the **Do,** the supervisor must motivate the person. This is done with good observation, follow up, and feedback. Finally, in the **Check, Action** stages the supervisor can evaluate the work of the person and the two can discuss progress toward desired personal growth and future action needed to meet each of their goals. Supervisors are taught in the class that it is their responsibility to train their subordinates and that it is Toyota's goal for them to personally "care" for each of their subordinates and his development. They are also taught that the development process must be tailored for each individual. Each person has different values, personalities, and abilities, and the training must be customized accordingly.

Toyota improves products and processes through the PDCA process. When there is a quality problem or team members are having difficulty achieving takt

---

[8] Internal Training Document, Toyota Institute, "OJT—The Toyota Way," Toyota Motor Corporation, January, 2005

time, this will show up in a large number of andon cord pulls on a job. This leads to problem solving. Part of this problem solving process is to look at the standardized work and how well team members are trained to follow the standardized work. Sometimes this can be solved easily by retraining team members locally on the standardized work. If this is a repeated problem across jobs and people, the entire system of training is reevaluated. The example given in the next section on identified training needs was an actual case where a problem led to reevaluating the training processes—in this case the need for clear identification of competencies needed by team leaders.

# WORK-RELATED TRAINING NEEDS IDENTIFICATION (THROUGH COPA)

We discussed training on how to do the specific details of a job; but in a more general sense, how does Toyota identify training needs beyond the specific mechanics of the job? In keeping with the Toyota Way people-development philosophy, the Critical Output Analysis system (COPA) offers a rigorous method that starts with understanding the purpose of the job and then translates this into specific competencies needed. At Toyota, when someone begins to solve a problem, often their supervisor will ask: What *is* the problem? We need a clear understanding of the objectives before we dive into problem solving. In the case of training, before committing to such development, we need to understand the intended outputs of the job and then translate these into training needs.

Consider the following brownfield situation in which the COPA method was used. A new production line was installed and started up. The team leaders involved became uneasy with their work, as well as that of the team members they supervised. Together they asked their group leader for a meeting to address their concerns. The group leader recognized that they were raising issues that related directly to their responsibilities as team leaders. She decided to hold a COPA session to identify training needs for the team leader role so that they could be addressed both for the group and for the individual team leaders. Her method involved the following steps:

## Step 1

Gathering the group together in a training room, she asked the group as a whole the following five questions and wrote the answers on a flip chart for all to see:

- What are the *critical outputs* of your job? What are the completed processes/pieces of work that you are responsible for performing?
- What are the *major tasks/activities* that make up, result in, or contribute to the critical outputs? What are the actions that the critical outputs are dependent upon?

- What are the *informational competencies* or the knowledge required in order to perform the major tasks? What must you know to do the actions that produce the critical outputs?
- What are the *interpersonal competencies* of relating to others to perform the major tasks? What must you do to work with your colleagues effectively on the job?
- What are the *intellectual competencies* or mental abilities and operations required in order to do the job? What kinds of thinking skills are involved?

## Step 2

Completing this task, the group leader asked the team leaders if the information recorded was reasonably comprehensive and accurate, and recorded in language they recognized. She then worked with the group to improve the list and get agreement. The session lasted about one hour. The philosophy of the system is that for the business to be successful, the leaders need to produce certain outputs that require certain tasks be done successfully in order to produce the outputs. It follows then that there is a need to identify what competencies are needed to perform the tasks. These are what will be addressed with training and development. The summary of the session is shown in Figure 5.9.

## Step 3

Equipped with this job content information, the group leader transcribed it into a COPA format for the next step. An example of a COPA form used to assess interpersonal competencies is shown in Figure 5.10.[9] Gathering the group together a second time, she reviewed the content and then focused on the three pages with the informational, interpersonal, and intellectual competencies. Beside each entry on the left are two scales marked one through five, from low to high, respectively. The scale on the far right, titled "Job Importance Level" allowed the group leader to circle her assessment of the job importance level of that specific competency. The middle scale, titled "Competence Level," allowed the team leaders in the group to circle their individual assessments of their respective level of mastery of the competency item. This step yielded three valuable results: an opportunity for the group leader to emphasize her view of the priority of work-related competencies; an opportunity for the individual team leaders to self-assess their own abilities and an opportunity to pinpoint the individual and aggregate training needs for curriculum development purposes.

---

[9] Figure 5.10 is a generic example of an intrapersonal competencies form that does not correspond directly to the example in Figure 5.9.

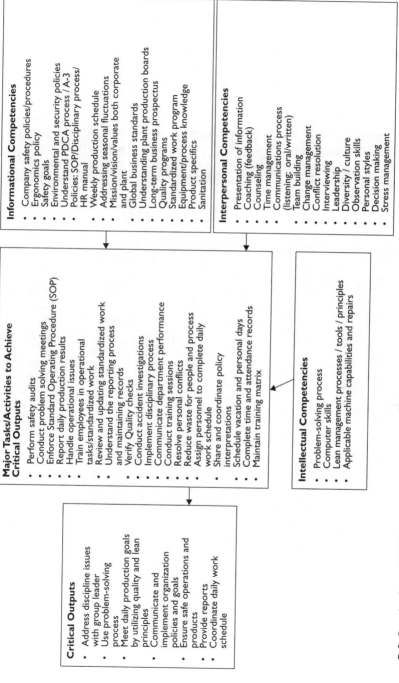

**Informational Competencies**

- Company safety policies/procedures
- Ergonomics policy
- Safety goals
- Environmental and security policies
- Understand PDCA process / A-3
- Policies: SOP/Disciplinary process/ HR manual
- Weekly production schedule
- Addressing seasonal fluctuations
- Mission/vision/values both corporate and plant
- Global business standards
- Understanding plant production boards
- Long-term business prospectus
- Quality programs
- Standardized work program
- Equipment/process knowledge
- Product specifics
- Sanitation

**Interpersonal Competencies**

- Presentation of information
- Coaching (feedback)
- Counseling
- Time management
- Communications process (listening; oral/written)
- Team building
- Change management
- Conflict resolution
- Interviewing
- Leadership
- Diversity / culture
- Observation skills
- Personal styles
- Decision making
- Stress management

**Major Tasks/Activities to Achieve Critical Outputs**

- Perform safety audits
- Conduct problem solving meetings
- Enforce Standard Operating Procedure (SOP)
- Report daily production results
- Handle operational issues
- Train employees in operational tasks/standardized work
- Review and updating standardized work
- Understand the reporting process and maintaining records
- Verify Quality checks
- Conduct accident investigations
- Implement disciplinary process
- Communicate department performance
- Conduct training sessions
- Resolve personal conflicts
- Reduce waste for people and process
- Assign personnel to complete daily work schedule
- Share and coordinate policy interpretations
- Schedule vacation and personal days
- Complete time and attendance records
- Maintain training matrix

**Intellectual Competencies**

- Problem-solving process
- Computer skills
- Lean management processes / tools / principles
- Applicable machine capabilities and repairs

**Critical Outputs**

- Address discipline issues with group leader
- Use problem-solving process
- Meet daily production goals by utilizing quality and lean principles
- Communicate and implement organization policies and goals
- Ensure safe operations and products
- Provide reports
- Coordinate daily work schedule

**Figure 5.9** Results from COPA Session

135

| Major Interpersonal Competencies COPA Assessement Form |
|---|

On the left below list the major Interpersonal Competencies needed to complete the major tasks named on the task list. Do not be surprised if the same competencies are needed for more than one task. If this is true, do not list any Interpersonal Competencies more than once.

On the right are two rating scales. The first scale is for rating your particular competency level. The second scale is for rating the job need level for that specific competency. A rating from one to two is low, three is moderate, and a rating from four to five is high.

| INTERPERSONAL<br>COMPETENCIES | COMPETENCE LEVEL | JOB IMPORTANCE LEVEL |
|---|---|---|
| • Presenting information orally, in training modes, and response to questions | 1  2  3  4  5 | 1  2  3  4  5 |
| • Coaching, counseling, communicating one on one and in work settings | 1  2  3  4  5 | 1  2  3  4  5 |
| • Encouraging teamwork, trust and problem solving | 1  2  3  4  5 | 1  2  3  4  5 |
| • Resolving conflicts and misunderstandings | 1  2  3  4  5 | 1  2  3  4  5 |
| • Observing, interviewing, relieving stress | 1  2  3  4  5 | 1  2  3  4  5 |
| • Respecting diverse cultural practices | 1  2  3  4  5 | 1  2  3  4  5 |
| • Explaining change and enlisting support | 1  2  3  4  5 | 1  2  3  4  5 |
| • Leading problem solving efforts and continuous improvement | 1  2  3  4  5 | 1  2  3  4  5 |
| • Recognizing achievement and innovation in others' work | 1  2  3  4  5 | 1  2  3  4  5 |
| • Being able to recognize my own limitations | 1  2  3  4  5 | 1  2  3  4  5 |

**Figure 5.10** Example of Interpersonal Competencies COPA form for Each Member to Self-assess Competence

**Step 4**

Training sessions were held based on the needs identified. By having the actual members involved in the process, the buy-in for the training was greatly increased and by having the members report on their actual job and the gaps that exist in their own competencies, the training could be customized to address both their needs as a group and as individuals. In both cases, the training needs to be related both to the job as a whole, and to the more recent needs that occasioned the COPA session.

# TRAINING DIFFERENT LEVELS AT TOYOTA

We have focused most of our training examples on the team member, team leader, and group leaders on the shop floor. In this section we will focus on the manager and executive-level training. As you move up the hierarchy, jobs become less clearly defined and less repetitive, yet the same basic philosophies of TJI are ingrained in the Toyota culture:

1. Always prepare to understand who needs to be trained, for what purpose, and who will be qualified to do the training.
2. Do the core of the training in actual work situations by the supervisor who is well-trained to develop others.
3. Always use a repetitive process of showing the student, letting the student try, and then letting the student practice with supervision.
4. Never leave the student on her own until she is capable of reliably performing the work on her own.

In order to understand the training and development strategy in the Toyota culture, it is important to distinguish the roles and functions of each layer of the organization. There are four levels: team member, team leader/group leader, manager, and general manager/vice president (see Figure 5.11). The people at each level focus on level-specific work content and tools, but all levels connect through the problem-solving process.

## Team Leader and Group Leader Training

We have discussed training for the team leaders and group leaders in some detail. The foundation of the organization is standardized work at each level, for each member, for each process. Whenever there is a variation in the standardized work, the activity of the team leaders and group leaders comes into play, as they, and the team member, use their problem-solving skills to address the problem and bring the process back into standard. At the same time, in the spirit of continuous improvement, all three are identifying any opportunities to eliminate more waste in the process and further improve it.

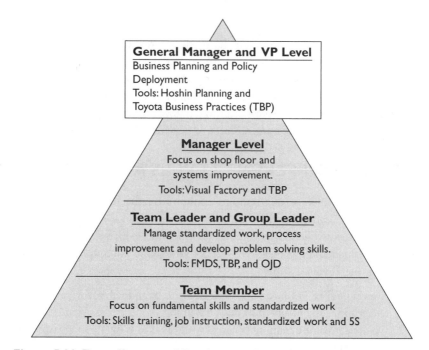

**Figure 5.11** Toyota Training and Development Strategy: Roles, Focus & Tools

With these considerations in mind, the training for team members, team leaders, and group leaders focuses primarily on workplace organization, standardized work, TJI, problem solving, and more problem solving. Training at Toyota builds upon itself layer by layer. The team member learns the basic foundational tools, and more are added as she moves through the people value stream. The team leader adds Toyota Job Instruction as a tool, and begins to coach the problem-solving process. Communication and teamwork skills are also integrated into the teaching of these tools in order for the values of respect and trust to be reinforced during the improvement process. These communication skills go beyond the "HR approach" of "being nice." It is a fact that problem solving is improved when there is an established relationship of mutual respect and trust. The communication skills also act as a "lubricant" during the problem-solving process to address issues as they arise. As one team leader put it during an OJD problem-solving exercise: "Our team went to an area to solve a problem and the group leader was real closed and defensive about us being there 'in his business.' We practiced our listening skills and validated his concern about outsiders coming in to change his process. Before we knew it, he was answering all of our questions and giving us information we didn't even know we needed."

Accordingly, training underscores a perpetual cycle: perform standardized work, encounter variation, conduct problem solving, set a new standard, train everyone to the new standard, and perform to the new standard. That sequence is the core of the daily activity for the team members, team leader, and group leader. Without this sequence there is never enough stability in the process to make improvements, and there is no system to standardize them and share them after they are made. It is mind boggling to go into organizations that have been on a "lean journey" for some period of time, reducing inventory, creating work cells, etc., but they have no standardized work or problem solving at the floor level. It has been shown that top and middle management only spend 2 to 15 percent of their time on the floor at the process level (Toyota's managers spend much more time on the floor), and they make up about the same percentage of the organization's workforce. Meanwhile, the team members on the floor make up about 80 percent of the workforce and spend 99 percent or their time right at the value added part of the process. By focusing on the systems and training of these individuals Toyota is able to positively impact their key business indicators.

By having clear roles and responsibilities for each job level, Toyota is able to first train the person to be able to perform his current role and then begin to train the person to work "one role up" from his current role. This is done by identifying the skill, projects, experiences, etc., that the person must be able to master in order to be ready to work at the next level. These skills are put on to a matrix chart similar to the team member "multi-function worker chart" so that the member and coach can clearly see the current status and make plans to address any gaps. A group leader at Toyota will work to develop each team leader through proper delegation in order for each team leader to be able to perform the role of "acting group leader" while they are still team leaders. Figure 5.12 shows an example of a team leader development chart that would include cross-training and rotating all the team leaders to different teams so that they are eventually proficient in all the teams of a group. At the same time group leader "tasks," such as participating in each "area of Toyota management" like safety, quality, productivity, and cost, are rotated across all of the team leaders. This rotation will be for at least a year in each area, where the team leader will represent the group leader on the safety or cost committee.

Group leader job tasks, such as processing scrap or tracking time and attendance, will also be taught to each team leader. The way these tasks are taught is using the same method described earlier for training team members on their process. Standards are prepared for most every task one can learn at Toyota. There is a standard for how to calibrate an air tool or wrench in order to get the right tightness, there is a standard on how to properly maintain a piece of equipment to prevent breakdowns, and there are standards on how to process scrap. By having these standards, it makes the task of training that much easier and then the trainer is able to follow up the training by comparing the student to the standard. This follow-up process is the trainer's confirmation that the students are able to perform the task on their own. They are then given a full 100 percent circle on

| Group Leader | | Team Leader | | | |
|---|---|---|---|---|---|
| **Name:** Jeff | | Mike | Mary | Mark | Margaret |
| **Dept.:** Assy | | | | | |
| **Date:** 01/02/08 | | | | | |
| | **Process or Skill** | | | | |
| 1 | Team 1 Processes | ● | ⊕ | ◐ | ● |
| 2 | Team 2 Processes | ◐ | ● | ⊕ | ● |
| 3 | Team 3 Processes | ⊕ | ● | ● | ● |
| 4 | Team 4 Processes | ● | ◐ | ⊕ | ● |
| 5 | Time/Attendance | ● | ◐ | ⊕ | ● |
| 6 | Safety Task Force | ● | ⊕ | ⊕ | ● |
| 7 | Lead Quality Circle | ⊕ | ◐ | ● | ● |
| 8 | Cost Committee | ● | ⊕ | ⊕ | ● |
| 9 | Scrap processing | ● | ⊕ | ⊕ | ● |
| 10 | TPM on equipment | ● | ● | ● | ● |

Key: ⊕ 0%   ◐ 50%   ● 100%

**Figure 5.12** Team Leader Multifunction Training Chart to Prepare for Future Group Leader Role

their training chart and are considered ready to move on the next task. By the end of four or five years, the team leader is already developed and trained to perform most of the tasks that would be expected of a group leader. This will give them a good foundation to step into the role of the group leader when they get promoted.

## Manager Level Training

In most cases, the best managers at Toyota were first developed as the best group leaders. They have proven themselves competent in using tools like standardized work and TJI, and they are adept at problem solving and at maintaining trust and respect. In the early days of the Georgetown plant, there was little formal classroom training for the manager level. Each manager was assigned a full-time coordinator from Japan for several years as a teacher and daily mentor for how to do business the Toyota Way. This coordinator literally shadowed the manager, continually asking questions about what the manager was thinking, and then teaching and challenging him to see the situation differently than he was accustomed.

For example, the first manager in the Assembly Plant was Mike Daprile, who had many years of experience at General Motors. When he was setting up the new assembly plant, he questioned the set-up of the repair area at the end of the line. He wanted to know why there was no key-making machine in the plant. All of his plants at GM had key-making machines for the cars that were missing keys at the end of the line. He questioned his coordinator, Art Nimmi, about the issue, explaining the recurring problem that would occur by having a car get to the end of the line without a key and, thereby, not being able to make a key to start it. Nimmi asked why there would be a key missing. Mike responded that they often got lost, they got taken, or they were just missing. Nimmi simply stated, "Then spend your time finding out why they are lost or taken, and fix that, instead of spending time and money making keys." This is a simple, common-sense approach, yet a very different way of thinking for managers not brought up in the Toyota Way.

This day-in-day-out coaching developed the managers' ability to think and behave. Meanwhile, the basic tools of the Toyota Production System already described were put into place at the beginning. These were advantages that the Georgetown plant experienced as a new greenfield start up. Brownfield organizations often must battle poor work habits as they try to transform into the lean ways of doing business. Indeed, Toyota was similarly challenged recently to change some bad habits that were developing due to the rapid expansion and globalization it is experiencing.

Because of this expansion into other countries such as India, China, and Russia, Japan no longer has the resources and ability to send more than a handful of experienced managers to the United States to act as coordinators. After about 15 years with guidance from Japan, TMMK managers were asked to take responsibility for teaching others. They were sent to the other plants in North America, such as Baja and Texas, to act as coordinators for the new managers there, and the Georgetown facility was named the "sister plant" for the new plant being built in Tupelo, Mississippi. For this reason there are also more formal training curricula and coaching programs being developed to fill the gap left by the paucity of Japanese coordinators.

## Manager Rotation—Cross-Training

Toyota rotates every level of their organization as a development tool. This same tool is used for managers. Rotation is considered an effective way to train both the technical and interpersonal/leadership skills of managers. Obviously, going to a new area in the organization will expose the manager to new technical skills, and many times the production manager is rotated to administration and vice versa.

It is not uncommon to have an assembly manager going to accounting or a human resource manager going to production control. In addition to learning the "new" technical side of the area, they are also put into a position where they will be more successful leading in the Toyota Way than depending on "old" styles of management. If someone is the "technical expert" and put into a position of leadership, it is very easy for them to manage in a top down, dictatorial manner. As one Japanese coordinator put it, "When managers are rotated to a new area, they are forced to do two things. One, they have to humble themselves and depend on the subordinates to give them the technical information they need, and two, they must rely on their Toyota Way of managing using PDCA and problem solving. This increases their skills in this area and those they manage."

Manager rotation is highly valued at Toyota, and almost all people promoted to the General Manager level have spent time rotating to at least two different areas of management.

## General Manager and VP Level Training

Executive training at Toyota utilizes a similar strategy as the manager training. It sounds cliché, but Toyota executives are expected to continue to learn throughout their careers. Rotation takes place at the vice president level as well. Don Jackson, the senior vice president at Toyota's truck plant in San Antonio, Texas, started his Toyota career at Georgetown and was developed up the management ladder from a specialist to the position of General Manager of Quality and then to Vice President of Manufacturing. He was then rotated to Texas and given the responsibility to start up that new plant. In this position he has responsibility for the "overall hiring and development" of his management team and, in a sense, the entire organization. At the same time, he is being developed by the current Japanese President and by the experience he is gaining starting up a new plant. When asked about his development into his current role, Don quickly named his past Japanese coordinators and credited them with transferring the "Toyota DNA" to him.

*Keith Takanami[10] was my coordinator when I was a general manager of quality and he had a tremendous influence on my learning and career. He taught me that I was going to hit road blocks along the way, but when I hit these walls I would need to not give up and to persevere through them. He*

---

[10] Keita Takanami passed away in a Comair plane crash in 1997. He has supported TMMK on two different rotations. His coaching, friendship and messages live on within Toyota.

*taught me that every "event" at the plant is an opportunity to learn and to teach. He used an event, where production and quality would have to come together to discuss a quality issue as a way to teach stabilization, standardization, containment, data collection and decision making. First I watched him facilitate these "events." He would always use a white board to get all the facts out in the open. He would also ask questions around first the "whats" and then the "whys" and get the whole team involved in the problem identification and countermeasures and confirm "who will do what by when." He then coached me to lead the meetings. One time, after the meeting, I asked him why he let me struggle so much. He said, "I can't just give you the answer. It is better to let you discover for yourself; that way it is much more powerful." He then placed two objects on the table and motioned as he talked. "The quickest way from point A to point B is a straight line, but it is not the only way. You can zig and zag a little and still get to point B. It is OK for you to zig and zag a little bit. It is my job to not let you fall off the table."*

*I remember another time as an assistant manager at TMMK I made a significant mistake in working on an issue we had at the plant. I worked all night on an A–3 problem solving report, focusing on prevention of reoccurrence, to present to our President, Mr. Cho the next day. I was pretty nervous, due to the tremendous mistake I had made. As I went to the meeting, there was Mr. Cho, with hands folded and a big welcoming smile on his face. His only words to me were, "What have you learned today?" What had been a big fear turned out to be a great learning experience. It so happened that very early in our start up in Texas there was a team leader who had some miscommunication with a paint contractor which resulted in a big spill. It was a major incident and even though we confirmed there was no environmental impact, the financial cost was significant. I went to the floor to observe first-hand the problem and there were people everywhere and right in the middle was the team leader responsible. He was obviously nervous and I quickly realized all eyes were on me and not him as I approached. Call it the Toyota Way or DNA or whatever you want but the words were leaving my mouth, as visions of Mr. Cho returned, as I asked "What have you learned from this?" The team leader was relieved and excited as he walked me through the countermeasures. I ran into him again the other day and I saw that he was wearing his paint stained bump cap. I asked, "why don't you get a new bump cap?" He said that he plans to always wear it as a reminder of his error, and how he was treated, and how to treat his people in the future.*

Don learned most about the Toyota Way from direct experience mentored by Japanese coordinators and he will pass on much of that learning one-on-one to people who report to him. Learning is considered as ongoing or forever in a Toyota environment. In addition to these more informal learning opportunities, there is a good deal of formal training for managers.

The Toyota Institute in Japan takes the lead in developing management courses and then they work with each continent to certify trainers to be able to deliver the classes in their respective countries. In the United States the training is done through the North American Production Support Center located on the same site as TMMK. This organization is divided into production training (for team members through group leaders) and management training (for assistant man-agers through presidents). The Manager Support Center is staffed with training specialists, all of whom have management experience in the organization. They are not necessarily executive level because they do not need to be, but are acting more as facilitators of the information and the activities necessary to share the information and the homework assignment. One example of such a course is "Advancing the Toyota Way," which teaches the executive to see the big picture of the entire organization, and then stresses tools to evaluate it in terms of the standard.
Topics include:

- presence of a long-term strategy based on the values and principles of the Toyota Way,
- workplace ethics and social responsibility,
- leadership system with understanding of top management thinking and the role of each department in the organization,
- establishing and deploying hoshin,
- value creation through human development,
- value creation through work process improvement and supplier improvement,
- managing daily results, and
- benchmarking, information sharing, and utilization.

These topics are looking at the larger value stream, all the way from suppliers to customers, and include even broader topics, such as the community, environment, and assessing the competition. True to the Toyota method of development, each of the categories is spelled out and given an objective standard from which to compare the current situation. The assessment of the plant's current situation is spread out over all of the key areas, such as Administration, Safety, HR, Cost, Production Control, and the overall plant. An example of one of these is Safety. The key factors are shown in Table 5.3. Standards are set for each other.

**Table 5.3** Management System Assessment—Safety

| | How Customer Requests are Gathered | Competition Related Factors | Related Internal and External Suppliers | Evaluation Indicator |
|---|---|---|---|---|
| Safety | Plant safety and health meeting | Safety and health at other plants | Safety and environment committee | Number and frequency of major disasters |
| | | Utility systems | | Amount of accident-free time |
| | | Environmental systems | | Amount of pollution and $CO_2$ generated |
| | | Equipment management systems | | Percentage recycled |
| | | | | Amount of energy used |

Once each of these standards is identified, the executives' assignment is to go back to their locations and "grasp the situation" of each indicator. The main components of grasping the situation are to use an external team's consensus ratings, then go directly to the customer and get feedback, and then go to the team members through a survey of their input. The executives put all of this feedback together in order to clarify strengths and improvement points. Using practiced Toyota methods, a plan is developed, implemented, and followed up with the PDCA process until standards are met and business needs are addressed.

The executives then come back together as a class to review their results and get feedback from their class peers. The activity utilizes the classroom only to share the information, coordinate assignments, and get feedback. The real work is done "on the job" in each of the executive's organizations.

## Making Available Training Resources

Training is a broadly distributed responsibility in Toyota, and trainers themselves get certified to teach. Human resources is responsible for human resource development classes at the company level, but the responsibility for most teaching is broken down and given to each manager and supervisor in their respective areas.

The preferred and most common approach is to use the actual line-side production managers and supervisors (group and team leaders) as trainers for these classroom subjects. Of course, it is a challenge to free up line managers and supervisors to provide training during production time, but there are two ways Toyota addresses this issue:

1. Have classes between shifts or on Saturday—this provides flexibility for both the instructor and the students.
2. Utilize "off-line" managers and supervisors to help with training. Many managers and supervisors are freed up to work "special projects" off-line through kaizen efficiency improvements. These supervisors are working on projects such as pilot teams (preparing for new model introductions), kaizen teams (working on future efficiency improvements), safety teams, or quality team. In these roles, the supervisor has the flexibility to be a trainer for identified classroom training.

These two approaches help involve production people as trainers in the classroom, but there are still occasions when it is necessary to utilize other resources to teach classroom subjects. Toyota's strategy in these cases is to make sure the instructors have production experience, or provide them with an opportunity to understand the actual workstations through on-the-floor activities.

Toyota hires a core group of trainers as full-time instructors, and utilizes contract instructors to fill in at peak training times or for specialized training. Even with contract trainers, Toyota follows the same philosophy of hiring persons with production experience, or provides them with the on-floor opportunities. Since Toyota has been in the United States for more than 20 years, there is a growing resource of Toyota retirees that are available to be trainers for these classroom subjects at peak times. This is an ideal situation since the trainers have credibility with the students, and they are not pressured with the demands of production.

## SUMMARY

Toyota has standards and systems for every aspect of training and development for every level of the organization. The orientation of a new member includes training in values, physical fitness, fundamental skills, and finally their production processes. The fundamental skill training is coordinated across the globe to collect all the best practices and deliver them simultaneously via Web-based video manuals. The training of each production process is via a standardized method that is also consistent across the company. While there is more classroom training than in the past, due to rapid growth, the focus of Toyota's training and development is still "on the job" for every level.

# KEY POINTS TO CONSIDER FOR YOUR COMPANY

1. There is a clearly articulated orientation curriculum and corresponding schedule of sessions aimed at initially familiarizing new employees with all significant company policies, procedures, work expectations, and programs. The training and socialization process at Toyota starts during selection.

2. The roles of all members of the organization are established and communicated throughout the organization. Each role includes problem solving at all levels.

3. There is a standardized instruction method (Toyota Job Instruction) to train all operators on standard work processes throughout the organization. The process is followed up by both line management and human resources.

4. There is a process to match on-the-job related learning, behavior, sequences, and performance standards to individual and team training needs.

5. Classroom training is becoming more common in Toyota to address global expansion and the lack of Japanese coordinators to go around. This classroom training is almost always coupled with the gemba projects to reinforce the training and develop real skills.

6. Job rotation is used to provide broad based skills and force people outside their comfort zones. Moving members outside their expertise also forces them to rely on other people and develop Toyota Way leadership skills.

7. Human resources coordinates training, but most of the training is done by team leaders, group leaders, and managers who have been certified in Job Instruction training.

# Chapter 6

# Engaging Competent and Willing People in Continuous Improvement

*There is a way to do it better—find it.*

—Thomas A. Edison, inventor

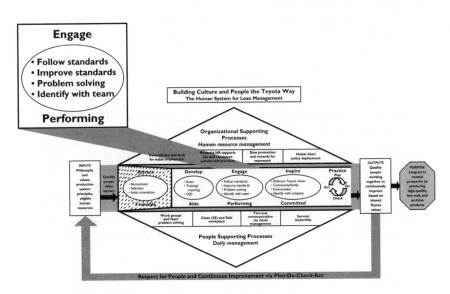

## PROBLEM SOLVING MAY BE THE SILVER BULLET

It is clear that there are no silver bullets in the Toyota Way in the sense of absolute, universal quick fixes, but if there is one key it is problem solving. When a student came to Taiichi Ohno to learn the Toyota Production System, the first lesson was in problem solving. He would sometimes literally drag his students to the shop floor, the gemba, and make them stand in a circle he drew on the floor and observe to understand the real problems. He asked them to look with a blank mind and ask why five times. When Ohno happened upon a student working on something, he would challenge them by demanding to know why they were working on that problem and not another. He would sometimes yell and scream to force them to think deeply about the problem, where it occurred, and what the true root cause was. The next step was almost always a walk to where the problem occurred to observe first hand. Eventually the method Ohno taught implicitly was called "practical problem solving," though it continued to be taught one on one through daily tutelage on the shop floor. By the 1980s practical problem solving was formally taught through classroom training and shop floor exercises, mostly outside Japan, as the standard problem solving methodology for Toyota.

More recently Toyota has made a breakthrough—for Toyota—introducing a new problem solving method. The intent was to formalize one common methodology since there was a perception that there are different views of practical problem solving as well as to kaizen the improvement methodology. Problem solving is seen as such as critical part of the culture that Mr. Cho, as vice chairman of the board of Toyota Worldwide, personally introduced the new global standard method entitled Toyota Business Practices. Consider the following directive as quoted by Fujio Cho in a Toyota Internal Document, *The Toyota Business Practices, 2005*:

> *For all Toyota members: Why the Toyota Business Practices now?*
>
> *We are aiming to be a global company in which members worldwide can work with a sense of enthusiasm and achieve their dreams. Today, Toyota members of many different cultures are working around the globe, and it is the Toyota Way that joins us all together as one. Toyota desires to be a true global company where all of us from different nations understand and implement the values of the Toyota Way, are recognized for our efforts, and achieve our dreams through the fulfillment of our roles within the company.*
>
> *Since the foundation of our company, an accumulation of all Toyota members' wisdom has been synergized in providing the best products and services to society and our customers, and the Toyota Way was developed based upon that wisdom. While the Toyota Way principles have spread throughout the company, I have heard that it is still not easy for individuals to fully understand and practice the Toyota Way. Thus, I would like to introduce the Toyota Business Practices (TBP), which explicitly outlines practical business applications, based on problem solving. In order to put the Toyota Way values into action, all of us are expected to master the TBP and practice them in our daily work. This will enable us to contribute to society, our customers, and Toyota itself, which will lead to our continuous personal growth and satisfaction as professionals. Such a standardized approach is not intended to limit an individual's way of conducting business. Rather, the standard approach provides a basic framework from which the individual can express his or her unique talent.*

Toyota Business Practices (TBP) is a standard approach to problem solving, but like standardized work, rather than limit people's creativity, it aims to be a vehicle for its development. The diagram in Figure 6.1 summarizes the new formulation of the Toyota Business Practices.

Toyota's new TBP method has two parts—the method described as "concrete actions and processes" and the approach described under "drive and dedication."

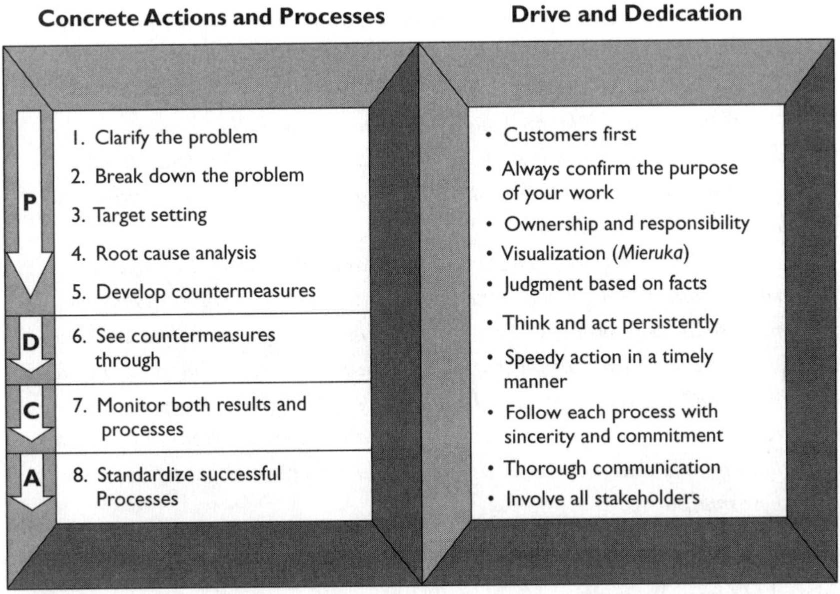

**Concrete Actions and Processes**          **Drive and Dedication**

| P | 1. Clarify the problem | • Customers first |
| | 2. Break down the problem | • Always confirm the purpose of your work |
| | 3. Target setting | • Ownership and responsibility |
| | 4. Root cause analysis | • Visualization (*Mieruka*) |
| | 5. Develop countermeasures | • Judgment based on facts |
| D | 6. See countermeasures through | • Think and act persistently |
| | | • Speedy action in a timely manner |
| C | 7. Monitor both results and processes | • Follow each process with sincerity and commitment |
| A | 8. Standardize successful Processes | • Thorough communication |
| | | • Involve all stakeholders |

**Figure 6.1** TBP is the Revised Problem Solving Process

There is a lot in common with the older practical problem solving method. Both are based on the PDCA model and on management by fact but a few subtle differences make a big difference in some cases.

One major addition in Toyota Business Practices is in clarifying the problem the team is encouraged to define the ideal state of the process. This pushes the team to look beyond a small, incremental change to the process and think bigger and more long term. Envisioning the ideal state also creates a large gap with the current approach. Even if the current process is achieving today's targets, by considering how it compares to an ideal state it will be clear that there are many opportunities for improvement. The risk of the ideal state is that it can seem overwhelming to achieve. Where do we start?

To get to action a second step was added—break down the problem. Henry Ford made the wise observation: "Nothing is particularly hard if you divide it into small jobs." Cheryl Jones, vice president of manufacturing at TMMK, learned this lesson during a visit to Japan and relates it to the Toyota Business Practices step that is designed to break down big problems into small chunks:

*Something we are stressing through the Toyota business practices—breaking the problem down—are the many levels of problems and gaps we are trying to close. If the project is too large or too overwhelming the advisor's role is to break down the elements—man, material, machine—and perhaps encourage the group to focus on one aspect only and make some improvement. There may be a 50 percent gap but do not start with that focus and instead start working on a two percent gap and make the improvement and focus on the next part as you are starting to improve problem solving.*

*When I was in Japan I suggested some big items that were not really doable and tried and failed and then broke it down. They said "let's start with the hand motions and just save one or two seconds." You continue to look at that and it adds up.*

*Last year I was in Japan to do benchmarking to see what we need to be working on at Georgetown. One plant made a presentation all about how many small improvements team members implemented. They had books of suggestions each team member tried to implement. I was so impressed by all those small improvements and how they were recognizing every one of the team members for that contribution. At my level I am always thinking about that big item that needs to be different. And the presentation was all about those small items.*

Gary Convis also emphasizes breaking down big problems into smaller, actionable pieces. He proudly explains how it might appear from outside Toyota that large improvements are the result of a big bang effort of a few individuals whereas they are really a collection of many smaller innovations. Then through improvement ideas at all levels, the innovation is refined and further developed to the level the outsider sees. For example he speaks about the Global Body Line that in the late 1990s revolutionized the way Toyota made car bodies through a system of robotics: cutting floor space in half, new product launch time in half, and allowing Toyota to make virtually any body in any sequence without changeover. It was globally deployed to all plants. It follows the Toyota policy of simple, slim, and flexible in that it is not the result of the most complex technology, but a very simple use of robotics. Convis stated:

*We are always taking one step at a time—look at any innovation and there are many smaller innovations within it. For example, the Global Body Line was a major innovative step forward for Toyota but there are many smaller innovations that allowed it to happen. As you build bodies in the old line the hard points where you had hard technology to maintain were very inflexible and led naturally to technology that is simpler and inexpensive based on robotics. Then technology and knowledge can blend toward a better way. It was not a breakthrough but a lot of learning points that led to an image of what it can really do. Breakthrough thinking is not totally innovative. You have to have a foundation and the world looks more clear and you evolve a different picture of it based on advancements in technology and your experience or intellectual property as a company.*

Another technological leap forward for Toyota was in the way they paint the car body. Through a cartridge system in which each cartridge holds the paint for one car body Toyota can paint cars a different color for each body on the line without batching colors and without any interruption during the changeover from color to color. Convis continues:,

*Another example—cartridge robotics systems in the paint shop. The use of tubes that deliver paint stepped up to cartridges and dramatically cut down on cleaning expense. We simply put a little solvent through the bell to clean out between colors. The new system had many moving parts but it saved $15 a car. The next breakthroughs—reduce the many moving parts—created the next level of cartridge robotics. Sometimes it looks like huge steps but actually is a lot of little steps.*

Daily and virtually constant problem solving activity is the key to the Toyota culture and to its success. Often people talk about the Quality Circles and the Suggestion System as keys to the success of Toyota. We talk about them also, because they are part of the system and culture, but they are not the foundation. For example, the Quality Circle program in the Toyota culture is focused on developing the problem solving culture at Toyota, not just specific results. It is process-driven rather than results-driven. In other words, the focus is on building quality team members, and developing both their problem solving skills and their team relationships, more than it is about X amount of savings. The president of the Georgetown plant at the time of this writing, Steve St. Angelo, who came from General Motors, saw this difference as perhaps the most critical difference between the two cultures. In an interview he said:

*Problem solving is very important here at Toyota. I have been here almost three years now. Some differences I see at Toyota are that we are very process oriented and traditional companies are very results oriented. Obviously Toyota cares about results—profit, etc. But we spend more of our time discussing the process that gets you results. In our Quality Circle program we have a lot of personal contact and friendly competition. Each shop has its own QC circles of team members and support from management. In competition the circles are rated NOT on how well they solve the problem but how well they went through the problem solving process. Rated by the management team (break down problem, genchi genbutsu, etc.) we select bronze, silver, gold QC circle award winners. Gold are judged by the President and staff and one of these is selected as the platinum winner—twice per year. One winner will compete against all American plants once per year. This year the ceremony is at NUMMI and next year it is here in Georgetown. There are two platinum's per year, one in Spring and one in Fall. In Spring, the platinum winners go to Japan to compete against platinum winners from around the world. There are prizes for gold and silver, but not money—five to six laptop computers, small prizes, gas cards, DVDs. We do not want people to do it for the money. We want them to do it because it develops them and gives them an opportunity to participate in the business, encourages teamwork, and implements diversity by having cross-functional teams. Getting feedback is the best part of Quality Circles— anyone who is gold or platinum meets with me as the president and I go and see what they did and have a first class lunch and talk about whatever they want to talk about and it is just them and me."*

# AT TOYOTA EVERYONE IS A PROBLEM SOLVER

The first step for any new team member, or a team member assigned to a new job, is to learn the job. They must develop the skills necessary to perform specific jobs through Toyota Job Instruction training. Through repetition, performing the tasks eventually becomes natural and the team member can consistently perform the job within the allotted time. We might think that they are performing adequately by doing the job to standard with high quality. In Toyota this is only the starting point. The full Toyota team member must develop ideas for improving the job.

Why is it so important for all team members to be critically evaluating their jobs and coming up with ideas for improvement? Is it because it makes them feel good about themselves or that it generates commitment to changes management wants to make? There is some truth in both these results but the real reason is different. Going back to Asian culture and the Toyota thinking that evolved in this culture there is an underlying premise: *People can never know in detail what will happen in the future.* The world is dynamic and complex and we have to learn to read and adapt to the environment as we go. When an engineer first sets up the process she has an image of how the process will operate, what the conditions will be, and what people will do. Once that process is in operation the real world does its best to confound all the great thinking of that engineer. The process is bound to fail in many unexpected ways. We can learn from past failures of the system and the engineer can try to develop the next one better but there will be new, unexpected failures. We cannot anticipate the world as fast as it can confound us. What is the solution? Place an attentive, thinking individual at each process to monitor the process and quickly adjust to all those disruptions. Imagine assigning an engineer to every process to stand and watch the process and the person operating it so they can see first hand every deviation from standard and immediately stop the problem from passing to the next process (contain) and later develop a long-term countermeasure (root cause

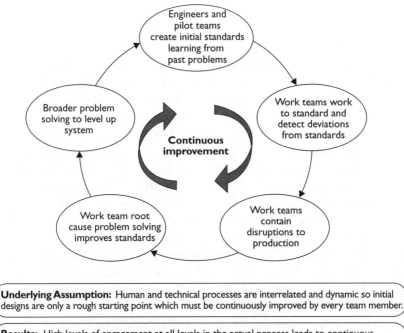

**Figure 6.2** Toyota Continuous Improvement Culture

solution). This would be very expensive indeed and not very lean. But wait, we already have people there operating the process. Why not use the team member to act as the engineer—get two people for the price of one?

For this to work we need (see Figure 6.2):

1. Engineers, getting input from people working in the processes, doing the best job they can to set up the processes by solving past problems.
2. Team members on the floor need to see deviations from the standard (with the help of visual management).
3. A process for immediate containment of any problems so defects cannot be passed on to later processes and get compounded.
4. A process to reflect on the problems that have occurred over a period of time and through root cause problem solving establish long-term counter-measures—more frequent reflection means more problems being solved before they can do continuing damage.
5. A process for managers to identify larger system problems and achieve new levels of performance.

Fujio Cho, chairman of Toyota stated the principle behind this simply and elo-quently, when he said, "The soul of the Toyota Production System is a principle called kaizen....its essence is the notion that engineers, managers, and line workers *collaborate continually to systematize production tasks and identify incremental changes to make work go more smoothly.*"

The five-step process seems simple enough and it is hard to imagine anyone objecting to the notion that we want to improve at every level and then learn from past mistakes. Unfortunately most of the companies we work with outside Toyota do not have consistent improvement even though opportunities for improvement abound. The common one-week kaizen workshop has become popular because there is such a large impact, mainly just cleaning up the chaos—tools out of place, lots of extra material sitting here and there, every worker doing the job differently, equipment breaking down routinely, quality problems that go undetected until final inspection, and supervisors who do not know where to begin in prioritizing problems to solve. The underlying problem is that the culture is working against systematic problem solving at the point of attack—the actual processes where the problems are occurring. We have established layers and layers of management, procedures, metrics, and general bureaucracy that seem to be designed to isolate those responsible for improving processes—managers and engineers—from the actual problems.

When we work with companies wishing to learn from Toyota we are often brought in by middle managers who have been ordered by the top to get lean projects going to reduce costs. Figure 6.3 summarizes in a flow chart the usual process of top-down problem correction in these companies. The underlying assumption is that the system being managed is mainly a set of technical processes that are static and with clever manipulation management can get whatever output they request. Top management has a dream of what they would like to see accomplished, of course grounded in metrics, and issues orders. Middle management working with technical specialists develop solutions to problems with the biggest impact and order supervisors to follow the new system or use the new technology. Supervisors supposedly train and motivate workers to follow the new process. We say "supposedly" because training is usually of poor quality and the worker's attitude is often: "Here we go again."

When we work with these companies one of the first questions that they ask us is: "What are your lean metrics and do you have data to convince management they are getting a return on their investment from lean?" One of our colleagues likens this to the Star Trek model in which all the important decisions are made from the bridge of the ship based on remote sensing of what is going on (though actually on Star Trek Captain Kirk and his team always beamed to the surface to investigate at the gemba).[1] In the traditional enterprise, the top executives rarely

---

[1] Personal communication from Michael Balle, author of *The Gold Mine*, Cambridge, Mass: Lean Enterprise Institute, 2005.

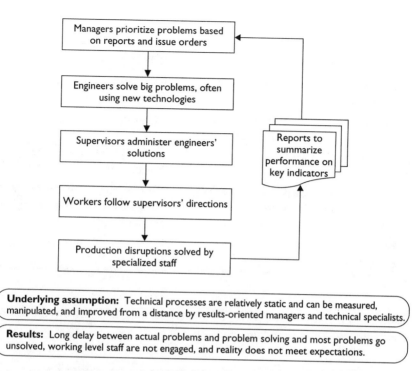

**Figure 6.3** Culture of Top-Down Measure and Correct

see the actual situation up close except when it is a carefully orchestrated tour where managers show them what they want them to see. The result is a strong disconnect between understanding and decision making at the top, what technical staff are trying to accomplish, and what actually happens at the gemba.

Toyota starts with a different underlying assumption, rooted in Eastern culture. They believe the world is dynamic and complex and people matter more than technology. To capture the learning from all the different situations that occur, Toyota managers want people closest to the process to act as signal detectors identifying problems which they then help to solve. They realize that problem solving at all levels of the organization—from solving little problems to major projects to leveling up the system—will continually strengthen the human and technical systems. Investing in ways to involve people in problem solving is not an option to be decided upon by cost-benefit analysis. It is integral to the culture and the main competitive advantage of Toyota.

The starting point of any serious effort to turn around this culture of isolated problem-solving specialists is to directly connect thinking and doing at all levels of the organization. In this chapter we will give examples of the systems Toyota has developed to make steps one through five a reality by connecting problem

**Table 6.1** Example Toyota Continuous Improvement Approaches in Plant

| Plant Improvement Process | Main Method |
| --- | --- |
| 1. Engineers and Pilot Teams Create Initial Standards Learning from Past Problems | New Model Launch Process |
| 2. Team Members Work to Standard and Detect Deviations from Standards | Andon System |
| 3. Work Teams Contain Disruptions to Production | "Event Type" Problem Solving to Maintain Standard |
| 4. Work Team Root Cause Problem Solving Improves Standards | "Setting Type" Problem Solving at Local Level to Improve to Higher Standard |
| 5. Broader Problem Solving for Leveling Up System | System Kaizen Through Toyota Business Practices |

detection to problem solving to organizational learning. Table 6.1 lists these steps along with the main method used for each step.

# 1. ENGINEERS AND PILOT TEAMS CREATE INITIAL STANDARDS LEARNING FROM PAST PROBLEMS

## Engineers Begin the Development of Standardized Work

When a new plant is launched or a new vehicle is launched in an existing plant, engineering is responsible for developing the product and the manufacturing process. They then turn over responsibility for building a quality product to the plant. Toyota is a manufacturing company first and it is drilled into all engineers that they must always support manufacturing. This support starts early in the development of the new vehicle in what Toyota calls simultaneous engineering—simultaneous engineering of the product and manufacturing process. There are a variety of computer tools to support this and Toyota uses them all but the real focus is on people, capturing the knowledge from past vehicles, including getting input from those who build the car. Toyota has been steadily moving simultaneous engineering earlier and earlier, to the point where manufacturing representatives are now part of study groups looking at artistic renderings in the form of clay models of the vehicle. They are commenting on what aspects of the style will make manufacturing difficult and helping with solutions.

Product engineers are somewhat distant from the shop floor but they experience manufacturing first hand within months of joining the company. In Japan,

Toyota hires a "freshman class" of engineers in the Spring every year. All of these engineers will spend two to three months of their first year working in production doing the jobs of hourly team members. They will be part of a work team and assemble or stamp body parts or make bumpers. The goal is to start to learn that engineers should get their hands dirty and the products or processes they develop should support the team member on the line. Gary Convis explains the development of the young engineer this way:

> *In Toyota's evaluation of engineers we highly evaluate and put people in positions of working on the plant floor. Our engineers are dirty-handed engineers. If they are going to excel in Toyota, they have to respect, appreciate and find ways of adding value to the actual production operations and the plant floor. That is a prerequisite to be successful as an engineer. This floor experience— you live on the floor for eight hours—you have to have a special character to do that. If you don't you are in the wrong kitchen. We try to tell them what it will be like, but some may or may not appreciate it. But that does not change the fact that that is what it takes to be successful at Toyota.*

In addition to working on the production line the young engineer spends several months selling cars and learns first hand what the customer is looking for. After this the engineer is assigned to an engineering department and a mentor will supervise a "freshman project." This is always a challenging project as the young engineer has never designed anything for real. One production engineer was asked to design a checking fixture for a body panel—a complex fixture that holds the panel in place at precise points so it can be checked for quality. The mentoring style at Toyota is that of giving a challenging assignment and asking difficult questions and then sitting back while the student struggles. If the young engineer goes to the right people and asks good questions she will get answers. Periodically the mentor will ask the young engineer what they are working on. A natural question will be, "When did you go to the shop floor last to observe the process?" Genchi genbutsu—going to see—is drilled into the young student. Go to the test lab, go to the shop floor, go see the supplier's process. This becomes second nature to the Toyota engineer and makes working with production much more natural.

Product engineers are in the R&D division, while production engineering is located within the manufacturing division. Production engineers actually develop all the manufacturing processes in the plant. They are very hands-on compared to most manufacturing engineers we know of—and often will even learn to build actual equipment. Most of them could design a robot from scratch. The production engineers have their offices and labs at a plant site so they are directly connected to daily manufacturing operations. The production engineers work closely with product development engineers and represent production in the development of the vehicle and in the manufacturing system that will produce it. They are involved at the earliest stages of the conception of the product and take the product into production. A key part of their job is to review all of the production difficulties with the past model and develop countermeasures for the new model launch working directly with team members taken off the production floor.

Learning from the past is captured formally in engineering checklists that are kept part by part by both product engineers and production engineers. The senior engineer in charge of each part of the car maintains this checklist and updates it after each new program. For most of Toyota's history these checklists were paper documents in notebooks. For each program the most recent version of the checklist was prepared, from the point of view of product engineering and production engineering, and the engineers checked off that they considered that issue or they were in the bounds of that curve on a graph. Now the checklist is captured in a know-how database but the process is still the same—checking off on the computer for each item that it has been considered. This is a way to accumulate knowledge and be sure the knowledge is used from program to program.

## The Pilot Team Is a Way to Involve and Develop Team Members

A key part of the Toyota culture is giving responsibility for making up the production processes to the team that does the work. At a major model change or new model start up for example, a team leader or team member is taken out of the group (usually freed up by improvements made by the group), and given the responsibility of representing that group in the new model start up team; it is known as the pilot team. This person works with engineers to "build each production process" with the input from the rest of the group. This initial involvement and "buy in" into the process is the foundation for the team members to not only follow the standardized work, but also to make improvements. There is ownership in the process. Improvement is focused on reducing all the waste of the process.

The launch of the 2006 Camry was the smoothest launch in the history of that plant. There were only about three hours of downtime between models and the quality at launch was the best ever. Gary Convis had lived through a number of model changes and had a simple explanation for the comparatively smooth launch. He said they finally got it right in involving all the people on the floor in creating the standardized work. In the past the pilot team played too strong a role often creating standardized work in the office and then sending it out to the floor where the teams did not own it. For this launch the teams themselves worked on finalizing the standardized work.

Cheryl Jones supported Gary Convis' view on the 2006 Camry launch:

*With a new model launch we get the opportunity to make improvements in all parts of the process. There were big improvements when we launched the*

*new Camry; we worked on it for at least 2 years. We worked on the follow-*
*ing types of things: inefficient layout, parts flow, parts presentation, build*
*sequence, and difficult parts to install. And, in the early stages of design for*
*the new model Camry, the savings were huge. The benefits for team members*
*were that the cars are so much easier to build! The new cars were very well*
*designed, and early involvement of many team members in the plant, that is*
*members of the pilot team (who are constantly rotating through), made a*
*huge difference.[2]*

## 2. WORK TEAMS WORK TO STANDARD AND DETECT DEVIATIONS IN AN ATMOSPHERE OF NO BLAME

### Without Standards There are No Problems

At Toyota, standards or standardization are the focus of all systematic improvement. The most visible standards are those associated with the 5S Program—Sort,
Straighten, Shine, Standardize, and Sustain. Sometimes we associate 5S with neat-
ness and tidiness. Through 5S we can go beyond this and identify visually the standard and deviations from the standard. For example, if there is a garbage can with
tape around it, and it is labeled Garbage Can, then there is a clear standard set.
If this garbage can is missing, then it is very clear to everyone that there "is a problem." If there was no square on the floor with a label, not everyone would know
that there was supposed to be a garbage can there, and therefore it would "not be
a problem" if it were not there (see Figure 6.4).

Often someone from Toyota will go to a supplier and ask them to do 5S
throughout the workplace before they will teach them anything else. This does

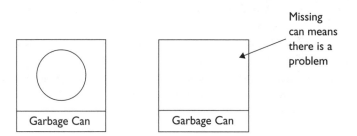

**Figure 6.4** Toyota's 5S Program Is about Visual Standards

---

[2] The quotes in this section all came from one interview with Cheryl Jones, at the time vice
president of manufacturing for the Toyota, Georgetown plant.

provide some visual standards but more importantly it starts to emphasize to everyone the importance of basic discipline. At Toyota plants, 5S is also used as a teaching tool to emphasize the importance of standardization. At TMMK, the basic 5S Program is consistent in the work place and extends to all parts of the shop floor and the support areas. The team member's break areas are all organized in a neat and organized manner. It is clear, and there are visible standards for where team members are to hang their coats, where the lunch boxes go, and how the break area should look when the bell rings for every one to go to their respective production process work stations. There is a picture in the break room showing all the tables clear (with no magazines or newspapers), and all the chairs pushed in ready for the next group to use.

In the production area, supply cabinets are also to be set up this way. The team members know where to go to get their gloves or ear plugs, and the cabinet is neat, organized and labeled. It is also set up with a mini "kanban" system; that is, with minimums and maximums set for each item in the closet, so that if the team member takes the tenth pair of gloves with a minimum of ten, they would follow the standard of taking the order card from its spot, and placing it in the ordering box. This is a simple example of a relevant standard to follow that insures that there will be the right amount of gloves available for the next person, the next day.

When Hiroyoshi Yoshiki was hired by Toyota in Japan he was taught that standards were the basis for kaizen. If you have a standard and it is not being followed you have a problem. If you have a problem you have an opportunity to improve. According to Yoshiki, this was extremely difficult to teach the Americans when they started up Georgetown:

> *Even though you think you have a problem, if you do not have a standard, it's not a problem. It is just a phenomenon. A standard needs to be set first. Then check the facts. If there is a gap between the standard and the actual situation, there is a problem. I learned this early. My first supervisor asked me to make a problem solving report in my first year at Toyota. I picked up an issue and conducted some investigation. Then I told my boss I found a problem and had some ideas to solve it. He was not convinced. He said it was only my opinion because I did not show any deviation from the standard. This is my first and most impressive lesson in problem solving at Toyota. You may think things are not going well, but without having any standard, that is just your opinion. If you cannot show what is the standard and what is the fact deviating from it, you cannot say there is a problem. It is an opinion.*

The basic 5S Program is a teaching tool in the Toyota culture, and a building block toward more advanced standardization and problem solving. The most important application of this program in the Toyota culture is standardized work.

## Standardized Work is the Basis for Improvement by the Team

Standardized Work is a concept that is often misunderstood in the context of the lean journey. Many times we have heard the comment that standardized work is going to make a bunch of robots out of us, and take away our ability to think. Our response is, on the contrary, standardized work in the Toyota culture does just the opposite. It is the baseline for improvement.

The fear of becoming like a robot that we often hear in Western culture is a reflection of Western individualism. We do not want to do it like everyone else. We want to do it our way. We want to have freedom of choice on how to do the job. We want individual innovation and creativity. That is fine if the work is individually oriented.

Now let's consider a Toyota plant. The worker is called a team member because the team performs a set of tasks. Job rotation is expected within the team with every team member learning all the jobs. The team has a team leader. The team and team leader are responsible for defining the standardized work and then updating it when there is an idea for improvement. The idea for improvement might come from a quality issue that arises more than once. The line stops for this problem several times and the team members go into a problem-solving mode. What is the root cause? Why did it happen? Why? Why? Why? The countermeasure is tried and refined. Then the standardized work is updated to reflect the new countermeasure. Or perhaps some steps are taken out that increase productivity of the team. The team shares responsibility for the standard work and shares responsibility for following the standard work.

What happens if team members decide they will each do the job their own way? They each come up with what they think is an improvement. They each do the job at a different speed. They each have different quality problems when they do the job. Then can we have a systematic approach to kaizen? Individuals might be learning a different way to do the job that they think works, but maybe the wrong way. Even if it is a better way nobody else will learn from the idea. And will the individual feel good about their improvement? They may individually benefit by having a few seconds less work per cycle. But the product has not improved and productivity has not improved. So they do not share in the satisfaction that comes when the whole team is performing better.

A useful indicator for leaders in the Toyota culture is to see how current the standardized work is at the process. If the standardized work is old and outdated, it is a clear sign that there has been either a lack of improvement at the process, or there has been improvement and it has not been shared with all team members and made into a new standard. Something about the team dynamics or the team leader role is not working. The standardized work must be owned by the team and seen as a tool to record and teach the newest ideas.

## Use of Standards Does Not Mean Every Operation Is the Same

The natural inclination for large corporations that culturally are top-down, coercive bureaucracies is to grasp onto the sameness of Toyota plants and make all their plants look the same. They assemble large corporate groups and invest in consultants to identify "best practices" and develop the corporate standards. They seek to use the power of the executive office to "tell everyone they have to do it this way." Unfortunately they miss a key point. They do not understand the concept of kaizen. They do not understand that by telling the plants how to do it they kill any chance of developing a true kaizen culture.

Cheryl Jones explained a subtle but important aspect of Toyota's view of top-down standards:

> *If we try to simply get everyone to the current standard you are missing opportunities to get better. You are not taking into account how times are changing. There has to be lots of flexibility in allowing creativity along the way. Some take a little different path and learn a little bit differently.*

Obviously when a technical standard that works is developed, Toyota wants to communicate that standard and make sure it is uniform across the world, right? Cheryl went on to explain how this was not really the case. Standards are not developed and then communicated from headquarters to all the plants. Rigid standards will only kill kaizen.

Toyota's kaizen process includes the concept of *yokoten*. To *yokoten* is to spread across or propagate. In nature this is the multiplying of saplings and grafts from a large tree into many new trees. These new trees will thrive with properly prepared soil and weather conditions. However, each new tree will grow differently in its own unique way and adapt within the new environment. They are not clones, but take on a life of their own. The same is true with *yokoten*. It is not just a "go and see and then copy." For Toyota, it is "go and see and then improve upon." To allow the individual manufacturing plants this kind of latitude requires a different perspective on diffusing best practices. It is not so much moving a piece of equipment into a new location as providing input to an organism that is encouraged to grow in its own way. Cheryl employed the Japanese concept of "*yokoten*" when we asked how Toyota communicates new standards. She explained:

> *It is yokoten every time—share best practices. But there are different avenues for this. In North America we have NAPJM [A consortium of North American Producing Japanese Manufacturers] meetings in a different plant every 3 months. Each department shares with other departments what they are doing and what others can look at. We had a big sheet from the last NAPJM saying who did what from the last one and where gaps were still*

*open. It is not mandated. We must let individuals from plants decide what they will do to fix their problems and close gaps. We cannot have someone from corporate saying you need to do X, Y, Z because this is completely contrary to Toyota problem solving.*

## Team Members Serve as Problem Detectors

From a technical point of view we think of signal detectors as devices that detect a deviation from a standard and alert people that there is a problem. The idiot lights in a car come on when oil pressure is too low or there is some engine malfunction. Sakichi Toyoda developed an automatic loom that could detect when a thread broke and immediately shut itself down and signal for help—an example of an andon system. The andon started out as a metal flag that popped up. Toyota engineers do their best to develop many kinds of automatic signal detectors, particularly on automated equipment, but many problems cannot be automatically detected and a human must diligently watch for these problems. The andon system then gets triggered by the person pulling a cord or pushing a button.

The first step in continuous improvement is problem identification and every team member must be willing and able to call attention to the problem. As discussed in Chapter 3, Nate Furuta headed up human resources when Toyota first started NUMMI and eventually became vice president of human resources for North America. He explained what the Toyota Production System meant to him: "The whole system to me is about identification of problems. They want to call it an opportunity. No, I say it is a problem. With an opportunity you have a choice. You can take it or not."

Why do we often prefer to use the term "opportunity" in America? The answer is in our culture. When we say problem we automatically assume that someone is to blame. This was the problem Toyota faced when starting up production in the United States and has been one of the major challenges in every plant startup globally.

Hiroyoshi Yoshiki was originally trained in human resources in Japan. He was involved as early as the site selection for the Georgetown plant. We asked him what stood out most about the difference in culture between Toyota in Japan and what he saw when starting up TMMK. He did not hesitate:

*We were most surprised by the reaction of the people when we asked them about problems. In Toyota we always ask what is the problem? The reactions from Americans were very, very negative. We were surprised. It does not have any negative connotation for us in Japan. What is the problem? When we asked that question of a person it was like "Oops" in the United States. People think "I messed up." "What is the problem" was the first thing I experienced when I joined Toyota. You hear this everywhere, everyday at Toyota. How can we make the word problem a positive word rather than negative word? It is very much a unique example of Toyota culture.*

We asked what the countermeasure was to this dilemma. He explained further:

*At first we did not know how we could remove the negative connotation from "problem." We worked hard to separate the problem from the person. We are not accusing you, we explained. We just want to know the fact to resolve the undesirable condition to you and the company. It is not for accusation of any human beings, we tried hard to convince the people. That took time, repeatedly going to the production floor and encouraging the team members to come forward with a problem rather than hide it.*

The cultural assumptions about problems in traditional Western culture compared to Toyota culture are summarized in Table 6.2. When there is a serious error or performance is below the expected level traditional Western management goes into action to place the blame. Who did it and what is the proper punishment? The assumption is that problems are caused by people—ask the 5 Whos to find the cause. Here is a mock example:

Problem: In a shop that makes kitchen cabinets there are rejects due to inconsistency of the painted surface.

Who? The painters are incompetent and messing up.

**Table 6.2** Western Versus Toyota View of Problems

| | **Traditional Western** | **Toyota** |
|---|---|---|
| What is a problem? | Result of someone messing up | Deviation from standard |
| What is the cause? | Individual (5 Whos) | System (5 Whys) |
| Who is responsible? | Person who makes mistake | Management |
| What should individual who makes mistake do? | Solve problem on own if possible | Call attention to problem for assistance and to avoid the problem in the future |
| Assumptions about People | They will not accept blame unless forced to | They will feel empowered if they get positive support for solving problems |
| Problem Solving Skill | Some have it, some don't | It can and must be taught |

Who? The painters are not well trained on how to use the new paint gun and it is the supervisor's job to train them.

Who? The supervisor says the old paint gun worked fine but engineering specified a new complex gun that is erratic.

Who? Engineering says they did not pick that gun because it was known to be unreliable, but purchasing got a good deal on it and insisted.

Who? The purchasing agent says his brother-in-law works for the company that makes the gun and swore by its quality.

Useless Conclusion: The root cause is the brother-in-law of the purchasing agent.

Toyota simply views a problem as a fact—there is a deviation from the standard. The first assumption is that some failure in the system has a root cause that can be discovered by asking "why?" five times. In the above case we might ask what in the purchasing system allowed the buyer to purchase a new brand of tool without proper testing and validation? Perhaps more important what in the system caused each of the other people to know that there was a problem with the gun and not immediately bring it to the attention of management? The system will not be improved if people doing the work fail to report problems, so people must not fear admitting problems. So how did Toyota deal with the American cultural tendency to hide problems at Georgetown?

We know that culture is developed gradually, over time. It evolves more from experience than from what people say. It depends on complete consistency by leaders. The Toyota leaders were already part of a culture in Japan where the role of a manager is to be a teacher. It is understood that teaching requires patience, modeling the behavior desired of the student, and constantly finding opportunities to coach the student. This seems to have been a particular skill of the Toyota leaders sent to the U.S. from Japan—patiently encouraging the Americans, coaching the American managers on the importance of encouraging team members to surface problems, and absolutely making sure nobody was punished for surfacing problems.

The most important thing is that the Toyota leaders from Japan did not compromise on the importance of surfacing problems and did not give up. This was essential to making TPS work in America and they had no choice but to be successful. The future of the company was depending on being able to replicate this aspect of Toyota culture in other countries. With time and patience and continually demonstrating that people who pulled the andon were not punished, the culture at TMMK started to develop a willingness to share problems.

Roy Jay, a former manager of the TMMK Plastics Department, came from General Motors. He describes a time where his coordinator taught him this lesson first hand:

*Early in the production stability phase of the Georgetown plant I had an experience that helped me understand how to think as a manager at Toyota. At the time I was a production assistant manager of operations and excited about the challenge of handling the whole plastics operation when my manager took a trip to Japan for new model preparation. A section of the plastics operations produced instrument panels made of a sandwich of decorative vinyl skin, urethane foam, and a plastic reinforcement. The plant was producing vehicles at a 57 takt and so the supplier shops like Plastics produced at the same rate to match the line demand. On this particular day the instrument panel molding area was having trouble shooting the urethane foam leading to quality issues. As a result the in-process and emergency stock (~2.5 hours) was consumed because of the foam quality issue. At that point the assembly line had to stop because they had no instrument panel pads to install in the vehicles.*

*My heart dropped and my general manager had already been at my side asking the inevitable question: "When will this operation be able to supply product?" (I already knew the cost of stopping the plant was around $20,000 per minute.)*

*I was in close contact with the recovery team on the shop floor and tracking the corrective activity history on a flip chart (which proved very valuable later), but this activity was just a way to convert my nervous energy into some value-added action and show my fellow team members and my general manager the status of what, how, and the result of our shop team problem solving. At this point our recovery team dumped new material in the system and made a fresh blend after many unsuccessful tweaks of the existing material. Once the new batch was blended and loaded into the foaming machines the subsequent products were of acceptable quality and we soon began shipping product to the assembly line 64 minutes after we shut the line down.*

*You can do the math, but with this kind of cost impact I expected to be fired as soon as my manager returned from his business trip. But to my surprise my executive coordinator, a Japanese man named Kayzioshi ("Karl") Takeuchi and one of the best mentors of my career, asked me what I had learned from this experience. I almost stuttered and said "Well, one it's not good to shut the line down. Two I should have been able to troubleshoot the problem more quickly since that was my previous operational area of responsibility, and three, do I still have a job?" His response was truly remarkable: "What should we do to prevent reoccurrence?" I studied him for a few moments and then finally got past the shock of not being relieved of my responsibility and responded: "We have to identify the actual problem to solve, then analyze deeply for root cause(s) and develop corrective actions that would be used to minimize or eliminate the impact of this abnormality in the future."*

> *I worked the next two days on problem identification, analysis, and countermeasure development with numerous reviews with my mentor Karl until we were both satisfied with the comprehensiveness of the problem report (one side of A-3 paper) and then was asked to explain it to the president, Mr. Cho. After that review we began our countermeasure activity to reduce the chance for another incident of this kind.*
>
> *I was so relieved when I got through this situation and my manager didn't fire me, but the final comment from my coach Karl really gave me another level of understanding of the deeper meaning of the Toyota Way. He said "Roy-san, it's okay to shut down the assembly line for a few minutes a month when you are challenging the shop inventory level to bring the next problem to the surface. That's TPS. In fact, for the next couple of months I want you to actually stop the plastics shop from delivering parts to show your management team and your team members that it is okay to stop the line." Now that's what I call a different way to think.*

This is not to say that the only way to create an environment in which team members feel free to share problems is to hire a bunch of Japanese trainers from Toyota. This was done in a plant in America with Americans. Over time the American managers learned to encourage openly discussing problems without blame and became mentors to other plants. Mike Hoseus shared his "making the scratch" story back in Chapter 1. That helped him to learn this culture of trust in Japan, but now there was the challenge of instilling the same trust in Kentucky.

In fact the problem of scratches was a big problem for the assembly plant in the early years and most of the scratches were found by inspection, not tagged by a team leader indicating where a team member admitted their mistake. To encourage team members to pull the andon in this situation, the name of the scratch ID tag was coined an "I made it" ticket. The best situation is to have all scratches with "I made it" tickets on it, because this insures that no scratches will make it past inspection and for problem solving the problem identification and point of cause are already completed and all that is left is determining the root cause and countermeasure. If there is no "I made it" then there is much time and effort spent on determining what section of the plant the scratch came from and which process or part of the process is the point of cause.

When the data showed that most of the scratches that reached assembly did not have "I made it" tickets, the American management team got together and decided to do something to heighten the level of awareness that it was okay to make a mistake. They decided to print hundreds of "I made it" drink tickets and for the next month anyone who pulled the andon, admitting their mistake, was awarded a soft drink ticket in front of the group to cash in at the plant cafeteria. The awareness campaign helped to reinforce the culture of trust between management and the team members. There were some managers who were afraid that some team members would deliberately cause a scratch to get a free Coke, illustrating there was work to do in establishing mutual trust. As it turned out the percentage of "I made it" tickets increased dramatically over the course of the next month and there was actually a decrease in total scratches over the course of the month because of the ability to problem solve the root cause quicker and better.

# 3. WORK TEAMS *CONTAIN* DISRUPTIONS TO PRODUCTION THROUGH "EVENT-TYPE" PROBLEM SOLVING

Toyota considers problem solving as the main activity for all levels of the organization. There are two types of problem solving: "event-type" problem solving uses individual events that are deviations from the standard to achieve and maintain the standard, while "setting-type" problem solving concentrates on setting a new standard. To understand event-type problem solving think of a thermostat. You set it for a fixed temperature and when you are either too hot or too cool the thermostat adds or turns off heat to bring you back to the original setting. The setting itself is not questioned. By contrast, setting-type problem solving actually changes the setting and this is how we can significantly improve the system. You set a target of 25 parts per million (ppm) defects and you have been able to achieve this and the company challenges you to meet a new competitive standard of less than 10 ppm.

These two types of problem solving drive the daily activity of the team member, the team leader, and the group leader. We will discuss event-type problem solving in this section. When a problem occurs during the day, the first step is to contain it so production can continue and then work to be sure that the rest of the day and tomorrow the standard can be maintained. Event-type problem solving is sometimes called "maintenance kaizen."

If the standardized work is set (i.e., the team member is to perform the steps of an operation correctly, in a certain sequence, and in the requisite amount of time), that is the plan for the day. The check step is to verify that the team member actually accomplishes the task. In reality there are many variations throughout the day that may make it impossible for the team member to follow the STW. Consider the following example:

If a side mirror on the door is not attaching to the door properly, and there is a gap between the mirror and the door, the team member is not able to follow standardized work, and he pulls the andon cord. This prompts problem solving activity by the team leader. He is not initiating activity for improvement; at this point his activity is just to get back to the standard. The team leader works to find a temporary measure to close the gap that the non-fitting parts present. He involves the group leader, the inspection department, and the quality department to confirm that the temporary method will meet the shipping standards, and that there is no danger of the gap coming back once the customer buys the car. The temporary measure may include a different installation method or adding a shim to offset the gap.

The team leader and team member then work together to solve the problem of the gap. The team member is involved in clarifying the problem by collecting data. The team works to break down the problem, identifying whether the gap is on a particular model, a particular side, a particular color, a particular destination etc. The team member, even within his busy work time, would welcome the opportunity to put a tic mark on a flip chart, in order to help get rid of the problem. The chart offers a simple but useful way of breaking down the problem (see Table 6.3).

With this information at hand, the team can observe the standardized work of this particular type of car to specifically identify what in the process is out of standard. They will obviously observe just those models and places where the problem has occurred. They then can identify a countermeasure, try it, and follow up to ensure it solved the problem.

There is a good deal to teach and organize in order to accomplish this relatively simple process of detecting and correcting deviations from standard work. Let's consider what has to be in place:

1. The standards must be taught thoroughly to the team members so they can detect deviations.
2. The team members must be on the alert for deviations.
3. The team members must be motivated to pull the andon without fear of reprisal.
4. There must be someone near enough to respond to the andon before the car moves to another station (typically less than 45 seconds response time).
5. The person responding, generally the team leader, must be trained to quickly determine what the problem is and the appropriate way to respond.
6. The team leader must understand the standardized work well enough to audit the team members to determine where there are deviations.

**Table 6.3** Example of Maintenance Kaizen to Bring Back to Current Standard

|  | Passenger Side | Driver Side |
| --- | --- | --- |
| Camry | ✓✓✓ |  |
| Avalon |  |  |
| Solara | ✓✓✓✓✓✓✓ |  |

The Japanese trainers taught the American group leaders and managers a key visual management tool to be able to confirm standardized work was being followed and to be able to confirm and encourage the team members to pull the andon so event-type problem solving could be initiated. Mike Hoseus recalls lessons learned with the red line and yellow line:

## LESSONS ON THE RED AND YELLOW LINES

As a group leader, the first thing the Japanese trainer did was to make sure I knew all of the jobs on my teams. He taught me how to construct a STW sheet that showed the person's foot movement from the parts rack, to the car, back to the rack if necessary, back to the car, and then back to the rack to pick up parts for the next car.

Our starting takt time was 60 seconds and if it took 6 seconds to pick up parts for the next car at the flow rack, I knew that the first part went on at the right hand front fender. We put a red line of tape down on the floor at that exact location where the team member would get to the car. We were instructed that the standard was that the operator had to stop and wait at the red line until the front fender got there. We quickly found out that it was "human tendency" to not wait at the red line and for the team member to build ahead by crossing the red line to get a head start. My trainer noted that in Japan there seemed to be more of a cultural norm to follow the standard. For example, if the light is green but the crosswalk light is red, no one waiting on the street will cross the street until the crosswalk sign turns green, even if there is no actual traffic in sight. In Japan it was almost always enough to just tell the operators "not to cross the red line, and they would not." In America, he suggested, we need to give the reasons why.

He taught me both the big picture and the hands-on reasons to not cross the red line. From a philosophy point of view it was a standard and as a baseline for improvement it had to be followed. In this case, if the red line was "jumped" we were building a car before "just in time" and we would be building ahead and breaking the even "*heijunka*." (leveling). Practically speaking, if we jump ahead and the line should stop on that car, we would be caught right in the middle of standardized work and it would mean that the operator would either have to stop in the middle or finish the entire car and be a full minute ahead. Breaks like this in the STW make defects more likely to occur.

Another key reason we taught the team members to stop and wait is to highlight problems or areas for improvement. If they are getting to the red line ahead of time that means that they are finishing the prior car in less than 60 seconds so there is "extra time in the process." If there is extra time in the process, we want to look at how to reduce even more waste and then work as a group to consolidate all of the "extra time" from all of the processes to reduce the number of operations in the group. We were able to explain this all to the team members, tying in the purpose of long term mutual prosperity and the ability to reach this through providing the highest quality car at the lowest possible cost, in the shortest amount of time right down to following standardized work and waiting at the red line. This explanation worked for all of my team members except one. I observed him working ahead of the red line, with sweat pouring from his forehead because he was working so hard. I asked a team leader to take his place so we could talk in the break area. When I asked him why he was working ahead of the red line he explained he didn't want to fall behind and he was trying his hardest.

Because of the knowledge the trainer gave me, and the fact that they had me actually write up the initial standardized work sheets, I was able to show him how all of the parts were set up in the parts rack according to the red line, as well as all of the tools. I was able to show him first on paper and then at the process, that if he waited at the red line and then followed standardized work his walking distance (and therefore time) was reduced because it was timed according to the red line and he would be right at the next part as he finished the prior one. By working ahead of the red line he was adding two or three steps each time he went to the flow rack. We timed his walking time when he "jumped the red line" and it actually added five seconds of time to his 60 second job. By trying his hardest to not get behind and jumping the line, he was only adding to the problem. When he started from the red line, with 5 less seconds walking, he had no problem keeping up on his job. From that day on I never saw him go past the red line again. I was beginning to understand why Toyota had me learn all of the processes in my group and why I actually wrote out the standardized work. It was not my job to "be the boss" and order my team members to follow standardized work. It was my job to "be a teacher" and teach them why it was important to do so and to follow up until each person understood the reason why.

The other "tool" the Japanese shared with TMMK was the yellow line. This was known as the 70 percent line. Just as the red line was put on the Standardized Worksheet and on the floor to show the start line, a yellow line was put on each STW sheet and on the corresponding place on the floor to signify where the operator should be when they are 70 percent done with their jobs. For example, if I had a process where the team member installed a part in the front wheel well, and then under the doors and then in the back wheel well, we had to determine where they would be at the 42 second mark (70 percent of 60 seconds). In this case, the team member would just be finishing installing the part under the doors before hitting the yellow line. So we taught all of our team members where they should be at that time and to pull the andon if they were past the yellow line and they weren't yet finished with that step. The reason for this is that it gives the team leader plenty of time (18 seconds) to see the andon board, get to the team member, find out the problem and make a decision on how to fix it, all before the line would need to come to a stop. It would also get the team member help quickly and not cause them to have to try to "rush and catch up" which can lead to safety and quality issues.

This yellow line was a great tool for the team members and the team leaders and group leaders. The team members had an easy to follow standard and the leaders had an easy tool to follow up on. By knowing each job the TL's and GL's all knew where each team member should be in their process by the yellow line. The trainers taught all of the team leaders and group leaders to walk up and down the line and observe the team members and to encourage them to pull the andon in order to get help at that early point. The red and yellow lines were tools used to create and sustain the culture to follow standardized work and to ask for help when needed.

## Toyota's Suggestion System Supports Event-Type Problem Solving

The Suggestion System at Toyota is famous for its team member involvement and its payback in company cost savings. It is not uncommon to get over 90,000 suggestions in a year at TMMK and over 90 percent are implemented. This does not mean that all of these suggestions are breakthroughs returning huge cost savings. In fact, one reason why the number of suggestions is so high is that management will try almost anything unless it is known to be harmful. If we were to analyze the results of the many suggestions we would classify most as event type in that they help maintain the current standards. Sometimes the suggestions lead to a change in standard but we are more likely to see a change in standard when team members take on a bigger project through quality circles.

The formal Suggestion System will be used when a team member has an idea that is self-initiated on how to make an improvement. At Toyota, the role of the team member goes much further still. The Suggestion System at Toyota is not the "box on the wall" system where a member makes a suggestion and turns it over to "management" to implement and waits and hopes for a big monetary reward. We have seen these types of systems cause nothing but frustration for both parties. For the managers, they are left with a long laundry list of items and a shortage of resources available to implement them. They get frustrated over not being able to implement everything and of course the originators of the suggestion are frustrated because they have this great idea and "management is doing nothing about it."

In Toyota culture, the Suggestion System is completely team member driven. When the member has an idea, he initiates a suggestion form (one side of one piece of paper) that clearly and simply outlines the problem in terms of the current situation, the goal, and the gap between the two. Then he shows the potential causes and narrows down to the root cause. Once the root cause is identified, he can show potential countermeasures and the cost, effectiveness, and feasibility of each. Finally he can predict the results based on these countermeasures, show how they will standardize the countermeasure and follow up to insure implementation. Once he has completed this step, he goes to his group leader and proposes his plan with a strategy to "pilot" or trial his idea. The group leader confirms the situation and the team member's "thinking" within the problem solving process, and either approves the trial or coaches the team member in his thinking and process, and steers him toward the Toyota Way of handling the problem.

If the trial proves successful, the team member confirms the savings in terms of key resources, for example, time saved in process. If the team member has made an improvement in the process, like moving a part rack or building a shelf to improve his reach, and saved two seconds, he is able to go to the Suggestion System Manual to calculate the corresponding dollar amount he is due in reward. He then completes the suggestion form, with the implementation complete and his reward amount filled in. The group leader confirms the implementation, the results, and that it is standardized across all team members and all shifts, and then approves the suggestion for payment. The form goes to the human resources section responsible for payment, which spot checks some of the forms to confirm implementation, and insures consistency and fairness across the plant. Once confirmed, they issue payment to the team member.

While team members are getting paid for suggestions the system is different from most we have seen which pay for ideas. In most cases there are small dollar amounts for small suggestions which get progressively larger up to huge awards such as getting a new car. At Toyota, the payments to the members are designed to be weighted toward the small improvements and not to the large. In other words, the savings of two seconds in a job would most likely be paid in an amount such as $20–$25. Noticing a safety hazard and taking care of it would also result in a similar payment. The majority of the money paid out is in small incremental improvements whereas; a large dollar savings for the company of tens of thousands of dollars may only result in a $100 payout to the team member. This is part of the Toyota culture, not just for the Suggestion System, but for problem solving in general. They are after the singles and walks to first base as opposed to the grand slam home runs. They know that all of these small things will of course add up to large improvements and savings.

# 4. WORK TEAMS IMPROVE THE STANDARDS THROUGH "SETTING-TYPE" PROBLEM SOLVING

Generally the andon call will lead to immediate containment of the problem. At the end of the day there have been many such calls, easily exceeding 5,000 within one major department like assembly. The group leader is able to see a summary of the andon calls by job and then has decisions to make about which ones should move to the next level of problem solving. Some events will automatically trigger more detailed problem solving, such as a safety incident or a critical quality incident which could require either type of problem solving.

Setting-type problem solving may be a reaction to difficulty in meeting the current standard and then a new standard might have to be considered. It may be that the standard has exceeded the capacity of the operation and must be relaxed, for example the inventory buffer was set too low and needs to be adjusted upward. As you can imagine Toyota leaders are not inclined to accept relaxing the standards and more likely to suggest that the process needs to be improved. Improving the process might involve a change to the standardized work which is itself a form of setting-type problem solving. This does not necessarily mean that the team will go through a major problem solving process that takes weeks and involves filling out an A-3 problem solving report. It might simply involve observation of the job compared to the standard work and a change agreed upon by the team and group leader.

In other cases of setting-type problem solving, the current situation already may be currently stable, but in the spirit of continuous improvement, a new goal is "set." When the new goal is determined, a new standard has been set and a new gap is created and there is a new cycle of problem solving. For example, the team may decide that it is time to reduce a process in the line. If a group has 20 processes and the current time to build a car is 60 seconds, the challenge may be for each process to find three seconds of waste and problem solve to reduce it. The net gain of all the activity will be 60 seconds, and, with some rebalancing, a process may be removed.

The types of problem solving are pictured in Figure 6.5. This diagram shows these as stages. First the standard must be reached which may require solving some

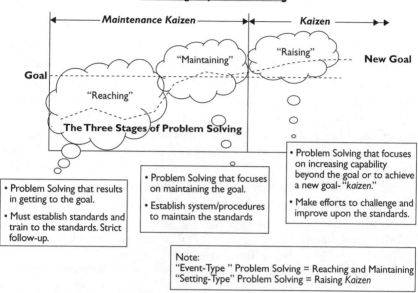

**Figure 6.5** The Three Stages of Problem Solving

problems. Then event-type problem solving is used to achieve the standard and then fix disruptions in order to maintain it. Setting-type problem solving is then used to achieve a higher standard. This generally is the sequence of events over a long period of time, though in any particular instance of a disruption, event-type problem solving might be used on its own to return to the standard without necessarily working to change the standard immediately.

Team members at Toyota are taught to be able to think and solve problems in all three stages. An example of these three stages would be the use of an air tool at an assembly process. If the standard is to use a certain level of tool at a process in order to shoot four bolts at a certain tightness (for example 750 kg/cm$^2$) in 20 seconds then the first task is to be able to consistently reach that standard. If the air tool wears down to where the installation time is taking longer than 20 seconds or if the 750 kg tightness is not being obtained, there would be an event-type problem to be solved. The problem solving process would kick in and the team leader and team members would go through the process in order to get back to the standard of 4 bolts at 750 in 20 seconds. If the team found out that the gun was not able to meet the standard because there was an air leak and not enough air was getting to the gun, they would do a short-term countermeasure to fix the air leak in order to get back to the standard, but their job would not be complete. They would need to do "maintenance" problem solving in order to identify what caused the air leak in the first place and what daily maintenance they would need to perform in order to keep the gun in good working order.

Setting-type problem solving would be the next step once the process is stabilized to achieve improved performance. In this example, the team may be working on reducing a process as mentioned above and need to decide how to reduce time in their processes. The standard of four bolts at 750 kg in 20 seconds would need to be improved upon. The team may set a goal of 15 seconds. The most likely countermeasure would involve finding a new and improved air tool that could reach the same tightness standard in 3.5 seconds. This would set a new standard, reducing the time needed to get the four bolts to 750 kgs to just 14 seconds.

All three levels of problem solving are important and while it sounds like a progression, the real situation admittedly at Toyota is that most of the problem solving taking place is at the first level, getting back to standard. This is not to say that this is trivial problem solving because in many cases it is very difficult to find the root cause of falling below the standard.

## 5. BROADER PROBLEM SOLVING TO LEVEL UP THE SYSTEM

### Roles in Problem Solving by Level of the Organization

Continuous improvement is done throughout the organization at different levels of the business, in different roles, and with respect to different needs. Everyone uses the same process and vocabulary but applies it to different situations. Generally speaking broader systems problems are the responsibility of managers.

When Toyota Business Practices was first presented to the company it was done in the Toyota Way. It was first taught to the most senior executives of the company by master trainers. They had to do more than listen and actually identify a significant systems-level problem to work on. These senior executives humbled themselves by presenting their A-3 reports to the master trainers for feedback. Over 80 percent failed the first time and had to go back and rework some aspect of the problem solving process—usually in the early stages of problem definition. Then these executives participated in teaching the next level of the organization working all the way down to the work teams.

Sometimes the words "continuous improvement" are misunderstood to mean only small changes made on individual processes on the shop floor. The term *kaikaku* has been used to refer to more radical changes of the overall system. At Toyota, continuous improvement means that everyone at all levels is constantly looking for opportunities to improve. These might be big changes—system

kaizen—or small, incremental improvements at the work station—process kaizen. The entire range from huge to tiny changes follows the same problem solving process, but big changes generally use a more formalized process with rigorous data collection, analysis and rigorous reporting using A-3s. Generally speaking, senior management takes the lead on major system changes and work groups focus on smaller, localized improvements. However, Quality Circles are one mechanism that allows hourly workers to get involved in larger kaizen projects that cut across individual processes.

The roles and responsibilities of different levels in the organization in problem solving are summarized in Table 6.4. In reality roles are more blurry and there is involvement of all levels in all types of problem solving. For example, we saw that hourly team members through the pilot team are involved in the launch of an entire new product line.

Starting with the team member, the chart shows that the primary focus of their role is individual process improvement and suggestions. Since all regular team members rotate between jobs they work on each job in the team. The strength of this job rotation for problem solving is that they all have in common all of the jobs on the team. We often see in companies in which workers have one fixed assignment that they have no interest in discussing improvements of other jobs on the team since they do not personally perform them. Also, when discussing improvements in their own job they are very protective: "This is my job and I am the expert so do not suggest to me how to improve it." The subtext of

**Table 6.4** Role in Problem Solving by Level

| JOB CLASSIFICATION | Process Problem Solving | Systems PDCA | Business Planning |
|---|---|---|---|
| Department Head | Pattern Problem Solving | System Kaizen | Identify Company and Department Priorities |
| Manager—Asst. Manager | Process Performance Problems | Process Performance Management | Identify Section Priorities and Improvement |
| Group Leader/ Specialist | Operations Management Problems | Operations PDCA and Improvements | Annual Plan Projects |
| Team Member | Individual Process Problems (Suggestions) | Process Standards and Target Management | Daily Work |

this message is: "I like this job because it has some easy elements and I do not want you to mess that up and add work to the job." With job rotation there is a high level of interest in discussing all aspects of the jobs in the team and we rarely see this kind of protectiveness.

The types of changes to the job at the team-member level include presentation of parts, positioning of tools, and various types of job aids. When giving a public tour of TMMK the tour guides love to point out the devices team members came up with to make jobs easier. For example, there are chairs that team members sit on that slide in and out of the vehicle so the team members do not have to reach in, hunched over. One chair was constructed by a team member in his garage from something off an old fishing boat. There are flat beds on wheels to lie down on and slide in and out of the bottom of the car. (It is obvious the team members enjoy line stops when in the reclining position.) Note the importance of job rotation so no individual team members get these less physical jobs to themselves.

Most of these small projects can be approved and completed within the team with only group leader approval. Maintenance help can be requested and approved by the group leader as well. At the same time, this doesn't mean that they are not aware of and involved in the other two levels of improvement as well.

The highest role of problem solving in the company is referred to as business planning, which includes the *hoshin kanri* process that we have briefly discussed and will cover in detail in Chapter 15. As the chart shows, the amount of time and focus for the team members on business planning is small because this is not their primary role. At the same time, they are connected to the process in both its development and implementation.

The group leaders and engineering specialists work on individual process problems as well as operations management problems. An example of an operations management problem may be a parts shortage that occurs. When there is a part shortage the group leader will mainly focus at the individual process level. For example, is there a problem with visibility of the parts that allowed the team member to miss the fact that parts were running short? The team leader should have noticed and pulled the andon cord before it got to the point of a shortage. Or perhaps training on how to use the andon is needed. However, at Toyota the group leaders will also work at the systems level of problem solving. For example, at the systems level the material handling route may need to be rebalanced so that the material handler can handle the volume of work during peak periods. This is the responsibility of the material handling group but the group leader may participate in a team to help work on this problem. At an even higher level the group leaders will also have a role in the annual planning (or *hoshin* process), but mostly as it relates to setting the targets for improvement for their group and working on the daily projects to achieve the plan.

The development and coaching of problem solving at the team leader and group leader level is a core part of every manager's job. The day is spent with the system highlighting problems and coaching people through the process of solving them. Most often it is done informally as problems occur. Systems are also set up in the plant to facilitate this process formally. For example, Toyota has an internal auditing process that takes five cars off-line each shift and inspectors go over the car with a fine-tooth comb to find out if there are any defects. Team leaders and group leaders are called immediately if a defect is found from their area. They go right to work to put in short-term countermeasures at the process and to "contain" the problem using event-type problem solving. Then after second break a meeting is held at the audit area everyday for all group leaders and above to come together, review the defects and to allow the group leaders to "report out" their problem solving investigation, their short term countermeasures, and their long term countermeasures (if they have any already). Managers take this opportunity to question and coach the group leaders to go deeper into the problem solving process, shifting to setting-type problem solving.

The Japanese taught the American managers important lessons in using this time as a way to coach and develop problem solving not to degrade or embarrass the supervisor. They did not want the audit "meeting" to turn into an audit "beating." The Japanese also taught the leaders to "go and see" the process and to not always give the answer or specifically direct the next step. The Toyota method is to ask questions to get the student to think. In "customary Ohno" fashion (minus the drawn circle) group leaders were taught to stand and observe the process where the defect occurred in order to "learn to see" what the real causes of a problem were. This taught the group leaders to go much deeper than giving the standard response to a defect as "the cause was the team member not following standardized work" and the countermeasure is to "retrain the operator."

You can see from Table 6.4, as a person moves up to the role of manager at Toyota, she will spend less time on process problems and more time on systems PDCA and even more time on the business planning for their section. The department head or general manager will still be involved in process problem solving but they will be looking for the "pattern" in order to quickly look at it as systems-based PDCA, which may even end up as part of the business planning company priorities. An example of this is that a general manager is trained to "go and see" problems at the source if they are "lifted" up by the system. If the general manager identifies a pattern of errors made by new team members they will work with the section manager on the system of training a new hire in their area. If this happens with a few of the manager's areas, it will most likely become a priority to be addressed by the entire company on the next annual plan.

## *Jishuken*—A Kaizen Event or Way to Develop Leaders?

The kaizen event has become a popular tool for implementing lean at many companies. It is typically structured as a five-day event starting with training Monday, analysis and problem solving Tuesday, implementation and experimenting Wednesday and Thursday, and presenting results on Friday. Improvement events are common at Toyota but they take on a different twist than we are used to seeing at other organizations. The kaizen event has become the cornerstone of lean implementation for many companies. They want a way to quickly use the lean toolkit to drive change in the operation and achieve aggressive metrics. Some organizations even measure the number of events held to judge lean activity level and dollars saved to impress the board of directors that the lean effort is paying off.

Toyota kaizen events are done with the primary purpose of developing the leadership and problem solving skills of the managers. Certainly, a side benefit is to improve the business indicators, but this is not the driver. More recently these events have been referred to as *jishuken,* which means voluntary self-study. A *jishuken* event at Toyota is facilitated by the internal coaching group and generally takes place in one week. At TMMK, this group is known as the Operations Development Group or ODG. For the first decade and a half of the plant's history, the group would identify a bottleneck area of the plant and then gather a group of managers who were identified by their supervisors as needing this experience. Most people in the group were from different production areas and non-production areas as a way to give a new experience to these individuals. The ODG group then facilitated the activity focusing the development of the managers not only on the technical aspect of the job, but also their leadership and facilitation skills. They were taught how to better communicate with and involve all the team members in the area and to integrate everyone's input into the improvement actions.

In the early 2000s, the supply chain of Toyota was showing some weaknesses due to the rapid growth of demand. Toyota used this as another opportunity to develop manager skills. Every manager in the company took turns going to a supplier company for two weeks to take part in a *jishuken* activity. The first week was to focus on individual process improvement. The Toyota managers and the supplier managers worked side by side to work on the process to interview team members, identify wastes, and make improvements. The days were long and included learning how to coordinate support departments such as maintenance and engineering. At the end of the week the team presented their process improvements and results to both presidents. Gary Convis, president at TMMK at the time, was faithful in his attendance and support, not only at the presentation, but also back at the plant where the managers were expected to continue leading *jishuken* activities in their areas of the plant.

Don Jackson recalls participating in one of these process-level events when he was Vice President of Manufacturing at TMMK. This was in Japan and separate from the TMMK management jishuken but it illustrates the intense learning that can take place:

> As a vice president I was able to take a Toyota management course that included a week long TPS/kaizen activity at a supplier in Japan. I was teamed with two other executives and we were guided by a TPS expert at the supplier. He took us to the work cell that was assigned to us to kaizen. We were all told to stand there and observe to find the waste in the process. Visions of the "Ohno circle" came to mind as the hours passed. Mr. Cho told us often at TMMK that waste is not always easy to see. After four hours of observing I was convinced they had given me a process with no waste left just to "have fun with the new vice president." My trainer informed me, "no, there is plenty of waste in there, keep observing." Finally, after two more hours, it was like the lights came on and the waste was jumping out at me. I was able to list over 20 items to address and when combined with the other two students we were able to kaizen out an entire process. There was even a "wild kaizen idea" that we wanted to do but we could not implement it by ourselves. Our main focus was motion kaizen that we must do with our hands. The TPS leader requested support from the third shift maintenance group and the kaizen team supported the team member during implementation and reduced additional waste. In the usual Toyota teaching fashion, we weren't given the answers, but were left to struggle through it and discover for ourselves. It was a powerful lesson and one that I can use here in Texas as we embark on a takt time change after only six months after our initial start of production. My goal throughout it all is to keep developing my people and pass on the Toyota DNA as it was passed on to me. It's most rewarding to see new Toyota team members and supplier team members learning the Toyota Way. With "On the job development" it is important to walk the talk.

The second week of Jishuken training for TMMK management involved looking at the larger processes of running a manufacturing plant—system kaizen. In this activity a facilitator from Toyota North American headquarters, taught the managers how to develop "material and information" flow diagrams. This is the original version of what has come to be more commonly known as value stream maps. Once again the managers spent long days mapping out current and future state maps and then implementing improvements. This week was also followed up with a presentation and then assignments back at each manager's home plant to continue leading kaizen activities.

## LEADERS ENCOURAGE AND DEVELOP KAIZEN THROUGH GUIDANCE, TRUST AND DISCIPLINE

The mistrust philosophy we see in many companies leads to the strategy of having a special group of process engineers and "expert" managers responsible for thinking through the operation, and for imposing their ideas on the employee "doers." This was the original basis of Frederick Taylor's scientific management theory early in the twentieth century. He believed industrial engineers would find the one best way to do any task. This approach creates the "us versus them" culture we characterized in the first chapter. Then we hear complaints that the improvements taught to the people on the floor are not being sustained. Since there is no ownership on the floor the only way to sustain these coercively dictated changes is through further coercion—constantly monitor and offer rewards and punishments to keep the imposed standard alive.

We see this culture still alive in many organizations, even those on a lean journey. We have heard many stories about this type of culture, even with helpful tools such as six sigma, or the common kaizen event. In the case of six sigma, based on statistical quality tools, we have seen several organizations focus on the number of Black Belts or Green Belts they have certified and the number of projects they are working on. They are creating the expert teams to go out and solve all the problems for the organization. The question we ask these organizations is this: "Would you rather have a team of a few experts out there solving your problems, or an entire army made up of every member of your organization? And, which one do you think is more powerful, and likely to gain the competitive advantage?"

This "expert" strategy seems flawed from both a numbers and a continuous improvement standpoint, and it also makes no sense from the perspective of mutual trust and respect. If the expert is not to be involved at the process with those doing the job day in and day out, then valuable information will be missed and we are not likely to gain the team members' buy-in supporting the improvements.

In Toyota culture, the kaizen event is done "with" the members, not "to" the members. Extra manpower will be brought into the group in order to take members off-line to interview them for their perspective on problem identification and problem solution. The managers of the event help to gather information, the team members coordinate all the information, and the resources needed to address the problems, such as maintenance and engineering support. It is truly a team effort in which the members get their ideas on the table for consideration, and managers get open minds to try out some of their improvement ideas. Both parties are working in partnership, and trust each other to try out their ideas and improvements on each other. Both continuous improvement and mutual respect are alive and well.

Compare this to some of the "events" we have heard described: the team of experts come to an area and identify all the things the team members are doing wrong, quickly implement the improvements tapping into resources normally not available to team members, report out on the dramatically improved process on Friday and leave. Anything they cannot get done in the week goes on a homework list. They wonder why, when they come back a week later, the improvement ideas are not being used in the process, and it is back to the original state and condition. The homework list is still homework and is growing longer and longer with each kaizen event. Neither continuous improvement nor mutual respect is alive or well in this scenario. The Toyota kaizen events work because they are a continuation of the kaizen culture already alive and flourishing. It is not an artificially imposed blitz of kaizen driven top down with the people in the area left to follow the new directives afterwards.

The development of effective problem solvers does not happen overnight, even with all of the support systems discussed in this chapter. It is a constant struggle and battle and takes a lot of hard work to make it happen. The Japanese trainers passed this discipline on to the early American managers. Mike Hoseus recalls a lesson learned from his trainer in regard to problem solving.

*We were at full production and demand was exceeding our capacity so everyone was working hard to meet our production targets. There was a breakdown on a piece of equipment which stopped the line for over 10 minutes. The maintenance group and engineers were able to get it going again and we were beginning to discuss some of the 5 whys when a call came over the radio that another piece of equipment was down and had already stopped the line for another few minutes. Like "super manager" off to the rescue, I began to set off to the next emergency (or fire fighting as it is called). My Japanese trainer literally grabbed my shirt sleeve, stopping me in my tracks and instructed to me to stay right here with this maintenance and engineering team, go into the group area and do a full problem solving activity with an A-3.*

*"But the line is down," I pleaded. "The line stopping is okay, he explained, but not getting to the root cause and countermeasure is not. Someone else will get the line running again on that one; you get to the root cause on this one." That was not easy for me to do either psychologically or functionally. I wanted to be where the action was, but deep down I think I knew that at the time I really wasn't a very good problem solver and it was a lot easier to direct a breakdown activity than it was to lead a group of engineers and maintenance people through a problem solving process. The group struggled through it, with my trainer "checking in" on us periodically to make*

*sure we weren't too far off track. The team found the root cause and was able to put in some effective countermeasures to correct the issue, but more importantly, I learned to stop running around and "fixing things" and instead to go through the discomfort and take the time needed to solve problems.*

*In teaching these lessons to my team, I found out that I was not alone in my phobia of problem solving and that we had to make it safe for people to practice problem solving. The Japanese taught us that there are no experts in problem solving because you can always get better at it the more often you actually do it.*

It is this constant coaching of the problem solving process that develops the culture and level of skill that Toyota has been able to achieve. They refer to it as using problem solving to improve problem solving. You have to use PDCA in order to improve your ability to PDCA. Having the opportunity to practice and develop daily problem solving is the Toyota culture. Every deviation is seen a chance to problem solve.

## SUMMARY

The continuous improvement cycle that stretches from standardization to continuous improvement, over and over again, is virtually relentless for Toyota members. They carry this thinking with them to other aspects of their lives. There are numerous stories of how members have taken this approach and culture and have utilized it in their families, churches, and community groups. In the next chapter we talk about this next level of development in which team members go beyond kaizen in their individual jobs and how it becomes a personal way of life that they bring to their families and communities.

## KEY POINTS TO CONSIDER FOR YOUR COMPANY

1. Standards and standardized work are established for all jobs and visual methods are used to highlight deviations from the standard.
2. Problem identification methods are in place and used and then improvements are captured and maintained in the new standard.
3. Team members are performing problem solving on a daily basis as part of their jobs.
4. Employees at all levels get exposure to problem solving training in multiple classes which in all cases include practice in solving real problems.

5. There is a system to document and share (*yokoten*) best practices of problem solving with the entire organization, though best practices are not imposed but rather selectively adopted and adapted by each unit.

6. Supporting programs such as Quality Circles and a Suggestion System are in place to both develop and recognize team member problem solving and improvement.

7. At a deeper cultural level, the kaizen process and associated learning is often emphasized more than the particular results achieved by projects or events.

8. Both small process improvements and large system improvements are made but, if anything, there is more appreciation for the many small improvements than for the few large improvements.

# Chapter 7

# Inspiring People to be Committed to the Company, Family, and Community

*Individual commitment to a group effort—that is what makes a team work, a company work, a society work, a civilization work.*

—Vince Lombardi, football coach

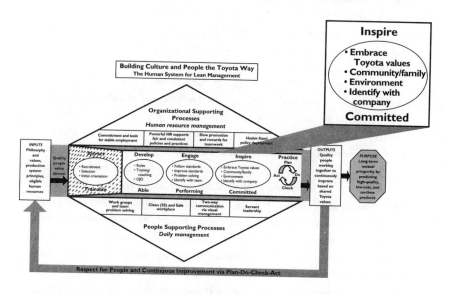

## WHAT IT MEANS TO BE COMMITTED TO TOYOTA

Toyota's development of its employees is not limited to minds alone: hearts are considered equally important. Since its beginnings, Toyota has seen itself as a social institution as much as a money-making company, with a role to play in regards to its employees, the community which surrounds its plants, and society at large. Toyota shows its commitment to its employees is by inspiring them through offering unique learning opportunities. Here is one such story. Upon being assigned to the Operations Development Group (ODG, the internal consulting group) from the assembly department, Charles Luttrell had to face the following situation:

> *We had just completed a huge kaizen project in our material handling system. Our goal was to produce and fill parts as close to "one piece flow" as we*

*could. With this current improvement, known as the lane system, the parts for the car were taken right off the truck, put onto delivery dollies (staged in lanes) and then taken directly to the line side flow racks. All of the parts racks that had previously been in the receiving areas had been eliminated. This drastically reduced the inventory and "safety stock" of all the parts. The TPS group was worried about the part shortages this might produce, but we were surprised when instead we found ourselves in the middle of huge amounts of excess stock piling up at the line side flow racks, overflowing onto the floor and into the aisle.*

*A working team quickly formed and we came together on the floor to grasp the situation. In addition to myself, there were representatives from assembly, material handling, parts ordering, and suppliers on hand to tackle the problem. Emotions were running high because of the problems being created for assembly workers with all of this extra stock piling up around them. Meanwhile, I was also remembering my instructions when leaving assembly for my rotation to ODG from my Japanese trainer, "You are non-value added, Charles," I was told. "Your sole job is to take care of the team member who is creating the value." With this foundation, I was teaming up with the assembly representative in pushing back the problem to parts ordering and the suppliers, instructing them to recalculate their delivery amount and times, etc.*

*After the group dispersed, my mentor Watanabe quietly took me aside and asked me, "What problem are you working on?" "What do you mean what problem am I am working on" was my quick response. "I am working on all of this overflow stock." His only response was "no" and again, "What problem are you working on?" For the next hour this continued as his only response as he patiently and quietly waited for me to give one incorrect response after another. "The problem is the wrong amount of stock order from PC." "No." "The problem is that the flow racks have too little capacity for what is ordered." "No." "The problem is the box size and amount of parts in each box." "No" The amount of time that he would quietly and with no emotion wait for my next wrong answer was one of the most frustrating experiences of my career. He would not stop until I got the right answer and it was obvious that he was not going to just give it to me. Finally the light bulb went on and I said, "The problem is the operation rate for assembly. They are not running to the planned rate." "You are correct, **that** is the problem to work on."*

*What a breakthrough. I felt a sense of empowerment and commitment with my new revelation. I would have spent a lot of time on these other 'problems' that were really just symptoms of the real problems that were causing the operation rate to be too low. The assembly line does not run continuously according to plan because of line stops when the andon is pulled. Parts were being ordered to a plan of assembly running at 96 percent of the schedule but they were running at only 93 percent. This difference is what was accounting for the extra parts accumulating line side.*

*Our group spent the next year supporting the assembly team members, not by ordering fewer parts or more flow racks, but by identifying and eliminating all of the barriers and problems they were encountering in their processes. By taking care of these issues, the number of andon pulls was reduced, the operation rate was increased, and the parts stacked up at the side of the line disappeared. The assembly team members and both of my mentors were satisfied with the improvements that were made and my understanding of the Toyota Way was continuing to grow.*

The unique feeling of hard work, empowerment, and commitment generated by such experiences is hard to find in any other industrial setting, and indeed, those few Toyota managers who get lured away by the competition seldom find the same kind of motivational environment.

Up to this stage in the people value stream, Toyota has developed people who follow the standardized work, help improve the standards through problem solving, and identify with the team. Why would Toyota need anything more? If Toyota was simply a business based on financial transactions this would probably be enough, but Toyota is more like a social institution. Toyota wants people to be committed to the company and to be inspired to take what they learn to positively benefit their families and the community. One definition of commitment is: "devotion or dedication, for example, to a cause or relationship." This is a cause, not just a business, because Toyota is dedicated to adding value to customers and society. Toyota's goal of mutual prosperity between the company and team members suggests a partnership, which is a type of relationship. Toyota wants all team members and partners to be committed to the cause and the relationship, by choice. Henry Ford said: "Quality means doing it right when no one is looking." If the company wants employees to do the right things—treating people respectfully, admitting mistakes, passionately working to solve problems, and investing themselves in the company—they need to inspire true commitment.

We are not suggesting that a company focused on the short term has no hope of making money. A company with the right patented technology, in the right industry, at the right time can be extremely profitable whether or not the owners invest heavily in the long-term development of the people. Many people have retired rich by building a business to a certain point then selling it. We are not trying to judge whether this is right or wrong. However, if the leaders of the business want to build a legacy that withstands ups and downs in the market and lasts for generations, they need to think more like Toyota by attempting to inspire a high degree of commitment in employees at all levels who work to improve the business as if it were their own.

There is a good deal of evidence that external rewards, like money, do not produce true commitment. True commitment requires what psychologists call "intrinsic motivation" meaning that the person is driven from within themselves. People have to get satisfaction and be energized through an enriching job, without managers rewarding them for specific behaviors. If a person performs the desired behavior for the sake of the reward, whether it is monetary or simple praise, then logically they will stop as soon as the reward runs out. Unless you can follow the person around every minute of the work day they will only do what is necessary to get the reward. Toyota has very explicit expectations about how the production system should operate, how people should identify and solve problems, how people should contribute to 5S, how people should work together as a team, and how people should take responsibility. For Toyota to truly get these desired behaviors from their employees, they must be really self-motivated and able to think for themselves.

In the final step of the development process, the goal is to inspire a high level of commitment to the company, its values, as well as incorporating the Toyota Way as natural guidelines for thinking and behaving. When the Toyota Way is taken for granted by team members as simply the right way to do things, it fosters a cohesive culture. *The Toyota Way 2001* training was one step toward this goal to teach a common set of values, daily rules of management, team member behavior, but obviously training by itself does not lead to true commitment. To inspire commitment, team members must see their leaders model Toyota values in action every day on the job. By contributing to the community, making charitable contributions, and being environmentally conscious, team members are inspired by the feeling that they are a part of an important institution that has a positive impact on other people.

## THE CHALLENGES OF INSPIRING COMMITMENT IN A WESTERN SETTING

When Toyota started up operations in the United States, there was concern that the desire for employee commitment might clash with Western social values. One might argue that a business is a business and should not expect commitment from its employees beyond doing a fair day's work for a fair day's pay. As we discussed in Chapter 1, one of the strong underlying assumptions of Western culture is a separation of work life and personal life. We do our jobs to make money so we can live, and then we live outside of work. Compartmentalizing our work lives and our personal lives seems quite natural. In fact, those who have a difficult time doing this are talked about negatively with terms like *workaholic*. It is seen as unhealthy and unnatural.

If we go back to Toyota's origins in Japanese society we have to understand Eastern logic to comprehend what this is about. When someone from Japan introduces themselves in a business setting he does not say his first name then last name and then where he works: it is the opposite. For example, he might first say Toyota, then his department, and then his name, because he is defined by the company and the groups he is part of.

Anthropologist Edward T. Hall distinguished this West-versus-East tendency calling it a "low-context" versus "high-context" society.[1] In the low-context Western culture we are all separate individuals—separate from each other and separate from any particular social group. At different times we might participate in some group or even say we belong to a group, but we are always separate. In high-context Eastern cultures the individual is not defined apart from memberships in groups and institutions. Leaders are not just doing jobs but are personally responsible for the actions of everyone in the organization who report up to them. Team members are part of the larger whole first, and do not think of themselves purely as individuals. In a sense, the company becomes an extended family. When employees go into the community and do good work—or bad for that matter—they are reflecting on the company, positively or negatively.

In highly individualistic cultures like the United States, we do not strive to put the company first. To many Americans today, the very idea of strong identification with the company is downright frightening. However, nothing in our experience of Toyota suggests its culture is built on people acting as a mindless piece of a collective unit, all thinking the same way. In fact, diversity of thought is encouraged and necessary to get the creativity and innovation required for Toyota's success. What is important is a common work culture that is spelled out in *The Toyota Way 2001* as two pillars: respect for people and continuous improvement. So far we have talked mostly about continuous improvement. People have been developed up to the point of knowing the job and improving the job. The "respect for people" pillar is more about relationships, and this last step of inspiring members to become committed is about that respect for people. In Chapter 1, we described the two foundational elements under respect for people: "respect others," which asks team members to make every effort to understand each other and "build mutual trust and teamwork," which requires that Toyota stimulate personal and professional growth that maximizes individual and team performance.

From the beginning of setting up operations in the United States, Toyota believed these features of respect for people were necessary to be successful. To get Americans to buy into this, they had to accept that Americans were individualists but still sell them on the importance of identifying strongly with the team and the company. They did not need to become a "Toyota man" or a

---

[1] Hall, Edward T, *Beyond Culture*, Anchor Books, 1976.

"Toyota woman" to the full extent that might happen in Japan, but they had to behave according to Toyota core values. According to *The Toyota Way 2001*, team members need to:

- respect other people,
- respect themselves and strive to become better people,
- work cooperatively with others to continuously improve products and processes,
- do this through *genchi genbutsu*: through actual time spent on the floor and direct interaction with others,
- always think about how to serve the end customer,
- treat all team members and suppliers as partners in the business,
- work to make others on the team better, and
- work to positively impact society.

This goes beyond doing the job at work and extends to be being a good family member and contributing to the broader community. The Toyota principle of adding value states: "We make possible improvements in global living standards by utilizing human, financial, and material resources in ways that make productivity greater and add value, benefiting both our company and our host communities."[2]

In this chapter we will talk about how Toyota has worked to inspire people to become committed and behave in ways consistent with the core values of respect for people and continuous improvement. We will discuss how Toyota stimulates personal and professional growth in team members and how as team members grow they are in turn expected to contribute what they have learned to their family and the community. Most recently, this has even expanded to having a positive impact on the physical environment through going green.

## DEEPENING THE CYCLE OF LEARNING AND COMMITMENT

The human systems model gives the impression that there is a one-time, linear process to develop a quality person. It appears that each person goes through each phase of development once and at the end is completely committed and indoctrinated into the Toyota Way. It was convenient to draw it this way, but the reality is that learning and developing commitment is an ongoing process. It is more realistic to view this as a spiral process in which the individual goes through these phases more deeply over and over. For example, a team member can be recruited into a job, learn that job, improve on how it is done, and develop a level of

---

[2] *The Toyota Way 2001*, Toyota Motor Corporation, Japan, Internal Company Document.

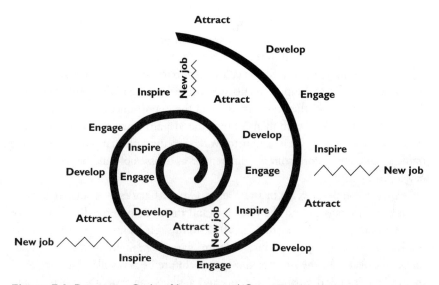

**Figure 7.1** Deepening Cycle of Learning and Commitment

commitment, then get moved to a new job, start to learn over again and experience a broader view and even deeper commitment (see Figure 7.1).

For instance, the career of Charles Luttrell whom we met at the beginning of the chapter closely mirrors this repeating and deepening cycle of learning and commitment to maximize his potential. Charles grew up in the small town of Somerset in southeastern Kentucky. He went to the University of Kentucky to study engineering but after hearing about the new Toyota plant being built in Georgetown he decided to put in his application before completing college, not wanting to miss the opportunity to start on the ground floor of the new facility. He went through the recruitment and selection process and was hired as an hourly team leader in 1988 in the assembly plant to work on the chassis line. He worked directly with his group leader and Japanese trainer to learn all of the processes in his team, learning the Toyota Production System step by step.

In 1989, Charles went through the plant-wide promotion process for group leaders and was promoted to group leader for Chassis 1 on second shift. Here his foundation of TPS and Toyota Way training was built on again through the training and development he received in the classroom and on the job. Once again he had an American assistant manager to mentor him as well as a Japanese trainer. Charles recalls, "I have always remembered what my first Japanese trainer taught me: 'When you are building the car, take care of the quality for the customer. When you are no longer building the car, take care of the people who are.'"

As a group leader he was rotated to lead the Kaizen Group in 1992. This group is staffed by people freed up when their team makes productivity improvements.

As groups make productivity improvements in their area they are able to eliminate processes. The people that are freed up as a result of these improvements are used primarily to fill attrition and in the process reduce headcount without anyone losing their job. But, part of the Toyota culture is also to use some of the freed up people to help make more improvements that will eventually reduce more processes. As the group leader of this team Charles had the opportunity to work with all of assembly and interfaced with many of the other departments to work on improvements. He also was in the position to work directly with many of the Japanese trainers and coordinators from the different areas of assembly and be coached and developed by them.

After a couple of years in the Kaizen Group, Charles was rotated back to a production group to lead the door line and then was promoted to the role of assistant manager of trim assembly in 1994. In this role he was responsible for five production groups that added various "trim" parts (e.g., upholstery, carpet, headliners, and seats). In the spirit of the Toyota culture he was still being developed by his American and Japanese mentors and at the same time was coaching and developing those he was supervising.

Once again as part of the continuous cycle of development at Toyota, Charles was rotated to ODG. In this role, Charles was able to put to work his experience in the assembly Kaizen Group and the technical knowledge he had gained about the process of building a car: but just as important were the personal relationships he had developed in working with the other departments. As an assistant manager in this TPS group, Charles was mentored by both Japanese and members of a new generation of American TPS sensei, Glen Uminger and Roy Jay. Charles respectfully points out his direct TPS lineage back to Taiichi Ohno as a result of this learning assignment, which is illustrated in Figure 7.2. Ohno would often say if we leave the production system to its own natural tendencies, it will act as water and find the path of least resistance to rest in stagnant pools. There needs to be a catalyst to keep initiating improvement. For this reason OMCD (Operations Management Consulting Division) was started by Ohno in Japan to facilitate the sustaining and growth of TPS.

From ODG, Charles' next rotation was back to production, but this time he was asked to go to the Paint Shop. With this assignment Charles' development in the Toyota Way continued to build. Paint is a complex technical process requiring knowledge of chemistry, but what Charles learned much more about was Toyota Way leadership.

*When I rotated to paint I learned the hard way that I needed to be patient and teach and coach my new subordinates as I was taught by my mentors. Unfortunately I went in not always trusting my team to come up with the right answers and many times I rushed the process of learning. I also learned*

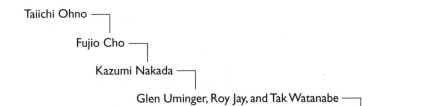

**Figure 7.2** "Family Tree" Leading to Development of Charles Luttrell

*that there are differences in problem solving in different areas of the organization. We are taught to look at the 4 M's when we solve problems at Toyota—Man, Method, Materials and Machine. In assembly, there are many people and few machines. I found here that most of my problems and subsequent improvements were with the team members and the standardized work methods. In working with the paint shop I learned that most of the problems were with the materials and equipment. I had to work more with the engineers and the maintenance department and focus on process control and repeatability. I credit my different mentors and different rotations with giving me the foundation and broad experience in the Toyota Way. I needed to be prepared for my current role as assistant general manager back in the assembly department. With having responsibility over the production members of one assembly plant and the engineering and maintenance of both assembly plants I have two goals. It says "TOYOTA" on that sign in front of our building and I take pride in that. My first goal is to continue to learn and to go deeper in my understanding and practice of the Toyota Way. My second goal is to pass this culture on to others that I work with.*

In Charles' 20 year career with Toyota up to this point, with his rotations and promotions, he has been in over nine roles with the company. He demonstrates the ideal spiral of deepening understanding and commitment that the people value stream of Toyota produces.

## CHALLENGE TEAM MEMBERS TO GROW AND DEVELOP

An important part of being in the Toyota culture and of being committed to the company for the long term is the opportunity and even obligation for an individual to continuously improve himself. In *The Toyota Way* (2004*)*, Liker stated Toyota's approach to people is to respect, challenge, and grow them. In this cultural context, respecting an employee means you want them to grow to their fullest potential. People will not grow if they get too comfortable doing a routine job with no challenges. When Toyota asks an engineer to take on a project to reduce quality defects by 70 percent they are challenging that person to work and think hard, which will ultimately lead to personal growth.

A general manager from Toyota's die engineering and production organization in Japan explained he had just completed a project to reduce, by half, the time it takes to design and make a casting die as part of the engine development process. "I was challenged to achieve this difficult target. We were already quite good at designing and making dies compared to our competition, but my boss wanted me to try harder. My team worked many weeks on this and achieved the goal. We were very happy. The day after we succeeded on a pilot project my boss asked me: 'So what is your next improvement target?' This is the Toyota Way. It is about kaizen mind."

Later over a beer and sushi, coauthor Jeff Liker had an opportunity to talk to this manager in a more informal environment, and asked him if there was a lot of pressure because he is always so challenged. When the manager replied that there was indeed a lot of pressure, Liker continued and asked whether he was happy working for Toyota or whether he just felt pressured all the time. The manager replied, "Yes, I am very much pressured, but when I achieve the objective I feel very good. That is what makes me happy."

This is obviously very good for the company. In the name of developing team member they get an army of people who are making major process improvements that lead to cost reductions and competitive advantage. A critic might say the whole discussion of respect for people is a ruse to disguise Toyota's exploitation of employees. Instead of expecting an employee to come to work, do a good job, and then go home and enjoy his personal life, Toyota is driving him toward higher and higher levels of performance which require long hours of work and being intellectually and emotionally involved in these improvement projects. The general manager of die engineering and production casually stated, "Sometimes I have dreams about my project and can't get it out of my mind. I have gotten some good ideas from my dreams."

Has this man's level of commitment gone over the top and become a psychological obsession? In the Toyota way of thinking, working on a challenging project, stretching yourself, and learning from success and failure is the essence of respect for people. Getting so wrapped up in a project that you even dream about it is the ultimate in passion about one's work: it is what we would expect of great artists or writers. In this sense, this general manager was living the Toyota Way. We also asked him what would happen if he tried very hard and made big strides but did not meet his 50 percent target for lead-time reduction. He answered without hesitation," Even if I achieved 49 percent I would be asked to reflect on what happened and identify the root cause of failing to meet the objective. My boss would want to know why I could not meet 100 percent of the objective. Did I need more help from him? Did I put in enough effort? Did I get support from other departments? Do I need better training in kaizen? At the end of every year we reflect on what happened that year and it would come up again: Where did I fail to meet the objectives for the year? What was the root cause? What are the countermeasures?"

*The Toyota Way* (2004) included as a principle the Japanese concept of *hansei*, or reflection. This is less a Toyota-specific concept than a part of Japanese culture. There are three key components of hansei:

1. The individual must recognize that there is a problem—a gap between expectations and achievement—and be open to negative feedback.
2. The individual must voluntarily take personal responsibility and feel deep regret.
3. The individual must commit to a specific course of action to improve.

Within Toyota culture, *hansei* is considered essential for kaizen. What drives kaizen is individuals voluntarily striving to improve, based on an inner drive. They are not satisfied with the way things are, they set objectives for improvement, and they are not satisfied with anything less than 100 percent success. Even a successful outcome does not mean a 100 percent perfect process. There is always something to learn from reflection. A Toyota executive explained it this way, "To me this is the biggest difference between Toyota and some other companies. I have had the opportunity to work with some companies in America. If they ask for a 20 percent improvement and the member achieves 15 percent that is okay. They have made an improvement and their boss acknowledges a good job. In Toyota we are not satisfied with anything less than 100 percent."

Toyota team members are not only expected to achieve challenging objectives—which become more challenging as they are promoted to higher levels in the company—they are also expected to do it in the Toyota Way. The process is as important as the results. They should personally go and see to get the real facts of the situation (i.e., *genchi genbutsu*), get key stakeholders involved through *nemawashi* (broad input into the decision), rigorously follow each step of the problem-solving process, and, perhaps most importantly, work effectively with a team of people to get the best from the team and develop others while developing themselves. Gary Convis explains what Toyota expects from leaders who must go beyond getting results and do things right in the Toyota Way,

> *We believe in hands-on knowledge and not someone who comes out of college and becomes the boss. We look for someone who has ability, personal drive and appreciation for team members' work itself. A person who is humble and can respect the work others can do, and can use their problem-solving skills*

*as they slowly go up the ladder, can have greater influence. First, I need the right kind of people that I am challenging with daily operations. TPS people have to really understand it, and it takes years to develop. I look for the person who manages the Toyota Way naturally when we hire them and when we promote them. We do not promote the smartest guy on the block who can make a great presentation. That may be valuable and fit certain parts of our business. In manufacturing we also need the personal touch—respect for individuals—and the ability to motivate and truly partner with people at all levels.*

A common theme through the history of the Toyota Way is the importance of getting your hands dirty. The founder of Toyota Motor Company, Kiichiro Toyoda, expressed distrust of any engineer "who did not have to wash his hands before dinner." Gary Convis explained further how Toyota views the importance of working on the floor and adding value as part of a team and then learning to lead the team as the engineer matures.

*The success of the group is more important than individual personalities. People have to understand that and put it all together. You have to put "we" before "I." Certainly we have very successful brilliant young people and some decide to go to another company and many are very successful for it. But many, many, many make a successful career with us. You have to be comfortable on the plant floor, with dirty machinery, and you have to understand that you have to add value to be the kind of person that will be successful. It is not a place for a big ego. If you have a big ego at Toyota, you do not make it far or fast.*

This gives us a picture of what it means to become committed to the Toyota Way. It is more than believing in the company and espousing the principles of the company. You have to dive in, get your hands dirty, lead teams to make major improvements; but when you accomplish this heroic objective you should not boast about your personal accomplishment. You must be humble enough to give credit to the group. We see the rules of engagement adding up and it starts to sound more and more like Eastern culture and contrary to Western culture. Yet, as Convis said, Toyota has successfully developed many, many, many committed people in their North American operations who learn the Toyota Way.

There is no question Toyota has created a high-pressure environment where the stakes are high. Some people fit in while others do not and these people often leave. They leave stronger and more capable than when they came and go on to do good things elsewhere, but there is a limit to how many people Toyota can afford to lose. We discuss employee retention later in the chapter.

# FAMILY AND COMMUNITY FOCUS

Astonishingly, for a company so focused on results, cost reduction, and line improvement, Toyota also expends a lot of effort and energy on building solid ties with the communities hosting its plants and offices. The outreach department at Georgetown is a good example of Toyota's commitment to members and their families, even though there is not a specific return on investment. The sole goal and purpose is to help team members in need. It is a group of five people, separate from HR, with its own manager, whose full-time role is supporting this goal. They do things such as locate and provide housing for out-of-town family members visiting an ill child; provide zero-interest loans to members who have a house damaged due to fire or flood; help a member with a deceased spouse or the spouse of a deceased member to make funeral arrangements; and ensure death benefits are applied for and processed properly. Some of this may sound like what a typical human resource department might do, but goes beyond this in giving a sincere personal touch that includes attending the funeral and visiting in the hospital.

One of the members of the outreach group recalls a story of when a team member suffered a death in his family and experienced the "outreach" help. He was a team member with a reputation for being an "anti-company" guy with a hardened, negative attitude. At the end of the process, he was sitting in the cubicle with tears rolling down his face, expressing appreciation to the outreach person and explaining that his whole outlook and perspective about the company had been changed as a result. This type of personal touch can go a long way to encouraging people to commit to the company, even though Toyota doesn't try to put a dollar figure on the benefits.

We talked with Shelby Shepard, a skilled-trades team member, about his service to the community as a result of working at Toyota. Shelby started with the company in 1989 as a production team member and was promoted to team leader in 1990. In 1993 he entered a skilled-trades training program that was a three-year classroom and hands-on training program for production team members to have the opportunity to work in skilled trades. At the end of three years, he earned his associate degree in Industrial Maintenance Technology and a new higher-paying job in the facilities department. He was enjoying work and life as usual until September 11, 2001.

*After 9/11 hit, I felt compelled to get involved. I was not sure how to do so, so I made a 9/11 tribute video. The company allowed me to give them out to fellow team members and collect donations. We collected over $500 and donated it to the local food bank for the homeless. We did other fund raising in our team as well, and one time used the money for a fellow team member* *to take his wife on a trip and to buy a computer and internet access so we could keep in touch with him while he was in his last days of fighting a losing battle with cancer.*

*In 2001, I joined my local Rotary and became involved in the Woodford County Repair Affair. This is a program that repairs houses for people who can't afford to or are unable to repair it themselves. The program has repaired over 170 homes in the area with the help of over 1,160 volunteers. I am able to put my skills from maintenance, problem solving, and teamwork to good use because I have been both a team captain and a team captain coordinator for the program. I can tell you the best part of the program is not seeing the house with a new roof or new paint job: it is seeing the impact on the owners and their lives. One house we fixed was for a blind 71 year-old lady who was told she had to leave her lifelong home because it was in such a state of disrepair. She didn't want to leave, and after our work she got to finish out her life in her own home. It seems only natural that with all the success that Toyota has had as a company and in turn shared with the team members, that we would in turn share it with the community.*

Shelby is a good example of a quality person engaged in the work with his team and committed to the company and community. We also learned that Shelby has had 18 years of perfect attendance, is a blood donor, works with Habitat for Humanity, fundraises, walks in the Relay for Life for the American Cancer Society, and rings the kettle bell for the Salvation Army at Christmas time. Shelby is hard at work in Figure 7.3.

Indeed, the committed team member is expected to strongly identify with Toyota values at work and to live those values outside of work. The importance of matching potential members' personal values with those of the company is a big part of the selection process. Another key point of the Toyota culture is to go beyond the relationship with the member and company to include others as stakeholders in the process. Toyota seeks to make its "circles of influence" as big as possible, so these circles expand to include family, community, and society as a whole, which also includes the environment.

Toyota looks at the maturation of companies in internal-external terms; that is, by how well they are focused on the outside higher-level circles. An immature company focuses exclusively on itself and its profits, while a more developed company sees itself in a larger context. Figure 7.4 illustrates this process.

The progression of this sharing of values offers a win-win situation for all stakeholders. Very often, successful companies like Toyota are targeted and questioned for doing things that appear to benefit society for the sake of hidden motives that really benefit the company with comments such as, "They are only giving to the community in order to get their way politically," or "They are only worried about

**Figure 7.3** Committed Toyota team member helping out in the community

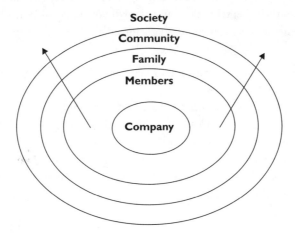

**Figure 7.4** Expanding Toyota Values

the environment because it is good for business." The best way that Toyota knows to answer such criticism is to return to the original purpose that reflects the Toyota culture: mutual, long-term prosperity. Toyota never denies the goal to be prosperous in the process, but it goes further in order to involve all stakeholders. This alignment of values is much appreciated and effective for stakeholders who agree with the idea of doing the right thing that will be rewarded in the long haul.

## Family Focus

As we discussed earlier, the expectation for the role of the company in personal and family life is different in Japan compared to the United States and the expected sacrifices of the individual for the company are different. For example, it is common in Japanese companies for team members when first joining the company to live in company-owned dormitories and later to live in company-provided family housing. There are company hospitals and company fitness facilities. The company is integrally involved in many aspects of life outside of work. The individual employee is expected to work long hours, and salaried employees are often expected to move within Japan or take overseas assignments to help the company. Often that means leaving the family behind, particularly if children are in the critical years of high school preparing for entrance to the Japanese university system.

It became clear to the Japanese expatriates who were sent to establish TMMK that Americans valued family and personal time more than the expatriates did, and the Americans expected a clearer separation of work and family life. This resulted in many human resource policies at TMMK that focus on family. Stated simply, they do not sound much different than things that are present in other good companies, though they would be very unusual for Toyota in Japan. Some benefits that Toyota offers their American counterparts include:

- on-site child care facility;
- family fitness center with full exercise facilities, including tennis, softball, and basketball leagues;
- flex time for office workers to balance family life;
- part-time salaried work for members taking care of small children or for those who are parents again;
- summer and part-time work for family members in school;
- family picnics at Kings Island (the local major amusement park); and
- an outreach department.

## Community Focus

In Toyota culture there are two aspects to involvement in the community. The first is to contribute to the community with financial resources from a company perspective. The second is to encourage and provide team members with the opportunity to contribute their time and talents directly to the community.

With the first, Toyota is actively committed to being a part of the community, contributing money and resources, but they also actively avoid being in the spotlight. Contrary to the cynic's view that Toyota uses community involvement to gain power and get their way, in fact they work to avoid unduly influencing community politics. They strive to find a balance between having good public relations and blending into the background. Over a twenty-year period, TMMK contributed over $29 million to the local community as illustrated in Figure 7.5.[3] By design, this was in small donations of between $500 and several thousand dollars to United Way, community colleges, Urban League, universities, and other nonprofit organizations that serve those in need. Some of the gifts have been larger as well, in the $250K–$300K range, targeted to specific projects. One example is the "Central Kentucky Riding for Hope" program, which serves challenged youth by providing them opportunities to ride and care for horses. The problem was, with the fickle Kentucky weather, the program couldn't function over half of the year. With the help of Toyota, they were able to build an indoor arena and now are able to serve the youth all year long.

Tom Zawacki, general manager of administration for the Georgetown plant, is responsible for this program and described how Toyota avoids becoming the "four-hundred pound gorilla." He said TMMK is "very cautious about being perceived as a leader of anything." For example, the local water company is a public corporation that was struggling financially. The city wanted to condemn it and take it over, so the water company came to Toyota and asked for support in arguing that it should remain an independent corporation. TMMK, with its

**Figure 7.5** Cumulative Corporate Gifts for TMMK, 1987–2006

---

[3] http://www.toyotageorgetown.com/commdex.asp, 10/09/07, Toyota and the Community

size and clout, could easily have steered things in the direction it wanted, but they believed that it was a controversial community issue that the community should work out. Zawacki explained Toyota's position by saying,

> We are a very conservative company. We could easily use influence to get things accomplished, but rather than take the direct approach, we want to have consensus as we do internally and want leadership collectively rather than individually. In Toyota we do not look for individual excellence but organizational excellence. This philosophy applies externally, too. We do not want a boastful presence in the community, just like we do not want one in the company. We could easily steer things because of size or influence, but we would rather be behind the scenes and not get credit for everything.

In this regard, part of the Toyota culture is to share its management resources with the community. Earlier we discussed the process that took place to develop the Toyota manager: focus on values, teamwork, and problem solving. These are qualities that serve a community well, and that is how Toyota seeks to use them. At the Georgetown plant, there is an explicit company goal to have 95 percent of managers and above—manager, assistant general manager, general manager, vice president, and president—personally involved in the community. This goal is tracked as part of the company's key performance indicators just like other production metrics. Tom Zawacki adds, "We have over 92 percent participation: coaching little league serving as deacons in churches, and many board members for nonprofit organizations, including the current chairman of the Lexington Urban League."

Another part of Toyota's focus on community is in the form of encouraging all team members to be part of the community by way of volunteerism. The main vehicle for this is the Volunteers in Place or VIP program. It is a program administered through the Community Relations Department that includes over 1,200 Toyota team members, who logged over 31,000 volunteer hours in 2006. The members link to a network of ongoing community projects throughout the year and volunteer on their time off to serve however they choose in the community. These team members are involved in youth leadership activities such as coaching little league sports teams and serving as leaders for the boy scouts and girls scouts. There are also day projects that include anything from participating in walk-a-thons to painting at the local homeless shelter.

The participants in the VIP program accumulate hours and "cash" them in for real money to be donated to charities of their choice. A special awards ceremony is held once a year for the Toyota President to recognize the outstanding volunteers, and additional money is awarded to the five volunteer leaders ($1,500–$3,000 each) to be allocated to their selected charities. The representatives of those charitable agencies are invited to the event and are presented the donation from the VIP. It is a win-win for everyone involved: the agencies receive practical assistance for worthwhile civic work, the company earns good local public relations, and the members contribute their time and talents to the community while deepening their dedication to the company.

There are countless other company projects and activities that give members an opportunity to serve their community. Last year over 100 team members participated in an annual "volunteer day" that gives team members a paid day off to go out and work with community agencies. The company takes great pride in the fact that they are the number one blood donors and number one in United Way total corporate giving in the community. When talking with Nila Wells and Kim Sweazy, Community Relations Specialists for TMMK, it was obvious they were proud of the dollars and numbers involved with the support to the community, but it was more obvious that they were proud of the impact Toyota was making in the lives of people in the community and the lives of the team members as a result of their service.

This may all sound like a commercial for Toyota, but the philosophy lived out in the company really is that building quality cars, quality people, and a quality community all go together, and as Figure 7.4 shows, they are all intertwined. Just as "what is good for Toyota is good for the team members, and vice versa" we can say, "what is good for Toyota is good for the community and vice versa." An example of that is another community outreach program called the Toyota Scholars. This is a national program that awards 100 scholarships a year, valued at $10K or $20K each, to outstanding high school seniors who exemplify outstanding academic excellence, leadership, and commitment to community service.

TMMK also gives a scholarship each year to a graduating senior at Scott County High School, in Georgetown, Kentucky to attend nearby Georgetown College. In 2003 Scott County High School nominated Ashley Ray for the award. Ashley completed the application and essay and ended up getting a full scholarship to Georgetown College, where she studied Communications and Media. As part of her college studies she took an opportunity to co-op at Toyota for a semester. She says she was "hooked" on her very first day.

*I was given an orientation tour by my new supervisor and I could feel the environment of success and teamwork. Everything was so neat and organized, and then, when I saw the president of the company sitting in a cubicle in the middle of everybody else, I knew I wanted to work there after graduation. The participative management style and open communication were things I wanted to be a part of. I was so intrigued by the culture there that I wrote a semester-long "mini thesis" on the topic and upon graduation came to work here. Having been born and raised in Georgetown, I really appreciate what they do for the community and how it affects people's lives. I never could have afforded to attend a small, private, liberal arts school, one of the best in the country, had it not been for the Toyota scholarship I received. Now I have a Bachelor's degree and a job working at Toyota. What a blessing.*

The Toyota Scholars program affects people's lives nationwide, and while not every scholar graduate goes to work for Toyota, this is a good example of how the values of the company intertwine and "what is good for the community is good for Toyota."

# THINK GREEN: POSITIVELY IMPACTING THE PHYSICAL ENVIRONMENT

Toyota's mission of adding value to customers and society is now extending to the long-term health of the planet. A policy that many people can enthusiastically get behind is Toyota's Earth Charter, which spells out the goal of having zero negative environmental impact. Fujio Cho stated the challenge in his usual positive tone of an opportunity to benefit society and the company simultaneously: "Environmental action is one of the most important issues that business must address. However, they should not look at it as something negative; but rather, they should view it as a prime opportunity for continuing growth."

## Green Buildings in Toyota Motor Sales

Toyota's goal of zero negative environmental impact was taken seriously by Toyota Motors Sales (TMS) when they decided to expand their Torrance Headquarters, building a LEED®4 compliant green complex, while making the project economically viable and helping several suppliers grow their business based on green principles. The Leadership in Energy and Environmental Design (LEED) Green Building Rating System™ is the nationally accepted benchmark in the United States for the design, construction, and operation of high performance green buildings. Toyota chose this path not to win any building awards but to develop much needed office space economically, while complying with the global mandate. They did it in the Toyota Way by stretching the thinking of team members who volunteered to help out while all feeling good about their contributions. Sanford Smith, corporate manager of Real Estate and Facilities, explained the goal: "Our goal was not to build a green building but to house our members and do it in an environmentally responsible way. Every decision had to make good business sense."

The $87 million, 624,000 square foot South Campus expansion was designed from the ground up to be lean and green. A cross-functional team was assembled, and they agreed the objective was to meet the intent of the Earth Charter

---

4 LEED® is the nationally recognized voluntary standard in the United States created by the U.S. Green Building Council.

while cutting costs in construction. They would rely on a simple but powerful principle they borrowed from TPS: They would make the building green by eliminating waste.

The TMS group could not find a construction company that knew how to do this. They selected Turner Construction as their partner. Turner Construction did not have experience with building a green building and at first suggested that making it so environmentally friendly might add cost. Instead, by collaborative problem solving between the Toyota team, skilled in problem solving, and Turner Construction with their in-depth construction knowledge, they found ways to actually make it cost less.

One pivotal decision early on that set the framework for the entire project was to use a concrete tilt up structure and build it like you would build a warehouse, instead of the way you would build the typical skyscraper. When you build a skyscraper, you erect a structure from steel girders and then concrete is layered on top of that structure. One approach to building a warehouse is to make panels out of concrete and treat these panels as the structure, eliminating much of the use of steel. This considerably reduces the cost of construction and with some clever architecture, they could still make the building look more attractive than a warehouse (see Figure 7.6).

This central idea was pivotal, and, among other things, saved enough money so the team could spend more on some other items to make the building more thermally efficient, such as double-pane glass, highly efficient insulation, and a

**Figure 7.6** Inexpensive Concrete Structure yet Attractive

highly reflective cool roof. The result was a significant reduction in operating costs of this energy-efficient building. Building on this decision, there were many smaller innovations that collectively made the project work, including:

- Panels were cast in forms and produced on-site as they were needed just-in-time.
- They needed to cast the panels on a concrete floor and there was not enough space, so they constructed a temporary concrete slab. Normally the concrete slab would be broken up and sent to a landfill, but instead it was ground up and used under the asphalt parking lot. Other parts of the concrete slab were cut into pieces that look like slate and were used for making patios and walkways.
- By getting very organized about sorting waste using a process similar to 5S, they actually reduced the cost of disposing of the waste. They arranged bins and sorted waste (e.g., remnants of dry wall) as the construction progressed, which reduced the normally high cost of removing all the waste at once at the end of the project.
- In the construction process, 95 percent of all waste was recycled or reused.
- The building was designed and oriented to maximize East and West exposure and minimize Southern exposure. This was planned to give the interiors light with minimal heat gain, while sun screens and translucent panels were used on the Southern facade to protect the interiors from glare and minimize heat gain.
- Using 53,000 square feet of solar photovoltaic roofing provides 20 percent of base electric needs (see Figure 7.7). This was viewed as a pilot for other Toyota facilities. One thing they learned, for example, was that they needed to spend some extra money to clean the roof annually, but overall it exceeded performance expectations. At current energy costs this feature should pay for itself in seven years, and perhaps sooner as energy costs rise.
- Every small detail was considered. For example, they switched to all green-seal certified cleaning supplies and started buying larger containers of concentrate.

There were also countless small decisions made in the design of the interior, mainly to recycle and to maximize the healthfulness of the building. For example, the cubicles were of a panel construction. Much of it was brought over from the old rental offices they no longer needed, but for all the additions, Toyota wanted them to match the older interior yet still be 100 percent recyclable and have low emissions (i.e., no clean-car smell). They challenged their existing office furniture supplier, Knoll, to provide this without raising costs. The company succeeded and now is using low emissions and recyclable panels as a key part of its marketing.

**Figure 7.7** Solar Panels on Roof

They also chose low emissions carpeting and paint. The result was another interesting lean benefit. Normally, LEED requires that you must add about two weeks onto the building process just prior to occupancy to air out the building with large fans so the air is safe for employees. Since there was nothing in the building to produce the harmful emissions to begin with, Toyota requested a waiver of this rule. They asked the U.S. Green Building Council (USGBC) government agency to test the air instead. Doing this saved considerable time and money and in fact, the USGBC changed requirements to include the possibility of air testing as an alternative to the two-week airing out process.

Art on the walls is recyclable; there are chairs made of recycled seat belts; everything used in the building is recycled or incinerated creating zero waste; recycled water is used for all nonpotable uses; water-efficient yet lush landscaping adds beauty and reduces heat around the building, and the list just goes on and on. Many Toyota employees have gotten involved by volunteering to act as "Think Green Champions" and continue to spread best practices.

Overall, the results are stunning:

- 94 percent less potable water than a conventional building, has saved 11 million gallons annually;
- energy costs for South Campus are about 30–50 percent lower per square foot than some of TMS' older buildings;
- less construction waste saved over $35,000;

- using environmentally-friendly construction approaches helped get government credits;
- achieved the original goal of a 10 percent return on investment compared to the cost of the rentals;
- overall construction costs per square foot internally and externally low by standards of the area;
- lots of favorable publicity and an opportunity to positively impact society, and;
- awarded LEED® Gold Certification, which was the largest privately developed office complex to earn this honor.

The other benefits were the growth and environmental awareness of Toyota team members. The project was an exercise in teamwork, problem solving, and partnership. The group also exercised leadership in the environmental movement having a positive impact on society. Robert Pitts, Toyota group vice president for administrative services explained: "We wanted to show that building an environmentally sensitive office complex does not have to be limited to small or unique projects—or ones with inflated budgets."

## Environmental Safety

In Toyota culture, the company looks beyond the safety of its members to environmental impacts on the surrounding communities. Its intention is to commit time and resources to maintaining and improving the environment where it locates plants. For example, when Toyota located in Georgetown, the local naturalists were concerned that air and water quality would be compromised. Toyota was able to demonstrate that through its commitment and improvements, there was not only no negative impact, but that the water quality actually improved. A list of some of the environmental improvements at the plant include:

- Toyota vehicles are now 85 percent recyclable. Huge shredders allow steel and non-ferrous metals to be recycled, and new processes also enable the recycling of car materials like urethane foam, copper, glass, and plastic bumpers.
- About 99 percent of all scrap steel generated by Toyota plants is now recycled. In addition, many waste materials, like plastic wrap, paint solvents, used oil, packaging materials, and cardboard are recycled. Even engine block modules are recycled, which annually keeps 500,000 pounds of material from ending up in landfill.
- Total recycling at TMMK—Toyota's largest plant outside Japan—has now exceeded 100,000 tons per year, which includes over 45,000 light bulbs each year.

- At all Toyota plants, the use of returnable packaging serves as a major means of conservation, as wood pallets and cardboard boxes are being used less frequently in the shipping process. Over 90 percent of the North American parts at TMMK are currently received in returnable packaging. This direct reuse of containers helps to conserve our natural resources and keeps the waste out of the landfill.

- In addition to activities like recycling, Toyota looks for ways to redesign the process itself in order to produce less waste. For example, anti-chip paint is now applied to the wheel-well with a roller, rather than a sprayer. This saves paint, reduces emissions, eliminates the need for plastic masking, and holds down cleaning costs. All told, this redesigned process reduces waste by 40 percent.

- TMMK environmental efforts even extend to its construction sites, where thousands of construction workers follow strict guidelines for everything from hazardous waste disposal and storm water control to recycling of construction materials.[5]

Positive environmental impact has become even more of a priority in Toyota culture in recent years, and many changes and improvements have been made in the plants as a result. We have already discussed the Key Performance Indicators (KPI) scoreboard focusing on Safety, Quality, Productivity, Cost, and Human Resources; now Toyota globally has another indicator for Environment. Goals have been set for zero landfill use and zero emissions.

## Zero Landfill Goal

As is the custom, once a standard is set in the Toyota culture, many people get involved in the problem-solving process and improvements result. For example, with respect to the zero landfill goal, every department in TMMK started to track how much trash was being thrown away and not eliminated or recycled. Obvious improvements were made in the plant with huge benefits. Cardboard and plastic "dunnage"—materials left over from the delivery of all the parts—were captured and recycled instead of being thrown away. These improvements led to many of the boxes being changed into reusable plastic containers, which in turn were sent back to the suppliers on returning trucks and reused.

This recycling has carried over to every area of the plant: there are no trash cans in the office areas, meeting rooms, or cafeterias. Instead, there are big rows of recycle bins with graphical illustrations for sorting items in terms of compostable food scraps and paper, plastics, glass, etc. The compostable food is turned to soil

---

[5] From http://www.toyotageorgetown.com/envirodex.asp

right at the plant in a huge compost bin. From there the compost is taken to an onsite greenhouse and used to grow vegetable seeds. The next step in the cycle is the onsite garden, where the seedlings are grown into vegetables for the local food bank. In a single year, the garden produces over 2500 pounds of produce, representing about 1,571 meals.[6]

## Paint Waste Improvement

Other environmental improvements have been directed at the production process. The paint department is a big focus because the painting process involves numerous chemicals and waste products. One such waste product—paint sludge—is the leftover "gunk" from painting 1,000 cars a day. Previously, this waste was loaded into 55 gallon drums to be sent to the landfill. One countermeasure was to partner with a landscaping company and to mold the harmless gunk into landscaping bricks for residential use. The idea worked, saved costs, and a huge amount of space in the local landfill.

In the plastics painting area a new type of "bio filter" was developed that uses lava rock and pine bark mulch to produce microorganisms that consume the volatile organic compounds (VOCs) that are currently being filtered and exhausted in the air. This improvement keeps the air cleaner and saves energy as well. One unit has been calculated to save Toyota nearly $350,000 per year, and there are several units in the plant adding up to literally millions of dollars of savings a year.

It is quite common for these kaizen activities to improve the environment and also have a positive impact on safety or cost. There is efficiency in having all six indicators on the same scoreboard: everyone is looking at all six at the same time and conflicting initiatives are quickly identified and stopped. We are aware of stories from other organizations where the cost department or engineers may be cutting product costs, but at the expense of safety or quality. With Toyota's matrix organization, and everyone having the same six indicators, the opposite happens: improvements have a positive impact on more than one of the indicators.

This multiple benefit is illustrated by the improvements made in the painting area of the plant. The story starts long ago with Henry Ford's famous line for his model T: "You can get any color you want, as long as it's black." Giving customers any color they want is part of any car maker's plan, but with Toyota and its pull system of production, the goal is to build the cars as the customers are buying them, and not produce them in batches.

This customer-driven goal has always posed a challenge in the painting area because switching from one color to the next involves flushing and cleaning the

---

[6] http://www.toyotageorgetown.com/enviro2.asp, 10/10/07. TMMK's On-site garden.

lines and nozzles with solvent. It is expensive and a waste product for the environment. When the Georgetown plant first started, the paint was all enamel based, so the waste product was more expensive to process. During this phase the cars in the paint shop were painted in batches of 20 in order to balance the pull of the customer with the expense of changing the paint colors. In other words, 20 white cars were painted, then 20 black, and so on.

In the 1990s, there was a huge engineering improvement that came out of Toyota in Japan, and Toyota was able to switch over to water-borne paint. This can be thought of in terms of switching from enamel to latex. As any home improvement painter knows, the latex paint chemicals are less harsh, and clean up is easier and cheaper. The same was true for the paint department at Toyota: the lines were easier and cheaper to purge in between colors and they were able to reduce their batch size to 10 cars at once.

Currently, Toyota has implemented a new "cartridge system" of painting; the color of each car is held in a little cartridge about the size of a pineapple. It is basically a bag of color that is mixed right in the lines with the water base to paint the car. When the next car advances on the line, the cartridges rotate on a carousel and the next color bag is chosen and processed. The lines do not need to be flushed because there is no color going through them: the color is being added to the water, one car at a time, at the last moment. This process has been a huge technological breakthrough: it has saved flushing and cleaning costs since the lines do not need to be purged with solvent, and it has saved material and handling costs since there is no need for solvent and none to be disposed of. Accordingly, because of the flexibility of the system, Toyota is able to paint cars for each customer, in any color, at any time.

Toyota's experience of improving scoreboard metrics through environmental waste reduction is substantiated by a recent study on the environmental practices of lean manufacturers recognized by the prestigious Shingo Prize for Manufacturing Excellence.[7] The study found that there was a positive and significant correlation between the plant's efforts to reduce environmental waste and lean scoreboard metrics. This study dispelled the "zero sum gain" myth that by focusing kaizen teams on environmental waste reduction lean metrics will suffer. The result of this study indicates that there are synergies between efforts to reduce environmental wastes and traditional lean wastes that result in positive improvements in all scoreboard metrics and to the overall health of the value stream.

In this new area born by the Earth Charter, Toyota's value stream now extends from natural resource extraction to the return of products either back into the

---

[7] Bergmiller, Gary, *Lean Manufacturers Transcendence to Green Manufacturing: Correlating the Diffusion of Lean and Green Manufacturing Systems,* University of South Florida, unpublished Ph.D. dissertation, 2006.

value stream or safely back into the earth. This "cradle to cradle" approach to the value stream improvement is exemplified by Toyota's high vehicle recycling rates, clean water processing in facilities, green buildings, hybrid vehicles, composting, and bio-filters. Improving the flow of the value stream, that Toyota holds sacred, now goes beyond reducing the obstacles to achieving instantaneous customer fulfillment (i.e., lean wastes) to reducing obstacles to returning materials back into the value stream and safely to the planet (i.e., green wastes).

# KEEPING THE DEVELOPED TEAM MEMBER THROUGH HIGH RETENTION

Attract and retain the best and brightest is the mantra at many companies. At Toyota it would be more accurate to say attract, *develop*, and retain the best and the brightest. Gary Convis notes Toyota has indeed lost some of its best and brightest. In fact, this is a testimony and compliment to the value stream components of selection, development, and engagement, but honestly a challenge to the "committed" component. Mike Morrison, Vice President and Dean of the University of Toyota at Toyota Motors Sales in California, is an example of a Toyota senior manager who developed a strong commitment to Toyota. He came out of a top university with an MBA energetic and ambitious, and expected Toyota to be one stop on his career path. At that time Toyota was hardly a star company others were trying to emulate, yet he was attracted to the culture of respect for people and never left despite external visibility and many opportunities. He said:

> When you look at the opinion survey results, Toyota is always through the stratosphere among Fortune 100 companies in employee satisfaction. When they come in and give you the results, you never think you are that good because when you are inside you see all the blemishes too. But it always has had a very positive culture, and I credit Toyota for always practicing the fundamentals of respect and CI. When I came here out of MBA school we were selling silver cars with brown interiors and these were the small Japanese cars you bought as a second car for economy purposes. I thought it would be a good first job and did not think I would be here this long, 28 years later. What kept me here is values. Toyota has tremendous relationships with its vendors, its suppliers, its dealers, the community, and its members. It is unique in that way.

Morrison is one example of a long-term employee but how does Toyota do on retention overall? Employee retention issues are best understood by looking at Toyota members in three categories: production members, supervisors and middle managers, and executive level.

1. Nonexempt production members (made up of production team members and team leaders, and skilled trades team members and team leaders) account for nearly 6,000 of TMMK's 7,400 members (as of 2007). As mentioned earlier, the annual attrition rate for this group has consistently run less than 3 percent. As of the year of the writing of this book, the annual attrition rate for this group of members for all of the North American plants put together is only 2.5 percent, while the rate at TMMK is running at 1.7 percent. This group is indeed the best and brightest, and Toyota has been successful in selecting, developing, and retaining 98 percent of them. It is important to note that because of the high pay in the auto industry this group is also among the highest paid in manufacturing in the country and cannot usually go somewhere else for higher pay.

2. The group leaders, assistant managers, and managers for Toyota have been a highly sought after population in the field of lean consulting and for positions as lean champions in organizations transforming their operations to lean. Since coming to the United States over twenty years ago there has been a continually growing interest in Toyota and its production system, now commonly known as "lean." With everyone from healthcare to supermarkets studying lean, people with direct Toyota experience are in high demand, which translates into high income levels. Even with this situation, Toyota still retains more than 98 percent of this level of management and the number is increasing with time. Even though the "lean wave" and demand for experienced lean managers has been increasing, the current management group at Toyota remains largely intact. It appears that these managers have stayed throughout the years, despite more lucrative offers, because they are "committed" to Toyota and value the culture in which they work and the communities in which they live. They continue to forsake the higher dollars for higher principles. Should a manager consider leaving, Toyota refuses to match offers to retain that manager because they do not want to distort pay structures.

3. The executive group at Toyota has also had some attrition at its level, but retained an unusually large percentage, particularly among those who grew up with Toyota. When Toyota came to Kentucky, the agreement with the state incentive package was that Toyota would hire 95 percent Kentuckians and could hire 5 percent from outside the state, so that it could hire managers and executives with automotive manufacturing experience. The latter was a high-level group who more than likely left their former company to advance to a higher level with Toyota, and they were later happy to step from Toyota to yet a higher level with a different company. They had not really been through the People Value Stream for any amount of time or repetition. During the peak of "lean leaders demand," the turnover

of this group at TMMK was a problem, but this problem has since leveled off and the attrition rate is below 1 percent.

From the overall experience it appears that the "home-grown Toyota men and women" retention rate was much higher than that of those who entered the company at later stages in their career and then used their experience at Toyota as a stepping stone to further their personal careers. There have certainly been exceptions—and some highly visible executives have left Toyota—but the majority of the leaders started their careers at Toyota and have been raised through the system and have personal values that correspond with the company's. One thing they often say is that at Toyota they are continually challenged and keep learning to a greater degree than they expect would be the case at other companies. They are in the "people value stream" for the long term and appear at this time to be committed to the company for the length of their careers.

Despite the loyalty of many managers, attrition and growth has been a real challenge for Toyota throughout the years. In the early years of TMMK, for example, there was a commitment and communicated goal to promote from within. The belief was that the supply chain of the people value stream would keep up with the demand, but two factors hit at the same time to complicate matters: as the demand for "lean leaders" was luring Toyota managers to other organizations, the demand for Toyota products continued to grow in the United States, and Toyota continued to build plants to meet the demand. The population of Toyota in North America has risen quickly from the first few thousand at Georgetown in the early 1990s to close to 40,000 people at the time of this writing.

With the need for new managers increasing and with some of the group already leaving, Toyota looked to the outside for the first time to fill some of its management ranks. A top Japanese Toyota executive explained that the gap in management ranks was not in the skill sets of the two we have talked most about—problem solving and leadership—but with the actual technical competencies of building a car. For this reason, Toyota went back to the auto industry and its suppliers to look for managers with all of these skills. The technical skills had to be there for the building of the car, but the Toyota Way leadership skills were also important because of the challenge the new managers would face by coming into the Toyota culture in mid-stream.

TMMK has successfully found and hired managers from the outside, mostly from GM and Ford, who have demonstrated all of these competencies in their past careers. Leaders like Steve St. Angelo, the current President of TMMK, came from a long career at GM that included time at the Toyota/GM joint venture at NUMMI. Another executive from GM includes the current Vice President of Manufacturing, Pat D'Eramo. The current General Manager of Assembly, Barry Sharpe came from Ford Motor Company. An example of an executive coming from a supplier is Phyllis Crume, who is the current assistant general manager of assembly and was hired from Johnson Controls, a supplier of seats to TMMK.

These executives have been able to assimilate into the Toyota culture by their own hard work to "learn the system" and by demonstrating the competencies they were hired for. There appears to be a healthy balance of promoting from within and from without, with executives like Phyllis working alongside home-grown talent like Charles Luttrell to manage the Assembly Plant. The key business indicators of the plant continue to improve, while the attrition of the executive team is increasingly limited to retirements instead of job hopping.

## COMMITTED TOYOTA MEMBERS CAN BE DEVELOPED OUTSIDE JAPAN

We are often asked whether the Toyota system is peculiar to Japanese culture. Can this work in companies that are not Japanese? As we have noted the Toyota Way started in Japan and heavily reflects Japanese cultural tendencies. In some ways it is very alien to the West. On the other hand, we have given examples of Americans who are highly committed to the Toyota Way and fit into the culture very nicely, and there are many, many more.

Our experience is that this actually works in the West for Toyota. It works in the United States, Canada, and Mexico. We have seen it work in various European countries. We spend time with seasoned Toyota members at various levels and locations and our observations about Western Toyota members are:

- They are highly engaged in their jobs.
- They are confident in their abilities.
- They have an extraordinary capacity for solving problems and improving processes.
- They have many soft team skills—listening, presenting, facilitating, encouraging, supporting, and positively dealing with conflict.
- They feel a part of Toyota and take pride in being part of this great enterprise.
- They are driven to reflect on their weaknesses and improve themselves.
- They feel obligated to teach others what they have learned from the Toyota Way, both inside and outside of work.

## SUMMARY

The people value stream is a continuous cycle that deepens team member capability, confidence, and commitment to the company. A member's success equals the company's success and vice versa. Toyota is not satisfied with just being a successful company. If that were the case the successful loom maker would never have begun building automobiles. Toyota sees the maturity of any company based on its contribution not just to the bottom line, but to the team members, their families, the community and the environment. As a company it also judges itself on the team members' commitment to the same. Toyota continually challenges team members to grow focusing on problem-solving capability. Team members who develop the ability to objectively look at the facts and improve any process use this profound skill to benefit their families and the community. More recently Toyota has made it a priority to improve the environment through the global mandate.

## KEY POINTS TO CONSIDER FOR YOUR COMPANY

1. The highest level of development is commitment to Toyota, its values, and taking what is learned to family and the community.
2. The quality people value stream is not a linear, one-time process but is more like a spiral repeating over and over leading to deepening understanding and commitment.
3. In the United States, there are systems in place to support a "work–life balance" and include the member's families as part of "the team." This is largely an adaptation to American culture.
4. There are systems in place to contribute both financial and human resources to local charitable organizations.
5. Environmental improvements are included as part of the organization's "key performance indicators" and are practiced throughout the organization.

# PART TWO SUMMARY

This concludes the discussion of Part II, the Quality People Value Stream. As noted in the Culture Diagram at the outset of the chapter, the continuous improvement PDCA process wraps around each of the systems discussed. The Toyota culture is in a continuous cycle of reviewing and improving these systems. This perspective on the People Value Stream acknowledges that the systems described are not perfect; they do not always achieve their intended results. Toyota's goal is 100 percent commitment by the employees, and aims for lifetime employment. One can see the continuum of investment that Toyota makes in each and every employee: from the sponsored school programs to improve teamwork and problem solving, to the selection assessments, to the six weeks new hire training, to the quality circle and suggestion system payouts, to the support of volunteering.

With this type of investment, one of the goals is to avoid losing active, full-time employees. As mentioned earlier, the team member turnover is less than 3 percent per year. There were a few years when the management turnover was substantially higher than this. In the mid–1990s the Big Three auto makers and many other manufacturing companies were starting their lean journeys. They were willing to pay a lot of money through targeted recruitment strategies to help their cause and Toyota was a key resource for them. Mike Hoseus recalls his frustration when he was assistant general manger of Human Resources,

> *It was very frustrating to spend all the time and money that we do on training and development of our managers, and then to have them leave for other companies, much less competitors. I went to my Japanese Coordinator with some turnover data and much frustration, asking his advice on how to handle the situation. He simply said, "Do the right thing and keep your eyes on the long-term vision of the company. Don't let the choices of a few individuals affect how you practice the Toyota Way. Of course, make sure you are doing everything you can to improve our management systems of development, succession and compensation, but do not even consider reducing the investment we make in our people."*

Visitors to Toyota see evidence of something special. For example, in the daily tours offered at TMMK it is common to hear visitors remark on how neat and clean the place is and also notice that employees seem friendly and engaged in their work. This seems surprising when we consider the jobs in that plant repeat about every 55 seconds. The assembly line is supposed to be the ultimate mind-numbing job. What visitors cannot see is all of the years of work and development that led team members to feel good about their jobs, the company, and themselves. The investments pay off in mutual prosperity.

For Toyota in Japan it seems self-evident that long-term investments in developing people are not negotiable. It is essential to long-term competitiveness and it is the obligation of senior management. As Figure II.1 illustrates, what is seen on the surface reflects at deeper levels long-standing values and basic assumptions about the nature of humans and their relationship to the company. These "Eastern" philosophies have been drilled into Americans and represent the company culture wherever Toyota operates globally.

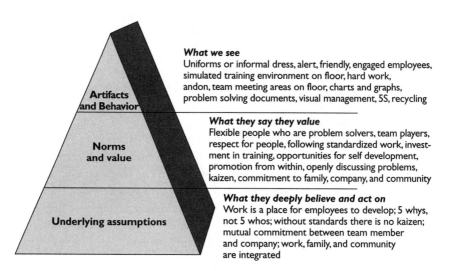

**Figure II.1** Summary Cultural Analysis

# Part Three

---

# People Supporting Processes

*If you had to identify, in one word, the reason why the human race
has not achieved and never will achieve its full potential, that word
would be meetings.*

—Dave Barry, columnist and humorist

At the core of the Toyota Way is the development of people who are willing and able to continually improve the way work is done. We call this the people value stream. While the development of people who are capable and committed is at the core, this does not happen in isolation. Development of people who learn their jobs, take initiative to surface and solve problems, and become committed to the company is an ongoing process. In this section we will see that there are daily processes supporting this development and growth, including:

- Work groups to support daily learning and team problem solving.
- A clean and safe workplace to have the security needed, physically and psychologically, so team members can focus their attention on higher-level production issues.
- Two-way communication to listen to and give feedback to team members and leaders so they can improve themselves and operations.
- Servant leadership that supports, teaches, and is open to input.

The "people-supporting processes" support the team member in learning the job, performing the job safely, and solving problems. At Toyota, support comes most frequently from the team leader and peers in the work team. This work-group structure is a conduit for communication and development for both team members and leaders.

Why are these types of support important to Toyota? If team members are so carefully selected and trained in such detail to do the work, why do they need additional support? The Toyota system is built around strong daily support and ongoing development for a number of reasons:

1. Lowering the water level raises the pressure level—The concept of eliminating waste has been described using the analogy of lowering the water level. As inventory is removed, the water is lowered, and the rocks (problems) are exposed. Any serious problem can shut down the whole production line. This pressure helps develop the team members as they are confronted with daily challenges and are expected to help solve these problems. At the same time it could put a lot of pressure on the team member to work very precisely, possibly risking health and safety, and to cut corners risking quality problems. Fortunately the team leader through the andon system is there to jump in and help, as a pressure release valve, which allows the team member to follow the standard work and openly identify these types of problems.

2. Team problem solving—There is a strong belief in Toyota that the team is better at problem solving than any individual. This is because teams have more insights into the cause of the problem, will come up with more ideas for improvement, and can work together to implement the solution. The role of the leader is to facilitate team problem solving and develop the problem-solving capabilities of team members.

3. People develop at Toyota by learning from each other—Team members develop by learning from team members and the team and group leaders. The team leaders and group leaders are formally trained in job instruction and can provide ongoing guidance to team members. Ongoing safety audits are used to coach team members in safe methods. Since team members rotate jobs, they all are performing each job and contribute ideas for improvement as incorporated in the standardized work.

4. People enjoy social activity—People are not happy or motivated if they have to work in isolation, and the selection process at Toyota favors those people who enjoy working in groups. Toyota invests heavily in the development of people, and teamwork helps to create a better working experience which is more likely to lead to high retention rates and is necessary to develop truly committed members.

At Toyota, direct support is provided by the work team. Unfortunately, people do not always work efficiently and effectively in groups, as the opening quote from

David Barry illustrates. Many people do not believe that groups can be efficient or effective. "They simply slow us down and complicate otherwise simple tasks," some might say. This may well be an accurate assessment for many organizations, but as we will see in Chapter 8, Toyota has worked hard to develop highly effective groups and to make meetings productive. Part of making groups effective at Toyota is a culture of clear roles and responsibilities for individuals within the group.

# Chapter 8

# Work Groups and Team Problem Solving

*Never doubt that a small group of thoughtful, committed people can change the world. Indeed, it is the only thing that ever has.*

—Margaret Meade, anthropologist

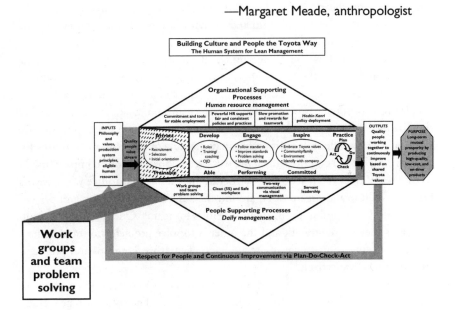

## TEAMS AND WORK GROUPS ARE THE BASIC UNITS OF TOYOTA ORGANIZATION

Toyota is famous for its teamwork, from work teams to quality circles to its more recent "modular development teams" in product development.[1] Teamwork may seem to be one of those concepts like problem solving, that is a lean silver bullet. The idea of the team structure, in and of itself, is not a panacea that is going to solve all the "lean transformation" challenges. Nonetheless, this has not stopped people from trying: "Let's form into work teams and improvement teams and it's bound to help us get leaner."

There is a clear tension in the way most companies think about teams. On the one hand it is sacrilegious to say anything negative about the importance of

---

[1] Morgan, James and Jeffrey Liker. *The Toyota Product Development System: Integrating People, Process, and Technology*, New York: Productivity Press, 2006.

teamwork. Every year senior executives advise the administration for the College of Engineering at the University of Michigan, and the most frequent comment is that engineers need to be taught to work in teams. On the other hand there is an irritating itch around teams, meetings, and committees: they are perceived as wasteful, inefficient, and reducing brilliant individuals to mediocrity. After all "a camel is a horse made by committee." We see particularly strong management resistance to the role of the hourly team leader. Add in a formal team leader who is not doing a production job and they become an immediate target for the finance group to cry: overhead, overhead—kill the indirect labor! It is interesting that the team leader within Toyota is considered the lynch pin of TPS and few companies "going lean" have this role.

At Toyota there is also recognition that groups and meetings can become inefficient and reduce the effectiveness of individual work. So there are counter-measures in place to prevent this, including leaders highly trained to facilitate the simple problem-solving processes that keep the teams on track. It is safe to say that the Toyota Production System would not function without high performance teams on the shop floor. It is also safe to say that one of the main mechanisms for transmitting Toyota culture is the basic work team. So, while one company might see the team as an inefficient social structure they are forced to live with, Toyota builds its culture and organization around the basic unit of the work group.

We find it helpful to think about two roles for teams. One is to support individuals as they do their work and the other is to solve problems to improve how the work is done. Sometimes, these are referred to as work groups and problem-solving groups respectively.

*Work groups* get the daily work done and in the process are finding opportunities to continually improve the way the work is done. They often can be seen on the organizational chart as part of the formal reporting structure. On the shop floor at Toyota a small group of five to seven people report to a team leader and several of these small groups report to a group leader. There is a similar structure in product development with a small group of engineers reporting to a lead engineer. When we watch people work we see individuals performing tasks. We usually cannot see a group working. But, in fact, the work group makes important decisions about how the work is done, and their roles and responsibilities and must support each other in various ways through the workday.

*Problem-solving groups* are often temporary and usually do not show up on the organizational chart. These are teams like task forces, Quality Circles, temporary cross-functional teams to solve a particular problem, and standing committees. They often deal with problems that cut horizontally across different departments in the organization, such as a problem of bad material flow across stamping, welding, and assembly.

These two types of groups are not mutually exclusive. Work groups also have meetings, and solve problems and at these times act as problem-solving groups. Some problem-solving groups may be full-time such as Toyota's pilot teams of hourly employees that spend years together preparing for a new vehicle launch.

We should note that within a culture there is a third type of team (beyond work teams and problem-solving groups). There are teams that people form for themselves that are not officially sanctioned by the organization. Sometimes these are called "informal groups." They are not part of the formal structure that management created, but rather, people on their own get together and form a group. One type of team might form around a hobby such as owners of antique cars or a group that forms a sports team. Informal groups can be threatening in an organization that is obsessed with control. For example, a group that formed to organize a labor union would often be perceived as a direct challenge to management. When the company culture is weak, often the informal structure grows strong filling in the vacuum. Often these informal groups are a counter-culture to management. Originally unions were formed from informal groups of people who felt that management was acting against the interests of the worker and only through banding together could their voice be heard and taken seriously. Over time, these informal groups may become formally recognized parts of the organization, for example, if the informal group working to organize is successful in bringing in a union and becomes formally part of that structure. Another example, that would fit well into the Toyota culture, would be a group that forms around issues of environmental consciousness that eventually becomes a formal work group to do environmental projects in the plant.

For Toyota all of these types of teams are essential. People need to feel a sense of belonging and small groups help us feel connected. Both formal and informal groups provide this essential function. Ideally the groups one belongs to are cooperative and not antagonistic. But even employees meeting informally to complain about the inevitable frustrations they feel with management can serve a function. It can make members feel a little better that their frustrations are heard and others care. At Toyota the support structures strive to provide formal vehicles to address these frustrations before they become destructive to the cohesiveness of the formal organization. We will see in Chapter 13 how an issue of sexual discrimination at TMMK raised the awareness of human resources that team members did not trust HR to represent their concerns to management and were obviously talking about this "informally." This led to a plant-wide kaizen effort that eventually completely reorganized HR to create formal vehicles outside the usual HR channels to voice these concerns which greatly improved employee trust.

Teamwork is particularly important when the problem cuts across departmental boundaries. At Toyota it is also recognized that as humans we become invested in particular points of view and interests. Production control wants to optimize the production schedule. Stamping managers want to optimize stamping performance metrics. Human resources is interested in safety, health, and welfare of team members. One person may have a great idea to solve a problem from her perspective supporting her interests, but if all the stakeholders are not involved in the process of helping to develop and implement the countermeasures, the solution is not going to get far. Former Toyota Chairman Eiji Toyoda said, "Whenever you decide to start something new or something necessary, coordination among many divisions and departments always becomes necessary. I want you to think for the entire Company rather than yourself alone, coordinate with other divisions, and lead on, no matter what, to concrete results."

Toyota wants to build strong individuals through job instruction training and individual problem-solving training. But the strong individuals must work collectively toward a common goal. Each person must identify with the Toyota enterprise. Building this identification begins very early in the career of a new hire as illustrated in Mike Hoseus' experience when he first joined Toyota:

> When I first went to Japan as a group leader, we were given two days to see the entire process of building a car. We visited a steel mill, a casting foundry for engines, the stamping facilities, body weld, painting, and so on. We were taken to the world headquarters to see the administration of the worldwide operations. We saw a sales dealership and even spent time at the Toyota Museum where we saw the looms from the original loom works factory and all of the original Toyota automobiles. I experienced a real sense of pride and an understanding of the big picture. I realized that we were being oriented into the Toyota Team without even knowing it. We were given this big picture and welcomed into the big team so that we would always know the direction and focus of the smaller teams that I was a part of.

Mike was a trainee, and, in fact, there was no guarantee he would work for the company long term or work out as an effective group leader. Yet Toyota invested the time and money to bring him to Japan and orient him to the entire company's history as if he were a senior executive. This same philosophy carries over into everyday action at Toyota today. New hires are given a walking tour of the entire Georgetown facility by senior managers for the same reason. It gives them a sense of the entire "team."

Teams are not only necessary to solve complex problems and effectively implement solutions, but the problem-solving process reinforces teamwork. The methodology of solving problems establishes a standard or a goal and a purpose for getting there. This approach gets everyone on the same page and going in the same direction. It also entails a "go and see" requirement and relies on facts not opinions. Without this framework, there is nothing less efficient or more destructive of genuine teamwork than a group of people sitting around sharing unsubstantiated opinions.

Toyota sincerely believes that teams are more effective and efficient than the sum of individuals, and that when they are given the skills and systems of problem solving, the sky is the limit. When the team and the "process" come together the balance between creativity and discipline is achieved. Ideas are great, but there is neither time nor money enough to just randomly try these ideas to see which ones work and which ones do not. By having team processes that rely on facts and consensus, the team is able to weed out the ideas that have a better chance to make an impact and create improvement.

Perhaps the most important role of teams in Toyota is in developing team members, maintaining the discipline needed for following standardized work and continually improving. Many companies we work with ask how to sustain the great changes that result from lean projects or kaizen workshops. They set up a wonderful looking cell and write out beautiful multi-colored standardized work sheets and before they know it inventory is building up in the cell and the standardized work is largely ignored. The answer to their question is in the work groups.

At Toyota the work group is the context for employee development and training and the mechanism for daily discipline. Team members are coached daily by their team leaders who audit jobs to confirm that the standardized work is followed. Group leaders wander the floor and a build up of inventory is an occasion for coaching. Day in and day out the process is observed in detail and coaching is used to maintain the standards. Team members rotate jobs and because of one-piece flow it becomes very apparent if someone cannot keep up or is making quality errors. The system comes to life at the work-group level and that is how the great tools of lean become institutionalized in daily practice. *Without the work group functioning at a high level, Toyota's people value stream collapses and continuous improvement will stop in its tracks.*

To help illustrate teamwork in this chapter, we bring the concept to life through examples of actual teams at work. We illustrate both work groups and what a typical day might be like as well as examine problem-solving groups and how they worked on an actual problem as a Quality Circle.

# TOYOTA ORGANIZATIONAL STRUCTURE: FLAT AND OPTIMAL SPAN OF CONTROL

The Toyota culture works to reinforce the feeling and fact that employees are all members of teams and do not function as isolated islands. The organizational structure is designed to support teamwork. Toyota was not the only organization to discover the power of coordinated team structures. Let's consider the case of a PT (Patrol Torpedo) boat. These are fast vessels the Navy used in World War II to attack larger surface vessels. They were nicknamed the "mosquito fleet" since each one was tiny and not very powerful, but when a group swarmed around a much larger ship they could do incredible damage in little bites that added up. Teams could operate each individual PT boat patrolling in a specific area and do a fine job, but in World War II when they were called together to attack a far larger surface vessel the key was teamwork across all the PT boats. Each individual team must be aware of and coordinated as part of a larger team that has individual assignments but are integral to the success of the larger plan, otherwise they will be blown out of the water.

When we think of an organizational structure, we often think of a hierarchy designed to control individuals and to keep them on target producing the largest quantities of work possible for the least cost. At Toyota, teamwork is about solving problems shared horizontally. The goal for Toyota in setting up the ideal organizational structure is to be able to:

- have complete understanding of the purpose and objectives of the organization by everyone, especially managers and supervisors;
- integrate effectively across functions, divisions, departments, groups, and so on;
- organize functional specialists together so they can develop depth of expertise and standards for their specialty;
- have prompt decision making and smooth flow of information; and
- meet mid- and long-term business objectives.

Toyota strives for a relatively flat organizational structure while still maintaining the right group size so people can effectively work together in solving problems. Toyota wants the team members experiencing the problems to be the ones able to solve the problems. It is *muda*, or waste, for a team to have to go up a level or two, or to have to go to maintenance or engineering, in order to solve a problems that they have the skills to solve themselves. This is a distinct advantage of a flat organization. Another advantage of a flat organization is the flow of information. The fewer levels that information has to go through, the quicker and more accurately it can be passed on.

When actually designing the organization there can be a conflict between the desire for a flat organization and the needs for work groups small enough to effectively solve problems together. The easiest way to make the organization flat is through a large span of control. In an organization with 800 people we could have 799 reporting to one leader, assuming we need a leader at all. This is very flat, but this model would completely dismiss the importance of leadership in the organization. By contrast, Toyota's system is heavily dependent on teams led by highly skilled leaders. They do not believe in leaderless work groups. In fact, Toyota believes the ideal work group has five to seven people. Each small work

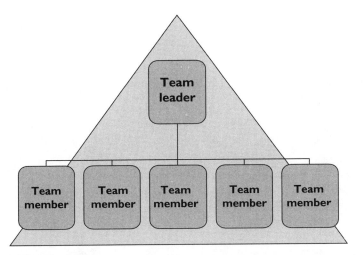

**Figure 8.1** Ideal Span of Control for Work Team

team has a team leader who has many important roles including responding to andon pulls, auditing the standardized work, ensuring safety and ergonomic procedures are followed, and facilitating the process of solving problems. This involves not only the technical aspect of these tasks, but also maintaining trust and respect within the team. In order to be able to spend the time with each person, to establish a relationship of trust, to gather input, to facilitate and coach problem solving, Toyota has found that 5 is the ideal span of control for a work team (see Figure 8.1). In reality there is variation in team size within Toyota plants and many teams have 6 to 8 members.

A broader view of the work team in the context of the work group is shown in Figure 8.2. The team leader is an hourly employee and has learned all of the jobs in the team and has a set of off-line responsibilities (e.g., quality checks, audits, training) but the first duty is to respond to andon calls. The group leader is the first-line supervisor and is a salaried position. The group leader has broader planning responsibilities as well as overall production responsibility for several work teams. Notice that we show the typical hierarchical pyramid upside down to reflect that the team members are doing the most important value added work to support the customer and all others are supporting them.

Typical corporate departments like HR, quality, and engineering must also be deeply involved with the work teams providing daily support to help them better add value to the customers. The entire organization is focused on delivering customer value, which occurs through the team members. There are many daily management systems to support the team member every day and we will be discussing many of those in the coming chapters on safety, communication, and

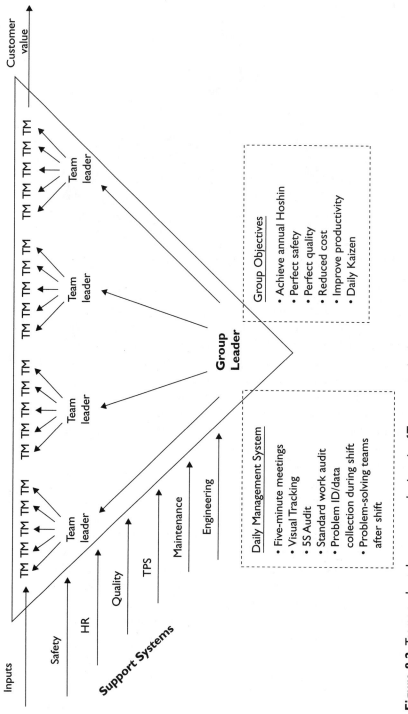

**Figure 8.2** Teams and work groups are basic unit of Toyota organization

234

the role of the leader. Interestingly, there are a few key differences between this structure and those we see in most other organizations:

1. The team leader role as practiced at Toyota is virtually nonexistent in most companies. There may be a "utility" person who can substitute for others when absent, or on break, but there is no functioning team leader role to respond to andon and support daily production and problem solving.
2. Support departments mandate and enforce policies rather than providing the daily support we see at Toyota.
3. First-line supervisors act as fire fighters, disciplinarians, and the arm of management rather than providing leadership, coaching, teaching, and planning support for team members.

The work group refers to the everyday reporting and supervisory structure of the organization. One group is made up of several small teams that work day in and day out to develop their standardized work, solve problems, improve the standards, and create new ones. This does not mean that other teams will not have more than five people. For example, problem-solving groups, such as Quality Circles or Safety Committees often have more than five members. However, even in these situations, the number is recommended and controlled to be no more than six to eight. If the number of members gets too high, the flow of information and ability to work through the problem-solving process get hampered. A maximum number of 12 people are placed on problem-solving groups because it was found that the team dynamic with more than 12 people tends to split and become two groups.

With a work team the size of five to six people, the 800 person organization is not flat, but quite tall, requiring five levels total including the working level of over 600 people at the bottom. How can Toyota balance its rule of five with the concept of having a flat management structure? On one hand they are saying that fewer levels of management are needed in order to be fast and efficient, and on the other they say that a small span of control and small work teams sustain trust and problem solving. These two concepts can appear to be in opposition and must be balanced.

For Toyota, the key is to be able to have the span of control needed to have trust and coaching, yet still have the prompt decision making and flow of information. Toyota does three main things to make both of these happen:

1. use a matrix organization,
2. distribute decision making based on clear decision-making standards, and
3. clearly identify the role and function of the team leader.

Toyota's matrix organization has two dimensions as illustrated in Figure 8.3. Looking down are the line organizations that makes the product such as plastics,

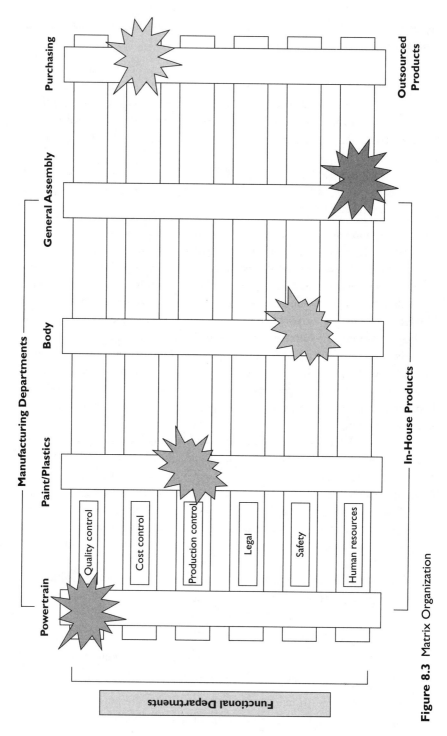

**Figure 8.3** Matrix Organization

body, and assembly. Looking across are the different specialty supporting departments, such as, safety, quality, HR, and production control. Toyota's matrix organization gives the line departments a great deal of responsibility for daily decisions (i.e., Safety, Quality, Productivity, Cost, etc.) that lead to quick decision making, while still balancing out the need to have information flowing across the organization. They do this by having the specialty support departments truly support the line organization with standards and policies, on the one hand, and active on-the-floor communication on the other. The practice of genchi genbutsu means even specialists do not simply manage from the office but are active on the floor understanding the actual condition and developing relationships.

Another key point is to support distributed decision making by the line organization with clear standards that enable most decisions to be made in real time, without interference from support groups and higher management levels. If this process is not flat, the lower levels will have the tendency to leave the decision making to management. These "invisible" levels of management are present in many organizations, even if they have large spans of control and could be considered flat. For Toyota it is more important to be flat in decision making, even if there are layers present for the sake of creating a smaller span of control. An example of flat decision making can be seen in the area of cost accounting. The goal is to provide each level of management the flexibility within their respective areas of control to make the decisions to buy what they need to make improvements (within boundaries). For the sake of purchasing new equipment or services, there will be a set dollar amount up to which each level is able to approve. A group leader, for example, will have the freedom to approve up to $10,000, a section manager $50,000, while a general manager will be needed for $100,000. These standards are set and known by everyone and decisions are made accordingly.

The last way to balance having a flat organization and optimal span of control is the team leader structure. When we describe Toyota's team leader structure to other companies the immediate reaction is something like: "That is not lean. We are leaner than Toyota. We have 35 people reporting to our first-line supervisor." Actually Toyota will typically have 25–30 people reporting to the first-line supervisor. The team leader in Figure 8.2 is a working level person. In Toyota's American plants, the team leader is designated "hourly" and the group leader is the first level of salaried supervision. When we explain the team leader is working level the next response is typically: "Now I understand. Yes we have working level people who are performing a full-time production job but also have some leadership responsibilities. So our structure is pretty similar." Then we must explain that the working-level team leader at Toyota is actually not working production full time, though they do spend some time doing production jobs.

The Toyota standard is that the team leaders spend 50 percent of their time online, working on a process and the other 50 percent of the time off-line answering andon pulls, coaching, supporting the team members, and solving problems. So, if there is a group of 20 members and four team leaders, there will be two on line and two off-line on any given day. The off-line team leader will really be supporting ten processes while the line is running. So for sake of cost and efficiency, the ratio could be considered 1:10. But during breaks, and after the shift, the two online team leaders will resume their role of coaching and support and the ratio immediately goes back to 1:5. This team leader structure is a great example of how to balance the need for a flat organization while at the same time having a small span of control. In the next section we illustrate how the team leader structure actually works with a real case example.

## WORK GROUPS AT WORK: CASE EXAMPLE

In *The Toyota Way Fieldbook*[2] we described Toyota's work group structure in some detail including a five-page table that lists the typical tasks in a day in the life of a team member, team leader, and group leader. This gave a detailed picture of the formal roles and responsibilities. In this section we want to give a richer picture of Toyota culture through a story told by an actual team leader about one day in her life at the Georgetown plant. Tracey Richardson was a team leader for five years and at the time of the story was responsible for assembly of the instrument panel which is built off-line and sent to the assembly line. She continues to support Toyota through the Center for Quality People and Organizations.

As a team leader she was an hourly employee who had learned all the jobs on the team and showed leadership ability. She went through extensive training to learn to be a team leader. Tracey was outstanding by most standards in her dedication and enthusiasm for Toyota and TPS, but not out of the ordinary for Toyota team leaders. Notice, as Tracey tells the story how in an emergency team leaders flexibly responded sharing roles and responsibilities; the group leader, the salaried "boss," jumped in and started building parts; quality was always at the forefront; even in a crisis there were clear operating rules and visual management systems to help determine what to do in the situation; the team did not panic and fall into chaotic fire fighting; the team was well trained in how to execute all the procedures and pulled together as a true team even sacrificing break time; and the feeling of the team members acting as one was exhilarating.

---

[2] Liker, Jeffrey and David Meier, *The Toyota Way Fieldbook,* New York: McGraw-Hill, 2006, Table 10.1, pp. 227–231.

# A DAY IN THE LIFE OF A TEAM LEADER AT TOYOTA, BY TRACEY RICHARDSON

"There are not many people in the automotive industry who understand what it really means to work for Toyota Motor Manufacturing Kentucky (TMMK). Not only do you feel fortunate to be part of a unique team, but each team member understands exactly what it takes to live through a day of production where 2,200 vehicles a day is the norm. It's much more extraordinary than most can fathom.

Toyota has such high quality standards for their vehicles, and with that comes extremely high expectations that each team member must know, understand, and follow rigidly. If any one team member falls short of those expectations during production it takes the entire team to pull together to countermeasure the out-of-standard condition. At times this has to happen in a matter of minutes or even seconds due to our demanding takt time to meet our customer's needs.

It's amazing what you can accomplish when your team members have an understanding of one another's strengths and developmental areas that contribute to the quality of the parts we ship to assembly. That is living the Toyota Way at its best; what one person can accomplish doesn't compare to the various tasks a synergetic team can achieve. When everything goes as planned, it is harmonious and almost peaceful, but the true strengths of the team and the Toyota Production System come out when things go wrong.

I can remember being newly promoted in the team leader position on second shift, feeling very anxious inside determining whether I would be able to handle all the responsibilities that would come my way when the pressure was on. How I define pressure is when you have several out-of-standard situations occurring and how quickly you prioritize what to do first and who is going to assist you in accomplishing it, all without missing a part to the assembly line. I often wonder how I was able to get so much done in so little time but as I look back, I believe it was my leadership style and my ability to know my people which allowed me to quickly delegate when I couldn't be in two places at once.

A typical team member ratio online at Toyota is approximately five to seven team members per one team leader, so when you had 100 percent of your team members crossed-trained and present each day, you were able to do more proactive problem solving to improve those day-to-day issues that tend to plague you when you least expect it.

I can remember one particular day that I felt like our team pulled together and conquered the adversities. I was the team leader supporting part of the IP Trim Line (Instrument Panel, some call dashboard) and we had one last process to trim, inspect, and repair the IP's before they went to the assembly shop. We tried our best to ensure built-in quality at each process, but we are human, and, at times, were known to overlook defects during the inspection processes.

At that time it took us approximately 60 seconds to fully inspect the IP and do minor repairs. Our standardized work sheets had close to 50 seconds of inspection time and 10 seconds for the optional type work to repair minor items. Any time longer than that went into the official repair process. Each repair was then documented on a check-sheet, and feedback was given to the preceding process to support them in counter-measuring their process parameters, therefore decreasing that type of defect the next day. That is what we would consider to be the 'ideal' situation. In the Plastics department many of the parts were either injection molded or mono-foamed with polyurethane substance in order to get that 'nerf ball' feel to your instrument panel. It is actually a pretty sensitive process. For example, certain weather conditions can be detrimental to our process parameters and defects can be created if the team leaders and group leaders aren't fully trained on how to handle these fluctuations.

This particular production day I remember it being a very humid summer evening, with a high degree of moisture in the air. When these days occurred, which was often in Kentucky, it was counter-measured by various types of temperature adjustments and chemical adjustments to cure the foam within our takt time period. If any of those items were tweaked too much, it could create havoc for our inspectors and repair team members on those processes.

It was a Friday, and as many know in the industry, it's a day you prefer to have few issues. At Toyota, as well as other companies, many team members take off on Fridays and Mondays to get in three day weekends. When this occurs normally the team leader will fill in on line until that team member returns. The Toyota Production System seeks to eliminate waste and that includes not designing in extra team mem-bers standing on the sidelines waiting to fill in. The team leaders and group leaders become the safety relief valve and have to go work on the line when there are unplanned absences. Of course, we try to minimize these situations but they do occur often in those vacation-coveted spring and summer months.

So, during this particular Friday production evening we were short two team members in our group and one of them was on my line, so of course I was working on the line. Along with those responsibilities I had certain team leader jobs to keep up with throughout the night. As a team leader your ability to "multi-task" was a prerequisite for the position. At any given time you could have ten things that need your attention especially when andons are involved. When I was online normally we had one team leader in the group off-line who was covering her team and mine and our group leader was always close by to jump in as well. We all also had Motorola radios in order to communicate very quickly with one another when issues arose. We also were in constant contact with the assembly groups we fed parts to which enabled us to respond quickly when they needed our assistance. Because we were building directly to the line with very little inventory any problems could very quickly shut down the assembly line.

As the evening was about to start, it was duly noted within our shift-to-shift log that first shift had had some problems with IP wrinkles most of the day, so we had an inkling that we would fall under that same fate as it was a very humid night. We started production at 5:15 P.M. dead even with the assembly line since first shift had run one hour overtime to compensate for the scrap they had with the IPs during the day. We started out running fairly well, not seeing any wrinkle scrap for the first hour of production. It was about 45 minutes till our first break at 7:15 P.M. and I noticed we had three wrinkle defects on line.

These defects occur when the polyurethane foam is injected into the IP mold and it expands under pressure as the IP makes it way around the carousel. At times when the IP mold closed, it could have a tendency to pinch the skin under humid conditions and create a wrinkle. These would normally occur on the ends of the IP. Many small ones were repairable within the takt time, but some of the larger ones were not and had to be reworked at the end of shift. To minimize costs as much as possible we would use some of the scrap parts that were not repairable to practice new repair techniques to improve the skills of our team members.

When these defects occur back to back, it is standard procedure to give feedback to the mono-foam team leader to communicate that we are seeing defects and to pull the andon and make adjustments accordingly. The mono-foam team leaders immediately started to make process adjustments in hopes to countermeasure the defects as soon as possible; this can be a time-consuming process when there are other elements involved with the chemical setup. We continued to lose production since the line had to be shut down to make those adjustments. It was normal to be down 15 to 20 minutes when these situations occurred so you could take various temperature samples on the current polyurethane foam shots.

As they were trouble-shooting the mono-foam process, I was documenting our downtime and repair ratios using various flip charts to help our management visualize our current situation. This too, was a common practice for all groups when your line was down past 20 minutes. I began delegating various responsibilities to team members to ensure the quality of our emergency stock. In emergency situations most of the time the parts needed to be wiped down and quickly inspected for any defects that could have occurred in storage. While this was occurring, other team members were preparing their areas to ensure flow-rack stock levels and our equipment was ready when parts would begin to flow again. We had several large trim presses that required hourly cleaning to maintain the quality of our cutting processes, so several team members were cleaning our equipment during the downtime. Most of the time when we were in these situations my team members would keep themselves productive either cleaning or helping me in one way or another as each minute that is lost is a potential minute everyone will have to work overtime.

As the mono-foam team leaders were continuing to make adjustments and we were preparing for parts, I got a call on the radio from assembly stating we had let a wrinkle defect flow out of our process. This is a condition that you train for, but hope never occurs. When this situation happens we have to replace the IP with a good part so assembly doesn't miss a vehicle. They have a planned buffer of two colors of line-side stock per IP type, so this is what we have to replenish quickly. It was approximately $^3/_4$ of a mile to the assembly line, so walking an IP up to the line was unacceptable and considered muda. Each group is assigned a bicycle for general purposes and our group, in a kaizen, had built an IP transport rack on the back of our bicycle; this allowed us to transport two IPs to assembly very quickly to ensure minimal downtime.

As I was determining the color needs of assembly, I had one team member locate our bike and another team member prepare the IP's for shipping. I also asked two team members to check our current process carts for any other potential defects, since one had slipped through unfortunately. I would then do the same with the carts next to the assembly line to confirm there were no other defects. We call this 'walking the line' or 'tracking back' to ensure you've caught your discrepancies and quality is once again maintained. Being accountable and taking ownership was something our Japanese trainers instilled in us from day one; it wasn't something I took lightly, nor did my team when we caused assembly to be out of standard.

As I was returning from the assembly line, the mono-foam process restarted so my group leader took my place on the line till I returned to ensure our processes would run smoothly at restart. When I returned my group leader told me to catch up on my production numbers and emergency stock levels and he would continue to work on the line until break time. As it turned out, we were about one hour into emergency stock with all our line-side stock depleted. It was very common during those hectic production evenings when things aren't going as smoothly as they can, that team members pull together to run through their breaks to help us catch up a bit and to ensure we replenished our line-side stock in case the defects continue.

The process of break rotations normally takes about 45 minutes since we rotate breaks feeding team members in and out of the break room as the other team leaders and group leader cover until everyone has had their break time. Often we will continue this through lunch if the situation warrants it. It shows teamwork at its best, for the flexibility it takes for many to do more than their process may call for, in a 15 minute time frame, but normally everyone understands why it needs to happen and chips in working extra time on a more difficult process to prevent part shortages.

We continued to receive sporadic wrinkle scrap throughout the night which created a lot of extra work for our repair team. When there is a high ratio of repair, you have to rotate your set-up team member over there during their optional type work to grab a part every few minutes when the line-side racks were full. There were many visual and auditory cues for this and our team members understood what they needed to do to maintain line speed.

Our setup and repair team members were somewhat specialized in their responsibilities so it took some maneuvering of our manpower to free up those individuals to remain on those processes till our situation improved. As a team leader, you are very appreciative when your team goes outside of their standardized rotation or work extra to help others showing their flexibility.

As our night progressed past second break the night air cooled and our wrinkles seemed to slow down; the team leaders in the mono-foam process did everything they could to minimize the scrap as well as document all chemical parameters to better prepare for the next humid evening. We also spent time in our five-minute meeting at second break recapping how we could improve our repair methods and any techniques found throughout the evening that could assist us in training team members down the road. At Toyota we document all we can to ensure we get past the symptoms to the root cause.

Some of those evenings I spent in reactive mode I wouldn't have traded for anything; that's when your team learns how to handle the unthinkable and one team member seems to split into two when the going gets tough. It's as if you read each others' minds when tasks need accomplishing, all without missing a single beat to assembly.

In conclusion, the night ended with about 1.2 hours overtime, all emergency stock was made up and accounted for, and our IP repair team gained a little more experience out there honing those skills for tomorrow. We all learned a little more about understanding the environment and how small changes in the air can be detrimental to our process capabilities. Lastly, we gained mutual respect and trust for one another knowing when problems came up everyone would play a role in keeping the cars rolling down the line. Those days on the line were priceless to say the least."

Any Toyota team leader can tell you similar stories. These are the days that they will remember for the rest of their lives and that make them realize why they wanted to come to work at Toyota. These experiences bond the teams together and develop confidence in all members. They are the equivalent of the big soccer match, when you have practiced and practiced and finally it all comes together in a game situation when your team is threatened with a loss, but you pull together and win. For lean consultants of outside companies, these are the days we live for—when all the systems we have helped develop and all our coaching comes to life and the team executes like we described in class. It is unfortunately all too rare. For football, soccer, basketball, and hockey teams, the coach puts people though the entire people value stream—selecting, developing, engaging, and inspiring. Every individual learns all the skills and goes through exercises and scrimmages to learn how to handle many situations. There are set plays that are taught and practiced. A top team can execute almost flawlessly and then improvise when needed. This is much like the Toyota team, and much different than teams in most companies that are very poorly prepared; improvisation means a lot of yelling and shouting and running about. For Toyota, this is where all the investment in preparing people pays off.

# MANY TYPES OF PROBLEM-SOLVING GROUPS

Apart from doing the daily work, there are many different types of teams that meet to communicate issues and solve problems. These teams develop both formally and informally, at every level, and in all directions of the organization. Examples of the variety and focus of these teams include:

- work groups holding team meetings
- Quality Circle teams
- various working committees (teams)
- teams of group leaders
- department teams
- plant teams
- continent company teams
- worldwide company teams

Project teams are also a common tool that Toyota uses to get people from across the organization (and value stream) together for an improvement initiative. The best known example of this type of initiative is the pilot team that Toyota uses for a new model start up. Design engineers, production engineers, production members (at the team leader level), quality engineers and supplier representatives are all brought together in order to see a new model launch through, from concept to production. This is obviously more efficient and effective than the common "throw it over the wall" approach, where the engineers design a new model and pass it on to the production folks leading to multiple rework cycles before the design is buildable.

Toyota continues to improve this process as new models are launched. Mike Hoseus recalls an example of this progression:

*The Toyota Production System depends on a smooth flow of parts just-in-time, and this was particularly challenging as Toyota started up the Georgetown plant and was transitioning many of its part components to American suppliers. In some of the earlier models of the Camry, the parts were not always up to the ideal standard (even though they passed the customer quality standards). The team members on line worked through many part problems that caused them to push or pull with extra physical force in order to get the part to meet the customer standards. As a result, there were a number of cumulative trauma injuries to our team members. In Toyota fashion, the problem solving started. There were short-term countermeasures implemented at the process, such as tools, new installation methods, and the temporary rework of parts.*

*The root cause was that the standards that safety had set for pushing and pulling (the amount of force necessary to push or pull a part on a car) were not known and not understood by the design engineers. For the next model change, the safety department was part of the horizontal pilot team. They were present not only to interpret the standards to the design engineers, but also to actually measure and confirm that the parts could indeed go on the car within the standard. If the standard was not met, the engineer had to work with the supplier to make changes to the part until it did. The new model was launched with tremendous improvements in the workability of the parts for our team members; the injuries (and cost) went way down, while morale and trust increased.*

Another example of tools and processes in use to support horizontal coordination is the cross-functional meeting. These are standard meetings facilitated by the administrative function to coordinate the teamwork and improvement across all of the functional departments. These meetings are held at different standard intervals and are a vital tool for problem solving, communication, and sharing of best practices. There are many standing meetings at Toyota. We give a flavor for the broad range of teams and meetings at TMMK in Table 8.1[3] and even this long list is only a subset.

# PROBLEM-SOLVING GROUPS AT WORK: CASE EXAMPLE

Like the work group, it is difficult to envision what a Toyota problem-solving group does from abstract descriptions. The problem-solving groups are carefully put together, well trained in problem-solving methods, and follow an unusually rigorous process. To illustrate this we selected an exemplary Quality Circle project that won an award and follow it here from start to finish. The work of a Quality Circle is usually summarized as an A–3 report.[4]

Quality Circles are voluntary. Someone or a small group must recognize a need and be motivated to want to work on an improvement project. They must formally request support for the activity and need a sponsor in management who will guide them, clear the way for data collection, and get them the resources needed for countermeasure implementation. For team members the sponsor is usually the group leader. The teams designate a leader who must go through

---

[3] From Internal Toyota Class, "Advancing the Toyota Way," Toyota Engineering and Manufacturing, 2005

[4] See *Toyota Way Fieldbook*, Chapter 18 on the A-3 process.

**Table 8.1** Example of Range of Meetings at TMMK (*Continued on next page*)

| Responsibility | Type | Chair | Participants | Frequency | Objectives |
|---|---|---|---|---|---|
| Crossfunctional | Plant Presidential Hoshin | President | General Managers, Managers | 3x per year | Creation and checking of Hoshin |
| | General Manager Meeting | President | Plant, General and Dept Managers | Monthly | Review and decision making on plant-wide strategies |
| Safety and Environmental | Plant Safety Meeting | President | Plant Manager and General Mgrs. and Safety Manager | Monthly | Information, review and problem solving on Plant Safety issues |
| | Department Safety Meeting | Department. Gen Manager (GM) | Section Mgrs. and Asst. Mgrs. and Safety Manager | Monthly | Information, review, and problem solving on Department Safety issues |
| | Section Safety Meeting | Section Manager | Asst. Managers, GLs and Safety | Monthly | Information, review, and problem solving on Section Safety issues |
| Quality | Plant Quality Meeting | Quality GM | VPs, General Mgrs. & Section Mgrs. | Weekly | On the floor review of customer feedback and problem solving |
| | Daily Audit Meeting | Quality Manager | Section Managers, AMs and GLs | Daily | Information review and problem solving |
| Productivity | New Model SOP Meeting | Production Control GM | Pres., VPs, GMs | Monthly | Project Status and decision making on new model SOP |
| | PEFF Meeting | PC GM | Pres., VPs, GMs & Mgrs. | Monthly | Review of plant efficiency and problem solving |

**Table 8.1** Example of Range of Meetings at TMMK (*Continued from previous page*)

| Responsibility | Type | Chair | Participants | Frequency | Objectives |
|---|---|---|---|---|---|
| | Production Meeting | PC Manager | GMs and Mgrs. | Monthly | Adjustment and decisions on production plans |
| Cost | Plant Cost Meeting | President | President, General Mgrs. & Acct. Mgr. | Monthly | Information review, and problem solving on Cost Acct. plant issues |
| | GM Cost Meeting | Department GM | Section Mgrs. and Asst. Mgrs. & Acct. Mgr. | Monthly | Information, review, and problem solving on Cost Acct. Dept. issues |
| | Section Cost Meeting | Section Manager | Asst. Mgrs., GLs and Acct. Rep. | Monthly | Information, review, and problem solving on Cost Acct. section issues |
| HR/Administration | HRD Meeting | HR GM | Pres., VPs, GMs & Mgrs. | Quarterly | Review and decision making on HRD and workplace environment |
| | Manpower Meeting | HR and PC Manager | Section Workforce Coordinators | Monthly | Monthly adjustment of need/have for workforce numbers |

special training in group facilitation and the Toyota problem-solving process. The leader of the quality circle in this case was Renee Brown and it was her first time in this role. She worked at the local hardware superstore as a customer service manager and came to work for Toyota as a temporary at the end of 1999, and then was hired as a full time employee in 2002 for the Assembly Department. In

# THE LIFE OF ONE QUALITY CIRCLE BY RENEE BROWN

I wanted to learn something new, and there was a job in my team where people were getting hurt and we thought we could do something about it. People were having shoulder problems on this particular job and we got approval to form a Quality Circle to work on it. We all watched each other do the job and we took the best from everyone and made a new standard that would prevent injuries. We then followed the job to verify we had in fact solved the problem. This positive impact on the health of our team excited me about Quality Circles, and so I decided I wanted to try my hand as a leader.

Then the new Avalon model was ramping up in Assembly and there was a problem with getting the rear reinforcement (the metal part to which the rear bumper is attached) to fit properly into the car. We had to use a hammer to "bang the parts" into the car (see Figure 8.4) which was really avoiding addressing the root cause of the problem. Some team members from a few different lines were together talking about it and someone suggested getting a circle together to solve the problem. We took some folks from an existing circle called the "Fab Five" and added a few others and unofficially became the "Fab Seven." Our team was made up of Crystal Brewer, Renee Brown, Steve Dennis, Chris Harris, Carl Hogg, Dave Gafford, and Marvin Robbins.

We started through the problem-solving process by clarifying the problem. In addition to a lot of frustrated team members, the problem was objectively stated as:

- We had bad fit condition on the rear reinforcement on 442 Avalons per day.
- We had one acute injury as a result of the process.
- We had to scrap seven rear lights due to the problem for a cost of $323.28.
- We averaged 650 andon pulls per shift.

**Figure 8.4** Does the Hammer Solve the Root Cause of the Problem?

We set a goal to reduce the bad fit on the rear reinforcement by 90 percent over the next three months. From here we did *genchi genbutsu,* or as we call it "get your boots on," and we all went to the process in order to see first hand what was going on. By observing the problem at the source, we were able to make a fish bone diagram of all the potential causes (see Figure 8.5) and then began to narrow the possible ones down to a manageable number.

We narrowed down all the possible causes to five potential causes we wanted to investigate so everyone in the team took one to go and see and determine if theirs was the root cause (see Table 8.2). I had responsibility to check the standardized work, and make sure that everyone on the job had been properly trained and were following the correct installation procedure in the same way. We were, so we went on to the next potential cause. This time the whole team investigated the brackets of the part that first attaches to the car, and then the rear reinforcement attaches to them. We needed help with this, so we went to the production engineering group that is responsible for the quality of the incoming parts, and they did their measurements and the bracket turned out to be okay.

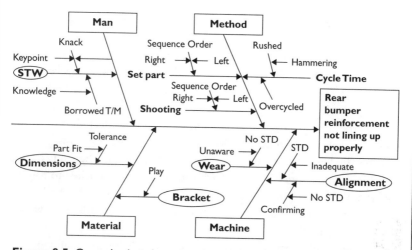

**Figure 8.5** Cause Analysis Investigation

**Table 8.2** Potential Cause Investigation Matrix

| Potential Cause(s) | How Investigated | Who | When | Results | Eval. | Rank |
|---|---|---|---|---|---|---|
| Reinforcement Bracket Support out of Alignment | PE REP | Fab Five | 10/15 | Misplaced Guide Pin | X | 1 |
| Lower Body Panel Tolerance | QC Group | Crystal/Steve | 10/4 | Bad Parts Shipped | X | 2 |
| Bumper Reinforcement Alignment | RI Rep confirmation | Marvin Robbins | 9/29 | Confirmed | 0 | 3 |
| Reinforcement Bracket Play | PE Rep chks specs | Fab Five | 9/26 | To Standard | 0 | 4 |
| T/M's Doing STDWK | Signatures on JIT | Renee Brown | 9/19 | All TM JIT | 0 | 5 |

Activity plan to investigate potential causes
Evaluation Key: 0 = acceptable, = needs improvement, X = poor results
Rank Key: (1) most likely potential cause, (2) next most likely potential cause, (3) next likely, etc

Then Marvin had the assignment to check the rear reinforcement alignment. He worked with an inspection team to have it checked. It was put into a checking fixture and it too measured as okay. We weren't sure where to go next so we asked the advisor of the Quality Circle for some more ideas. Our group leader was our advisor, and he suggested that we go back to body weld to see how the parts were put together. For us assembly folks it seemed like another world back there, but Steve and Crystal went over and 'walked the line back' until they found where they welded the body weld bracket to the body. They checked this part and found a problem. The lower body panel was out of tolerance.

In the process of trying to see how to have it corrected, they found out that there was another problem to deal with. The actual bracket that was on the lower body panel was also out of standard. The studs on the bracket were misaligned causing each subsequent part attached to it to be off as well. When trying to find out where that part was made a body weld team leader spoke up and said, "that part is not even made here; we get that from a supplier." So the team took a sample bracket and went to the production engineering group that was responsible for the quality of that part. The engineer, John McCoy, actually visited the supplier to see with his own eyes what the situation was. He found that guide pins on the supplier's dies were actually out of alignment, which caused the studs to be out of alignment. We did a 5-Why Chain to make sure that we had the root cause, which we did (see Figure 8.6).

We worked with John in order to come up with some countermeasures. We came up with three main countermeasures the supplier needed to implement. The actual stud was tall and bent easily, so it was decided to make it .2 mm thicker so that it did not move easily. It was also decided to make the hole that the stud went into smaller so that the stud could not move as easily. Finally, the supplier set up a preventive maintenance program to make sure their die fixture stayed to the standard and they even sent us some of the weekly and monthly logs to confirm their activity (see Figure 8.7).

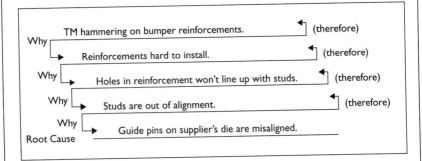

**Figure 8.6** 5-Why Analysis of Causes

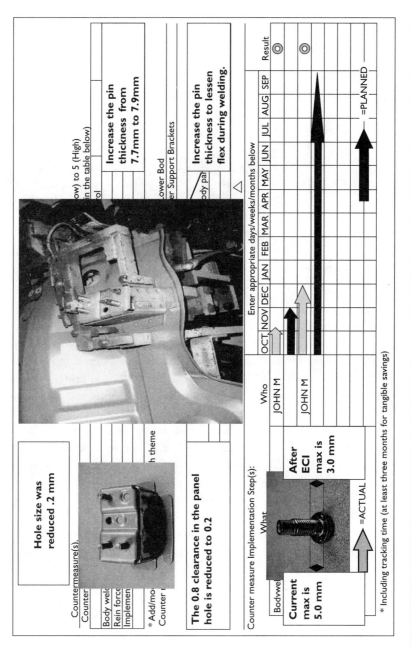

**Figure 8.7** Countermeasures

253

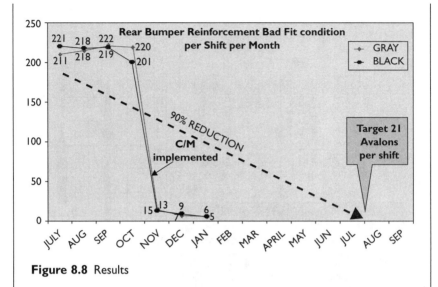

**Figure 8.8** Results

We worked with John and the supplier in getting the good parts to the line and working through the remainder of bad parts. The countermeasure worked great (see Figure 8.8), and we retired the hammer back to the tool cabinet. The bad fit on the reinforcements dropped like a rock. We went from over 400 bad a day to less than 20 right away. We also had no more injuries on the job, no more scrap rear lamps, and the andon pulls in the group went from close to 1500 pulls a day to less than a 1000. The team felt great about this because we did the detective work needed to properly identify the problem. The rest of the team members who ran the process were also very appreciative. Even though it was up to the supplier to actually countermeasure the problem, they would have never known it was a problem, and it would not have been addressed if it were not for us.

We also found out that actually solving the problem at Toyota is only the start. Then the Quality Circle worked on documenting the problem solving on an A–3 problem-solving report. This is done so that the countermeasures can be standardized and shared with others. Our advisor helped us and suggested we do a better job at telling the story. We presented to the managers of assembly with each one of our team telling a part of the story, or problem-solving process, that they were most involved with. We were picked by our managers to represent assembly and present our problem to the plant's general managers and vice presidents.

We wanted to win the Platinum Award so we could go all the way to Japan to represent our plant, but another team won that. We won the gold. The team was disappointed for a brief moment because we didn't win the Platinum but it didn't last long. The team was so fired up because we were making a difference. We didn't only get rid of the hammer, we directly impacted the key performance indicators of our group and our plant. We wanted to keep going, and in the past two years we have solved five other problems and have won a silver award and three bronze awards.

There was one example when the team was working on a problem with door locks getting lost when the doors traveled from trim line over to the door line. We videotaped the door all the way through its travels and found out that up in the conveyor the door carriers banged each other and the locks were actually being thrown out of the door. We did a lot of trials to find some way to keep them in the door and nothing worked. The team had the idea to add a PVC cup to the door carrier in order to hold the lock in place. We put six dummy locks in the cup and ran a trial for a whole month to make sure we could prove its effectiveness. The same locks were all there in the cups a month later, so we had the proof we needed to move forward.

We went to the team at the beginning of the line and explained the problem to them. They didn't like the idea of having to add a second to their job in taking the lock from the door to the PVC cup, but when we showed them the data on both the amount of lost and scrapped locks and the effectiveness of the countermeasure, they agreed to the change. We went to Lowe's and bought the PVC pipe, cut over 1400 three inch pieces and glued them to the door carriers ourselves on a Saturday. We have not lost or scrapped a lock set since. I believe if we hadn't had our facts together we would not have been able to convince them to implement the countermeasure.

a personal interview Renee told the story of her first time leading a Quality Circle. Renee was later selected to perform a new role in the assembly department. The Georgetown plant has been focusing on increasing participation in Quality Circles and the circle members told the management that they needed help with the circle activity, especially in coordinating all the cause analysis and countermeasure activity. Assembly decided to assign two team members (one for each assembly plant) to perform this role on a full-time basis. This allowed Rene to work directly with new circles and coach them on how to do all the paperwork and documentation. She guides them through the problem-solving process, and how to get buy in through face-to-face contact instead of relying on written messages. She has a team of people in the engineering and maintenance sections that actively support the quality circles. As a result, the participation rate in Quality Circles in assembly has risen from 18 to 34 percent. While the increase in numbers and KPIs are satisfying to Renee, she says her biggest satisfaction comes from working with someone and seeing a fire start within them when they too see they can make a difference. Clearly this experience has greatly broadened Renee's view of Toyota and deepened her understanding of problem solving. As a result of her Quality Circles experience, she has moved to a much deeper level on the quality people value stream, becoming even more valuable to Toyota.

Quality Circles was a trend, or some would say fad, in the 1980s in America. It was brought over from Japan as part of the quality movement. Unfortunately, it rarely succeeded and was generally dumped by most companies. If we were to go to those companies now and suggest that to get to a new level of lean they need to commit to Quality Circles they would probably laugh at us—been there, done that, it does not work! Yet what is Toyota working on in 2008? They are working to broaden participation in Quality Circles to deepen the training of team members and strengthen kaizen. Toyota considers a vigorous Quality Circles Program in which team members are volunteering to work on problems to be one of the best signs that respect for people and continuous improvement is alive and well. We believe the problem that the American companies had in the 1980s was that they "implemented" Quality Circles as a standalone method without developing the infrastructure and culture to make this powerful tool work. They were viewing it as a quick fix tool for quality improvement and cost reduction instead of part of a quality people value stream.

## NATIONAL CULTURE AND TEAMWORK

Obviously national culture plays a role in how people work together in teams. As we described in Chapter 1, Japanese culture measures out to be near the top of collectivist thinking, while the United States is toward the opposite extreme of strong individualism. Teamwork doesn't always come easy in America. In fact, American culture can even promote a different connotation of teamwork. We frequently hear comments in American companies that teamwork means competition, with each team trying to one up the other. Each individual wants to be part of the winning team. We even see this American tendency in simulated classroom exercises when there is nothing at stake. Mike Hoseus comments:

*When teaching Toyota culture to American organizations, we use a simulation exercise in which teams of executives and managers work to improve a process. It often involves several days and multiple rounds of improvement. Each team of individuals is trained to build a model car with the highest quality, lowest cost, and in the shortest amount of time. We divide them into two teams that are part of the same company but each makes their own set of cars like two different factories. It is normal to see the two large factory teams literally hiding their improvement ideas from each other. When I ask them, "Why are you hiding your ideas from your own teammates?" They look at me like I am crazy and respond: "They aren't our teammates. They're the competition!" This prompts a teaching moment to explain to a group of executives and managers, all from the same company, that they are on the same team and part of the challenge and goal is to know that and learn to communicate and share best practices with each other.*

Obviously teaching people to work cooperatively both within teams and across teams is easier said than done, whether in the United States or elsewhere. Americans generally value independence and the sense of competition is strong. That fact occasions the question, How is Toyota able to influence this independent mentality in relation to the Toyota team culture? Fujio Cho, the first president at TMMK articulated the first vision: "We are not going to change the American Culture. We are going to take what is best from the Americans and what is best from Japanese (the current Toyota culture), and have a new and improved version." In other words, Toyota seeks to utilize the independent/individualistic American style; that is, thinks for himself, and doesn't just do what he's told because "it's been done that way for years."

While this independent nature works and can be useful in some kaizen and improvement processes, it tends to emphasize the competitive: "I will do it my own way and all by myself" tendency and does not fit into the Toyota culture. Here Toyota utilizes strength from Japanese culture. It involves a more disciplined approach, and the willingness to be part of a team and share with each other what is working and not working. Remember, the simple-problem solving formula: Set a standard and follow it (Japanese strength of discipline), improve the standard (American strength of innovation), set the new standard, and then share it with the rest of the team (Japanese strength).

This entails taking the best of both worlds. But one may well ask: Is there such thing as healthy competition between sections, departments and plants in Toyota culture? The answer is certainly. The key distinction embedded in the formula is that there is a system to share the improvements that the competition creates, and the system rewards the managers who share their success (and failures).

We should note that the spirit of competition is one of the sub principles of *The Toyota Way 2001* stating, "competition further improves our organization and its ability to add more value." The key here is that Toyota wants most of the competition to be with other companies and not within different departments of Toyota. Toyota also uses healthy competition internally, for example, stamping departments across Toyota plants focus on benchmarking and competing on key performance indicators. However, at the end of the day Toyota also wants those same stamping departments to share practices so they all can be strengthened to the benefit of the company. Obviously developing a culture with the right balance of competition and cooperation is challenging, even for Toyota.

## NO SOCIAL DIFFERENCES

A key part of Toyota culture and another example of intentional HR processes to build teamwork relates to minimizing social distinctions; that is, the philosophy that all are part of the same team, and that there are no differences between managers and employees, other than their roles within the company. As discussed in Chapter 2, the goal is to have a "we" attitude and atmosphere, not an "us versus them" outlook. There are several ways that Toyota practices what it preaches in this area, including:

- Everyone has the same dress code.
- There are no executive parking spaces or areas; members who arrive earliest get the closest parking spaces.
- There are no executive restrooms.
- There are no executive dining rooms or cafeterias; everyone eats in the same areas (except for dining rooms for special outside guests).
- There are no executive offices; all desks are in an open office environment.
- All members have the same basic benefits.
- Special offices, like a beautiful office for the President, are mainly to entertain outside guests and rarely used by the executives.

In the three-tier culture model from Chapter 1, these are all visible artifacts at the top-most surface level. It would be perfectly possible to copy all of these features and not get true teamwork. But when coupled with the organizational structure, and the consistent messages being sent every day by Toyota leaders, these visible organizational features send the message: "We are all part of the same team." In addition to the symbolic benefits of eating together, sitting close together in open offices, and managers going to the floor to manage, all these arrangements provide many opportunities for informal communication. This improves the quality of communication and provides opportunities to build trust. When everyone eats together there is opportunity to interact, communicate, and build trust. Open door policies are nice, but if there is a door, the "subordinate" still knows when she is entering the office of the "superior." Open office means there are no thresholds to cross.

Mike Hoseus recalls his experience as a human resources assistant general manager sitting in an open office:

*There was literally no place to hide. Any team member could walk up at any time during the day with a question, an issue, or a concern. It really held me and our management team accountable for the policies we enforced and the decisions we made. I looked at every "walk up person" as an "andon pull" for our Toyota people systems. Most often, there was some breakdown in the system or communication process that caused that person to need to come to me. It was then my job to do the same root cause-countermeasure problem solving that I did in production in order to prevent it from happening again. For example, the issue could be a complex one dealing with a person's corrective action process (Toyota's discipline system focused on problem solving not punishment), or something as simple as, "What time does the company picnic start on Saturday?" Each question or issue is part of a system, and part of it may have broken down for a team member to come to me. The open office also helped communication within the department and across departments. Sitting in the middle of 100 HR members was conducive to hearing and seeing what was going on at all times. Problems were easily identified and communicated.*

These conscious and intentional no social difference polices and practices do not mean there are no differences. Leaders at Toyota should not act as though they are higher status than team members, but they must still lead by example. Mike continues:

*My Japanese trainer taught me as a group leader to consider myself as working for my members and not the other way around, and not to treat myself any different than what I expected from them. For example, he said, "If you expect your members not to drink cola during production time, then you should not drink cola during production time. If you expect your members to use the restroom during break time in order to minimize disruption when the line is running, then you use the restroom at break time and not while the line is running." This turned out to be good basic management advice and the kind of example of practical, everyday behaviors that reinforced Toyota culture.*

## SUMMARY

Teamwork is an easy concept to talk about at seminars and in strategy meetings. In the Toyota culture there are intentional policies, processes, and practices that both support and encourage teamwork. The Toyota difference is that once a concept is part of the system, it is a practical expectation. It becomes part of the PDCA cycle of the organization. This means that it will be intentional, planned out, and implemented daily with corresponding observable, measurable actions and behaviors, and that its status will be checked regularly and any identified gaps addressed.

# KEY POINTS TO CONSIDER FOR YOUR COMPANY

1. The organization is intentional about instituting teams at every level in all directions of the company.
2. The every day work is divided into teams, and the standard is five to seven direct reports to each team leader. There are clear roles and responsibilities, but when a problem occurs the teams are trained to flexibly respond while still following defined procedures.
3. Work teams are engaged in daily work and problem solving, and the leaders of the teams play a key role in understanding the concerns of team members, facilitating problem solving, auditing standard work, and directing the team toward achieving measurable team objectives.
4. Problem-solving groups are temporary and set up to solve specific problems or lead specific projects. There are formal processes in place for training leaders of problem-solving groups, getting agreement on the goals of the group project, coaching and mentoring the groups, and using them as a vehicle for developing team members. Development of team members is at least as important as achieving specific targets.
5. There are processes and practices that support both vertical and horizontal teamwork in the organization, such as planning, cross functional work teams, and administrative departments that cut across all the functional departments.
6. Competition is encouraged as a way to motivate the company and individual teams to do their best to win, but at the end of the day the teams need to share what they have learned with other teams and work for the betterment of the company.
7. There are intentional policies and practices that minimize social differences between managers and members, but managers must still lead by example.

# Chapter 9

# Clean and Safe Workplace

*Undoubtedly the physiological needs are the most potent of all needs. A person who is lacking food, safety, love, and esteem would probably hunger for food more strongly than anything else.*

—Abraham Maslow, humanistic psychologist

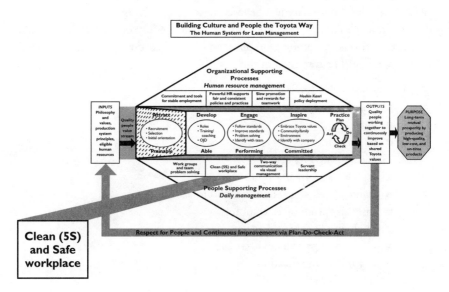

## A HOLISTIC APPROACH

A common story that is part of the Toyota lore is of a Toyota Japanese sensei who goes to a supplier to teach them the Toyota Production System. After a long trip to the plant he visits the rest room. Upon coming out he informs the plant manager that he is leaving. "The toilet is a mess," he says angrily. "Until you have the discipline to keep your toilet clean you are not ready for the Toyota Production System."

Whether or not this story is exactly true as told it reflects a fundamental value within Toyota culture placed on cleanliness and orderliness. Probably the easiest way to start our focus on a clean and safe work environment is to reiterate our earlier discussion of the basic 5S program. We explained that 5S sets the standard for the first step of problem solving and that it was the foundation for setting a proper work environment for all team members.

In Japan, Toyota refers to this as a clean and "pleasant" work environment. It is part of the continuous improvement cycle that weaves through the entire culture. It acts as a standard for problem solving, but also characterizes the larger company role and responsibility to ensure this type of environment for its employees and for continuously looking for ways to improve it.

The 5S program is considered as the foundation of safety by keeping everything organized and in its place, and properly labeled for everyone to see and know the standard. Indeed, many companies in their lean transformation have even made Safety, the sixth-S, which supports this important integration of cleanliness, organization, and safety. Toyota does not spell this out, in large part because safety is a given. Without safety it is believed nothing else matters.

A clean, pleasant, and safe environment in the Toyota culture is a holistic concept. It covers the entire workplace and is broken down into the following topics, which will be discussed in turn:

1. Physical Work Environment
   - cleanliness
   - lighting
   - temperature
2. Physically Safe Processes
   - ergonomic jobs and rotations
   - standardized work, training, and follow up
   - early symptom investigation
3. Psychologically Safe
   - safe and respectful environment
   - cognitive simplification
   - safety culture
4. Personal Health and Safety
   - effectively deal with work restrictions
   - easy access to quality medical care
   - easy access to proper medication

## THE PHYSICAL WORK ENVIRONMENT: CLEAN, WELL LIT AND COMFORTABLE

Thousands of people tour the Georgetown Toyota plant each year, and the most common comment heard after the conclusion of the tour is: "I can't believe how clean it is for a factory." The common paradigm of a factory is still one of an old dirty sweat shop. In contrast, 5S is part of the overall Toyota culture, and not just on the plant floor. It extends to all areas: administration, the contents of supply cabinets, and even the appearance of personal desk areas. And, of course, this priority must be balanced with the other business indicators: safety, morale, quality, productivity, and environment.

One example of balancing these indicators occurred in the Georgetown plant with regard to lighting. As part of efforts to take care of the environment and reduce energy costs, the goal in the plant was to reduce the cost of lighting. There are two types of lighting in the production areas: sets of large overhead lights and sets just above the cars in the work areas. The first step was to turn out every other high ceiling light and to turn off every other fluorescent bulb on the lines.

This step cut the cost of the lighting by 50 percent, but the team members responded negatively to the change. They identified some quality concerns as a result of not being able to inspect for defects with the dimmed lighting. Following the Toyota Way of problem solving, a kaizen team utilized member ideas by replacing the normal white fluorescent light holders with highly reflective mirror-like aluminum holders that provided the sufficient illumination needed. They maintained keeping every other light turned off. This improvement kept the energy costs for line-side lighting at 50 percent and brought the lighting results almost back to the level of two bulbs.

This situation was adequate for a time, but then experimentation and problem solving indicated that the brightness of the lighting had a direct relationship to better quality and increased team member satisfaction. Accordingly, Toyota set a new standard for the minimum amount of lighting of a team member work area.

Following this standard, both types of lights, including those directly over the work area, utilized the new reflective holders yielding crisp, bright work areas that facilitated improved quality and morale. Meanwhile, the cost reduction from the large overhead ceiling lights was increased by turning them off in unused areas, and continuing to reduce them in many others. Also, all but minimal lights were automatically turned off when the line stopped and team members went on break or lunch. The result of these efforts was continuous improvement with increased trust and respect. Employees were listened to and ultimately developed creative solutions that satisfied quality, safety, morale, and energy efficiency.

Toyota culture seeks a balance between cost reduction and team member comfort, with team member comfort often getting the priority. Another example of this approach is the temperature of the plant. Heating and air conditioning are expensive in a large plant but being too cold or hot is not a safe, pleasant work environment for team members. The improvement activity started with a standard. Using research, surveys of employees, and trial data, the standard set for temperature in the plant was that it goes no lower than 65 degrees in the winter and no higher than 79 degrees in the summer. (The standard set point refers to the equipment settings, similar to a thermostat in a house, while the standard actual temperature maximum in any work area is set at or below 82 degrees.) With the standard set for team member environmental comfort, the challenge was to achieve those levels while reducing costs if possible!

Similar to the lighting improvement, the key to temperature efficiency was to ensure that the heat and cooling reached the team members but not the non-work areas of the whole plant. The idea implemented, known as "wind socks," took air from large overhead vents, that had previously heated and cooled the entire plant, and funneled the air directly to the team member on the line. The result was improved working conditions with a net decrease in temperature maintenance costs.

# PHYSICALLY SAFE PROCESSES

The team members' most basic need is to be physically safe in their everyday activities. A key part of the Toyota culture is that safety is first. If a team member's job is not safe, the company can forget about establishing an atmosphere of trust and respect.

This is easier said than done in an automobile factory that involves much manual labor. There is heavy duty equipment and machinery that can cause serious injury and even death. Hazards include chemicals (e.g., paint), weld sparks, multi-ton dies stamping out parts, hot plastic, and more. Even in the more benign manual assembly jobs there are physically demanding, repetitive motions that can cause serious cumulative trauma injuries which are invisible on a day-to-day basis. What are the steps that address these hazards?

## Design in Ergonomically Safe Jobs

Designing in safety is always the goal for Toyota. Many times the root causes of issues can be traced to the design of the part and the assembly process. Assembling an automobile is a complex task with thousands of parts coming from hundreds of first-tier and lower-tier suppliers. As discussed in the last chapter, the key to safety is to set standards for parts and the assembly processes, and then to continually apply the PDCA improvement process until all standards are met. One source of safety problem is from the design of work that leads to strain and stress on the body, a dynamic addressed by the applied science "ergonomics." An example of an "ergonomic design guideline" is shown in Table 9.1[1] with setting the maximum push force on assembling any part that requires pushing with the thumb to not exceed 3 kg and ideally to be less than 1 kg. This maximum force

---

[1] Sources TMMK uses for ergonomics knowledge include: *TMC Ergonomic Manual, 2001; Hand Wrist Cumulative Trauma Disorders in Industry* (Silverstein, 1986); Corlett and Clark, *The Ergonomics of Workspaces and Machines*, 1995 Bodyspace, Pheasant, 1998; Ergo Design for People at Work, E. Kodak, 1986; MOD 00–25, *UK Military Standards Handbook of Human Factors*, Bullinger, Kern, & Braun, pg. 703; *Handbook of Human Factors*, Schmidtke TMMK/University of Louisville Study, 2001.

**Table 9.1** Example Ergonomic Guideline for Push Force for Part Assembly

| Item | Sketch | Criteria | Purpose | Design Application |
|------|--------|----------|---------|--------------------|
| Push with thumb | | Pushing with thumb where surface area <30mm² (approx area of a finger tip). If a digit cannot be supported, a limit of I kg push is recommended. | The structure of the finger/thumb tips is not suitable for absorbing high contact stresses, which can result in injury to the nerves, tendons and ligaments. | Where forces exceed guideline alternatives may be used to reduce the required force or to improve the grip or surface area so greater force may be generated safely. |

| Should Not Exceed | Ideal Value | Typical Part/ Example | Measurement Criteria |
|-------------------|-------------|------------------------|----------------------|
| æ 3 kg | ≤I kgf | Single clip Grommet | Measured using a push/pull gauge or load cell. Measure should reflect as closely as possible production conditions such as time required to complete and line of force. |

of 3 kg equals about the same amount of pressure needed to push a thumb tack into a bulletin board.

The Japanese from Toyota made sure that these ergonomic guidelines were just that, guidelines and not standards. As we have said, standards at Toyota are powerful and the idea is that the company works to get there and won't stop until it does. So, for example, if a part took more than 3 kg to push in then it is out of standard and the engineers would have to work until the part was able to be assembled with 3 kg push or less. This is not always the case with part design and ergonomics so it is considered a guideline. The design engineers' goal is still to meet the 3 kg guideline and they are accountable to do so. However, when it is extremely difficult to do so and cost prohibitive, the "out of guideline" condition will be passed on to the manufacturing engineers. Their job will be to work with the team members and design a tool or jig to assist the operator in pushing in the part such that it puts less than 3 kg stress on the thumb. The positive effect is the same to the operator, but it is done through process improvements instead of product design.

In this context, the PDCA process is never ending: the goal is to keep improving the standards. Once they are met with respect to one model, the process must anticipate a major model change happening every four to five years. With that schedule the design and manufacturing of parts and corresponding assembly occur all over again. Understandably, the goal in these major model changeovers is to use them as additional opportunities to improve all the major indicators: safety, quality, productivity, cost, and HR.

One of the tools that allow Toyota product engineers to design in safety is the digital assembly process. Engineers use software to build 3-D replicas of the person doing the assembly task work station by work station. The person is in animated form. This is used for a virtual design review which includes engineers from product development, production engineering, and people from the plant including hourly employees on the pilot team.

One example Georgetown members are particularly proud of is an innovation in the engineering of the Camry. There are a set of jobs in which the team member does assembly tasks in the engine compartment under the hood such as installing fluid reservoirs. The team member had to bend over the front grill to do this work in an awkward posture that could over time damage the back. Team members suggested that the front bars and grill be added after all assembly under the hood was complete. This allowed the team member to walk into the engine compartment and do the assembly work without bending over. It also improved productivity. It required an engineering change to the vehicle and a change in the process so that the front radiator and structural supports are attached late in the process allowing team members to walk into the engine compartment to work on the engine. This was done well before the launch of the vehicle as a result of cooperation between production and product engineering.

## Ergonomic Ratings and Rotations

Toyota devotes a great deal of effort to preventing injuries, especially those involving cumulative trauma and these are identified through the use of ergonomic ratings. Toyota did have some serious problems with cumulative trauma in the past and as a learning organization made it a priority to solve these problems. Since cumulative trauma is cumulative and also somewhat specific to the individual, you cannot judge at a point in time exactly what exposure will lead to long-term problems for any given individual. Ergonomic ratings provide an indication of potential problems and jobs lower on the ratings have a lower risk of long-term problems. Toyota works to minimize the risk and tracks the improvements made on the ratings, as well as using them to set up a proper ergonomic rotation for each team and team member.

The ergonomic ratings identify unnatural or overburdened positions for either the upper or lower body. By assigning objective rating numbers to each process, Toyota is able to set a standard that takes into account industry standards and internal plant history, and labels a job as red (a high burden), yellow (medium burden), or green (least burden). Based on these ratings, standards can be set for rotating team members.

Job rotation is a vital part of the Toyota culture; we talked about it in the teamwork section as being the key framework of continuous improvement. Job rotation is also a key to prevention of repetitive motion injuries. This was highlighted at the Georgetown Plant during its maturation. As Mike Hoseus explained in Chapter 8, there were many injuries during the ramp up of the second plant at that location, as the first plant was running at full production. The designing in of safety standards helped during future models, but an additional factor that helped improve the safety record was the power of the ergonomic rotation.

Mike explains: "It was one of those things that we learned for ourselves as part of our plant maturation. We were experiencing many cumulative trauma injuries at our facility while the plants in Japan were not. It was an issue we had to solve together locally since the Japanese trainers couldn't give us the answer. We found some key differences in the plants. One was a part fit issue with the new suppliers, and the other was the difference in body type diversity between American workers and those in Japan."

The workers in Japan are very similar, with body type heights and weights in a close range. Therefore, when a job is set up in Japan to work on part of a car, nearly everyone is working with the same angles and burden. In the United States, there a big variation of body types; there can be a 5-foot, 90-pound female doing the job, and then a 250-pound, 6-foot male. These differences accentuated the ergonomic issues and resulted in an increase of injuries. Many countermeasures were tested to address the injuries, but the main solution came from identifying short- through long-term countermeasures.

- Short-term: Set up ergonomic rotations
- Mid-term: Design work stations to adjust to any body type or height
- Long-term: Design vehicle and parts with safety standards in place

Design standards are powerful, but it became clear they needed to be supplemented by job rotation. Basically, this means that if a team member is working on a job reaching over his shoulders for two hours, then the next job he does will not be an upper body burden. He will go to one where he works at or below the waist. Likewise, if he is working on any red, heavy burden job for two hours, he will not go to another red job for the rest of the day. Figure 9.1, taken from a TMMK Process Diagnostics Manual, shows an example of four muscle groups that are under burden in four different jobs. You would not want to burden the same muscle group three times or even twice during a day.

Similar to other aspects of Toyota culture, the standard has to be set and then improvement activities start. For example, the assembly department had to look at

**Figure 9.1** Four jobs Using Four Muscle Groups

the rotation of almost 1,000 people in order to see what was actually happening at the work stations. Of course, before the awareness and standard was set, there were imbalances all over the place. So, one by one, the team members studied their job in terms of ergonomic ratings, and the team designed rotations that met the standard. In some cases, no changes were made other than adjusting the rotation as shown in Figure 9.2. However, it quickly became apparent that red jobs had to be reduced to no more than one per team so that every team member would perform only one per day. Some groups were able to be creative with short-term countermeasures and worked together, in situations where there was one team with two red jobs and another with none; they switched jobs and made up new teams so that each team had one red job each.

These changes helped reduce risk in the short term, but the real key to increasing long-term safety were to get to the root cause by reducing the number of red jobs in the plant. Two examples of this activity are some improvements that team members and support groups helped to implement. The first was known as the "Wal-Mart Bass Boat Improvement." The team members were working in the wheel well of the front of a vehicle and running wires through it that attached to

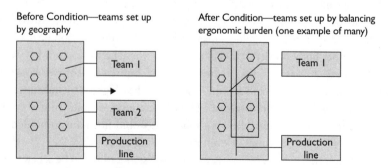

**Figure 9.2** Adjustment to Job Rotation to Balance Ergonomic Burden

other parts. Prior to the improvement, they had to bend over at the waist for the entire job to perform the tasks. The team worked on improvement ideas and brainstormed the idea of riding on a chair, sitting down the whole time they did the job, they wouldn't have to bend over at all.

With the power of teamwork and support from the skilled trade's maintenance group and engineering, the simple track and seat design was planned. During the building of the seat, the team searched through trade catalogs to find a seat that would function. They could not find a suitable one, they were all expensive, and the delivery schedule would take weeks. Another member of the team, who was an avid fisherman, suggested that a seat for a bass boat would do the trick: it was built to sit in all day, it had a head rest, and it had swivel action capability. The team agreed and the next day he brought in a bass boat seat, and they were able to implement their new sit down job countermeasure. It was the envy of many teams; they could sit down, improve the safety of the job, and improve the value-added time of the job.

Many other sitting devices have been continually improved over the years from Japan and elsewhere and then shared with other plants. These seats can handle virtually any size person and position them in and out the car, or ride alongside and prevent the need to crawl in and out, kneel down, bend over, or stretch to do their work. They have been a tremendous help in reducing ergonomic risks, red jobs, and injuries (see Figure 9.3).

Another example of a simple improvement in safety at the Georgetown plant used adjustable platforms. The chassis areas of the plant have always had many jobs that required the team member to reach overhead in order to perform the jobs. By making platforms that move up and down at the push of a button, any size person can perform the task between waist and shoulders at a safe level (see Figure 9.4). This ability to adjust the working conditions/job configuration reduced the ergonomic risks and the injuries that high-risk jobs create.

Strong leadership and engaging team member ideas have lead to virtually the elimination of all ergonomically red jobs in the plant. Instead of rotating around the red jobs the management team set the goal and the standard that there would be no more red jobs, in the plant. This is easier said than done and is a never ending process. Small changes in jobs, like team members rebalancing tasks from job to job for other improvement reasons, completely change the ergonomic rating of the new job. Part of the standard in doing so is to complete a new rating to confirm it is not red, and to make improvements if it is. The same activity is done plant wide for each model change, when the parts and processes all change. Other times there are subtle changes that are not always recognized. A small deviation in a part from a supplier can have a big impact, and is not always detectable by the operator. For this reason, it is also part of the plant safety standards that all processes will be reevaluated twice a year to confirm that they are still out of the red.

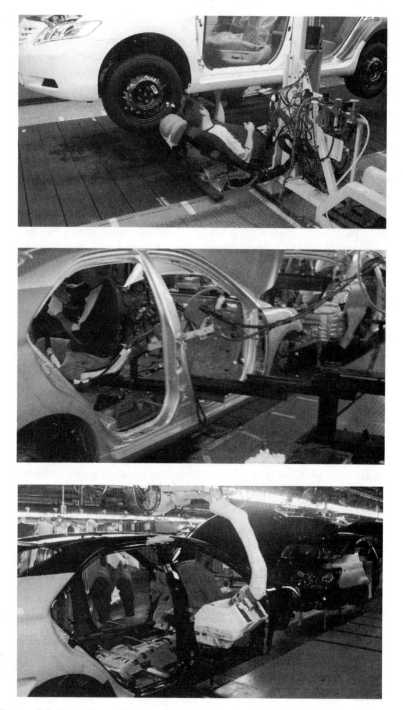

**Figure 9.3** Examples of Seating Devices to Reduce Awkward Postures (*Continued on next page*)

**Figure 9.3** Examples of Seating Devices to Reduce Awkward Postures (*Continued from previous page*)

## The KYT Meeting

The Kiken Yochi Training meeting, referred to at TMMK as the KYT meeting, is a routine daily five-minute meeting that takes place with each work team for the purpose of keeping all team members focused on safety. Kiken Yocki can be roughly translated as "danger foresee." The idea of the meeting is for team members to be aware of the environment and to anticipate any unsafe hazard that is present in the workplace. It may be an unsafe behavior that is related to oneself or other teammates. The problem is identified, discussed and countermeasures established as part of the meeting.

This daily meeting is a quick huddle for the team, like a time out in a basketball game for everyone to stop, step back, and gain perspective. This keeps safety first and part of the everyday behavior and culture. It also demonstrates the company's safety priority for the team members by stopping the line for five minutes everyday, on company time, to discuss safety.

## Standardized Work, Job Instruction, and Safety

When Toyota manages safety they look at both the process and person in order to make sure there are no injuries. It is often the case that standardized work is a cost reduction tool to improve worker productivity. At Toyota it is also a key safety tool. Standardized work means setting up the job so safety hazards and risk factors for cumulative trauma disorders are eliminated. The next step is to train the worker properly so they do the job safely. A process may be set up safely, but if a person is doing it unsafely, then an injury can still occur. For this reason, safety is integrated into the fundamental skills training, standardized work sheets,

**Figure 9.4** Example of Adjustable Platform for Different Sized People

job instruction training, and follow-up systems. We do not believe a company can do a great job on safety without having all of these elements (and few do).

The computerized fundamental skills training area (GPC), discussed in Chapter 5, is where all new members are taught how to shoot bolts and make electrical connections, such as in the assembly area. The computerized visual manuals also include general, but important, safety key points involved when using an air tool and making connections. For example, it is very common for new hires to be nervous and excited about doing a good job so they inadvertently squeeze the air tool so tightly that veins are obvious in their wrists and arms. Unless they are told and trained not to do so, they will continue this until they finally suffer an injury. As part of the video training and human follow up, they are taught to hold the gun very gently and to squeeze the trigger with the base of their finger instead of the tip, and to let the gun do the work. This avoids injuries to the wrist and index fingers.

As part of standardized work, the safety key points are always noted on the work descriptions and highlighted with a shaded cross (see Figure 9.5). This particular job is to install a "register duct." The standardized work outlines the steps in sequence to perform the job to takt time. It also shows the movement of the team member as he performs the steps. Certain steps have been found to have potential safety issues. These have been marked with a green cross. For example, when you secure the register ducts with five screws in step 8, there is a potential safety issue. Down at the bottom in the comments section we see that you should be keeping your wrist neutral as you shoot the screws with an air tool. Twisting your wrist downward or upward (flexion or extension) over repeated cycles over the long term can lead to carpal tunnel syndrome.

Whenever there is a green cross on the standardized worksheet description, the associated job breakdown sheet used for job instruction training will include the details of the correct way to perform the job, along with an example of an incorrect approach. These details are usually shown with a visual and include such things as the correct angle to stand, or the correct angle or height to hold the air tool so that the team member's wrist is not in an unsafe position (see Figure 9.6). We should note that in this particular example in Figure 9.6, working overhead is itself not great, but at least holding the air tool with a neutral wrist position is much better. Job instruction training is the missing link in turning well-designed standardized work into daily practice in the work place. We call it the missing link because even those companies that have adopted the lean practice of standardized work, rarely have developed the disciplined process of job instruction training.

Once a team member is trained to follow the standardized work and perform the job safely there is one more step—follow up. At Toyota it is expected that team leaders, group leaders, and even assistant managers audit jobs daily. In the group leader's domain of about 20 team members, one job per day is observed so each

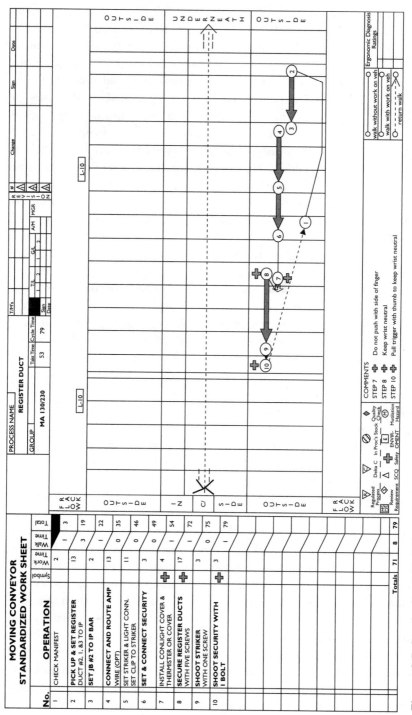

**Figure 9.5** Standardized Work Example Highlighting Potential Safety Concerns

**Figure 9.6** No Good and Good Way to Perform the Job

job is observed each month. The group leader uses the standard work sheet and possibly the more detailed job breakdown sheet to observe workers performing that job and looks for deviations from the standard. The team leaders also do this within their smaller teams and observe each team member more frequently. As a key part of these daily standardized work checks, the team leaders and group leaders confirm that the team members are following the safety key points. Deviations can lead to coaching the team members or reconsidering the physical set up or the standard work itself to prevent unsafe practices from occurring.

We have already discussed the power of standardized work and training for the problem solving and continuous improvement process. It is the system to take what has been learned from a problem and standardize it so that all who do that job follow today's best practice. The same is true for safety. By utilizing standardized work, and training systems for safety, it is integrated into the Toyota culture; it is not a stand alone, safety department initiative. It is the way to do business.

## Early Symptom Intervention

When Ernie Richardson was rotated from his position as manager of the Georgetown powertrain plant to the manager of safety and medical management for the entire plant he had a challenge. As a manager in a plant he had responsibility for the safety in his section, but now he was responsible for medical management of the entire plant. This type of rotation is not uncommon within Toyota and is designed to broaden the individual as well as bring fresh ideas to the job. Ernie was thoroughly trained in the Toyota problem-solving method so he started at the beginning—What is the objective? He did some *nemawashi*, discussing safety with many parties, and identified the goal as to never hurt anyone—not a single person and if they get hurt it is a significant event.

On further investigation Ernie discovered he should go even further. Fortunately serious injuries were a fairly rare event at Georgetown but emphasizing them as significant events was not enough. He needed to prevent these events just as one would do in quality—zero defects comes from prevention not detection. So he began to focus on Early Symptom Intervention (ESI). Why not fix the process before it gets out of control?

It did not take long to justify any cost of ESI. The Georgetown plant took $25 million out of workers compensation reserves in two years. The plant happened to be up for renewal for short-term and long-term disability at the end of this period. For the first time there was no rate change. Usually if Toyota stayed the same they would see at least a 15 percent increase per year, but they have actually been decreasing the costs annually since ESI. The goal is decreasing overall medical expenses each year. For example, worker compensation costs (work related injuries), short-term personal leaves, and long-term disability costs were reduced by 40 percent under Ernie's watch. With a plant of 7,400 workers, that equals millions of dollars a year.

The ESI is a system built on the assumption that the earlier a problem is identified, the better chance to put in preventive countermeasures. Cumulative trauma injuries build over time; they start with a team member having difficulty on a process, building to discomfort, experiencing pain, and finally a resulting injury. The goal is to educate the team members to pull the andon (figuratively) and identify the problem at the earliest stage, solve the problem, and prevent the problem from causing the team member to go to medical services (IHS) to be treated for an injury (see Figure 9.7).

When the andon is pulled for team member discomfort and an ESI is opened, the system begins. It sounds like common sense to say that when a team member is experiencing discomfort, pull the andon (figurafively) and solve the problem. In reality, while this is true, there are many obstacles that can get in the way of that

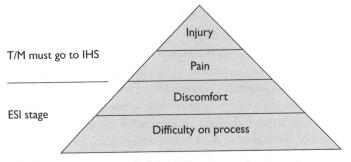

First prevention, then identify abnormality at first opportunity

**Figure 9.7** Early Symptom Intervention Program

**Table 9.2** Early Symptom Intervention Operating Guideline

| Summary of Key Steps | Timing | Lead | Support |
|---|---|---|---|
| 1. T/M first report of discomfort/difficulty | | T/M | |
| 2. Initiate "New Case" and gather basic information | ≤ 24 hours | G/L | T/M |
| 3. Investigation | ≤ 2 working days | G/L | ESI |
| 4. Countermeasure Plan | ≤ 5 working days | G/L | ESI |
| 5. Countermeasure Implementation—Short Term/temporary | ≤ 10 working days | G/L | Sect Mgmt |
| 6. Assessment by Rehab Consultant for all cases open >10 days* | >10 ≤ 15 working days | Rehab | ESI |
| 7. Countermeasure Implementation | ≤ 20 working days | G/L | Sect Mgmt |
| 8. Countermeasure Confirmation | ≤ 20 working days | T/M | ESI/G/L |

* Up to the 10th day assessment by the Rehab Consultant is optional. All cases open greater than 10 days must be assessed before the 15th day.

**Definitions**
ESI Case—T/M who has reported signs of discomfort/difficulty as the result of cumulative stresses.
ESI Team—A T/M or T/Ms designated by a section's management to support the ESI Program.
Rehab Consultant—A medical provider assigned to support the ESI Program.
Cumulative Injury—Injury or disorder arising over time from repeated exposure to physical stressors.
Acute Injury—Injury resulting from a single traumatic event.
(Source: Internal TMMK Document on Operating Procedures for ESI)

sequence actually happening. In a PDCA system, there has to be awareness, support, accountability, and standards. The ESI system has all of these. Table 9.2 shows the milestones of the response once the team member has pulled the andon. There are clear standards for the response time leading up to establishing countermeasures, implementing them, confirming they have worked, and closing the case within 20 days.

Once the ESI is opened, tracking and accountability start, and soon after the investigation problem solving begins. The first step is to talk to the team member who is the expert on what is happening, and gather his or her perspective on the situation and problem. She will be able to identify key things, such as when the discomfort started and whether anything changed in the process, or in the required movements near this time.

Group leaders and members of the ESI team are trained to be able to identify certain symptoms. Table 9.3 shows an example of one such symptom in the hands and wrists. The full table includes a number of these symptoms for all parts of the body, including neck and shoulders, shoulder and forearms and so on.

**Table 9.3** Example Symptoms in Hands and Wrists

| Symptoms | Postures/ Movements | Forces/ Loads | Check For |
|---|---|---|---|
| Pins and needles/numbness to the medial aspect (little finger side) of the hand/finger | Prolonged flexion or extension of the wrist | Hammering with hand pressure around the base of the thumb or side of hand | • Poor parts fit<br>• Tool not used or unavailable<br>• No fixtures to hold work steady e.g., pushing in fuses while holding box |

Next, the team member is observed, and in many cases videotaped, to allow for more focused analysis of potential causes. There may be job elements at fault, or specific team member movements or postures. The team has training and resources at its disposal to be able to identify postures that will lead to injury if repeated and sustained for a long time. An example of "no good postures" for the neck is shown in Figure 9.8

Finally, the ESI program sets performance and process indicators to initiate a continual PDCA process for tracking the process, (e.g., ESI case opened and closed, countermeasures implemented, team member compliance, and so on) and its effect on the specific business indicators, such as the OSHA Recordable Incident Rate, which looks at the rate of injuries per employee. These results are then reviewed as part of each department's safety meeting each month, and then shared at the plantwide safety meeting with all department managers present. These meetings serve to facilitate accountability for the managers and group leaders, and allow

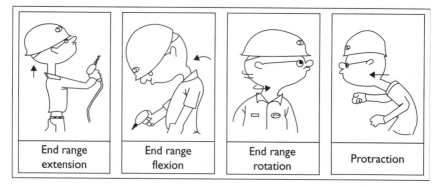

| End range extension | End range flexion | End range rotation | Protraction |
|---|---|---|---|

**Figure 9.8** Illustrating Posture Risk Factors of the Neck

sharing, or *yokoten* (Japanese term for sharing practices), of good ideas across the entire plant.

Ernie is proud to report that as a result of strong leadership and continual improvement of these safety processes, the plant has improved dramatically in its safety results. The industry standard for measuring safety is in the OSHA Recordable Incident Rate. In the late 1990s, the plant was up in the upper 20s for its recordable incident rate. This was average for the industry but Toyota's goal is not to be average in anything. The incident rate now is consistently below 10 and on its way down toward five. This is among the best in the industry and Toyota will not be satisfied until it hits zero. This company challenge has also translated into a continued personal challenge for Ernie. Because of his acquired experience in safety and his leadership in facilitating such improvement, Ernie was assigned as the manager for safety and medical management for all North America Manufacturing.

# PSYCHOLOGICALLY SAFE IN THE PLANT

Safety includes more than just physical safety; it is also means feeling safe psychologically. This starts with a respectful environment where team members do not fear psychological abuse. It also refers to protection from an overly stressful job. We have emphasized that Toyota challenges employees, but there is a difference between challenge and psychological stress. Finally, the culture itself must be openly based on the value of a safe and secure environment for team members as the highest priority.

## Safe and Respectful Environment

We have already discussed that a team member must feel secure in the act of bringing up a problem and that the company or the supervisor will not punish him for it. This same concept carries over into the larger context of the culture. Mike Hoseus reflects back to his early years at TMMK:

> *I remember early on in the Georgetown plant's history that as supervisors we were given the message that we were not to tolerate any disrespectful actions, messages, or symbols of any kind directed at any person or groups of people. I was told to think about the plant, and specifically my team, and to act as though my mother or my daughter were working here. That's how I was to expect it to be. Correspondingly, there were to be no "pin-up calendars" or lewd pictures in the plant or the locker rooms. Cussing of any kind was not to be a part of the conversation on the plant floor, in the management meetings, or anywhere. I think this kind of disrespectful behavior is less common in workplaces today, but twenty years ago, Toyota was breaking new ground*

*in the factory culture with these types of expectations. I remember hearing Cheryl Jones, current vice president of manufacturing at the Georgetown plant, answer a question from a visitor about what surprised her most about working for Toyota. She answered that she always felt safe, as a woman, working here, and that she appreciated the culture of respect and trust demonstrated by no cussing, no offensive pictures of women, and the capability of women to be promoted upward in the organization. She had prepared herself for the "rough" environment of a factory and it is not what she found at Toyota. As a man, her answer was one I would not have thought of, but hearing it expressed from a woman made me appreciate it as part of the culture, and I no longer took it for granted.*

## Cognitive Simplification: Challenging but not Stressful

In Toyota culture, there is a concept that a person's work should be challenging but not stressful; everyone is expected to follow standards, improve their process, and solve problems. This improvement process allows members to tap into creative gifts and unleash the potential of their imaginations. However, if a person is under stress, his potential is hampered. As part of the Center for Quality People and Organization's work with improvement in schools, we became aware of current brain research showing that if a student is under stress, from home or at school, the fight or flight area of the brain is activated, and when this area is activated, it shuts down the other areas of the brain, including the front area which is responsible for creative thinking.

In school culture they talk about making sure the student is relaxed during the day, in a trusting environment free from stress, in order to promote the best learning. These findings seem to echo some of the values and practices of Toyota culture. The same principles of relationships built on trust and reducing stress at the process appear to be beneficial in education and industry. The team member is healthier and more prone to develop creative ideas which are good for the individual member and for the company.

Early on in the Georgetown plant's history, group leaders were coached to make sure the processes were not stressful, and to allow the team members time to think. One philosophical Japanese trainer referred to it as "Allowing the Zen to happen." He explained that if the team members' minds were full, there was no room left to do the job of creative thinking. The group leaders had to make sure the members were able to have a free mind. The trainer also observed that the same problem can happen on the other end of the spectrum. If the process is too light and not challenging at all, the team members are likely to spend time thinking about everything other than improvements to the job. The key was to find the balance.

This has been put into practice in the Georgetown plant as a cognitive simplification process. Charles Luttrell, assistant general manager of the assembly plant in Georgetown, explained the simplification process as a system to achieve three things: to develop the process to. have smooth flow, to keep memory requirements simple, and to make the motion simple. As Charles explained:

*It is all about reducing the burden on the team member by setting standards and then making improvements in order to meet those standards. This activity has been the focus of improvement for the last couple of years. Even with adding the hybrid Camry, that increased the complexity of build, we have been able to meet these simplification standards. We have redesigned jobs to keep the member in one area of the car, and the biggest success has been realized by reducing the number of decisions a member has to make to build each car.*

*In Assembly, for each car the member has to decide which one of many parts goes on the car based upon whether the car is an Avalon or a Camry or Solara, whether it is six cylinder or four, a standard model or deluxe, and what color it is, etc. Our system found that most internal defects came from processes that required making over three decisions on selecting parts. That's understandable since, at 55 seconds a car, the member doesn't have much time to choose. We set the standard (or goal) to get 80 percent of all Assembly processes to a "green simple" rating of having less than three decisions to make for each car. The most work and improvements have come in the area of part presentation. We have moved the decisions for selecting the parts to the part area off-line, and have taken it off the member on the line. This is done by sequencing parts in their order of build for the online member, or actually making a kit for the member by putting the parts for an entire process in one box, therefore, all the members on line have to do is go to the same place each time and pick the part or the box.*

*They still confirm that it is the right part, but no longer have to take the time to make the decision and go and find the part. In many cases, we now give this freed up time to the member to confirm the installation, and make quality checks. We are placing more emphasis on reducing team member burden and improving quality than achieving productivity. We have gone from 36 percent "simple green" processes to 64 percent and meanwhile we have added new models that have increased complexity. We have reduced our internal defect rate by over 30 percent in the entire plant. We are continuing our plant-wide improvements and there are worldwide meetings with designers in order to simplify components and get the best part structures to simplify the decision for the members on the line.*

This simplification process in Toyota culture starts with the attitude that the team members on the line are the experts and, since they represent the only value-added work in the company, we have to take care of them. One Japanese trainer told Mike Hoseus that the member online is to be thought of as a doctor performing surgery. The material handler's job is there to support the expert and to hand them the tools and supplies they need, right when they need them, without them having to think about it, so they can free up their mind to focus on the important part of taking care of the vehicle.

## Safety Culture

Ernie Richardson credits TMMK's dramatic improvement in the plant's recordable incident rate with a few key systems: early symptom intervention, management support and accountability, and instituting a safety culture. He describes how the plant progressed from a behavior-focused method to a culture-focused system.

> In the past we focused on behaviors of people and it was a list of do's and don'ts that centered around individuals looking at other individuals and pointing out what they were doing wrong. We saw some early positive results, but we were not able to sustain them. Instead we decided to look deeper at our core values as a company and as a team. We chose to focus on our culture and how we thought and the reasons we did what we did. This is a more internal approach as opposed to the external, behavior-based approach.

Ernie credits Gary Convis and his coming to TMMK as the impetus for the change.

> He was a real champion for our safety. He basically said that we were good, but not good enough and that we were going to improve. With his leadership we were able to involve the entire executive team in changing our culture. The first thing we had to do as an executive team was to admit that we weren't where we needed to be and we had to change the management culture before looking at the team member culture. The team agreed and made a long-term plan to go department by department, based on the total incident rate, to go through the process to change the culture. The team agreed to dedicate a full-time safety specialist to coordinate the initiative.

Early in the launch of this project the safety specialist assigned to the area transferred to another position, so the team had an opening to fill. They decided to look internally to find the right fit for the job. They wanted somebody from the production floor with hands-on experience who also had some safety knowledge. They selected Terri Manning who was working as a team member in the body weld area. She had experience working with the Section Safety Committee, and she was part of the Early Symptom Intervention team. She is another example of the "People Value Stream" in terms of the way she was trained, engaged, and committed in her job as a team member and had taken initiative to be involved in extracurricular developmental opportunities. Now she was put into the position to continue to grow as a former team member, responsible for a plant-wide initiative, aimed at changing the culture of each department's management team. Terri described to us the four-phase process she was taking every department through in order to implement a Safety Culture.

- Phase I involves educating the department management team: TMMK decided to include everyone from the group leader up. This phase helps everyone understand how culture affects safety. It is at a general level.
- Phase II is divided into three steps with the first being a team member assessment. The assessment asks questions directed specifically at the culture and the way things are done around here with regard to safety. In order to promote honest answers with the team members, it is done anonymously yet at the same time the answers are displayed for all to see. Second, there are focus groups held in order to go over the results of the survey and have open, honest discussions with all the team members regarding what they think the problems are. The team members are able to be completely candid and often name names of managers they think are not helping in the area of safety. The third step is for Terri to summarize the team members' comments from the focus groups and prepare a report for the management team's review. This is a difficult but powerful session and gains the buy in and commitment to take action.
- Phase III involves putting together grassroot's teams designed to include and empower team members to get involved. In order to support the grassroot's teams a management guidance team is also formed. The guidance team at TMMK is made up of seven to nine members from every level in the section from the general manager to the team member. These members are also a part of each grassroot's team with one person going to all meetings as a coach. This helps build in a level of accountability to the process for both management and team members. The grassroot's teams then enlist other volunteer team members to take action.

The team uses their assessment results (from Phase II) in order to prioritize where and how to take action. A common theme for all the teams was to not invent anything new, but to look at the current programs and see how to create a better culture of safety around them. One small example: a team didn't want another newsletter but they also didn't want to get rid of the one they had. It had good information but the current culture didn't see it as important or meaningful. They partnered with the department general manager to spend a couple of hours at the plant's doors to personally hand a newsletter to each team member and thank them for taking safety seriously. It was a small gesture but a significant event that quickly became part of the lore and culture of the department.

Another grassroots example goes even deeper into problem solving. This team was looking at the ESI program and found that the number of new cases was declining while their incident rate was not. They found out, literally at the grassroots level, that team members were reluctant to raise their hands and say they had a problem early because they found out their two year "workers compensation clock" got started at that point. They were actually being penalized if they followed the early detection process. This was unintentional by management and the policy was changed immediately to start the clock the first time the member went to the clinic for treatment. Now the members are rewarded for early detection and correction.

Another example of how the culture has changed is with the group leaders. It was found that so much administration and daily checks had been added to their role that it was difficult for them to accomplish them all. The role of the group leader was reviewed and many of the daily tasks were found to be non-value added and were therefore eliminated. The goal was to focus on the processes and checks that made the most positive impact. These included the ergonomic ratings and rotation, the ESI program, and a daily standardized work posture confirmation. The daily posture confirmation is done by the group leader observing one team member per process per day and verifying that all of their body postures are correct. They note any deviation and what was done to correct it. Within the current safety culture this is done as a partnership with the team members and not as a police action to catch somebody doing something wrong.

■ Phase IV is focused on sustaining the teams and the improvements that occur. It works toward the long term downward trend, taking out the peaks and valleys. This is currently the case at TMMK, with grassroot's teams meeting once a week, some during production time. The improvements keep coming and the incident rate continues to fall. Ernie cites incident rates for departments implementing this safety culture that are literally being cut in half within two years.

Ernie and Terri are very encouraged with the progress made over a few years in the safety culture of the plant and are working hard sharing the lessons learned with other Toyota plants.

# TEAM MEMBER CARE—PERSONAL HEALTH AND SAFETY

While the goal is zero injuries, things happen. They happen at work and they happen outside of work. There is still a need to care for team members.

## Dealing with Workers on Restrictions

What do you do when a team member does develop some sort of work restriction? The conventional response is send them home. Ernie Richardson discovered that, in fact, sending them home may not be best for the company or the injured team member:

> We made a big improvement in how we treated the team members who did get hurt. We found sending them home was not good for the member or the company. The members were away from their teams and productive work, and many times suffered depression in addition to their physical injury. We also found that it cost about $1.80 an hour more for the company to send someone home rather than remain at work because of insurance costs, and the cost of replacing them with a temporary worker. Our goal became: keeping them working and finding them productive work somewhere in the plant that was acceptable given their injury. This was a mind shift for everyone involved: insurance carriers, group leaders, managers, and the team members. We work harder on restriction management. We now have computer programs with lists of jobs that people with certain injuries are able to perform. We punch in the person and their injury and up comes all the jobs in the plant that the person can do.
>
> The first goal is to keep them in their section. So a member in assembly may work most the day in their team, but be able to work for a two hour rotation in another part of the assembly plant. This is considered a non-rotational job and is temporary. The goal is to get them back to a full rotation of jobs in their team. For restrictions that are more serious and where we can't find a way for them to keep working on the line, we have developed an Extended Job Placement (EJT) program. This program is designed to find the restricted members an off-line, value-added, productive job for the team member to work, and receive a reduced amount of pay while they rehabilitate their way back to the line. We have 22 team members in the program right now, and have already sent five back to their old normal rotations.

## Medical Clinics on Site

From the beginning, Toyota has always had medical clinics on site at TMMK that are staffed with contract doctors and nurses to take care of work-related medical care. They have made two big improvements that have allowed expansion of these services. The first is that with all of the safety improvements already described, fewer members require the services of the clinic for work-related issues. The second is that improvements to the clinic itself, in which Toyota managers helped apply Toyota Way principles to the clinic's operations. Ernie explained:

> We held kaizen events focusing on eliminating waste. We posted Yamazumi charts (time balance charts) for every employee in the clinic and how they spent their time during the day. The team implemented improvements that made things more efficient for the staff and the team members while they were serving and improved the quality.
>
> "In just one clinic of 10 people, the team was able to reduce the manpower needed by 2.6 people. As part of the Toyota Way, we did not want anyone to lose a job because of making improvements. We could have waited for attrition to happen, but looking at the big picture, the company decided to use the freed up staff to start offering services to team members for personal medical issues such as colds, the flu, and so on. This is more convenient for the members and it saves them the co-pay at an external clinic, and saves the company money in paying the rest of the claims for personal medical care.

## An Onsite Pharmacy: Getting It Wrong, Then Getting It Right

We mentioned in Chapter 1 that Toyota is not perfect. We were serious. Toyota makes mistakes like any other companies, but they are better than most at responding and fixing the mistakes. One well intentioned "improvement" at Georgetown that was designed to save costs backfired the first time. Management decided to add onsite pharmacies for the members to fill their personal prescriptions. This seemed like a great costs-saving idea, but there were immediate negative reactions from team members. This was a case where management did not listen as well as they should have. Pete Gritton, vice president of Human Resources for both the Georgetown plant and Toyota Engineering and Manufacturing of America, explained the situation, "When we put in an onsite pharmacy some team members thought it was negative. Some thought of it as an inconvenience and negative. You could go to Kroger's [a local grocery store with a pharmacy] and pay $3 and now your wife will have to go to the plant to do that. I thought of it as positive to keep the company viable long term for job security."

As it turns out, the team members had a reason for concern. There were very long lines and members had to get to work early to get online to get their prescriptions filled. As usual, Toyota responded with vigorous problem solving. Gritton explained further by saying, "Originally we were not prepared for the pharmacy, and had people in the parking lot lined up. So we tried to figure out how to make it more efficient. One guy walked up to me and said that he always supported the company staying union free, but having to come over here and wait on line to get his prescription filled, he did not know if he could do that anymore."

It was clear that management, overall, thought that it was best for the plant to have the onsite pharmacy. Clearly, it was a significant cost reduction for the company, but instead of reacting defensively to criticisms or abandoning the concept, they used rigorous problem solving to improve the process. The problem was not that an onsite pharmacy was a bad idea. The problem was that it was inconvenient for team members to get their prescriptions filled and they had to wait too long. Gritton explained how the problem solving was used to address the concerns:

*We did a lot of kaizen to make it more convenient. We sent TPS specialists to the pharmacy to reduce waiting time and turnaround from prescriptions called in to when ready. We made some layout changes to reduce motion waste. We implemented machines that can sort pills; they are equipped with software and sort the pills—more automated—for common pills.*

*Also, that allowed for a person cost reduction and we negotiated a better price; but the real story was lead-time reduction. Then we went further than this. Now you can drop off a prescription in a drop box on the way to the workplace (entrance). Someone will pick it up and deliver the drugs to different cafeterias or take it right to where the team member works and drop it off. You can use a fully automated system to call it in anytime and pick it up on the way home. We now fill 10,000 prescriptions per month, and complaints are way down. How does cost compare? We save a couple of million dollars a year. Only 60 percent are filled through the pharmacy. If you are using generic drugs there is zero co-pay in our pharmacy for some drugs (e.g., Claritin, Prilosec, Nexium), but if you go outside then you pay 20 percent or up to $30 for the same drugs. Even with over the counter generic replacement, you do not have to pay anything. I've never heard of a plan that pays for over the counter.*

*There is also a half-tab program. The cost for a certain number of pills is the same regardless of size. If you need 30 mg we will give you 60 mg and you can cut it in half yourself (first prescription we will give you a pill cutter and you cut in half) and you save the entire co-pay. It has been good for both the company and the members and there is still plenty of room for improvement.*

## SUMMARY

This chapter illustrates the holistic way in which Toyota looks at the safety of all stakeholders. It involves providing for the physical and psychological safety of each member and their families. It is an intentional value that drives subsequent action. It is part of the Toyota culture that involves the ideas and input of all the members to create positive results in which all can take pride.

## KEY POINTS TO CONSIDER FOR YOUR COMPANY

1. The organization has a system that provides a positive work environment that includes effective 5S, proper lighting and comfortable temperatures.
2. There is a system to identify the safety standards and problems with all work processes, and to quickly address issues for the short term, while providing feedback for longer term redesign of the part and process.
3. There is a safety culture established whereby management is intentional and accountable for practically putting safety first in terms of their actions, their facilitation, and their support of getting all members involved.
4. There are systems to recognize and reduce mental stress and burden and each specific work process is designed to reduce this stress.
5. Detection and response to safety problems has shifted upstream to early symptom investigation and prevention.
6. Safety and ergonomics are designed into the product and the job.
7. Safety and ergonomic considerations are part of the standardized work and job instruction training with follow-up audits to turn the standardized work into actual behavior.
8. There is a company commitment that goes beyond immediate work-related safety to develop a culture of personal safety and well being of each member.
9. The defects in health and safety are intentionally targeted at zero.

# Chapter 10

# Two-Way Communication and Visual Management

*I know that you believe that you understood what you think I said, but I am not sure you realize that what you heard is not what I meant.*

—Robert McCloskey, U.S. State Department
spokesman, March 31, 1984

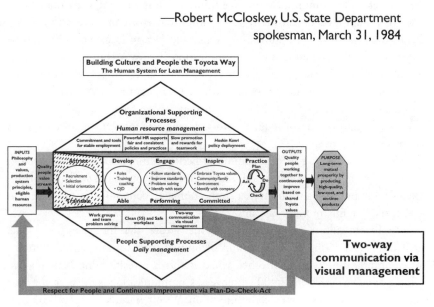

## COMMUNICATION IS FRAGILE

Can you think of anything more fragile then communication? By fragile we mean it can break down easily. As the quotation at the beginning of this chapter suggests, there are many opportunities for a breakdown. We think about what we want to communicate, translate it into words we hope reflect what we intend, the listener has to hear it accurately, then decode it correctly, then translate it into thoughts from his point of view. At every step there is plenty of opportunity for communication to break down.

The biggest problems in communication seem to come when we are absolutely certain that what we are saying is so clear anybody should understand it as we intend. As Robert Sommer said in his book, *The Mind's Eye*, "Misunderstandings can result when people automatically assume that others think as they do."[1]

---

[1] Robert Sommer, *The Mind's Eye: Imagery in Everyday Life*, New York: Delta Books, 1978, p.67.

How often do we assume others understand what we are saying? Or if they do not understand, that they must be simpletons or intentionally twisting our words. Effective communication starts with truly believing in the fragility of communication. One-on-one communication is difficult enough. Communication from one to the masses is even more challenging. Then add to that language and cultural differences and you have a recipe for a high level of defects.

Toyota believes in zero defects as a core value. Have they solved the problem of defects in communication? We think not, but within the Toyota culture there is a high level of sensitivity to the importance of communication, and a belief that two-way communication, especially face-to-face, will generally be far more effective than one-way communication. Two-way communication provides opportunities for feedback: We can test our assumptions about what we think is heard and understood. With one-way communication there is no feedback and no testing. The PDCA cycle depends on feedback and if we apply that to communication, it requires two-way conversation with repeated PDCA loops to be effective.

It is impossible to reach the summit of perfect communication; like kaizen, it is a never-ending cycle of continuous improvement. Toyota builds systems for communication, but then surrounds that connection with continuous improvement in order to constantly monitor and improve it.

In Toyota culture, communication is the "grease" that lubricates the engine. It is impossible to have a relationship of mutual trust without effective means of communicating with each other, whether this is a relationship between two people or at TMMK with 7,400 employees. Communication is the basis for trust and trust is the basis for open communication. We often think that good communication means we are good talkers, but one of the best ways to build trust is to actually listen to concerns and to address them as they are spoken. Mike Hoseus recalls:

*I remember one of my first manager Town Hall meetings in which I, a green, newly promoted 28-year-old manager, stood in front of a couple of hundred team members fielding touchy questions and concerns. One of the members voicing a concern could be best described as a rough guy. He was an older man, and quite honestly intimidated me. He voiced a somewhat personal concern about his process equipment and, not wanting to take time away from others' more general and common concerns, I asked him to wait until the end of the meeting and we would discuss it then. I could tell he took it as a brush-off and didn't expect me to follow up with him. In fact, he didn't even wait around at the end, and started to head out to the plant. I caught up with him and got a surprised look when I asked him to show me his concern out on the plant floor.*

*He enthusiastically took me to his process and explained the issue and his frustration with no apparent countermeasures being taken. I got the group leader there, and was able to get the right support people there, on-site, to work on the equipment, incorporating the member's ideas. In the middle of the interaction he turned to me with a serious look and said, "You really give a #@\*&, don't you?" It was one of the best compliments I could get, and from that day forward I had a friend on the line that I could smile at, wave to, and touch base with.*

Toyota interprets communications and its systems in three ways, as illustrated in Figure 10.1:

- **Formal communications** both vertical and horizontal; these involve information sharing from the company (or management) to the employees, from the employees back to the management, and between the employees.
- **Human Resources activities** that are designed to keep the communication channels open and effective.
- **Informal activities** that are designed to facilitate and improve communication.

Communication is an important enough part of the Toyota culture to warrant its own chapter. At the same time, it is a concept that overlaps and integrates with many of the other concepts (and chapters) in Toyota culture. Certainly a case could be made that communication is part of the people value stream and all

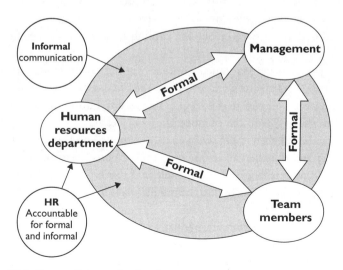

**Figure 10.1** Toyota Communication Systems

the supporting systems in the Human Systems Model. It is integral to orientation, training, on-the-job coaching and development, engagement in problem solving, gaining commitment, teamwork, leadership, hoshin kanri, and so on. This chapter will focus on the formal and informal communication systems.

# FORMAL CHANNELS OF COMMUNICATION

## Top-Down Communications

At the center of the Toyota culture is the assumption of partnership. All members, and even outside companies like suppliers, are partners in the business and must share common goals. In order to maintain a partnership relationship with the members of the company and the extended network, top management must literally include all the members in the workings of the business by sharing with them the status of the business. This communication includes education on the auto industry in terms of its cyclical and competitive nature. There are charts and graphs showing how the trends in quality, productivity, and sales are going for Toyota and the rest of the auto industry. The communication is intentional, aiming to educate members about the state of the company, and the need for partnering in the Toyota Way in order to continue to prosper.

Most companies would say that they communicate their business status to their employees, and that is probably the case. From what we have seen, Toyota does this more frequently, more intentionally, more accurately, and more long-term than others. An example of this in TMMK's history happened during the mid to late 1990s when Japan suffered a long-term recession. Meanwhile, the plant in Georgetown was booming; sales were increasing, team members were being hired in droves, and everyone was earning a lot of extra money from over-time work.

The Japanese managers started working with the American staff to communicate with and educate the workforce about the situation. Every channel of communication we will discuss in this chapter was used to inform the team members how bad it was in Japan: the number of cars decreasing, the number of plants reducing hours and then idling. Everyone was educated on the yen and its value to the dollar and the effect of its value on their exports. Everyone was told that Toyota made more money with cars built in America, but TMMK would be giving up some of its production to the mother plant in Japan, Tsutsumi, in order for them to keep working.

These production shifts were gradual, and demand in the United States was still growing, so it was hard for team members to see any cause for concern when everything was still going strong for the plant. But the Japanese persisted in painting a bleak picture, and they forecasted an eventual effect in America. The

American management team put together videos updating everyone on the situation. They put together a financial planning and management class and offered it to all the employees with the main message being: Do not get dependent on your overtime earnings to pay your bills. Be careful about making purchases with overtime money that probably will not be there in the near future.

It was a hard message for team members to understand because growth was still going strong in the United States, but most did listen. Sure enough, in the early 2000s, the Japanese recession came to America and it was TMMK's turn for a slowdown. The plant's production numbers decreased and overtime at the plant reduced to zero. The warning that had been communicated for literally five years had now come true. All team members had been informed, and many took the steps needed to weather the storm. It was a great example of early, consistent, repetitive, and intentional communication. It built a lot of trust with team members and made them feel like they were all in this together.

The communication system at Toyota is vast and multi-faceted. There are typical forms of communication, including company newsletters and bulletins, mailings, bulletin boards, emails, and the like. These methods emphasize distribution of information and are important in any organization. Two other effective tools have been closed circuit TV systems and computerized kiosks. Consider the following examples.

In every break area and in the office areas there is a TV set on at all times. It runs general information, such as the amount of overtime necessary to meet the monthly production goals, safety tips, times of the next blood drive, benefits fair, and many other topics. The real purpose of the system is to reach all 7,400 employees simultaneously (or at least half of this on one shift). For example, when TMMK was chosen as the production site for the Hybrid Camry the system was used to simultaneously connect Washington D.C., Tokyo, TEMA (headquarters) in Erlanger, Kentucky and TMMK to announce the news to all team members at one time. The presidents of the company are also able to use the system for major communication issues of quality or safety, and for sharing a consistent message to all team members reliably, accurately, and quickly.

The other technological system streamlining communication and processing information is the computer kiosk. These are placed strategically throughout the plant, but mostly in the cafeterias. Many routine HR informational transactions are now processed by team members themselves instead of via paperwork or with HR administrators. These types of transactions include benefits changes, transfer requests, and applications for job openings.

At Toyota, there is an entire section of the administration dedicated to corporate communications: they are in every plant and major unit, such as headquarters, the Toyota Technical center, and Toyota Motor Finance. They are responsible for the internal communications of the organization. At TMMK, there is a long list of communication tools they manage in order to keep the lines of communication open with all team members; these are summarized in Table 10.1, including the purpose, the intended audience, whether or not it is voluntary or mandatory, and

**Table 10.1** Toyota Communications Tools Matrix

| Tool/Option | Purpose | Audience/Frequency |
|---|---|---|
| TMMK Today **Mandatory** | Plant-wide info and safety alerts | To GLs and above for team members Daily |
| Inside Track **Voluntary** | Plant-wide news, production updates and team member recognition | All Team Members Weekly |
| News to Use **Voluntary** | Inform T/Ms about auto industry | All Team Members Weekly |
| Toyota Topics **Voluntary** | Topics of plant-wide and family interest | All Team Members and Community—Mailed Bi-Monthly |
| Toyota Times **Voluntary** | Inform T/Ms about Toyota business and financial results and industry and economic conditions | All team member's families— Mailed semi annually and on the Web |
| Plant-wide Memos **Mandatory** | Plant-wide announcements and organizational changes | Group Leaders and above to be read to all team members As needed |
| Group Leader Key Messages **Mandatory** | Topics of plant-wide interest for Group Leader education and interest | GLs and above As needed or by plan |
| E-mail **Mandatory** | Time sensitive notices, memos and surveys | Plant wide or GLs and above As needed |
| Bulletin Boards **Voluntary** | Plant wide notices, announcements, job postings, activities etc. | All team members Monday – Wednesday |
| Headline News **Mandatory** | Topics of plant interest, recognition, company and industry news | All team members Weekly |
| Discover Toyota **Mandatory** | Heighten T/M awareness and understanding of Toyota | All team members Weekly (Tuesday) |
| TNN Slides **Voluntary** | Concise plant wide reminders, announcements and activities | All team members Daily |

the frequency. It includes the daily and weekly newsletters (*TMMK Today* and *Inside Track*) as well as the larger publications that are done bi-monthly and semi-annually (*Toyota Topics* and *Toyota Times*). Finally, there is a publication entitled *Driven*, that is put out by Toyota national headquarters on a quarterly basis to the entire nationwide team of 45,000 members.

All of these publications are professionally designed. The first two go through the group leader, while the latter two are mailed to team members' homes. These are useful tools for recognizing team member achievements like groups or Quality Circles that have had good results following the problem solving process, as well as for educating team members on the plant's status, the auto industry, and the economy in general. Some of the headings of the sections in *Toyota Topics, Times,* and *Driven* are: "About the Team Members and Business of TMMK," "Industry Watch," "Our Business," "Toyota Global Production," "Global Toyota Financial Information," "U.S. Auto Industry," and "U.S. Overall Economy." In addition, there are team member photos and articles about recognition for team members and their achievements, but the focus is on educating and sharing business information with the team members who are, in every sense of the term, business partners.

As Table 10.1 shows, there are two main audiences for the tools—team members and their supervisors. It is important to emphasize the extent of time, effort, and money Toyota invests in both in order for them to live the Toyota values in the context of the company's business purpose. The use of formal communication media by management is powerful, and many companies have them, but they are typically one-way communication. There is no dialogue, and thus no opportunity to detect and correct misunderstandings. Probably more important than these messages that come down from the top are the various ways Toyota uses face-to-face communication.

## Meetings, Meetings, Meetings

In Toyota culture, the preferred method of communication is face-to-face. Toyota strives to set up as many structured opportunities as possible for management and members to come together to have open and sincere communication. While these meetings are meant to provide an informal atmosphere, the meetings are intentional and part of an overall system and strategy. The daily communication system is a good example of how HR and Manufacturing work together in order to get the word out to people. In the last chapter, we talked about the daily KYK safety meeting where the line is shut down an additional five minutes after every first break in order to communicate safety information to everyone. At the second break, the same thing occurs, in order for the group leaders to have time to communicate with their team members. The line shuts down for 15 minutes, but the team member break is only 10 minutes. This gives all of the group leaders five minutes with their members. What usually happens is that the team members spend the 10 minutes going to the restroom and getting drinks and snacks, and then return to the break area for the meeting.

These group meetings last five minutes every day. While the morning meeting is focused on safety, the afternoon meeting is focused on everything else. The quick huddle allows the group leader to update the group on its current business scoreboard, to give out company information, and to find out if there are any questions, comments, or concerns.

Human resources and manufacturing work together with team members to identify what information is most needed and desired on a daily, weekly, and monthly basis. With this data, a standard was developed for a communication wall for each group break area in the plant. At the TMMK plant, that consists of more than 300 areas. The wall is organized and labeled with headings and corresponding key information, both generic and group-specific.

We cannot emphasize enough the high value Toyota places on face-to-face communication. As in anything, simply saying something is important does not translate into action: it must begin with a formally defined goal or standard, and that standard is to have every level of management meet face-to-face with team members on a regular basis. The actual standard varies by topic and purpose. Table 10.2 illustrates the type and frequency of various meetings.

Each of these formal meetings is an opportunity to share vital company information with team members and to sustain their motivation to stay engaged in their work. They also provide an opening for management to hear what is going on with the team members for quick identification and correction of issues. These meetings act as an andon system for the human systems of the culture, and the environment must be safe to encourage expressing concerns without fear of retaliation.

Mike Hoseus recalls a key incident regarding communication, "We learned the hard way in some of the manager lunch box meetings. If a member brought up an issue with the group and then we followed up with the group leader in an insensitive way, the group leader would throw it back to the team member: 'Why did you have to go and air our dirty laundry?' It didn't take many of those comments to stifle any real discussion and sharing at those meetings. We had to be extra sensitive to both the members and the supervisors in order to keep the environment safe and encourage problem identification."

It is also important to underscore the point that the communications taking place with team members are open and honest; that is, Toyota trusts their team members enough to share the bad news along with the good, the challenges along with the recognition. Other organizations we have worked with have talked about their practices of protecting their team members from the bad news. Even done with the best intentions, this can be a serious mistake that undermines true partnership between management and team members.

**Table 10.2** Types of Meetings and Standard Frequency and Length

| Management Level | Meeting Type | Frequency/ Length | Purpose |
|---|---|---|---|
| TL | KYK | Daily/5 minutes | Safety |
| GL | Huddle | Daily/5 minutes | KPI's and discussion |
| GL | Lunch Box | Monthly/1 hour | Identification snd PDCA of group issues with assignment and tracking |
| Assistant Manager and Plant Manager | Town Hall | Monthly/1 hour | State of the Department and open discussion, with tracking the countermeasures of identified issues |
| Assistant General Manager and General Manager | Lunch Box | Monthly/45 mins | A random selection of 5–6 team members at a time to build relationships and ID and resolve issues. |
| VP and President | Roundtable | Quarterly/90 minutes | A random selection of all team members, with 25–30 members at a time, meeting with the President for sharing of company information and open discussion to ID member issues |

Nan Banks, the Manager for Corporate Communications at both TMMK and TEMA, emphasizes this partnership in all company communications.

*We really focus on communications from the team member perspective. What is the "core benefit" to them? It is natural for everyone hearing information to listen to it through "their own viewpoint". We all tend to listen to "WIIFM" (What's in it for me). We want every team member to know, and they want to know "What do I need to do differently as a result of this information?" Our goal is to be the plant of choice in North America for Toyota so we have to connect our team members to our Key Performance Indicators.*

*It is easy to connect behaving safely with staying healthy. Our bigger focus is connecting quality, productivity, and cost to job security and the Toyota value of long term mutual prosperity. We now connect all of our communication messages to the five KPI's of Safety, Quality, Productivity, Cost, HR, and recently we have added Environmental. We know what percentage of our communications is directed at each one and we can increase the percentage of one if improvement is needed.*

## Meeting Facilitation and Communications Training

HR and the communications section have assisted in formalizing and standardizing the five-minute meeting to make it effective and efficient for both the leader and the members. Newly promoted group leaders are trained in how to facilitate these meetings in the most effective way. The training includes role playing and addresses basic communication principles, such as body language, eye contact, standing up to deliver, moving about the room, active listening, and more complex issues, such as conflict prevention and handling a disgruntled employee. To make the training more credible and effective, the trainer is typically a former group leader who went back to college to get a degree in communications.

At Toyota, there is also a meeting facilitation standard that all leaders are trained to use during meetings. The standard was developed for Quality Circle leaders in order for them to be more effective with their time, and it was such an effective tool that Toyota decided to expand its use to include all team and group leaders. The facilitation standard is basic and simple, yet extremely effective in involving everyone in the meeting, coming to decisions, and making an action plan. The standard involves four steps, as shown in Figure 10.2:

**Step 1: Preparation.** The standard in this phase is for the leader of the meeting to spend at least as much time on preparing for the meeting as the meeting length itself. For a one hour Quality Circle meeting, the leader is expected to spend one hour preparing so that when his members come to their meeting, their time will be worthwhile. The key points of preparation are making an agenda and getting materials ready for the meeting. The use of flip charts is highly recommended and utilized at Toyota because they provide good visual control and allow all members to be a part of the action.

**Step 2: Conducting the Meeting.** This is the core of the meeting and the key here is involving everyone in the meeting and using facilitation tools. There are key roles that are used and everyone in the meeting takes turns with these roles—facilitator, recorder, time keeper, and gate keeper. The gate keeper maintains order in the meeting by holding everyone accountable to the agreed-upon ground rules of the group. For example, if there is a side conversation going on, the gate keeper will remind the group

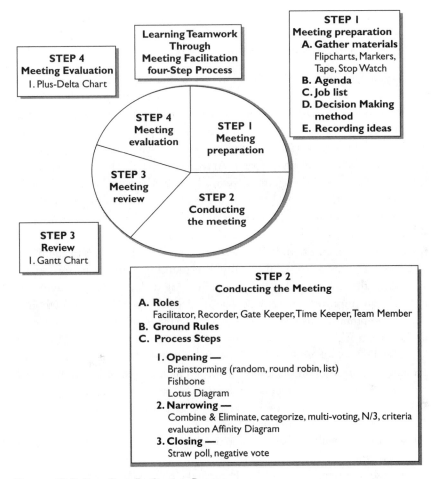

**STEP I**
Meeting preparation
A. Gather materials
Flipcharts, Markers,
Tape, Stop Watch
B. Agenda
C. Job list
D. Decision Making
method
E. Recording ideas

Learning Teamwork
Through
Meeting Facilitation
four-Step Process

**STEP 4**
Meeting Evaluation
1. Plus-Delta Chart

STEP 4
Meeting
evaluation

STEP I
Meeting
preparation

STEP 3
Meeting
review

STEP 2
Conducting
the meeting

**STEP 3**
Review
1. Gantt Chart

**STEP 2**
**Conducting the Meeting**
A. **Roles**
Facilitator, Recorder, Gate Keeper, Time Keeper, Team Member
B. **Ground Rules**
C. **Process Steps**

1. **Opening —**
Brainstorming (random, round robin, list)
Fishbone
Lotus Diagram
2. **Narrowing —**
Combine & Eliminate, categorize, multi-voting, N/3, criteria
evaluation Affinity Diagram
3. **Closing —**
Straw poll, negative vote

**Figure 10.2** Four-Step Facilitation Process

of the standard, no side conversations, rule. The task of the meeting is accomplished by utilizing the facilitation tools of brainstorming to get everyone's ideas out, and then narrowing and deciding on tools to get the group to come to a consensus around a problem, its cause, and the countermeasure actions.

**Step 3: Meeting Review.** Just as the name suggests, this is a review of all the to-dos agreed upon by the group. A simple chart of "What, who, and when" is used to facilitate, record, and follow up on the agreed upon action steps.

**Step 4: Meeting Evaluation.** This is a review of how well the group did with the meeting itself. Did the group follow the meeting standard? Were the ground rules followed? A simple Plus/Delta chart is used to capture what the group did well that they want to continue, and what they need to change in terms of stopping things that were not effective or adding things that would allow them to be more effective the next time.

Toyota has found that presentation and facilitation skills are important for leaders to communicate effectively, but it is also necessary to teach leaders to communicate effectively one-on-one with an individual, especially a subordinate whom the leader is coaching. For this reason, newly promoted group leaders are also trained in a two-way communication model that teaches them to put Toyota Way values into daily action. Anna Marie Eifert, the developer of the Group Leader training program, developed the model with her team in order to teach basic interpersonal skills such as empathetic listening and integrate them with the Toyota PDCA method of solving problems. These two sets of skills correspond with the pillars of the Toyota Way—mutual respect and continuous improvement. In order to maintain respect, the leader has to communicate in such a way as to build a trusting relationship with the person. At the same time, the two need to accomplish something such as solving a problem or planning an improvement activity. The model utilizes the PDCA method in order to accomplish this. Figure 10.3 shows how these two sets of skills integrate in the Toyota Way.

The first set of skills is based on the Toyota Way value of respect for people, and it focuses on the leader's ability to build a relationship of trust with individuals. The key checkpoints that leaders are trained to practice are:

- Understand needs and shared goals.
- Respond with empathy. Express understanding, not agreement; seek solutions.
- Use common language. Use simple and clear speech.
- Encourage accountability and personal ownership. Seek ideas before sharing yours to encourage ownership and buy-in.
- Demonstrate confidence and respect for abilities. Believe in the creative power of the human spirit and the ability to achieve personal goals.
- Address behavior using "I" messages. Speak in terms of your own thoughts, feelings and observations.
- Share the facts to build trust. Gain cooperation by sharing relevant insights and perspective.

The second set of skills is based on the Toyota Way value of continuous improvement. These focus on the ability to follow the PDCA process in solving a problem or initiating improvement. The key checkpoints for the leader to address are:

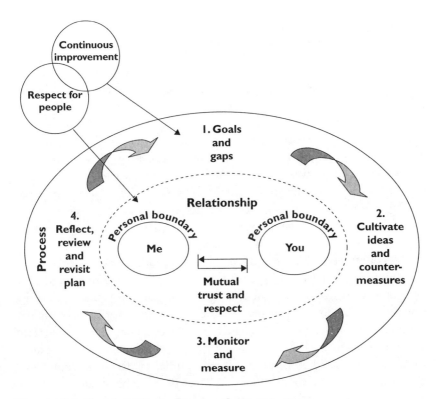

**Figure 10.3** Model of Effective Two-way Communication.

- **Customer First** What is the impact from the customer viewpoint?
- **Shared Goals** Define success for both parties. What are my goals, what are the other party's goals, and what do we both need to do to succeed?
- **Genchi Genbutsu** Go to the source and get the facts.
- **Visualization** Express the situation simply and explicitly.
- **Strengths and Challenges** Identify points to leverage and possible barriers to success.
- **Partners and Support** Insure that the required financial, technical, and organizational resources are available.
- **Measure and Monitor** Determine what to start, stop, or continue doing based on data and monitored progress.

New leaders practice these skills with each other with the help of video cameras. They use a Communication Planner form as a tool to document key points and plan for the discussion. It is based on a problem-solving A-3 form, but customized for two-way communication.

## Clear Roles and Responsibilities Make Meetings Efficient and Effective

With all of the meetings that Toyota holds it would seem everybody is in meetings all day. How can anyone get other work done? Toyota meetings tend to be very efficient. Most standing meetings, such as the quality meeting, are 30 minutes long. They start on time and end on time and the objectives are accomplished.

One example of a meeting that is unusually efficient in Toyota is a major design review for a vehicle in the process of being engineered.[2] Whenever a prototype is built, a design review is held where all project people come and look at the vehicle. The lead evaluation group organizes the meeting. The chief engineer, program managers, evaluation engineers, and design engineers responsible for each part of the vehicle (e.g., interior, exterior body, chassis, etc.) look at the completed vehicle and list problems they see. The facilitator puts up flip charts on the walls or passes out sheets with categories—problem and countermeasure ideas.

The vehicle is reviewed by those who know it best, and they write down everything wrong with the vehicle along with initial improvement ideas. For example, let's say 50 people come to a two-hour meeting—not every engineer but at least one person per department. For an American-engineered vehicle this would happen separately in America and Japan—50 people at a TTC session in the United States and 50 in a parallel session in Japan. This is scheduled for a specific period of time, for example 10 A.M. to noon—a two-hour window and not everyone needs to be there the whole time. Each person comes in and reviews the vehicle and test results, writes comments on the flip chart, maybe discusses the comments with program management, who is there for the whole time, and then leaves. Then the evaluation group gets the results typed and puts the items on one tracking sheet organized as problem, countermeasure, person responsible, and due date.

In some cases, clear countermeasures are decided right in the meeting, and if not, the evaluation engineers follow up with designers to see what the countermeasures are and implement them in the next phase. Follow-up review meetings might be held several times with around 20 people per meeting, and when all is said and done, 50–100 issues are clarified. At the prototype stage, 100 percent of the items must have a countermeasure. These are all real problems. That's the philosophy of the zero open-issues policy—zero remaining issues are to remain at the end of pro- totype phase. The goal of the initial design review meeting is simply to identify the problem—the point of cause. The complete PDCA process happens outside the

---

[2] This description of design reviews was based on an interview with Andy Lund, program manager, Toyota Technical Center, Ann Arbor, Michigan.

meeting and is led by responsible individuals. The follow-up meetings are mostly for status reporting, or in some cases, to ask for help from other functions.

With a meeting as complex as one in which many functional specialists review an entire car, we could imagine days of 10 hour meetings with extensive debate. Most people in the meeting would be laying back and observing while a few individuals discussed each problem. Toyota would view this as a tremendous waste of resources and probably of limited effectiveness. There are a number of things that support the efficiency and effectiveness of Toyota meetings:

1. The time consciousness of Toyota affects meetings which generally start on time and end on time.

2. The preparation that goes into the agenda facilitates a smooth flow of the meeting. This starts with a clear purpose for the meeting.

3. Specific roles and responsibilities make it clear for each issue who is responsible and will follow up to make sure the issue is resolved. We saw for example that not everyone comes to the design review and not everyone stays even for the entire two hour meeting.

4. Specific roles and responsibilities also support a balance between teamwork and individual responsibility. While the team is working together there are clear individual assignments and each individual takes responsibility for presenting the status of action items and follow-up on ideas that come out of the meeting. The complete PDCA cycle is not going to happen in the meeting. In the design review case only the issues are identified. The actual countermeasures, implementation, checking, and further action take place outside the meeting and progress is reported in follow-up meetings.

5. Much of the two-way communication takes place outside of meetings. Many Toyota meetings would appear to the outside observer to be rather sterile, with mostly one-way communication as individuals report out and perhaps take a few questions and comments from others. There is intense discussion and debate occurring before and after the meeting. The process of *nemawashi* is about building those agreements and resolving issues and that happens best among two or three people most familiar with the issue. By the time the meeting is held, the most challenging issues are usually already worked out and agreed upon.

6. There is a norm of focusing on deviations from the standard. In many meetings individuals report out on the status of their projects using green-yellow-red status updates. The green items are not discussed, while the most intense focus is on those items behind or that need help. If all of an individual's action items are green they will generally pass on reporting.

7. There is a norm of standup meetings, especially on the plant floor. The information is posted on walls and each individual has a section of the wall

with their data reporting on yellow or red items. Meetings seem to flow more quickly when people are standing up. Also movement is encouraged from place to place to review information or objects.

The underlying root cause of much of what makes meetings work at Toyota is specific roles and responsibilities. It is clear who is responsible for preparation, facilitation, and follow-up for the meeting itself. It is clear who is responsible for reporting on specific projects and who is responsible for follow-up on action items. The expression "if everyone is responsible, no one is responsible" seems to characterize the thinking of Toyota leaders who decades ago evolved the norm of clearly articulated individual roles and responsibilities.

## Human Resource-Facilitated Upward Communication

As mentioned earlier, HR plays many important roles at Toyota, including making the work environment fair and positive for all employees. Listening to management is one thing, but employees need a voice. In unionized companies, the union plays a role in providing members with a voice to management. In a Toyota non-unionized plant, the HR department plays that role.

One such communication system is the Hotline, in which any member can call anonymously straight to a phone recorder system. These messages are documented and logged by HR, and then followed up with the section management responsible for the issue. HR and the section management work in partnership to solve the problem. These human relations issues are dealt with the same way that the problem-solving steps are used for production issues. In other words, the problem is broken down, a root cause determined, short-term countermeasures are put into place to fix the immediate problem, and longer-term countermeasures to prevent reoccurrence. Mike Hoseus describes an example of this:

> An example of this occurred when I was the manager of Assembly. It involved the issue of overtime and was a concern that made it to the Hotline system often. Each month, depending on the customer demand and the current operating rate of the plant, the daily "forecasted overtime" is scheduled for the month. From the team member's point of view, they plan their days according to the scheduled overtime, but then have to adjust according to the plant's needs each day. Each day the plant must produce the scheduled number of vehicles and that usually involves some amount of overtime. The plant's overtime call is based on numerous factors, including feeder plant capabilities (such as body weld, paint, power train, and plastics) and the number of stops when team members pull the andon cord. Team members can understand when things have gone wrong on their shift that prevented production, but it is often not that simple.

*Usually, when there is a breakdown, the section that had the breakdown is not able to support the extended overtime.*

*Then, with each shift, a decision has to be made about how much extra overtime can be run to make up for the deficit. Team members on second shift may be working overtime because of problems in first shift. These decisions did not always make sense to the team members without them knowing the reasons behind the decisions. It didn't take many specific explanations on the Hotline system to figure out we needed a standard and a system to communicate these reasons to the team members on a just-in-time basis. We established the standard that whenever the overtime was reduced or extended from the plan we would call all the group leaders together to give them the reasons for the change and then, shortly after the overtime was communicated via the signboard, the group leaders could share the information and answer questions at the 5-minute meeting held at second break. This standard and procedure eliminated the calls to the Hotline system questioning why a certain amount of overtime was called.*

Another system that functions as an andon for team members to voice concerns and have them corrected is known as the Concern Resolution Process. This is an appeals process for team members to communicate that they are not happy with how they are being treated, either due to their disagreement with a particular policy or a member of management. The concern is logged and tracked by HR as it progresses through different levels of HR and manufacturing management. The team member meets face-to-face with the members of management in order to voice his concern and his suggestions for resolution. If the member is not satisfied with the answer he receives as a result of the meeting, he can appeal the decision to the next level of management and this can go on all the way up to the vice president level of the organization.

The system is used often, and there are many examples where management decisions have been changed as result. Human resources policies have also been altered as a result of the process. The first example is with a team member being called as a witness in a jury trial. He had witnessed an accident on the way to work, and was required to take a vacation day, since being called as a witness did not fall under the jury-duty policy. The team member believed that being called as a witness was the same civic duty as serving as a jury member; it was a requirement over which he had no control. A concern resolution was prepared and submitted. Through the resolution due process, the policy for jury duty was changed to include being called as a witness.

Another example involved a female team member who was Amish. The dress code policy for the company stated that there were to be no shorts, skirts, or dresses permitted while working on line. This team member's beliefs included that she not wear pants. She initiated a concern resolution process, and the dress policy was changed to allow for members to wear long skirts and socks, as long as no skin was exposed. This met both her needs and the plant's safety and modesty needs, and both parties were happy.

An additional tool that Toyota Human Resources uses is a morale and opinion survey; it serves as an indicator and way of improving communication and the human systems. It is a questionnaire administered to all team members every 18–24 months with the purpose of grasping the status of employee morale. The survey is substantial, with more than a hundred questions focusing on communication and trust between team members, their supervisors, and the company.

Completing the survey is a voluntary paid activity for the members. It was originally completed on overtime, but as we've seen, team members do not always appreciate taking time away from their personal lives, even though they get paid extra. The company found that the rate of participation was higher if the line was shut down, and members were given the time to complete it during their shift. The choice is still voluntary for the members; they are able to stay in their group and perform other work, if they so choose. Participation is more than 90 percent, and the information gathered is invaluable. The questions are similar to the example questions in Figure 10.4.

The survey is conducted anonymously, with at least five people participating in a designated group in order to maintain anonymity. This allows the data to be analyzed by work group for feedback to the supervisor. The data is broken down in this detailed manner, not to beat up the supervisor or manager with the results, but to identify a problem needing to be solved.

When the results come back, each group leader meets with her members, and the group goes through the problem-solving process to prioritize problems that the team has the ability and desire to work on and improve. The group is given an overtime and financial budget to develop ideas and countermeasures to address the issues they have identified in the survey. Items can range from concerns about team member training taking place in the group, to the need for more room on the coat rack. These are items that the group can take care of themselves without outside help. Other items may require help and/or plant-wide coordination. One example of a problem identified in the opinion survey was the lack of microwave ovens and refrigerators for team members to use for breaks and lunches. For safety and plant-wide consistency purposes, this concern had to be addressed at the plant level, with HR coordinating. The decision was made to get a consistent number and type of refrigerators and microwaves at many different locations throughout the plant in order to better serve the team members.

The results of the opinion survey are also used to identify any communication and interpersonal skill gaps of any of the leaders in the organization. The opinion survey is a key performance indicator for leadership in the functional area

**RELATIONAL — Involving Two or More Parties**

66. Employees treat one another with respect and dignity
67. The organization is committed to helping me develop professionally
68. Our leaders help me view my mistakes as opportunities for learning and growth
69. There are opportunities available to communicate with senior management
70. The role I have in the organization is clearly understood by others
71. People are encouraged to apply new skills and ideas to their jobs
72. Good ideas are approved quickly without having to go through layers of management for acceptance
73. The organization shares rewards of productivity with me and my fellow employees
74. The organization has systems in place for members to focus on reducing work related inefficiencies
75. The organization and its members focus on cost reduction instead of price increase as a way to increase profit

**TRUST IN MY SUPERVISOR / MANAGER**

76. My supervisor/manager maximizes individual responsibility for how my job is done
77. My supervisor/manager provides flexibility in work hours, when applicable
78. My supervisor/manager provides opportunities for me to grow as an employee through training and promotions from within the department
79. My supervisor/manager allows me to learn from my mistakes and encourages taking responsibility for my own actions
80. My supervisor/manager cares about my work/life balance
81. My supervisor/manager rewards and recognizes my efforts both as an individual and as a member of my team
82. My supervisor/manager understands what my responsibilities are outside of work and helps me to accomplish a better work/life balance
83. My supervisor/manager treats me the same way s/he treats my peers

**TRUST IN ALL SUPERVISORS/MANAGERS**

84. All the supervisors/managers expect the same level of performance and commitment from all their employees
85. All supervisors/managers recognize and reward positive behavior
86. All supervisors/managers treat each employee the same when policies and/or procedures have not been followed
87. All the supervisors/managers treat each employee with respect and dignity

**Figure 10.4** Example Questions from Employee Morale and Opinion Survey

of HR. The score a manager receives on this survey is as much a key indicator as is the quality or production numbers they produce. The results are considered in terms of performance evaluations, yearly wage increases, and promotions. It is humbling for a manager or group leader to go in front of her subordinates and admit a problem they are having with communication, but it is also a powerful way to build trust with the team and correct the problem.

Managers will get feedback directly from their subordinates in order to make an action plan to improve their skills. Human resources specialists support the manager with training. The specialist will shadow the manager and observe both group and interpersonal interactions and be able to give live feedback. Executive coaches are contracted if needed to help the leader improve.

We have emphasized throughout this book the importance of mutual trust. Nowhere is this more important than in upward feedback to management. It is very sensitive to both the team members and their supervisor to give this kind of feedback. In many companies, team members fear retribution, or at the other extreme, that they will be ignored or supervisors will react defensively and lash out at the group if they receive negative feedback. At Toyota the goal is to always establish an environment of trust and openness in which the goal is to get the facts and improve. If it becomes a blame game then this type of survey feedback is not productive for problem solving.

## INFORMAL COMMUNICATION CHANNELS

Part of the Toyota culture includes intentionally setting up as many opportunities as possible for management and members to interact in work and non-work settings. We discussed a number of these types of interactions in Chapter 8 on Teamwork. These same interactions, such as daily recreation activities in the plant, sports leagues, and company picnics, are all ways for team members and members of management to relate to each other on a nonbusiness level, without the barriers of titles and hierarchy.

These same types of informal interactions are encouraged during work time. The well-known idea of management by walking around is similar to what Toyota calls *genchi genbutsu*, or go and see; go right to the source and find out for yourself. Genchi genbutsu is practiced for other reasons in problem solving—to grasp the situation and deeply understand the problem firsthand, but also to bring leaders in direct contact with team members to deeply understand their current concerns.

We have had students of lean systems question us on this principle of walking around and going and seeing as suggesting *distrust* of team members. They saw it as checking up on them and not trusting them to do their job. Certainly in an atmosphere of distrust it is possible to use walking around as a form of monitoring and control. The difference is the way the leader communicates with the members as they do these activities. If the communication is one of respect, sincere questioning, and sincere interest in gathering and utilizing team member input, the result will be increased trust.

Wil James is (at the time of this writing) the president of Toyota Auto Body in Long Beach (TABC). He recalls his earliest times as a leader at TMMK, in

Georgetown. Wil started as a group leader in 1987, was promoted to assistant manager in 1988, to manager in 1991, to assistant general manager in 1994, to general manager in 1997, and to vice president over all of manufacturing at TMMK in 2003. In 2006, he was offered a move to TABC, and was then promoted to president in 2007. (This was unusually fast promotion for Toyota where gradual promotion is the norm as we discuss in Chapter 11.)

What was particularly unusual in Wil's case was that most of his career was spent in maintenance and facilities engineering, both support areas to manufacturing. When Wil was promoted to assistant general manager, he was challenged with taking over management responsibilities for the entire Assembly Department—over 2,000 members—with no prior experience in assembly. Given the importance of cross-training and rotation that Toyota practices at all levels of management, and of rotating managers to new areas and putting them in a position to depend on the their team, good communication is essential. How did Wil respond to being thrown into the deep end of the pool with little prior experience? He turned to his instincts to understand the concerns of team members by immersing himself in their issues. As Wil explained,

> *Becoming the assistant general manager of assembly was my turning point. I was responsible for a couple of thousand people, and I had never been in assembly before, let alone managed it. I met with all of the team leaders, group leaders, and assistant managers and interviewed them one on one. I asked them four questions:*
> 1. *I will tell you a little about myself and ask you to tell me a little about yourself. It could be about your family, your job, or anything.*
> 2. *What do you believe are the top three or four things that prevent your department from being what it needs to be?*
> 3. *What do you personally hope to accomplish in your career; that is, what are your individual aspirations?*
> 4. *What else should I know that I did not ask you?*

Based on interviews with 270 people, Wil went through all his notes and classified underlying problems. There were a few common problems that stood out.

One was about replacing attrition and it became clear the plant did not have a good manpower planning system. Another was about varying group sizes: some groups had seven or eight people, while others had as many as 40. There needed to be standards for group size. There were also many little problems that Wil found he could easily fix. Wil explained: "That is why genchi genbutsu is so important: you see little things that are systems barriers that you can fix quite easily while leaders of individual groups cannot."

Wil learned the biggest concern was that this critical group of leaders believed they were not being listened to and that there was inadequate individual coaching, training, and development. They did not have a clear understanding of their role and what they should do. Wil had been at the Georgetown plant long enough to know the history intimately. It became clear to him that at the start-up of the plant—when there were many Japanese trainers—the leaders all had good coaching. In fact, it was one-on-one personal trainers teaching the Toyota Way of leading. But eventually the trainers had to go back to Japan or be redeployed to other parts of the world as Toyota grew. In the meantime, the Georgetown plant was growing, including adding a second assembly line and hiring many people, while losing well-trained leaders to other companies who had an insatiable appetite for Toyota-trained leaders.

Unfortunately, nobody put a lot of effort into writing down what they learned. That was fine in the early days, when so many people had directly gone through that immersion coaching, but when they reduced the number of Japanese coordinators—without the luxury of having everything written down, and without the personalized attention—some important things got diluted. Wil soon began training programs and coaching to clarify roles and responsibilities. As a longer-term countermeasure, in the early 2000s a lot of effort was put into documenting the teachings so people now have material to start from.

Wil attributes learning the importance of intimate face-to-face contact to the great Toyota leaders at Georgetown who taught him personally. One was Fujio Cho. Wil fondly recalls running the facilities group, which was far from the central core of daily production, and having an opportunity to spend time at Mr. Cho's home:

> When Mr. Cho was president of TMMK, he opened his home to different departments. On Friday nights he would invite us to his home on a rotating schedule: he would invite team members too, and we'd all do karaoke, or play ping pong, basketball, or tennis, and socialize for the evening. He would wander among the group and talk with anybody about anything they had on their minds. I personally talked to him about the Toyota Way and asked why things were the way they were. I asked pretty specific questions about different departments. It appeared to me the facilities group experienced more frequent opportunities to visit with him.
>
> I asked Mr. Cho why the special attention and he explained: "In a manufacturing department the supervisor gets to see his people every day and often sees them one by one each day, but with the facilities role, your people have to trust you and care for you, and want to support you. It is really important you support them because there is no way in the world you can see them all when they are spread all over the plant, so it is important that you get to know each other, and here is an opportunity to get to

*do that." He had a method behind what he did, and he took the time to explain what he did and why.*

This is a prime example of how a Toyota leader, in this case Mr. Cho, teaches by example the importance of personal communication. Wil learned this lesson and when he became president of TABC he demonstrated his understanding by personally interviewing hundreds of people. Wil summarized well what he was taught: "I think the one-on-one personal contact is everything in the Toyota Way. I have always quoted one of its main ideas: 'People do not care what you know until people know that you care.' If you take the time to ask them their concerns and then take time to communicate that you have heard them, and then put plans in place to meet their issues, there is no reason for them not to give you their best."

# VISUAL CONTROL AND A-3s AS COMMUNICATION SYSTEMS

We have been emphasizing communication as a way to inform team members and treat them as partners as well as surface concerns. Communication is also integral to the daily functioning of the production system. In the first two chapters we discussed the importance of problem identification in the system. A main foundation tool of the Toyota Production System is visual communication. The purpose of the system is to be able to communicate the status or condition of a situation simply and clearly to all observers.

We might think of visual control as purely a technical issue, but in reality it is embedded deeply in the culture of Toyota. It reflects the value placed on shared information that surfaces problems to all team members, and the practical understanding of the human information processing limits of people. Through that practical understanding there is skepticism that information a person has to look up in a book or on a computer screen will be used broadly for problem solving.

We will discuss two kinds of visual communication which are deeply embedded in Toyota's culture. The most well known are the myriad of visual indicators in the factory and the offices that include graphs, charts, andon, and kanban. These indicators all have in common that they visually indicate a standard condition as well as when something is out of standard. The purpose is to surface problems so they can be solved. More recently there has been a good deal of notoriety in Toyota's visual approach to problem solving called A-3 reporting.

## Visual Indicators of the Status of the Process

The goal of visual management is to communicate the problem for all to see. Note that a problem is defined as the gap between the current situation and the standard. We see in Figure 10.5 four different ways of visually communicating this gap. In

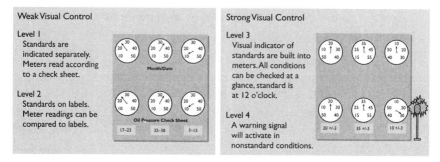

**Figure 10.5** Four Levels of Visual Control

Level 1, each meter must be read separately and has its own calibration. If you look at a separate checklist you can tell which of these meters is out of standard. This is the weakest form of visual control, since you need a separate reference to interpret the results. In Level 2, we have added the standards on labels under each meter so you do not have to refer to a separate document. This is a bit stronger. Level 3 orients each meter so the standard is at 12 o'clock. Now any deviation from 12 o'clock is out of standard and we can see this at a glance without reading numbers and interpretation. The strongest version, Level 4, adds a warning signal when out of standard. It might be even stronger to lock out the process or shut it down automatically when the meters reach some specified gap from the standard; for example, any meter that reaches 2 o'clock or 10 o'clock shuts down the process.

Unfortunately, there is a lot of information that is poorly communicated in manufacturing plants. Either the purpose of communicating the information has not been clearly thought through or good communication skills are lacking. In many company cultures that are more technocratic there is an assumption that any information that is available on a computer should be found and utilized in an optimal way. There is also a lack of understanding in many companies that a standard is necessary to define a problem.

On a visit to a non-Toyota plant, Mike Hoseus recalls seeing a communication board set up in the name of lean that actually communicated very little of value:

*As I was touring a facility that has been going through a lean transformation for the last couple of years, the lean champion took me past the new "Production Communication Board" located at the entrance of the plant for all members to pass on their way in and out of the plant. On the board was listed "Yesterday's production = 505." I asked him if that was good or bad. He said he wasn't sure, but the team members all know what the goal is. So I suggested we ask the next employee who walked past. He answered that last month the daily goal was 500 a day, but he wasn't sure this month. There are two points to emphasize: Obviously, the organization had taken steps to communicate better with the employees and to involve them in the process, however, they missed the simple principle for communicating effectively. Include the standard, the actual, and the gap, clearly identifying the problem in all communications.*

Table 10.3 illustrates an example of how Toyota might communicate the same information to team members. At a glance, everyone can look at the board and grasp the current status. Colors could also be added in the example to show in red the 4/15 and Month-to-Date data because of the minus condition exceeding five.

**Table 10.3** Production Status Board Example

| Date | Goal | Actual | Daily +/– | Month to Date +/– |
|------|------|--------|-----------|-------------------|
| 4/15 | 500  | 490    | −10       | −24               |
| 4/16 | 500  | 505    | +5        | −19               |

STANDARD 5 is Acceptable

## A-3 Reporting to Visually Communicate Status

The key to visual communication and control is that it is designed to drive action, and at Toyota that usually means problem solving. We have already covered Toyota problem solving but no discussion of this would be complete without discussing the A-3 tool. A technical explanation of the A-3 as a problem-solving tool is covered in *The Toyota Way Fieldbook* and *The Toyota Product Development System.*[3] Our goal here is to look at the A-3 as a communication tool and how it is used in Toyota culture.

The A-3 is not seen as just a problem solving tool but as a key Toyota communication tool. All vital, important information is put together in the form of an A-3. It took a couple of years to "break the code" of the term A-3 at the Georgetown plant. Team members were constantly told to put information onto an A-3. They thought it was some sort of secret Japanese code until one day someone came back from the copier machine with the observation that A-3 stands for the size of paper it is written on (11x17). Maybe they went to the large 11x17 size because one of the tenets of the A-3 is that whenever you communicate to someone at Toyota, the standard is to put it on one piece of paper.

---

[3] For a description of the A-3 tool see Liker, Jeffrey and D. Meier, *The Toyota Way Fieldbook,* New York: McGraw-Hill, 2005 (Chapter 18). The A-3 is presented in the context of product development in Morgan, James and Jeffrey Liker, *The Toyota Product Development System,* New York: Productivity Press, 2006 (Chapter 14).

The A-3 is used for problem solving, proposal writing, and status summaries. It is designed to communicate information in many directions. The tool is used informally to *nemawashi* with others to "prepare the soil" with them before presenting the problem or a proposal in a formal manner.

The A-3 is also known as a "bashing draft." This is a critical part of the Toyota culture in that the author presents the information in order to be "criticized." It is a very productive and helpful technique, but cannot be done unless there is a culture of respect and trust already present. The author is saying, "I am not personally or emotionally tied to this information and I am laying it on the table for everyone to take a shot at it." At the same time the bashers are saying (silently), "Do not take this personally; we are critiquing the information, not you as a person." With this mutual understanding, they are able to cut through the formal, polite, superficial feedback usually given at many organizations and get to real communication.

Communication at Toyota is based on three factors, which include reporting, informing, and consulting or as the Japanese call it *hou-ren-sou*. These three can be broken down into the categories: need to agree, need to know, and need to consult. Communicating to people who need to agree would include supervisors, plant managers, etc. It could also include accounting and finance if necessary. Communicating to people who need to know includes other related groups and depending on the subject could include the entire plant. This stage would also include communicating as a form of *yokoten*. As we already discussed, the last stage of problem solving is *yokoten* in which the problem and counter measures are communicated to related departments in order to learn from others problems and to prevent the problem from occurring in their area.

The final stage of communication, needing to consult, would include talking with all related stakeholders on the subject. This could include other affected groups and anyone who is expected to contribute or be involved in the activity. When applicable, this would also include the Japanese coordinator. The Japanese trainers teach all Toyota members to practice these three forms of communication whenever there are important issues to communicate and especially when an A-3 is involved. Many times, the Japanese trainers remind their students to "eat their spinach." *Hou-ren-sou* loosely translates into spinach.

The A-3 is a tool designed for all three of these communication functions during the problem-solving activity and afterwards. At anytime during these three stages, especially during the report and consult, the A-3 also becomes a developmental tool. When the A-3 is bashed the feedback is taken as developmental feedback. The supervisors and managers at Toyota welcome this developmental feedback from their supervisors and trainers and expect to get feedback either verbally or written. Initially, all the feedback is done in person, one on one. As the relationship between the trainer and the supervisor deepens then the feedback on the A-3 might come in the form of red ink on the A-3, similar to a school paper in need of much proofreading. This correction is taken as a sign by the trainee that the trainer cares about them and takes the time to give feedback. It is taken as a bigger concern by the trainee when the A-3 comes back with no red ink.

Once again, the A-3 is just a tool and can be used to help build a culture of trust or to quickly destroy it. There are already many war stories in organizations which have implemented the A-3 or problem-solving report and it has quickly become a tool of punishment. "Go and do your A-3" becomes a demerit, an assignment to a bad employee as their penance for doing wrong. In other cases, the A-3 is merely a way to check the box to signal we are doing something lean like Toyota. In terms of culture, these become part of the underlying beliefs that won't be said out loud by the leadership of the organization, but will be well known by the internal organization and sometimes shared with others outside of the organization.

## SUMMARY

It should come as no surprise that Toyota spends so much time and money on communication when they value developing people, trusting relationships, and continuous improvement. The key point to building a Toyota culture is to be intentional about both the formal and informal communication systems that take place in and out of the workplace. These systems should foster open and honest discussion, where members feel it is safe to voice concerns and ideas for improvement, and then contribute in the process of corrective action.

## KEY POINTS TO CONSIDER FOR YOUR COMPANY

1. The company clearly communicates expectations, objectives, and current events to employees.
2. The company establishes the environment and systems where employees feel comfortable expressing their opinions, ideas, and concerns which are viewed as data used for improvement.
3. Human resources acts as a bridge for communication between the members and the company, and measures key performance indicators, including a team member trust audit to track progress.
4. All leaders practice *genchi genbutsu* to stay in touch with the concerns of team members firsthand and respond by reducing barriers to growth and performance.

5. Training is mandatory for leaders to develop real skills in facilitating meetings and communicating with team members.
6. Visual methods are used to clearly communicate the gap between standard and actual.
7. The A-3 report is one form of visual communication used as a development tool to teach the problem-solving methods, as a tool to simply inform others of the status of a project, and to get support for a proposal or idea. Successful use of the A-3 depends on an open and respectful process of sharing information and accepting feedback.

# Chapter 11

# Servant Leadership

*If you are out there observing at the gemba, do something for them (the workers). If you do, the workers will think, "He's watching us but he comes up with some good ideas." That way when the workers see you they will look forward to your help again, and as a result they will begin telling you what makes the work hard to do and ask you to think of ways to make it better. If the workers think, "There he is again just standing there. He must have a lot of time on his hands. He never does anything for us," then nobody will come to you with their problems.[1]*

—Taiichi Ohno, creator of Toyota production system

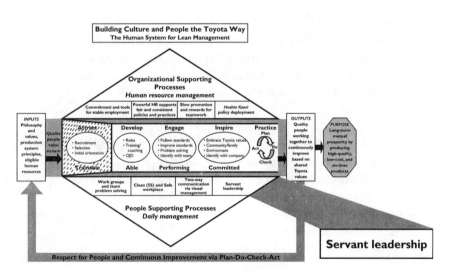

## LEADERS DEVELOP CULTURE

What does it mean to be a leader? Obviously, a leader needs followers. People follow a leader because they want to—they are drawn to the leader. We must remember, however, that managers are not necessarily leaders. Managers have tasks to get done, with deadlines and budgets and rules governing them. They make sure the tasks get done in the right way, on time, and within budget. The distinction between management and leadership can be made clear in this way: workers do not necessarily want to follow the lead of a manager. They may even find their

---

[1] Ohno, Taiichi, *Workplace Management*, Mukilteo, WA: Gemba Press, 2007, p. 95.

manager uninspiring and his or her rules cumbersome. They may think they have a better way, but the manager is in charge, so they follow the rules.

To better understand the differences between leadership and management, we can draw from the example of push-versus-pull systems. Traditional top-down management is a push system in which workers are pushed to follow the orders of managers. Leadership, on the other hand, is a pull system. Followers feel a magnetic pull that compels them to follow the direction of a leader. They seek the leader's direction, believe in the leader, want to learn from the leader, and relish the time they spend with the leader. We speak of charisma as a special quality some people have that makes them attractive. People are drawn to charismatic leaders.

Leaders have power. One of the first sociologists, Max Weber, defined power as the ability to influence others, even against their will. Convincing someone to do something that they wanted to do anyway is not a great demonstration of power. A person exhibits real power when he or she is able to get someone to do something that they would not ordinarily prefer to do.

What the most effective leaders actually do with their power is build a shared culture. A charismatic leader can certainly influence people one-by-one, but this is both inefficient and ineffective. A group of people all moving in the same direction at roughly the same time is a far greater force. And while a manager may be able to get people to move in the same direction by making rules and rewarding people for following those rules, effective leaders develop common goals and common beliefs about the right ways to achieve those goals among a group of people, which leads to far longer lasting commitment to high performance.

When Toyota sends a contingent of Japanese coordinators to other countries to start up operations, they are looking for leaders, not managers. The Toyota Way is designed to cultivate leaders. Of course, not all people selected to be leaders work out, but the success rate is quite high. Principle 9 of *The Toyota Way* states that Toyota wants to: "Grow leaders who thoroughly understand the work, live the philosophy and teach it to others."

We are often asked how to sustain lean changes. A kaizen event produces many positive changes, a lean project reduces inventory, and we want to gather up the gains and hold them tight so we do not lose them. Without effective leadership at the site where we have made those changes, we will with certainty lose those gains. Very few self-maintaining systems exist. In fact, the second law of thermodynamics covers entropy, which means chemical systems will tend over time toward the state of least energy—things tend to decay over time. The concept of entropy also applies to culture. Culture tends to decay over time unless there is continual new energy being fed into the system to keep it going. In the case of societal systems, leaders provide that continuing source of energy, which allows them to maintain, develop, and grow the culture in which they live and work. Pull out the leaders at any point and the system will resume decaying.

Toyota leaders must do more than merely understand the company's philosophy if they expect to maintain and continue to evolve Toyota culture; they must live it and teach it to others. To get the Toyota culture into their DNA, they have to grow within Toyota and experience it firsthand. For this reason, Toyota cannot easily recruit leaders; they must take people who have some natural leadership abilities and develop them to think and act in the Toyota Way every day—a process which easily can take ten or more years.

At their best, Toyota Way leaders should be able to integrate the production and people value streams, identify the key competencies, hire the best people, train them to follow standardized work, and instruct them on how to identify and solve problems. Toyota Way leaders are part of a team, model the behaviors they desire from subordinates, practice safety first, and are not only good talkers but active listeners. At the end of the day, Toyota leaders do their best work through developing in others the values, beliefs, and capabilities to be personally responsible and accountable. They invest authority, responsibility, and accountability in others.

## SERVANT LEADERSHIP

Toyota's internal document, *The Toyota Way 2001* talks about "thoughtful leaders," who are defined as "[having] the ability to energize and invigorate others, willingly giving realistic challenges and development opportunities and fostering a sense of accomplishment in subordinates. Thoughtful leaders monitor individual and team performance, holding people accountable for their actions and taking responsibility for their activities."

Thoughtful leaders who monitor individual and team performance can sound a lot like traditional management. When we think of monitoring, we think of externally measuring and controlling. Isn't that what we said managers do? They set targets, communicate what is expected of people, monitor people to see that they follow the right procedures and are on track to achieve the targets, and use formal rewards and punishments to keep people on task. A key difference between this image of the manager as a monitor and controller and the Toyota view, however, is that Toyota leaders focus on "confirming the process," not catching people making mistakes. Every process has a set of defined rules of operation—standardized work, 5S, standard work-in-process inventory, well-trained people, safe ways of performing the work, metrics, takt time—and the leader is confirming that all these things are up to date and operational. Anything out of standard is subject to problem solving, not finding someone to blame.

Thoughtful leaders do not assume that the right rewards and punishments will automatically produce all the behaviors they desire from subordinates. In fact, they do not even think of the people they are leading as subordinates; rather, thoughtful leaders develop a culture in which they can effectively delegate to and *trust* their team members to produce excellent results as long as they are working in a well-designed process and system. They have developed a culture in which their team members share the right values and beliefs and are well trained in how to do the job so they can focus their attention on helping to solve problems when there is an out-of-standard condition. This is captured in a companion leadership principle in *The Toyota Way 2001*:

> ***Development through delegation***—*We trust our team members and have confidence in their ability to originate ideas, create opportunities, and find solutions. We value the savings in time and effort made possible by investing authority, responsibility, and accountability in other individuals.*

Before the publication of *The Toyota Way 2001*, Toyota's leadership principles were passed down by word of mouth from generation to generation. One key aspect that was communicated to the American leaders at the Georgetown Plant from the Japanese leaders was the concept of "Servant Leadership." Its ideas were articulated and drilled into the minds and hearts of leaders at Toyota. They included statements like the following:

"The team member is the expert."
"Focus on the problem, not the person."
"Mistakes are okay as long as people learn from them."
"Take care of the people building the cars."
"You work for your team members."

TMMK's second president, Mikio Kitano, formalized this perspective and taught all Toyota leaders its main ideas. He would begin by drawing an upside down pyramid, and then would put himself at the bottom of it and the team members at the top. His key point was that the team members are in the value stream of connecting the suppliers to the customer. Since Toyota is a manufacturing company that builds cars, the key value-added work is the process of building cars. Team members doing the production work are building the sellable product; hence, they are the ones that matter most, and everybody and everything else is here to support them and give them what they need to do their job. Figure 11.1 illustrates this leadership perspective.

The key insight of servant leadership is that the further someone is from the value stream, as in the case of upper management, the less that person can directly add value. As leaders, we only add value by supporting those who are most actively adding value to the stream, and therefore, the closer we are to the bottom of the pyramid, the more people we are responsible for supporting. When team

**Leadership develops the capacity that allows team members to improve what needs to be done**

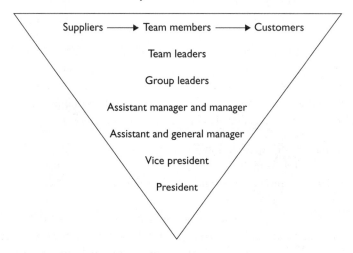

Suppliers ——▶ Team members ——▶ Customers

Team leaders

Group leaders

Assistant manager and manager

Assistant and general manager

Vice president

President

**Figure 11.1** Servant Leadership in Toyota Plants

members are at the top, the organization can draw on the collective capacity and imagination of a much larger pool of individuals. In a traditional top-down organization, the capacity and imagination is limited to a few leaders at the top.

It is important to bear in mind that Toyota didn't adopt this leadership approach so that it could simply hand over the reins of the company to the team members in order to have self-directed work teams. Toyota leaders are highly developed and seen as the key to energizing the organization, actively coaching, and evolving Toyota culture. The leaders' roles are to support the team members with what they need; in Toyota culture, this includes business strategy, long term planning, training, and continuous development. Leaders who delegate to the extent of abdicating responsibility are not leaders at all. As Ohno's quote at the beginning of this chapter suggests, "If the workers think, 'There he is again just standing there. He must have a lot of time on his hands. He never does anything for us,' then nobody will come to you with their problems."

Servant Leadership is an important value in the Toyota Way leadership culture, and it transcends or blends with the cultures of all the Toyota employees, regardless of their national or religious background. When teaching managers in America, Toyota President Kitano sometimes shifted into talking in spiritual terms, noting that service is a critical value in all religions, including Buddhism, Hinduism, Islam, and Christianity. Jesus himself said, "Let the greatest among you serve the most."

# THOUGHTFUL LEADERS LIVING THE TOYOTA WAY VALUES

In the Toyota culture, Toyota Way values drive the leadership's daily actions. Throughout this book—and in Chapter 2 specifically—we have discussed the core values of the Toyota Way, with respect and continuous improvement serving as the foundation of the Toyota culture. We also looked quickly at the supporting values of the Toyota Way, which are worth revisiting in greater detail due to their connection to Toyota Way Leadership. The five supporting values of the Toyota Way are:

1. *Challenge*—forming a long-term vision and meeting challenge with courage and creativity.
2. *Kaizen*—improving the business continuously and always driving for innovation and evolution.
3. *Genchi Genbutsu*—going and seeing; go to the source to find the facts to make decisions, build consensus, and achieve goals at the best speed.
4. *Respect*—taking responsibility to do our best to build mutual trust.
5. *Teamwork*—maximizing the personal and professional growth and performance of both the individual and the team.

## Challenge

*We form a long-term vision, meeting challenges with courage and creativity to realize our dreams. (Toyota Way 2001)*

Imagine the challenge that Toyota faced in its transition from running a loom factory to competing in the auto industry in the aftermath of the devastation of World War II. Toyota has always taken pride in being the underdog and working through the challenges it has faced. This is part of its history and culture.

The Toyota Georgetown plant is visited by thousands of people a year who marvel at the efficiency and orderliness they observe. They learn about the tens of thousands of suggestions that shop floor workers give to their managers. They can see that the people working throughout the operation are highly—and unusually—energetic. It is easy to assume that Toyota's attainment of high levels of efficiency and energy was an easy feat, but according to the leaders who started the operation, it was anything but easy—it was a major challenge. When Toyota first opened the Georgetown plant, the Japanese who were sent over to start it up were under great pressure. They had the success of NUMMI under their belt, but TMMK was the first fully owned Toyota plant. Hiroyoshi Yoshiki, former Vice President of General Administration at TMMK, was involved from the earliest stages and talks about the planning and preparation that was involved in Toyota's move to Kentucky two decades ago:

*Every day was a serious struggle for us. We did not plan a grand experiment. We thought if we fail here, then Toyota Japan itself would be in serious trouble. We did not want to create any artificial thing. We wanted to establish a good car operation, period. We knew what worked in Japan. We could not change our approach, so we tried to do the same thing as much as possible. The most important thing was to produce quality cars. If something could not be well understood by local people, we tweaked and twisted. We tried to articulate what Toyota did; that is, making tacit or implicit knowledge into explicit knowledge. We still have to experience, struggle, and learn.*

The spirit of challenge could be seen in the teachings of Taiichi Ohno. His approach to teaching was to challenge students to achieve a major improvement in a production area. He might ask them to double productivity, for example, after which he would not be satisfied with anything less than doubled productivity. When Ohno himself, after World War II, was charged with catching up to the productivity of gigantic and mighty Ford Motor Company, then eight times more productive than Toyota plants, he accepted the target and achieved it in three years. That is the spirit of challenge.

One of the former students of Ohno who later became the president of a Japanese supplier to Denso, (Toyota's largest supplier), explained that his biggest lesson from Ohno was learning to never be satisfied with less than 100 percent achievement. He had been trained as an industrial engineer to gain efficiencies, but when he encountered Taiichi Ohno, who came to his plant to teach TPS, he said that Ohno's teaching changed his whole way of looking at the world.

*Before I met Ohno-san, I would practice industrial engineering and had been taught to try to load up production jobs to 85 percent of the cycle time. I was told that, practically speaking, 85 percent is the maximum because of natural variation and that perfection was not possible. Ohno-san challenged me to achieve 100 percent of the cycle time. Anything less than this is a compromise, and we should always aim for perfection.*

We often think of NUMMI as the first operation using TPS in the United States, but actually Toyota started Toyota Auto Body (TABC) in 1972. That operation was set up with the sole purpose of making truck beds for the Tacoma truck so that, when the rest of the truck was imported from Japan, the truck would have some local content. Of course, the truck beds had to be painted to match the rest of the truck.

TABC had a senior Japanese advisor who had been a student of Ohno. He came to the plant in its early years and was very unhappy with the large batch sizes in paint. The paint shop manager explained that changing over from one color to another was costly: it took time to clean out the oil-based paint from the hoses, and paint was wasted as they flushed out the paint system, so they had to make a lot of truck beds of one color before they changed to a different color.

The Japanese advisor was not sympathetic. He requested that they reduce the time it took to changeover between paint colors and reduce the batch size. They worked very hard to please him, and by his next visit, they had cut the time in half. He still was not satisfied and asked them to try harder. By his next visit, the changeover time was cut in half again and the batch size was a fraction of the original size. He challenged them to achieve a batch size of one truck bed between changeovers. They worked really hard and got the changeover time down to a few minutes, changing colors after every truck bed, even though it was costly in lost paint and time. When their advisor visited, he was obviously pleased by their dedication and accomplishments. He said, with obvious delight, "You have done well. Now that you can achieve a batch size of one, please set the batch size to the optimum from a business point of view."

He recognized that, even with the changeover time reduced to minutes, it was not economical to change colors after every truck bed, but he did not want them to learn to compromise. After they had proven to themselves it could be done and had learned an important lesson, he was happy to let them compromise to a higher batch size. Today Toyota can paint with a batch size of one, but that was after several breakthroughs in paint technology such as moving to water-based paint.

## Kaizen

*We are relentless in our pursuit of improvement, never easily satisfied, constantly making improvement efforts and steadily encouraging innovation. (Toyota Way 2001)*

The spirit of challenge is closely related to the value of kaizen (continuous improvement). Throughout its history, Toyota leaders have embraced the value of kaizen:

- "We are working on making better products by making improvements every day." (Kiichiro Toyoda)
- "Don't think mechanically. Even a dry towel can produce water when ideas are conceived." (Eiji Toyoda)
- "Kaizen activities are the incubator of innovation. This is because kaizen activities create an atmosphere of change." (Akira Takahashi)
- "Be ahead of the times through endless creativity, inquisitiveness, and pursuit of improvement." (The Toyota Precepts)

While these quotations paint a suggestive picture of the leadership values at Toyota, putting these values into action is essential. Cheryl Jones, vice president of manufacturing at TMMK when we interviewed her, describes how these values drive everyday activity. She illustrates how Toyota keeps the spirit of competition going, even when they are dominating the auto industry and are first in the world in terms of overall automotive sales. She also explains how Toyota balances the spirit of challenge with nurturing and development so as not to discourage those being led.

*I just came from a Quality Circle presentation of a tool and die group; they have had a hard time and struggled to get team member involvement. A group of three members reported out on an analysis that focused on gaps in efficiency between TMC (Toyota Motor Corporation in Japan) and ours. It laid out three reasons we have the gap. We focused on one area and did kaizen to make some improvements. There were small kaizens, but it was the process they used and the satisfaction they experienced that has led to making bigger improvements. They ended up, after making a lot of small improvements, yielding six minutes of savings, where the gap is 1.2 hours. I challenged them to come up with other ideas with bigger savings. Sometimes we might think that six minutes is not a lot, but it is using the process to encourage the team members to see that this is a start and keep going.*

The values of kaizen and teamwork are reiterated in Georgetown President Steve St. Angelo's description of leadership at Toyota. "In a typical plant, it is looked upon as management's responsibility to make it successful. At Toyota it is our responsibility to take care of the team members who are making improvements. We foster the kaizen mentality. Team members are responsible for setting up jobs and doing time studies on them. They know how to eliminate waste."

## Genchi Genbutsu

*Go to the source to find the facts to make correct decisions, build consensus, and achieve goals at our best speed." (Toyota Way 2001).*

The value placed on learning directly—by hands-on experience—is deeply engrained in Toyota culture. Founder Sakiichi Toyoda's words are still quoted throughout the company: "Never try to design something without first gaining three years hands-on experience."

Genchi genbutsu is one of those values, like kaizen, that is found throughout all of Toyota. There are some concepts, such as pull systems, that are more difficult to translate directly to management and the office. Genchi genbutsu is alive and well in every nook and cranny within Toyota. For example we are often asked how Toyota understands the market when they design a new car. Does the marketing department determine the customer requirements? Do they use a tool like "quality function deployment?" The most important tool for understanding the customer is the chief engineer and his deep training in genchi genbutsu. There are many famous stories of chief engineers going to extremes to understand the customer first hand like living in Beverly Hills to understand potential Lexus owners and going to places where young Americans hang out to see how young people live to design a Scion vehicle.

Jim Farley, former Group Vice President and General Manager of Lexus, described some of the ways the Toyota team developed the requirements for the Lexus by renting a house in a wealthy part of Southern California:

> *The design team rented a house on the coast in Orange County, the designers and the chief engineer, for a month while they were designing the vehicle in Chelsea—our West Coast design studio. On the weekends they hit the country clubs and I think probably Toyota engineers are accused sometime of being weird people, because they tend to hang out at parking lots and take pictures of people while they're loading stuff in the back of their car.*

Mamie Warrick, Corporate Manager and Dean of Education, Planning and Business Operations, University of Toyota, told a story that has become part of the lore of chief engineers at Toyota Motor Sales:

> *They (Japanese coordinators) told us to go and see. They wanted us to escort them out there to go see. And there are some funny stories related to that. When the first RAV4 arrived for our markets, it did not have any cup holders. To help the chief engineer understand the situation, one of our distributor members picked up the chief engineer in the current RAV4 model, took him to the local 7–11 and bought the guy a 32 ounce hot cup of coffee. The purpose, of course, was for him to discover there was no place to put that cup. So the American team member helps the chief engineer into the car and gives him the cup of coffee. The chief engineer is so delighted with the coffee, he doesn't bother to put it down and just downs it. It's steaming hot! (The Japanese have a higher tolerance for hot liquids). And at that point he has the empty cup and realizes, ah! there is no place to put it, there is no cup holder. And then the point is made.*

## Respect

> *We respect others, make every effort to understand each other, take responsibility, and do our best to build mutual trust. (The Toyota Way 2001)*

It is little-known that the early name for the Toyota Production System was the "Respect for Humanity" System. When we think of TPS and the leanness it denotes, we may think of eliminating waste, making operations more efficient, reducing numbers of people from the production line, and major reductions in cost. Efficiency and respect for humanity do not always naturally go together.

In fact, lean is often associated with fewer people, especially because we sometimes hear managers talk about using kaizen workshops to cut heads. In Toyota's view, the focus is not on cutting heads but rather eliminating waste. Eliminating waste will eventually lead to higher productivity through careful planning of staffing levels.

If we think back on the origins of *jidoka*, one of the two pillars of the Toyota Production System, it started as a way to achieve efficiency gains in the use of Toyota automatic looms. Sakichi Toyoda developed a method by which automatic looms would stop themselves when a thread broke. Before its invention, workers would sit and watch so they could manually stop the loom when a thread broke, but by building looms that could stop themselves, a single worker could tend to many looms at once, which greatly increased productivity. Sakichi did not regard this only as a productivity gain; he had succeeded in "freeing the person from the machine." In the old system, the person was, in a sense, serving the machine. In Sakichi's mind, people should not serve machines; machines should serve people. So the term *jidoka* was used, which had to do with automation, but a character was added that symbolized a person. So Sakichi Toyoda had put the human into automation. Any waste of a person's time—even a mere second—is intolerable, as that time can never be given back to the person. Eiji Toyoda later expressed this philosophy well: "A person's life is an accumulation of time—just one hour is equivalent to a person's life. Employees provide their precious hours of life to the company, so we have to use it effectively; otherwise, we are wasting their life."

When people eliminate wasted motion through kaizen, it is considered a great human achievement, as he or she is developing their ability to think deeply about problems—one of the most highly-valued human accomplishments within Toyota. As we have discussed throughout this book, that does not mean their job, or the job of a teammate, is threatened—that would be completely disrespectful. Instead, it means that Toyota is more competitive, which raises the level of security of all employees.

Respect for humanity extends beyond Toyota employees to respect for the broader environment. When Toyota finally was given permission to build their first full-scale mass production facility, to be built in Koromo (now Toyota City), Kiichiro Toyoda said in a famous speech, "I have made every effort to see that there are no flaws in my plans—and I have complete confidence. Should Toyota fail in this venture, however, there will be other entrepreneurs to take advantage of the plant and the facilities that we are going to build. Our endeavor is certain to benefit Koromo, we will never turn against its interests."

Later, in the 1990s, Chairman Okuda said, "We must be a company that is accepted wholeheartedly by people around the world, who would think it natural if Toyota became No. 1 in size, since we provide attractive products that excel in environmental protection, in safety, and contribute immensely to local communities. That is the goal of 'harmonious growth' and what I regard as corporate virtue."

## Teamwork

*We stimulate personal and professional growth, share the opportunities of development, and maximize individual and team performance. (Toyota Way 2001)*

Alex Warren was one of the early Americans who, after years in the American auto industry, joined Toyota and rose to the executive ranks because of his intuitive grasp of Toyota's Culture. Looking back over his career in American companies and Toyota, he concluded, "Until senior management gets their egos out of the way and goes to the whole team—goes to all of them and leads them all together—then senior management will continue to miss out on the brain power and extraordinary capabilities of all their employees."

We are working with an American company that is in the midst of lean transformation and that recognizes the cultural challenges involved. They have found the biggest change in culture (and results) coming when they implemented the practice of huddles. The senior leadership decided that if lean was going to work, they were going to have to include all the members, so they decided to start asking them what they thought about problems they were experiencing and ways to correct them. They were astounded by the quantity and quality of the problems and solutions identified. With this energy, the company made it a daily practice for all managers and supervisors to meet with their people and to discuss problems that were occurring and incorporate ideas on how to solve them. Huddle success stories range from correcting customer complaints that had been unresolved for years to countless time-saving ideas. One manager said that the teamwork huddles had made more difference than anything else in their lean implementation. When asked why all the plant managers were not seeing the same success he replied:

*Because they don't all get it. When some heard about the huddles, they saw it as more work that they would have to do, and they wouldn't have enough resources to deal with all the problems the team members identified. Those plant managers missed the point that, given the opportunity, the team members themselves can become the resources to solve the problems they identify. The plant managers who recognize this are excelling.*

Interestingly enough, this manager's reflection on the next step for his progression as an organization was to improve the problem-solving capability of the entire organization—managers and employees. This is just what Toyota Leaders are working on in order to continue to lead the organization toward mutual prosperity. As discussed in Chapter 5 on problem solving, Toyota developed the Toyota

Business Practices in order to have a global standard with which to teach and develop their leaders to implement the Toyota Way on a daily basis.

One of the practices we have used in many contexts is the visual metric board and daily problem solving. We have done this in office environments, iron ore mining, research and development centers, aircraft repair facilities, and at rental car sites. It is amazing. Simply create some form of visual management where you track progress every day and flag deviations from the standards and teach the team basic problem solving and you will start to see whole new levels of kaizen in the organization. Of course, management must believe in the power of kaizen and enthusiastically implement any good ideas, and even some not so great ideas.

The key to effective visualization is to keep the information simple, current, and to make deviations from the standard stand out. The most common approach is to have some form of green, yellow, and red indicators, like traffic signals. On some boards in Toyota plants you will see a list of current problems organized by function, with a big red magnet by those problems that are critical and need immediate attention.

Like many Americans, Mike Hoseus had learned to present detailed information to impress the boss. He had to learn the hard way the value Toyota places on simple, visual presentations:

*As a plant manager, my team was preparing presentations for a VIP visit from a high-level executive from Japan. I had worked with my team to put together big display boards with all of the information, being sure to include as much detail as possible, to answer any questions he might have. He looked at it and said, "No good!" I asked why. He said, "It is too complicated for someone with fresh eyes to understand. It is your job to make any problem or communication simple and clear enough that a preschool child could walk up to it and understand what you are trying to say; whether it is for a new hire or the president of the company." I remember thinking that this is just the opposite of what we were taught in school, especially college. I was taught to use big complicated words and keep things esoteric. Now, I was being taught to think like a kindergartner.*

It is hard to find many people who would argue against the value of teamwork. It is the foundation of popular sports, music groups, the military, and for many people, their most exhilarating experiences were when solving problems as part of a team. Yet, we saw in Chapter 1 that there is a problem. Some cultures naturally embrace the team, while others are more naturally individualistic. Western cultures tend to embrace the individual. Even today in America, its seems that about one-third of CEOs are fired within a two-year period, and the new CEO, as an individual, is expected to ride into town and save the company. We embrace teamwork, but we love the lone hero who comes in and saves the day. We value the long-term employee who gets the gold watch after 30 years of service to the company, but we are much more impressed by the fast-tracker who rises quickly through the ranks then is recruited by the next company for twice the money, dazzling managers as he climbs the ladder. Peter Drucker, one of the greatest management thinkers of all time, said:

> *The leaders who work most effectively, it seems to me, never say "I." And that's not because they have trained themselves not to say "I." They don't think "I." They think "we"; they think "team." They accept responsibility and don't side-step it, but "we" gets the credit.... This is what creates trust, what enables you to get the task done.*

What drives teamwork is not necessarily good will and management goading. It is part of the broader Toyota Production System, which places such a high value on leaders working on the floor and adding value through team members. When you have the tools of standardized work and visual management, and the system is set up where you must work through teams to meet your objectives, teamwork becomes as much a business success factor as a core value unto itself. Gary Convis has lived through the many challenges of teaching Americans the value of putting the team first and makes an interesting connection between teamwork and *genchi genbutsu*:

> *You cannot change the fact that we are Americans and we are individualistic people. But inside yourself you have to find the balance of what satisfies your personal, individual needs, and yet you have to be hands-on on the floor, and solving real problems; you must be physically out of the office and on the plant floor. You spend hours of every day like that. The human being needs to adapt his own individual characteristics to what it takes to do the job properly. By and large, people find that common ground some way. In Japan, based on the cultural characteristics of team first, individuals come into that naturally and naturally work as a team. In our American culture, it probably takes some adaptation. The common ground is hands-on involvement and the need to work on the shop floor. You need to have personal pride and feel connected to team members, to the success of that team, section, and the product they make. You start to see your value is the result of a group of people, not necessarily because of "me."*

# HOW DOES TOYOTA SELECT AND DEVELOP LEADERS?

We heard optimism from Gary Convis about Toyota's success in developing American leaders that fit the Toyota culture, but we also heard him acknowledge the challenges and how some exceptional individuals simply leave Toyota out of frustration. Arguably, the biggest challenge Toyota has faced as it has rapidly expanded globally is to develop Toyota Way leaders as fast as needed to lead operations being launched all over the world. How does Toyota do it?

The most important thing we learned from Toyota in this regard is the power of commitment and patience. Toyota leaders have such a strong vision of the Toyota Way culture and are so committed to maintaining and growing that culture that they have the patience to let it grow; they are simply not willing to compromise. Crash courses in the Toyota Way simply do not work—it takes time and patience. Gray Convis explains:

> *Toyota by its nature is not a very fast-track company. We are not the same as Japan, but the principles we value at Toyota, North America, and look for in a leader, are very similar. You will not get up the ladder unless you can manage the Toyota Way and can manage that way in your daily job. If you cannot make that transition, and people do not want to follow you because they know that you don't care, you will not be successful. It is not a fast-paced promotion system here in America. Look at me; look at almost anybody. You have to develop the capability and demonstrate it and grow with it. Each step requires new capability development. It is all around, this Toyota culture.*

One example of a true success story in growing a Toyota leader from within is Cheryl Jones, who at the time we interviewed her was vice president of manufacturing for the Georgetown plant, with approximately 6,000 people reporting to her. While this is an enormous responsibility, when you talk to Cheryl you feel like you could just as well be talking to a team leader on the shop floor. That is because she worked her way up from the shop floor and has the passion for developing people and the humility that are so highly valued within Toyota.

Cheryl never worked in manufacturing before joining Toyota—she was a supervisor at Kroger's grocery store in the Lexington, Kentucky area. When the Toyota plant was announced and they advertised for people she took a chance and felt confident that "If I got my foot in the door, I could move up." It was obvious that HR saw potential in Cheryl because they hired her as a group leader, with a significant amount of responsibility in the Toyota system.

She went to Japan and began learning TPS. When she was just getting comfortable in that role, she was asked to go to the pilot team organization, which is set up to get shop floor input into new models working directly with product development. It is a multi-year commitment, and at first Cheryl said she would rather work her way up in manufacturing. Her supervisor suggested otherwise: "Never say no to an opportunity—always take an opportunity to learn." She then agreed and has never looked back.

The pilot team gave her opportunities to work one-on-one with many trainers from Japan and learn how to set up prototype builds and set up processing and new assembly jobs. Bringing the product over from Japan also gave her a more up-close look at the processes in Japan. She was then moved to help start up the new assembly line (number 2) before there was even a building. She helped set up the processes, hire people, and train new people. She worked her way up to assistant general manager within assembly and was next invited to lead the paint department, of course with no prior experience in paint. By now she knew better than to ask questions, and spent the next seven years running the paint plant—a highly technical process with tremendous learning opportunities.

She was soon looking for more learning opportunities, and she was asked to move to the new truck plant in Baja, Mexico for one year. Georgetown had been selected to be the "mother plant" to teach TPS to the new startup. This was a first: In the past, all the mother plants were in Japan. She agreed to take on this major challenge, which also meant getting support from her husband to have a commuter marriage for one year. She learned much in Baja teaching them from scratch. Since it was a smaller plant, she could see the whole process from start to finish.

After the Mexico experience, Cheryl came back to Georgetown and was appointed vice president for all of manufacturing. She had learned all aspects of manufacturing technically, but what she learned that was more important was how to develop people:

> It is critical to establish a culture where people feel comfortable bringing up problems and see them as opportunities to make improvements. It is a real challenge to make the environment comfortable and yet challenging. How do you create a safe condition? In order for people to continually engage in kaizen, it has to be a safe environment. I had to feel that in my own development as I was continually taking on new assignments without a lot of background. I always felt comfortable that as long as I was learning from each experience and acknowledged learning points it was always a positive, and that others view it as positive. My job was not at risk.

In Chapter 10 we described how Wil James rose rapidly in Toyota, North America, first at the Georgetown plant, and then as president of TABC. Wil points out that his fast rise up the ladder was unusual for Toyota, and he was pushed a bit faster because of the urgent need for leadership as Toyota grew rapidly in America. Toyota executives obviously saw something special in Wil that caused them to push him along. Wil explained it in this way:

> I have really internalized Toyota's philosophy and live it every day—the concepts of continuous improvement and respect for the individual. I believe these were principles of mine before I joined Toyota. I happened to find a place that felt as strongly about respecting the individual, and I am always looking for a better way. I was frustrated with practices in

*corporate America outside Toyota because they were not taking the opportunity to involve people in the process, so Toyota is like a dream to me because I have always lived that way.*

# SUMMARY—BEST OF BOTH WORLDS

The goal for any new start-up plant for Toyota is to take the best of the Japanese Toyota Way and to blend it with the local culture to create that plant's Toyota culture. TMMK's General Manager of General Administration, Tom Zawacki, explains:

*From the very beginning, Mr. Cho said that the goal was to take the best of Japanese and American management techniques to create a new and unique management system. I am sure he was referring to the softer side of managing Americans and not saying we will change the TPS. That was firm. We will do things according to TPS. There are things we should never change—respect for humanity, standardized work, JIT; the things that are so key to our DNA—kaizen, genchi Genbutsu, preventing problems from occurring, and so on.*

*These are definitely engrained in Toyota in Japan and are fairly well in place here in TMMK. Continuous improvement is hard for Americans. We want that—to do a better job today—but it is related to not being satisfied with what we have done. We want to celebrate. For some Americans who have not embraced that, or who have not been able to understand it from a cultural viewpoint, it is hard. Those who do understand are able to say—that is Toyota; the best of the Japanese way is TPS. The best of the American way is in knowing how to manage Americans successfully in a TPS environment—diversity, working from home, helping single mothers be successful in the workplace—flexible hours—other things that relate to American values and lifestyles.*

While Toyota wants the best of both cultures, there is a Toyota Way of leadership, and in many respects it is contrary to many Western tendencies. Table 11.1 summarizes some of the key differences. American managers want quick results, have great personal pride and want to climb the ladder of power and prestige rapidly. They regard results as being much more important than approach, and people are seen as a means to achieve results. A successful American leader should overcome barriers, not make excuses. Results are judged by the numbers.

A Toyota leader is expected to be patient and humble. Slow development by learning jobs deeply at each stage is preferred over rapid ladder climbing.

**Table 11.1** Traditional Western Leadership Compared to Toyota Leadership

| Traditional Western Leader | Toyota Leader |
| --- | --- |
| Quick Results | Patient |
| Proud | Humble |
| Climb Ladder Rapidly | Learn Deeply and Horizontally and Gradually Work Way up Ladder |
| Results at All Costs | The Right Process Will Lead to the Right Results |
| Accomplish Objectives Through People | Develop People |
| Overcome Barriers | Take Time to Deeply Understand Problem and Root Cause Before Acting |
| Manage by the Numbers | Deeply Understand the Process |

Toyota leaders are often moved several times horizontally to get a broader perspective before climbing higher in the organization. Toyota leaders are encouraged to follow the right process and have faith that doing the right things will lead to the desired results. Toyota leaders are teachers who develop people. A barrier is a problem to be deeply analyzed and understood so appropriate countermeasures can be developed and carefully evaluated. Deep understanding of the process is more highly valued than managing by the numbers.

Once again culture rears its ugly head. We want a culture to support lean, yet it is our culture that seems to be getting in the way. A recent study suggests the "servant leadership" perspective is much more natural in the East compared to the West. A group of psychologists[2] compared how Eastern cultures view leadership compared to those in the West. First they looked at how World Cup soccer teams select captains. National teams from Western countries chose more midfielders and strikers (i.e., offensive players) as captains, and East Asian teams chose more goalkeepers and defenders. Then they conducted a controlled experiment using a projection test in which participants looked at diagrams and identified the leader; they found Americans assumed the person at the front of the group was the leader while those from Singapore tended to view the person in the rear as the leader. Their interpretation:

[2] Menon, Tanya, Jessica Sim, Jeanne Ho-Ying Fu, Chi-yue Chiu, and Ying-yi Hong "Blazing the Trail versus Trailing the Group: Culture and Perceptions of the Leader's Position." University of Chicago Working Paper, 2007: p. 11.

*American participants perceive leaders as agents and give them credit when they find opportunities for the group (consistent with a "Democratic" model), by contrast, Singaporeans who see leaders as agents blame them when they fail to protect the group from threats (consistent with a "Paternalistic" model). Members of both cultures share the view that the leader in the front is an innovator and the leader in the back is the protector.*

The implication is that the American leader is charging ahead, blazing new trails, and the team members are following along, while the Singapore leader is standing behind to protect and support the group. From behind the leader can see the group and understand what they need, while the leader out ahead does not know in detail what is going on with the group. Working with these natural cultural tendencies of Americans has been a challenge for Toyota. While the goal is the best of both worlds, the reality is that some basic American tendencies can get in the way of developing the kind of culture Toyota believes is essential to its success. Developing a strong and positive blended culture will take time, and if there is one thing Toyota leaders have, it is patience. Gary Convis agreed that the management culture is much slower to develop than the techniques of TPS:

*How close are we in America to the Toyota Way? In terms of the practical operations level, very close. Self-reliance and establishing plants in the United States really helped us a lot. At the operations level we are very close, but not at the management level: It is not as easy. In practical operations we can see and feel better why the Toyota approach works; the cycle is short so they can experience it. It makes sense and people are willing to do it. The management cycle is longer, not as clear, and not as crisp to experience. It will take more time. On the operations level we are close. That is why we can do the Camry launch now with zero assistance from Japan. During the last launch we had 200 Japanese members, and this time, zero.*

# KEY POINTS TO CONSIDER FOR YOUR COMPANY

1. Leaders develop culture, so Toyota invests years to develop leaders who carry the DNA of the company in their thoughts, words, and actions.
2. Toyota leadership is sometimes referred to as "servant leadership." The higher leaders go, the less direct power they have and the more they have to work hard to support the value-added workers.
3. Toyota wants thoughtful leaders who live the core values, including the spirit of challenge, kaizen, *genchi genbutsu*, respect, and teamwork.

4. Toyota prefers to develop leaders from within through slow development, rotating them broadly but with deep experience at each step.

5. When it is necessary to hire from the outside, the selection procedure is rigorous, searching for the kind of technical awareness characterized by *genchi genbutsu* and the "soul" of the Toyota spirit.

6. While Toyota in America has achieved a high level of TPS at the operational level, despite several decades of developing Americans into Toyota leaders, the management culture of Toyota in America still lags behind Japan in understanding and practicing the Toyota Way.

# PART THREE SUMMARY

The people-supporting processes include both formal structured processes like scheduled meetings, quality circles, and early-symptom investigations and the unscripted daily behavior of leaders and team members working cooperatively to get the job done. Without this formal and informal support it would be impossible for individual team members to develop to their potential in the people value stream.

If we step back from the long list of practices we have described in this section we can see a reflection of Toyota culture. At the surface level, if one were to hang around a Toyota operation, it would be clear that there are many meetings, lots of writing on white boards, well kept up metrics on charts and graphs, and audits done of member safety. We often hear people comment even from a short tram tour of the Georgetown plant that people seem engaged and energetic. The meetings would look a bit peculiar because so many are done standing up on the shop floor rather than in cushy chairs in conference rooms.

What these practices really reflect are norms and values about supporting team members in a physically and psychologically safe environment, servant leadership to develop and engage team members, and the importance of clear and frequent communication (see Figure III.1). The strong belief in objective problem solving that focuses on improving systems instead of blaming individuals underlies a good deal of the daily kaizen.

All of these contexts aim to sustain the individual team members and work teams in their coordinated efforts to add value. Each also offers ample opportuni-

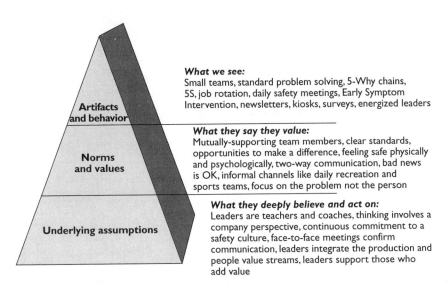

**Figure III.1** Section III Summary Cultural Analysis

ties to surface problems that become the subject of the PDCA problem-solving method. The ultimate goal of these supporting processes is the practical well being—physical and psychological—of all team members as they engage in their work daily.

We are often asked why Toyota will often talk about quality, cost, and delivery and leave out safety and morale. The reason is that safety and morale of the work-force seems like such an obvious priority that it may not even be mentioned. For example, every management quality meeting begins with a report on safety. Without safety nothing else matters. The concept of servant leadership also seems obvious because of the strong belief in value-added work. Managers do not add value so they can only contribute through those doing the value-added work. Whether the activities involve holding daily team meetings, highlighting ergonomically-correct bolt-shooting techniques, presenting a problem analysis to other team members, or speaking up in a manager-led cross-training session, the emphasis is on encouraging participation, in keeping with the values, and actively supporting the commitment to continuous improvement.

# Part Four

# Organizational Supporting Processes

*The first type of bureaucracy is the more familiar one: it serves the purposes of* **coercion and compliance.** *Here, the role of the authority hierarchy, procedures manuals, and staffs is to assure that potentially recalcitrant, incompetent, or irresponsible employees do the right thing. The second type of bureaucracy serves the purpose of* **enablement.** *Here bureaucratic structures and systems function to support the work of the "doers" rather than to bolster the authority of the "higher-ups." When bureaucracy takes this form rather than the more traditional, coercive form, then even a highly bureaucratic structure will be experienced by employees as a tool with which they can better perform their tasks, rather than a weapon used by their superiors against them.*[1]

—Paul S. Adler, professor of management,
University of Southern California

Now we are shifting gears from the daily support team members experience every day to the formal supporting processes that enable team member development and high performance. The topic of formal organization has been taught since the beginning of management courses. "Organizational structure" is often thought of in terms of the organizational chart. The term bureaucracy has become a pejorative term that means "red tape." If you ask most employees about their visit to the human resources department, they would describe going to fill out long and

---

[1] Adler, Paul S. "Building Better Bureaucracies," *Academy of Management Executive,* 13, 4, Nov. 1999: 36–47.

complicated paperwork to change their benefit plan or add a beneficiary—about as much fun as going to the dentist. It would be unfair to claim that Toyota has no burdensome bureaucracy that employees find frustrating, but we can say that many of the formal organizational processes are absolutely essential to support Toyota's culture of respect for people and continuous improvement.

*The Toyota Way* (2004) drew on Paul Adler's distinction between "coercive bureaucracy" and "enabling bureaucracy" to explain how Toyota is different from many other large bureaucratic organizations. Toyota is very bureaucratic in that it has a strong division of labor, clear roles and responsibilities, and rules and standard operating procedures for everything. In this regard, it is arguably one of the most bureaucratic organizations in the world. However, there is something different about Toyota's brand of bureaucracy compared to what we see in most other large organizations. While the typical bureaucracy is designed to provide the hierarchy with the power to control others, Toyota's "enabling" bureaucracy seeks to assist team members to creatively solve problems, improve processes, and continually learn. Rigid bureaucracy that creates an inflexible structure to control people would stifle continuous improvement and have the exact opposite effect desired by the Toyota Way.

In this section we will begin in Chapter 12 by looking at how Toyota carefully plans and controls employment levels to provide stability and security to team members. In Chapter 13 we argue that at Toyota human resources is far more hands on, and in some ways far more directly controlling, than most human resources departments in order to ensure a fair workplace that supports team member morale and growth. The reward system is one of the favorite topics of visitors to Toyota; in Chapter 14 we will show how monetary rewards and fast track promotions are very much deemphasized at Toyota in favor of slow and deep learning and growth. There are many types of rewards and recognition, and these need to be tailored to the local culture. Corrective action when there is a performance issue is viewed objectively based on the facts, and the goal is to solve the problem and bring the team member back to the expected performance level. Finally in Chapter 15 we discuss the famous system of *hoshin kanri* (policy deployment) which is how Toyota channels the energy of highly developed team members to achieve long-term mutual prosperity for the company and employee.

## Chapter 12

# Commitment and Tools for Stable Employment

*It's up to us, in management, to create an environment in which every team member on the line takes control of quality, and works to stream-line production without ever worrying about his own job security.*

—*The Toyota Way 2001*

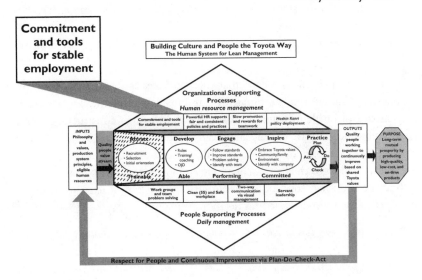

## LONG-TERM PARTNERSHIP OR DISPOSABLE LABOR?

After years of top Western companies proclaiming "people are our most important resource," their actions suggested otherwise. Human Resource departments develop extensive training programs and career paths, mission statements extol the virtues of people continually improving processes, and at the same time the executive office plots the next plant closing. Leveraged buyouts put companies in huge debt and a cadre of CEOs move from company to company cutting costs through restructuring and outsourcing to take the company public. There seem to be sincere desires to invest in people at the working level, but they are continually undermined by the chaos caused by decisions from the top. In the meantime, these same CEOs, who are cost cutters, have proclaimed their commitment to developing people and processes, and, at some level, seem genuine in their desire.

The American mindset on the workforce is still that the employees are expendable resources to be added and subtracted based on the ups and downs of the business. The only thing that seems to slow them down are legal requirements and labor unions. We have heard all kinds of justifications for this from executives participating in Toyota culture workshops:

- "We have to lay off some employees while times are bad. It is the only way to save the company for the employees that are left, and the stock-holders."
- "It is our responsibility to cut people in the short term to save the company in the long term. It is not easy, but it is the responsibility of management to do so."
- "The car business is different than ours, we have cycles that make it impossible not to lay off employees."
- "We have the pressure of our shareholders demanding improved quarterly earnings; Toyota does not seem to have that."

As an example, one company that engaged Liker as an advisor had begun to do one-week kaizen events facilitated by an outside consultant. The events were very successful in identifying a lot of waste and through constructing cells and rebalancing the work there were significant productivity gains. As a result of the productivity gains employees were immediately laid off.

Liker challenged the wisdom of asking employees to participate in kaizen only to find the team had contributed to eliminating the jobs of team members. The manager of the shop defended his decisions explaining:

> This is not the Toyota culture. It is not uncommon here that we work on a productivity project, and, as a result, lay off workers. We do not get credit for the productivity gains until we lay off the workers or transfer them to another shop if there happens to be an opening they are qualified for. In my case, I was using the kaizen events as a way to get rid of the dead wood. The other workers all know these people were dead wood, so they also welcome getting rid of them. They are on board with the lean program.

Referring to people as dead wood is disrespectful and using kaizen events to get rid of poor performing employees is avoiding due process and responsibility. We should note that not every worker left behind did agree the laid off workers were dead wood. Pretty soon word spread that when there is a kaizen event there will soon be layoffs. Lean got the reputation of being mean. While workers complied with the management directive, they did not do so enthusiastically or with any degree of commitment.

Albert Einstein defined insanity as "doing the same thing over and over again and expecting different results." Somehow many managers who have bought into a lean vision seem to think they can keep treating employees as variable costs and buffers yet create an environment where employees are deeply committed to the company vision. In reality, they will keep on getting employees who see the company as a short-term place to hang out and make some money until they move to the next gig.

Toyota truly believes that people are its competitive strength and makes investments accordingly. Even if senior leadership desires highly capable and committed employees and people at the working level are happy to carry out these wishes, we still need something in the middle to connect the executive desires and what happens on the shop floor. That something is a planning system. Toyota has converted their values into practice through a detailed and carefully thought out workforce planning system that proactively adjusts requirements to avoid the need for layoffs of permanent employees.

As discussed in Chapter 2, in the 1950s, after their labor crisis, Toyota decided that they were going to value the trusting partnership with their employees and manage the company in such a way as to prevent the need for any more layoffs, making it "the last thing we do." The starting point of Toyota culture is the underlying assumption of the partnership between the company and the employees toward a purpose of long-term mutual prosperity. Toyota values the trusting relationship with the employees and "treats them as assets" instead of commodities. As a result, many actions and behaviors support these values and assumptions. The three-level culture model can be used to illustrate how this works in the case of workforce management (see Figure 12.1).

Toyota does not leave much to chance and to support the long-term commitment to employees, they have developed detailed methods for stable employment. Figure 12.1 shows just some of the daily processes and behaviors that Toyota puts into practice in order to actually make the job security commitment a reality. It is how Toyota "manages the company" in such a way as to prevent the need for layoffs. This is a critical piece that most American managers miss in the implementation of lean. They credit Toyota with valuing employees but often say

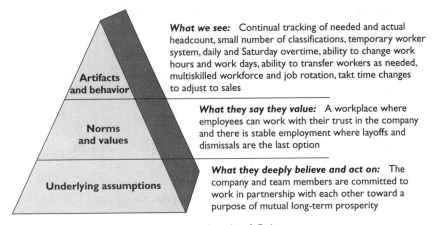

**What we see:** Continual tracking of needed and actual headcount, small number of classifications, temporary worker system, daily and Saturday overtime, ability to change work hours and work days, ability to transfer workers as needed, multiskilled workforce and job rotation, takt time changes to adjust to sales

**What they say they value:** A workplace where employees can work with their trust in the company and there is stable employment where layoffs and dismissals are the last option

**What they deeply believe and act on:** The company and team members are committed to work in partnership with each other toward a purpose of mutual long-term prosperity

Artifacts and behavior

Norms and values

Underlying assumptions

**Figure 12.1** Workforce Management Levels of Culture

"it is easy to offer job security when you are growing and making bucket loads of money." The fact is they are part right, but also wrong. They are right in the fact that Toyota does value this. They are also right in that Toyota has accumulated a great deal of money and this does help them to weather the storms. They are wrong in thinking that Toyota does not need to worry about this. Toyota is expert at worrying and therefore has evolved many systems to "manage" the business to deal with both upswings and downswings in the market.

We talked to Mark Daugherty in his role as manager over Staffing and Workforce Control for all of Toyota's North American Operations. At Toyota, the production control department is extremely important as they set the schedules for the plants. They are very sophisticated at what they do and use algorithms to level the schedule, while using a variety of methods to work with sales to jointly optimize production and customer service. Daugherty is doing the same thing with staffing—considering many factors to decide on the right staffing levels, for plants to ride out ups and downs in the market. His Toyota career started in the Georgetown plant where he was responsible for its staffing levels, and he later was moved to do it for all of North America. He explains Toyota's perspective on workforce management:

> Toyota values stable employment—it is a unique characteristic that we focus so much on. It goes back to key Toyota values of mutual respect and trust. My belief is that if you really want to develop trust and maintain mutual respect you have to take away fear about my job for the future. That comes with a bit of a price in the short term.
>
> We obviously have better years than others, as does the auto industry overall. Some of the pitfalls of others' workforce management is that waves and trends dictate how they treat their people. Profits are good, more people are hired, profits get shared with employees, and in the short term everyone feels good. But when the downturn happens, profits go down and employees are let go, impacting that person's ability to provide for their family. By cutting out the highs and lows as it comes to employment, Toyota is able to get a stronger commitment from employees. There is a cost for us to pay for this—to deal with highs and lows, has to do with the way we manage.

This chapter will look in detail at how Toyota manages their workforce before, during, and after an upswing and a downturn.

## STABLE EMPLOYMENT DEPENDS ON A FLEXIBLE WORKFORCE

The first way Toyota manages natural fluctuations in demand is internal to each plant. This requires a system that coordinates the key stakeholders in the plant associated with staffing. Toyota Motor Company's internal manual, *Human*

*Resources Management Guiding Model,* states the objective of Toyota's workforce control systems as:

*Through precise allocation, optimized fixed headcount and a lean and efficient workforce, we ensure the ability to adapt flexibly to fluctuations in production and secure stable employment. In order to realize stable employment, it is necessary to keep fixed headcount to a minimum level, establish mid- to long-term hiring and workforce plans and then make fine-tuned adjustments based on fluctuations of production, sales, and so on.*

In Chapter 13 we will go into some detail on how Toyota HR takes on the role as "guardian of the trust" of team members, but they also take on the role of coordinating the plant wide planning and adjustment systems for staffing. The planning stage for Toyota is critical for everything that they do, but it is even more critical and practiced for staffing. The key stakeholders involved and their role in the process at Toyota are:

■ Sales—Grasp the market condition and develop, adjust, and communicate sales plans.
■ Production Control—Develop and adjust production plans to level the schedule across time and plants.
■ Manufacturing—Workforce adjustment and production management at the front-line level based on flexible mixed-model production systems.
■ Human Resources—The central role of coordination of all stakeholders and adjustment of plans for workforce allocation including hiring and transfers of staff.

It is ironic that stability depends on flexibility. A flexible workforce allows Toyota to ride out the ups and downs of the market without laying off permanent employees. Sometimes this leads to some inconvenience for the team members and some additional cost for Toyota. Both parties must understand the high value of employment stability and thus the necessity of planning and working for it. The methods that lead to a flexible workforce include:

■ temporary and permanent transfers to other jobs in the plant (small number of job classifications that allow flexibility for transfers),
■ cross-training and multifunction workers,
■ flexible daily overtime (two shifts of production and three shifts of maintenance),
■ planned production Saturdays,
■ temporary workers, and
■ freshman jobs.

We will discuss each of these methods in turn.

## Transfers (Flexible Movement)

We already talked about the importance of having the ability to move workers when and where needed in Toyota culture in Chapter 3. This is one of the non-negotiables of the Toyota Way. Remember, Nate Furuta (Chapter 3) would not go any further in the union negotiations with NUMMI, until this point was agreed to. Other important HR considerations for this flexibility are "few job classifications" and nobody "owning" a job. Everybody is considered to be part of a team. This is the reason that at Toyota there are so few job classifications. For example, at the Georgetown plant there are over 6,000 hourly workers, but only four hourly classifications.

- production team member
- production team leader
- skilled team member
- skilled team leader

This structure at Toyota sets the foundation for flexibility in moving people where they are needed.

## Multiskilled worker (Flexible Skills)

Cross-training like so many other practices in Toyota has many purposes and benefits. To have members know as many skills as possible and to rotate among the team helps teamwork, ergonomics by rotating muscle groups, and helps the team make improvements in order to raise their capabilities and improve productivity for the company. It also helps the flexibility of workforce management when there is a need to transfer. If a person already knows four or five jobs in the department, and is proficient in the fundamental skills we have talked about, the person will be able to move to a new team and set of jobs and quickly and efficiently learn to perform them. On the other hand, if a person only learns one job and gets wedded to that job, or spends years developing the seniority to get assigned to an easy job, they will not want to move, thereby reducing flexibility.

## Flexible Overtime

This is another foundation of Toyota culture, and everyone learns coming into the company that overtime is a very flexible and fluid thing. Except under very unusual circumstances, there are two production shifts instead of three in order to allow a window of opportunity to work overtime on each shift as needed. Table 12.1 shows an example.

The process used at Toyota is to set the production schedule based on the sales need and the current production capability. Under normal production situations, this will include some scheduled overtime in order to build some buffer in for

**Table 12.1** Overtime Capability to Provide Flexible Production

| Shift | Production Time | Overtime Capability |
|---|---|---|
| First | 6:30 a.m. – 3:15 p.m. (with 45 minutes unpaid lunch) | 3:15 p.m. – 5:15 p.m. |
| Second | 5:15 p.m. – 2:00 a.m. | 2:00 a.m. – 4:00 a.m. |
| Third | None—utilized for Preventative Maintenance | None |

when sales demand drops. For example, if the assembly department is currently running at a 95 percent run ratio, the takt time is 53 seconds, and the sales division is asking for 40,000 cars this month with 20 production days, then the schedule might include one half hour of overtime. If the assembly plant runs better then that, overtime may be reduced slightly, or they will go a few units over production. If there is a production problem during the day in assembly, any feeder shop or supplier, then the overtime will have to be increased that same day in order to meet the production schedule. This will be posted on an andon board by second break (for the day shift at 1:45 in the afternoon). When OT is posted on the andon board before break, it gives the team members the chance to make arrangements for day care, transportation, and so on.

Flexible lunches and breaks are another tool that Toyota uses on a periodic basis to be able to adjust immediately to production issues in order to help meet production goals. For example if there is a conveyor problem with transferring cars from one line to another, the entire assembly line will eventually come to a stop. If this happens near a break or lunch time, production control, manufacturing, and human resources will all work together in order to call for everyone taking an early lunch (up to one half of an hour), to allow for the problem to be fixed, and downtime for the entire line reduced. This, and daily overtime adjusting, is a lot of flexibility to ask of the team members, but it is part of the partnership culture that helps achieve the purpose of mutual long-term prosperity.

Planned production Saturdays are another tool Toyota uses as a buffer for increased sales demand and/or production capability issues. It is common for a Toyota plant to pencil in 18 potential production Saturdays a year for this very reason. Then, month by month, sales, production control, manufacturing, and human resources can review the current situation and decide whether or not the day is needed and to communicate the decision to the team members at least two weeks ahead of time. In Georgetown, for example, this process alone gives the plant the ability to add up to 36,000 units a year in "flexible units."

Scheduling only two shifts, with an the opportunity in between for daily production overtime and occasional Saturdays, is part of the overall strategy for

Toyota that is contrary to the thinking of many of the manufacturing executives we talk with. Their first question is, why wouldn't Toyota set up continuous operations, running a plant 24/7/365 at straight time if their demand is exceeding their supply? If all Toyota was considering was pure production numbers and profit, without considering the flexibility of the operation and avoiding the need for layoffs, they would be correct. What Toyota gives up in the short term, they more than make up for in the long-term gain of team member trust, loyalty, and commitment. Of course, running two shifts also allows time for preventative maintenance, which increases production output of equipment during work hours.

## Temporary Workforce and Freshman Jobs

Toyota's temporary workforce provides flexibility in reacting to changing customer demand, while balancing long-term employment security for its full time team members. The use of the temporary workforce is the secondary strategy to deal with increased customer demand. The first adjustment is by utilizing the processes just reviewed. If there is still demand needed, the plant will decrease its takt time (i.e., faster line speed) in order to increase vehicle capacity, but then staff the additional operations using temporary workers.

Toyota is sensitive about maintaining the proper balance of production flexibility with team member trust and morale when using temporary workers. The Georgetown plant has set a standard or goal of having no more than 15 percent of its workforce as temporary in order to find that balance. It becomes a full-time team member concern, for example, if they are working second shift and feel that someone is taking "their position" on day shift and they are a temporary, so there has to be constant communication about the purpose and long-term strategy of the use of temporaries. The morale of the temporaries is also an issue, if they feel that they are not part of the team and they are being treated as temps. To balance this issue, Toyota has made the decision to purposely include the variable workforce (a more sensitive name given to the temporary workers) in as many of the company activities as possible. They are given the same orientation and training as full time members and are able to participate in and even lead Quality Circles. Toyota has also set the assignment limit at two years for the variable workforce. At the end of two years, if there is still a production need and they are qualified, they are converted to full-time employment. This is the goal for both the company and individual as long as the company is growing, as has been the case for over fifteen years since Georgetown started up. At Georgetown, for example, at the time of this writing all variable workforce members who have successfully completed their two-year assignments, with their supervisor's and HR's approval, have been converted to full time employment. Mark Daugherty explains how the two-year standard came about:

> *The standard was 18 months to two years of converting to regular but after 9/11 when the market was a bit soft, we were going out to three, four, or five years. Some felt we were being overly cautious. It was a trust issue. "You said 18 months to two years and we are hanging out here and it is not fair." But the fact of the matter is, if we sit down and talk to folks, they appreciate that we manage that way. They understand this is the price to be paid for employment security.*
>
> *There is no legal requirement in the United States for how long we can keep people as variable. The only requirement we have is that we have to provide service credit as it relates to vesting for pensions—401k. There are no Toyota contributions made but from a vesting standpoint we have to give credit. There have been issues on the legal definitions of contractors and employees. That is a tax issue with withholding.*
>
> *The Japanese government cracked down and imposed a two-year period. Recently we agreed in North America that at the two-year mark we will make a decision one way or another—a firm decision at two years. From a technical standpoint it is a matter of how many employees go out every month and we have to visualize what kind of kaizen we will have to reduce workforce needs, expected turnover of workforce, planned sales and this begins to give us a picture about what we need to do.*

With the strong emphasis on quality at Toyota, there is certainly some risk in using temporary employees. Toyota minimizes that risk through a number of mechanisms:

■ *Freshman jobs*—Throughout the plant specific jobs have been designated as freshman jobs. These are the jobs that temporary employees start on when they are first assigned to a group. They are easier than others in a number of respects, in terms of not being as heavily loaded with work in each cycle, little decision making, and no major manual dexterity.

■ *Limited rotation*—The temporary workers generally do not initially rotate in the same way as the permanent team members, so permanent team members need to rotate around them.

■ *Excellent training*—through the GPC, standardized work and job instruction training, the team can feel confident that the variable workforce can perform high quality work to takt time.

■ *Oversight within team*—The variable workforce is spread out among teams so on each team there are permanent team members to watch out for them and help if needed.

# PLANNING FOR UPS AND DOWNS IN THE MARKET

Workforce plans are developed for larger changes in demand or more permanent ones. The planning is done in two stages for staffing, a mid to long-term plan, which is a one to three-year plan and then a short-term plan which is a quarterly to monthly plan. These two stages are then put together with a simple equation similar to Toyota's definition of a problem.

Remember, Toyota defines a problem as the gap between the standard and the actual, and then they address the gap. The same concept is applied in staffing. It is simply referred to as the "need–have." Toyota looks at what the upcoming need is from both a short and long-term perspective. Then they look at how many they currently have, what the planned needs are, and then they address the gap. Table 12.2 shows how Toyota's workforce planning integrates the long term, short term, and the need—have into one process.

**Table 12.2[1]** Toyota Workforce Planning Comparing Need and Have

| Strategy | Calculate Workforce Requirement | Grasp Current Workforce Level | Workforce Plan |
|---|---|---|---|
| • Long-Term 3–5 Year/ Yearly | • Mid – long range <br> • Forecast—production, profit, product development, sales and economy, and productivity gains | • Current head count <br> • Attrition forecast | • Finalize regular T/M hiring <br> • Draft transfer plans <br> • Draft temporary worker plans |
| • Short-Term Monthly/ Weekly | • Forecast short-term production needs and nonproduction needs such as training, new model preparation and current overtime levels. Determine required T/L online percentage and productivity goals. | • Grasp current head count and a detailed forecast of attendance, calculating vacation, absences, military and medical leaves and restricted workers | • Monthy meeting to finalize transfer and temporary worker plans for the next month |

[1] Human Resources Management Guiding Model, Global HR Division, Toyota Motor Corporation, 2005.

The three-year plan is based on a forecast negotiated between the sales and manufacturing divisions. The trends for forecasted sales are overlaid with the production capacity forecasts and the resulting workforce needs are forecasted. Volume forecasting for each plant is done on a three-year rolling basis and thus plans for workforce size also are on a three-year basis. Toyota's building of new plants is planned out in 5–10 year blocks, but they are based on somewhat sketchy forecasts. The workforce planning goal works to make three-year commitments in building people and capacity plans. The company is pessimistic in dealing with volumes, so it looks at best case and worst case scenarios.

As an example, TMMK was making the Sienna minivan and the Camry on one line. A decision was made to move minivan production to Princeton, Indiana and move the Solara two-door coup from the Canadian plant to TMMK. Mark Daugherty explained that he had a three-year planning window to make the change:

*We were going to lose 100,000 Siennas and pick up on about half of that with the Solara, so the net result was losing about 10 percent of total plant volume (most volume is Camry). This translated into needing about 300 people less in transition. Sienna had unique processes requiring more staff not necessary with Solara. By having three years we planned to absorb the loss through natural attrition, but we knew we would need to have people to cover the jobs temporarily before losing all the jobs (and the need for people) all at once. We stopped back-filling attrition right away and were able to cover the first couple of years through reduction of processes and increasing the team leader online percentage. But the last year we needed people short term to fill the gap because we didn't want to burden the workforce for an entire year. We decided to create a special short-term temp position just for this occasion. We called them family temps. We went to our team members and said we have an issue. We are going to lose the need for three hundred people in the next year.*

*We need people for nine months and then their jobs will go away. If you know any people who can help out for nine months that is great and would help us to not hire. The team members, through word of mouth, went out and literally found us 300 people to bring in on a short-term basis. It is a good example of how to manage. Granted, it was not ideal because we had to keep 300 temporary people motivated for nine months, but it was a success. There were no significant quality, safety, productivity issues. More importantly, by managing to maintain stable employment with detailed planning, we did not put anybody's job at risk. With our competition, if they need 100 people they will run to grab people even if that is a very short-run need. Toyota has two key paths. First is the short-term need based on firm volume for up to a three-month peak sales period. We will make short-run decisions such as moving people around, overtime, accepting more team leaders online, and pulling people from other projects as opposed to bringing in the 100 people. So it is a short-term matter of reassignment for months. Long-term decisions are based on three-year volume forecasts. We want the decision to hire people to be based on the long-term three-year plan not the short-term plan. We never want to be in a position where we say we do not have a job for you to regular employees.*

## Short-Term Planning

The short-term planning and balancing of resources within the plant is necessary on a continuing basis at the plant level. The executive and manager levels work on the long-term plans, while the manager, group leader, and specialist levels work on the short-term planning and carrying out the day-to-day activities. Once the three-year plan is made, the plants are able to put together their annual plans. From there the work starts in balancing out the needs and haves in order to properly maintain the balance between having too many people, which is costly in the short term in labor hours per unit and in the long term with overhiring. Having too few people can also negatively affect the labor hours per unit if the operation rate goes down and have a negative effect on the people because the lack of people puts extra burden on everyone.

Production control, HR, and each section of manufacturing have assigned workforce coordinators that work with their respective areas in capturing the needs and the actual number of people present or the haves, which literally changes daily. They have to work with each group leader to confirm who is "out" on different types of short-term issues such as:

- Absences
  - □ Military leave
  - □ Family Leave
  - □ Short-term medical leave
  - □ Long-term medical leave

- Team leader on-line percentage
- Labor hours per unit
- Plans for kaizen in the near future
- Current overtime levels

All this is put together on planning sheets and discussed in a group meeting once a week in order to work out how to balance amongst themselves for the short-term needs and/or to request an increase in variable workforce labor in the short term. The information gets worked up into a monthly summary and is brought to the monthly workforce planning meeting that is attended by all production departments, HR, and production control. To help illustrate this course of action, we have provided an example of the entire process using a new model startup.[2]

# CASE EXAMPLE OF WORKFORCE PLANNING FOR A NEW MODEL STARTUP

Step 1: Calculate the Takt time to Determine Production Rate Based on Customer Demand

The takt time is calculated by dividing planned work time by expected customer demand and is expressed as the amount of time per unit of production. It is the most fundamental representation of what the customer needs and the basis for much of the design of the production system (see Table 12.3).

Step 2: Calculate the Number of Processes Needed.

This will be based on the model being produced with a planned productivity improvement. This number refers to the number of process positions or jobs needed to set up and is not the number of people needed to cover these processes. The target attendance rate is 95 percent which includes unexcused absences (should be less than 1 percent), vacations, military leaves, medical leaves, family leaves and people present but on a work restriction. It is also important to consider attrition at this point and forecast a monthly number based on past history. Table 12.4 is an example of a Need/Have report that would be filled out by the production department and then brought to the monthly meeting in order to determine necessary action.

**Table 12.3** Example Takt Time Calculation

| | |
|---|---|
| Time worked in a shift (two 15-minute breaks per shift) | 7.5 hours (450 minutes) |
| Efficiency per shift (percent of planned production expected within the shift) | 95% |
| Demand per shift | 480 vehicles |
| Takt* | 53.4 seconds/vehicle |

* Takt Time (Available time/demand) = (450 minutes × .95 × 60 seconds)/480 vehicles

---

[2] Toyota Human Resources Management Guideline, Toyota Motor Corporation, 1997.

**Table 12.4** Example Need/Have Monthly Report

|                                            | Body | Paint | Assembly | Quality | Total |
|--------------------------------------------|------|-------|----------|---------|-------|
| Needed number of Employees                 | 299  | 199   | 398      | 100     | 996   |
| Actual number of Employees                 | 304  | 208   | 410      | 100     | 1022  |
| Forecasted long-term Absences              | 5    | 6     | 10       | 2       | 23    |
| Forecasted Attrition/transfer Promotions   | 2    | 1     | 3        | 1       | 7     |
| Need/Have Gap                              | −2   | +2    | −1       | −3      | −4    |

The key to the monthly workforce planning meetings is the ability to be flexible with some of the systems mentioned earlier in the chapter. For Toyota, there is a three-step process in workforce management:

1. adapt with the current headcount utilizing overtime, temporary transfers, kaizen, and permanent transfers,
2. hire temporary employees, and
3. finally, hire full-time employees.

With the bottom line for the plant standing at -4, there will be a need for people. The committee will have to look at the transfer situation to see if it can first be accommodated with team-member initiated transfers. For example if a paint transfer is scheduled to go to quality, obviously this will help the short-term situation to make this move. The workforce management representative from each department would also be in contact with both the team members and the company doctors to check on the status of the long-term absences and their scheduled return.

For example, in assembly, if any of the 10 are scheduled to return the following month, they wouldn't act on filling their -1 condition. If there are no long-term absences scheduled for return, the team may decide to bring in temporaries to cover the minus condition. The team would also be looking at the plant standard of 15 percent temporaries when making this decision. If they are already at this maximum number, the decision might be made to bring in regular full-time employees.

The actual results of this planning process are then tracked daily, weekly and summarized in a monthly report in order to check action of the accuracy of the forecasts. An example of an actual report from the sections is shown in Table 12.5. The table shows that the agreed to target was to have 157 people there each day. The first shift ended up just shy of their goal, averaging less than half of a person below target. The second shift was not as accurate with their forecasts, ending up with four people over their target. The goal is to be as close to the target as possible, because if a shop is far below their target, their productivity targets may be obtained, but there is a burden placed on the people and morale will suffer. If they are way over their target, the burden will be lifted, but the productivity targets will not be met and if this continues, it could affect Toyota's competitiveness. The goal is to balance the two.

**Table 12.5** Example of Tracking of Actual Need Versus Have

| | WORKING AVERAGE SHIFT BREAKDOWN | | | | | | |
| --- | --- | --- | --- | --- | --- | --- | --- |
| | Monday | Tuesday | Wednesday | Thursday | Friday | Average | Target/ Need |
| 1st Actual | 155.2 | 158.3 | 158.8 | 154.9 | 155.3 | **156.5** | 157 |
| 2nd Actual | 162.8 | 162.5 | 164.9 | 160.9 | 155.3 | **161.3** | 157 |
| 1st +/− | −1.8 | 1.3 | 1.8 | −2.1 | −1.7 | **−0.5** | |
| 2nd +/− | 5.8 | 5.5 | 7.9 | 3.9 | −1.7 | **4.3** | |

# THE UPS AND DOWNS OF WORKFORCE MANAGEMENT

This process is easier said than done. Mike Hoseus recalls the struggles that hit the plant as they were bringing on the second plant. He was the plant manager for the first assembly plant and its workforce coordinator.

*The workforce for the first shift of plant two was basically going to be coming from the second shift of plant one. We had to give everyone on second shift an opportunity to come to first shift before giving those positions to new hires even though most of the people on second shift had less than a year's service. The people on second shift could also request to go to other areas of the plant on first shift such as paint, plastics, or body weld. The problem was that the transfer system was set up to first allow the day shift*

*people to transfer to fill any opening on days, and then the second shift
person would fill the remaining openings on days.*

*Next, all the second shift people could choose to fill the resulting open-
ings on second shift. When all those moves were done, new hires were put
into the final openings on nights. The process became known as "daisy
chaining" because having one opening on days could "daisy chain" out to
become as many as a dozen moves. The fairness of the transfer system was
outweighing the business need to be able to get the right person to the right
place in the right amount of time. There were many discussions among
the workforce coordinators because filling an opening with so many daisy
chains could take months. Instead of fighting amongst ourselves, we decided to put together an A-3 problem-solving report to show the executive
management the problem and the recommended countermeasures. Because
of the coordination of all of the sections, it was agreed to limit the daisy
chain moves to a maximum of three openings. This is what was determined
as the right balance of being fair to the team members and considering the
needs of the business.*

The car industry has its cycles of ups and downs just like everyone else and
Toyota has experienced both. The goal is to have clear strategies and plans in
place to handle both. TMMK experienced nothing but growth and ups the
entire decade of the 1990s. Even with growing from 1,500 employees in the late
1980s to over 8,000 in the late 1990s, there was extreme care and planning
given to each increase in head count. The already described buffers of temporaries and overtime were put into place to literally absorb up to 25 percent
market decrease with no effect on the regular team members. With a recession
going on in Japan in the late 1990s, there was extreme care given to not over-
hiring in Kentucky. As a result, overtime was maxed out. There were shops
working two hours of overtime every day and Saturdays in order to reach their
production goals.

In the past, overtime had always been a popular thing with the team members, providing extra discretionary income to many. Overtime was now beginning to become an overburden issue for the team members, who were willing
but physically tiring out.

The plant had been communicating the workforce management mantra that
long-term job security requires flexibility and sometimes short-term overburden.
The problem was that the recession in Japan lasted for more years than expected
so the overburden at TMMK was going also into multiple years. The leadership
of the plant got together with HR and discussed how to handle the situation.
The first step was to set a standard for all shops and all team members on the
maximum amount of overtime that could be worked, because there could be

no problem without a standard. The standard was based on keeping the average overtime to less than two hours per day (including both production and non-production overtime) and no more than two Saturdays per month. The actual number was calculated each month (according to the number of days and Saturdays in the month) and then given to all the section managers. Their first goal was to reduce the overtime and then balance the remaining so that no one person was outside of the standard.

All team members were engaged in kaizen and improvements were made in both the production overtime and the non-production overtime. For non-production overtime, the team members were able to make improvements in many of the daily tasks. Many of the daily tasks, like calibrating wrenches and guns that had not previously been standardized now were, resulting in reduced time needed. They also found that many of the tasks could be done during the shift instead of waiting until after. Hundreds of these small improvements added up all throughout the plant, resulting in drastic reductions in non-production overtime; this allowed for more production without adding people.

For the production overtime, team members made improvements to the process that improved the run ratio of the plant (percent of shift actually making cars), resulting in less need for overtime to hit the daily production targets. These improvements took more time to implement than the non-production overtime and the plant's improvements were not able to keep up with the sales. Toyota Motor Sales kept increasing their requests because of the demand for the products TMMK was producing. With the demand being greater than the supply, TMMK's plant leadership pulled the andon and requested no more increase of units based on the plant's current level of overtime per team member. Toyota Motor Sales agreed. It was an important day in TMMK's history, which had up to that time always been able to say, "Okay, we can do it," to any request for increased production. The short-term overburden/morale and the long-term job security needs of the team members were considered more important than selling more units. The values had lead to a real decision.

In typical Toyota fashion, the balance of mutual trust and continuous improvement quickly kicked in and there was major emphasis on improving the run ratio in each section. The strategy here was focused on finding out what problems the team members were having and working together to countermeasure them. This helped the daily team member morale and gradually the run ratio improved, which allowed TMMK to build more cars in less time, satisfying the requests from sales.

The same time TMMK was experiencing these problems of too much demand and balancing overburden and keeping workforce management in check, Japan was facing the opposite problem. Their recession was dragging on for years and the "tenets" of the 1950s pledge for no layoffs were being challenged. They had gone through the stages of overtime reduction and then elimination. They increased their takt time, stopped hiring new members, and reduced their temporary workforce to zero. They reduced shifts and formed kaizen improvement teams throughout the plant to make improvements in the areas of safety, quality, cost, and productivity. Finally, plants were being shut down and the workforce shifted to plants still running to balance out production. The problem was there were still more people than needed to meet demand, and the short term improvements had all been exhausted.

Instead of justifying layoffs, which could have been done, with the worst extended recession in Japan's history since WWII and the 1950s layoffs, Toyota sought other options. Toyota used the available manpower to staff a huge R&D division. Dozens of competitor vehicles were purchased and disassembled part by part. Then each part from the various vehicles was displayed as a group. An army of team members, team leaders, and group leaders spent days going through the thousands of parts, coming up with ideas on how to improve the design of the current Toyota parts in terms of safety, quality, productivity, and cost. Hundreds of ideas were submitted to and implemented by the design engineers. The activity reduced the number of parts on the car by eliminating or combining brackets or wire harnesses. Quality was maintained or improved while the cost was decreased. Because they were design changes, the changes were not actually seen in the plant or to the customer for several years. It was a long-term investment that paid off in the long run both in terms of financial return and team member trust.

# PUTTING IT ALL TOGETHER GLOBALLY

In the early days of establishing plants in North America, each plant was on its own for workforce planning. Over time, more plants were added and each plant began to make multiple auto models, which provided challenges and opportunities for more complex planning. The planning was moved to the North American corporate headquarters (TEMA). Mark Daugherty provides an insight into the thinking process using the example of how to deal with rising demand for Camry and falling demand for trucks and minivans. One solution for the need for more Camrys was to make a deal with Subaru. They had idled a plant in Lafayette, Indiana and Toyota purchased 10 percent of Subaru in Japan. So Toyota wanted to help Subaru be profitable and utilize the facility in Indiana. Lafayette is reasonably close to Georgetown, Kentucky, and both are within the region of Princeton, Indiana, that was losing volume. Mark Daugherty explains further:

> We have been working hard to figure out allocation of people between TMMK and SIA (Subaru). We are now seeing three-year plans and worried whether we can deliver the high volumes of Camry and Camry hybrid.

*Yesterday, I was at the plant in Princeton, Indiana, and all forecasts are going down—Tundra and Sequoia are big gas guzzlers and Sienna is in its third year. Texas has to have volume for Tundra and Princeton, as the more seasoned mother plant, has to suffer if the volume goes down. TMMK has more volume requests than it is capable of.*

*From the point of view of headquarters in Kentucky, the mission has to be to share resources so employment stability is maintained at every plant. How do we use the available opportunities we have? We are starting to make people decisions on a regional basis. This place (SIA) will need 300, and Princeton, Indiana, has a need for 300 fewer people. The discussion is two-fold: Indiana variable team members have been there for two years. We have to consider who will go to the SIA new Camry line as full timers. For variable folks, we can provide them with a full-time option if they move to the Lafayette, Indiana plant. We are negotiating with SIA to make that happen. The second option is to make opportunities available here at TMMK. We can make the same offer to regular employees currently at Princeton, Indiana. It may be a geographic opportunity if they were originally from the Lexington, Kentucky area and want to move back.*

*Princeton, Indiana is three and a half hours from SIA and Georgetown so those coming from Princeton would have to move. Obviously, the challenges of distance in North American facilities for Toyota and the plant in Japan are different. It is very easy to move team members between plants in Japan due to their close proximity. We will continue to have geographic challenges to regional staffing flexibility; however that should be a challenge we accept and are quickly working to find a countermeasure. We are driven by our commitment to long-term employment security for our team members.*

To make things even more complex, Japanese capacity enters into the mix. The ultimate 'mother plants' are those in Japan. They are the most mature and also the most flexible. One of the beauties of the Toyota Production System is the emphasis on flexibility. Some Japanese plants can produce six cars on the same line. At this time there is a new highly flexible next-generation line being piloted in Japan that can handle eight different cars on the same line. That allows the plants to change volume mix quickly to compensate for ups and downs in the global market. So for example, if Sienna minivan volume is down in the United States, Toyota may decide to reduce minivan volume in Japan to maintain the volume in Princeton, Indiana, and increase volume of another higher-selling model. The Japanese plants are mature enough to act as shock absorbers juggling the mix of vehicles made to compensate for fluctuations in demand in other parts of the world. This global juggling adds complexity but also adds a great deal of flexibility.

Another example can be seen with what happened in Indonesia in 2006. Indonesia suffered a big hit in automotive demand when the government decided to reduce subsidies of gas prices and prices went up by about 40 percent with demand for vehicles going down by almost that percent. Almost overnight one of the Toyota plants in Indonesia saw a 30 percent drop in demand for the product it produced, which was a car unique to the Indonesian market. That plant was relatively new so it had not matured to the point of making multiple models—it only made that one vehicle. Rather than eliminating a shift and laying off 30 percent of the workforce, the plant slowed down production on both shifts and used the extra workers to do kaizen on existing production and prepare for accepting a new model. Thailand is a much more mature country in terms of Toyota production and was producing vehicles that were shipped to Indonesia, so it was determined a car model would shift from Thailand to Indonesia and Thailand, which was already stretched for capacity, would adapt. Within less than a year the new line in the Indonesian plant was prepared and production was launched. Toyota benefited from the experienced workers they had kept on the payroll in Indonesia during the down times, and the plant responded successfully to a major challenge and was strengthened as a result.

When we are in plants of companies outside Toyota and they say they have no choice but to lay off employees because sales went down, we are sympathetic because we know that this is true based on the current system of planning and the current policies of the company. We also know from Toyota that it is possible to avoid layoffs in most cases through a combination of carefully thought through workforce planning, flexible production lines, flexible team member policies, looking at volume and demand globally, standardized work, and excellent training of team members.

Many companies we have worked with have been challenged to manage their workforce like Toyota. A few have gotten past the initial defenses and justification of "We don't have the bankroll Toyota has, so we can't do this," or "We aren't the auto business, our cycles are more drastic," and so on. One company's paradigm shift was initiated by the middle managers. They had a workshop on Toyota culture and agreed with the Toyota concepts of mutual trust and long-term prosperity for the company and employees. Personally, they felt the trust break down as they had to personally sit down with any employee and tell them that their job was coming to an end.

They decided to form a problem-solving team designed to present the entire business case to the executive team. Their mission was to treat employees as the valuable assets they are and not as commodities. The data collection phase proved to be enlightening for the team. Their key findings were:

- Looking at the last 10 years the "cycles" of the downturns lasted no more than two quarters.

- Every time they laid off employees they had to go back to the market within six months to hire more. Many times this was bringing back the laid off ones, but many times they had found other jobs and they had to hire new employees resulting in thousands of dollars of training and ramp-up costs associated with hiring a new employee.

- They found that these costs and others associated with unemployment benefits were actually greater than if they had just kept the employees through the six-month down cycle. It was cheaper to keep them there, doing nothing, than to send them home.

Of course their countermeasure plan included them doing more than sitting in a room doing nothing. It included training all the team members in problem solving and forming kaizen improvement teams during these down times in order to invest in the future. Yes, the short term plant productivity numbers would not show as positive during these times (because there was the same number of people producing less product), but the overall costs wouldn't be negatively affected. Then when the up cycle returned, both the plant productivity numbers and the overall costs would show improvement based on the problem-solving results.

The executive team was open but hesitant at the first meeting of the group to discuss the proposal, wanting further verification of the cost data. Once they got a second confirmation on the accuracy of the data, they agreed to a strategy to have phases of actions based on the length of the down cycle. They agreed to no layoffs of employees for at least six months to allow the up cycle to return and to form problem-solving teams in the meantime. The plan was to evaluate this short term plan in order to keep taking steps to improve the flexibility of the plants and to keep lengthening the time committed to no layoffs. The entire management team felt it was a good first step in the right direction and is out to prove the theory correct in actuality. As of the writing of this book, they are experiencing a down cycle and have not yet laid anyone off. They just shut a plant down for a whole week (four days surrounding a holiday) in order to have the entire workforce focus on improvements instead of just a few teams. The improvements are taking place and the trust is being built. Time will tell if the cost improvements will outpace the down cycle and if the company will stick to the plan.

# SUMMARY

The topic of employment security seems to be a stumbling block for many companies we talk with. It unfortunately demonstrates the current perspective of looking at the short term instead of the long term and looking at employees as expendable commodities instead of as assets. It will be difficult to go too far with learning from the Toyota Way and Culture until organizations tackle this topic.

The time to tackle this topic is not when there is a downturn and you are faced with too many people. It is up front, with first establishing the value, and then establishing the systems to prevent over hiring and to promote flexibility of the organization and workforce. Once the value is agreed to by the leadership team (including support from the Board of Directors), then the organization can work out the details by using Plan-Do-Check-Act. Changing the mindset from "we can't do this in our industry" to "we are going to do this in our company, let's figure out how" is the first step.

## KEY POINTS TO CONSIDER FOR YOUR COMPANY

1. The organization is intentional about long-term job security for its employees.
2. Long-term and short-term plans are created and implemented to forecast and deal with the ups and downs of the market.
3. Workforce planning is multi-plant and even global to balance work across regions and plants.
4. Many policies and practices exist to promote organizational and team member flexibility, such as daily overtime, company initiated transfers, multiskilled workforce, and takt time changes.
5. A flexible temporary workforce is used to balance out ups and downs in the market with opportunities for flexible workers to become permanent when business increases.
6. People are trained to work on kaizen and problem-solving activities to keep them productive through a severe downturn.

# Chapter 13

# Fair and Consistent HR Policies and Practices

*The precepts of the law are these: to live honestly, to injure no one, and to give every man his due.*

—Justinian I, Byzantine emperor (483–565 C.E.)

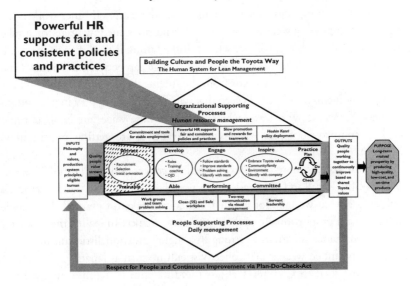

**Powerful HR supports fair and consistent policies and practices**

## WHAT IS FAIRNESS?

Fairness seems like a pretty straightforward concept. We want the treatment we deserve in a way that is equitable compared to other people. Ask the next person you run across if it is important to them that they be treated fairly and guess what they will say. Who wants to be treated unfairly? Whether we are in a family, in a community organization, or on a sports team, everyone wants to be treated fairly and desires consistency in how they and others are treated.

Academic researchers even have a theory of motivation about this. John S. Adams called it "equity theory." It is sometimes put in equation form to make it look scientific, and it says that your outputs (rewards) divided by your inputs (performance) should be the same as the ratio of rewards to performance for others in a similar position in your local environment (see Figure 13.1).

In other words, if you perceive that you have done more for the company than your peer and you get rewarded less or the same, you will see the process as unfair and your motivation will go down. Life is, of course, more complicated than this simplistic notion. For example, it is not clear to whom we are comparing ourselves.

$$\frac{\text{Rewards}_A}{\text{Performance}_A} = \frac{\text{Rewards}_B}{\text{Performance}_B}$$

Key: Theory says if person A receives the same ratio of rewards to performance as person B to whom they are being compared they will see the system as fair.

**Figure 13.1**  Equity Theory View of Fairness

Adams says it is "comparable references in the marketplace." If other workers are all being paid a poverty wage and we are also paid the same low wage for similar work, we should see this as fair, yet what will they think if the CEO at the top is pulling in millions of dollars in bonuses? Will a huge gap between the bottom and the top be perceived as fair? It seems from the Adams theory that workers will not be comparing themselves to a CEO, so that will not come into play in perceptions of fairness. Yet we know of cases where workers whose wages are being cut in a struggling company cry foul when senior executives are getting multi-million dollar bonuses.

To make matters more complex, we believe conceptions of "fairness" are culturally specific. Recall in Chapter 1, when we talked about how the deeper levels of culture are what we take for granted. Americans take for granted that people want to be paid proportionally to their own performance. In reality, the desire for pay for performance is extremely strong in a highly individualistic culture—as in America—and much weaker in a collectivist culture such as Japan.

We also talked in Chapter 1 about the difference between a high context culture and a low context culture. In a low context culture like America, we expect things to be highly explicit. For example, we want all the terms and conditions of our employment spelled out in detail both in verbal and written contracts. In the low context culture of Japan, there is much more that is implicit and thus not stated clearly and not written clearly. Even contracts tend to be much vaguer in Japan.

Hino Motors Manufacturing is majority owned by Toyota Motor Company and recently has been expanding into America, making trucks and parts for Toyota factories. A Hino manager, on an expatriate assignment from Japan, found the assignment to bring the Toyota Production System to the United States particularly challenging because of the cultural differences. He explained:

*America is a contract-oriented society. There are clear job descriptions for everyone. Each person asks: What exactly is my job? What are my responsibilities? In one U.S. plant we have a number of manufacturing cells. If a person is assigned to Cell A, they will only concentrate on the performance of Cell A. In Japan our job descriptions are vague. We are trying to create an atmosphere where teammates will work together to make improvements. Japan is a small mountainous country with a population of over 100 million. It may be said that we are like a family living in an Indian's tent. An Indian's tent is small, and seven to ten people may be living in it. People get to know each other so well that there is no need to express everything loudly and explicitly. There is a strong value placed on mutual trust, and we will support each other without expressing everything very clearly.*

Toyota is growing the truck business very quickly and Hino provides truck components for Toyota in America. It seems quite natural to this Hino manager that everyone would pull together and do whatever is necessary to achieve the challenging targets set by Toyota:

*As a Toyota group supplier, we believe if we work hard and follow the Toyota Way, in the long term, Toyota will return the benefit. When we have a problem, Toyota is really there to send help—production managers, human resource specialists, cost reduction specialists. They are always friendly, but often very strict. They set challenging targets and want us to be independent and solve our own problems. That is the only way we will learn. But in the end, if we are really struggling, they will be there to help us. They will not give up on us.*

This way of thinking also characterizes the workforce inside of Toyota and Hino. The feeling is that each individual must do their best for the team and the company. At times, they will have to make personal sacrifices, but in the long term they will benefit and the company will be there for them. They are not calculating ratios of rewards to performance in their heads every day as equity theory suggests. They are contributing all they can and working to improve every day with the trust that the relationship is fair and equitable *over the long term.*

Hino's manager went on to ask an important question that greatly concerned him: "How can TPS be introduced in other countries with different cultural backgrounds? In the TPS culture, roles are not clear and everyone has to sacrifice for the team, but in individualistic cultures, each individual wants to get their individual rewards based on individual performance."

This is a challenge for Toyota as they are globalizing and addressing different cultural concepts of fairness. Toyota managers who came from Japan to make TPS successful in America were forced to confront Americans' concept of fairness. In this chapter we describe mostly what was done in Toyota in America to create a system that team members believe is fair, but that also meets the TPS requirements of teamwork and support beyond the boundaries of a narrowly-defined job.

# TRUST ECONOMY VERSUS COMMODITY ECONOMY

With a foundation of trust, the Toyota culture can flourish. While Toyota culture and the results it has produced stand on their own, it is reassuring when other research validates the principles. In the book *A Great Place to Work*,[1] Robert Levering researched a number of companies where the employees reported that they worked at great places. He found the common denominator among these companies was that they all emphasized relationships built on trust. He also found that these relationships ebb and flow, based on the amount of trust in the "trust bank." The policies, programs, and processes, and how they were communicated and carried out by the leaders in the organization, determined how much trust was in the bank account. Wil James, president of Toyota's TABC plant in California uses a similar metaphor when talking about Toyota Way leadership: "If you do not give them your best, there is no reason for them to give their best to you. You have to make deposits before you can make withdrawals."

Companies like Toyota build their trust accounts through daily interactions between members. They build a culture of interaction that enables the members to feel as though they are part of a family or partnership, rather than just of a business or a job. Robert Levering describes two types of interactions in companies. First, the typical ones where there is a "this for that" mentality; that is, of clocking so many hours and earning a paycheck. The second is a type of "gift" economy where things are exchanged without direct compensation based on trust and partnership. He uses as an example the relationship between neighbors: One neighbor goes on vacation while the other willingly collects newspapers and mail and waters the flower garden. There is no exchange of money, just an exchange of assistance and social support. The next time the other neighbor starts a project, say, building a shed, the first comes over and spends the day helping her out.

The Quality Circle program described in Chapter 6 is an example of a trust interaction. Toyota has had active Quality Circles for over 50 years. They are part of the Toyota culture. When the Quality Circle "fad" hit America in the 1980s, American managers were looking at the circles in terms of the "commodity" economy: "If we pay workers overtime or stop our line for these activities, then we'd better see the return on investment." This results-driven mentality, based on "I give you this in return for that," was one of the main reasons that the Quality Circle program failed in so many American companies. The reason Quality Circles are still going strong in Toyota is that they are based on the long-term "trust economy"

[1] Levering, Robert. *A Great Place to Work*, New York, Random House Inc., 1988.

perspective. Managers at Toyota are not seeking a one-for-one return on investment. Rather, they are looking at the long-term development of the members' problem-solving and teamwork skills, and trusting that these skills will be applied in many future situations, resulting in long-term mutual prosperity for both the company and the members.

We want to emphasize the importance of the trust economy in the Toyota culture before getting to specific "terms and conditions" of employment in Chapter 14. Of course we do not want to pretend that the Toyota employment relationship is like a big commune—Toyota is a company where people come to earn a living and both commodity and trust types of transactions are present and have to be considered.

Table 13.1 compares and contrasts these two types of interactions. Like many things about the Toyota Way, trust interaction is much more challenging to sustain and make work for you compared to commodity interaction. Commodity interaction is pretty simple: I offer you a clear cut compensation package; each year I clearly point out how you will be measured and what you will get if you achieve the measures, and we let the year play itself out. It is even better if you can get a reward for every instance of good behavior, like a sales person who gets a commission for every sale. Then the system is pretty well self sustaining: You are on your own, I measure you, and, if you do well, we all win.

The problem is that we cannot measure everything we really want. In manufacturing we want quality, safety, low cost, on-time delivery of the right products at the right time, and low inventory. We have seen companies with piece-rate systems pay employees by the number of pieces they produce and they get a lot of pieces but not necessarily the right pieces or high quality pieces and they definitely do not get employees stopping to work together and solve problems. In another company that wants to use a kanban system to produce only what is needed when it is needed the supervisors are measured based on daily production and equipment utilization and the supervisors refuse to stop producing even when there is no kanban and enough of a particular part has been produced. We can try to patch up the holes in the measurement system by adding or deleting metrics, but it is a bit like putting your finger in one hole in the dyke when you know the water will find fifty other places to break through.

Trust interaction requires trust by both parties that the other will, in the long term, hold up their end of the bargain (see Table 13.1). If trust breaks down it can erase years of fair play in the mind of the person who feels wronged. The two-way daily communication we discussed in Chapter 10 becomes critical to maintaining a trust economy. At Toyota there is a formal body set up to maintain the trust economy and that is the human resources department.

**Table 13.1** Two Views of the Company–Employee Relationship[2]

| Commodity Interaction | Trust Interaction |
|---|---|
| One-for-one exchanges | Fair exchange works itself out over time |
| Low risk | High risk |
| Easy to rectify bad exchange | Betrayals hard to repair |
| Relationship must be renewed after each exchange | Open-ended relationship |
| Terms available to all | Terms highly personalized |
| Each side maximizes its advantage at the expense of the other side | Both sides give up something for the common goal |
| Goal is individual advantage | Goal is mutual growth |
| Currency is money | Currency is trust |

# FAIRNESS AND CONSISTENCY IS HUMAN RESOURCES' MANDATE

Fairness and consistency are easy concepts to talk about, but much harder to effectively achieve. It is easy to say "set the standard and be consistent for everyone," treating everyone the same way every time and that there will never be a case where anyone could feel like they are being treated unfairly. This is practically impossible but is the ideal vision for the employee-relations process in Toyota.

The philosophy for Toyota is to manage by values and to work toward having all the members of the organization living those values. This is a different approach from most organizations that have a stack of manuals with detailed procedures that people rarely even look at. Toyota's team member handbook is very small in comparison and contains only descriptions of key policies like vacation and medical leave. The expected behavior of TMMK team members is summed up in simple and clear language:[3]

> *Every team member is important and each person has a significant role to play in the TMMK organization. TMMK believes that team members care about their work and will act responsibly when given responsibility, sufficient information, and training. All team members are expected to take part in developing and designing new ways of doing their work that continue to*

---

[2] Based on Levering, Robert, *A Great Place to Work*, New York: Random House Inc., 1988.
[3] *TMMK Team Member Handbook*, internal Toyota publication, Georgetown, Kentucky, 2006.

*improve the job and productivity as well as the quality of our product. In the process, team members also learn to work effectively as a team and to help their fellow team members, when necessary, to perform their job duties.*

*Team members are expected to come to work on time, produce an established quantity of quality product, maintain good housekeeping in their work area, avoid disruption of the work flow and exercise good safety habits.*

*We want our team members to:*

- *Be a good "TMMK Citizen"—refrain from any actions which have a disruptive or negative effect on other team members or on the efficient operation of the plant.*
- *Maintain a good attendance and punctuality record.*
- *Follow all safety rules—always work in a safe manner.*
- *Perform good work—maintain acceptable standards of quality and production.*
- *Support and abide by TMMK policies.*

In Toyota, the human resources department is the official guardian of fairness and consistency. HR is structured to work with management and the team members in order to balance the needs of the company with the needs of the team members. The organizational structure is not unlike other large companies, including:

- Payroll and Benefits (Compensation)
- Training and Development (HRD)
- Safety
- Strategic Planning
- Employee Relations

What is unique about Toyota is what happens within each of the units. The role of the employee relations unit is to bridge the management of the organization to the team members. Within this group there are full-time jobs assigned to specialists known as HR Reps (Representatives). The role of this group of people is to be the team member advocate. They are to be on the floor, accessible to the members, and there to hear their issues and then facilitate the rectification of the issues.

The role of the HR Rep is defined by Toyota as a "designated human resources representative who monitors the workplace and supports human resources and management in each workplace." Their primary roles include:

- providing information to, and advising, managers and supervisors,
- proposing methods for communication between managers/supervisors and team members, and arranging venues for the same,

- supporting the implementation of and complete adherence to HR measures, and
- collecting and passing on employee opinions and concerns, along with handling grievances through cooperation with managers/supervisors.

Requirements for implementing their roles include close communication with managers/supervisors, employees and union representatives (when applicable), creating an easily-accessible and cooperative atmosphere; knowing members of the workplace for which the HR representative has responsibility; clear knowledge of HR and company rules and procedures; and accurate comprehension of company conditions and production, quality, and working attitudes.[4]

The position and role of the HR rep is critical to Toyota culture. They are the *genchi genbutsu* of human systems: they are present right on the floor with the team members and have the ability to quickly identify and solve employee-relations issues.

Kiyoshi (Nate) Furuta played a critical role in launching the HR system for Georgetown, which ultimately became the blueprint for Toyota in North America. Perhaps most critically, he insisted that HR play a neutral role in the plant and have the final decision on any change in employee status, whether it is to hire, fire, promote, or demote:

*In the very beginning our concern was how we can make the worker not be afraid of management and freely tell us the problem. TPS requires that we make things visible, so we have to convince people that their job is secure—that if they admit to a mistake it will never be the cause of being fired. I explained to Cho-san (then president of TMMK) that we need a strong HR department. We must have the final decision to change employee status. Supervisors can recommend but cannot make final decisions. Even then people in HR did not believe in this kind of concept because they were so used to being the processor after department managers make decisions about hiring, firing and promotions. Our system says HR can say no.*

As a plant manager, Mike Hoseus saw his HR Rep as an important member of his management team and a mirror or pulse check for how well his team was managing the people side of the business. At first Mike had the American inclination and defensiveness of hiding problems and initially seeing issues as a team-member problem and not a management one. Mike learned over time

---

[4] *The Human Resources Management Guiding Model*, an internal Toyota publication, Georgetown, Kentucky, 2006.

not to get defensive when a rep brought him a problem and to look at it first as a management problem and not a team member one. Mike recalls one incident that brought this to light:

*There was a time our HR Rep brought to our attention the way we were allocating our overtime for non-production items such as updating our performance charts and calibrating tools for the next shift. We had always done it on a voluntary basis, and the first few years most everyone was willing and able to pitch in and support what needed to be done. After a time, the group of volunteers got to be smaller and smaller, and eventually they were telling the HR reps that not everyone was part of helping out with the needs of the group and a few members were accepting an unfair burden. Apparently the extra money for the overtime was not important enough to the team members who preferred personal time to the extra cash. My first reaction was to feel defensive. After all, I was responsible for overtime allocation and thought I was doing it right by giving everyone an opportunity. Those who volunteered more often were not doing so under any pressure from me. Then I started to think about how this would be viewed from a Toyota perspective: It became clear that I should seek out the system causes and not assume it is the fault of individuals.*

*We put together a team of supervisors, an HR Rep, and some team members and were able to develop a system in which all the responsibilities of the group were listed out in the form of daily, weekly, and monthly activities. Then we put together a system of tracking to make sure that everyone got trained on how to do each activity. Finally, a big visual board was put together with every duty having a responsible person assigned and a visual control system to confirm that the task had been completed. These tasks were known and rotated at the beginning of each month so everyone got a turn doing every task. Also, by knowing the expectations up front, everyone was able to work on the tasks throughout the day, whenever there was some production downtime, so that the amount of overtime could be reduced.*

*The result was a system that accomplished what the company needed to have done and at the same time was fair and consistent for the team members. The reduction of overtime was a win-win for both the company and team members as well. In retrospect, I learned an important lesson: it is not enough to give individual employees a choice, and if it seems unfair, blame the team members for their bad choices. We must put in place a system that makes the problem visible to all and then find ways to eliminate the problem at its root cause.*

# RESTRUCTURING HR AS A RESULT OF A CRITICAL PROBLEM

## Understanding the Problem

With Georgetown being the first wholly-owned Toyota plant in the United States, it was looked at as an important source of learning for future overseas plants. In 1997, the plant had its first real human resources problem that showed major improvements had to be made.

The problem that finally came to the attention of management was a sexual harassment situation that was taking place in the paint department involving supervisors and members of management. As soon as the HR Reps and management team found out about the problem, it was attacked in the standard Toyota fashion. The HR Reps started to interview team members to get the facts, but were quickly told that they were not trusted, and that is why nobody had come to them earlier. The HR Reps were seen as members of management, and therefore part of the problem and not the solution. HR management decided to hire an outside investigation team to do interviews with paint team members and management.

Through this process the facts came out, and they were not pretty. There were a number of supervisors and members of management that were not behaving according to the values and standards of the Toyota Way. Disciplinary action all the way up to termination for some was initiated. It was ten years into the plant's history, and all the news had been positive up to that point. Many thought the company was going to downplay the problem, try to minimize it and justify their actions. It was testimony to the Toyota Way that this large HR issue was handled just like Toyota handles the smallest of production issues: be honest, get it out in the open, and tackle it head on. The message to the press and the team members was the same: We messed up; the systems we have in place to highlight and deal with these issues failed us; and we are going to investigate, find the root cause, and correct the problem.

That is exactly what took place. The company hired outside consultants to help because part of the problem was that team members had lost trust in HR and the reps in their area. There were special team member meetings and focus groups held to talk with the team members and get their perspective on the cause and possible countermeasures.

Two main themes emerged. The first was that the plant had to get back to following Toyota Way values, and the management team had to be held more accountable for doing so. The second was that the plant needed to address the HR organization and the fact that the reps did not have the trust needed to be told about the problems early on.

Notice that the problems defined were much broader than the specific incidents of sexual harassment. In Toyota problem solving, the five-why process leads to continuing to dig into root causes until you arrive at the underlying system causes. Simply fixing the proximate cause—like sexual harassment and the individuals involved—would not prevent the problem from occurring again. Beyond this, there are other problems that occur when management is not living Toyota Way values and HR is not trusted, and those problems would still exist if only the sexual harassment issue was addressed.

## Back to the Basics—Values

For the improvement activity of following the values, more management and member focus groups were held, the values of the company were specifically defined, and then ideas were generated on how to better hold everyone accountable for following them. The team members and managers mutually agreed to a vision and a specific set of values that would define the Georgetown plant. They are (with key points included):

### Our Vision

*Be a company respected worldwide for producing the highest quality vehicles at the lowest cost in a safe environment. We will achieve this by following the principles of TPS, promoting mutual respect, living our values, and by maintaining an environment of continuous learning.*

### Our Values

- **Safety:** *To make safety and health the priority. We accept individual responsibility for our own safety as well as others'.*
- **Customer Satisfaction:** *To gain and hold our internal and external customers' respect and loyalty. We live by our philosophy that the "next process is our customer."*
- **Respect:** *To achieve an environment where all team members treat others with dignity, trust each other, and care about the work we do. We foster initiative and creativity.*
- **Integrity:** *To demonstrate the highest ethical standards in all interactions. We deliver on our commitments, admit our shortcomings, and act as an environmentally, socially, and economically responsible corporate citizen.*
- **Teamwork:** *To ensure the success of our company, each team member has the responsibility to work together. We communicate honestly, share ideas, and ensure team member understanding.*
- **Continuous Improvement:** *To contribute to our competitiveness and long-term success, we take responsibility for improving ourselves, our processes, and*

*our products through innovative thinking. We continually challenge ourselves to improve, take pride in our work, and play an active role in making TMMK a better company.*

Then everyone agreed to follow the systems already in place to "pull the andon" in case these values were not up to standard. The systems already in place included the regular communication channels such as team member meetings and the Hotline Call system. Because of the mistrust of the HR department, a new hotline was also set up which was known as the "Corporate Compliance Hotline," and it went directly to the office of the president. In effect it became a check and balance on the HR division.

The team members also came up with the idea to institute a values "card system" in order to give immediate feedback to anyone in the company, including mangers, if they were not following the values. The cards worked like those that are used for a soccer referee. Each team member had a pocket-sized booklet that included a set of the values, the expected behaviors, and three cards in the colors green, yellow, and red. Whenever anyone observed anyone else demonstrating the values of the company, like stopping what they were doing to help a teammate, they were greeted with a green card. A yellow card was used to "warn" another person or the whole group if they were getting close to the "line," while the red was used to let the others know that the "line" had been crossed. It was not uncommon to be in a meeting and see yellow or red cards come out if there was some gossip starting, or some derogatory comments or even jokes that were at the expense of others. It sounds a bit corny, but the system was a great tool that was serious, but also fun. This is not a permanent tool and has a clear lifespan after which people get tired of it, but that is the reason why continuous improvement is needed.

## The HR Reorganization

At the same time the values activities were going on, HR was also looking at itself in the mirror to determine what needed to be done. In proper Toyota fashion, there was an honest look at the situation as compared to the standard. The standard for HR is to uphold the company's values and to partner with manufacturing in order to reach the business goals. The reality of the situation was that neither of these two was being accomplished. There was much data from the company indicators to substantiate this, including data from the Hotline Call system, the opinion survey, and the team member meetings. With this gap identified, it was time to get to work on problem solving.

As we have discussed, in Toyota Culture the problems identified are solved by getting a team together and allowing them to use the problem-solving process and empowering them to make the decisions necessary to take care of the problems. In this case senior management developed the goals of the activity and guidelines acting as a "steering committee" to a working team. The goals or outcomes of the activity were identified as:

- improved teamwork within HR and with Manufacturing,
- development of individual skills in HR,
- integration of HR principles into each section,
- greater flexibility in the workforce,
- improved communication and access to HR for team members, and
- improved consistency of policy applications across manufacturing areas.

The working team was made up of the assistant manager and specialist levels within the HR department. They were given the following directions:

- gather input from customers (the team members and manufacturing management),
- benchmark other organizations,
- map out all current processes and flow,
- list all current member roles,
- identify the key roles of HR, and then align the organization accordingly, based on a formal A-3 report, and
- operate within budget constraints.

The working team spent a couple of months getting input from the customers, benchmarking, doing research, and then a couple more months of analysis. They looked at the current structure of the HR organization as shown in Figure 13.2. The team found that the biggest problem with the current layout was that HR was literally and figuratively apart from the manufacturing sections and not doing a good job in partnering with them or being available to the team members and building the relationship of trust.

The team also found a problem with the structure and the role of the HR rep. TMMK had the rep being the team member advocate one day, but if the team member went into a corrective action situation, the same rep may be sitting on

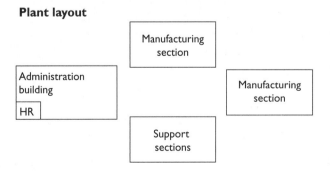

**Plant layout**

**Figure 13.2** Past Layout of HR at TMMK

the other side of the table from the team member as part of the investigation and disciplinary process. It was a logical consequence for the team members to see the HR rep as more of a management advocate than a team-member advocate, and, as a result, they were not confided in when there was a problem.

The last thing the team discovered was that the reps were spending the majority of their time with administrative issues from the team members. They were answering questions about picnic dates and funeral leave benefits for a sister-in-law, but not solving issues and problems that the team members were having. Responding to administrative questions is a common role of HR in traditional companies, but not what Toyota was looking for.

As a result, the team then proposed that the "new HR" organization be structured around four key roles with the corresponding functions:[5]

1. Strategic Partners
   - Act as an integral part of the business team.
   - Engage the business team in systematic organizational audits resulting in clear priorities.
   - Provide HR resources to the business.
   - Possess clear understanding of current business conditions (internal and external).
2. Administrative Experts
   - Develop and manage guidelines, plans, and policies for effectively managing human resources.
   - Act as consultants in fields of expertise, supporting other HR professionals and other HR clients.
   - Take responsibility for continuous improvement in programs and operations.
3. Employee Champions
   - Speak for employee needs and management concerns about employee relations.
   - Know the employees and anticipate their concerns and issues.
   - Be available and approachable by employees.
   - Be experts in assisting employees with concerns.
   - Provide employees with the resources they need to commit themselves to meeting company objectives.
4. Change Agents
   - Influence and drive organizational change strategies in support of business objectives.
   - Manage the process to ensure successful change management.

---

[5] These four functions based on book by, Ulrich, Dave. *Human Resource Champions*, Boston, MA. Harvard Business School Press, 1997.

- Continuously take the organization's pulse regarding both internal and external matters.
- Remain current about tools and practices of change in order to effectively and efficiently manage change and respond to the organization's requirements.

The team proposed that the new HR structure be set up in order to facilitate these four roles. The new structure is illustrated in Figure. 13.3.

This new structure had a "mini-HR team" set up in each of the manufacturing areas (at the *gemba*) in order to do a better job of both partnering with manufacturing management and performing the role of team member advocate. This team performed the HR roles of both employee champions and strategic partners. The roles of the teams included:

- Development—OJT, process improvement, section-specific training, coaching, and strategic planning
- Employee Relations—employee advocate, concern resolutions, peer reviews, safety & health—accident follow-up, early symptom investigation, ergonomics
- Salaried HR Systems—salaried promotions up to assistant manager, salaried relations, training for salaried members

The change resulted in a mutually beneficial partnership between manufacturing and HR. HR and manufacturing now work on the hoshin plans together (see Chapter 15), resulting in better collaboration and integration of the two departments, while at the same time preventing some of the team member concerns from coming up like they used to.

The move also addressed the problem of having silos in the organization and at the same time, the design was meant to prevent just taking the HR and manufacturing silos and turning them horizontally and creating "sewer pipes." In other words, if HR and manufacturing are two silos and Toyota splits HR

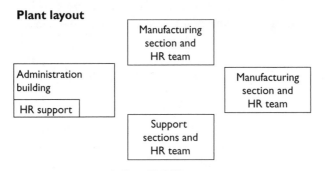

**Figure 13.3** Revised Layout of HR at TMMK

into mini-teams to work closer with management, it will help the collaboration of each but make it harder to ensure fairness and consistency across all of the departments. For this reason, the team recommended that there still be a central HR administration group that would be split into certain functions in order to address the issues that were highlighted.

This central HR group was formed in order to connect the rest of the teams for consistency and fairness and to be the window to Toyota North American headquarters. The group consisted of the following functions:

- Personnel—comp/benefits, payroll, staffing and recruiting, transfer system
- Safety/HIS—MLOA, FMLA, ADA, data reporting, new hire program, health assessment, workers compensation
- Employee Relations—policy development and training, communications, recognition
- Training—Promotion process, Quality Circles and suggestions, plant-wide training

This central group now had the ability to focus on planning and policy setting and become the experts of their respective areas. For example, in order to address the issue of the HR Reps spending most of their time with administrative issues, the group recommended setting up a central call center which all team members could call or stop by to ask their general questions. All concerns were tracked by computer for two reasons. One was to make sure that the question or concern was brought to closure within a standard time. This rebuilt the trust team members had in HR and did not leave them waiting for an answer. The second reason was for continuous improvement.

The computer tracking enabled the group to track the most frequently asked questions and then apply the problem-solving methods to countermeasure the system breakdown that necessitated the team member having to make the call. Every call was treated like a defect, with the assumption being that there must be a problem with some system, training, or communication that is causing the team member to have to ask the question. One of the most frequently asked questions was about the transfer system and where a team member was "in line" to transfer to another department. Another major question concerned benefits, which things were paid for and which weren't.

The team solved the bulk of both of the problems by implementing computer kiosks in all of the cafeterias. These were designed to be simple to understand and use so that the transfer system became a paperless "self-service" process. As a result, the team members could sign themselves up and then check their own status anytime without needing help from the rep or the help desk. By taking the calls on a priority basis and solving the issues one by one, the HR group was able to greatly reduce the number of issues the team members needed help with, thereby resulting in fewer HR specialists needed to answer these concerns. These specialists were then freed up to perform more "value-added tasks" as described in this section. The number of calls reduced from a monthly average of 7864 in 2001 down to 3052 in 2003. The time needed to answer and "close" the call also went down reducing the demand on the service center which went from being open 13 hours a day with six HR members to being open $3^1/_2$ hours a day with two HR members ($4^1/_2$ hours on Friday). A summary of the results is shown in Table 13.2.

Two other teams were put together as part of the central administration group to address the needs highlighted. In order to prevent the need for the HR Rep on the manufacturing teams to be a part of the investigation or discipline of a team member, a separate "I" (Investigation) team was formed. By having a team of four to five specialists perform this role for the entire plant, it not only helped build back the trust with the HR Rep in each section, it also improved the fairness and consistency of the investigation process because there was only a handful of people doing it instead of 20–30.

The final team in the central administration group was set up to be a projects and planning group. Their role was designed to be the "change agents" of the company, partnering with the manufacturing sections in order to work on improvements in areas such as:

- management and organizational development,
- internal TPS development,
- supplier development, and
- safety benchmarking and interfacing with affiliates as part of a global network.

Pete Gritton, vice president of HR for TMMK and TEMA, summarizes how this restructuring helped the Georgetown plant with developing and sustaining the Toyota culture:

*Who is the customer of HR? It is everybody. Our mission is to make sure that we get the maximum utilization out of all of our people whether it is a team*

**Table 13.2** Improvements Resulting from Implementing the Team Member "One Stop"

|  | Before Kaizen | After Kaizen |
| --- | --- | --- |
| Average number of calls per month | 7864 | 3052 |
| Number of hours per week needed to handle all the calls | 65 | 18.5 |
| Employees needed to cover | 6 | 2 |

*member on the floor, or a VP, or whomever. Everybody is the customer and we are trying to achieve a successful business, which requires everybody operating at the maximum level. It is company success that we are after. With HR there is a potential danger of bureaucracy, but if HR is set up correctly, it does not have to be that way. The restructuring has taken us out of the role of "HR police" and has put HR on the floor where we need to be. Instead of managing from the "administrative ivory tower," we sent HR people to the floor to work directly with management. We had gotten to the point in our maturity that it was time to work more closely with manufacturing, and it was time to share with manufacturing that authority—to partner with manufacturing. It gave the manufacturing people one-stop shopping.*

*Before, we were set up here within silos. If a performance problem occurred, a person may start out talking with employee relations people and might be told the problem was with training and then they would go to the training person and be told it may be a skills issue and be told they need to go to the development people, and the manager is going from group to group, and this is where the bureaucracy comes in. Now, all the manager has to do is talk to a team that is sitting right near him and the team covers all the functions, and they have the connection back to central HR, and the manager does not have to worry about that.*

*At the same time, our role is that we are the employee advocates, making sure the team members get a fair shake. There are systems to make sure values are being followed correctly. In many companies, that is the extent of that, but we also want to make sure systems are set up to make high quality cars—staffing, training, motivating, and so on.*

At Toyota, HR plays a key leadership role in the improvement process toward the never-ending goal of producing the highest quality car at the lowest possible cost, in the shortest amount of time, while respecting those who do the work. As we have discussed, there are many internal systems that are designed to deal with these issues. One big external check on how well the management team is implementing Toyota culture is whether the work force feels a need for a union to represent them as an outside, independent agent.

# UNION INFLUENCES: IS A THIRD PARTY NEEDED TO REPRESENT THE INTERESTS OF LABOR IN THE TOYOTA CULTURE?

When we think of unions, the first thing that comes to mind is conflict with management—strikes, grievances, bargaining. In the traditional view, the union is on one side of the conflict, representing the interests of the workers, and management is on the other side representing the company interests. Workers want a safe environment, good working conditions that include not being overworked, pay that they view as fair for the work done, competitive benefits that take care of their families, and job security. Management wants to maximize profit. Management cares about the image of the company, but profitability is the primary goal. Within this context, it is difficult to talk about a single company culture. At the very least, there is a worker culture and a management culture, and maybe even more subgroups represented in the company.

Toyota in Japan is a unionized company. The Toyota union is a company union connected to a broader industry union. The union does care about annual pay increases and watches how Toyota pay and benefits compare to the industry standard. They see their job as to protect the interests of the workers. But they also see that in many respects worker interests coincide with management interests. If the company is strong, all will prosper; if the company is weak, all will suffer, so the union contributes to productivity improvement. In many respects, the Toyota union is like an internal human resources department that cares for workers' interests and benefits and also works collaboratively with management on productivity improvement. To a traditional union advocate, this relationship between the union and management is all too cozy. There is an old union expression: "When the union and management get into bed together, nobody gets any sleep."

Toyota experienced American-style unions for the first time when they entered into the joint venture with General Motors (NUMMI) in Fremont, California. While Toyota accepted the role of the UAW, it was clear they were not sure exactly what they were in for. GM recommended three closed-down plants as alternatives for the new joint venture, all with strained union-management relations, and it turned out Fremont was the worst. In a typical year when it had been a GM truck plant, they had 4,000 grievances, 20 percent absenteeism, and wildcat strikes. Some basic assumptions of the Toyota system in Japan were challenged by the UAW—team member involvement in setting production standards, multiskilled workers, and even mutual trust between management and the worker. Kiyoshi (Nate) Furuta drew the job of negotiating for Toyota, and on the other side of the table was UAW President Dick Shumaker.

Before starting negotiations, the Toyota team thoroughly studied the background of the UAW, going back to its formation. Nate described the challenges Toyota faced.

*Once they (UAW) agree to a production standard they cannot change it. If management wants to change it, there is a struggle. That is a very rigid system. When we develop the original standard work, we want the team member involved. We then want the team member involved in improving the standard. We need multiskilled and not single-skilled workers. We say we do not need so many job classifications—too many—we collapsed them into one production classification and then a minimum nine skilled trades and the goal is two.*

Eventually Nate and NUMMI management won over the UAW leadership. They did it by demonstrating through action that their commitment to team members meant something. NUMMI started out only making Chevy Novas, and in its second year sales were about 30 percent below plan. Instead of laying off workers as General Motors had done in the past, Toyota kept the entire workforce together. They developed a major training program and did kaizen as well as providing extra vacation days. Toyota then quickly rushed a Corolla into production at NUMMI and sales volume increased to the planned amount. At that point Toyota had earned high levels of trust with the work force and the UAW leadership. Years later, when the UAW had a disagreement with NUMMI management, the UAW president proposed that they ask Nate Furuta (who had moved to TMMK) for his judgment and agreed to abide by whatever he recommended. You cannot buy this trust and all the benefits it brought to NUMMI. The result was among the most liberal UAW contracts including broad job classifications, the right to move workers around based on capability rather than strictly seniority, and even latitude to use temporary employees.

The Georgetown plant has never been unionized. Toyota learned a great deal from NUMMI and put in place many of the same human resources systems at TMMK.[6] Without a union, the human resource department has to play some of the roles of the union in looking out for worker interests. We saw earlier that gaining the trust to do this has not always been easy for HR.

The UAW has been at the door of the Georgetown plant for more than a decade attempting to unionize the workforce. Some Toyota team members have signed a union card calling for a vote on the union, but there have never been enough cards to hold the election. To say that Toyota's hourly employees have a single culture in total harmony with management would be a gross overstatement. As in any relationship it has been up and down.

The plant got used to success in the early 1990s, capturing five straight J.D. Power Plant Awards (1990, Gold; 1991, Silver; 1992, Bronze; 1993, Gold; and 1994, Gold). The next five years were not as fruitful, producing only one Bronze award in 1997. This period was one of rapid growth of volume at the Georgetown plant, combined with extensive use of temporary employees, combined with

---

[6] An excellent comparison of the human resource systems of NUMMI, Georgetown, and a Toyota plant in Japan is provided by Paul Adler, "Hybridization: Human Resources Management at Two Toyota Transplants," in Liker, J.K., W. Mark Fruin, and P.S. Adler, *Remade in America: Transplanting and Transforming Japanese Management Systems,* New York: Oxford University Press, 1999.

major cost reductions, and significant turnover of management which created a great deal of pressure on salaried and hourly team members. This is not to say that Toyota management gave up on the principles of the Toyota Way, but the reality was that the Toyota Way was strained with subcultures forming based on disenchantment with directions away from the early years of building a Toyota culture. A great deal of effort has helped to rebuild that culture starting with leaders like Steve St. Angelo and Cheryl Jones. The plant added two more plant awards in the 2000s with a Gold in 2000 and a Silver in 2001. The large majority of the plant is focused on recapturing the Toyota culture of the early 1990s and the "winning ways."

According to the national press, they have their work cut out for them. On May 26, 2007, an article appeared in the *Washington Post*:[7]

> *Dissident workers at the Toyota plant here gather at the Best Western Georgetown on Wednesdays between shifts to shape a battle plan. The workers are angry at conditions at this flagship Toyota site, where the best-selling Camry is built.*
>
> *The United Auto Workers has launched a big new push to organize the plant, trying to capitalize on fears of lower pay, outsourcing of jobs, and on Toyota's treatment of injured workers…The UAW and the workers have seized on leaked business documents from Toyota that detail a plan to put a lid on manufacturing wages in the United States. At a new factory being built in Mississippi, Toyota plans to pay workers about $20 an hour in a region where many people earn $12 to $13 an hour. The average Toyota worker at Georgetown makes about $25 an hour.*

Toyota is perhaps experiencing its own predictions about dealing with being the newly crowned "number one automaker in the world," and it is natural for the press to go after the giant and look for weaknesses. It seems the union and some of the team members see this as an opportunity to cash in. Meanwhile, the management of the plant works hard to keep the treatment of the employees fair and consistent and maintain the essence of the Toyota Way in the plant's culture.

Toyota Motor Corporation in Japan (TMC), which is responsible for worldwide operations and new-plant start ups, has a stance on unions based on these main points.

■ Managing the Toyota Way and establishing a Toyota culture is not negotiable.
■ The local management should establish a stance toward labor unions, taking into consideration local culture, laws, labor movements, and so on.

---

[7] Sholnn Freeman, "In Kentucky, Toyota Faces Union Rumblings: Downtrodden UAW Makes New Push" the *Washington Post*, A1, Saturday, May 26, 2007.

■ If the company does have a labor union, both should recognize that the prosperity of the company is the common objective and both must use thorough communication in order to resolve any differences of opinions and build a relationship of mutual trust.

■ This relationship of mutual trust can ensure the long term prosperity of the company and thereby stabilize employee lives by maintaining and improving working conditions.

In summary, the key to keeping things in balance is that as long as the union operates within the Toyota Way, with mutual trust and respect and facilitates continuous improvement for the company's long-term prosperity, then it will be a positive situation for all the stakeholders. Problems will arise if the union interferes with the relationship of mutual trust between team members and management or if they put restrictions on flexible polices and practices that help the company adapt to business needs. If they are out of balance, and simply request changes in working conditions without regard to the company and business needs, then the long-term prosperity of the company (and therefore all the stakeholders) will be in jeopardy.[7]

In one of our discussions with Pete Gritton, he shared insightful observations about Toyota in America and the way they view unions:

*The main argument of a union organizer is that without a union the company can make decisions and announce them, and you do not have a voice. Our greatest strength is thinking long term and problem solving, that means flexibility and change and doing things differently. When I was interviewed by Toyota, I was an employee relations manager and came from a nonunion company with 1,000 people. Our philosophy was that we were a nonunion company. There were many things under that to manage to keep a union out. I came out of interviews with Toyota executives, and they never mentioned unions. They asked me if I had any questions and I said, "You never mentioned your union philosophy, and what is your position?" They said, "We do not know—what is yours?" I said that if we manage the company in the right way the issue of unionization is a nonissue. Unionization is a byproduct. They said, "We are not sure what our position is on unions in this country, but there are certain things we believe and we will manage that way whether there is a union or not."*

*After I was hired, we spent months studying the labor climate in the United States and visiting the Hondas and Nissans and talked about what*

---

[7] The Toyota stance toward unions is summarized based on: *Human Resources Management Guiding Model,* internal document, Toyota Motor Corporation, Japan, 2006.

*our strategy should be. Should we have a visible statement that we do not want a union at Toyota? We decided not to do that. We have a certain way we want to manage this plant and then everything else will take care of itself. Our goal is to manage this plant according to Toyota philosophy and then the team members will decide.*

*You want to treat people right because you get a huge payback from that. Toyota does that and probably better than anybody else. Heaven forbid that I ever did something because I want to avoid a union. We are going to manage the way we think is the right way to manage.*

Being perfect is not one of the tenets of the Toyota Way, only the continued pursuit of it. For over 10 years, David Meier, coauthor of *The Toyota Way Field Book* and *Toyota Talent* had worked for TMMK, and he has spent the next 10 years working with other manufacturers. In a personal communication with Meier, he commented on the *Washington Post* article cited earlier:

*One of the issues is that many people at Toyota NEVER worked in an industrial environment outside Toyota and have no point of comparison. They have no idea how good they have it. The jobs are hard, but most people don't know it is just as hard or harder at other places. I do not see any impending implosion, but I expect that there will be a trend to discuss the bad news about Toyota because of their new status as number one. We all love to knock down the top dog. There are also the CAVE people (Citizens Against Virtually Everything) and in any company there will be dissenters, but management needs to spend time working with the people who are there to do well and succeed.*

*A union will NOT reduce any of these problems except maybe allowing people to lay out of work with pay. The union will not reduce the outsourcing of jobs, nor layoffs, or plant closings. Look at how many jobs have been "lost" in the Detroit Three. The union will not prevent anyone from getting hurt. Detroit has the same issues with cumulative injuries as do most manufacturers. I know as an organization, Toyota spends more time on the preventive side—trying to design the work to prevent such injuries—than most other auto makers.*

# SUMMARY

It is clear that what motivates Toyota's philosophy is to do the right thing in a quest for a culture of respect and trust. The long-term benefit is mutual prosperity. Do the right thing (process) and you will get the right results. It is their philosophy in both the product value stream and the people value stream.

Fairness and consistency in this partnership does not mean giving the team members everything they want, whenever they want it. The result of this would be short-term satisfaction, but longer term would create a culture of entitlement which would eventually lead to a culture of unemployment. Nor is the goal to give management complete authority to decide on the future of team members. Managers are not perfect and have their own idiosyncrasies.

In a sense, Toyota agrees with the argument of union advocates that fair and consistent management is essential and managers of work groups cannot be counted on to always act in a fair and consistent way. There needs to be a mechanism for all employees to be heard. Being heard is the foundation of the Toyota culture of continuous improvement. So, Toyota sets up mechanisms through the HR department to allow team members to be heard. We saw that even the HR department can be viewed as biased. The countermeasure was to set up a separate "I" team representing a cross-section of the plant to investigate employee issues. Do we believe that the management of most companies is mature enough to police themselves and protect the interests of the business and the workforce? Unfortunately, the answer is no. Yet a lean enterprise depends on surfacing problems. That depends on employees trust that the system is fair and consistent. Companies striving for a lean enterprise will have to change to be adequately seen as fair and impartial to workers or work cooperatively with a union representing both the workers and the long-run success of the company.

With Toyota's partnership relationship the focus is always on the team members and the business at the same time, which sometimes means doing what is hard in the short term, in order to be around for the long term.

## KEY POINTS TO CONSIDER FOR YOUR COMPANY

1. Toyota strives for fair and consistent treatment of people.
2. Toyota does not believe that supervisors left on their own will all have the same criteria for promotions, rewards, and discipline so it puts this responsibility in the hands of human resources.
3. HR plays a much stronger role at Toyota than we typically see in other companies, including final approval of all promotions, even at the executive level.
4. HR is very hands on at Toyota with representatives distributed throughout the organization getting to know people individually and actively listening for concerns.
5. Toyota views fairness in relational terms looking beyond formal contracts to more personalized terms and long-term exchanges.

6. Toyota's culture is based on "trust interaction," which assumes fair exchange works itself out over time, versus "commodity interaction," in which I do this for you only if you do that for me in return.

7. In commodity interaction, each side seeks to maximize its advantage at the expense of the other side, whereas in Toyota's trust interaction, the goal is mutual growth and prosperity.

8. Toyota works to create an environment of mutual trust and sees HR as the "police" of fairness, reducing the need for another third party to represent the interests of labor.

# Chapter 14

# Slow Promotion and Rewards for Teamwork

*The secret of joy in work is contained in one word—excellence. To know how to do something well is to enjoy it.*

—Pearl S. Buck, author

## DO YOU GET WHAT YOU MEASURE?

By far the most questions we get when Americans visit a Toyota factory are about the reward system. Ears perk up when we talk about how performance is measured or how pay and promotions are used to motivate people. How does the performance review work? What does it take to get promoted fast in Toyota? How does Toyota reward team members for suggestions? How does Toyota motivate team members to follow the standardized work? How does Toyota measure how much people contribute to teams? Measure, measure, measure, reward, reward, reward!

It seems obvious that if we pay people proportionally to their performance, they will be more motivated to do a good job. Often times what seems obvious is far from reality. There is a long series of research studies in social psychology that deal with this issue. Some of the main findings are:

1. Simply setting challenging but realistic goals and measuring performance relative to the goals almost always increases the chances of achieving the measures, whether there are monetary awards attached or not.[1]
2. Generally speaking money motivates people to direct their energy toward doing exactly what is needed to make more money. For example, if a cab driver gets paid by how many miles he logs driving passengers, the cab driver will drive faster to maximize how much money he takes in.[2]
3. Pay someone to do a job that is otherwise intrinsically interesting and they will not find it so interesting and will be less likely to do it again unless they get paid.

Neither point 1 or 2 is surprising but point 3 suggesting that you can make an activity less interesting by paying for it is certainly not intuitive. A famous set of social psychology experiments by E.L. Deci in 1971 called into question the simple assumption that we should always pay people to get the performance we want.[3] When people performed an engaging task for no special reward—no special money, awards, praise, winning the contest—they found it interesting and enjoyable in its own right and were more likely to do it again "for free" compared to the condition where they received some special reward. If they were given some special reward, it seemed they believed they were doing it for the reward and not because it was interesting. This counterintuitive, but powerful finding set off decades of further research that have found somewhat conflicting results about delayed rewards and immediate rewards, but there does seem to be agreement that external rewards can actually reduce intrinsic motivation. For example, a study in 2002 followed people to see how often they used spare time to play computer games that were either very engaging or pretty boring.[4] Boring games were more likely to be played if people got immediate rewards. The opposite was true for interesting games—they were played more often if people got no extrinsic reward.

The implications of this research are important, suggesting that managers need to be very careful about what they measure, what they do with the measures, and what they single out for rewards. In the last chapter we compared the trust economy to the commodity economy. We argued Toyota is very concerned about

[1] Locke, Edwin A. and Gary P. Latham, *Goal Setting: A Motivational Technique that Works*, Englewood Cliffs, NJ: Prentice Hall, 1984.
[2] Staw, Barry M, Bobby J. Calder, Randall K. Hess, Lance E. Sandelands "Intrinsic Motivation and norms about payment," *Journal of Personality* 48 (1), 1980,1–14.
[3] Deci, E. L. "Effects of externally mediated rewards on intrinsic motivation." *Journal of Personality and Social Psychology*, 18, 1971, 105–115.
[4] Tietje, Brian C. "When Do Rewards Have Enhancement Effects? An Availability Valence Approach." *Journal of Consumer Psychology* 12:4, 2002, 363–373.

the harmful effects of a commodity economy. The commodity economy is based on "extrinsic rewards" for everything the employee does. Why should I come to work on time? Why should I push myself to work hard all day? Why should I take the initiative to call attention to a problem if nobody else notices? Why should I help out my struggling teammate who is having a hard time keeping up if that is not my job? If the company can measure all these things and pay extra every time the employee does the right thing, then perhaps everyone can win. Unfortunately there are so many different situations a person faces in a day it is impossible to monitor and measure everything they do. Take the cab driver scenario. If a company is interested in high quality customer service for executives, do you want a taxi driver gunning it whenever the light turns green and making the passenger in the car sick? If we want quality in this case, we may have to consider a broader concept of rewards.

Toyota pays people well and motivates people by setting challenging targets, but Toyota prefers to create a trust economy based on a longer-term view of the exchange between employee and employer. They realize people come to work to make a living but wish to create a long-term social contract—if you do your best for the company over the long haul, even in cases where you are not being watched, the company will be more successful and you will share in the prosperity. That is all well and good, but is it realistic? Can we really expect people to put their faith in the company to eventually reward them appropriately?

As we will see in this chapter, there are vast differences between the way rewards and recognition are viewed in Japan compared to the United States, and Toyota struggled to find the right balance when they started up operations in the United States. For example, it is unusual in Japan for your boss to listen to a presentation on a project you accomplished and tell you what a great job you did. If you achieved 100 percent of the objective they may say "good job," but in fact that is considered to be your job and not worthy of special recognition. It is even a little insulting to be singled out for praise if all you did was to achieve the objective you had agreed to in the first place. Effusive praise would be embarrassing and the individual being praised would almost certainly say something like: "You are too kind but I must tell you that this was the work of the entire team. I just happen to be the one making the presentation." Certainly that does not mean that everyone on the team contributed equally and there may even be a slacker or two, but the person presenting would not admit that in a formal setting. In reality, in Japan it is rare that the project was perfect and more likely some objective was not 100 percent achieved. It is almost a given that the boss will identify a weakness in the project and point it out. In this case the individual presenting would take full responsibility, bow, and say: "Thank you so much for that useful feedback. I must try much harder next time."

The early Japanese coordinators whom Toyota sent to America quickly learned the Japanese way did not sit well with Americans. Americans felt unappreciated, criticized, and said that they deserved better treatment. Yet, as we have seen, Toyota was not willing to compromise on the basic assumptions about people and work that had been so successful in Japan. The Japanese coordinators agreed to try to give more praise for satisfactory work, but stuck to the principle that teamwork should be encouraged over individual aggrandizement. Celebrations and public recognition are much more frequent for Toyota in America but the emphasis is always on group accomplishments. Cheryl Jones, manufacturing vice president, Georgetown, gives an example of this from TMMK:

*We have a total plant-wide competition to get back to the basics and get plants cleaned up (5S). There are standards to meet, with all office supplies on kanban, desks very clean and crisp and everything where it needs to be. Then the VPs and even the President go around to check the condition to standard and "certifies" the group if they are to standard. We had our first group certified in plant 2. We knew that not every individual in the group contributed on an equal basis—some worked more weekends and overtime and spent more of their time to accomplish this project. But when we recognized the group we recognized the whole group, not individuals. Doing that total recognition for the group, people sort of had it on their conscience and on their shoulders that "I did not pull my weight, but next time this comes around I am going to do better in pulling my weight". Maybe they will try to do it next time around. This would more than likely happen within the person and the team itself and if not, there would be some coaching and encouragement that they need to step up this time around from the team leader and group leader.*

This is a good example of using recognition and celebration to help build the Toyota way, for both teamwork and 5S. At the same time, it respected the Japanese tradition of not being singled out for substandard performance and relying more on the power of the team (peer pressure) than the power of the supervisor. We would not claim that this system is perfect and those individuals who did the bulk of the work were happy to see their teammates who were loafing get the same treatment. We can say that it seems the benefits of this approach in America have outweighed any negative consequences. Toyota leaders work hard to emphasize the importance of the team and the success of the company for every individual member. They also have opportunities over longer periods of time to single out individuals who show a lot of initiative and accomplishment through promotions. Like everything in Toyota, understanding how to use rewards and corrective action in different cultures is a process of continuous improvement and learning—in this case learning how to maintain the global principles of the Toyota way, while adapting to local culture and individual needs.

We will start our discussion of the way rewards and recognition are used to support the people value steam by setting the baseline with a brief overview of how this works in Japan. We will then go into some detail about how this has been adapted to the West at TMMK. After the description of the policies and procedures, we will stop and consider the underlying thinking behind rewards and recognition.

# TOYOTA'S REWARDS AND RECOGNITION SYSTEM IN JAPAN

Before looking at how Toyota created a new "hybrid" rewards and recognition system in the United States, it is important to first understand what the original looks like. As just discussed, the divide between Eastern and Western views of rewards and recognition is more like the Grand Canyon than a small ravine. A good example of this is in Toyota's philosophy of "slow promotion." For Japanese members of Toyota it is common to work 5–10 years in each position before moving on. In production, it is not uncommon for a person with 25 years experience to finally "work their way up" to being a supervisor. Although not as drastic, the same is true for the white collar managers. It is typical for a new engineer at Toyota to work 5 years before supervising anyone else and even then it is likely to be in the form of a "lead engineer" on a team before actually getting a promotion to a formal supervisory position. In each of these cases the team member may be performing at a high or even exemplary level. They may one day become an executive vice president, but they are expected to be patient and wait their turn. Job hopping is almost unheard of. The individual is committed to the company for the long term and the company is committed to the development of the individual. Both parties do their best and wait to see how it works out in the long term.

Whether it is a cause, effect, or simply a correlation, this strategy works well in the Japanese culture, where the employees are "employees for life" and are willing to be patient, valuing long-term commitments to peers and company. This, in turn, lines up directly with the Toyota way value that Toyota managers are leaders and know the breadth and depth of their organization. In *The Toyota Way* (2004), the Toyota leader was shown as much more than either an in-depth mechanic or one who empowers and delegates everything. Toyota managers are expected to know how to do, in depth, all the processes they are supervising. A team leader can perform every job in his team, a group leader every job in his group. A plant manager has spent years managing a number of the subareas of the plant (i.e., trim, chassis, final assembly). Whether it is maintenance, engineering, or human resources, this same multifunction, cross-training is a vital part of the development/rewards and recognition of every job and person in the organization.

Let's consider the careers of two Japanese members who happen to be sent by Toyota to the TMMK plant as trainers. For Toyota in Japan there are two career paths for manufacturing management. One is through the production floor side and the other is via engineering. On the floor side, new production team members actually go to a Toyota High School where they finish their academic studies and learn the manufacturing process. It is determined at this stage whether they have competencies toward manufacturing, skilled trades (such as welding, electricity etc.), or engineering. If their competency better fits manufacturing, upon graduation (at approximately 18 years of age) they will be assigned to work for a Toyota plant.

The goal for Toyota as a company is that all team members hired at the worker level should be developed to be able to progress to be a group leader. Progressively smaller percentages will move up to the assistant manager and manager level, with a few going all the way to assistant general manager. The company will provide training along the way to prepare the person for the next level. Some of this training will be formal training with classroom and homework assignments to be completed on the floor. Most of this training, however, will be "OJD"—on the job development.

The culture in Toyota Japan is very conducive to making OJD effective. There is not much movement (internal transfers and promotions etc.) so most people will have the same boss for years. They consider it a family environment and refer to it as "staying in the same house" for a long period of time. The group leader is considered like the father of the house, and it is his responsibility to take the team members and team leaders under his wing and prepare them for the next level. The typical amount of time for a team member to progress to team leader in Japan is 10–12 years. This is much different than the average 2–3 years we often see in Toyota operations in the United States.

## Production Side

Shunji Endo, currently a coordinator at TMMK in assembly is a good example of a production person's career path. Endo, who is known as "Eddie" at the plant, started his career at Toyota upon graduation from high school at 18 years of age. He went to the Tsutsumi plant in the assembly area. He stayed in the same group for years with the same group leader. He attended some "small group training" provided by HR that included supervisory training at about the ten-year mark. Also at this time he was given the opportunity to be an "acting team leader" for a year, in order for him to get a feel for the job and decide if he wanted to continue on that path or not. This also gave the company an opportunity to see him in action to decide the same. Finally, after 12 years, Endo was promoted to team leader at the age of 32. Most all team leader promotions will occur between the ages of 30–35, after 12–17 years with the company.

Endo went through the same process on his way to become a group leader. The step to group leader goes a little quicker, with most occurring between the ages of 35–42. Endo was promoted to group leader at the age of 40, after 22 years with the company. His step to being promoted to assistant manager was even quicker, happening at the age of 46, after only 6 years in the group leader position. Most production people at TMC would not make it to this step, but those who do would be in the range of 43–53 years old.

As mentioned earlier, a very small percentage of production people would progress to the manager level. In order to do so, there would be more OJD training in the form of some alternate assignments in the organization. This may be in the form of acting manager or rotating to a different area. Again, this gives both the person and the company an opportunity to experience the role and decide if it is a good fit. Endo's current role as coordinator in the assembly plant is one of those roles for him. He has been an assistant manager for 4 years and was assigned to TMMK for a three year assignment at the age of 50. If Endo is successful with his role in TMMK and desires to keep going, he may well be one of the few production people to be promoted to Manager upon his return to Japan.

## Engineering Side

The other career path in manufacturing management is on the engineering side. This is the more traveled path to management at TMC in Japan, especially at the higher levels of executive management. This path starts with going to one of the top universities in Japan and then joining Toyota as an entry-level engineer. Their path is sometimes quicker and always more diverse than the production side. They will still spend 8–12 years as a working-level engineer with various assignments along the way. They may get an acting supervisor role over a team along the way to test their competency and desire to move into management. If both are a yes, the first promotion will usually come between the ages of 30 and 35. From there, they will have another 10 years of developmental assignments meant to grow both their breadth and depth of experience and knowledge. It is the company's goal that all engineers progress to at least the manager level. This will happen usually between the ages of 36–45 but may take all the way to 50–55 years old.

The manager level at TMC is difficult to translate because there are many grades and roles performed by managers in Japan. There are three levels of managers. The first is number three, then number two, and finally number one and they perform roles of managing a work team, such as in engineering. At the number three level, this would be with a small group of people, while at the number one level this could include up to 50 engineers, with the direct supervision of five or six other managers. There are also project manager roles, where there are not direct reports, but the person is responsible for a project such as a specific model change. Finally, these managers can go into the production side role as a manager and have responsibility for an entire plant.

A good example of this career path is an executive coordinator at TMMK, Yoshihisa Nagatani. An executive coordinator is the highest level of Japanese trainer at the plant. They coordinate the general manager and vice president level on the American side and supervise the other Japanese coordinators. Yoshihisa joined Toyota at the age of 22 right out of college. By the age of 25 he was assigned to the Overseas Production Engineering Department. As the name suggests, he was responsible to support overseas operations and had a long line of assignments that got progressively more complex, with larger plants and more people. His assignments over the course of the next six years included the Philippines, Malaysia, South Africa, Venezuela, and Turkey. These were all engineering assignments that gave him both depth and breadth in his development. The role also included some supervision of small teams.

At the age of 31, Yoshihisa was promoted to assistant manager. He spent two years back in Japan and then was assigned a five-year stay back in Turkey. Here he went deeply into the manufacturing process to learn the entire plant. He spent extensive time in assembly, paint, and the engine plants. He did well with these assignments and was promoted to manager at the age of 39. In the five years up to the time of this writing he has already had four different assignments:

1. one half year as group manager in engineering;
2. three years as a production manager at the Tsutsumi number two plant, supervising over 800 people;
3. one and a half years in a role of manager of assembly production engineering where he was responsible for the supervision of seven section managers; and
4. one half year to date in his current assignment at TMMK as executive coordinator at the age of 43.

His current role could be his last on the developmental path to number 2 Manager. This would correspond with giving him an opportunity to become a General Manager on the production side. Generic career paths on the floor side and engineering side are shown in Figure 14.1

## T-Type People

President Watanabe of Toyota Motor Corporation refers to these as "T-type people." Toyota works hard to develop people who have depth of knowledge and breadth of experience. He explains:

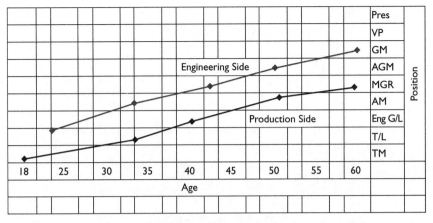

Note: "Production side" are usually hired out of high school as hourly workers called "team members." "Engineering side" are hired from the university with engineering degrees.

**Figure 14.1** Generic Career Paths of Production Side and Engineering Side for Toyota Motor Corporation, Japan

*Toyota develops T-type people... The vertical stroke of the T stands for the fact that employees must intensify or deepen what they do, and the horizontal stroke indicates that they must learn other jobs. Creating T-Type personnel is a time-consuming process. However, in many countries outside Japan it's tough to employ people for the long term. The moment we start operations, employee turnover begins. So we are learning how to retain people.[5]*

*The Toyota Product Development System*[6] describes an upside down T model for product development engineers. In product engineering technical depth is very highly valued. The narrow part of the T at the bottom is the initial breadth in the first one to two years working for Toyota when product engineers spend months performing production jobs in the factory, months at the dealer selling cars, and time performing basic computer-aided-design work. By the third year, the engineer is immersed in his technical specialty (e.g., instrument panel engineering, exterior body structures, or control systems engineering) and likely to stay within that specialty until retiring. A small number of engineers are groomed to become chief engineers or executives and are rotated more broadly after about ten years. Figure 14.2 depicts T-type development as well as the inverted T.

It is unclear whether the slow development and promotion concept originated as the Toyota Way and coincided with the Japanese culture or the Japanese culture created opportunity and/or necessity to make this part of the Toyota Way. Toyota

---

[5] "Lessons from Toyota's Long Drive," *Harvard Business Review*, July-August, 2007, pp. 74-83.

[6] Morgan, James and Jeffrey Liker, *The Toyota Product Development System*, New York: Productivity Press, 2006.

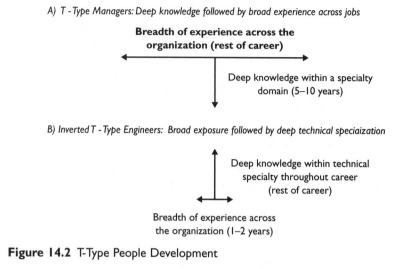

**Figure 14.2** T-Type People Development

has had good steady growth in Japan since the 1960s, but most everyone hired by the company has stayed until retirement, limiting positions at the top and upward mobility. Perhaps to prevent disenchantment Toyota chose to use horizontal mobility and cross-training. In the end by going both deep and broad, they created a highly effective team of managers. Now that has become the preferred pattern in Toyota.

# A HOLISTIC APPROACH TO REWARDS AND RECOGNITION

Perhaps it's the Eastern holistic approach to life that influenced Toyota's broad approach to rewards and recognition, but the perspective is that all the factors of rewards and recognition are tied together into an integrated system. Figure 14.3 shows the parts of the system and how they link together in the Toyota approach.

The holistic recognition and rewards system at Toyota includes linking all the key systems such as:

- Formal compensation system
- Performance evaluation
- Slow promotion
- Corrective action
- Informal recognition and rewards

These systems in Toyota Japan are a blend of both the Eastern culture in general and the Toyota Way culture. For example, in Chapter 1 we talked about the

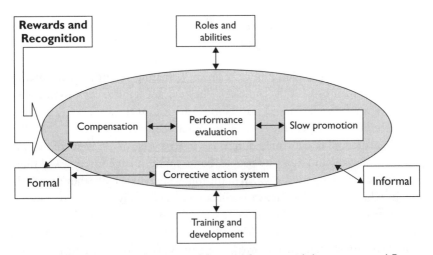

**Figure 14.3** Holistic Recognition and Reward System with Interconnected Parts

"mutual long term prosperity for all stakeholders." It is the guiding principle for the compensation and benefit program at Toyota in Japan.

We might think of mutual prosperity from the point of view of employees—the company does not simply try to maximize profit but seeks to share the wealth. Mutual prosperity actually goes beyond this and puts some responsibility on employees to think about their compensation as being part of a team. Pay is the same for all within a given classification, and bonuses (as a percentage) are the same for all members. The "long term" part of the equation figures into the strategy where members are given slow steady increases over the long haul. There are also parts of the Toyota Japan system that reward people for their long term commitment. The compensation however varies with levels in the company, and promotions are based on skills acquired and demonstrated as opposed to just time in position. Moving up the hierarchy, there are pay grades and different pay levels. At the executive level there are special bonuses; however, the multiplier in pay from the top of the company to the bottom is very small compared to what we see in the United States.

We have also talked about the Toyota "competencies" that flow out of the Toyota Way values of mutual respect and continuous improvement. The individual competencies flowing out of each of these (i.e., communication skills for mutual respect and problem solving for continuous improvement), also are very much a part of the holistic rewards and recognition system. Respectful communication and problem solving, for example, are parts of the performance evaluation, the promotion system, and the compensation system. Individuals in any position who are excellent problem solvers, strong communicators, treat others respectfully, use *nemawashi* to develop consensus, and generally fit the Toyota way leadership model are those who will advance in the company.

# EAST VERSUS WEST VIEWS OF REWARDS AND RECOGNITION

Toyota has a strong philosophy of teamwork, sharing rewards, and expecting people to do their best for the company. They did not want to compromise these principles when they expanded into North America. At the same time, they had to understand and respect the realities of Western culture.

There are well-documented differences in East versus West views of the proper way to reward and motivate people. For example, a large survey asked thousands of managers to indicate which of the following types of jobs they preferred:[7] jobs in which personal initiative is encouraged and individual performance is rewarded; versus jobs in which no one is singled out for personal honor but in which everyone works together. More than 90 percent of American, Canadian, Australian, British, Dutch, and Swedish respondents endorsed the first choice—the individual freedom alternative—compared to fewer than half of the Japanese and Singaporeans. The preferences of Germans, Italians, Belgians, and French were in between.

The same study finds important East versus West differences in views of disciplining people.[8] They asked, "What would you do if an employee whose work for a company, though excellent for fifteen years, has been unsatisfactory for a year. If there is no reason to expect that performance will improve, should the employee be dismissed regardless of age or previous record, or is it wrong to disregard the fifteen years the employee has been working for the company and one has to take into account the company's responsibility for life?" A total of 75 percent of Americans and Canadians said fire the employee. Only 20 percent of Koreans and Singaporeans agreed with this and 30 percent of Japanese, French, Italians and Germans agreed. It was clear that the Americans and Canadians believed in universally applying a simple and fixed set of rules—once the contract is agreed upon, violation with a few warnings leads to dismissal, regardless of the history of the relationship or the specific conditions. The Eastern view is to consider the long-term loyalty of the employee and the importance of the relationship in the decision.

The individualism versus collectivism distinction discussed in Chapter 1 is a powerful, even foundational, cultural difference between the Japanese context in which the Toyota Way was formed and the Western countries in which Toyota is developing local operations. A summary of observations about the modal way

---

[7] C. Hampden-Turner and A. Trompenaars, *The Seven Cultures of Capitalism: Value Systems for Creating Wealth in the United States, Japan, Germany, France, Britain, Sweden, and the Netherlands*, New York: Doubleday, 1993.

[8] Ibid.

Westerners think about what people want from life and at work is directly at odds with basic tenets of the Toyota Way:

- Each individual has a set of fixed distinctive attributes. Moreover, people want to be distinctive—different from other individuals in important ways.
- People are largely in control of their own behavior; they feel better when they are in situations in which choice and personal performance determine outcomes.
- People are oriented toward personal goals of success and achievement; they find relationships and group memberships sometimes get in the way of attaining these goals.
- People strive to feel good about themselves; personal successes and assurances that they have positive qualities are important to their sense of well being.
- People prefer equality in personal relations or, when relationships are hierarchical, they prefer a superior position.
- People believe the same rules should apply to everyone—individuals should not be singled out for special treatment because of their personal attributes or connections to important people. Justice is blind.

Table 14.1 summarizes these differences in how rewards and recognition are viewed in Western and Eastern culture.[9] These are not quaint differences in custom, but foundational differences that qualify as fundamental assumptions about the relationship between the individual and the organization.

If we look down the list of what people in the West want, we would expect that Westerners will find this to be obvious and even "human nature." Is it a big surprise that people want to be recognized for their accomplishments or that they want to control their own fate? Isn't it natural to want positive assurance that we are valued and doing well? Don't we all want the same rules for everyone and clear metrics to figure out what will make us successful and eligible for a raise?

While these may seem like obvious human characteristics, they are not so obvious in the East. In fact those in the East will feel much more comfortable with the list of what is desired in Eastern culture. The Western list, in fact, seems unnatural in the East and vice versa. The Eastern culture would influence how managers and supervisors recognize daily performance of their employees. In the East, people do not expect recognition for just doing their job. It is seen as part of their duty and they would feel embarrassed if they were called out for doing so. At the same time,

---

[9] Nisbett, Richard E. *The Geography of Thought: How Asians and Westerners Think Differently... and Why*, New York: Free Press, 2003.

**Table 14.1**  Differences in East-West Views of Rewards and Recognition

| Western Culture: What People Want | Eastern Culture: What People Want |
|---|---|
| Individually recognized for their accomplishments. | Give the group credit for success and take personal blame for failure: individual recognition is embarrassing |
| Control over individual choices and determine own fate. | Fit into a group and through teamwork accomplish team goals. |
| Relationships and group memberships often get in the way of accomplishing personal goals. | Relationships highly valued and most business is with long-term partners. |
| People "job hop" for the highest pay. | Will accept short term losses for long term stability and gain. |
| Personal assurance they have positive qualities and are doing well. | No recognition for just doing job and seek critical feedback so that they can improve. |
| Equality in personal relationships or in unequal positions be the one in power. | Accept position in hierarchy and seek direction from wiser people at higher levels. |
| The same rules should apply to everyone based on simple categories and systems of measurement of success and failure. | Positive and negative behavior are highly situational and attempt to understand in detail the context of the situation. |

they respect their elders (supervisors) and seek out critical feedback on what they are doing that is not up to expectations, and how they can improve. During the reflection process or as the Japanese call it, *hansei*, the team will be focusing on all the deficiencies of both the technical process and their team process. They will not be patting each other on the back for all they did well. These interactions would be done respectfully, but still Americans will quickly become disillusioned by hearing constant "criticism" with little praise.

How does this same interaction happen in the West? In the West, people do want personal assurance for doing their job to expectations. At the same time, people in the West are not as respectful of elders or the boss and culturally want to be in control, so as a result, in many cases they see themselves as smarter than the boss. This translates into "tell me everything I am doing well, but I don't really want to hear what I am doing wrong." This obviously does not fit the Toyota culture and as we have already heard from the first trainers at TMMK, it was the biggest challenge to overcome to bring the Toyota way to America.

# BLENDED AND BALANCED REWARDS AND RECOGNITION SYSTEMS IN TOYOTA USA

The Japanese and American HR professionals worked together to blend the cultures. For coaching and development, supervisors are taught to give positive feedback, but to also be specific about the exact behaviors they are praising. Instead of just saying "good job," they are taught to say things such as "I noticed when Joe was behind in his job you stepped right in without being asked which helped him finish on time." Similar to the behavioral interviewing discussed in Chapter 4, the feedback is designed to focus on the situation, the action, and the result. The supervisors are taught to give critical feedback in the same way—focusing on the specific behavior and not the person. They are also taught that it is important (since it is America) to give more positive than negative feedback (a 4:1 ratio) in order to increase their chances that the critical feedback will be accepted and acted upon.

Although the coaching and development systems are formal, these daily interactions between supervisors and their employees are considered informal. There is formal recognition, both in Japan and in the United States, often in the form of celebrations for achieving some milestone. These relatively modest celebrations in Japan are at the plant, group, and team levels and rarely recognize individuals for their achievements. These plant and team celebrations quickly became part of the Toyota culture in TMMK and other U.S. plants. The first part, first car, 1000th car, Millionth, 10 Millionth, first Avalon, first Solara, first Hybrid, and so on, were all opportunities to bring the team together to celebrate. On occasion these celebrations would include celebrities like Rick Pitino, the University of Kentucky Basketball coach from 1989 to 1997, to help recognize and to reinforce the importance of teamwork.

## Compensation and Benefits

The compensation system at Toyota USA is based on a combination of standard pay scales and practices in the auto industry in the United States and Toyota values. The philosophies and strategies it is built on include:

- support long-term employment security through a pay and benefits program founded on good business judgment;
- provide a stable pay program;
- avoid severe fluctuations in total cash compensation;
- reflect overall company performance; and
- reward during good times and protect during bad times.

This philosophy obviously reflects the Toyota way philosophy in general. It aims for the long term, and builds a partnership with employees; yet it is tied to the results of the business. During good times every team member receives a substantial, yet not overwhelming, bonus related to how the business is performing. The effort to avoid severe fluctuations is an example of being fair in the short term and protecting the long term. Often we have seen other companies paying exorbitant bonuses in good times, and then laying off thousands of workers when the market goes down.

Toyota's philosophy is to be stable, long term and have slow and steady continuous improvement over the long haul. This is based on the common goal of long-term, stable employment. If Toyota has record profits, they will not give all those profits to the members as a short-term reward. Some will get paid out as bonuses, but the bulk of the profits will be banked and reinvested in order to provide for the members in the long term. Granted, this is not the common mentality or practice in the West so Toyota has to go to great strides to communicate with and educate their American workforce on the Toyota philosophies. Consider the following communication by Art Nimmi, president and CEO of Toyota Motor Manufacturing of North America. It was sent out to all North American employees in 2003 at a time when the company was breaking records for profitability in the United States, while struggling in a tough market in Japan.

*Dear Toyota Team Members,*

*Toyota has achieved tremendous success and yet we face severe global competition and demanding customer expectations in North America. Toyota must be flexible and responsive enough to adjust to the ever-changing market, and the Toyota Way is the guidepost to our activities and strategic choices.*

*Business decisions are made from the mid- to long-term viewpoint to ensure our continued success which is why profitability is so important. Toyota's financial growth is a result of our sound management, the dedication of our team members, and our focus on long-term planning. Profitability allows for ongoing research into technological advancements, additional capital investment in new plants, renovations to existing facilities, and improved wages and benefits for team members. As a company, we also have responsibility to our customers, shareholders, business partners, and local communities.*

*I sincerely hope that each of us will continue to demonstrate commitment and enthusiasm. Together we—Team Toyota—will realize our goal as global leader.*

*Thank you for your contributions,*

*Art Nimmi, President and CEO, Toyota Motor Manufacturing of North America*

This formal, nationwide message to over 40,000 Toyota employees is the same informal message that Nimmi shared with the assembly plant group leaders in the Georgetown, Kentucky, Plant in 1992 when he was in the position of executive coordinator. The philosophy and the message are both timeless.

## Hourly Employee Compensation

We will use TMMK for specific examples of the components of pay for hourly employees which include base pay, a performance award, and a discretionary bonus.

Base pay consists of the regular hourly wage received, not including shift premiums or overtime. It is adjusted semi-annually to maintain the targeted position in the industry and adjusted for local conditions. This is considered a fixed portion of the total compensation that is meant to provide for the livelihood and stability of the members. After a "grow-in period" of three years, all team members and team leaders get the same pay. This is not a pay for performance system as Americans might desire, but at least it fits the Western culture mentality that the same rules should apply to everyone.

A performance award (also called T.I.E., which stands for "Targeted Improvement Extra Earnings") ties plant performance to compensation as additional income that can be earned by achieving plant-level KPI targets in safety, quality, productivity, cost, and attendance. The T.I.E. is completely tied to the plant's internal "key performance indicators." They are completely within the members' control, and do not depend on external things such as sales, the economy, value of the yen, and so on. All hourly employees receive the same percentage bonus. This fits the Western culture of rewards that are within control of the employees though it is not tied to individual performance. It also combines the Eastern (and Toyota) philosophy by making it the same amount for all members across the plant and not pitting sections against each other.

A discretionary bonus is based on company-level performance, and it is up to the discretion of the company to take into account all the external factors that are not within the control of the members, yet, nevertheless, to allow a way to share success. These types of factors include high sales, a good economy, and a favorable exchange rate for the yen, and so on. This is also paid semi-annually to maintain the competitive market position in total cash compensation. For this also, all hourly employees receive the same percent bonus. This part of the compensation fits well into the Eastern culture philosophy to look at the entire situation and context without a simple formula. It gives the company a chance to consider the total situation beyond simple "results," like profits to reward the team members when the company is very healthy as a whole. From the point of view of the Americans, it is extra pay that they are happy to get, so they are willing to have some component that they actually cannot control, especially since Toyota has performed well enough to consistently pay out a bonus.

The percentages of the three compensation components for TMMK hourly members in a typical year are illustrated in Figure 14.4.

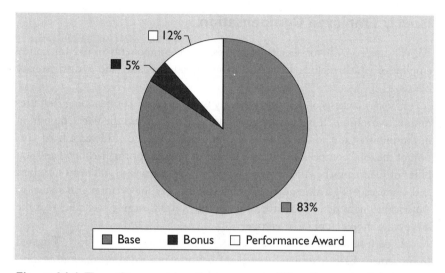

**Figure 14.4** Three Compensation Components and Their Respective Percentages of Total Pay for Georgetown Hourly Team Members in Typical Year

## Keep It Simple and Communicate It Often

Toyota's goal in compensation is to ensure that the system is understandable to all the members; that is, to be transparent and to communicate how the system works, and where everyone currently stands. The internal document quoted for much of this topic is taken from a team member communication packet that was delivered and discussed for this very purpose. Toyota's initial compensation goal, since the start up in this country, was to be consistently among the highest paid in the American auto industry, and to be the employer of choice in the areas where they are located. This position in the auto industry is reviewed twice a year, and graphically depicted in a bar chart; everyone is able to see where Toyota stands in comparison to the rest of the auto industry across the country. HR puts together this graph through industry sharing. All of the union plants under contract have public disclosure of the information, and the non-union auto plants share information with each other.

At the time of this writing, Toyota was number two in production compensation, and number one in skilled trade's compensation. Even with this high standing, you still hear the occasional "we should be number one making as much profit as we are." This comment validates the need to have a long-term, consistent philosophy and strategy in compensation, and to communicate it often.

In the spirit of continuous improvement, Toyota just recently revisited and revised its compensation goals. After 20 years of building cars in this country and seeing the plight of the Detroit Three, Toyota is now more focused on being the employer of choice in the local area rather than competing against the Detroit Three on a national level. They see "chasing" the high union wages as a threat to the long-term job security of its members. Combining high union wages with the increased health care and retirement benefits costs, they see it is leading to more and more instability and layoffs in the industry.

It is not in the best interest of the company or the team members "for the long term" to go down that road. However, as discussed at the end of Chapter 13, this is a tough sell for some team members, and when we see the short-term thinking of the Western culture, we understand why. Toyota's strategy will be to keep communicating with and educating the team members on the big picture for the long term and keep paying competitively locally for the short term.

## Salaried Compensation

The philosophy and much of the practice of compensating salaried members is the same as for hourly members. The base salary is approximately 75 percent of the total with the other 25 percent variable pay in the form of bonus. The size of the bonus percentage for salaried employees is for the same reason as it is for the production members, to have flexibility to reward in good times and to protect in bad. The main difference in the salary structure is that there is more room for individual performance bonuses in the structure. Figure 14.5 illustrates a typical breakdown for a salaried member.

The bonus component of the salaried compensation is an example of Toyota's strategy to blend the Eastern and Western cultures. With a percentage linked to the overall plant performance, it links everyone to the "big team" as an entire plant. This took some "healthy conversation" with people in support areas (for example a specialist in the HR department), who asked, "How does my work affect the plant performance?" This is exactly the question Toyota wants everyone in the organization to ask, giving the supervisor an opportunity to explain how everyone's job is to support the team members on line and the product value stream.

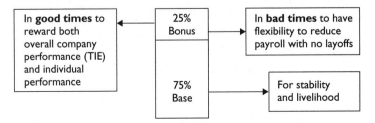

**Figure 14.5** Salaried Employee Compensation Strategy

Unlike Japan, where the entire bonus would be based on company performance, the bonus in the United States also has an individual pay component. This fits the traditional Western culture of recognizing and rewarding individual achievement. However Toyota has put their twist on this component as well. Each manager works to develop an Individual Development Plan (IDP) that supports the overall company annual plan. The Toyota difference is that this plan (and outcomes) is focused on the process in addition to the results. They are evaluated according to the Toyota values and competencies as to whether or not they have demonstrated them in obtaining the results. The supervisor has many avenues of feedback to get this information. The company "opinion survey" discussed in Chapter 10 is part of the manager's individual performance input, as well as the hotline calls or concern resolutions initiated by team members concerning the manager.

The salaried wage system is also meant to attract and keep high quality people in the company, and to be part of the system that seeks the person's commitment to Toyota for the life of their career. The base pay of the salaried compensation has a "time in grade" component to support this long term commitment. This means that the person gets rewarded for spending more time at a particular level. Nevertheless, as discussed with the team member strategy, Toyota wants to be competitive without giving away its profits. As discussed in Chapter 8, the strategy has lost some good managers to other companies willing to pay more in the short term, but Toyota has also kept the large majority of managers whose values match theirs.

## Benefits Encourage Long-term Security and Trust

The last area of compensation is the benefit program. Benefits are also a form of reward and recognition for the employees. The Toyota Human Resources Management Manual states: "Benefits should be applied as a means to provide stability to employees, further enrich employees' lives, as well as enhance the image of the company."

These are three key points that signify the practical application of the Toyota Way and culture. Stability for the employee is connected to the long-term security and trust that the company seeks to maintain with all its members. At the same time, in keeping with the partnership agreement and sharing success, the company desires to go beyond meeting the basic need of security. It aims to provide benefits that enrich and fulfill the employees' lives. Finally, as part of being an employer of choice, it is important to have a positive image within the community.

Benefits directed at stability and mutual trust include such items as: vacation time, paid personal time off, short and long-term medical leave, retirement plan (401k), pension plan, and so on. Benefits that are directed toward improving life include things such as tuition reimbursement, flex time, vehicle purchase discounts, no interest loans, and more. Toyota reviews these benefits twice a year with reference to local and industry benchmarks to remain competitive.

A final type of benefit goes beyond both of these and are "signature benefits" of Toyota (in Georgetown), including the "Perfect Attendance Ceremony," and the on-site child care and fitness center. These are benefits that are talked about in the community, and in the industry, and are considered industry-leading efforts. The Perfect Attendance Ceremony has been described in many other writings proving the point about enriching the company image. Annually, the company recognizes all team members who have achieved perfect attendance for the year. Perfect attendance means not one day of unexcused absence. They are all invited to a huge party at the local sport and concert facility. Big name entertainment acts are booked, such as Bill Cosby, David Copperfield, or Keith Urban. Team members and guests, usually numbering near 6,000 people, enjoy a deluxe dinner, activities, and a show. Prior to the show, 12 new cars (Camrys and Avalons) are given away to randomly selected perfect attendees. The company pays the taxes and all fees up front, and the winning team members are given the keys and encouraged to drive the car home that night. This is a great event and everyone is proud to be a part of it.

Toyota puts a lot of emphasis on its recognition and rewards program toward attendance because it is so important to the overall system. One of the most critical components of operating a lean system and getting the highest quality product at the lowest cost in the shortest amount of time is to have the least amount of people there as possible. This is part of the overall continuous improvement philosophy and part of the day-to-day management of the culture. In Chapter 12 on stable employment planning, we said the goal is to have just the right amount of team members there each day, neither too many nor too few at any given time. For Toyota, good planning is only as accurate as the attendance of the team members dictates. The system can plan for vacations and people out on family or medical leaves, but does not plan for unexcused absences and if a team member is absent, it puts a burden on the rest of the team and the overall system.

Two other benefits that are practical, used daily, and are certainly signature are the on-site child care and the fitness center. The child care is provided at below the local market prices, is state of the art, and open around the clock for use by team members on all three shifts. It is appreciated by parents, and also helps the company by assisting the stability and attendance of the members. By being so close, it is very common for moms and dads to visit their children on their lunch time. It is a prime example of a benefit that contributes to the stability, the quality of team members' lives, the image of the company, and the bottom line.

## Performance Evaluation System: Individual Development Plan

Performance evaluations are very important at Toyota because they provide an opportunity to provide feedback necessary for the development of each member. It is critical that the evaluation process and criteria support the Toyota way philosophy and values. Key points include:

- balancing appraisal of both process and results,
- evaluating the doing of the job and the improving of the job,
- checking system in place for fairness,
- focus on development—daily observation, coaching, and feedback.

These factors are all intimately connected to the Toyota Way and are adapted to integrate into the Western culture. As mentioned earlier, Westerners like simple formulas for measurements of success and failures. By adding to the formula, process as well as results, Toyota is able to blend the western way with the Toyota Way.

At TMMK, hourly team members do not go through an annual review. In the early years of production at TMMK, there were yearly performance appraisals done for each production team member. There were a few problems that surfaced in this process. For one, we already explained that after the new hire grow-in period, all production members receive the same pay. Without the ability to directly link the evaluation to pay, coupled with the Western view of supervisors, it was agreed that the evaluations did not add any value and were eliminated. TMMK did keep an abbreviated form for temporaries and new hires (as discussed in Chapter 3). This is a basic evaluation that includes attendance, following standardized work, learning to do at least four processes with good safety and quality, and making improvements in their job. These are an important part of the temporary and new hire training period and a good opportunity for the group leader and employee to build their relationship and make plans for improvement. Keeping in mind that the temporary program is two years and the "grow-in period" for new hires is three years; there are still five years of performance evaluation for hourly employees. As a check and balance system the evaluation must be reviewed and signed by the supervisor of the group leader and by an HR specialist.

TMMK also began with a fairly traditional American performance evaluation system for salaried employees and then modified it to better align with the Toyota culture. In fact, Toyota doesn't even call it an "evaluation" because this would denote a "hierarchal" relationship in which the boss acts as a judge. The result of this type of evaluation is often a subordinate feeling resentment toward their supervisor. Instead, as mentioned earlier, it is called an Individual Development Plan (IDP) because its primary function is one of development.

Toyota has set this tool up to be more of a partnership and a strengthening of the relationship. The way it is structured is that the tool is designed to "develop" both process and results and give the individual responsibility for the process, not the supervisor. Before meeting with the supervisor, the individual fills out his development plan to support the company hoshin process which will be described in detail in the next chapter. This is the results side of the equation. Then on the process side of the equation there is a list of competencies for the individual to rate himself. For those that he or she rated as "needing improvement," they can then work these into their plan to address the *hoshin*. For example, if a person rates herself as needing improvement in the "teamwork and collaboration" competency, and she needs to improve results of her "cost" indicator, she may make a plan that will include organizing and leading a task force, with members from each department, focused on lowering cost. This will give her an opportunity to work on developing her competency while at the same time improving her results.

When the individual finally meets with the supervisor, it is in the form of reviewing the plan with them for support moving forward, not evaluation of the past. This puts the supervisor in the position of a resource, not a judge. This is not to say that there is not reflection and evaluation. At periodic intervals (quarterly to semi-annually), the pair will meet formally again for *hansei* or reflection. The individual will first bring their summary of both process and results and will be addressing it in terms of PDCA, asking such questions as, "What is there to learn from the process and results so far and what do I need to do differently moving forward?" Again, the supervisor acts as a confidant and source of support as the individual is developed through the process and the relationship between the two is strengthened.

## Slow Promotion Process at TMMK

We have already discussed the slow promotion process in Japan. This practice had to be modified in the United States. The practical reason for the modification is that with the rapid growth in this country and the principle of promotion from within, many people have been promoted within very short time frames. The unintended result was that this helped Toyota with the more subjective problem of "keeping up" with Western counterparts who consider two years without a promotion to be a dead end job.

Toyota was able to pull off this "quicker promotion" strategy in the United States with the help of the Japanese trainers and coordinators. People like Wil James, Cheryl Jones, or Mike Hoseus who were promoted every two to three years were able to be successful because of the support they received from their Japanese counterparts. Mike Hoseus recalls his promotion to manager of assembly.

*Art Nimmi, our Japanese executive coordinator, came to me and said 'we will need you to be the manager of plant one. With our expansion of plant two, doubling our size, our management team will be cut in half and we will need to fill many positions. We know that you only have four years experience in the company (two as group leader and two as assistant manager) and this is way too little to become a Toyota manager. It is not the Toyota Way, but we must do. We would prefer you to spend more time to grow your roots horizontal before you grow vertical. We will make sure you have the support you need to be successful.' At the time, and with my current inflated ego, I did not appreciate his suggestion that I was not ready. Of course, I thought I was ready. Soon our first major model change came for the plant, completely restyling the Camry and changing the entire assembly line. I quickly found out that Nimmi was right; I was not ready to be a manager at Toyota. If it were not for the help of my Japanese coordinators (Jomen-san and Yokoi-san), I would not have survived the demands of the job.*

As Toyota matures in this country they are implementing other strategies to "slow promotions" to be more consistent with the Toyota Way. For example, when the new truck plant opened in Texas, the decision was made to hire no team leaders off the street. This was not the case in the earlier startups in this country like Kentucky and Indiana where team leaders were chosen from the initial applicant pool alongside the new team members. Using *hansei*, it was determined that even though the assessment process used (described in Chapter 4) was good, it was not as good as having time and experience on the production floor. Instead they asked support from their "mother plant," Toyota Indiana, and TMMK to supply experienced team leaders and group leaders to start up the plant. This method was much more challenging and stressful for all three plants. Team leaders are the backbone of the production process and all three facilities were "running thin." This "short-term" struggle gave way to long-term benefits, allowing both the company and the team members more time and experience with each other and the role before making decisions on who would finally be internally promoted to be the first team leaders.

The process used to promote the team leaders at the Texas plant is similar to the ones used at the other U.S. Toyota plants such as TMMK. The principles underlying the promotion system at Toyota are built on fairness and strictness. The promotion system is similar to the hiring system described in Chapter 4, in that no one person can promote someone. A plant manager at a Toyota plant does not have the power to decide who gets promoted. If they did, personal biases could/would enter into the system and other team members would incorrectly or correctly perceive the system as unfair, eroding the trust between the company and themselves.

The other component of the system, strictness, is to ensure that the system is indeed promoting the best person for the job. We have to go back to the Toyota values and competencies to define the "best." The best will be determined by their ability to demonstrate the Toyota Way values of mutual respect and continuous improvement, through competencies such as communication and collaboration on the respect side and problem solving and project management on the continuous improvement side.

The team leader promotion process can be visualized in terms of the same selection process. The key competencies are identified; the company must attract, select, orient, and ensure the progress of the team leader through the people value stream.

Attraction

- Team leaders are paid a premium of 5 percent more than the team members.
- All first line supervisors (group leaders) are selected from the team leader pool.
- All interested team members are invited to a two-hour orientation that includes a realistic job preview and a self-insight inventory.
- Team members decide if they want to proceed to the next step of the process.

Selection

- Step 1: Criteria to be qualified to enter this step of the process include
  - no serious corrective action (discipline process) in the last six months and none at any level for the last year,
  - at least one year experience in the current department (after hire or transfer), and
  - acceptable current performance review from current supervisor.
- Step 2: A behavior-based interview is conducted by human resources that is similar to the new team-member interview using behavioral examples based on Toyota experience.
- Step 3: Two competency demonstration activities are given.
  - Individual problem solving. The applicant is assessed on her ability to solve a problem; and
  - Employee-development exercise. The applicant is assessed on her ability to coach a problem employee through a conflict situation.
- Step 4: Management interviews are conducted.
  - Behavior-based interview, this time including the production department that has the opening (facilitated by Human Resources).
  - Only one candidate per opening moves on to Step 5.

- Step 5: Promotion preparation training begins.
  - All candidates go through an in-depth three-week training program that includes classroom, simulation, and on-the-floor activities.
  - Curriculum includes
    - Toyota Way Values and TPS principles;
    - the role of the team leader;
    - personality instruments and discussion;
    - interpersonal skills, including listening, oral communication, and conflict resolution (utilizes videotaped role play sessions and group feedback);
    - diversity training;
    - basic computer skills (Word, Excel, and PowerPoint);
    - problem solving with a three-day assembly line simulation activity for sequential learning and improvement implementation;
    - going to the floor in teams of three, picking up an actual, current problem, and working through the problem-solving process for four days, coached by instructors;
    - A-3 completion and presentation of the on-the-floor problem-solving activity; and
    - team presentation on the key learnings from the entire three weeks to management.
- Step 6: Decision
  - HR and production review all information on the candidates.
  - Candidate's work performance (supervisor evaluation) is factored in.
  - Promotion offer is made to the candidate.

This is a long and intense process for both HR and the candidates to go through in order to make a promotion. It is certainly not the easiest way to promote someone, but Toyota would say it meets the requirements of both fairness and quality of team leaders selected.

## Corrective Action System at TMMK

Toyota would love it if its selection, development, and rewards and recognition systems were foolproof and there was never a need to address any deviations to standard. Just as perfection is an ideal but not achievable in the product value stream, the same holds true for the people value stream. In fact, Toyota prides itself in surfacing and solving problems in this arena just as they do in the product arena. The system has to be quick to expose, as in the case of the product value stream, any behavior that falls below standard.

The foundation of the corrective action system at Toyota is designed to focus on the behavior and not the person, and it is focused on problem solving and development as opposed to discipline. We have talked about Toyota hiring someone for life, and with that value comes responsibility and work. It would be much easier (at least in the short run) to just fire anyone who falls below standard. It fits in better with the short-term, Western assumption that employees are not to be trusted, are not loyal to the company for any length of time and that the company should not trust employees.

The Toyota method in the United States is consistent with that of Japan—do everything in your power to correct any problem and develop any employee to be successful in the long run. This philosophy applies to both the hourly and salary employees. The company is committed to working with the person to make them successful This does not mean that people don't lose their job at Toyota: it means they really have to give up and stop trying in order to actually be fired.

Using attendance as an example, we will take a look at hourly corrective action at TMMK. We have already discussed the importance of attendance to Toyota to running lean, and the importance of it being communicated to applicants before they are even hired. We have also discussed how TMMK recognizes those with perfect attendance, with a huge celebration and giving away cars. For Toyota, it is important to communicate the standard up front, before the corrective action, so that failure to meet the standard is clear to all parties, as is behavior that goes above and beyond the standard.

The Toyota principle of corrective action, especially attendance, is to be swift, fair and consistent, and solve the problem. Being fair and consistent is more difficult than being just consistent. Attendance is an emotional issue for people, especially when it involves their health or the health of family members. TMMK's attendance policy has never had "sick days" as part of the standard. The rationale is that if people are given a certain amount of sick days per year, they'll hit the standard and be sick that many days. Toyota chose instead to make perfect attendance the standard and then treat every occurrence of tardiness or absence as an occurrence.

This does not mean that Toyota encourages people to come to work if they are sick. They are encouraged to come to work if they do not feel well because many times just getting up and out will help. If a member still doesn't feel well when arriving at work, he can go to the medical services at the plant. If the team member is sick, he can call in before the start of the shift and the next day he can request an emergency vacation. The group leader then has a standard criterion upon which to evaluate and decide the approval. The factors that are considered include the team member's attendance history, the reason, and if he gave notice before the start of the shift. If these factors are all positive, then the group leader is able to grant the emergency vacation and the team member is still eligible for the perfect attendance recognition.

Let's walk through the process if a team member misses work for an "unexcused reason."

## Step 1—Coaching

The group leader is trained to address every occurrence of a team member missing work or being late as a defect. Just as in a product defect the response is the problem-solving process. The group leader and team member have a discussion on the absence and apply the same problem-solving process that they would if there was a defect on part of the car. If a team member was late, then the group leader would ask the five whys to get to the root cause and help the team member countermeasure the problem to prevent reoccurrence. The conversation may go as follows

> GL:  Hi Tom, I noticed you were late this morning, are you okay?
>      (The first why.)
> TM:  Yes I am okay, I overslept.
> GL:  Oh really, what happened? (The second why.)
> TM:  My alarm clock did not go off.
> GL:  How come? (The third why.)
> TM:  It has been acting up.
> GL:  Do you know why? (The fourth why.)
> TM:  There was a storm last night and it must have knocked out
>      the electric.
> GL:  What can you do to ensure you'll be here on time, even when there is
>      another storm? (The start of countermeasure selection)

And so on.

The group leader would use this opportunity to address the absence as well as coach the problem-solving process. The group leader could stop asking why at this step because it is the place where the team member can take personal responsibility and implement a countermeasure, such as buying an alarm clock with a battery back up or a wind up alarm clock. He may even joke with the team member that there is no need to ask "why" there was a storm or go any further to investigate the changes in barometric pressure, seasonal changes, or rotations of the earth. By using the problem-solving process, the group leaders are applying the same principle to these personal issues as they do the production issues. They are separating the person from the problem and working to address the process, giving the team member the benefit of the doubt, and trusting that they are doing their best to be in attendance every day.

## Step 2—Written Reminder

If a team member has four occurrences (the standard) in a rolling 12 months, then official corrective action kicks in. The group leader will sit down with the team member and write up a formal reminder. This is official documentation for the group leader, team member, and company that there is a concern with the attendance of this team member and there is a place on the form for the team member to write up his countermeasures to improve.

## Step 3—Corrective Action Conference
If two more occurrences take place in the next 12 months, after the written reminder, then a corrective action conference takes place. Present at this meeting would be the group leader, an assistant manager of production, a human resources assistant manager, the team member, and a HR specialist whose role is to act as the team member's advocate. The intent of the conference is to make sure the team member knew the expectations of Toyota concerning attendance, to communicate the seriousness of the situation, and most importantly to find out how to support the team member in correcting the problem.

## Step 4—Decision Making Leave
If the problem continues and the team member continues to have absences (two more in another 12 month period), he will be given a Decision Making Leave (DML). With a DML, the team member is sent home for an entire day in order to have time "to decide" if he wants to continue to work for Toyota, and if so, what actions he will take to demonstrate it. He writes a letter that is presented to the DML committee (a group similar in composition to the Corrective Action Conference). If the committee decides to allow the team member to return to work, the team member is paid for the time spent at home.

## Step 5—Termination
The DML committee may recommend the team member for termination at the time of the DML, or if they bring him back to work, he is "on probation" for the period of 48 months. If there are any absences within this time frame, the DML committee will review the circumstances and reasons and may, at any time, recommend the team member for termination. It is the goal of Toyota to never reach this step, and to solve the problem within the first four steps. Indeed it is extremely rare that this step has ever been reached.

A concern and goal for Toyota in terminating any employee is making sure he was given every chance to correct the problem and to make sure that he was treated fairly and consistently. As a final check and balance in the system, Toyota also has a Peer Review Process.

## Step 6—Peer Review Process
Not every case of misconduct is subject to the corrective action process, including the peer review process. Serious misconduct such as fighting, stealing, being under the influence of drugs or alcohol, selling drugs, or possession of firearms

go directly to termination from the company. However, with other misconduct such as attendance, the company can only recommend termination. Then it is up to the team member whether or not he would like to take his case to a peer review committee.

The peer review committee is made up of three fellow team members (chosen randomly, not from the same work group) and two managers. The five-person committee comes together for a meeting that lasts several hours, in which the company (the group leader with his HR rep) and the team member (along with his HR advocate) present their respective cases. The committee listens and asks tough questions to both, confirming that they both did everything possible to take their share of responsibility to solve the problem. At the end of the meeting the five cast votes on whether or not the team member is to be terminated or allowed to return to work. It is a simple majority decision. If three members recommend that the team member stays, that is what is recommended to HR. Even though by policy, the decision to terminate the team member rests with the company and not the committee, in 20 years so far at TMMK, there was not a single case where the company has not followed the recommendation of the committee.

This may seem like a lot of work to go through in order to fire someone. Mike Hoseus was skeptical and had the typical "Western view" of this when he first started with Toyota.

*I remember thinking "this is crazy. First we're going to pay someone who misses work anyway to stay home another day and then we are going to send him to a panel of five, made up of three other team members who are not going to rat out a coworker. At least there could be three managers and two team members." But I was wrong on all accounts. I found over the years, both in production and HR, that the team members worked hard to correct their problems through the stages of the corrective action, and many were "saved" along the way. Very few made it to the peer review committee, and when they did, the three team members were much harder on the person than the managers. The managers were wiping their tears at the sob stories while the other team members were saying, "That same thing happened to me, or Tom, and we made it to work." The committee did terminate some people, but over half were allowed to return to work. When they did, the committee would do so under certain conditions. These conditions were usually very strict and unless the team member had truly solved the problem and corrected the situation, they would end up being terminated in the end. By that time there was never any question from anyone else in the plant about the fairness of the termination. I also realized this process was as much for the 6000 team members who are doing their job so they can know that if they have difficulties they will be given every chance to improve.*

The corrective action process for the managers has the same philosophy but it is not quite as lengthy as it is for hourly employees. While the intent is still to coach and problem solve the manager through any issues, the standards and expectations for managers at Toyota are high. Craig Grucza, the general manager of HR at TMMK explains:

> *The core of Toyota is respect people, and we are obligated to follow that value. We have ongoing training of everybody in the company on our values and what it means to treat people with respect—it is about behavior and not beliefs. That has been reinforced at the management level—ethics training, legal training—it is always in front of us. We constantly remind everyone "Here are Toyota's expectations of behavior." This was really reinforced by Toyota Way 2001. We go through it every year—values and diversity training. In the last five years we have had five different training sessions with managers to reinforce our expectations. We have had Diversity 1, 2, 3, Ethics training, and Toyota Way 2001. We have the training and then there are internal systems to insure the behaviors are being implemented on the floor.*
>
> *We have HR teams with roaming employee relations representatives who are on the floor for people to talk to about any deviations. If they are not comfortable with that they can call the hotline anonymously. If they are not comfortable with that there is also a legal compliance hotline, which has been in place for about eight years. This is a check and balance on the HR systems. Our method is to make sure everyone understands the expectations and the process. It is not an option in our environment to continue sub-standard or bad behavior. Our salaried and performance system is results and process driven and includes respect for the individual. Getting results because of a bad process is not acceptable. In terms of our plant, we have had problems over the years— harassment, and cover-ups. We are transparent about it—we will bring in third parties to conduct investigations, and we will hold people accountable. We use problem solving and coaching with the individual and then look at the system as a whole. If problems are not corrected immediately we have little patience and will terminate people who do not follow our principles.*

# WHERE EAST MEETS WEST IN PERFORMANCE MANAGEMENT

There is a very high correlation between the ways East and West view recognition and corrective action and how this is viewed by Toyota culture compared to Western companies. In Toyota, each individual is a part of a broader collective and expected to contribute to the whole. Standardized work, for example, starts with the assumption that if the organization wants to learn and improve, we all have to follow the standard until we come up and verify a better way. Standardized work is often met with horror by Westerners who see this as an affront to their personal freedom and creativity.

We have added two columns to what we earlier presented in Table 14.1 and in Table 14.2 summarize how rewards and recognition are treated for Toyota in Japan and the blended East-West system of Toyota in the U.S. We see that Toyota's approach to rewards and recognition are very compatible with Eastern cultural assumptions and at odds with many Western assumptions. For example, Westerners want and expect individual rewards, and they expect to be recognized for their individual contributions at work. At Toyota, pay is the same for a given job classification and grows with seniority; any individual recognition is deflected to "we did it as a team." We also see that in the U.S., Toyota mostly carried over its recognition and reward system from Japan, but added individual bonuses for managers.

For example, in the Eastern culture people identify with their company and work group as if it were an extended family. Their identity is intertwined with being part of the company. "I am a Toyota man" is commonly heard among Toyota salaried workers and the implication is that they are a card-carrying member of this collective called Toyota and will be until they retire. This allows the company to think of promotion paths and compensation over the career of the employee. Slow promotion is quite natural when there is a mutual commitment over a 30–40 year period. Similarly, suppliers are partners in the business seemingly forever and even employees in an independent supplier might view themselves as a member of the Toyota group. Contemporary Americans are used to the individual freedom to job hop and therefore their time horizons for promotions and pay increases are much shorter. Toyota has tried to develop long-term committed employees in America, but has had to make some compromises such as more rapid promotion for some and more individual recognition. An ongoing kaizen activity is to work on improving employee retention.

It is interesting to note how individuals in the West are likely to see themselves as performing above average and view problems as being someone else's fault, while in the East the individual is more likely to take personal blame for any failures and view it as the result of personal weakness. The concept of *hansei*, or reflection, is very much about individuals taking personal responsibility, and deeply reflecting on their weaknesses, feeling very bad, and vowing not to let it happen again. As we saw in the United States, Toyota has worked to build a culture of praise with more occasional criticisms and even set a standard of 4:1 between positive and negative feedback. Yet, they have also worked hard to build a culture of responsibility where individuals take personal responsibility for projects and achieving objectives and reflect on themselves when the goal is not achieved. This culture of responsibility takes a decade or more to develop.

**Table 14.2** The Toyota Way and East-West Differences in Rewards and Recognition (*Continued on next page*)

| Western Culture: What People Want | Eastern Culture: What People Want | Reward and Recognition Toyota Japan | Blended and Balanced Reward and Recognition Systems in Toyota USA |
|---|---|---|---|
| Individually recognized for their accomplishments. | Give the group credit for success and take personal blame for failure: individual recognition is embarrassing. | Pay is the same for a given job classification and grows with seniority; any individual recognition is deflected to "we did it as a team." | Pay is based on job classification, seniority, company performance, plant performance for production workers and adds individual bonuses for management. |
| Control over individual choices and determine own fate. | Fit into a group and through teamwork accomplish team goals. | Rewards and recognitions go to team, including small funds for team activities, quality circle awards, group performance bonuses. | Some group awards and some individual based bonuses but consider how work with others in individual bonus. |
| Relationships and group memberships often get in the way of accomplishing personal goals. People "job hop" for the highest pay. | Relationships highly valued and most business is with long-term partners. Will accept short term losses for long term stability and gain. | Individuals stick with the company and company sticks with suppliers for long-term and will make short-term sacrifices for the good of the long-term. | Design a system that both rewards individual achievement, competitive with the industry, while recognizing and rewarding long term commitment to the company |
| Personal assurance they have positive qualities and are doing well. | No recognition for just doing job; seek critical feedback so that they can improve. | Through hansei individuals are expected to reflect on deficiencies (*hansei*); supervisors seldom praise doing the job well. | Daily coaching system focusing on both positive and critical feedback. |

**Table 14.2** The Toyota Way and East-West Differences in Rewards and Recognition (*Continued from previous page*)

| Western Culture: What People Want | Eastern Culture: What People Want | Reward and Recognition Toyota Japan | Blended and Balanced Reward and Recognition Systems in Toyota USA |
|---|---|---|---|
| Equality in personal relationships or in unequal positions be the one in power. | Accept position in hierarchy and seek direction from wiser people at higher levels. | Pay is seniority based. Individuals are expected to be very patient about individual promotion or movement to favored assignment and accept wisdom of elders. Some people keep advancing to higher management while others stop at a certain level. | Seniority based pay but room for some with less seniority advancing faster than others more senior. |
| The same rules should apply to everyone based on simple categories and systems of measurement of success and failure. | Positive and negative behavior are highly situational and attempt to understand in detail the context of the situation. | Performance data only one input into performance appraisal; positive and negative performance evaluated through intense discussion and investigation of situation. | Balance a system that rewards the entire organization's performance consistently based on an objective system (the same pay and increases for everyone) while also having ability to reward more subjective and situational factors. |

The challenge to Toyota, and certainly to Western companies seeking to learn from Toyota, is how to take the best of the East and integrate it with the best of the West. With a successful system in Japan, Toyota's first choice would have been to simply transplant its system into the Western soil. Who wouldn't want people working in teams, toward team goals, putting the team and the company first for the duration of their working careers? Toyota was not naive enough to think this "culture" would transplant in its entirety to America. Toyota also saw some value to diversity. We will see in Chapters 16 and 17 that particularly in Toyota Motor Sales, Americans' understanding of what American customers want and a certain individualistic boldness in innovating has very much helped Toyota's success in America. At the same time, there were certain non-negotiables of the Toyota Way that they would not compromise. As we discussed in this chapter, Toyota has effectively transferred much of its core values to the West and made modifications as necessary to accommodate these different cultural expectations.

# TREAD CAREFULLY IN CHANGING REWARD SYSTEMS TO IMITATE TOYOTA

Toyota has already had over twenty years in the United States to continually improve and update their rewards and recognition systems. TMMK did not immediately start with the individual development plan for salaried employees. It was implemented after 10 years of learning the culture in the West and in the local plant. All of the processes we have described have undergone gradual, incremental changes and updates throughout the years. There has been a similar learning process in other parts of Toyota in America, such as Toyota Motor Sales and the Toyota Technical Center, and each has a different variation of rewards and recognition systems that fits its location and type of employee. Toyota has different practices in other countries as well, but all based on the same underlying philosophy:

1. Support the values of respect for people and continuous improvement.
2. Emphasize the process as well as the results.
3. Make the system transparent to all team members.
4. Emphasize the group and the company over the individual.
5. Develop T-type people, particularly at higher management levels, with deep expertise and inverted T-people for technically challenging engineering jobs.
6. Make heavy investments in training and development with the goal of retaining employees over their careers.
7. Use corrective action as a problem-solving process to help develop the individual and address any disciplinary issues.

We have two key recommendations to organizations that are going through lean transformations and would like to learn from Toyota's rewards and recognition programs.

1. Don't change anything you don't have to early in the process, but do address the barriers to lean.
2. Go slow and adjust as you go.

The reason we suggest avoiding major changes to the reward and recognition systems early on is because you are already going through a lot of change and to add more would more than likely produce adverse consequences. Employees care deeply about any changes in compensation policy and some will be unhappy no matter what changes you make. We do not see a good reason to add this source of uncertainty to an already complex and uncertain process. At the same time, you will need to review your reward-system policies and procedures to identify anything that creates barriers to implementing lean.

For example, we were working with one company and helped them implement a pull system in which parts were stored in a supermarket and kanban were used to communicate when to build parts and when to move parts. The employees were instructed to follow the standards and to quit producing when they no longer had kanban coming back because the supermarket was up to its maximum. The waste of overproduction is the most fundamental waste in the Toyota Production System, and we were trying to teach them not to overproduce even if it means shutting down production. The plant manager was away from the plant on business, and they wanted to impress him with following all of these new lean standards. Their pride was short lived. When the manager called in to check the numbers for the day, he grew angry as he learned that they had stopped production earlier and were not reaching the daily production goal set by the MRP system. You can imagine the conversation.

*Plant Manager: Why didn't you hit the production numbers?*
*Answer: We filled all the kanban orders and got up to the maximum levels we had worked out in the supermarket and according to the standard, we are not supposed to overproduce.*
*Plant Manager: I don't care about any kanban. I am judged according to how well we meet the MRP schedule which says we should still be producing and you are making me look bad. Go back to producing to the schedule.*

Obviously there is something wrong with the performance evaluation system of the plant manager that is leading him to reject the pull system and the new standard. He will block implementation because he is being judged based on hitting his daily numbers (no matter how he hits them). This is something that has to be changed quickly, and the plant manger must be educated on the philosophy of the pull system and assured he will now be judged based on following the new standard.

There are many other common barriers we have seen that at some point will stop progress toward becoming a lean organization:

- Rewarding individuals for achieving their own individual goals even at the expense of team or company goals.
- Using a discipline/punishment system instead of the corrective action problem-solving approach. This is the best way to discourage employees from surfacing problems.
- Executives and leaders focused on short-term results instead of committing to a set of values and principles and focusing on the process that will deliver the results, for example, going after headcount reduction even when the process is not capable of operating with such low numbers of people.
- Rewarding executives and leaders using large, short-term bonuses that encourage them to hit and run to a new job or company instead of providing long-term incentives that will slow down the constant "churning" of leadership in the organization. If the incentive structure is to achieve certain headcount and inventory reduction targets by the end of the year, they will get you a one shot reduction without creating a robust, capable process and encouraging people to continually improve.

Some of you may be able to identify with some of the above examples, which brings us back to our second key point. If you plan to address any of these, we recommend that you go slowly. Of course, there may be cases where you have to make a statement in your organization and completely dismantle some "sacred shrine" in order to rally the troops. One office furniture company fought for years and finally eliminated the piece-rate system that had dominated its culture for decades. The piece-rate system led to overproduction, discouraged teamwork, discouraged following standard work, led to quality problems, and created ergonomics problems. Breaking the piece rate system was like taking down the dam. The flow of improvements that followed was earth shattering. However, the company needed to work with the union to gradually phase out the old system which took about three years. In certain rare cases a complete overhaul can be very effective.

In most cases it will be more effective to tread carefully, selecting some particular offending metric that should be eliminated or adding a few metrics that reflect your goals for the new lean system, for example, adding inventory turns as a metric and dropping machine utilization. In general, Toyota will focus on singles, bunts, even walks in order to get on bases, with all of them adding up to runs scored. They do not believe in "swinging for the fences" and trying to hit the home runs. We recommend the Toyota approach, which treats the change like a journey, using the principles of Plan-Do-Check-Act and *hansei* along the way in order to make adjustments as you go. We will return to this theme in Chapter 18 and recommend ways to think about culture change.

We have focused in this chapter on the philosophy and thinking behind Toyota's reward and recognition system with some examples from TMMK. We emphasized the process is as important as the result, but do not mean to imply Toyota does not care about results. In fact they care intensely. Everyone in Toyota can recite to you their targets for improvement and they are all challenging. Where do these targets come from? The answer is the *hoshin* planning process which is the final piece of the Toyota culture model as discussed in the next chapter. In this case, last is certainly not least since *hoshin* planning is what directs the entire organization toward common goals.

## KEY POINTS TO CONSIDER FOR YOUR COMPANY

1. Managers and leaders are developed slowly giving them both deep vertical experience and broad horizontal experience across functions (i.e., T-type people).
2. Toyota works to grow managers from within, including from the hourly workforce, and promotes people who learn how to develop other people and live the Toyota values.
3. Recognition and rewards are based on the team and not just individual accomplishments.
4. Recognition and rewards are focused on the process as much as if not more than the results.
5. Corrective action processes are aimed at problem solving and coaching rather than discipline and punishment.
6. The philosophy behind rewards and recognition has remained consistent with the Toyota way, though specific details are adjusted to fit the local culture.
7. Fairness in administering rewards and recognition is emphasized by involving human resources and various types of review committees, even using peer committees in the corrective action process.
8. Changes in reward and recognition programs are done with a step-by-step methodical approach as opposed to a scrap and rebuild approach.

# Chapter 15

# Hoshin Kanri and Floor Management Development System

*Our goals can only be reached through a vehicle of a plan, in which we must fervently believe, and upon which we must vigorously act. There is no other route to success.*

— Vincent van Gogh, artist

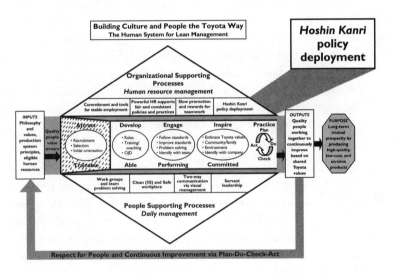

## THE HOSHIN SYSTEM MAKES INVESTMENT IN CULTURE PAY OFF

Throughout this book, we have emphasized the benefits you will get from patiently investing in people and culture. We have been critical of lean and six sigma programs that use the toolkit to drive out short-term costs. How can Toyota keep investing without getting a return on their investment? We realize that few companies are structured to take a view as patient and long-term as Toyota and need to get results more quickly. *Hoshin kanri,* also known as policy deployment, is the system that focuses the energy of quality people toward corporate objectives.

Hoshin kanri translates into "direction and means management." One Japanese trainer translated hoshin to mean "compass" and kanri as "control." It is Toyota's corporate planning process. We will summarize here some aspects of the system, but we do not claim that this chapter is a how-to manual. There are many entire books on the subject that go into great detail of how to implement the system.[1] This chapter is meant to summarize some highlights of the system and to describe how the tool connects to the culture.

The experience of typical business planning is not pleasant for many people. Non-connected and top-down directives are handed down then followed up by those dreaded "sit down follow-up meetings" with the boss where the managers try to fudge the numbers and use statistics to show how good things are going while the boss tries to figure out what went wrong. It took a while for the Japanese trainers sent to America to create the Toyota Culture of focusing on the process instead of the results and using process checks to provide support and coaching instead of punishment. Two general managers remember their "early days" experience at TMMK with their "formal overall plant check" with then president, Mr. Cho. In this meeting, the president would check their progress on hoshin objectives. A circle meant the action was on target in meeting the objective, a triangle was just below the objective, and an X indicated a significant gap.

Ken Kreafle, a 20-year veteran at Toyota, currently a general manager for TEMA and a former general manager at TMMK over Body Weld and Stamping, came to Toyota through General Motors and remembers his first "Check" meeting.

*My report looked like one big X. It had X's all over it. I have never been so nervous in all my life. I remember calling my wife before the meeting and telling her to be prepared to move because I will more than likely lose my job when they see how I am doing. When I went into the meeting, what I got was a smiling Mr. Cho, asking me what I was learning and how he could help. It was one of those days I'll never forget, because it started to form in me the real life Toyota Way.*

Mike Hoseus had a similar experience with his first hoshin check with Mr. Cho as the assembly plant manager.

*I had two circles, mostly triangles and a few X's. I went into the meeting ready to make myself look as good as possible. I wanted to make sure they knew they made the right decision when they promoted me. I put the X's toward the bottom of the pages and toward the back of the report and of course the circles were out front for everyone to see. When I started the meeting I was quick to start discussing the circles and the activities we did to achieve them.*

---

[1] Jackson, Thomas L. *Hoshin Kanri for the Lean Enterprise: Developing Competitive Capabilities and Managing Profit*, NewYork: Productivity Press, 2006.

*Mr. Cho just as quickly was flipping to the back of the report and started asking questions about the X's. I wouldn't give up that easy and once again tried to "get my points" in on the circles. Again he asked about the X's. A slow learner, one more time I tried to share some circle information. Finally, he interrupted and said, "I do not want to take time to talk about the circles. If you have a circle it means to me you are doing well and do not need my assistance. I want to discuss the X's so I can hear about your struggles and we can talk about how I can help you." That was not the response I was expecting, and I thought about all the energy I wasted trying to cover my behind and make the report look good when all he wanted was the problems and to help me improve—a much better use of our time.*

The chapter will also describe Toyota's Floor Management Development System (FMDS) because it is the system that connects the hoshin to the everyday activity on the floor. We will give an example of a year in the life of hoshin to show how the system starts in Japan and quickly translates to activity on the production floor at Toyota's plants across the globe. We have emphasized throughout this book that the activity on the floor is more than just producing the product. The activity is also centered on the development of both the leaders and the team members, and how they are driven to continually improve their level of skill, in part through the challenging stretch objectives set through the hoshin kanri system.

# WHAT IS HOSHIN AND HOW DOES IT RELATE TO THE FLOOR MANAGEMENT DEVELOPMENT SYSTEM?

"The origin of Toyota's strength is to be able to maximize performance as an organization through teamwork and to develop the people through the job," said Shunichi Kimura, general manager of Toyota Institute and global HR.

Kimura explains that hoshin is the process that does both of these, and more. Hoshin is a key component of the Toyota Management Framework. It connects leadership's vision, values, and philosophies (the Toyota Way) to the daily activity on the floor (developing people in problem solving to reach business goals).

Toyota Motor Corporation defines the hoshin process in a bit more detail as a system that aims to:

■ create an organization capable of sustained high performance, and
■ produce results

by:

- setting mid-to-long-term management plans and annual hoshin,
- prioritizing activities and resources,
- involving all members in targets/means to achieve,
- maintaining PDCA, checks and follow-ups during implementation

so that:

- the whole organization goes in one direction, with the *members taking initiative.*

Toyota uses the hoshin to get the entire organization on one page, which translates into a big competitive advantage. A common response heard at Toyota Culture workshops from executives and mid-level managers is that their company has planning processes, but no one below the top executive level is really involved. "We are told what to do, and then it seems like different departments have different priorities, and we are never on the same page. The worse case is that the activities actually conflict or contradict each other. We have a lot of good problem solving going on, but it is in pockets and they are not connected to one another." Figure 15.1 shows how the hoshin process connects everyone in the organization, both vertically and horizontally.

The hoshin process follows these key points as it progresses down to each organization:

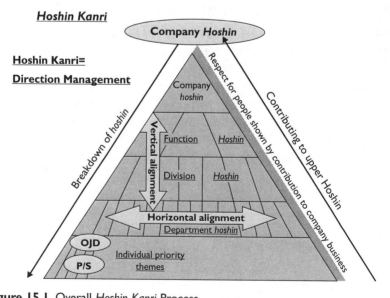

**Figure 15.1** Overall *Hoshin Kanri* Process

1. based on top management thinking, with understanding of mission and vision
2. mainly "target setting" problem type (as opposed to the "event type")
3. prioritizes major activities
4. is broken down to each workplace/group
5. has "catch-ball" for understanding, quality, ownership
6. has PDCA follow-up
7. standardizes good processes to build stronger organization

In general, the hoshin is focused on process and results, it is circular, using PDCA methods and it involves the team members in the process as well as with their development. Figure 15.2 illustrates how the hoshin cascades down the organization but also flows back up from the individual on the floor.

No one can argue against these concepts, but even Toyota has had challenges implementing hoshin in America. At TMMK for example, with the quick growth and everyone working very busily, it was sometimes a challenge to have the hoshin be the driver of daily activities, instead of the "firefighting" that can take much of a supervisor's and manager's time. The system Toyota developed to prevent this is called the Floor Management Development System.

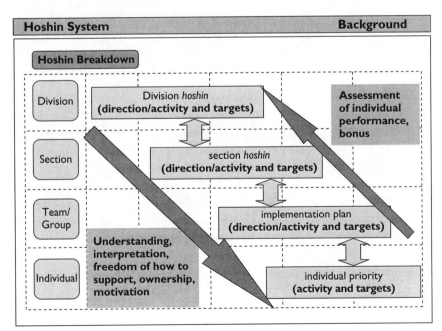

Adapted From Toyota Motor Corporation/Toyota Institute presentations of *hoshin* and Toyota management.

**Figure 15.2** Hoshin Goals Cascades Down through Company and Results Flow Up

## The Floor Management Development System (FMDS)

As the name describes, the FMDS is the system Toyota currently uses to teach group leaders and managers to manage the floor. Toyota describes the key points as a system that aligns floor management and development activities to achieve company targets by:

- Visually demonstrating the management condition of the shop and alignment of daily activities to hoshin targets.
- Promoting two-way communication, creating the environment to address abnormal conditions through targeted problem solving, determine needed support and resources and develop team members.

It is set up on the foundational principles of the Toyota Way and runs in four stages. These four stages are similar to our overall discussion of the Toyota culture model: Set a purpose and agree to measurable goals, establish standards, make problems visible, and then develop people to solve the problems and improve in order to reach the business goals. (See Figure 15.3)

Phase I starts with the hoshin and then breaks down the yearly activities to support the hoshin. The hoshin establishes clear purpose and direction for the organization and then breaks it down to measurable goals. For the Japanese, the

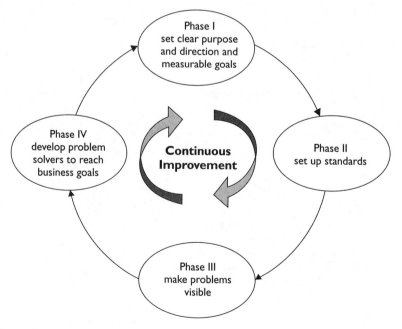

**Figure 15.3** Phases of FMDS

hoshin usually is related to a longer term, "breakthrough" project that takes at least three years to accomplish.

Phase II is focused on standardization, starting with 5S, reinforcing the principle that without standards and organization there can be no improvement activity. At TMMK, it took several months and even up to an entire year for groups to get certified through phase II because the standards are so stringent. In fact, Steve St Angelo, the president of TMMK who oversaw this transition, personally toured each area in order to certify them in order to go on to phase III.

Phase III is about setting up the plant, section, and group visual control boards in order to highlight problems. Where Phase I was looking at the big picture, this is how the big picture translates for each group in the plant. It translates accident and defect ratios and percentages into understandable indicators for each group. It makes it clear for everyone in the organization where the problems are.

Phase IV is where the Toyota Business Practices, or TBP, kick in. Supervisors and managers are trained and then train others (OJD) to use the go and see with the 8 step global problem solving (P/S) in order to address any gaps in the indicators. People are developing their problem-solving process skills while progress is made toward reaching business goals.

## Connecting Hoshin—FMDS and the Quality People Value Stream

The integration of hoshin with FMDS and TBP was new at the start of the 2000's. Toyota started to use hoshin as far back as 1961 while introducing Total Quality Management (TQM) in the company in pursuit of the Deming Award. In 1999, there were problems both inside and outside of Japan that made the system less effective than desired. There were found to be too many individual interpretations of the system resulting in unclear priorities for everyone. Also with the rapid globalization of Toyota, there was a need to share and coordinate the global corporate vision in order to get all overseas plant actions in-line with the global vision.

The hoshin and FMDS connect many components of the quality people value stream. We started the book with the discussion of how Toyota connects the product value stream, (i.e. building a quality car, at the lowest possible cost, in the shortest amount of time) to the people value stream (building a quality person). The FMDS is the daily activity that supports this connection. The hoshin is the "what we need to do?" and the overview of "how should we do it?," while the FMDS details the specifics of the "how?" and then gives daily feedback toward "how are we actually doing?" See Figure 15.4.

The hoshin process connects to the Toyota Way on a larger level. It is in line with the core values of mutual respect and continuous improvement by connecting team member development and problem solving. Many times organizations

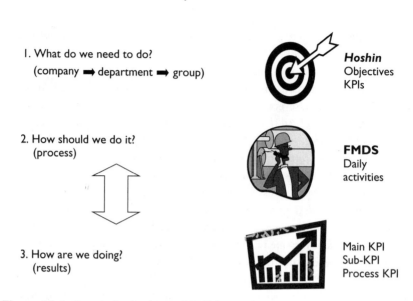

1. What do we need to do?
   (company ➡ department ➡ group)

   *Hoshin*
   Objectives
   KPIs

2. How should we do it?
   (process)

   **FMDS**
   Daily
   activities

3. How are we doing?
   (results)

   Main KPI
   Sub-KPI
   Process KPI

**Figure 15.4** Connecting hoshin and FMDS

implement the hoshin planning tools without the respect for people part of the equation. One executive, on joining a new company after a Toyota Culture workshop explained, "This company had those 'on the floor meetings' that you talked about at Toyota with their FMDS and problem solving. They had the big wall and the indicators and then would bring everyone together every morning to review. But there was one big difference. At the plant, everyone referred to 'The Daily Meeting' as 'The Daily Beating,' because it was management's way to get everybody together to tell them how bad they were doing, that they were below target and needed to do better...as if this was going to really help anyone actually meet their target."

The problem solving component of hoshin is almost every time considered a "setting type" of problem. As discussed in Chapter 6, that is one in which Toyota has met its goal and then tightens it again in order to set a new gap and create another problem to solve. This is the purpose of hoshin, to continually "stretch" the organization and hence individuals, to constantly improve. However, the hoshin should be stretch objectives and the stretch objectives should fit the capability of the team for performing the job at a high level with high problem-solving skills. Giving a group a stretch objective they are not prepared for is stressful and unfair. So the hoshin will get progressively more challenging as the group and plant gets stronger. The younger plant in Mexico will not have the same challenges as a plant like TMMK.

There is a fine balance between stretching too far past the breaking point and stretching to the point of challenge. The hoshin reflects the Toyota Way value of challenge. Challenge is how team members grow. They must be stretched a little beyond what they think they are capable of, and when they reach the new level they are stretched some more. This obviously solves problems but also helps team member satisfaction. The hoshin is how the work stays continually challenging and intrinsically rewarding. Without it, progress would stop and the teams would begin to lose energy after a few early wins.

Hoshin helps maintain the quality people spiraling value stream so that individuals go deeper and deeper through the four stages. They are continually developing, engaging in problem solving and being inspired by the process. Just as the hoshin is a large PDCA cycle that repeats itself, it facilitates the same repeating process for the team members.

# A YEAR IN THE LIFE OF HOSHIN KANRI AT TOYOTA

Following is an example of a year in the life of Hoshin.[2] The hoshin process starts at the top executive level of TMC in Japan, flows down to the global affiliates and goes all the way from the president to the team member on the floor. The entire picture is shown in Figure 15.5. There are seven steps shown in the diagram in which the hoshin cascades throughout the organization. Our example will take one hoshin year (2006) and describe how this process takes place with each of the seven steps.

## Step 1. TMC Selects a Hoshin Theme (a priority to focus on)

Like everything else within Toyota, there is a system in order to make a decision. Figure 15.6 shows the "system or process" that Toyota uses to select a hoshin item. It resembles the SWOT analysis that many organizations use for strategic planning. Each company would follow this process in order to continue to cascade down the hoshin item. The hoshin starts general at the TMC level, moves to TEMA (Toyota North American Headquarters) and then cascades to the plants becoming more and more specific at each step.

### *Top Management Thinking and Vision and Values*
Before actually selecting a focus item, there is the foundation and background. The foundation is to support the purpose of working toward long-term mutual

---

[2] This example of a "year in the life of Hoshin" is a culmination of stories and activities taking place over the course of the last few years at Toyota and TMMK. The early hoshin objectives and most of the pieces of the story are true but some details have been filled in based on years of experience with the process and how it works.

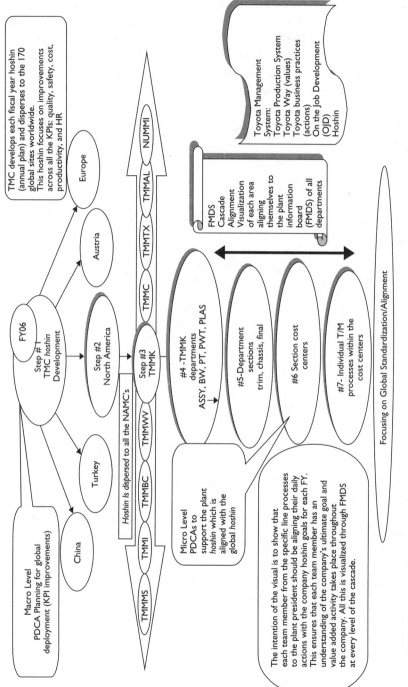

**Figure 15.5** Cascading *Hoshin* from Japan through North America to Floor Level (Developed by Tracey Richardson, CQPO 2007)

## Selecting a *Hoshin* Item

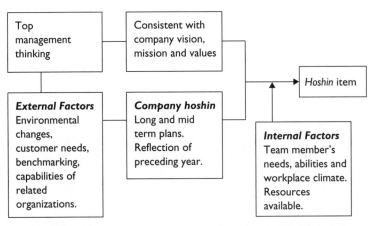

Adapted From Toyota Motor Corporation/Toyota Institute presentations of *hoshin* and Toyota management.

**Figure 15.6** Selecting a *Hoshin* Item[3]

prosperity for everyone involved. The mission and goals are translated into key performance indicators to support the goal of producing the highest quality car, at the lowest possible cost, in the shortest amount of time, while respecting those who do the work. These KPIs (Safety, Quality, Productivity, Cost, and HR) make up the business results side of the equation for the hoshin process. The hoshin process will always include all five of these indicators, but the top management will decide which of these need special focus depending on the other factors shown in Figure 15.6.

## External and Internal Factors

Toyota starts with on customer needs, the competition, and the capabilities of external organizations, such as, suppliers as key factors in determining hoshin priority items. For example, in 2005, Toyota looked at the competition and saw the trends as demonstrated in Figure 15.7.

By looking at the competition (as measured by J.D, Power's initial quality study), Toyota was able to see that they were losing their competitive edge in quality during the first three months of ownership. The wide gap that had previously given them their competitive advantage was shrinking. Not only was the competition getting better, as Hyundai illustrates dramatically, but Toyota was also suffering some of their own quality issues. During this same time period, there were

---

[3] Concept and material for figure taken from "Advancing the Toyota Way," internal Toyota North American course, and a TMC Hoshin manual.

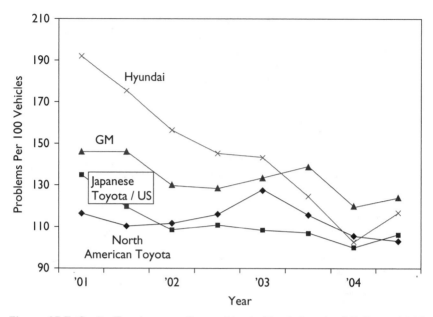

**Figure 15.7** Quality Trends versus Competition in North America (J.D. Power Initial Quality Study)

multiple recalls of Toyota automobiles that were tarnishing their reputation of high quality. Certainly, there were both external and internal factors contributing to these blemishes. For one, industry experts point to Toyota's growth in the five years of 2000–2005 (in adding almost 3 million units of production to their capacity) as the second largest in automobile history, behind only that of the Ford Motor Company in the early 1900s. From the decade of 1995 to 2005, they had more than doubled the number of plants, from the starting point, of 26 to nearly 60.

At the same time cost and volume pressure increased on external partners, the suppliers, who were also struggling to keep up with Toyota's rapid expansion and increased demand for parts. You will never hear Toyota point fingers, but the fact is that most all of the recalls were due to supplier produced components and not Toyota facilities. However, Toyota's name is on the car and they take full responsibility for any problems with the vehicle. Because of these factors, TMC selected quality as a hoshin priority focus item for all global plants to address for the next five years. The stretch goals to be achieved by 2010 were:

■ have zero recalls,
■ obtain J.D. Power Number One award for Initial Quality Survey (ISQ) for all Toyota Models produced in America at least once between 2005 and 2010, and
■ reduce warranty claims by 60 percent.

These global goals are broad and cut across all plants and Toyota organizations. The goals are also challenging. In accordance with Toyota's problem-solving process, the "zero recall" and "number one award for all vehicles" would be considered ultimate goals within the Toyota Culture. It is not expected they will be completely achieved, but striving for anything less would be a compromise. The 60 percent improvement in warranty claims is a concrete goal for the plants to drive toward, with the thinking that if this number is achieved, the other two will follow. To make the process more concrete, we will see how these long-term, broad goals are broken down into specific yearly targets for each level of the organization.

## Step 2. Cascade to TEMA

TEMA, Toyota's North American headquarters, leads the process of translating the quality as a hoshin priority to specific goals for North American operations in 2006. This does not mean that TMC will lose contact with the process once they hand it off. They are still connected to the plants through the quality division and through manufacturing via the "mother plant" network. TEMA, as the North American headquarters, has two responsibilities: First, to address the quality goal as part of their own company hoshin, and second to communicate, coordinate, and support the quality focus with all North American affiliates, such as the manufacturing plants, and the Toyota Technical Center.

TEMA gives hoshin goals to all department heads. Remember these department heads (i.e., quality, HR, legal, engineering, production control, etc.) are responsible for horizontal communication of their functional responsibilities across all of North America. We will not discuss how this is cascaded to suppliers in detail here, but TEMA works through its North American Production Support Center (a division of HR) to help suppliers with their part of the hoshin. Several supplier conferences are held in order to train suppliers in the Toyota Way and the Toyota business practices (the eight step global problem solving). Suppliers will also take on hoshin responsibilities as Toyota cannot achieve their goals without supplier support.

For the second step, TEMA communicates the quality hoshin focus to all the North American affiliates (plants in Kentucky, Texas, West Virginia, Indiana, etc.). This is done through both vertical and horizontal channels. The vertical channels flow from the TEMA president to the plant presidents. The quality priority focus is communicated and discussed through the quality department since they are the coordinating department for quality, just as accounting is for cost. North American-wide activity in this area for the plants is coordinated through the quality division. There is also horizontally related activity taking place through the North American Production Support Center. They coordinate the

Global Production Center's fundamental-skills training, group leader training, and manager training and integrate the quality focus into their activities.

## Step 3. Cascade Down to Manufacturing Plants (TMMK)

TMMK picks up the quality hoshin goals of zero recalls, number one JD Powers, and 60 percent reduction in warranty claims from the TEMA president sharing the goals with all the plant presidents. The TEMA quality division supports the TEMA president in this meeting by supplying global trend information for both Toyota and its competition.

The President of TMMK then takes the information back to the plant and has discussions with the Japanese and American leadership team (this includes the president, vice presidents, general managers, and assistant general managers, as well as Japanese counterparts, totaling about 20 people). The quality item is one of a few that will be on the agenda for the discussion. Every year the hoshin includes all management areas of safety, quality, productivity, cost, and HR, and then there is a priority focus area. For this reason, this meeting covers all of the items, with most of the time being spent on the focus item of quality. For the quality portion, they would pick up the overall global and North American goals and then customize them for TMMK. They consider making these goals more challenging, but decide to stay with the same. They also add two plant specific indicators to their hoshin in order to support the warranty and J.D. Power's goals. Notice that these last two specific targets are based on one year, in this case 2006. While the overall hoshin focus may last 3–5 years, the plan is always broken down to a yearly plan at the plant level:

- TMMK to have zero recalls.
- Reduce warranty claims by 60 percent (warranty claims from TMS from 10 per month to 4[4]).
- Obtain J.D. Power Number One for Initial Quality Survey (ISQ) award for Camry, Avalon, and Solara between 2005 and 2010.
- Improve TMMK plant audit to less than 1.0 defect per car by the end of 2006. (The TMMK audit is a system where 5 cars per shift are taken off the sales line and gone over in great detail by highly trained inspectors, including riding on a test track. The number chosen is not an actual number.)
- Improve TMMK direct run ratio to 93 percent by the end of 2006. (The direct run ratio is the percentage of cars that go through all processes without coming off the line at any point for off-line repair and getting through

---

[4] Number chosen is not an actual number, but used here for illustrative purposes.

final inspection with no defects. Some minor defects may have been found and repaired online without reducing this score. This percentage would include defects from all shops, such as stamping, body weld, plastics, paint, and assembly. The figure chosen is not the actual number.)

There is some initial strategy discussion at this stage about general processes and activities that all will utilize to support the reaching of these quality goals. In reviewing the preceding year company hoshin, the group is able to connect current improvement activities to the hoshin.

## Step 4. Department Heads Play "Catch Ball" with Their Section Managers

This is the level where the hoshin gets down to the specific planning. Each plant general manager (stamping, body, paint, etc.) goes back to their department in order to "make their plan" to support the plant hoshin goals. The cascade continues within each department, for example, with assembly, the general manager calls together the assistant general managers, section managers, and Japanese coordinators. This group consists of about 10 people. This group of assembly managers strategizes about the hoshin, but have concerns over the amount of work coming at the same time with the major model change of the Avalon. This next year will be focused on new team member training and setting up the new processes. The group discusses and decides how to prioritize all that is expected of them. They decide to focus on the model change incorporating the quality focus hoshin items and safety. They request to add no new activites in the other hoshin items of productivity, cost, and HR.

This process is known as "catch ball" in the hoshin process. Hoshin is not a dictatorial process that says here are the goals and find a way to do it. That does not mean that the tendency does not exist to still do this, because in the short run, it is quicker and easier this way. However, without the input, and buy in from everyone involved, this advantage would be short lived. Toyota refers to it as "Tunnel Kanri" if goals are just handed down without the proper negotiation and buy in.

The executive team considers assembly's request and assigns the accounting and production control departments to take the request to the other departments. These two departments are the coordinating departments responsible to meet the hoshin goals for cost and productivity, respectively. Production control and accounting are able to work out goals with the power train, stamping, and plastics divisions. They too do not have to make as many changes to support the upcoming Avalon model and they all agree to make enough cost and productivity improvements for 2006 to offset assembly's request to wait until year 2007. With this teamwork, the plant is able to set realistic goals for each separate plant (weld, paint, plastics, etc), and still reach the overall hoshin request for TMMK as a whole.

**Table 15.1** Breakdown of Quality Hoshin Targets by Plant

| Item | Total Target | Body Weld | Paint | Plastics | Powertrain | Assy | Parts (QE) | Other |
|---|---|---|---|---|---|---|---|---|
| Audit (Defects Detected/Vehicle) | .9 | .2 | .15 | .1 | .1 | .2 | .1 | .05 |
| Direct Run (Percent through all Processes with Zero off-line Repairs) | 93% | 99% | 98.5% | 99.5% | 99.5% | 98% | 99% | 99.5% |

It is agreed within TMMK that the annual quality hoshin will be a 10 percent audit and direct and run improvement. The plant-wide quality department facilitates a meeting with all of the plants to determine specific targets for each. They brought with them the last year's audit and direct run data in order to have facts to start with. They also brought with them a draft of recommended goals for each plant. Quality had done the last year's average and then taken a 10 percent improvement from there. A minor game of catch ball ensued with some disagreement of where to take the improvement from. It was decided to take the 10 percent from the end of the year in order to have a better, more accurate chance to reach the overall 10 percent in the next year. The resulting targets, broken down by plant, are shown in Table 15.1. Note that to get the 93% direct run rate overall requires that each department has a much higher direct run rate as these get multiplied to make the total.

Assembly (and everyone else) now had specific hoshin targets for 2006 to take back to their sections. Now the section managers need to start planning the process improvements that would help them reach the targets. Because of all the changes to jobs on the assembly line and the training necessary with the model change coming up, the assembly team agrees to focus on two areas of improvement to address the quality hoshin: process diagnostics and FMDS.

Process diagnostics is a system that was created by TMC in Japan and then was further developed within TMMK. It is a system designed to simplify the work process for the team members working on the car, and, as a result, improve both the safety and quality of the process. The FMDS system is the Floor Management Development System that focuses on standards, visual control, and problem solving. The assembly management team believes that through these two processes they can achieve the quality objectives. They meet and discuss the best way to implement both of these initiatives in the next year. The managers of each area recommend to the general manager that they pick one area of the assembly line to start a model line that incorporates both the process diagnostics and the FMDS system. This would allow the rest of the groups to focus on the model change while concentrating the improvement activities and resources in one area to learn and develop a template. Then after the problems are worked out with both the model change and the model line, the rest of the groups would implement the improvements. The general manager agrees and the decision is made to have the model line be a section of the line in Assembly Plant 2.

## Step 5. The Hoshin Cascades Down to the Individual Plants

The assembly managers are now able to go back and work on their specific hoshin plans within their plants. The managers call together the assistant managers and hold planning sessions to complete the detailed planning.

The first activity to plan is the process diagnostics. It is based on the philosophy that the team members, on the line are like surgeons and everything should be focused on simplifying their jobs, providing just what they need, and reducing physical and mental stress as much as possible. There are many improvement factors. Some example factors are:

- amount of lighting
- temperature
- noise
- standardized work and training completed
- number of returns to the parts rack
- number of mental decisions needed to be made per car

All of these factors are given an objective, numerical score and, at the end, there is an overall rating for each process. All processes are given a score and a rating of green, yellow, and red. Green is a process that scores 90 or better (designated "good"), yellow from 70–90 (designated "level up") and red, anything below 70 ("bad). The maximum score, if all factors are at their highest level for the process is 100. Table 15.2 is an example of this objective scoring.

One principle of the Toyota way is that if you get the process right, the results will follow. A basic assumption of Toyota culture is a strong belief in the scientific method based on facts. By developing objective scores to diagnose the process, it provides an indicator of how well the job and workstation is designed. The process is the independent variable that is changed by the problem solver to investigate its effect on the dependent variable. In this case, the assembly team is hypothesizing (with samples and results already proven in Japan) that an increase in score on the process diagnostics will result in improved quality (in addition to safety, and therefore cost and productivity).

With this objective, measurable process, the managers can set process goals across the department to support the general manager's direction of focusing on

**Table 15.2** Hypothetical Process Diagnostics Example

| Item | Standard and Point System | Job # 3 Points before Improvement | Job # 3 Points after Improvement |
|---|---|---|---|
| Standardized Work | Up to date and followed = 5 | 0 | 5 |
| Ergonomic Ratings | Red = 0 Yellow = 1.5 Green = 3 | 1.5 | 3 |
| Rotation | 4 jobs per person = 4 2 or 3 = 2 1 or less = 0 | 2 | 4 |
| Lighting | > 380 lux[1] = 1 | 0 | 1 |
| Noise | < 79 decibles = 1 | 1 | 1 |
| Temperature | between 65 and 80 degrees = 1 | 0 | 1 |
| Total[2] | | 4.5 | 15 |

[1] The lux (symbol: lx) is the unit of *illuminance*. It is used in *photometry* as a measure of the intensity of light, with wavelengths weighted according to the *luminosity function*, a standardized model of human brightness perception. (Taken from http://en.wikipedia.org/wiki/Lux)

[2] The points here do not add up to 100 because these are just a portion of the total process diagnostics categories.

process diagnostics and FMDS. They first have to compile the data on the current situation and then set a target for improvement over the course of 2006. They decided their process diagnostic goals would be to improve diagnostic scores into the "level up" (yellow) zone for all of assembly, with the exception of the model line, which would target all processes in the good zone (green). For FMDS, they decided to complete Phase I across both plants and complete the first three phases in the model line.

With this information, they filled out the hoshin form to include KPI goals, process goals, and the responsible person. We emphasized the importance of teamwork in Chapter 8, but at Toyota, teamwork and individual accountability go hand in hand. There is always one name as a lead person assigned, even when there are many people/teams involved. Without this personal responsibility and accountability, even with good teams, there are problems with getting assignments completed. Then a timeline is laid out for the year, showing progress on the process indicators and timing for the official hoshin checks. When there is improvement, the team will evaluate the effects of improving the process diagnostic ratings on each process on the overall quality indicators of direct run and audit. Ultimately for the plant, the goal is to see an impact on the global goals of zero recall, obtaining the Number One J.D. Power award, and 60 percent warranty improvement.

## Step 6. The Plan Goes Down to the Group Leaders

While this plan is being drawn up, in draft form, the managers are meeting with their group leaders in order to get input and buy in. The Assembly 2 manager schedules a Saturday offsite meeting in a local hotel in order to have both shifts of assistant managers and group leaders present. All hoshin categories are discussed (safety, quality, etc.) and the manager communicates the course of the hoshin to date from the TMC down. There are committees organized around each hoshin category, with each having two assistant managers and six group leaders. This will be the team that facilitates the improvement activity throughout the year.

A quality committee is formed to support the focus hoshin activities for process diagnostics and FMDS. Their first assignment is to confirm KPIs for each group leader to take to their group, and eventually, the team and individual. In order to have the KPIs cascade all the way down to the team level, they need to determine new quality goals for each group. Part of the FMDS system is to take the general goals and convert them to an understandable set of targets for the team members. Their assignment is to take the audit and direct run goals and translate them for each group, both shifts. For example, with the direct run goal for assembly being 98 percent, it leaves a 2 percent defect rate—2 percent of 500 cars per shift = 10 defects per shift to go off-line for 13 groups. This means that some groups get less than one defect/shift. The group leaders play "catch ball" in order to finalize how many defects will be "allowed" for each group. It gets more complicated with .2 defects per car in the 5 cars per shift audit. With each of the two shifts working approximately 20 days per month, this would equal 100 cars audited for each shift per month, leaving only 20 defects for the 13 groups per shift for the entire month or 1 defect per day. More "catch ball" and then consensus.

Table 15.3 shows an example of how this breakdown might work out to allocate the allowed monthly defects by groups based on group size and past defects. It is much more meaningful to a group to know they have a goal of one defect per day for the direct run and two per month in audit, as opposed to telling them assembly's goals are .2 and 98 percent.

## Step 7. Hoshin Goals Are Taken to the Team Members on the Floor

The group leaders now have all the information they need to have hoshin meetings with their groups in order to share KPI and process goals and to make plans for their respective groups to support the hoshin. For example, the Trim 2 group leader calls a meeting of the entire group to finalize their plans. There is not too much "catch ball" at this stage in regards to KPI and process goals, but there is

**Table 15.3** Quality KPI Targets broken down for each group in Assembly

| Group/Team | Audit Defects per Month | Direct Run/Off-line Defects per Shift |
|---|---|---|
| Trim 1 | 2 | 1 |
| 2 | 4 | 2 |
| 3 | 2 | 1 |
| 4 | 2 | 1 |
| Chassis 1 | 1 | .5 |
| 2 | .66 | .33 |
| 3 | .66 | .33 |
| 4 | .66 | .33 |
| Engine | 1 | .5 |
| Final 1 | 2 | 1 |
| 2 | 2 | 1 |
| 3 | 2 | 1 |
| Assembly 2 Total | 20 | 10 |

much buy in, involvement, and discussion from the group in terms of how to support both of these. The improvements needed to raise the process diagnostic score will be made team by the team so a sequence must be agreed upon. The trim group agrees to the sequence of 2, 3, 4 and then 1. This is because most of the problems are coming from 2 and 3, and they are in a better staffing condition to support the kaizen right away.

The group selects volunteers, one from each team, to form a FMDS committee and be responsible for setting up the group board. Team 4 volunteers to be the first team to set up the Team FMDS visual board. All of this is captured on a hoshin planning sheet by the group and team leaders and then posted in the group area with a responsible person assigned to each task.

# THE PDCA PHASES

We have finished the planning stage of the hoshin process, and everyone now is on the same page and ready to move forward with the "DO" portion of the process. It is helpful to think of the hoshin process as many PDCA processes cascading down through the levels of the company (see Figure 15.8). An even more complex image is one of many sets of concentric circles with nested PDCA cycles from the company down to the work team level. The PDCA in this case is:

**Plan**—Standardization, generation, and confirmation of annual, mid- and long-term plans (by top management and all employees)
**Do**—Carry out scheduled plans (daily management)
**Check**—Review of processes and results (mid and end of year)
**Act**—Standardize the job

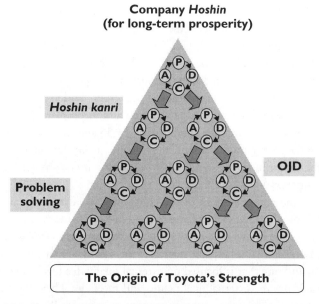

Company *Hoshin*
(for long-term prosperity)

*Hoshin kanri*

OJD

Problem
solving

The Origin of Toyota's Strength

**Figure 15.8** *Hoshin* is a Set of Cascading PDCA Loops at all Levels

Trim 2 works on their implementation items for their hoshin. The "DO" items for the Process Diagnostics/Simplification for 2006 include:

- Adding three process work dollies to reduce team member returns to the flow rack to only once per two hours.
- Adding "part kits" to their line, in addition to working with the parts handling group, so the option parts for eight processes are all sequenced off-line and brought to the car in order. This results in all processes reducing trips to the flow rack and the number of decisions needing to be made for each car to less than three.
- Adding lighting and airflow in order to reach both lighting and temperature standards.
- Exchanging out four existing work dollies with new and improved ones that eliminate the need for team members to physically hold or push them because they do so automatically.

Meanwhile the group also completed its Phase I and II FMDS processes for their second focus area of improvement. Phase I involves making clear quality goals for each team and person in the group. Phase II involves standardization and 5S. The team members agreed to work one Saturday a month for three months in order to set up all of the 5S systems in the group. They developed a board system that laid out the 5S responsibilities for the day, the week, and the month and then put them all on a large board. At the same time, they made picture cards of each team member. A rotating schedule was made for each task and each team member, and each day/week/month each individual team member moves their picture to the completed side of the board, to show that their job is done. The system improves their 5S tremendously because of the personal accountability and the visual control for the team leaders and group leaders who can look anytime and see the condition of work completed and incomplete. Each level of management comes by to check the condition of the 5S and the systems to maintain it. With some minor modifications, they finally qualify for the presidential visit, and, at the end of June, they receive their certification. The group leader buys a pizza lunch for everyone to celebrate.

Meanwhile, the executive team of the company has set up a visual control (FMDS) board for all of TMMK which is located in Plant 1 in order to focus on the quality hoshin for the whole plant. There are two separate areas set up, one that is focused on internal total plant management, (safety, quality, productivity, cost, and HR), and one that is focused on external quality feedback. The quality department facilitates the external quality area and meetings. They use it to post all of the J.D. Power information and the warranty claims to TMS. They facilitate immediate feedback from the customer directly to the processes that are responsible. The ensuing problem solving is then supported and items are closed when a countermeasure is in place and confirmed.

The internal management board is set up to visually show the condition of the entire TMMK facility in all five management areas (safety, quality, productivity, cost, and HR) at one glance. The hoshin "DO" items are posted for the process improvements as well as the daily results. Every morning at 8:40, the executive team comes together at the area to meet. The area is on the plant floor, right next to the end of the line and there are no chairs and there is a large timer to monitor the meeting so it stays at only 20 minutes per day. The meeting acts as a quick check of hoshin items and as a conduit for problem solving. It is not meant to be a problem-solving meeting, only to identify what the priority problems are and where they are coming from. From there the team puts together ad hoc groups of people needed to solve the problems. This group goes and sees the problem for themselves and works together as a team to solve it. They report back daily at the executive meeting. Difficult and repeating problems are prioritized and the president and vice presidents personally join the team, go and see for themselves, and join the pool of resources needed to solve the problem.

Two major repeating defects that were plaguing Trim 2 made it all the way to the executive level FMDS board. There was a visor issue and a headliner issue that involved both process and supplier engineers and without the focus of the executive the group was not able to solve the problem on its own. Solving these two problems had a big positive impact on their quality. The support from the

Points on deploying Hoshin Kanri

| Hoshin Checks | PDCA |
|---|---|

### Rapidly Turning Over the kanri Cycle

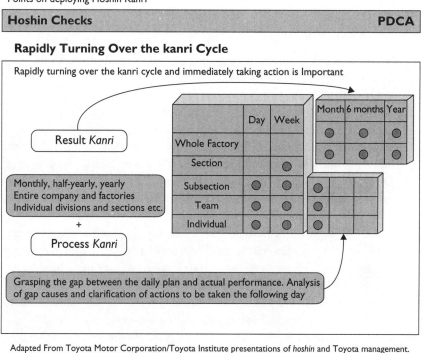

Adapted From Toyota Motor Corporation/Toyota Institute presentations of *hoshin* and Toyota management.

**Figure 15.9** Check Schedule for *Hoshin* Process and Results

executive team in coming out to the process and helping to solve the problem made a positive impact on morale and trust.

The Trim 2 group tracked their quality status daily and hoshin process items were followed up on weekly by the assistant manager. Once per month, all of the group's activities and results are rolled up to a monthly manager's report. These reports are then sent to the executive level area to be reviewed by the executive team. Quarterly formal checks are made by the general managers. At the end of October, the president is ready to do his bi-yearly check. Figure 15.9 shows the "check schedule" of both the process and results portions of the hoshin.

## Floor Management Development System

With the focus for the second half of the year on FMDS, the assembly manager team and Trim 2 updated a renewed plan to implement Phases 3 and 4 of FMDS. The manager team set up a section management board in order to show the hoshin items and all of the management indicators. Then Trim 2 and the team member committee set up a group board that also had the hoshin items and all of their management indicators. They followed the plant-wide standard in setting up the board and its categories and then customized the specifics and activities for each category. The committee came up with an idea to put big X's, O's, and triangles to visually show what needed attention.

The board's categories include:

**KPIs**—Key performance indicators for each of the management categories. The main KPIs for quality match the hoshin KPI's of TMMK audit and direct run ratio.

**SubKPIs**—Indicators that affect or impact the main KPI's. For quality, Trim 2 picked two internal inspection indicators of "trim inspection" and "final inspection." These were not items that made it off-line or to audit, but were found "in line" by inspection and quickly repaired by Trim 2.

**Daily Activities**—Items that need daily follow up in order to ensure problems are being solved. Trim 2 designed a simple problem-solving sheet, designating problem, cause, countermeasure, who's responsible, and results. Daily, they check the progress and even made red, yellow and green magnets to quickly see which items needed extra focus. These were "quick" problems to solve and usually did not require an A-3 or outside help to take care of.

**Process KPI's**—Results of activities that will ensure the achievement of sub and main KPIs. Trim 2 picked the process diagnostics hoshin indicators of the number of red, green and yellow processes for their first process KPI.

**Process Control Checks**—Daily checks to ensure the jobs are being done correctly in the group. Trim 2 developed a standardized work audit. This audit is done every day for one job a day by the team leaders in order to confirm that each team member has been properly trained and is practicing the standardized work steps and following the key points for each process.

**Theme Activity**—Targeted or long-term problem-solving activities. These are problems that are repetitive and could not be solved by the group as part of their "daily activities." An A-3 problem solving report is initiated and support from other related parties such as engineering, maintenance, part suppliers, and so on is facilitated.

An example of the group's board is shown in Figures 15.10 and 15.11. The first is an overall view of the area, with all five management categories, and the second is a close up of the quality section.

Three levels of management (executive, plant manager, and group leader) meet regularly at the FMDS visual management boards to cascade down the hoshin objectives and then help solve tough problems that bubble up at the working level. Trim 2 holds a daily afternoon meeting at their FMDS board to highlight any issues that need support and to assign problems to teams for solving.

An unexpected benefit of the FMDS system appears at the end of year hoshin check. Instead of doing it in a meeting room, the president is able to visit the plant boards and conduct the review right on the floor. For assembly, this includes a go

**Figure 15.10** Group Board for Floor Management Development System

**Figure 15.11** Quality Section of Group Board for Floor Management Development System

and see to Trim 2 in order to see the improvements made as a result of the process diagnostics and simplification as well as some examples of problems the group was able to solve using the FMDS system.

The reflection meetings for the end of year hoshin began generating actions for 2007. The assembly management team also demonstrated success from their model line so the focus for the following year was to *yokoten* (learn from) the simplification and FMDS systems across the department. Now they will be able to make the quality targets even more challenging for next year, and the Toyota hoshin cycle continues to turn.

The general managers and presidential level are able to demonstrate an encouraging trend of fewer warranty claims as a result of their hitting their internal goals. By mid-2007 they were on track to meet their 2010 warranty goals. The J.D. Power announcement was not in yet, but the warranty feedback is currently enough confirmation to keep moving in the direction already planned.

# IS HOSHIN PLANNING REALLY JUST MANAGEMENT BY OBJECTIVES WITH A JAPANESE NAME?

Hoshin is the strategic planning process for many Japanese companies, but like most other processes, Toyota has customized the process to fit the Toyota Way of doing things. When hearing about the process many people comment that it sounds like management by objectives. This is not the case. Table 15.4 contrasts the two approaches and shows major differences in philosophy and process.

**Table 15.4** Comparison of Process and Philosophy of Management by Objectives versus *Hoshin Kanri*

| Management by Objectives | *Hoshin Kanri* |
| --- | --- |
| Results-oriented evaluation of effort | Concerned with both results and process of getting those results |
| Top-down communication | Top-down direction setting and bottom-up flow of information and means |
| Directive | Participative |
| Primarily authority oriented | Primarily responsibility oriented |
| Linear—a one shot image of effort to reach the goal (no feedback, no second chance, just start over from scratch each time) | Circular/spiral image of how to reach a goal (add feedback loop and chance for improvement) |

Adapted from Toyota Motor Corporation/Toyota Institute presentations on *hoshin* and Toyota management.

The differences between these methods actually reflect general differences in top-down Western management compared to Toyota culture. In what we have seen of the practice of MBO, the main focus is on senior executives developing the specific outcomes they want, (cost, quality, perhaps safety), and asking their direct report at the director level to achieve these as a requirement for getting their annual bonus. The vice presidents then work with their reports to develop plans to achieve the objectives and roll out the plans. We rarely see the process of setting objectives go further down in the organization than perhaps the plant manager level, who then work through their reports in quality, engineering, safety, etc. to achieve the objectives. The executive level really does not care about the process as long as the results are achieved. It is very uncommon that these annual plans get down to planning at the work group level.

Toyota's hoshin reflects the values of respect for people and continuous improvement. It is a tool to align the total organization around corporate goals, and to provide challenges to develop people throughout the company. Toyota uses a participative process at all levels. Development and learning is just as important as achieving the objectives.

The PDCA cycle is integral to Toyota's culture and is the driver of the hoshin process. While the bottom sees goals come down from the top they have some influence on how to operationalize those goals at the working level. They then are very involved in the PDCA cycle at their level and progress is fed upward through reporting as well as hands-on involvement of senior management.

# FREQUENTLY ASKED QUESTIONS AND ANSWERS ABOUT HOSHIN

This chapter described the hoshin and FMDS processes and how they connect the values, business needs and team member development all together on a daily basis. It is a quick snapshot of how it works. The year in the life of a hoshin plan can by no means do justice to the planning, doing, and checking that take place at all levels throughout the year in order to make it successful.

Because hoshin is such a broad, integrated topic, it is difficult to explain it in an entire book, much less a chapter. Below are some frequently asked questions and answers that we've encountered when we explained hoshin at our workshops.

**Q.** *How general versus specific is the hoshin at the top level?*
**A.** As the example shows, the hoshin is general at the top in regards to results (i.e., Win J.D. Power) and almost nonexistent in terms of process, although at times general "process" types of hoshin goals are handed down as well. For example, when Mr. Cho became president of Toyota, one of his hoshin was to advance the Toyota Way globally.

**Q.** *If it is top down, how does it feel bottom up? How much flexibility is there in the catch ball by the time it gets to the shop floor?*
**A.** There is usually not too much "catch ball" on the floor in terms of results goals. As the example shows, this is done at the general manager, manager, and cross functional department level. The catch ball on the floor will be mostly in terms of who and how. Which team goes first, who is on the committees, and most importantly, the ideas of how to accomplish the goals.

**Q.** *How does the hoshin relate to the ongoing metrics of quality, cost, delivery, safety, morale? Is it in addition to these? Are there hoshin for each of these?*
**A.** There is a hoshin for each of these and these five areas of management make up the core of the hoshin, along with a special theme like the quality hoshin described earlier. Toyota managers warned the American management team to not get too many items. If it is more than a handful (five) then usually something will get dropped. There are times, however when other focuses will be added. Recently, environment has been added to the many hoshin KPIs.

**Q.** *How much data collection and reporting goes on for the hoshin and is this computerized?*
**A.** There is a lot of data collection and reporting done in problem solving and therefore the hoshin process. Toyota is still working on the balance of hand-driven data versus computerized. When others tour Toyota, usually their response is, "There is less data than we thought. We have tons of it and it all goes into the computer somewhere. Toyota has a few key items for all to see and it is done by hand." The Japanese believed that nothing should be done by the computer until you are first able to do it by hand. Once you understand what you are measuring, why and how, then you can consider using a computer to make it more efficient, but without losing visualization.

**Q.** *Is there really an attempt to roll up accomplishments quantitatively at all the bottom levels so the president of TMC sees that? Aren't some of these qualitative, such as, we did this or that activity?*
**A.** The roll up of hoshin in an inclusive manner will usually only be done at the plant level (i.e., to the president of TMMK). The roll up to the TMC president will be in the form of the main KPI's and some broad process summaries (made as quantitative as possible), such as the plant summary for process diagnostics. Usually, at least once a year, there will be a go and see visit by the president of TMC. This will be to walk the floor to see what process improvements have been made. A visit to TMMK, for example would include a tour of Trim 2, in order to see all the improvements made in 2006. They would be told, "We made these improvements (processes) and came up with

these results, and because of that we are next going to…(standardize, yokoten, and on to the next improvement)."

**Q.** *Many plants these days have KPIs presented in a standardized way in the plants or offices displayed for all to see. Should we assume they have hoshin kanri because they have these KPIs? What is different about Toyota's approach?*

**A.** The short answer is no. Just because there is visual presentation, does not mean there is visual management. It is relatively easy to set up nice display areas that are for show. The challenging part is making them "for go." Many people who visit Toyota openly voice the difference of their approach. We often hear comments such as "Now I see, the things that Toyota displays are actually driving action on a daily basis." This is indeed the difference, and Toyota would suggest that if it is not driving daily action, get rid of it.

**Q.** *Companies with six sigma programs are usually very good at measurement. In fact it is sometimes said that lean is weak on measurement and should be supplemented by six sigma. How is it that Toyota has all these metrics if they do not practice six sigma?*

**A.** Toyota's philosophy toward measurement is to only measure what you are going to use. It is "a just in time" type of thinking. If a process is critical then statistical process control will be used, but it is not needed on every process. The philosophy of the FMDS system is "let's measure less." Let's find those key processes and control items that will drive the results and get rid of the rest of the measurements. Drawing on a weight loss analogy, increasing the number of times you weigh yourself will not result in any more weight loss.

# DON'T RUSH HEADLONG INTO HOSHIN

We have received feedback from several companies reporting that they have tried hoshin and they struggled to find success with it. When questioned "why?" most cite issues related to company culture as the contributing detractors with comments like:

- We couldn't all get on the same page.
- People at the working level do not care about setting objectives; they just want to do their work and go home.
- Our leaders don't care about process, they just want results.
- We would never take the time to go down through all the levels like that, we don't have the time.

This is the reason we chose to put hoshin at the end of the model, even though it is the beginning of the process of planning and implementation. The fact is, without some of the foundation in place from the earlier chapters, the culture to allow hoshin to flourish does not exist. Just as we suggested in Chapter 14 to take your time in any major reward system changes, there are some strategies you will want to consider before embarking on a hoshin implementation. Without some of the basics such as visual management, employees skilled in problem solving, a strong group leader system, a safe and secure environment, a sense of mutual prosperity, and above all trust, hoshin will not work at the floor level. We have criticized top-down management-by-objective systems but until enough of the culture is embedded in the organization we suggest a more top-down approach to goal setting. Early on senior executives can develop hoshin goals and use a catchball process at the senior management level. As the culture matures the system can migrate down through the organization.

# KEY POINTS TO CONSIDER FOR YOUR COMPANY

1. There is a long-term/mid-term planning system in place that connects the mission, vision, and values of the company with the daily activities needed to obtain business goals.
2. The process is top down as well as bottom up, with systems of communication in place to allow for input and buy-in at all levels.
3. The planning system is horizontal as well as vertical, with a coordinating function taking the lead for facilitation.
4. The planning system focuses on process indicators as well results.
5. There are visual management areas present in the organization for the levels of management and team members to track key performance indicators and process results.
6. The focus of the planning system and visual management system is centered around problem solving and team-member development.

# PART FOUR SUMMARY

The organizational supporting processes are what some management experts would call the formal organization. It is what gets written down and issued in policy manuals, but at Toyota it is far more. Toyota has formalized and structured the support that human resources provides to ensure a safe and fair workplace.

Human resources at Toyota plays a true developmental role. Even at the artifact level one could sense something different is going on at HR in Toyota (see Figure IV.1). Look at employee data and there is unusually high employee retention and no layoffs. Absenteeism is also extremely low. If you look a little bit deeper you will find a lot of technical solutions that support employment stability along with detailed models to plan for numbers of full-time employment and variable labor. Like other parts of Toyota, HR is active in problem solving and visual management so there are telltale signs of both in conference rooms. Follow around and HR rep and you will find, unlike most companies, they are spending more time on the shop floor than in the office. One thing you will not see is an elaborate reward system. Companies with elaborate performance management systems with formulas for bonuses that you need a PhD to understand are far and away more sophisticated than Toyota's where promotions are slow and employees get simple bonuses mainly tied to company and site performance. Despite the lack of sophisticated performance-based pay systems you will see Toyota employees taking on stretch objectives cascaded from the top and moving heaven and earth to achieve them.

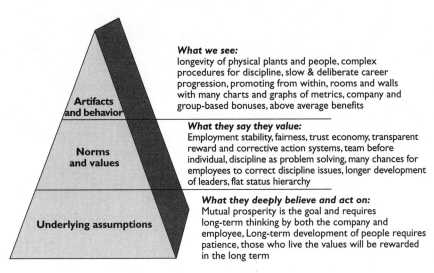

**What we see:**
longevity of physical plants and people, complex procedures for discipline, slow & deliberate career progression, promoting from within, rooms and walls with many charts and graphs of metrics, company and group-based bonuses, above average benefits

Artifacts and behavior

**What they say they value:**
Employment stability, fairness, trust economy, transparent reward and corrective action systems, team before individual, discipline as problem solving, many chances for employees to correct discipline issues, longer development of leaders, flat status hierarchy

Norms and values

**What they deeply believe and act on:**
Mutual prosperity is the goal and requires long-term thinking by both the company and employee, Long-term development of people requires patience, those who live the values will be rewarded in the long term

Underlying assumptions

**Figure IV.1** Organizational Supporting Processes Cultural Analysis

If you ask Toyota leaders what they value it will frankly sound like mother-hood and apple pie. They believe people must be treated fairly, they must feel psychologically and physically safe and secure in their jobs, they must believe that any concerns they have will be taken very seriously and given due process. They will speak of trust as the basis for the bond between employee and company rather than short-term reward systems.

If you studied the behavior of leaders over time and learned their deeply held beliefs you would find they are remarkably congruent with their stated values. They truly believe that mutual prosperity over the long run is the goal for the company and the employee and people will be willing to put their faith in the company to do right by them over the long-term. They believe trust is the basis for a partnership, and contracts and formally specified rewards are less important.

# Part Five

Learning from Toyota About
Growing a Lean Culture

*I dread success. To have succeeded is to have finished one's business on earth, like the male black widow spider, who is killed by the female the moment he has succeeded in his courtship. I like a state of continual becoming, with a goal in front and not behind.*

—George Bernard Shaw, playwright

What can another company learn from Toyota about becoming the lean enterprise that so many organizations around the world are dreaming about? We believe the answer is quite a lot. We also believe the answer is that it is impossible, and probably not even advisable, to try to imitate Toyota's culture.

Just after *The Toyota Way* came out Jeffrey Liker and associates at University of Michigan were organizing an annual lean conference and approached Toyota about keynoting the conference. The topic selected was "Learning from the Toyota Way." After long and careful deliberation by Toyota's external affairs executives they graciously declined to participate. Why? In their deliberations they questioned whether other companies can really understand the Toyota Way—their way. They also questioned whether other companies should be imitating their culture and concluded that other companies should be finding their own way. This deep and thoughtful answer shows great insight on the part of these executives. The conference title was changed to "Growing a Lean Culture" and some Toyota speakers participated.

We agree that other companies cannot imitate Toyota's culture. Toyota's culture is a unique confluence of historical events intertwined with Japanese culture and it is continuing to evolve today. Any imitation is only likely to be at the surface level of artifacts, not at the deeper level of values and underlying assumptions.

On the other hand, we have been intrigued by the way Toyota approaches building the Toyota Way culture in other countries. As Toyota has been globalizing, a new Toyota Way is being recreated in each country and there are even changes in Japan. Throughout this book we have focused on the United States, and mostly on TMMK. What we described is not exactly what we would see in Japan, yet Toyota has worked diligently to retain the core values and principles that make their company so distinct.

In this final section of the book, we have the challenging task of prescribing to other companies how they can learn from Toyota Culture. We believe there are many opportunities. Perhaps Nate Furuta (quoted liberally in Chapter 6) would say: "You want to call it an opportunity. No, I say it is a problem." He would have a point. Is this an opportunity or a problem? A problem means that there is a gap from the standard. The standard is where your company wants to be. If currently there is a big gap, it is a problem, and it is worth the effort and struggle to change your culture to support true high performance. If there is no problem perhaps this is just another interesting book about an interesting company.

We believe there is a problem. The problem can be phrased in a number of ways:

1. Organizations throughout the world have amassed large amounts of resources and are responsible for the well being of large numbers of people, and they are seriously underachieving in business and failing to develop their people.
2. Organizations wishing to become better and more efficient have been adopting lean and six sigma programs but will inevitably hit a wall unless they seriously work on culture change that is compatible with the technical and performance changes they desire.
3. People throughout the world are spending their most productive waking hours working in bureaucratic organizations that are shamefully wasting their potential as humans.

There were times in human history when as Abraham Maslow would note we were struggling to survive and get adequate food and shelter. Hunger and poverty certainly have not been eliminated and we have found increasingly sophisticated ways to kill each other, so perhaps we are not ready for the next level of evolution to start to become productive and cooperative learning organizations. Maslow said that self actualization cannot really happen until we sort out the lower level physical, egoistic, and social needs. We are certainly quite mired in all that sorting, but is it reasonable to start looking ahead to an age when we might function as cooperative societies working to make the most of our resources and time on this earth?

We admit this is an ambitious question but we also believe that Toyota gives us a glimpse at what a future organization can be.

The term "lean production" was coined in the book titled *The Machine that Changed the World* to refer to the next generation manufacturing company—a quantum step up from mass production. Toyota did more with less and continually improved. The focus was on adding value to customers at every step in the process from raw materials to finished goods, to give customers and society more with less. This is a noble vision but perhaps the story is even bigger. *Toyota Culture* gives us a picture of a new way of organizing a company that has an impact on the very fabric of how people work together. It is not esoteric but actually functioning in countries all over the world. Ordinary people are doing this in different languages with very different cultural backgrounds. Toyota has not erased national culture, but has managed to inundate people working for Toyota so they are swimming in Toyota culture every day at work.[1]

Given the noble goal of telling other companies how they can learn from this remarkable phenomenon we must humbly admit we are unworthy. We have no recipe for success. We are regularly asked to name other companies outside Toyota and a few other excellent Japanese companies that have successfully transformed themselves to become lean learning enterprises wall to wall, plant to plant, department to department. We admit that we do not know of any organization that fits the bill. We know of good companies that have been trying for some time to learn from Toyota, that have made great strides, and do not show signs of quitting. We have personally been involved in working with companies that have achieved remarkable transformations at local levels in parts of the companies through lean projects and active employee engagement—transformations that we would say have penetrated to the cultural level. We have also been involved with many other companies that have tasted some early successes, declared victory, and moved on without ever really penetrating the real management culture. Predictably, whatever gains they make in transformation are short lived.

We will start this ambitious undertaking in the final section of this book a bit indirectly. Instead of jumping in to telling other companies what they can do we will take one more look at Toyota. In Chapter 16, we are leaving the manufacturing environment and taking a look at Toyota Motor Sales, U.S.A. Inc., headquartered in sunny Torrance, California. Toyota Motor Sales is actually the oldest part of Toyota in North America celebrating its 50th anniversary in 2007. Parts of this organization have been working to more deeply adopt Toyota Way culture both internally in knowledge work environments and externally in the broad dealer

---

[1] "Swimming in the culture" are the words Toyota Vice President Jane Beseda used to describe how her people live Toyota culture every day in North American service parts operations as quoted in *The Toyota Way*.

network that directly touches customers. We believe there is much to learn from the journey of Toyota Motors Sales. In Chapter 17, we continue the in-depth case study of Toyota Motor Sales, this time looking at how the investment in quality people paid off in the innovations of Lexus and Scion brands. Finally in Chapter 18, we reflect on our own experiences working with many organizations and what we have learned from Toyota to suggest how others might think about culture change.

# Chapter 16

# Leveling Up Toyota Culture at Toyota Motor Sales

*The benefit from automobile sales should go first to the customer, next to the dealer, and then finally to the manufacturer. This attitude is the best one for winning the trust of the customers and dealers, which will consequently bring about the development of the manufacturer itself.*

—Shotaro Kamiya, first president of the
Toyota Motor Sales Company

## TOYOTA MOTORS SALES TURNS FIFTY

Toyota Motor Sales (TMS) is the oldest part of Toyota in America. In 2007 it celebrated its 50th anniversary. It was established to sell the imported Toyota Toyopet in 1957. In this sense, the Toyota Way should be most deeply engrained in TMS. The dual pillars of respect for people and continuous improvement were in fact part of the fabric of TMS long before this was written down in Fujio Cho's document in 2001. As an example of Toyota's respect for people in practice, we talked to the owner of a Toyota dealership who also owns a Detroit Three dealership and asked him to compare his customers:

*It is as different as night and day. When the Detroit Three representative comes knocking at my door, it is to pressure me to buy more cars and trucks that I will not be able to sell. It is like the loan shark coming to collect and threatening to break your kneecaps. When the Toyota representative comes, he wants to know what he can do to help. They give us amazing information on the local market. Look at this [he brings out a thick document full of data on the local auto market, competition and demographics]. I get this from Toyota every month. Look at those notebooks of materials from my training courses on how to sell in the Toyota Way. They are a remarkable company. They want me to be successful and help me do it.*

If you go around TMS, what you find is the type of teamwork, cooperation, energy, creative thought, and consciousness of being efficient that you would expect from a part of Toyota. In many discussions, business decisions will be balanced with discussions of value. What does this mean for the dealer? What does this mean for the customer? What does this mean for the image of Toyota as a good citizen? How can we retain customers for their lifetime? Very smart people are committed to the company and following Toyota Way values.

In some other ways, TMS in the United States has been slower than North American manufacturing to get indoctrinated into the Toyota Way. The Toyota Production System is a highly developed approach to manufacturing and the dual concepts of just-in-time and built-in quality are standard operating procedures throughout manufacturing and logistics. The problem-solving process is taught broadly and used every day in manufacturing. TMS is a much more broadly-based organization with functions ranging from service parts logistics, to marketing strategies, to developing advertising campaigns, to tax accounting, and managing the thousands of independent dealerships. Toyota Motor Sales in Japan was split from the rest of Toyota as a result of the American occupation forces desiring to avoid monopolistic practices. As such, it evolved as a separate corporation with a somewhat different management culture. Toyota Motor Sales in the United States was set up originally by Japanese executives, but there has been a great deal of hiring of American managers and executives as the company has grown rapidly, and the Toyota Way has not been ingrained to the degree it has in the manufacturing part of Toyota.

It is probably no surprise that service parts logistics, which supplies parts to the dealerships through a network of warehouses (part of TMS), follows Toyota Production System principles and is quite clear on its operational approach. Toyota regularly scores at the top of automotive companies for having service parts available when the dealer needs them (i.e., fill rate) and uses all of the principles of the Toyota Production System in flow-through distribution centers.[1] Since the *Toyota Way 2001* came out, other parts of TMS have been working to interpret what this means to them. In fact, Chairman Fujio Cho put out a separate document called "The Toyota Way in Sales and Marketing" (2001) to translate the Toyota Way for this group. Cho writes in the forward to this document:

> *Toyota's overseas sales have grown steadily over the past 50 years thanks to the establishment of a powerful sales network and meticulous marketing activities adapted to each market.... The experiences and expertise accumulated in selling Toyota vehicles have been systematized and organized into The Toyota Way in Sales and Marketing. Concerted efforts from dealers, distributors as well as TMC [Toyota Motor Corp.], in applying The Toyota Way in Sales and Marketing will enable us to successfully provide customers with the best purchasing and ownership experience. This will fortify our efforts to become the most successful and respected car company in each market around the world.*

---

[1] Toyota's service parts distributions centers are discussed in. Liker, Jeffrey, *The Toyota Way*. New York: McGraw Hill, 2004.

Toyota Motor Sales in the United States has been working hard to interpret and implement the spirit of the Toyota Way. It is no surprise that the basic model for the sales and marketing version is the same as for the rest of the company—respect for people and continuous improvement. The respect for people pillar is already deeply in the culture of the sales and marketing organization. Just as it is at the rest of Toyota, for TMS it means striving for perfection in customer satisfaction, developing team members, and dealing respectfully with all partners. Building a green complex for new offices in Torrance, California, described in Chapter 7, is another example of respect for people in TMS. Bringing the Toyota Way to TMS is not really the same as bringing it to a non-Toyota company that has never seen any of this before. TMS has decades of experience and it is in the blood of the senior leaders. For example Jim Lentz, president of TMS, had a hard time exactly putting his fingers on how they originally learned the Toyota Way:

*As a result of the influence of our parent company in Japan, Toyota's DNA is more prevalent at our TMS headquarters than at our field offices. The core values were taught first at headquarters and since have spread to the regional operations throughout the U.S. In the last ten years, Mr. Cho has played a pivotal role in strengthening Toyota's DNA. He recognizes the merit of formalized training to ensure that we never lose our core values.*

*While I have been with this company 25 years and have participated in formal classes, I have never had to pass, for example, an official "Toyota DNA proficiency test." The Toyota Way is in the mindset at the heart of the company. I could postulate that the people who advance in the company are those that understand and practice it the most. In truth, I cannot point to one reason to explain how the traditions and values are passed on. The Toyota DNA remains strong because it is who we are; it's how we do business.*

It is difficult for Jim Lentz to explain because it is culture, ubiquitous—just the way things are. An example of a Toyota sales executive who learned the culture in the trenches through direct mentorship is Jim Farley, former group vice president and general manager of Lexus. He learned some of his biggest lessons of the Toyota Way by accompanying the chief engineer of the second generation Lexus LS to competitions' dealerships:

*When I was the first product planner for Lexus in 1989, we had successfully launched the original LS 400 and we were trying to decide what the next group of products was going to be. I had an opportunity to travel around the world with the chief engineer. I was traveling with this guy, who probably had 5,000 engineers working for him, and we spent three weeks on the road at the time staying at far from upscale motels close to dealerships, renting cars, traveling, talking to sales people and visiting dealerships of competitive brands to talk to sales staff, technicians, and mechanics. We used all that input to design the next generation LS.*

*We would get up early morning and visit one or two more Mercedes-Benz or Cadillac dealerships. And we grilled them about everything—what they loved, what they didn't like, what their perceptions of our products were. If they had to sell against our product, what would they do? We asked the technician when he took the cars apart— what's good, what's bad? What frustrates you? What should be adjustable and what shouldn't be? How do you help the customer fix a problem if the alignment's off? By the end of the trip, it was pretty clear what to do. I guess the point was that he (the chief engineer) knew that the sales people and the technicians knew more than he did. And he respected them enough to spend time listening to them.*

In those early days of growing the company in America, many people had access to these special experiences and one-on-one tutelage by a mentor who grew up in the Toyota culture in Japan. That has changed and the challenge is to intentionally and formally ingrain that commitment into everyone working in the company without an army of Japanese mentors coming over. It is difficult to change people's thinking and behavior to "respect people" through formal training; so much of the training effort has focused on the problem solving methodology to support continuous improvement.

We believe TMS is a useful case study for many service organizations. It provides examples of extending lean thinking to transactional and knowledge work environments. It also, in some ways, is in a similar situation to other companies outside Toyota which are working to bring lean thinking to their organizations. Some of the basic tools and concepts of lean thinking and formal problem solving have only recently been introduced to certain parts of TMS and some dealers are just learning these tools and concepts for the first time.

In this chapter, we will provide a broad overview of Toyota culture at work at TMS. We will visit University of Toyota and also take a deep look at how the corporate tax group in TMS is learning lean thinking.

# TEACHING LEAN THINKING AT THE UNIVERSITY OF TOYOTA

How do you apply lean concepts to transactional processes like sales and marketing? The University of Toyota (UofT) was established in 1998 to teach a wide range of courses for TMS and has taken on the task of teaching, consulting, and coaching on Toyota business practices, lean thinking, and leadership training. They have had to go to school and figure out a lot of things such as how the basic tools of TPS in the factory can be adapted to a sales environment. Mike Morrison, vice president and dean of UofT has been struggling with this for years before *The Toyota Way 2001* even came out:

> *In a typical plant "kaizen project," you typically spend a couple of days in total—and have a small economic impact of a couple of hundred dollars, but enough of them make a significant difference through the continuous improvement culture. We rarely have those types of quick-hit opportunities in improving sales operations, developing new model launches and rolling out new dealer programs. Most of our projects have a wheelbase of three to six months and work with higher-level processes. As a result, we have had to change the toolkit. As we start to introduce people to it, we are trying to help them understand the difference in how the factory applies kaizen to a small discrete problem (an "in the room" problem because you can see it so you can optimize the solution)—compared to larger problems that are not "in the room," that may take years to solve. You may never know if you have optimized the solution because although you have picked a solution that you think will work best, the market keeps changing.*

The UofT is not exactly what we have come to expect of Toyota in manufacturing where we are used to modest facilities extremely focused on the factory. By contrast, visiting UofT is more of what you would expect from a booming Silicon Valley technology company. It is based out of a high floor of a building in sunny southern California surrounded by floor to ceiling windows with stunning views of the surrounding city. It intentionally has been set up as a place to get away and loosen up with clusters of colorful chairs in alcoves to relax in small groups, and artwork where Toyota management concepts are displayed as modern art.

Dean Morrison talks a little differently than those in manufacturing using terms like open-systems thinking and appreciative inquiry and he is tied into a number of universities and think tanks on innovation. Morrison himself wrote a book called *The Other Side of the Business Card*[2] that focuses on how people have to discover their true individual talents and passions, and companies must find a way to encourage and use what the individual has to offer. This sounds far different than standardized work and rigid process improvement protocols sometimes associated with lean.

One might think this is too ivory tower to learn lean thinking, but if we get below the surface of these artifacts, it does not take long to find the real Toyota. The work going on in UofT is anything but esoteric and as we would expect they are digging deeply into real problems. Over the years, they have struggled to

---

[2] Mike Morrison, *The Other Side of the Business Card*, New York: McGraw-Hill, 2007.

figure out what they should be doing to best add value. They went through a phase of teaching basic TPS and problem solving and got a lukewarm reception from sales organizations that did not see the connection to what they do. They also tried outsourcing teaching to training and consulting firms and found those firms could not speak a language that made sense within Toyota and the training was a bit too fluffy.

The UofT has many different types of classes ranging from basic orientations for new hires on the history and philosophy of Toyota, to teaching how to do on the job development (OJD), to teaching senior executives at a more strategic level. One of the clear winners in their journey is a short course called "lean thinking"; it teaches the basics of evaluating your processes for waste and developing a future state vision and acting on it. Those who have read Womack and Jones, *Lean Thinking*[3], would find great similarities to this course. The term "lean" is not one that historically was used in Toyota, but it was accepted within Toyota Motor Sales, U.S. and has become part of the local culture of this organization. Those in Japan saw that TMS was doing well—learning kaizen in a serious way—so they would not interfere with this effort. Morrison explained:

> *We grew up with that (lean thinking) in the early 1990s in TMS and it was beginning to emerge as part of our culture. At the turn of the century, Toyota Motor Corporation, with the help of a newly launched Toyota Institute [in Japan], has become more aggressive in launching Toyota Way management practices. We support these efforts and work closely with the Toyota Institute in promoting their Toyota Business Practices methodology [the eight-step process for solving problems] as the core model for our training and development efforts. Lean thinking, our adapted approach, is still part of the informal language, as it has been for 18 years. At the local level, TMC knows we are doing different things to make TBP work in our sales and marketing environment. Other parts of global Toyota come to benchmark us because they are interested in what we are doing and how. There will always be issues around the level of standardization required to both protect the consistency of our global practices, but at the same time allow for the flexibility needed to make things work at the local level. It's a healthy debate—one that we won't back away from.*

The lean thinking seminars are not all that different from what other companies are doing to learn to become lean. There are only a handful of instructors who teach this and they work to make sure lecturing is minimized and working on real

---

[3] Womack, James and Daniel Jones, *Lean Thinking: Banish Waste and Create Wealth in Your Organization*, New York: Simon & Schuster, 1996.

problems is maximized. They insist teams of people from an organization come to the course and bring a real problem. They will also go to the organization to work with a team on a real problem. In the early days, they tried to use a rigid Plan-Do-Check-Act process documenting every step in great detail and learned that many of the processes were not stable enough or repetitive enough to use the same degree of detail as in manufacturing processes. They chose to simplify this to Plan-Do-Learn (PDL) and are more interested in the thinking process. What is the problem? Let's get to the root cause by digging down and asking why. Now let's step back and creatively think of options, try them and learn from what we try. There is a bit more emphasis on divergent thinking in many of the processes at TMS, but basically it is much like the problem solving process used anyplace in Toyota. Morrison is always seeking to recognize the nature of the actual situation and not try to force fit methods that do not apply:

*I had a lot of experience trying to teach practical problem solving and PDCA in 1989 and we could not get the dog to eat dog food. It was dead on arrival. When Jack Welch was doing "Work Out," we had what you could call "Waste Out." We were struggling with the traditional toolkit and figured out we needed adaptations. So we started to focus on open systems and broader kinds of problem solving that would create more impact. The original PDCA class was five days. Practical problem solving was three days. It felt too manufacturing oriented and people did not feel it applied to them. It was around a problem solving and fix-it focus. You are growing up in a dealership where processes are not stable and you do not want to fix them, but you want to blow them up. At the University, we have been carefully using a very facilitated, customer-centered approach—adaptations to their needs not to our idiosyncratic insights. We are real happy with the success we have gotten in working with individual departments and the dance is aligning with Japan so we can have a common language. At the same time, we are being smart about using more structured problem solving but also allowing more unstructured think time. The training is catered to each individual group.*

Some of the instructors came from the parts logistics side of TMS, where they were rigorously trained in the Toyota Production System. That experience, with a more repetitive process, has helped them to see the opportunities for process improvement in less repetitive knowledge-based processes. The individuals selected to be teachers in the university have a sophistication that allows them to grasp the actual situation, whatever it may be, and adapt the teaching and problem solving to the customer's situation. Joe Kane, associate dean of UofT, is one of the original managers who started up the Toyota service parts distribution center in Ontario, California and moved on to teaching lean thinking to a broad range of sales and marketing departments:

> *Looking at less parts-oriented sales and marketing processes, I think our job is to help Toyota members make the connection as to how the Toyota Way and TPS applies in their area. If you look at manufacturing, it's very clear and evident in terms of linear, repeatable processes. You can see it very easily. What I think we are trying to do is help the people further down the entire product value stream, closer to the end customer, to understand that the principles still apply to them. It is a bit different because the nature of the work on the non-manufacturing side is more ambiguous and creative. It is more people-centered, not machine-centered. I do find they can make the translation of the seven wastes into the non-manufacturing environment and see right away what overproduction, waiting, and extra movements look like, but you have to stand back a bit and help them consciously make these connections.*

All of the administrators at UofT, including those with the title "associate dean" are hands-on instructors. They all grew up in Toyota Motor Sales and learned the Toyota Way informally through daily coaching. Will Decker, associate dean, remembers 23 years earlier when he had just come from an American company to join Toyota Way. He was amazed to see how often Japanese members were going out talking to dealers and talking to customers. He started in his first Toyota job in parts marketing administration and his eyes opened up in his first six months. "I remember my Japanese coordinator said 'you have to go look, you have to go see.' He did not refer to this as *genchi genbutsu*; it was a subtle thing. It was just kind of accepted that you go and you listen and you hear what's going on at the source."

One of the challenges of University of Toyota is staying true to the Toyota Way, yet making it understandable and teachable in the West as explained by UofT's Mamie Warrick, corporate manager and dean of education, planning, and business operations:

> *Prior to the Toyota Way in 2001, the Japanese coordinators came over, and through working with us daily, implicitly told us how to behave. It was through certain behaviors and practices that they showed us. We didn't have all the terminology down. The University's role now is to clarify the terminology. We need to localize some of this. One of the things we are trying to do is take the Toyota Way and put it into more of a teachable application to our members and dealers. That is the Toyota Promise. We have a formal manifesto and it is captured on a card on how we should behave toward our customers. For example, we respect their time and priorities as our customers and colleagues. We practice the belief that there is no best, only*

*better. That's the Toyota Way, but in language that our people can under-
stand, our suppliers can understand, and our dealers can understand.*

Now that Toyota Business Practices have been defined as the global standard
for implementing the continuous improvement pillar of the Toyota Way, the
University of Toyota has embraced that and sends members to the Toyota Institute
in Japan to become certified facilitators and bring it back. There are aspects of TBP
that are broader than the former practical problem solving and University of
Toyota is working to bring out the breadth for broader strategic thinking as
explained by Morrison:

*The UofT facilitates a leadership discussion in support of Toyota Business
Practices that precedes the very focused problem-solving approach. It is important to get the group leaders up on the balcony to get the larger, more strategic view of what their business unit needs to accomplish. In an operational
excellence environment like ours, problems take precedence. Unfortunately, in
our urgent response, we can frame the problem and the possible solutions too
small. Leaders have to be vigilant about guiding the process in a way that
will maximize value. We are continually looking at how to adapt the TBP
model to what we characterize as "open" systems problems—problems that are
magnified by their scope, complexity, and long-term time frames.*

There are many interesting points in the way Toyota approached bringing
lean thinking to Toyota Motor Sales that reflect the company culture:

1. The UofT was self-initiated by Toyota Motor Sales in the United States. It
   was not dictated from Japan. Toyota wants local operations and even individual team members to take the initiative to learn.
2. The executives in Japan have insight into their own strengths and weaknesses. For example, they realized they needed to adapt the Toyota Way
   message to the local culture and they needed help from the Americans in
   doing that.
3. The corporate office in Japan wants to encourage kaizen. There is a good
   deal of flexibility in exactly how the message is phrased and adapted. For
   example, Toyota Motor Sales in the United States could craft their lean
   thinking course and use terminology differently from that used in Japan.
4. The UofT figured out that they had to adapt the TPS methodologies to fit
   the sales and marketing environment which is less repetitive and not everything is "in the room."
5. The UofT also recognizes that there are routine transactional processes in
   the sales organization that can use much of the structure of the Toyota
   Production System and has facilitators capable of leading organizations
   through that application.

6. UofT is an internal organization that provides sensei support, but the individual units must pull from the university and take responsibility for their own learning and conducting the projects.
7. The values and principles taught by UofT are completely aligned with that of the corporation in Japan and the leadership of Toyota Motor Sales.
8. Over time, UofT is aligning more closely with the global training of Toyota Business Practices, but still working to adapt and improve it to fit the sales environment.

# BRINGING KAIZEN TO THE TMS FINANCE DIVISION

Every teacher has a star student and for University of Toyota, they have a star division—the finance division. As the name suggests, this division is responsible for all financial issues in TMS, including dealing with import duties, tax returns, and financial statements for Toyota Motor Sales. Like the rest of Toyota Motor Sales, the division has been around for decades and grew up living the Toyota Way. Yet, they believed there was more to it. They also had relatively new blood led by Tracey Doi, group vice president and chief financial officer, who came to Toyota from AT&T Wireless in 2000. The customs and taxes department is led by John Kennelly, vice president corporate tax and international customs, who came to Toyota from General Motors in 2004.

Tracey Doi has been immersed in the Toyota Way since joining the company. This includes a good deal of formal training. For example, along with all executives at her level, she went through a week long executive development program led by the Toyota Institute in Japan focusing on the Toyota Way. Doi got a great deal out of the session in learning about the history of the company and what the Toyota Way means conceptually through working deeply on case studies. The greatest benefit in the program was in networking with executives from many parts of the company. As valuable as the course was, she realized that she had only scratched the surface and the real learning came from living daily the Toyota Way and leading her organization to raise the level of kaizen. She explained:

*Having been with the company for just a few years, it was a great way to get indoctrinated. I was paired side-by-side with an engineer from engine development, the CIO from our Canadian distributor, the head of our plant in Turkey, and two general managers from our plants in North America. We were taught through case studies and asked to solve some problems using Toyota Way principles. Then we were given a group assignment to try to fix something that was relevant to our region. Through that process, I probably had a taste of the Toyota Way, but not necessarily an understanding of how to apply it. Within the TMS Finance Division, we had already started an effort to develop our people and improve our processes and systems to achieve higher profitability and stronger performance. We had our goals and objectives, but we still had not formalized kaizen. So when Mike Morrison tried to launch lean thinking, I could tie the two together. Prior to 2004, I had an initiative, when I was wearing the controller hat, on process improvement. But I still didn't have it connected to Toyota Way principles. So I think it was formally kicked off in 2004.*

While Toyota Motor Sales has been practicing the Toyota Way for decades, president of Toyota Motor Sales in 2004, Mr. Yuki Funo, felt that as a distribution company, TMS had not embraced kaizen anywhere near the level of manufacturing. Tracey Doi agreed that was a fair assessment. Funo passed down the hoshin through his executive committee to raise the level of kaizen. This became an internal hoshin for Doi and her group, which was linked to the general Toyota Motor Company directive to strengthen the Toyota Way. Each group vice president had to prepare their hoshin for raising the level of kaizen which then worked down to the department level. Tracey Doi, responsible for an organization of 152 members, worked out plans for the year with her direct reports and John Kennelly developed a plan for his 24 person tax and customs group. As Tracey Doi explained:

*The respect for the people part of the Toyota Way was here long before I came. The respect for people element is very clear. Other companies would make decisions based upon the financial impact only, the bottom line, and not think about [member] first or customer first or dealer first. That is a pronounced difference. I think it's probably part of the secret of why we have a strong relationship with our customer and high member retention. Sometimes respect for people means it takes longer to make a decision. You want to make sure if you're making a policy change or a system implementation that all the appropriate stakeholders are brought into it. Historically, I think I would have moved faster, but I would spend more time on cleanup. What was not as strong was continuous improvement and formalizing measurement of any improvements.*

John Kennelly took the lead responsibility for starting to develop a kaizen culture in tax and customs when he first arrived in 2004. As someone new to the Toyota culture he was very excited and recognized that the spirit of kaizen was stronger than at General Motors where he had come from:

*At GM, as executives, we never had formal process improvement objectives in finance. On a fairly regular basis, a new process improvement or "program of the month" seemed to come along, but it was not taken very seriously to be honest. Here at Toyota, the direction form our Group VP (Tracey Doi) is that kaizen is not just another "program of the month." This is an integral part of the Toyota Way. To try and institutionalize kaizen into the finance division culture, we incorporated very specific objectives into each person's annual performance plan by specifically making it into a requirement in HR documents and therefore, part of performance appraisal process. Also, we have formal and informal ways of making our process improvement successes visible and rewarding people for their efforts. Members are rewarded when they meet their individual or departmental objectives, and failures to meet these objectives negatively affect a member's performance ratings. Informally, departments are allocated funds to use as spontaneous awards to recognize member's kaizen efforts. In addition, we use non-monetary awards to recognize associate's kaizen contributions and keep our efforts visible. In fact, we have story boards up all over the department with A-3 format and have people believing that if you want to be successful here, you have to be really good at looking at your process and improving it. Here at Toyota, our process improvement efforts will always be "badged" as kaizen and the Toyota Way, whereas at GM every year or two a new program came along—along with a new vocabulary.*

The University of Toyota works on a pull system, delivering training based upon the customer need, and the finance division pulled and pulled. Phase I of this process is what John Kennelly refers to as "lean thinking lite." The finance division wanted to start to loosen up the organization, much as an athlete starts with stretching to loosen up muscles in the body. They decided to encourage many small kaizen projects focusing on problem solving. In 2004, every person had as a formal objective to go through the UofT lean thinking training and complete at least two Plan-Do-Learn projects documenting them through an A-3 format. The specific results were less important than just doing something to kick-start problem-solving skills.

As an example, one team selected as a theme to "eliminate non–value-added time and rework in the information gathering process of completing federal and state income tax returns." The "Current Situation" was:

- Separate information requests to separate Toyota companies and separate departments using different software (360 staff hours, 24 manager hours costing $20,000 per year).
- Information received is saved and printed. Information requests are cumbersome to track (16 hours/$1k per year).
- All unreconciled items from the General Ledger or payroll systems must be investigated and preparer information is often unknown (480 hours/$19k per year).
- Missing information (200 hours/$8.5K per year).
- TOTAL cost due to waste and rework about 1100 hours/$55k.

The "Problem" was stated as: "We are not getting the information we need that has to be complete, accurate, and timely to ensure tax compliance." The "Root Cause" was identified as: The information gathering process is a series of complex MACRO Excel spreadsheets that are often not user friendly and have not been updated since the ERP was implemented. The process is not centralized, or standardized, and there is little accountability.

Several alternatives were considered, but the first choice was to use Global Data Exchange, Web-based data gathering software to centralize and store all data for a period of ten years and link this data to tax return preparation. To accomplish the selected solution, a plan was developed, key stakeholders were brought on board to build consensus (accounting, financial reporting, payroll, and other Toyota-U.S. subsidiaries) and the progress was tracked until all items were completed. The entire project was documented on a single-sided A-3 report and all action items were closed out and the desired results were achieved and documented. Finally, further actions for improvement were identified. The complete PDCA process was followed and the group felt extremely proud.

The results of the many small kaizen projects completed by members in the finance division by the end of 2004 were impressive:

- 59 teams were created,
- 8 cross-department projects were created,
- 122 projects (66 completed, 39 in-progress by year end) were started,
- over $2.2 million in combined productivity and cost were saved, and
- more than 11,000 labor hours saved.

Not all of these projects were technically complex. In fact, the chairman and CEO of Toyota Motor Sales, Yukitoshi Funo, was encouraging quick and easy kaizen efforts to begin with to make it part of the TMS culture. One example was a project looking at duty payments. Every day many vehicles come to port, and each day Toyota pays duties on those cars and trucks totaling over $500 million per year. The customs kaizen team investigated the possibility of participating in a new pilot program that would allow payment of these duties on a monthly basis instead of a daily basis and they ultimately became one of the first companies to get governmental approval for this. The results: Over $1 million in annual interest was saved, as well as a significant reduction in the administrative burden associated with the old daily process and about $1.1 million in related annual labor savings.

Phase II in 2005–2006, the finance division moved to larger projects taking more time to flow chart them using what University of Toyota calls the "big paper process." This is also called value stream mapping. These projects focus on streamlining end to end processes. A major application of the big paper process was SOX

(Sarbanes-Oxley) compliance. Having compliance means ensuring high quality publication of financial statements which is taken very seriously since Toyota prides itself on integrity of numbers. They pulled together a PDL team and drew out flow charts in excruciating detail. In this way, they were able to see how inefficient the current documentation process was with many wasted steps. By streamlining the process they met their deadlines for compliance on time and passed their audit the first time.

Tracey Doi is excited that the intense focus on process improvement has created a new level of communication about how things are done and a higher level of excitement in finance:

> *The phenomenal growth that we've had has potentially masked some of the inefficiencies—now the reality is for the size that we are, we can't keep doing things the way we have for the last 20 years. That's a great opportunity for our team to reevaluate, step back and ask, "What can we do differently?" We are finding excitement when a team can see the waste by developing current-state process maps. There are a lot of "ahas" that people are finding. "I didn't know that was what you did! Oh! Had I known that that's what you were going to do with it, I could have done it this way." Everybody can play a part in this and feel good about what they're contributing.*

After three years, starting in 2004, the finance division knows they are far from done. They started with some rudimentary problem solving, focusing on more repetitive transactional processes and then moving on to larger projects requiring more sophistication. Tracey Doi was itching to get more deeply into measurement to track progress. After three years of developing problem-solving skills, she feels her division is ready for the challenge of taking on stretch objectives to really move the needle. In fact, she explained that her people are anxious to get started on this new level:

> *It's interesting. At a recent offsite, our managers said they'd like to see an umbrella challenge for our entire division so we have a stretch objective for our whole group. I want to have something which is an umbrella for the division so every member can say, "I can relate to that. I'm contributing whether I'm processing profit and loss statements, I'm planning tax strategy, or I'm in the investment group." That'll be probably part of our phase two.*

The role of the "experts" on lean thinking at University of Toyota has been very clear from the start—they are teachers and advisors. All of the improvement activities have been driven by the leadership in finance starting from the president of TMS. The projects have been led by working-level managers and members who already have a full-time job and the purpose has been as much to develop their level of skill and understanding as it has been to eventually start to get measurable results for Toyota. To maintain the enthusiasm and energy, Tracey and John have worked hard to make this fun. There have been many activities to make process improvement a bit playful and give simple rewards, like Starbucks gift cards. One example is explained by John Kennelly:

> *We did notice that if you don't keep the pressure on, what happens is projects get started and then you get this really big inventory of work in process, but they're not getting completed. Last November, we tried to break through this hurdle, with fun activity—what we called the "CFO Challenge Luncheon." In this challenge, if you completed your in-process PDL by a certain date, then your team would be eligible for consideration to join Tracey for a special recognition luncheon. We tried to pick a range of different completed PDLs and honor those people with a simple but fun lunch. We actually had a lot of fun with it—we took a lot of pictures, we had Kaizen team shirts made and each team did a brief report out of their project to our CFO. None of this was really expensive quite honestly, because we are finance, we're really careful with the amount of money that we spend in connection with trying to create our Kaizen culture.*

There are many things other companies can learn from the finance group of Toyota Motors Sales about getting started with lean thinking:

1. Lean thinking was initiated in an environment of respect for people that was part of the culture developed over decades.
2. The effort to raise the level of kaizen was driven by the president of Toyota Motor Company in Japan to the president of Toyota Motor Sales to the group vice president and continued to cascade down through the hoshin process.
3. Internal experts (University of Toyota) were used as teachers, advisors, and coaches, while the responsibility for improvement was completely owned by those managing the organization.
4. The initiative started with quick and easy problem solving and for the first two years there was little emphasis on major financial returns.
5. Rather than agonize over how to apply lean thinking to a service operation that is clearly different than manufacturing, the group simply started to identify and solve daily problems and worked their way up to larger end-to-end work stream improvement.
6. Relatively little money was spent on the process and rewards were intentionally kept small, symbolic, and fun.
7. Senior management had the patience to focus the first two years on development of people and teamwork rather than financial results.
8. Once the team members and managers started to mature in problem solving they were anxious to take on much larger stretch goals to drive organization-wide metrics. They were prepared and self-motivated.

# IS TOYOTA MOTOR SALES LEAN?

We are frequently asked as consultants if we have experience "deploying lean" in a service organization. The conversation usually comes from someone who is assigned to lead the service lean effort and goes something like this:

**Question:** We have done lean in manufacturing over the last two years and gotten very good results—inventory is way down, lead time is down, productivity is up, and quality is up—and now management has asked us to apply the lean methodology in our service organizations like product development, sales and marketing, and information technology. Have you seen any place that has done that well or has Toyota already done that?

**Answer:** First, we would have to question your assertion that you have "done lean" in manufacturing. We believe you have gotten started and begun to understand the tools. Second, you cannot simply take the solutions from manufacturing and copy them in services. Third, there are different service processes with some being very simple and repetitive and others being very complex and unique to a specific situation.

**Question:** Right, that is the problem. Manufacturing is easy to understand and see and we have done some kaizen events and each time we get big improvements that we can measure. It seems harder to do that in the service organization where people cannot see the results. Is there someplace we can go visit to get good examples of what lean looks like in a service organization and try to convince some of our service managers that lean can work for them too?

You can probably imagine the rest of the conversation. In this chapter we have learned several things. For one thing, you can now say that Toyota Motor Sales, at least in America, has also been struggling to figure out what lean and TPS mean in a transactional environment. University of Toyota has been teaching and consulting and struggling for years to figure out how they can best help various parts of the organization that face different problems. In some cases, they have concluded that they must go outside the Toyota toolkit to consider other perspectives and methodologies to get more "open-systems thinking."

You can also see that Toyota Motor Sales began with a very firm foundation in the Toyota Way—respect for people, continuous improvement, and the foundational elements like *genchi genbutsu*. There is a highly developed problem solving methodology in Toyota that has just gone up a notch from practical problem solving to Toyota business practices. There is a strong, common culture that supports long-term thinking, customer first, and investing in developing people. This culture leads Toyota Motor Sales to take a very patient and reflective approach to raising the level of kaizen through repeated experiments—try something, reflect, learn. They have been following their Plan-Do-Learn methodology and now include PDCA within the framework of Toyota business practices. Finally, the process and changes are owned by each separate organization they work with, not by the experts at the University of Toyota.

We will return to this theme of lean as a technical methodology to deliver specific results versus lean as a learning journey building a culture in Chapter 18. Before we get into that, we would like to dip one more time into the case of Toyota Motor Sales, this time from a different perspective. In this chapter, we saw there is a concerted effort to bring kaizen methods to Toyota Motor Sales to spread continuous improvement broadly. In Chapter 17, we will look at two case studies of radical innovation drawing on all the resources of the Americans trained deeply in the people value stream—the cases of Lexus and Scion.

# KEY POINTS TO CONSIDER FOR YOUR COMPANY

1. Toyota Motor Sales demonstrates that the Toyota Way values of mutual trust and continuous improvement translate well in a service organization.
2. TMS modified the Toyota Way and "tools" to fit its culture and industry.
3. The core values and ways to do business of the Toyota Way were taught from the executive level down, with the executives becoming teachers.
4. The Toyota DNA is transferred not through the classroom but through practicing and mentoring problem solving "on the job."
5. Top Executives lead the transformation with a focus on development and not financial "return on investment."

# Chapter 17

# The Lexus and Scion Stories

*Mission Statement: Scion Evolution (SE) was started to be an outlet for Scion owners to gather and share their passion for their Scions. It is with anticipation that SE humbly approaches this philosophy to enable Scion owners to contribute to the continuing belief in the Scion brand. Goal: To carry on as the premier Scion owners club, by our ongoing contribution to the Scion community through various events and projects. Car cruises, car shows, picnics, bowling nights, meet and greets, charity drives and club nights are among the many avenues we hope to promote a positive image. By doing so we anticipate that these efforts will continue to reflect the Scion brand in a progressive style.*

—Scion Evolution, Driven to Evolve, North Carolina
Chapter (a Scion owner's club)

## BEYOND CONTINUOUS IMPROVEMENT TO STRATEGIC INNOVATION

Toyota is most often associated with slow and steady incremental improvement, and Toyota leaders are proud to describe themselves as more like the tortoise than the hare. People are developed within Toyota to study every detail of the current situation from every possible angle and make fine-tuned adjustments to processes to get better. Certainly that is a good characterization of much or even most of what Toyota is about, but it misses the fundamental innovation that also characterizes the company. Toyoda Automatic Loom started with innovation by Sakichi Toyoda who became known as the "king of inventors" in Japan and technological innovation has always been highly valued within the company. Toyota leaders also think very strategically. Operational excellence is not enough unless it is strategically driven. In this chapter, we will see examples from Lexus and Scion on how strategy, innovation, and operational excellence all intertwine to create long-term competitive advantage.

President Jim Lentz does not see a contradiction between continuous improvement and innovation. He is pushing Toyota Motor Sales to achieve both, seeing a balance as necessary in today's rapidly changing world:

*In bottom-up leadership, members are empowered from the bottom to the top of the organization. They are empowered to find ways to improve the organization rather than wait for a manager to direct them. In this complex and evolving industry, in order to sustain our growth and ensure profitability, we must remain a lean organization. To do so, we must innovate, streamline, and focus on what's important—the customer.*

Two of the best examples of innovation in the customer experience in Toyota, and anywhere for that matter, are Lexus and Scion. Both arose out of a blend of Toyota's Eastern culture and the best of Western culture in America. Both started with Toyota teachers in Japan taking the time to develop Americans and teach them the meaning of the Toyota Way. These American leaders were able to use what they learned, skills like the power of *genchi genbutsu*, to deeply understand what American customers want and turn that into a remarkable customer experience. Through continuous improvement, Toyota dealers throughout the country continually assess customer satisfaction and develop innovative processes.

The Lexus and Scion brands were in many ways very unlikely for Toyota. How could a company known for highly reliable, but boring cars that appealed to middle-income and middle-aged people suddenly create competitive entries into the high-end luxury market and the lower end market of cars that excite young and trendy Americans? This chapter focuses on those stories. In the Lexus case, we discuss how the Lexus dealerships were grown using a people value stream that paralleled how all Toyota members are developed. In Scion, we use the analogy of a customer value stream—the strategic motivation behind the innovation was to attract younger people into the value stream that creates a Toyota customer for life. It is built on the vision of a lifetime relationship with customers rather than a short-term business transaction.

# LEAN CUSTOMER SERVICE THE LEXUS WAY

When Toyota decided to take the risky move of venturing into the luxury car market, they realized it would be difficult to compete against established names like Mercedes and BMW. Toyota was simply not a company customers associated with high-end luxury vehicles in the United States, even though the Toyota Crown was already a high-end vehicle in Japan. Ultimately, the first Lexus model was a major hit in its first year unseating all Mercedes models combined in U.S. sales. There were two pieces to the success of Lexus—a well-engineered and manufactured car of remarkable quality plus exceptional service at the dealership. The Lexus story is a great example of how investing in quality people leads to innovation and competitive advantage. It is also a great example of what Womack and Jones[1] call

---

[1] Womack, James and Daniel Jones, *Lean Solutions: How Companies and Customers can Create Value and Wealth Together*, New York: Free Press, 2005.

"lean consumption," which means deeply understanding what adds value to your customers, identifying the value stream that the customer participates in, and eliminating waste from the process so it is efficient and customers never have to wait.

When customers buy a luxury car they are partly buying a car with more expensive features and trim, partly buying status, and partly buying the right to be treated like a VIP. As the president and owner of a Lexus dealership in Ann Arbor, Michigan, Rosario Criscuolo explained: "Lexus owners fly first class and they stay at Five Star hotels in extra luxurious rooms—they are used to being treated special and willing to pay for extra service. We know their name when they come into our dealership, we have all the conveniences of an executive business office, and they never wait for anything. We go out of our way to give them extra special service." Here are some typical characteristics of any Lexus dealership:

- For any serious maintenance (e.g., beyond oil change), in most cases, the car is picked up from the owner's house.
- The owner gets a replacement car (which is a Lexus) even for an oil change.
- There is a well-furnished waiting room with a large screen plasma television, a refrigerator stocked with complimentary beverages, and wireless Internet.
- There is a window into the repair bay where the service areas are kept clean and organized.
- The car is waiting for the owner and if a charge card is on file the owner can simply switch cars and drive away.
- The car is cleaned each time it is in the shop, even for an oil change.
- Customers are referred to respectfully by name and members get to know each customer.
- There are generally some special services offered to the waiting customers that are unique to each dealership such as a manicure or massage.

In this section we will focus on how Toyota grew the Lexus dealer network in a way analogous to the people value stream—attract, develop, engage, and inspire. We will discuss the development of the Lexus dealership through these four stages using the Lexus dealer in Ann Arbor, Michigan, as a case example.

## Attract and Select Lexus Dealers

Toyota already had an established Toyota dealer network before Lexus, and the obvious thing to do was to offer them the opportunity to start up a Lexus dealership, perhaps using a bidding system. This would have been convenient, but would not lead to the breakthrough service levels Toyota envisioned. Toyota made a few key decisions:

1. Open the recruitment process to competition from the top dealerships in a market whether they sold Toyotas, Cadillacs, or Volvos.
2. Give them a realistic preview of what was expected of them which was a very large capital investment in a state-of-art facility, intensive training by Toyota, and a unique employee culture focused on customer first.
3. Look for wealthy, well-connected owners that were in the top two percent of their local market in customer satisfaction.

Jim Farley, former group vice president and general manager of Lexus, described the process that they used:

*First we looked at capitalization: does the dealer have the money to build the kind of facility that we're going to require because it was going to be completely different than the Toyota facility. No one had built Lexus-type facilities before. We have satellite connection with the factory. No one had had that. Everyone was still using telephones and big main-frame computers, and our computer system was through the satellite. We had a window to look into the service department. Every other dealership in the world hid customers from the service department. We wanted people to see because we knew that put pressure on the dealer to keep the service department clean. We had all these crazy specific requirements on the facility side and that all cost money, so we wanted dealers with the best capitalization.*

*Then we looked at their customer satisfaction levels and they had to be top two percent of whatever brand they represented. So you had to be the very, very best Cadillac dealer. That's how they got in. They were dealers with the best capitalization and the highest customer service. And then we looked at the management team. Who would they propose as the management team? Were they experienced selling luxury products? Did they have connections to the community so they were authentic to wealthy people? We looked at their plan for where they would build the dealership. Was it convenient for wealthy customers or was it near a piece of property they happened to own because their GM dealership was there? We sorted out ten things, and we graded everyone based on those ten things. Then we put the dealerships in order from high to low. And we also had different phases based on volume size. So first we hit the metro stores, and then we had phase two which was kind of like the Phoenix's of the world, and then we got to phase three which were the St. Louis' of the world.*

## Develop Lexus Dealers

Having selected owners of top existing dealers who already proved they could sell and get high customer satisfaction, Toyota still invested in teaching them how to be a Lexus dealer. There was another level of service beyond what these wealthy owners were used to. There was a different way of developing their people in the dealership as well. It started with the owners. Toyota selected wealthy owners, but did not expect they would spend most of their time on their yachts counting their money. They wanted owners who were passionate about their business and would get their hands dirty reexamining the entire business from the ground up. Then Lexus practiced Toyota Way principle number 10: *Develop exceptional people and teams who follow your company's philosophy* (Liker, 2004).[2] Jim Farley describes this intensive training from the owners to the person washing the car:

> *We showered them with training—spent crazy amounts of money—flew the owners to Japan and decided to train everyone in the dealerships—washing cars or reception. We developed a specific training program for every role: How do you answer the phone professionally? How do you put a customer on hold professionally? We developed our Lexus vocabulary—no one is a customer, they are all guests. We developed different certification programs and if someone is master's certified, we give them a subsidized lease to drive a Lexus even if they are a technician. We treat them all the same. Lexus treats everyone the same regardless of level. The lot boy has a huge impact on customer satisfaction. The service writer has more contact with the customer than sales. We wanted everyone to feel important because they were. When we had an event, we invited everyone in the store.*

Following Jim Farley's description and thinking back to Toyota job instruction training, we see that specific key points were identified for each position in the dealership. Essentially, Lexus developed high-level standardized work for each job. They did not have steps in sequence or times, but they had key points and trained to them. No job was unimportant. Even the lot boy who drove the car was trained in the details on the key points. When we interviewed Rosario Circsuolo, owner of the "Elite of Lexus" award-winning Lexus dealership in Ann Arbor, it was clear he knew all the key points for each job. He owned four dealerships at that time—two Lexus and one Toyota and another brand—yet knew every inch of the Ann Arbor operation and what each person should be doing. He had personally gone to every training course Lexus offers. For example, he described some of the key points for individual jobs as follows:

> *No manufacturer trains like Lexus. I just opened another brand dealership and no manufacturer does that. Our members go through training every year and then take tests online. That is part of the criteria for the "Elite of Lexus" award Lexus gives out—90 percent of members must go through the training and pass the tests every year. This includes the lane member who washes the*

---

[2] Liker, Jeffrey K., *The Toyota Way*, New York: McGraw-Hill, 2004, chapter 16.

*car then pulls up the car in the service drive at the right time for the customer returning to pick it up. He is making sure that the radio is on the right station, has gone through a check list to make sure the car is completely cleaned, and makes sure everything is working in the car. Every car is cleaned even if you come in just for an oil change. The switchboard operator learns she should introduce herself to the customer; she is the point of contact to coordinate and make the sales person know his or her customer called. Her other job is that she meets and greets the customer and shows them the waiting lounge and coffee and makes sure everything is taken care of. The switchboard operator is one of the key contacts to the customer and needs to get to know each one personally. For most customers, we have their charge card number and they do not need to deal with waiting for the payment process, but if they pay in cash, the cashier must learn to process it in a timely fashion and get the receipt into the car so it is on the passenger seat when it is delivered to the customer. If it is a check, make sure the receipt is in the car.*

Cirscuolo is one of the dealers who went to Japan to tour the plants that build the Lexus cars. He was struck by the devotion of the employees and how proud they were of the cars they built. He was also struck by their interest in hearing from him about what Lexus owners want in America. He explained: "At the end of the day they wanted to hear if we had problems with any of the products they built. Each plant manager in Japan had questions about what customers like in America. They really listened, which is a true partnership."

## Engage Lexus Team Members

Toyota's Lexus division began with a vision of a start-of-the-art dealership and how team members would be engaged, but many of the details of exceptional service evolved bottom up from the dealerships. Some of it is very basic starting with a clean and orderly dealership. Throughout the dealership, 5S is emphasized and most of it is open to the customer. There is a huge glass window in the waiting room, so the customers can see their Lexus being worked on, if they want to wait for their car in the luxurious waiting lounge. Cleaning the maintenance bays is a big job, so they contract this out and every major item in the shop is moved out to clean the floor every day. The qualifications of maintenance members are hung on big cloth signs from the ceiling for the customers to see. The service parts department is all laid out so that every part is in a particular place and the most frequently required parts are near the front.

The customer-first attitude drives the engagement of team members. The policy to pick up the cars for major maintenance applies in Ann Arbor even for customers 250 miles away in Traverse City, Michigan. One idea a team member came up with was to help customers avoid the need for their cars to be tied up at the dealership. For example, an antenna simply screws out and a new one screws in. Why have your car sit in a dealership if you break your antenna? Instead, Lexus offers to drop off a new antenna if you are willing to install it yourself. There are hundreds of different programs and nuances in every store that have been identified by daily kaizen at the dealerships.

In Ann Arbor, there are a lot of professionals who travel a good deal and drop off their car for maintenance at the dealership, then drive to the Detroit airport. So some team members came up with the idea of offering a delivery and pick up service. The customers bring in their cars and are driven to the airport, whether they need a repair or not, and the dealership tracks their flight and picks them up to bring them back to their car which has been inspected and washed.

Ann Arbor team members also came up with the idea of keeping the customer's snow tires off season. Snow tires are big and a nuisance to store. After the customer has had the great experience of being treated like a VIP at the dealership, it would be a let down to go home and drag dirty tires into the garage taking up valuable space. So, the Ann Arbor store will keep them in storage (in an area on the second floor) and come winter, they will have them ready to be put back on.

The Ann Arbor dealership does not have its own body shop, but instead of leaving customers on their own, they manage the process for no service charge. They do not want the customer to be on their own dealing with body shops that may not have the customer orientation of Lexus, so they coordinate the whole process. You bring in your car to the Lexus dealership and they take it from there. This is aided by the exceptional service parts capability of Toyota. At the dealership based on the VIN number, they can see every feature of the vehicle and its service history. The Lexus system for parts is to overnight all parts at no extra charge. They can get almost any part in two days, three at most. If you destroy the car body and have $20,000 of body work, the Lexus dealership will order all metal parts for repair and get them in two to three days. Usually, the parts arrive before approval for funds by the insurance company. It may have been the customer's fault that they damaged the car, but they are still considered a VIP and will be pampered.

The Lexus team is constantly thinking of ways to connect with the customers. For example, they regularly hire master chefs from the best local restaurants and have a private dinner for customers along with a silent auction. They also periodically hold elaborate brunches on Sundays.

A newer program Lexus introduced in 2007 was the Lexus Innovation reward to reward the best ideas nationally. As Criscuolo explains:

*It has to be something substantial, not giving away cookies and bottles of water. We developed the pickup and delivery service to the airport that no one had 15 years ago, but now everyone has that. The innovation program is*

*about a lot of little best practices and putting them into the dealership. We
are examining every position and looking at it—how can we improve this?
How can we improve the customer relationship and improve their satisfaction? It is not reinventing the car business—we are improving it.*

The innovations are evaluated by a panel of judges and they give awards for
the top three dealerships nationally.

## Inspire Lexus Team Members

Toyota as a company works hard internally to develop long-term, engaged, and
committed employees, and this is certainly as critical for Lexus dealerships. Lexus
measures employee satisfaction and finds it correlates to profitability of the dealership. Internal studies also show that customer retention is higher when customers
get to know a particular sales person whom they grow to trust and want to continue to come back to. Jim Farley explains: "There is a direct correlation between having long-term employees and profitability of the dealership, and longevity is related to employee engagement. Now Gallup and Lexus have combined forces and
every dealer measures engagement of each member to measure not only loyalty, but
more importantly, are the people working there fully engaged?"

The annual "Elite of Lexus" award for the top Lexus dealerships is based
partly on retention of employees. Toyota is looking for long-term commitments
starting with the owner. They do not want the dealership changing hands like
a commodity business. Jim Farley explains the strategy of focusing on a small
number of Lexus dealers that have the size and finances to make big investments
for the sake of customers—larger investments than they might make if there were
multiple competitors in the same town:

> *We wanted to be sure we had the right number of dealers. We watch com-
> petitors get too many dealers who are competing with each other and this is
> really bad for the customer and the company. There is a natural scale . . . we
> are going to have to develop more mega dealers and have separate offsite serv-
> ice locations because there is no more room at the dealer locations for further
> expansion. We are using TPS to streamline processes and make the best use of
> space in the dealerships. We want the owners to be so financially successful
> and incredibly fortunate that they will want to reinvest in the dealership and
> build state-of-the-art facilities.*

The comment about making Lexus dealers "so financially successful" is culturally interesting for several reasons. We have spoken to dealership owners from
other companies who complain that the car companies do not want them to make
too much money. If the dealer is getting rich, it is taken as a sign that the car company is not getting its share of the profits. It also seems to reflect envy by the car

company sales managers who themselves are not rich. Yet the Lexus executives feel part of their responsibility is to help Lexus owners become wildly successful. The result is that Lexus dealerships are growing larger and owners are growing richer and Lexus division supports this mutual prosperity. Cirscuolo has been well trained in the Lexus philosophy and works hard to select and develop people and grow them so they want to stay with the company:

*The person who pulls up the cars knows that this job is not a dead end job—with ongoing training he can become a service writer. If you hire a 9 or 10 out of 10, then he can grow with the company and move through the organization. We want him to understand the customer and to turn on the heat or air conditioning and to open and close the door for the client and say 'Here is your car Dr. Liker.' We want him to become loyal to the dealership and loyal to Lexus and loyal to the customer. It starts with hiring the right type of members, then training them to do the job and getting them to believe, and the next step is to show them a future in the dealership. It builds a very good bond. We have long-term members working with us from the day we opened the dealership—they know our customers and their needs. We have good relationships. The other night we had an upscale dinner for members for our winning the 'Elite of Lexus' award. It is not just a plaque: Everyone working here, including those who wash cars attended, and we rented an entire restaurant. We had sales people with managers and with mechanics and it is one big team—not separate departments.*

One of the most dramatic programs to encourage commitment is the one that enables technicians to purchase a Lexus. For those who are master certified (highest level certification), and keep up with Lexus' annual training for at least three years and have no disciplinary issues, they can get the subsidy to lease a Lexus. Lexus gives $200/month and the dealer matches that for a total of $400/month, until you own or release the car. A Lexus sedan as of 2007 was $500 to $600 a month, an SUV was about $450 a month. For the SUV, the technician would pay out of pocket about $50 a month. At the Ann Arbor dealership, eight technicians were qualified and five were using the program.

Lexus is an example of how strategy, intentional innovation, and operational excellence are interconnected in the Toyota Way. Figure 17.1 summarizes these connections. Toyota knew something exceptional was needed to attract wealthy customers who purchased luxury cars to buy something built by Toyota. The answer was a two-pronged attack—an exceptional car and exceptional dealer service. It started with sales and the chief engineer collaborating to deeply understand the target market through *genchi genbutsu*. Then the car was developed based on this understanding. Sales then worked to develop an exceptional dealer network in much the same way as exceptional people are developed within Toyota.

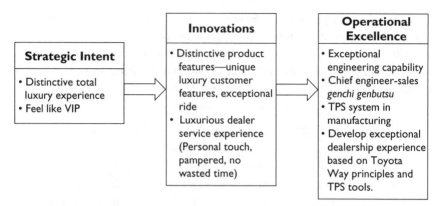

| Strategic Intent | Innovations | Operational Excellence |
|---|---|---|
| • Distinctive total luxury experience<br>• Feel like VIP | • Distinctive product features—unique luxury customer features, exceptional ride<br>• Luxurious dealer service experience (Personal touch, pampered, no wasted time) | • Exceptional engineering capability<br>• Chief engineer-sales *genchi genbutsu*<br>• TPS system in manufacturing<br>• Develop exceptional dealership experience based on Toyota Way principles and TPS tools. |

**Figure 17.1** Relationship between Strategic Innovation and Operational Excellence for Lexus

For Toyota to deliver on the vision depended on the operational excellence of TPS, Toyota problem solving, and exceptional teamwork.

We are often asked how to apply lean thinking to a service operation. Lexus exemplifies the philosophy of the Toyota Way—respect for people, continuous improvement, eliminating waste, just-in-time service parts, 5S, problem solving, standardized work, and job instruction training. It is all there to see, from the receptionist to the member who pulls up your car, to looking through the window into the spotless service bay.

# CREATING SCION TO ATTRACT YOUNG PEOPLE TO THE CUSTOMER VALUE STREAM

The Scion story is another example of a major innovation that is then refined through a series of small incremental changes. It also demonstrates the return on investment Toyota gets from investing in the people value stream; in this case developing Americans who understand the American market and live the Toyota Way.

Action at Toyota, whether small changes or big changes, starts with a problem. In this instance, the problem was that the average age of Toyota buyers in the United States was too high. The future is in attracting younger people who start with modest Toyota cars and become customers for life working their way up to higher end models. Was the answer new cars and price packages that appeal to younger people? That was not enough since young buyers' generally perceived the Toyota nameplate as a brand for their parents. The countermeasure was an entirely new nameplate, new vehicles, and a new way of marketing and selling cars.

We will push the metaphor of a value stream a bit further and talk about a customer value stream. Just as the goal of Toyota is team members for life, the goal is customers for life. In a sense the same process of attract, develop, engage, and inspire can be applied to developing customers for life. We are not going to push this too hard and go into detail about how each of these stages works for developing customers, but we will say that Scion would never have happened as it did unless Toyota had as a goal, attracting customers into this value stream at an earlier age. In fact, the goal of Scion was not to make a profit—a hard concept for many companies to grasp. If Scion broke even, then Toyota would still have profit over the long term by pulling more customers into their value stream, which would be the deal of the century from a long-term advertising point of view. In fact, the people leading this effort were quite evolved in the Toyota Way of thinking and were able to exceed the goal by making profits—a bonus. Mark Templin, now group vice president and general manager of Lexus, who was vice president of Scion at the time of the interview, explains the original objective in this way:

> The metrics we think are important are not about sales or profits—that's not what Scion is all about—it's about opening the door to Toyota. We try to reach young people. The median age of Scion owners is 30 years old, which is the youngest in the industry. We keep score about profits, but don't often talk about them. As it turns out, we do make money selling Scion products. Scion is three years old nationally and four years old from when first launched, and we have paid back the initial investment. It is not about making money though—it is about learning new ways of doing business. Even if we didn't make a dime, Scion would be valuable. The things we learn get passed on to the rest of the organization. We teach Toyota and Lexus how to think differently.

The main goal of bringing new customers into the Toyota family seems to be working according to Templin:

> We wanted to bring new people to Toyota dealerships in a way that was cost effective. So far, 80 percent of Scion customers are new to the Toyota family—that is, nobody in their household owned a Toyota. Most young people think of Toyota providing quality and reliable transportation, but not for them. We needed a different business model, a different sales process, different marketing, and different products. Early results show that we've been able to bring new people into the Toyota family and keep them. Among Scion customers who trade in their vehicle for a new one, 8 of the top 10 models they trade into are in the Toyota family.

Unlike Lexus where the solution was expensive customer perks like a loaner car driven to your home, high-end executive facilities, and expensive high-end product features, for younger Americans it had to be low cost, yet high value. It was further determined that younger Americans want to express their individuality through what they purchase so variety and customization had to be part of the package. In many ways the challenge of a built-to-order car at low cost was built to order for Toyota. After all, didn't the Toyota Production System evolve under conditions of low volume in Japan, with little cash, and the need to have very flexible production facilities? Here was a golden opportunity to stretch the best of TPS under modern conditions. Rather than spend a lot of money developing an entire new division and brand name, Toyota used an extremely lean approach and relied on the ingenuity of its people.

There was really a multilevel attack. First was the way the vehicle was engineered and built, which required collaboration between sales and the chief engineers for Scion models. The starting point was to take two small cars that were popular in Japan and rebadge them as Scion. For example, the Toyota bB in Japan (standing for Big Box for its boxy design) was a hit with young people in Japan and became the Scion xB.

The second was the way the vehicle was marketed and sold, which involved collaboration between Scion and the dealerships.

Jim Lentz was originally in charge of creating the Scion brand from a sales and marketing viewpoint. Toyota Motor Sales in the United States was given a high degree of autonomy in creating the concept while also considering TMC and dealer operation's input. The idea for the design-build model was partly inspired by a trip Jim Lentz took to a General Motors operation in Brazil.

> We spent a lot of time "going and seeing" different automotive operations all around the globe. Our purpose was to find out what works best for the respective customers. I traveled to Brazil fairly early in the process after learning about the Chevrolet Celta, which General Motors sold in Brazil. It was a fairly inexpensive car sold over the Internet and was built in only one configuration from the factory. The factory would hold the product in its yard until the dealer had a customer. Then, the factory would ship the vehicle to the dealer and the dealer would do all the final accessorization of the vehicle. Since the Celta had a fairly small margin from the factory, dealers relied on accessorization to make their profit.

This led to two key concepts at the foundation of the building and distribution of Scion. One is "monospec," which means there is one specification for the vehicle and the differentiation is done at the dealership. The other is the method of delivery which is "pooling" of orders. Ideally highly customized cars would be built to order for each customer, but this is not practical when cars are coming from Japan. Jim Lentz explains that they chose to build the cars at the factory with a few standard option packages and then pool them at the port, like a big supermarket, that allows shipping to dealers just what they want:

> At the time, using accessories to build the order and pooling inventories in a port operation were completely new ideas. At Scion, we allocate vehicles to

*our dealers, but rather than ship them directly to the dealerships, we hold them in a centralized port operation for up to 30 days. This process allows dealers to virtually trade with other dealers in that geographic area to provide customers the exact vehicles that they want much quicker. The key to the accessory piece is to limit the basic model for a car—the difference being color and transmission—and add the accessories either at the port operation or the dealership. We have the capability to add 50 to 70 different accessories, enabling customers to uniquely personalize their vehicles.*

There is quite a bit that buyers can choose from after the fact, such as LED-lit foot wells and cup holders, many types of sound systems, and even performance modifications such as lowering springs, sway bars, and cold-air intakes. Once this business model got started, many companies jumped on board offering other Scion-specific aftermarket enhancements. For example, there are a large range of bumper add-ons and side skirts that will create unique looks for your Scion. The goal was to give young people a lot for their money and also the ability to individualize the car. The package of standard features is remarkable for the money, and Toyota can do it because it is really a mass-produced plain vanilla car when it leaves the factory. Templin explained the business model based on the desire of young people to belong to a community, yet the need for individual expression:

*Young people aspire to drive luxury vehicles, so we give them all the features they want at a price point they can manage. They get automatic everything, like a Lexus, and great audio systems with i-Pod connectivity. You can normally only get those things in a luxury car. We're selling $15,000 to $18,000 cars with a great deal of standard content and safety equipment. Then comes the fun part—personalization. Young people have grown up in a world where they get to personalize everything they do. Think about the wallpaper and ring tones on cell phones, the color of the braces on kids teeth, the many different ways you can customize the coffee you order at Starbucks or the ability to buy custom Nike shoes online. At Scion, we want the personalization to take place as close as possible to the point of sale. People want to be noticed, but they first need to be part of a group in order to stand out. Their desires are being met by Scion owner groups.*

Toyota relied on the Toyota infrastructure to keep the cost down and the buying experience is very different. It starts with the concept of pure price. Toyota's in-depth study of young people found they are not enthusiastic about haggling and are more concerned about getting a fair price. They do not want to find that a friend got a better deal for the same thing. Scion's "pure price" is a little different than the single pricing of Saturn. There are opportunities for dealers to adjust prices somewhat for the local market, but once they set the price for a given model and accessories, it cannot change—the next buyer coming in will get the same price with no haggling. Cirscuolo, the Lexus dealer owner, also owns a Toyota dealer that sells Scion:

> *Scion is the only division that has the one price. It works well for Scion because it is a different clientele. Scion pricing also has to be consistent even on maintenance, such as on tune-ups—once we set the rate, it has to be the same. We price out accessories the same way. We sell 20–25 Scions a month. We do not send coupons out for Scion and do not discount the services—it is a one-price philosophy. Scion customers also get their first two maintenance visits (e.g., oil, fluids, check up) for free.*

On the advertising side, Scion challenged the traditional advertising and marketing structure. Normally they would contract with one agency to handle the entire contract, but in this case, used an unbundled approach with different staffs for sub-marketing plans. Lentz explained:

> *We had independent companies working on direct marketing, events, television, radio, and Internet. We completely unbundled the marketing approach to find the best vendors we could and have them work together as a team. It resulted in a unique style of communication with customers. At the time, Toyota spent approximately 95 percent of its advertising expenditures on television media while, Scion spent roughly 50 to 60 percent.*

Scion has gone beyond selling a product to creating a community of passionate owners. This has happened spontaneously for some products, such as Apple Macintosh users or Harley Davidson owners. Scion did this strategically. Scion has created fan clubs of people coming together to network and share their passion for Scion, as illustrated by the mission statement of the North Carolina chapter at the opening of this chapter. This is publicity that money cannot buy. Toyota also encourages this type of community building through marketing events that they and dealers organize. Each event has some sort of entertainment or theme tailored to the local area. Templin explained that the events have multiple purposes:

> *There are two kinds of events—on one hand we do events to reach taste makers in the marketplace because they tell others our brand is special. We try to support the creative community through art, music, fashion, and film events. There are also a large number of events that appeal to more typical Scion owners, and we do over 100 events per month. In addition to our national events, we give budgets to our regional offices to conduct events and to support dealer activities. Scion clubs also do their own events. For one taste-maker event, we rented gallery space where young people hang out, opened it up to young artists to show their works, and got the word out about Scion.*

*We didn't take any money. If fashion designers or artists sold their products, they got to keep the proceeds. Another example was a mass-market event at Knott's Berry Farm. We invited Scion owners and prospects during the Halloween season—for the annual Knott's Scary Farm. Last year owners driving more than 3,000 Scion vehicles showed up. An added benefit of events is they're an opportunity for our marketing staff and the chief engineers to talk to Scion owners and understand what they care about.*

They did not force dealers to make the seemingly risky investment in Scion but about 950 out of 1,200 dealers chose to participate. Part of the reason was intense communication with dealers. The Scion team got semitrailers designed so they could go on the road to educate dealers on the unique sales approach of Scion and the unique characteristics of the target market. Since the sales process is about creating a feeling of community among customers, it makes sense to start by building a community of dealers. After dealers came on board, they followed up with a national dealer meetings and 6,000 people came together to share stories about successes and new products coming up. They also developed a new concept called "Scion champions." Specific dealers agreed to identify sales people, especially enthusiastic about the brand, to play the role of Scion champions. Templin can barely contain his excitement about the brand, which for him is quite a lot of fun: "The champions are so passionate; they live and breathe the culture we are trying to create. The champions hang out with the customers. Most Scion champions are young or young at heart. We now have roundtables for dealers, and we pull the champions and other dealers together regionally."

Clearly this was a big investment by Toyota in an entirely new brand, with a new approach to building and distributing cars, and even new ways to market and sell the cars. The first thing a company should do in a case like this is staff up to get the infrastructure needed for this massive undertaking, right? The answer is not if you are Toyota and have developed exceptional people. A high-cost infrastructure leads to a high-cost product, which would not have met the goals of Scion. Templin explained the lean approach of Scion:

*Scion started as project Genesis that had five people and now we have grown a little. My whole team now is 17 people and will soon increase to 19 people—running an entire division with 19 people. We use teamwork. Nobody has blinders on and does one job. We leverage the rest of Toyota. We also have 40 people in field offices who call on dealers. The 19 people manage accessories, marketing, and calling on field offices. You will not find another auto brand with only about 60 people. It made sense to leverage resources in the rest of the company. Anything that does not touch the customer uses existing business units and gets more people involved in Scion.*

Scion is another example of how strategy, intentional innovation, and operational excellence are interconnected in the Toyota Way. Figure 17.2 summarizes these connections. A deep analysis of the customer led to the definition of the need and that was followed with broad investigation of options leading to the approach of monospec and late accessorization. Then the operational excellence of TPS and the ability of the sales organization to mobilize resources across the Toyota enterprise allowed Toyota to develop the Scion cars and brand at very low cost delivering exceptional value to young customers.

## Leveling Up the Total Customer Experience

Lexus and Scion were breakthrough innovations for Toyota Motor Sales. Clearly in both cases, once the big concepts were developed and introduced, there was a great deal of continuous improvement needed to keep on refining and improving. So what is next? The answer is to spread the learning across the entire dealer network in the United States as well as take the customer experience to yet another level.

Toyota is already working on the next level of improvement to keep customers for life. They are examining every aspect of the customer experience—no detail is too small. Jim Lentz explains the process in this way:

> *In a nutshell, it is really about grassroots leadership. We are asking everyone in the organization to consider thinking from the bottom up rather than the top down. In many cases, especially in the retail environment, there is a tendency to have a top-down management style.*

Toyota has been working for years to increase customer satisfaction and now is ready to move beyond static measures of satisfaction. They are much more

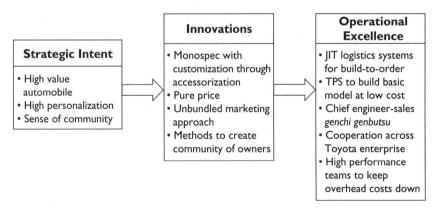

Figure 17–2 Relationship between Strategic Innovation and Operational Excellence for Scion

interested in long-term relationships with customers that go beyond crude satis-faction measures. Jack Hollis, vice president, Scion, explained this:

> *Customer satisfaction is really too small or is less than we want to be producing. Satisfaction can be a one-time experience, a one-time sale. We want to look at the customer's experience not only one time but over and over and over because our goal here is retention and loyalty. What we want to do is go further. How are we really creating relationships with our customers? Not just a purchase, but how about the whole shopping experience? How about after shopping and delivery? How about after delivery? Not only follow-up, but what's the relationship that we're building with them? So how are we getting them back in? This is just one example, but it really encompasses a lot of things which says that we're doing a really good job with our customers, cus-tomer satisfaction is improving, our delivery quality is improving—looking at it from a lot of surveys, we're doing very well. But how do we do better?*

Since the customer experience is most directly affected by the dealers, it would seem Toyota should create a dealer quality program of some sort, perhaps with different awards for the best dealers. Hollis disagrees and TMS concluded they should start with examining themselves:

> *We had programs like that in the past [different levels of awards]. This is as far from that as possible. Our message directly to the dealers is that we're eval-uating ourselves and we're not asking the dealer at this time to do anything different until we evaluate which things need to be done differently. What things are problematic? Which things are successful? And of course, dealers want to know: "Well, okay, what do you want us to do?" We answer: "Well, you go back, continue to be the best dealer you can be, but right now, we're working on what we can do to help you." So we're taking a really good look, a hard look internally at our people, processes, and policies to ensure we are prepared for the long term. This, I believe is a really unique message, and our dealers are telling us that they can't believe it, but greatly appreciate it. Any way you look at it, Toyota is growing and our performance, as based on sales and profits, is almost out of this world. That is what makes today the perfect time to be very critical of ourselves and rid Toyota of the waste that will hold us back in the future. Our relationships with our customers is the primary ingredient of our success and that is exactly where our focus is at today.*

This approach to Scion fits Toyota Way Principle number 9: *Grow leaders who thoroughly understand the work, live the philosophy and teach it to others* (Liker, 2004).[3] Until Toyota Motor Sales has leveled itself up to be leaders

---

[3] Liker, Jeffrey K., *The Toyota Way*, New York: McGraw-Hill, 2004, chapter 15.

who live the philosophy, they cannot expect dealers to follow their lead. That is all fine, but what about Toyota dealers that are not making the grade on customer satisfaction? Toyota certainly has the power to punish dealers who do not make the grade, but that does not fit their respect for people value system. Jim Lentz explains they would rather lead by example and inspire dealers with a positive vision:

> *We have a great deal of trust in our dealers. Since we share the future with them, we make sure to share information and useful tools with them. Rather than use a big stick with our dealers to say, "You'd better do this or else," we prefer to share what the future can look like if they choose to work with us. Ultimately, it's really up to the dealers to decide. Additionally, we're not focusing on the best nor the worst per say. The top dealers are doing great and we continue to learn from them. We believe it's the middle, the majority of the dealers upon whom we'll have the most positive influence. We want to assist these dealers to improve the overall customer experience. Our hope is that when those at the bottom see how successful the rest of the dealers are, they will choose to work together with us as well.*

One of the starting points for this intensive self-examination is the Lexus Covenant, which was developed when Lexus was first formed and reflects the principles of respect for people and continuous improvement. Since then, the Toyota Promise was developed which is similar, but applies to the Toyota brand. These are statements of values about how TMS wants to behave in regard to customers, such as:

- We must never stand still. Where others might rest, Toyota will move forward and seek out the opportunity to do even better.
- We honor our customers as welcome guests and serve them in the manner they desire.
- We respect the time and priorities of our customers and colleagues.

TMS is examining themselves in relation to these stated values and finding the biggest opportunities for improving themselves and the customer experience. They are asking what they can do to better support their dealers. Mamie Warrick, who has responsibility in University of Toyota for education, is supporting this effort and explains it as a reflection of Toyota culture:

> *The Toyota Promise is an expression of our culture. The Lexus covenant really started when Lexus was established. For them, it was really part of their culture from the very beginning. We're not in any position to tell a dealer how to behave differently if we can't even demonstrate it ourselves. The mission of the University is to keep that training moving in the organization, from the*

*new hire level to senior management, weighing customer vs. the needs of stakeholders. As you move higher in the organization, you get to some of the complex applications. We call this problem-solving to create a sense of urgency beyond just opportunities. Our facilitators, Joe and Will and Russ, guide business units through problem-solving sessions, using Toyota's values as a filter, and teach them how to solve their own problems. They come to us with a problem, but we help them frame it in a way that reflects these values and, in turn, gives them a model of practice.*

## SUMMARY

In Chapters 16 and 17, we took a deep look into Toyota Motor Sales and how they are working to deepen the Toyota Way internally and in partnership with dealers through continuous improvement and respect for people. It is a long-term learning process. There is no clear starting point or ending point. It is not a program. It is not a simple methodology to deploy. It is also not an act of charity—the bottom-line business results are stunning, continually increasing sales and profits, even when their competitors are continually losing market share and profits. If the way Toyota Motor Sales is approaching improvement sounds a lot like what your company is doing with lean or six sigma and you feel you are pretty much there, do not move on to Chapter 18. However, if you can see a considerable gap, then we recommend that you study Chapter 18 where we discuss what you can do to examine and work on your own culture.

# Chapter 18

# Developing Your Culture of Quality People for Long-Term Mutual Prosperity

*Never start with the idea of changing culture. Always start with the issue the organization faces; only when those business issues are clear should you ask yourself whether the culture aids or hinders resolving the issues. Always think of the culture as your source of strength. It is the residue of your past successes.[1]*

—Edgar H. Schein, professor, M.I.T.
Sloan School of Management

## LEAN TRANSFORMATION: TOOLS TO REDUCE WASTE OR CULTURAL TRANSFORMATION?

We learned from our Toyota sensei that before you can solve any problem you have to understand the purpose. What is the purpose of lean? Since the term "lean" was coined to describe the new paradigm of production and management, with Toyota as the model, we will start with the Toyota perspective.

Throughout this book, we have shown that Toyota Motor Company is much more than a business to deliver financial results to shareholders. It is a social institution. There are many entrepreneurs who start up businesses with the vision of getting rich and retiring young. That was not the vision of Sakichi Toyoda who invented more efficient looms so women in his farming community did not have to suffer from punishing labor around the clock. That was not the vision Sakichi Toyoda had for his son when he said: "I made my contribution to society Kiichiro, now it is your turn." It was not what Kiichiro was thinking about when he took responsibility and resigned from Toyota Motor Company after being forced to ask others for voluntary resignations. They were thinking about creating a social institution that outlived them and would lead to mutual prosperity for generations. They were passionate about contributing to society.

---

[1] Schein, Edgar, H., *The Corporate Culture Survival Guide*, San Francisco: Jossey-Bass, 1999, p. 189.

Since those early days Toyota has grown into a global powerhouse, but leaders have worked hard to retain the original values that started the company. As Fujio Cho later stated in the preamble to *The Toyota Way 2001*:

> *Since Toyota's founding we have adhered to the core principle of contributing to society through the practice of manufacturing high-quality products and services. Our business practices and activities based on this core principle created values, beliefs and business methods ... that are known collectively as the Toyota Way.*

Collectively these values, beliefs and business methods make up a culture. In Chapter 1, we investigated the concept of culture and it seems clear that the Toyota Way meets the requirements of this term. Not only is it a culture, but Toyota leaders have worked hard to make it very strong and pervasive globally.

Throughout this book, we have talked about the Toyota Way as, in part, a reflection of Eastern philosophy and thought. There is no denying that Toyota is a Japanese company and that it evolved in that country. We also know that Toyota leaders, over a period of about 20 years, learned a great deal about how to isolate what is essential about Toyota Way culture and successfully brought much of it to other countries and cultures throughout the world. It took a great deal of dedication and patience and Toyota is very much in the learning stage. This suggests there is something about the organizational culture of the Toyota Way that can be exported, though adapted to each culture. It is clear that Toyota leaders believe it is essential to develop and evolve this culture globally since it is the main source of competitive advantage.

The phrase "lean production" was introduced in *The Machine That Changed the World.*[2] That book mostly described the Toyota Production System and other processes of the Toyota enterprise, such as supply chain management, product development, and distribution. The conclusion was that Toyota had created a new paradigm for managing an enterprise. A "paradigm" is a fundamentally different way of thinking that filters how we see the world, what we accept as valid data, and what we believe. "Lean production" was a new paradigm replacing the older "mass production" thinking that characterized most industry in the West. This book suggested that either companies change to the new paradigm, or they would not be able to compete, since lean production better fits the modern rapidly changing society in which customers want increasingly greater value based on distinctive consumer tastes.

---

[2] Womack, James P., Daniel T. Jones, and Daniel Roos, *The Machine That Changed the World: The Story of Lean Production,* Harper Perennial; Reprint edition, 1991.

Since that seminal book was first introduced, the term "lean" has become a management buzzword and everyone has to have a lean program. In parallel, six sigma evolved, largely because of the success of companies like Allied Signal and General Electric and it was inevitable that the twain should meet as "lean six sigma." All of these efforts are aimed at improvement, but have we lost something along the way?

In this book, we argued that indeed we have lost something along the way. We have lost the essence of the Toyota Way—the soul of the company. We believe that for most companies lean six sigma has become a collection of tools to reduce cost, and in some cases improve quality as well. Lean six sigma is under the control of boards of directors who want regular reporting on short-term business results produced by the lean six-sigma program. The Toyota Way is not a program, though Toyota has used programs to reinforce the thinking. The typical approach to lean six sigma fits Western thinking about simple cause-effect relationships and the overall perspective that the business is a technical system that needs clever manipulation with the right tool kit to achieve financial returns. This type of thinking is totally alien to the human systems underpinnings of the Toyota Way.

Returning to our opening question, what is the purpose of lean transformation? Is it to apply tools to eliminate waste to make short-term improvements on key performance indicators? Is it to learn from Toyota how to become an adaptable and highly competitive learning organization for the long term? We believe the way that your company answers the question of the purpose of lean will set the course for how you want to approach the transformation.

For those who have a short-term need to cut costs or stop the bleeding of major quality defects or solve late delivery problems, and that is your only purpose for lean six sigma we would suggest this book is not all that useful for you. Sorry we told you at the end of the book instead of at the beginning. For those who are inspired to create a great enterprise that will outlive you, we have some words of advice in this chapter. It starts with understanding the challenges you face. We have said that the Toyota Culture that evolved in Japan is very difficult to reproduce by other companies, particularly in Western countries.

To understand why this is so hard, it helps to look back at what has been learned from the centuries of managing change, successfully and unsuccessfully; we will provide a very brief thumbnail sketch of this rich heritage. We know that building a culture is a challenge and changing an already entrenched culture is far more daunting, but we believe there is hope. We then have specific advice on how to introduce aspects of the human system model step-by-step. As Schein says in the opening quotation, trying to directly change your entire culture is a recipe for failure and also not a good idea. In this final chapter we hope to give some advice that will help other companies along on their journey to become successful learning enterprises for the long term.

# THE CHALLENGE OF BUILDING THE QUALITY PEOPLE VALUE STREAM IN THE CONTEXT OF TRADITIONAL WESTERN MANAGEMENT

We can vividly recall when the big realization finally came to American auto companies in the early 1980s that there was something different about Japanese quality. The flood of small car imports from Japan was taking over the low end of the market and American auto makers were crying foul blaming the success of these imports on unfair trade practices, low wages, and the insidious cooperation between the Japanese government and private corporations. Gradually it became clear that American customers really liked these little cars that had snuck across the border. They worked…and worked…and worked. The Japanese auto companies were doing a great job of building quality cars that had sensible features and required almost no maintenance.

This revelation ushered in the quality movement of the 1980s and gurus like Deming, Juran, and Ishikawa preached the virtues of the Japanese management system and its quality obsession. The journey that was launched from that realization is itself a reflection of American culture. Deming preached statistical quality control to understand and control variation and suddenly every American automaker was teaching statistics, even to shop floor workers with barely a high school education. Crosby later preached that "quality is free" and taught methods for measuring the cost of quality and executives raced down to Florida to learn how to make these calculations. The message was that if you invest in quality early in the process you avoid so many downstream costs that the early investments will pay off and you can measure the results.

American executives then went beyond this and took note of the high level of suggestions coming from employees on the shop floor in Japan and their careful attention to detail and this led to programs like "Employee Involvement" at Ford and "Quality of Work Life" at General Motors. True believers worked to change the culture from one of top-down management ordering aggressive head count reductions to investments in training of employees and problem solving groups that met on paid time to improve processes. The late 1980s and early 1990s were very exciting times around the auto industry, as management and the union began to cooperate in unprecedented ways, and employees began to develop talents even they did not realize they had. Many hourly employees who were underachievers in school flourished in this environment and took on new leadership roles, developing skills in organizing and analyzing data, facilitating team meetings, creating and giving presentations, and solving complex problems. These employees blossomed in ways that positively impacted their family lives and took leadership roles in community organizations.

Supervisors who were hired because they were big and tough and could intimidate people, were at first wary of their new role in "participative management." One Ford supervisor exclaimed in obvious dismay: "They trained us to be attack dogs, and now they are turning us over to our workers as pets." Some supervisors struggled, but others began to relish their new roles as facilitators and coaches realizing that playing tough cop was stressful and unfulfilling. Dare we say that culture was changing in old-line manufacturing plants built on years of tough adversarial relationships? Similar revolutions in the 1980s were taking place in purchasing where buyers who had been trained to be tough negotiators with suppliers seeking to maximize profits were now taught they should "partner" with suppliers and engineers to reduce total cost. The Japanese influence that began with American defensiveness started to loosen the fabric of the American auto industry and appeal to the softer human side of enterprises.

The experiments with employee involvement and natural work groups and supplier partnerships were real. For example, at its peak, Chrysler (prior to the buyout by Daimler) was achieving remarkable levels of innovation and at the same time, cost reduction through cross-functional platform teams, supplier partnering, and worker participation. Liker recalls proposing a study to Toyota in the 1990s comparing Chrysler's just-in-time logistics approach to Toyota's approach in North America. Toyota said no because they were afraid Chrysler was becoming too strong a competitor. Chrysler was becoming a learning organization, competing with Toyota at their own game. This abruptly ended when Daimler bought them, and all the leaders that were leading this learning journey were pushed out and the focus became rationalizing and consolidating and acting the way management 101 suggests large, rational corporations should behave. The impressive progress of companies like Chrysler, Ford, and General Motors, that was starting to get Toyota leaders nervous was short-lived.

One could say that the 1980s and much of the 1990s was a golden era for the American auto industry, but one that came to a predictable end as good business sense kicked in with mergers, acquisitions, and layoffs. This is not to say nothing was learned, but just as employee engagement in a plant started to really grow and come to life, a business decision would get made to cancel a program and lay off employees. Or a plant manager who was learning to become a great leader and had accomplished certain financial objectives was moved to a different position. Engineering leaders who led record-breaking vehicle development programs were soon offered early retirement packages to reduce costs when the auto market dipped. A myriad of changes, both external (e.g., competitive pressures, market conditions, betting on the wrong product), and internal (e.g., changes in the CEO, churning of management), made it impossible to sustain high levels of organizational learning.

There were peak periods of intense change and improvement, but each time followed by equally intense downward cycles. The downward cycle that started around 2003, when gas prices sharply escalated, seemed to push the industry over the edge and the bloodletting was on as tens of thousands of employees were let go or encouraged to leave voluntarily. It marked the end of an era.

We are often asked why Toyota so graciously opened its doors to its competitors and allowed public tours and even private tours of its plants. We have also been asked why the American car companies who saw the Toyota Production System in action, hired former Toyota managers as consultants and employees, and in the case of General Motors, owned half of NUMMI, have not simply copied the system thereby erasing any competitive advantage of Toyota. That question reflects underlying cultural assumptions about what makes a high performance organization work. The assumption is that there is somehow a set of technical systems and procedures which can be installed, and the main barrier is learning the technology and procedures. Since the American auto companies saw and learned the system they should be able to implement it if they simply tried. As the rest of the story has shown, the American companies failed to learn what was right in front of their faces. The answer must be inept management, so fire them and find new executives who can get it right.

We believe there is a deeper set of assumptions that blinded American management, or perhaps posed such severe barriers, that they could not act on what they learned. These assumptions are so pervasive that replacing executive teams was a hopeless strategy. We illustrate this through the simple model in Figure 18.1. The Western mechanistic assumption is that the key to success is making the right decisions to implement the right tools and technology. Who makes those decisions? It's got to be top management, of course. With the right senior executives developing the right strategy and making the right investments in the right products and technology, the company will gain competitive advantage and make shareholders more wealthy. Shareholders invest in the business to make money and if share prices are stalling, the only rational solution is to replace top management with executives who will make better decisions. We are not suggesting that these are always bad assumptions. History has shown that replacing the executive team with a new visionary group that makes aggressive business decisions to kill some products, close

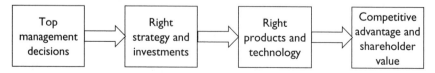

**Figure 18.1** Traditional Business Assumption—Smart Decisions and the right Tools and Technology Create Competitive Advantage

some plants, merge with or acquire the right companies, develop new marketing campaigns, and generally make solid business decisions can send share prices rising. We are not experts on the stock market, but we also have noticed a disturbing trend that what goes up generally comes down just as fast and furiously.

Toyota is not more successful at the game of mergers and acquisitions and rapidly accelerating shareholder value—they are simply playing a different game. For Toyota, the game is about steady growth of a human system through continually finding new ways to add value to society. Senior managers are grown from within and at any given time act as caretakers of the corporate trust. The corporate trust is shared among all stakeholders—employees, business partners, the community, and society. The underlying assumption is illustrated in Figure 18.2, which focuses on investment in quality people, systems that support the development of people, and a strong culture that ties goals together through shared values, beliefs, and goals.

On reflection, the core message of the Toyota Way goes back to what the quality gurus were preaching in the 1980s. It is about building in quality, not inspecting in quality after the fact. Quality products are what the customer sees but below the surface the Toyota Way is built on the unwavering belief that you get quality products from quality processes which are created and improved by quality people. Unfortunately, while it would seem that you can "implement" a

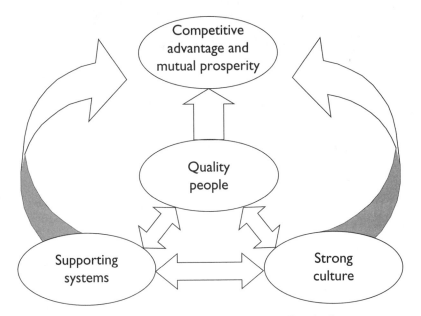

**Figure 18.2** Toyota Way Business Assumption—Quality People Create Competitive Advantage

quality tool or technology, you cannot implement a quality person. We believe that is why the American auto companies missed a great opportunity over the last 30 years. They had 30 years to make a major cultural transformation. They repeatedly began processes of building quality people and a supporting culture, but just as quickly destroyed momentum because of short-term business decisions. These business decisions did not reflect deeply held values of respect for people and continuous improvement.

One of our insightful learning moments came in a meeting with Nate Furuta when he drew a simple matrix to illustrate the difference between a process orientation and a results orientation (see Figure 18.3). He explained that everyone agrees that the X is bad—a bad process producing a bad result. They also agree that the ideal is the circle in which we use a good process to get a good result. He then explained that the difference between a good manager and a bad manager is how you evaluate a good process with bad results versus a bad process that produces good results. Most people, especially when asked what their boss prefers, would pick good results even with a bad process. The metrics and rewards focus on the results so that is what we aim for. Nate Furuta said with obvious emotion that results without a good process is just luck and not worth much. Toyota would prefer to have the good process without the results, because at least there would be a starting point for kaizen and improvement. The process is repeatable, and therefore it can be analyzed and countermeasured through PDCA. That is the only way to get repeatable results.

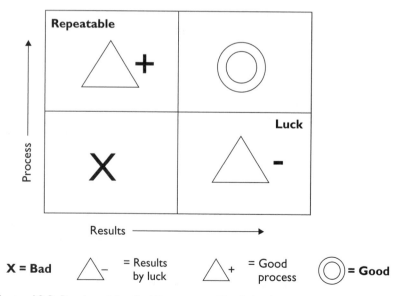

**Figure 18.3** Results with a Bad Process are Simply Luck

The question we finally turn to is whether Western companies, with such contrasting cultures to Toyota, can really learn anything useful from studying Toyota culture. Is it possible to change culture? Can Western companies learn anything from a company rooted in Eastern culture? Can short-term, individualistic Americans work cooperatively toward common goals? We remain optimistic. In fact, we believe that the experiments in the American, and also European, auto industries in areas of employee involvement, building in quality, cross-functional teams, and supplier partnering have already proven this is all possible in the West. The evidence through individual case studies is unequivocal. It can work, it has worked, and the results can be stunning. *The real question is not whether it can work, but whether we will let it work.*

We believe we know what companies need to do to build a quality culture. The answer is in the human systems model we have described throughout this book. It starts with the quality people value stream and requires that over time all the supporting systems and daily management behaviors evolve to support quality people. It is not easy, but it is possible. Unfortunately, what prevents the change in culture is the culture that needs to be changed.

In this chapter, we will discuss the culture change process that focuses on both the people and product value streams. Lean methods that take waste out of the product value streams play a key role in providing occasions for people to learn new roles and new skill sets. The cultural changes cannot be implemented through a culture change program but must be nurtured over long periods of time through better ways of doing work focused on developing and producing quality products. Senior management must be crystal clear on what they are trying to accomplish through these programs. Is it implementing a tool kit to get short-term cost reductions and favorable report cards from investors, or is it a commitment to building a learning, adaptable enterprise that will continually find new ways to add value to customers? We can suggest what should be done, but we cannot make anyone do it. The passion for change must come from within.

# DIFFERENT APPROACHES TO ORGANIZATIONAL TRANSFORMATION

What is referred to as "lean transformation" is certainly not the first attempt to create an organization that is improving and adapting to the environment. In fact, the way good companies approach becoming leaner builds on many other approaches. It is worth pausing to consider some alternative approaches to transformation and specifically contrast lean, six sigma, lean six sigma and the Toyota Way. We will illustrate this through two contrasting case examples—Big Ship compared to Small Ship.

## Lean Transformation at Big Ship Compared to Small Ship

Big Ship and Small Ship are pseudonyms for two actual shipyards that focus exclusively on repair and overhaul of large defense ships like submarines and aircraft carriers. They are both part of the same corporation. In 2001, the executive in charge contracted consultants who work in the Toyota Way tradition to help launch a lean transformation. This executive saw a need for change to become more competitive, but also did not have a sense of urgency. He did not want to aggressively order the shipyards to launch a lean transformation, but instead he wanted to expose them to the idea hoping they would then internally choose to invest in the program.

Even though these were both part of the same corporation, Big Ship and Small Ship took very different approaches to lean, and in fact, started off acting like competitors. Each wanted to do it their own way and prove their way was right. Big Ship tended to be bureaucratic and took a mechanistic approach to the transformation, starting by building a lean six-sigma academy and driving the program with metrics. Small ship had a culture of teamwork and problem solving and took what we call a more organic approach starting with a deep model in one ball-valve repair shop. Both did some good things and neither is a model of best practice that would fit the Toyota Way very well. On the other hand, in their own way they both illustrate very common tendencies when approaching lean and six sigma and also had some success. We describe each of these cases in the following pages.

## MECHANISTIC LEAN SIX-SIGMA TRANFORMATION AT BIG SHIP, BY ROBERT KUCNER[3]

Big Ship is a shipyard of 7,500 employees that repairs submarines and air craft carriers for the Navy. It is part of a larger corporation and is the largest and most influential shipyard in this company. In the past, it had a poor reputation for quality and efficiency and by modeling the Baldridge Award quality approach was able to make significant improvements getting some internal recognition.

[3] Abstracted from Robert Kucner, *A Socio-Technical Study of Lean Manufacturing Deployment in the Remanufacturing Context*, PhD Dissertation, University of Michigan, Ann Arbor, Michigan, 2008.

When the head of operations for the corporation announced an offsite workshop in 2001 to learn about lean methods, Big Ship was not enthusiastic because they already felt confident in the Baldridge-based Total Quality Management approach. They reluctantly participated and agreed to do one kaizen workshop with an external consultant. They seemed to want to sabotage the process, picking a project management problem with no real physical implementation and weak management support.

When it became clear that lean was going to be taken more seriously by the corporation, Big Ship developed an approach that fit their bureaucratic style, establishing a school to aggressively train "black belt" experts and senior managers through a newly established lean six-sigma academy. The strategy for deployment at Big Ship was to hire a six-sigma black belt from an automotive OEM to lead implementation of lean manufacturing and six sigma jointly via four to six month projects, led by the internal experts. Big Ship was successful in building a large infrastructure to support lean manufacturing and six-sigma and were lauded by the corporate office for their deployment approach. Walking through the yard one was hard pressed to find any visible evidence of lean, that is, little visual management, lots of inventory, poor 5S, no standardized work, and little evidence of employee involvement.

Over the next couple of years Big Ship continued to train black belt and green belt experts and they were deployed to each major department of the organization. There were many projects with reported savings but still little visible evidence of change. Finally, they decided to focus on machining as a pilot area conducting a building-wide 5S, one which reportedly removed more than 35 tons of waste, and made a visible impact. This was followed by kaizen events to strengthen targeted processes in the machine shop.

With this intensive effort the black belts assigned to the machine shop deepened their skill and began questioning the superficial training of the lean six-sigma academy. As the most senior black belt change agent stated at this point; "Employees go to the six-week training program and when they get back the first thing I have to do is retrain them." This rift began to exist as a divergence between textbook knowledge of the instructors and "deck plate" experience of seasoned change agents.

Over time, the corporate office decided they needed a common approach to lean six-sigma and adopted the lean six-sigma academy. They used extensive metrics and standard roadmaps and expected all the sites to carry out a cookie-cutter approach. Since the approach was largely modeled after Big Ship, that site was more than happy to comply. At Big

Ship a feeling existed that "now we can take lean deployment to the next level."

Big Ship now placed one of its most aggressive and respected managers to oversee the lean manufacturing deployment. He proceeded to implement, and oversee via command and control, the rigid implementation strategy laid out by Big Ship where quotas were established for each manager and department in terms of the number of improvement events, participants, and initiatives to be achieved. All departments at Big Ship were deploying lean in order to meet their management quotas; each was building internal examples and building internal expertise. However, the departments at Big Ship were working independently, not always willing to share resources, and top-notch personnel rarely participated in lean events outside of their particular department. Eventually there were so many initiatives the shops were getting overwhelmed.

After six years of lean their implementation and understanding was still limited. Big Ship began communicating with Small Ship and agreed there was a need to go back to basics to come out of the crisis. At Big Ship, back to basics led to focusing on the fundamentals of lean manufacturing. The experience to date was based on creating a bureaucratic infrastructure without the broad involvement and cultural change experienced at Small Ship. The organization reduced the number of ongoing initiatives and focused more on developing deep examples of learning starting by going back to the machine shop and making it a model.

## ORGANIC LEAN TRANSFORMATION AT SMALL SHIP, BY ROBERT KUCNER[4]

Small Ship, an organization of roughly 4,500 employees, is part of the same corporation as Big Ship but is like the little brother specializing in repair of submarines. It had the reputation for being the best in the company at submarine repair based on niche expertise.

When the lean initiative first started in 2001, Small Ship participated in the initial training enthusiastically and dived into the one-week expert-led kaizen event. At Small Ship, the first kaizen event targeted the process of ball

---

[4] From Robert Kucner dissertation, op cit, 2007.

valve repair, which was performing significantly above cost, beyond cycle time, and with significant quality problems. In one week the team was able to clean up the workspace, organize tools, improve work flow, and establish basic visual management in the workplace. Despite initial skepticism, the improvement effort was well received. However, Small Ship did not maintain energy beyond the kaizen event and the effort failed to take hold. In time, the work area regressed to the previous process and performance levels, and skepticism grew.

After a six-month layoff, and with continued encouragement from the corporate office, Small Ship placed a highly-respected senior leader, a production-oriented ex-project manager, as the director of lean manufacturing implementation and hired an outside consultant. With a lean manufacturing staff of only two, Small Ship attempted to rejuvenate implementation by working to make ball valve repair a true model. It was a small area with only 12 employees, in a relatively isolated section of a larger machine shop. In one year, the lean expert practically lived in the area coaching and teaching this group every day. In the course of twelve months, the team in ball valve worked with the consultant and made many iterative improvements, which added up to a major impact on the operation of the area and the results. Average cycle time for ball valve repair was reduced by 83 percent, schedules were being maintained, costs were reduced (e.g., overtime eliminated), quality was improved, employees were fully engaged, and the team was achieving continuous improvement through daily initiatives, both large and small.

Small Ship began getting high-level visits from executives and was awarded the honor as the best example of lean in the company. Top executives in the company marveled at the efficiency of the operation but particularly at the level of employee engagement.

After almost two years after starting the lean effort at Small Ship, multiple model lines began to develop based on a pull from other shops that were impressed by ball valve and similar results were achieved. Spontaneous lean initiatives began to develop as work leaders embraced the tools they saw demonstrated in the model line area. These follow-on areas were able to mature more quickly than the original model as senior leadership began to develop a deeper understanding of lean. Additionally, the application of tools such as workplace organization, standard work, and setup reduction began to "pop up" unexpectedly throughout the organization.

By the time the parent corporation decided to launch a formal, standard, bureaucratic program, Small Ship was relatively advanced in understanding lean and resisted participation. Its leaders saw the corporate program as superficial and even threatening to the continued progress of lean maturation. They decided to minimally comply, providing the reports requested, but did not accept help from the consultants contracted by the corporation and continued down their own path. They were, of course, viewed as renegades by the lean six-sigma office of the corporation.

During this time, a crisis had occurred at Small Ship when it was selected to be closed because the corporation determined there was too much capacity. Rather than simply give up, Small Ship became more determined to transform the shipyard, hoping if their performance was exceptional they might stay alive. Senior leadership at Small Ship held a two-day offsite meeting to strategize about the next level of lean manufacturing deployment. The big money to be saved was in moving from the back shops, like ball valve repair, to all processes conducted onboard an entire submarine more efficiently, but there were approximately 10,000 tasks executed on a submarine overhaul and nearly every one of those tasks was unique; how could techniques such as process flow, pull systems, work-in-process reductions, andon, and visual controls work in this environment?

An important revelation for the organization came when they realized that even though the 10,000 tasks were unique in work content and complexity, a common method existed in the planning and follow-up for each. Utilizing the same tools as were used in the original model line, the organization developed a value stream map and a strategy for managing the 10,000 tasks in a systematic approach, utilizing a wide array of lean production tools and techniques. With a focus on continuous flow and cycle time per unit, the organization was able to make tremendous strides in a short time. They established a supermarket for incoming work, visual communication boards, standard work instructions, significantly improved workplace organization, work-in-process inventory controls, andon systems, and pull systems. The deployment included all production shops, and required significant communication across multiple trades and functions. In many instances, as the strategy was both being developed and implemented, comments were made such as "well, we had a similar situation in the ball valve model line, this is what we did and this was the outcome... let's try that here."

Largely due to its innovation and process improvement initiatives, the parent corporation decided not to close Small Ship. The charismatic leader was promoted to the executive level at corporate headquarters, and the lean champion was assigned to a special project to take lean across the enterprise.

The honeymoon for lean deployment at Small Ship did not last long after being removed from the closure list. Complacency set in and without the drive of their charismatic leader, the lean program languished. The extraordinary energy and focus that was driving lean manufacturing deployment at Small Ship had dissipated and the organization had not built an infrastructure capable of maintaining the deployment. For example, there was only one person left in their lean office and occasional consulting support.

Six years after the first kaizen workshops were conducted and the lean effort had been up and down, "back to basics" became the goal and Small Ship began to refocus its efforts, cooperating with Big Ship and the corporate program. All senior managers at Small Ship were required to attend lean training and go on regular "waste walks" with the lean management team. The original charismatic lean champion returned to this role and a new shipyard commander was brought in who led the lean effort at another part of the corporation. New industrial engineers were hired and trained through the corporate lean six-sigma academy, as well as through spending time in each of the model line initiatives at the shipyard. Ultimately, Small Ship developed pockets of deep models and illustrations of lean manufacturing, they were adding to the infrastructure of their lean organization, as well as continuing to build support among managers, for long-term continuing success.

## What Can We Learn from Big Ship Compared to Small Ship?

Was either of these cases a successful lean transformation? Was one better than the other? What are some of the lessons we can learn?

1. *Need for Consistent and Committed Leadership*—Neither shipyard had consistent and committed leadership. Both had some excellent leadership in certain positions, but Small Ship was overly dependent on a small number of charismatic individuals and when they were transferred the lean process crumbled. Big Ship also had some strong individual leaders, but those running the lean effort were largely bureaucrats more interested in control than effectiveness.

2. *Top-Down Mechanistic Structures Do Not Drive Deep Change*—When we see a beautiful infrastructure on paper with certification courses, metrics, and great PowerPoint presentations, our first question is whether this matches what is actually happening at the gemba. In 90 percent of the cases, a walk of the process reveals superficial lean. Big Ship's lean six-sigma academy looked great on paper, and they received corporate accolades for it, but the reality was much less impressive.

3. *Arrogance Never Wins*—Perhaps the biggest barrier to change at Big Ship was the arrogance of the Baldridge leaders who believed they had it all licked. Their resistance to lean from the beginning was because of their pride in the elaborate system they had developed based on the Baldridge methods. They had training, metrics, projects, sophisticated statistical tools, a broad systems approach, and lean seemed like baby steps in comparison. What they lacked was deep implementation and the ability to develop people in the operation, but their arrogance prevented them from seeing this fatal flaw.

4. *Bottom-Up Organic Change is Powerful for Culture Change, but Limited Without Top Leadership and Infrastructure Support*—We will confess that we have been involved with great projects at the gemba, with people at the shop floor who "get it" and are rapidly learning. We can feel that something like Toyota Culture is starting to take shape, but without strong support from the top and a strong infrastructure it will never get beyond these isolated pockets.

5. *There are Natural Ups and Downs to Lean Transformation*—We have yet to experience perfectly linear upward progress in lean learning. We saw at several points in this book that even TMMK has had plenty of struggles. It seems natural to take steps forward and back, but the key to success is taking more steps forward.

6. *Stick With It and Progress Can be Made*—It would be unfair to portray either Big Ship or Little Ship as a failure or to say one was far more successful than the other. They both had their ups and downs but the good news is that at the time of this writing, six years after the 2001 event, both continued to work at it and they both have achieved some major improvements in processes and results. Ultimately, they converged in their approaches and began to share practices instead of competing. The important thing is using the plan-do-check-act process and both shipyards are still learning.

We can think about the different approaches that Big Ship and Small Ship took conceptually by thinking about all the key processes that were filled with waste back in 2001 (see Figure 18.4).[5] There was a lot of "low-hanging fruit."

Big Ship took a mechanistic approach to improvement, which is typical of lean six-sigma approaches. They saw the objective as to develop black belt experts who would do isolated projects. In Figure 18.5, we illustrate these projects through concentric circles. The more circles we have around a project the bigger the project. Big projects can deliver big financial results, but the learning does not go deep. In fact we can view the concentric circles like walls. The learning that

---

[5] Figures 18.4, 18.5, and 18.6 came from the dissertation by Robert Kucher cited in footnote 3.

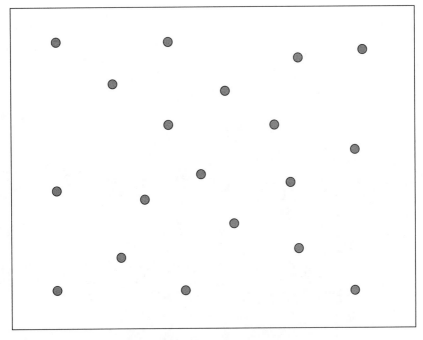

**Key Organizational Processes**

**Figure 18.4** Key Organizational Processes that can be Improved

takes place does not penetrate outside the walls of each isolated project. Most of the learning is individual learning by the black belt.

Small Ship took an organic approach to improvement which is more common with "lean transformation." If you watch how Toyota develops its suppliers for example, they will pick a process where there is a problem. For example, it may be a bottleneck preventing the plant from consistently meeting the delivery schedule. They will work and work and work in that area using all the tools of TPS and problem solving, or we should say that they will ask people at the supplier to do the work. The Toyota advisor will advise and challenge the supervisor in the area to take responsibility. The group responsible for the process may make mistakes but that is how they will learn. By digging deeper and deeper into that model area the learning is deepened. The spiral (imagine this is a view looking down) in Figure 18.6 reflects going deeper and deeper, burrowing down into the fine details of the process, uncovering even the tiniest wastes and creating true standardized work.

In parallel, other parts of the plant may decide to get started on projects and they, too, will begin to dig down in their own spiral fashion. In the case of the ball valve repair operation, they were working in isolation as a model but then other parts of the shipyard began to learn from them. The ball valve operation was a

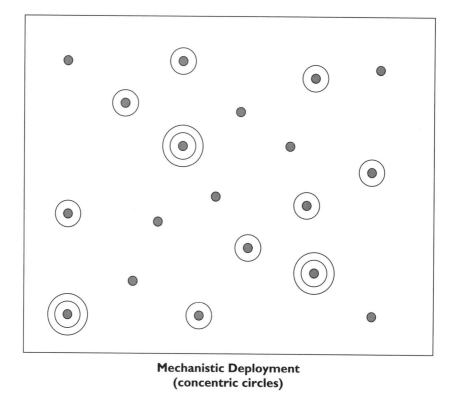

**Mechanistic Deployment**
**(concentric circles)**

**Figure 18.5** Mechanistic Approach to Process Improvement

small part of the machine shop and depended on other parts of the machine shop for specially made parts. With the success of ball valve, those other elements of the machine shop became a constraint and wanted to learn from ball valve. Over time, the upstream and downstream processes became connected and the spiral grew bigger encompassing the entire machine shop and ball valve. When the leadership agreed to tackle the entire submarine overhaul and repair with its 10,000 parts, the spiral of learning grew to encompass much of the ship repair yard. By digging deep in one area, driving technical and cultural change in that area, and then growing from there, we saw deep learning and real cultural change rather than superficial change at the physical (artifact) level only.

## The Cultural Assumptions Behind Lean Six Sigma Versus the Toyota Way

Lean six sigma appeals to Western managers because it is mechanical and results oriented. It fits the top-down, bureaucratic mindset. Figure 18.7 shows in a flow diagram the approach and thinking behind it. Six sigma was originally built on Total Quality Management (TQM), which was a deep philosophy to shift

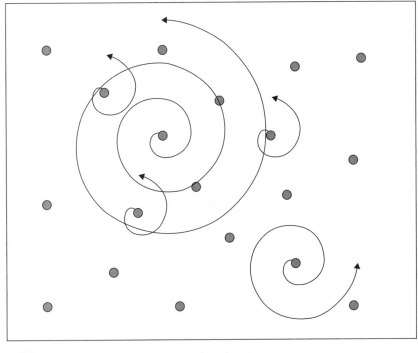

**Organic Deployment
(spirals)**

**Figure 18.6** Organic Approach to Process Improvement

organizations from a cost-only focus to a quality focus. Six sigma boasts bottom-line results that can be measured in dollars and cents. At its best it teaches problem solving throughout the organization. At its worst it reverts to the cost-only philosophy. Lean six sigma is a compilation of tools and training focused on isolated projects to drive down unit cost.

Because of the myopic focus on doing projects to drive out cost, the lean six-sigma approach rarely develops a total technical system of flow, pull, and built-in quality that we see in the complete Toyota production system. We see islands of solutions that are not tied together well, despite the lean toolkit. We certainly do not see respect for people and continuous improvement. Most of the easily measured cost reductions are headcount reductions that threaten jobs and people who quickly get turned off to these alien invaders with their black belts. The result is short-term cost savings that are not sustainable. Since the philosophy of the company focuses on short-term wins, true leadership is not valued and there is a constant churning of managers and an unstable culture.

The Toyota approach, illustrated by the flow chart in Figure 18.8, is far broader and far deeper. The starting point is the Toyota Way philosophy of respect

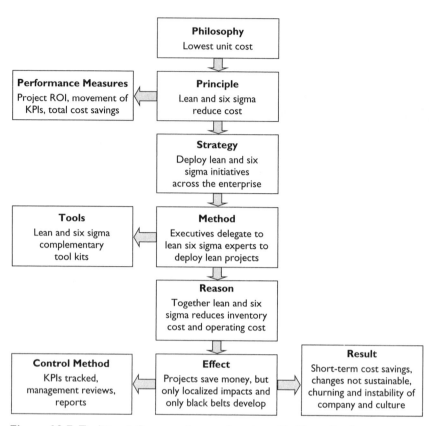

**Figure 18.7** Traditional Company Approach to Lean Six Sigma Deployment

for people and continuous improvement. The principle is developing quality people who continually improve processes. Performance measured is much broader than cost including quality, cost, delivery, safety, and morale based on long-term strengthening of the system and deepening of each person's skill set. A much broader tool set is used compared to lean six sigma and the tools are designed to surface problems and develop people. The responsibility lies, not with black belt specialists, but with the leadership hierarchy that runs the operation and they are the teachers and coaches. The result is continual waste reduction, competitive advantage, and mutual prosperity.

The difference between the tool-based lean six-sigma approach and the Toyota approach is more than methodology and reflects different underlying assumptions. Language reflects culture and the language is very different for these two different paradigms. Table 18.1 provides examples of key differences in language which once again reflect east versus west differences in culture. Lean six sigma is about deploying a methodology by black belts who collect data, lead events, conduct projects,

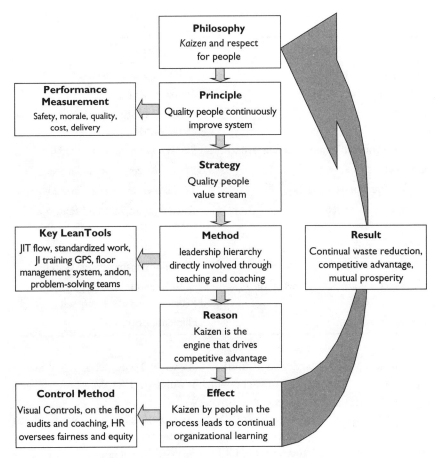

**Figure 18.8** Toyota Approach to Developing the Toyota Way

and achieve the targets on the metrics. When there is a success it is labeled a best practice that is deployed by the black belt. Consider the difference in Toyota Way language, which is about growing people's capability, teaching, going to deeply observe (genchi genbutsu), voluntary self study (jishuken), and providing ownership by work groups. The concept of yoketen (transplanting and tending the seedling) has a very different connotation than deploying the standard method. The work group is responsible for yoketen, for the transplanting, tending, and improving as opposed to black belts who are responsible for deploying lean six sigma.

We provide a still broader view of different transformation approaches and results in Table 18.2. TQM was really the foundation of what we now call six sigma. It had a very clear focus on quality consciousness throughout the value stream. Everyone has a direct customer and needs to understand what they need and how to achieve quality with zero defects. This philosophy is very engrained in

**Table 18.1** Language of Lean Six Sigma versus Toyota Way

| Typical Lean Six Sigma | Toyota Way |
| --- | --- |
| Deploy the methodology | Grow people's capability |
| Master black belt | *Sensei* (teacher) |
| Data collection | *Genchi Genbutsu* (go see actual place, actual part) |
| *Kaizen* event (rapid improvement event) | *Jishuken* (voluntary self study) |
| Conduct a project | System *Kaizen*/process *Kaizen* |
| Deploy the standard method | Teams own the standardized work |
| Spread best practice | *Yoketen* (transplant and tend the seedling) |
| DMAIC | Toyota business practices |
| Deploy the metrics | Shop-floor management system |
| Hold accountable for achieving metrics | *Hoshin kanri* (policy deployment, with focus on process and results) |
| Reduce headcount | Eliminate positions |

the Toyota Way and was developed in the 1960s when Toyota set as a goal to win the prestigious Deming prize in Japan (which it won twice). TQM is powerful and became one very central piece of the Toyota Way.

Contemporary lean and six-sigma deployment each have their own strengths and weaknesses. The strength of six sigma goes beyond the statistical tools and really is in the commitment at the CEO level to the program. Its weakness is the narrow, mechanistic focus on short-term results. Lean deployment is more organic and begins to build a culture of continuous improvement at the gemba but is often stopped short by lack of visibility to senior management.

The Toyota Way is not only visible to senior management, it is in the DNA of the top leaders. It extends from top to bottom and sideways and becomes a way of life.

We added into Table 18.2 "organizational development" as a methodology and philosophy. This is another seasoned methodology going back decades and the focus is on pulling people together to work toward a common vision.[6] The

---

[6] There is a lengthy and rich reading list on organizational development. One compendium of the field is by Schein, Edgar H. and Joan V. Gallos (Eds), *Organization Development*, San Francisco: Jossey-Bass, 2006. An excellent book that describes in detail an approach to large scale change of an entire organization is Jacobs, Robert W., *Real Time Strategic Change*, San Francisco: Berret-Koehler Publishers, 1994.

**Table 18.2** Comparison of Transformation Approaches and Results

| Transformation Approach | Target | Method | Focus of Activities | Leadership Level Driving Change | Role of Social Support Systems | Results if Successful |
|---|---|---|---|---|---|---|
| Total Quality Management | Quality throughout value stream | Cross-functional teams using statistical problem solving | • Statistical quality training<br>• Align metrics<br>• Team projects | CEO | Cross-functional teams | Large quality improvement |
| Six Sigma | Cost-reduction | Top-down structure with black belt projects | • Black-belt training<br>• Variation reduction projects<br>• Results metrics | CEO | Mostly individually based | Cost reduction and problem solving skills (especially for black belts) |
| Lean | Waste-reduction | Top-down direction and projects at gemba | • Gemba projects to reduce lead time<br>• Teach TPS to manage from the floor | COO or VP manufacturing | Work group | Local profound change and intensive local learning |
| Organizational Development | Social facilitation toward desired future | Facilitated group interventions | • Authentic communication<br>• Shared vision<br>• Teamwork<br>• Action plans | Executives or manager of unit (depends on scope) | Cascading team structure | Facilitate particular changes targeted employee engagement |
| Toyota Way | Long-term mutual prosperity via QCDSM | Top-down leadership challenges, teaches, and develops culture | • Leaders as teachers<br>• Daily management<br>• Kaizen<br>• People value stream | CEO and entire management hierarchy | Servant leadership and work group | Transformational business results (though few examples outside Toyota) |

practitioners view themselves as "process consultants." They do not attempt to be experts on the work itself, but rather help people to achieve whatever vision they desire through social facilitation of the process of change. In fact, many of the methods used by Toyota for teaching and facilitating change fit very well with the philosophical bases of organizational development such as:

- Participation and ownership by people who work in the process.
- Strong team facilitation to get groups to solve their own problems.
- Teaching through action, rather than telling people things.
- Leading through a shared vision.
- A positive outlook on the ability of a team to achieve their desired future if they all pull together.

As we talk about organizational and cultural change, we will see many elements of the organizational development approach. The Toyota Way adds a strong degree of content expertise and standardized practices as a foundation for continuous learning.

# WHAT DO WE KNOW ABOUT ORGANIZATION AND CULTURE CHANGE?

There is a long history of research and practice on organizational change and we can only hope to skim the service here. From the beginnings of human history, leaders have been using their skills to influence the masses. More recently, organizational development and organizational behavior have developed as academic fields, with tens of thousands of books and articles describing various practices. We will highlight a few key findings that will inform our advice on putting in practice some of the learning of the Toyota Way. We have summarized the lessons we have learned from our studies and practical experience as a set of four high-level observations with more specific recommendations below.

# SOME LESSONS LEARNED ON TRANSFORMATIONAL CHANGE

Leaders Must Lead

- It starts at the top.
- Leaders must change themselves to become lean transformational leaders.

- Progress depends on brutal honesty about the current situation at any time.
- Leadership living your values must be developed at all levels.
- Long-term change depends on continuity of leadership.

Change Requires a Reason and a Vision

- People need a reason.
- People need a future vision.
- You cannot copy Toyota's system but must evolve your own.

People Must be Taught and Supported

- People will resist change because they are human.
- Learning by doing is more powerful than learning by listening.
- To cope with the high uncertainty of change people need daily support.

Change Needs a Plan and a Process

- Attitude and behavior change must be supported by structural change.
- Metrics do not produce change but can be key enablers.
- Break up the journey into small steps.

# Leaders Must Lead

Throughout the book we have emphasized the importance of leadership and the tremendous investment Toyota makes in developing new leaders. The good news is that Toyota has been very successful in developing leaders who live their values in countries all over the world. The bad news is that it takes 5–10 years and that is under almost ideal conditions in an already established culture that supports all of the Toyota Way principles. Other companies cannot hope to dive into becoming just like Toyota, nor are we recommending this. We are suggesting that leaders need to develop a vision and lead from the very top of the company on down and make their top priority to develop other leaders.

## It Starts at the Top

It is easy to pick on people in the top positions of corporations and point the finger of blame at them. "The CEO does not get it and is only trying to make the quarterly results look good" is a common refrain. We have worked with CEOs, both kind and ruthless, but generally speaking we find them to be honest, smart, excellent leaders, and sincere in their desire to make a difference. What is sometimes not apparent is the tremendous pressures they are under to satisfy multiple constituents. As an example, we went through a presentation on Toyota culture with one CEO and contrasted the Western focus on short-term results with Toyota's patient long-term approach and he exclaimed: "I know what you are talking about, and I do not want superficial lean. But I am responsible as a leader to shareholders, customers, and our employees. I cannot simply ignore short-term results and be successful as a leader."

That is the reality for this thoughtful leader and the reality for most CEOs. We then discussed how we might work on high-leverage projects that both deliver short-term results and develop deep understanding among lean leaders. We agreed that the key is to always think about the long-term impact, even when working on projects with measurable short-term results.

It is possible to get significant wins at the department or plant level without the CEO being deeply involved in the transformation process. It is impossible to transform an entire company without absolute dedication and leadership from the top.

## Leaders Must Change Themselves to Become Transformational Leaders

There are different types of leaders and the type of leadership needed to maintain morale and direction is different from transformational leadership. A wholesale change in culture needs transformational leadership. We recommend the classic book by Tichy and Devanna called *Transformational Leader*[7] to get an understanding of the characteristics of this role. It takes energy, a sense of purpose, forging a vision, and the charisma to sell the vision every day.

In addition to being out front selling the vision, the transformational leader must eliminate barriers to change. This is impossible if the leaders themselves are the barriers. We have spent a good deal of time talking about Western culture and how it is at odds with much of the Toyota Way. Yet a leader from Western culture is expected to transform the organization based on the Toyota model. If the Western leader is strictly short-term oriented, results oriented, impatient, not very good at developing people, and wants to jump ahead to solutions without a good problem solving process, how can she lead others to a different way? Unfortunately, organizational change must start with individual change. We must develop ourselves to effectively lead others.

---

[7] Tichy, Noel M. and Mary Anne Devanna, *Transformational Leader*, second edition, New York: John Wiley, 1997.

Robert Quinn uses vivid imagery to talk about the process of "discovering the leader within" by "walking naked into the land of uncertainty." He writes these powerful words:[8]

> *We are all potential change agents. As we discipline our talents, we deepen our perceptions about what is possible. We develop a reverence for the tools and the relationships that surround us. We then bring a discipline to our visions and grow in integrity. Life becomes more meaningful. We become empowered and empowering to our context. Having experienced deep change in ourselves, we are able to bring deep change to the systems around us.*

## Progress Depends on Brutal Honesty About Where You Are

Ohno taught by asking his students to stand in the circle and observe with a blank mind. He was teaching them to understand the current reality without blinders. Unfortunately, one of the major barriers to lean transformation is leaders who seem all too willing to declare victory, move on and remain incapable of seeing the current reality.

When we are asked by middle managers to speak at senior leadership offsites, typically the request is to try to give senior leaders a dose of reality. A typical story goes something like this:

> *We started a lean program three years ago. We had a rocky start in a few plants trying 5S but getting little measurable result. Then our plant in Yugoslavia really took off with lean. They created cells, reduced labor by 20 percent, cut inventory by 70 percent, freed up half the floor space for new products, and greatly improved quality. They did that with the help of some consultants in one year. The plant manager was extremely aggressive and had led a lean transformation in another company. Now our management wants us to "lean out" all our plants and wants a plan for completing the transformation in two years. Please help us convince him this is a long-term journey.*

We suspect all the lean consultants out there will relate to this fictitious, but not unusual story. It is possible for an aggressive and experienced leader to blitz a plant and make major changes quickly using lean methods. However, the question is whether it is sustainable and whether the improvements will continue or end as soon as that aggressive leader lets up on the gas. We also do not know from this story the exact situation of that plant in Yugoslavia. It might have been a relatively simple process to turn with lots of easy opportunities for quick hits. It might have been relatively new with a young workforce that was hungry for good

---

[8] Quinn, Robert E. *Deep Change: Discovering the Leader Within*, San Francisco: Jossey Bass, 1996, p. xiii.

paying jobs that would obey any orders from the top. We can say with confidence that no leader, no matter how good, can build a strong culture of continuous improvement in one year. Ideally, the top leaders will understand this and actually visit the plant to stand in the circle and observe.

Organizational theorist, Karl Weick is the foremost authority on how people rationalize what has happened and paint it in an overly positive light. In a book written with Kathy Sutcliffe, they address how organizations deal with uncertainty and complexity. It turns out in many organizational cultures the answer is not very well: "The tricky part is that all of us tend to be awfully generous in what we treat as evidence that our expectations are confirmed. Furthermore, we actively seek out evidence that confirms our expectations and avoid evidence that disconfirms it."[9]

Tichy and Devanna find that true transformational leaders are aware of their own biases in seeing what is really going on. They have a strong point of view but realize they need other viewpoints to make the right decisions. For example, they suggest that "effective transformational leaders must develop mechanisms that provide dissonant information and surround decision-makers with people who can operate effectively in the role of devil's advocate."[10]

## Leadership Must be Developed at All Levels

Since most lean transformation starts at the gemba, lean change agents tend to be brought in at high levels, normally an executive in charge of manufacturing, and then immediately jump to the shop floor. Since there is almost reverence in the Toyota Way for the value-added worker, there is a tendency to spend a good deal of effort in winning over the operators. The operators get involved in the kaizen events and the senior management gets a kick out of talking directly to the operators.

This is all fine but the ones left out are often the so-called "frozen middle" (e.g., supervisor to department manager). We do not believe there is any reason to think people in middle management are any more or less resistant than anyone else. We do think there is something special about their position that makes large-scale change especially difficult for them.

An excellent book called *Life in Organizations*[11] vividly illustrates through stories the difference between life at the top, middle, and bottom of organizations. In most cases, organizational change is what the top tells the middle to do to the

[9] Weick, Karl, E. and Kathleen M. Sutcliffe, *Managing the Unexpected*, University of Michigan Business School Management Series, San Francisco: John Wiley, 2001.
[10] Tichy, Noel M. and Mary Anne Devanna, *Transformational Leader*, p. 53.
[11] Kanter, Rosabeth Moss and Barry A. Stein, *Life in Organizations: Workplaces as People Experience Them*, New York: Basic Books, 1978.

bottom. The middle is then stuck between following the orders of the top and alienating the bottom who they have to depend on everyday. Lean transformation can be particularly difficult because it is often the top working with external or internal consultants to directly change the bottom and then asking the middle to assume new roles and responsibilities.

We have emphasized the key roles of the group leader and team leader in the Toyota system. Obviously, the middle management level is not one we want to alienate in the lean transformation since they will be key to developing people, leading the transformation, sustaining the change, and leading continuous improvement. In reality this group of people will have to go through as much personal transformation as anyone in the organization, and it will be challenging. As we will see, coaching and developing this group needs to be done in parallel with implementing the tools and methods of lean.

## Long-Term Change Depends on Continuity of Leadership

It would certainly be convenient if lean was a one-shot transformation. Get the right transformational leaders in place, change the culture by unfreezing it, make the change, refreeze it, and it will go on its merry way beating the competition. This is far from reality. We discussed in Chapter 1 the concept of entropy. Without active daily leadership reinforcing the high-performance culture you desire, it will degenerate quickly to a low performance culture. Once you have worked so hard to establish the beginnings of a new culture it will be up to future generations of leaders to maintain and grow it.

Stagnation is a legitimate fear and the Western solution to this is a revolving door of leaders. The most exciting leader is the next one. In the book *Good to Great*,[12] we learn that in the top American companies that have consistently led the pack in financial performance by a large margin the top leaders are completely committed to the company and its product, humble, focused on the details of the business, and knock themselves out to develop several possible successors.

Toyota has managed to be very fresh and innovative despite growing leaders from within. One of the characteristics they select on and develop is the ability to constantly challenge assumptions and think fresh. The top executive of the company is actually an executive team. The president becomes the vice chairman then the chairman, and then a senior advisor. There is a very strong internal board of senior managing directors. Decisions are made by consensus though the president is on the hot seat and issues the annual hoshin. This could be a recipe for decision strangulation, but the culture so strongly supports challenge and

---

[12] Collins, Jim, *Good to Great: Why Some Companies Make the Leap… and Others Don't,* New York: HarperBusiness, 2001.

creativity that it works. Take out any one or even two top leaders at Toyota and the company will continue to function quite well. When the new president takes over they will have an agenda but continue to build the culture of the Toyota Way.

## Change Requires a Reason and a Vision

### People Need a Reason

It is often said that a burning platform is needed before any company will go through a major transformation. The implication is that unless the company is about to go out of business it cannot seriously be changed. This is of course extreme, and companies that are quite healthy financially that bring in a new CEO regularly go through quite major transformations. Often this is top down with parts of the business outsourced, others downsized, and the rest subject to strict new targets and policies in the name of increasing shareholder value. The point is that a burning platform can be created by an aggressive top executive.

If a top executive can create a burning platform in a negative way through fear and intimidation, is it possible to create it through a positive vision? One thing interesting about Toyota is that no matter how successful the company is, the feeling inside is that disaster is right around the corner. There is always a burning platform. Top leadership is constantly talking about competition and setting increasingly aggressive targets in the annual hoshin to keep everyone on their toes. This is all managed in a very positive environment.

There are two problems with launching a transformation to a new culture with a crisis like the burning platform. First, the crisis will take up all the effort and any leaning out of the operations is likely to be for short-term cost reductions rather than long-term culture building. Second, if the turnaround is successful, the crisis will be over before the serious culture change starts. A key role of a transformational leader is creating a sense of urgency by providing a positive vision of the future instead of waiting for disaster to strike.

### People Need a Future Vision

If there is one thing that all the books about leadership seem to agree on, it is that effective leaders are able to paint a compelling future vision. Perhaps the overriding benefit of Toyota as a benchmark is that your company can use it as a compelling positive vision for your organization. As we will discuss later, we are not suggesting that you should copy every aspect of Toyota. We are suggesting that having a real life example for inspiration is very powerful.

There are a number of ways that you can create a positive and compelling future vision and it is best to use several of these methods:

- Tour a lean plant (Toyota, a supplier, another successful plant that has been transformed).

- Create a study group and read books like this one.
- Hold an offsite workshop and get your leadership together to develop a vision for your preferred future.
- Invest in developing a model lean process or lean plant in your own organization and take leaders to go and see it.
- One company has used a very life-like simulation of a lean assembly line building trucks that participants work in and then improve.
- Require all senior leaders to participate in kaizen events...with cell phones off.

## You Cannot Copy Toyota's System, but Must Evolve Your Own

One warning about touring a lean plant is that sometimes we get confused between getting inspiration for a positive vision and copying. Copying does not work. We have been there and done that. We are often asked whether we know of a very specific lean example: "Do you know where we can go to see a lean flower shop, in a small community, that specializes in decorative center pieces?" We have a standard answer for these questions: "No, but what difference would it make if you saw one?"

We understand that there is some comfort in seeing a wildly successful operation that is just like yours, though a warning, they are likely to be your competitors. There is actually benefit to seeing a high performance operation with a strong, positive culture that is very different from yours. That may reduce the temptation to copy.

We say that you should not try to copy Toyota's culture or specific systems because they will not fit your current circumstances. Toyota has evolved a certain set of solutions to their problems that are today's best practice for them. They have the capability and expertise to use these systems. For example, Toyota has worked for decades to develop the capability to build cars to order instead of building to a thirty-day fixed schedule as they used to do. It took a great deal of maturity of the organization and some technological breakthroughs like the quick changeover paint system discussed earlier in the book. They have developed discipline in following standardized work and the ability to rebalance processes quickly to a new takt time. Suppliers deliver multiple times each day in small batches. Does that mean your company should strictly build to order to be like Toyota? Your situation may be different, your level of maturity may be different, and you may not have the technology or infrastructure in place. At the moment it may be advisable to build to a fixed schedule. As another example, Toyota has worked hard to develop systems for stable employment and makes certain promises to the work force that your organization may not be in a situation today to copy. While we do not suggest copying Toyota's solutions, there is nothing wrong with adopting similar general principles like respect for people and continuous improvement, as well as the production system principles.

## People Must be Taught and Supported

### People Will Resist Change Because They are Human

There are two tendencies that are very natural and cause a great deal of conflict. One is the tendency that when we get excited about something new we would like other people to get equally excited and change to our way. The other is that there is almost no chance the other people will want to do what we say. We should qualify this a bit as resistance will be highest if: (a) the people have to change a habit that they are comfortable with, and (b) they do not see a personal benefit in it.

Why do other people resist when we have such great ideas for them? Lean is about eliminating waste and won't everyone jump at the chance to do a job in a less wasteful way? We used to hear about resistance to change as though it was a personal flaw in a particular individual. "Older people resist change." "Jeff is very stubborn and refuses to accept new ideas." "Mike always wants to do it his way and does not want to consider my suggestions for improvement."

With the sophistication of imaging technology such as MRI that lets us monitor brain activity, a whole new line of neuroscience has helped demystify the phenomenon of resistance to change.[13] Unfortunately, it turns out it is all too human. One physical part of the brain, the basal ganglia or "habit center," is invoked by routine, familiar activity, while a different part is working memory that is active when you have to take in new information or learn a new skill. Using the basal ganglia to perform a routine activity feels comforting and good. There is a natural tendency to process any new task by rerouting it to the routine side of our brain, but if we have to learn something new it takes attention and leads to discomfort. A second problem with something new is that human brains learn to react to errors—the difference between expectations and actual— and when we detect an error our brain emits a strong signal which uses a lot of brain energy. Using extra brain energy for processing something new or when we mentally detect an error, actually hurts in our brain. It seems quite human to prefer what is pleasant and avoid the painful. At the very least we can feel comforted that resistance to change is natural rather than a particular person's personality disorder.

Does this sophisticated research provide any hope on how we can overcome resistance to change? One conclusion is that "focus is power." Intense attention

---

[13] See for example, Rock, David and Jeffrey Schwartz, "The Neuroscience of Leadership," *Strategy and Business*, Booz Allen Hamilton, Issue 43, May 30, 2006, pp. 2–10.

can change the patterns of the brain. Research has also found that our expectations as represented by "mental maps" affect how we interpret and react to situations. Mental maps can be changed by cultivating moments of insight. In reading about this fascinating research, we began thinking about some of the ways that Toyota trainers have taught new members, and it seems to fit these recommendations.

Take for example the Global Production Center. People are pulled off the job and put in an ideal environment to focus attention. All they are focusing on is learning the task using the video manual and the different exercises. They focus intently on learning the new skill and get immediate reinforcement from the trainer on hand when they accomplish the task. The tasks build so that once a lower level simpler skill is mastered, that skill becomes habitual and the higher-level skills draw on the reserve that may be starting to develop in the habit center of our brain.

On the other hand, developing new mental maps in Toyota comes from the mentor being there at the right time to cultivate moments of insight. We have described examples throughout this book of Americans working for Toyota who had some moment of great insight where they did something, and based on the guidance of their Japanese trainer, it shaped their way of thinking… or mental map. This research suggests telling someone how to behave is much less effective than helping them discover *a better way* to think and behave. One hypothetical example is a case of Mike who wants to increase entrepreneurial behavior in his organization. The recommended approach sounds very much like the way Toyota trainers developed American managers:

> *At the organizational level, Mike wants to change the way thousands of people think. A common approach would be to identify the current attitudes across the group through some sort of cultural survey. The hope would be that identifying the source of the problem would help solve it. Based on what we know about the brain, a better alternative would be for Mike to paint a broad picture of being more entrepreneurial, without specifically identifying the changes that individuals will need to make. Mike's goal should be for his people to picture the new behaviors in their own minds, and in the process develop energizing new mental maps that have the potential to become hardwired circuitry. He then needs to find opportunities for them to take concrete actions and get feelings of success that lead them toward becoming more entrepreneurial. He needs to be be around to reinforce these moments of insight.[14]*

---

[14] Rock and Schwartz, Ibid., p. 9.

## *Learning by Doing Is More Powerful Than Learning by Listening*

For many managers it seems the preferred method of changing behavior is telling people things. The neuroscience research just cited would suggest that is not going to be very successful. Robert Quinn also finds this is a recipe for failure in deep change:

> *In organizations, I watch managers engage in the strategy of change by telling. The manager knows that the people in the organization should make some important change, so this item goes on their "to do" list. At the appropriate time, the manager gives a speech or writes a memo instructing people to change. The manager then places a check next to the item on the "to do" list. The change has been implemented.[15]*

How can we avoid telling people things? The answer is to get them doing things and encourage a process of self-discovery. Recall the difference between a kaizen event led by experts who make a bunch of changes and then leave the work group to follow changes made by the outsider, and the preferred approach in Toyota where the team is responsible for making the changes. When we are being guided and the ideas are ours we are not only more accepting, but we are learning.

The principles behind job instruction training also assume people will learn by doing rather than by listening. The job instruction method starts with showing and telling but very quickly the student is doing, repeatedly, until the correct procedure becomes comfortable and habitual. The teacher does not leave until the standardized approach is being used regularly and comfortably.

## *To Cope with the High Uncertainty of Change People Need Daily Support*

A different look at resistance to change is in a book called *Change or Die*.[16] The author, Alan Deutschman, a physician, found that the large majority of people with potentially fatal diseases, when given a choice between changing their diets and daily behavior or dying, fail to change. In fact over 90 percent of the people failed to change. Even the threat of dying is not enough of a threat to change deeply entrenched behaviors.

Deutschman sought to increase the odds of behavior change, thus helping people stay alive. He was able to increase the success rate from less than 10 percent to almost 80 percent. He concludes that what many people think are the three keys

---

[15] Quinn, Robert E. *Deep Change*, p. 34.
[16] Deutschman, Alan, *Change or Die: The Three Keys to Change in Work and in Life*, New York: Harper Collins Publishers, 2007.

to success, the three Fs of facts, fear, and force, do not work. Instead he set up pilot cases and found through actual casework with patients over a one year period that the three real keys to success are three Rs:[17]

- Relate—Form a new, emotional relationship with a person or community that inspires or sustains hope.
- Repeat—The new relationship helps you learn, practice, and master the new habits and skills that you need.
- Reframe—The new relationship helps you learn new ways of thinking about your situation and your life.

Let's once again revisit what Toyota does when they set up a new plant and take employees, who have their own unique history, habits, and ways of thinking, into the quality people value stream. Toyota puts them into many situations where they form relationships that provide social support. These leaders provide opportunities to practice the job skills and behaviors desired in a safe environment. This starts in the job interview itself, such as in the simulated work environment, and continues through the fundamental skills training, job instruction training, and then their daily experiences as part of a work group. Over time, the Toyota team member or leader learns to reframe their way of thinking about dealing with situations. This new way of thinking is based on problem solving. Do not get mad and frustrated when something does not go well, but study the situation objectively, come up with solutions, and keep trying until the problem is solved.

## Change Needs a Plan and a Process

One of the hallmarks of Toyota's success is detailed, careful planning. No stone is unturned. Toyota leaders get many perspectives and in the process use a *nemawashi* process to get buy in. They lay out alternatives and get a lot of input on pros and cons. This does not mean that they produce hundred page reports, and in fact, one-page A-3s are preferred. One other key characteristic is that Toyota's plans are always provisional—until more is learned—so that they can learn from experience and adjust using the plan-do-check-act process.

Many other companies are good at planning in their own way. Some seem to love to plan more than to do. Others are impatient about planning and want to get on with doing. Few companies are very good at checking and acting. In our observation, companies that are going lean spend more time and effort developing structures for change, developing the right metrics, and planning who should move where in the organizational chart than they do on the softer side of developing leaders, creating a shared vision, and engaging people. This is backward. It is

---

[17] Deutschuman, Ibid, pp. 14–15.

particularly important in the early stages of lean transformation to get the soft side right and begin to make actual changes to processes to get successes and engage people. If this is truly a long-term journey there is plenty of time to make the structural changes in later years. The structural changes will have to be made and a step-by-step rollout plan will need to be developed.

## Attitude and Behavior Change Must be Supported by Structural Change

Returning to the cases of Big Shipcited and Small Ship cited earlier in the chapter, we saw two contrasting approaches to change. Big Ship had invested in the Baldridge approach and their focus was on establishing the lean six-sigma structure and process. They invested heavily in the lean six-sigma academy and trained many black belts. We described this as a mechanistic approach, and in fact, for years they did very little to drive real employee engagement on the shop floor and had very little impact as a result. Small Ship went right to the gemba and drove both local and cultural change in certain areas and then expanded step by step across the shipyard. Its main weakness was the absence of serious investment in infrastructure support for lean.

Our bias is toward the Small Ship approach which is more similar to what Toyota would do, but we also see a serious flaw in the lack of infrastructure development. If we go back to the human system model, Small Ship was starting to establish a people value stream in the shipyard but lacked the supporting systems to sustain and grow it. To go further, they needed to invest in all the supporting systems—the daily management systems and the human resource management systems. In fact as we saw at the end of the six year period, Small Ship was beginning to learn from Big Ship about the supporting structures and vice versa. We are going to return to the theme of how to stage the transformation of the supporting systems later in the chapter.

## Metrics Do Not Produce Change but Can be Key Enablers

Returning to the shipyard cases, we saw that Big Ship saw metrics plus training as the key levers for change. Training provides the skills and metrics provide the motivation. We believe this is the most common recipe for lean six-sigma transformation since it appeals to the Western mechanistic mindset. We also think it is a serious flaw in thinking. We have hammered away at the mistaken notion that lean is a technical transformation, that it is a matter of teaching skills in the classroom and then using a carrot and stick to lead the trained people. Even if this worked in creating skilled and motivated people, the only ones skilled and motivated are the black belts and top managers. The work groups have energizer bunnies coming at them from all directions who mainly want to get their tickets punched—we did this project, check, we did that project, check, and so on.

To get deep change that seriously penetrates the culture, the motivation for change must come from within. We saw the importance in Chapter 15 of the hoshin kanri system as a way to harness the energy of the work groups toward common goals. This is very powerful but can only happen after the people and organization are developed to the point that they have the capability to achieve stretch objectives. Toyota Motor Finance in Chapter 16 was a great example of an organization that first invested in developing teamwork and problem solving skills. The members were then anxious to sign up for aggressive organization-wide objectives.

We are not suggesting that you ignore metrics until the organization is mature enough for hoshin kanri. There are two ways that we believe metrics can be very valuable early in the process:

1. Study the overall organizational metrics, such as, at the plant level and department level, and work to balance them across quality, cost, delivery, safety, and morale. Generally they are imbalanced focusing mainly on cost and perhaps safety.[18]

2. As part of teaching problem solving in a learning by doing fashion, the teams will always want to measure key characteristics of the current state and set challenging targets for the project. This is part of the training and development process to understand how to set, measure, and achieve stretch objectives.

## Break the Journey Into Small Steps

This may be one of the most culturally challenging and most important steps for most companies. Toyota culture is based on concepts like continuous improvement, patience, slow and deep development, and follow-up to ensure real understanding before progressing to the next step. In *The Toyota Way Fieldbook*, Liker and Meier ended with a diagram of a stair step and suggested until you take a step you cannot see the next step.[19] This is easy to say and it fits Toyota culture very well, but it does not fit well with the Western culture of home runs and results tomorrow. We want a plan for the whole change, we want the results clearly spelled out, and then we want to head to the finish line as fast as possible.

---

[18] There is a growing literature on "lean accounting" with excellent advice. The overall movement is to fundamentally change, or even eliminate, traditional cost accounting. Some books worth looking at to get started are as follows: Huntzinger, James R., *Lean Cost Management*, Fort Lauderdale: J. Ross Publishing, 2007, and Stenzel, Joe (Editor), *Lean Accounting*, Hoboken, NJ: John Wiley, 2007. For a great lean accounting business novel read: Solomon, Jerrold, M., *Who's Counting?* Fort Wayne, Indiana: WCM Associates, 2003.

[19] Liker, Jeffrey K. and David P. Meier, *The Toyota Way Fieldbook*, New York: McGraw-Hill, 2006, pp. 461–466.

The typical Western approach sounds like a sprint. If we want to use a race analogy, it is probably more useful to think of the lean journey like the Tour De France bike race. The Tour De France is so long you have to pace yourself. No one individual biker can win alone but has to be helped by the team, while at the same time each individual on the team must have a high level of skill and be in great condition. The rest of this chapter is dedicated to help you plan how to break the journey into small steps and adjust and learn as you go.

# PHASING IN THE TRANSFORMATION PROCESS

The natural Western tendency when facing a challenge is to meet it head on. If the challenge is inventory reduction, let's create an inventory reduction program with lead individuals responsible, measurable targets, and a timetable. If the challenge is cultural change, let's train up the change agents and make them responsible with measurable targets and a timetable. We do not know how many times we have been asked how you can measure culture since we all know you cannot change anything you cannot measure. Unfortunately, culture is difficult to measure even at the most superficial level and simply measuring it does not change it.

We have found much wisdom in the words of our colleague, John Shook, who worked for Toyota for years and helped in the planning of the big experiment to bring Toyota culture to NUMMI. His conclusion: "It is easier to act your way to a new way of thinking than to think your way to a new way of acting."[20] This perspective fits very well with the Toyota way of thinking which highly values learning by doing.

We have not found any recipe for changing to a lean culture. We have summarized the philosophy of the Toyota Way of improvement as compared to approaches like lean six sigma. We have also gone through some of what we have learned about managing change. There are a few tips that we have found helpful in thinking about transformation of an organization:

- Most serious cultural change will happen as a result of specific experiences that cannot be planned out in advance. That is why Toyota planted Japanese trainers to be around all the time to opportunistically coach "moments of insight" as occasions arose.
- Lean projects provide an opportunity for learning and an occasion for changes in thinking.

---

[20] This is not the first time it was said but we heard it first from John Shook. A similar statement can be found in Pascale, Richard, *Managing On the Edge*, New York: Simon & Schuster/Touchstone, 1991.

- Culture change will be gradual and leadership needs to be persistent and patient.
- Leaders must be absolutely consistent in their words and actions in support of the culture desired.
- Leaders and change agents cannot do it alone but must engage first-line supervisors at the work group level to build the culture desired.
- As Schein indicates in the opening quotation to this chapter, build on the organization's strengths. Building on strengths is more powerful than trying to tear down the cultural weaknesses.

In Table 18.3 we describe a generic process for building the human system model in your organization. How long it takes will depend on your starting point, continuity of leadership direction, and seriousness, but think in terms of a decade or more and not a few years. It is a generic process, but we do not expect you to follow it in lock step sequence. The main point is to start with changes at the gemba, like we saw in the Small Ship case, then over time support this through personal change in leadership and gradually establish the supporting daily management systems and human resource systems. Do not force these changes too soon as it is likely to back fire.

## Use Lean Projects as a Vehicle for Developing People and Culture

With all of our talk about the difference between the lean tools approach and the culture change approach, much of the focus is still the same. Go to the gemba and do projects. Use the tools and drive change in the process. We saw that the centerpiece of action in the Toyota Way is Toyota business practices, which is basic problem solving.

We are not saying that a project is a project. What we have called the lean six-sigma approach is to drive results through projects led by black belts. Give them some training, let them loose to apply them, measure, and reward.

The main point of these lean projects from the point of view of Toyota Culture is to develop people. Figure 18.9 shows the process used to grow people.[21] Obviously not every person will be developed to the same degree, but the thought process is the same. The sensei is coaching the student to get her started with some basic learning in the classroom, or even better at the gemba. For example, Toyota business practice training starts with instruction and then

---

[21] Figure 18–9 and the points we made here were developed by David Meier, coauthor of *The Toyota Way Fieldbook* and *Toyota Talent*. A more in-depth treatment of how lean processes are developed and relate to people development will be presented in Liker, Jeffrey K. and David P. Meier, *Toyota Processes*, New York: McGraw-Hill, forthcoming.

**Table 18.3** Building the human system model in your organization

| What | How |
|---|---|
| Use Lean Projects as a Vehicle for Developing People and Culture | Sensei role is to challenge, support and teach by challenging student, not doing the projects. Projects must be viewed as teaching tool, not simply ROI. |
| Build deep models, while spreading tools broadly | Must commit to certain processes or mini–value streams to go deep building a system and developing people, while applying tools more broadly. |
| Senior leaders take a serious look at themselves and their motives | Senior leaders must change before they can expect others to change—requires reflection, offsites, leadership coaching. |
| Assess your current cultural strengths and weaknesses and develop your future state model | All key leaders must come together in organized and facilitated offsites using organizational development methods to assess the current state and agree on the future state. |
| Develop daily management systems starting in the models then spreading | A minimum of stability and TPS tools must be in place before the supervisors can be coached to the point of establishing a daily management system. |
| Change supporting HR systems at first to eliminate barriers to development | Start with very targeted changes in HR systems such as job instruction training, adding broader metrics and eliminating those obviously conflicting with lean systems, eliminating obvious disincentives in reward system, and adding symbolic awards like awards and ceremonies. |
| As the lean effort and organization matures add in hoshin at a high level | *Hoshin* requires sound plans at the top that are challenging, yet achieveable and the problem solving capability to achieve the stretch targets. This requires a degree of maturity. |
| As the organization matures add supporting HR structures | Structural changes such as career planning, pay and benefit systems, systems for fair treatment, active HR roles in all promotions and pay increases should be carefully considered and gradually adapted to the local condition. |
| Continue reflecting, planning, and improving | The goal is to make this a natural part of the culture. |

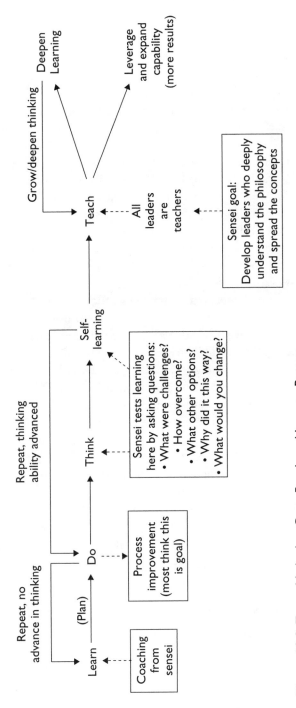

**Figure 18.9** Toyota Method to Grow People and Improve Process

quickly escalates to doing. The student must not stop after the one application but do this repeatedly, learning at ever deeper levels how to use the tools to drive improvement and change in the organization.

At some point, the student graduates from doing to thinking. The sensei wants the student to think independently and then begin to self-learn so the sensei does not always have to be around to initiate action and learning. The sensei will question and challenge, and not give answers. This is similar to the Socratic method of teaching.

An excellent example of this was the training of one of the early employees at Toyota's plant in the United Kingdom. Neil Smith[22] was hired to be part of a Toyota Production System group to help develop UK suppliers. As part of his training he was sent to a Toyota plant in Japan where he "stood in the circle" with some members for six days. Their task was to identify 240 improvements and make most of them on the spot with the help of one of the Japanese members from maintenance. The processes were already excellent after applying the concepts of TPS for over 25 years so it was tough work to find any waste at all. They had to search for seconds and even fractions of seconds of waste, looking at moving tools by centimeters so the person did not have to move his shoulders quite so far and cutting down flow racks with hack saws to reduce an extra couple of centimeters of bending. By the end 79 percent of their 247 improvement ideas were implemented. In another training session, Neil was sent to Japan to study one of Toyota's best suppliers to understand their heijunka system. When he returned from the trip, he found he had an assignment to implement a similar system at a supplier in the UK. When he struggled to accomplish it, his Japanese mentor bailed him out and sent him back to Japan to study the system for one week. This time, knowing when he came back he would be expected to implement what he learned, he studied intensively and was successful. There were no books to read or lectures by the teacher, but simply go and see and do.

TPS is often referred to within Toyota as the "Thinking" Production System. This is the real purpose and when you use TPS tools and methods to get people to think and teach others the effects of any individual project are leveraged exponentially. Unfortunately, when companies do one-off lean projects led by "experts" they lose that leverage.

## Build Deep Models, While Spreading Tools Broadly

There are many approaches to lean implementation as we discussed in *The Toyota Way Fieldbook*.[23] You can take a tools approach and spread tool by tool across the enterprise (e.g., 5S, cells, kanban), or you can take a "hot jobs" approach and go

---

[22] Neil Smith is a former manager of the Toyota plant in the U.K.
[23] Liker, Jeffrey and David P. Meier, *The Toyota Way Fieldbook*, 2006.

to where there is a serious problem right now, or you can take a model line approach and spend six months to a year on a model project like the ball valve operation at Small Ship. There are pros and cons to each approach, but we recommend you think beyond where you get the most bang for your buck and think instead about a plan for developing your people.

From the perspective of developing people, nothing can beat the one-inch wide, mile-deep approach like we saw in the ball valve area. There are deeper and deeper lessons learned. The first phase is simply to teach management and team members to use the tools, but when they become comfortable they can start to learn to think and improve on the systems. This takes time, and kaizen workshops or spreading individual tools does not provide the time or opportunity for this deep learning.

In a large organization, it could be many years before you get across the organization going one-inch wide at a time. A more shallow tool-based approach, one-inch deep and a mile wide, can get a lot of people exposed to the tools in a short period of time. We recommend a combination of the two. Pick model areas to develop people in the area deeply, and develop your own internal sensei and in parallel spread simpler tools like 5S using the one-inch deep approach (see Figure 18.10). It is also important to exploit the best of the lean tools when a burning issue needs solving, such as serious quality problems. One plant got way behind and had a backlog of customer orders. The lean sensei in the plant used this hot job as an opportunity to teach them visual management, team, work, and problem solving to eliminate the back orders.

## Senior Leaders Take a Serious Look at Themselves and Their Motives

Self-reflection by senior leaders is an ongoing process. We do not suggest that senior leaders have to perfect themselves before getting started. We have found that the organization needs some experience with lean before the senior leaders can understand what it is and what is needed of them. Even if a few of the leaders, for example, the director of manufacturing, already lean veterans, other executives such as the CIO and the CFO may not be.

**Spread lean across the organization**

**Develop depth of capability within the organization**

**Figure 18.10** Balance Deep Implementation and Broad Exposure in Lean Transformation

You can use facilitated offsites as one tool for reflection. We also recommend walks at the gemba with the sensei. One company has required that all executives up to the CEO participate in a one-week kaizen event with cell phones off and then reflect on that experience. Another company has assigned internal lean coordinators to be executive coaches. Every executive has a coach (an internal lean coordinator) and they have formal meetings biweekly.

## Assess Your Current Cultural Strengths and Weaknesses and Develop Your Future State Model

We mentioned the organizational development approach to change when we discussed Table 18.2. This is where we believe this approach will have a big payoff. At some point, when you have enough experience from lean-transformation projects to understand what this looks like in your organization, and when senior management has made a long-term commitment to building a culture to support, key lean leaders must come together to agree on a future vision for your culture. We are not sure of the exact timing, but we are sure it has to be done more than once. What does the organization stand for? What are your values? What is your desired future state?

This goes beyond business results to the way you will work together daily. Toyota developed *The Toyota Way 2001* decades after practicing it daily. They realized that as they grew and brought in new members they needed to agree on their values and write them down. You will want to do this as well.

In this step, you want to take an objective look at your existing culture, both good and bad. Recall that you want to embrace and build on what is good about your culture that got you this far. The organizational development approach is to use internal or external facilitators to interview and put together a picture of the current state. An offsite is planned in great detail with key leaders prepared to understand their roles. The Japanese concept of nemawashi is a useful one here. Toyota wants to prepare all participants prior to the meeting and get their input so there are no surprises in an important decision making meeting. The product of the offsite should be a future state vision and agreements on action items.[24]

## Develop Daily Management Systems Starting in the Models Then Spreading

This is another thing that takes maturity. There is nothing new to manage until the lean systems are in place and operational. Visual management, in-station quality systems, and standardized work are just a few of the lean tools that need to be in

---

[24] An excellent source that walks you through the organizational development process and the key tools you will need for large scale change is, Jacobs, Robert W., *Real Time Strategic Change*, San Francisco: Berret-Koehler Publishers, 1994.

place before an effective daily management system is possible. Problem solving capability is also necessary. At a higher level, job-instruction training, standardized-work audits, and job rotation will really bring daily management to life.

## Change Supporting HR Systems First to Eliminate Barriers to Development

We have preached caution in tampering with HR systems, particularly early in the process, but there are some fixes that can help eliminate obvious barriers to progressing with your lean efforts. You do not necessarily have to anticipate all the barriers but can work this out as you go. For example, in the process of doing lean projects, we often find that quantity is rewarded over quality and this is an obvious barrier that should be addressed.

Also, it is worthwhile to find creative ways to recognize and reward success with lean. These do not have to be elaborate or expensive rewards. It can be as simple as monthly recognition for the best 5S area, perhaps giving the best team a small allowance for a group lunch.

## As the Lean Effort and Organization Matures Add in Hoshin at a High Level

Hoshin is easy to do in the sense of getting managers together to establish objectives and telling people to meet them, but difficult to actually make work. The reason is that hoshin should be based on "catch ball." Each manager and subordinate level should agree on the target and method to improve and this requires that they understand their capability to improve. Understanding this capability, as well as having the capability, takes a certain level of maturity. There needs to be a certain minimum level of mastery of the lean tools and of problem solving.

We have seen many companies jump the gun on this one. For example, one organization got great results on lean model lines in two departments in the first year and then immediately expected the same level of improvement for the rest of the company in the second year. The problem was that the first two departments had a lot of consulting help, and the rest of the company was pretty much on their own. The result was a lot of scrambling and superficial effort to make the numbers without establishing stable processes or learning good procedures for problem solving. This top-down pressure did not show respect for people and sent the wrong message to the organization.

We suggest closely monitoring the capability of the organization to stabilize and make improvements. We saw that the finance portion of Toyota sales (Chapter 16) took two years before they were ready for a serious hoshin challenge. We also recommend starting at the top levels, for example, the vice president and direct reports. It takes more maturity to drive hoshin all the way down to the work-group level.

## As the Organization Matures Add Supporting HR Structures

This is another issue of maturity. You cannot change your HR structures overnight and what you really want is an adaptive organization that is continually improving as situations change or critical events occur. We saw in Chapter 13 how a sexual harassment problem at TMMK led to deep reflection and problem solving that ended up revamping much of the human resources system. This took exceptional leadership and a great deal of organizational maturity. It was prompted by a real and critical problem.

We are not necessarily suggesting you wait for a crisis, but it will take some years of learning problem solving and building trust before it is wise to tamper in a major way with the HR system. Generally speaking, people have come to accept the status quo. If you make a change to benefits or pay, people will notice anything they perceive as a loss ten times more than they will notice any increased benefits. Companies change pay and benefits regularly and have learned how to do it. We are only suggesting that as part of the overall lean transformation you tread carefully since any negative views of HR systems will be projected onto the lean effort itself.

On the other hand, there are less controversial things that can be worked on. Safety is always a good thing to work on at any time as is improving the physical environment. At some point you need to bring the standardized work to life with real job instruction training. We recommend you do this first in pilot areas and develop some internal certified trainers who can then train other trainers. A detailed approach to doing this is outlined in *Toyota Talent*.[25]

## Continue Reflecting, Planning, and Improving

Perhaps this does not have to be said, but whatever you do should be continuously improved. If the goal is to become a learning organization, you need to act like a learning organization as you take each step—reflect and improve and spread over and over.

# SUMMARY

Culture change is a challenge, and big culture change is a big challenge. Working to achieve all aspects of the Toyota culture laid out in this book can be an overwhelming task and is in fact not desirable. Every company has its own unique history and business circumstances and must develop its own culture. It is important to think deeply about your cultural strengths and your values and

---

[25] Liker, Jeffrey and David P. Meier, *Toyota Talent*, New York: McGraw-Hill, 2007.

how to build on those strengths to develop people who live your values. Toyota can provide a model for inspiration and ideas, as well as practical insights into the structures necessary to improve your people value stream.

There are many approaches to change. We contrasted a tools approach that characterizes typical approaches to lean six sigma with Toyota's approach to developing people and building culture. We argued that Toyota's approach is broader, deeper, and leads to more sustainable competitive advantage. Unfortunately it is not a one-shot implementation process. It is a continuous journey of improvement through problem solving.

Wholesale change of culture is nearly impossible for an established organization. Start with understanding your strengths, developing a positive future vision, and developing first steps. The journey to evolving your culture to the desired future state is long and you want to learn as you go, continually planning, doing, checking and acting.

Lean projects can be used in a mechanistic tool-based way to get short-term results, or in an organic way to develop people and build a learning organization. You need to decide on your purpose and whether you are ready to commit to a long-term journey to become a learning organization. The lean tools are well suited to making problems visible, challenging your people to grow, and supporting your development of a culture of continuous improvement.

The other side of the coin is respect for people. There is no reason why we would want to give our all for a company that does not treat us with respect. For Toyota, the foundation of respect is mutual trust and long-term security. This may be the most fundamental and challenging question for your leadership. Can you make the commitment to respect your people for the long term or are they disposable commodities? Making a commitment requires leadership stability which depends on developing successors and forging agreements with the owners of the business.

We have provided some evidence that building a lean culture is possible globally—Toyota has done it and many other companies have made progress in individual plants and organizations. This is possible. Do you want it enough to make it a reality for the long term? If the answer is yes, then there is nothing to do but get started, one step at a time. Each step is an opportunity to learn and strengthen your people and culture. We wish you well on the journey!

# KEY POINTS TO CONSIDER FOR YOUR COMPANY

1. You must have a very clearly articulated purpose for your lean transformation before you can plan your approach. Is it short-term results oriented or long-term building of a culture of continuous improvement?

2. If you are in it for the long term then the typical short-term tools orientation of lean six sigma will not get you to the culture you desire.

3. Leaders must deeply understand and embody the culture which will take serious personal growth aided by a coach.

4. Do not copy Toyota's model, but you might adopt many of Toyota's principles and values.

5. Culture change is necessary, but direct culture change is rarely successful. Lean projects, with strong sensei support, provide opportunities for focusing attention and moments of great insight to develop your people.

6. Start with an analysis of your own culture's strengths and weaknesses and build on your strengths.

7. Find the right balance between deep lean implementation to really drive culture change in local areas and broad deployment to spread it across the company.

8. Break the journey into digestible steps and view any plan as tentative and subject to reflection and adjustment.

9. Start by developing people through concrete improvement activities guided by well-trained lean coaches, and gradually turn over responsibility to the line organization.

10. Slowly build supporting human resource structures at first to respond to barriers to implementation, and then to build the structures to support respect for people and continuous improvement.

11. Invest in your quality people value stream because people are the source of your competitive advantage.

# Bibliography

Adler, Paul S. "Building Better Bureaucracies," *Academy of Management Executive*, 13, 4, Nov. 1999: 36–47.

Arvey, Richard D, *Fairness in Selecting Employees*, New York: Addison-Wesley, 1979, p. 114.

Bergmiller, Gary. *Lean Manufacturers Transcendence to Green Manufacturing: Correlating the Diffusion of Lean and Green Manufacturing Systems*, University of South Florida, unpublished Ph.D. dissertation, 2006.

Balle, Michael. *The Gold Mine*, Cambridge, MA: Lean Enterprise Institute, 2005.

Brannen, Mary Yoko, "Bwana Mickey: Constructing Cultural Consumption at Tokyo Disneyland," in *Remade in Japan: Consumer Tastes in a Changing Japan*, edited by Joseph Tobin. New Haven, CT: Yale University Press, 1992.

Brannen, Mary Yoko, Jeffrey K. Liker and W. Mark Fruin. "Recontextualization and Factory-to-Factory Knowledge Transfer from Japan to the U.S.: The Case of NSK," in *Remade in America: Transplanting and Transforming Japanese Production Systems*, edited by Jeffrey K. Liker, W. Mark Fruin, and Paul S. Adler, New York: Oxford University Press, 1999: 117–154.

Choi T.Y. and J.K. Liker. "Bringing Japanese Continuous Improvement Approaches to U.S. Manufacturing: The Roles of Process Orientation and Communications," *Decision Sciences*, Vol. 26, Number 5, Sept/Oct. 1995.

Collins, Jim. *Good to Great: Why Some Companies Make the Leap... and Others Don't*, New York: HarperBusiness, 2001.

Deci, E. L. 1971. Effects of externally mediated rewards on intrinsic motivation. *Journal of Personality and Social Psychology*, 18: 105–115.

Deutschman, Alan. *Change or Die: The Three Keys to Change in Work and in Life*, New York: Harper Collins Publishers, 2007.

Hall, Edward T. *Beyond Culture*, Anchor Books, 1976.

Hampden-Turner, C. and A. Trompenaars. *The Seven Cultures of Capitalism: Value Systems for Creating Wealth in the United States, Japan, Germany, France, Britain, Sweden, and the Netherlands*, New York: Doubleday, 1993.

Hofstede, Geert and Gert Jan Hofstede. *Cultures and Organizations: Software of the Mind*, New York: McGraw-Hill, 2004.

Huntzinger, James R. *Lean Cost Management*, Fort Lauderdale, Florida: J. Ross Publishing, 2007.

Jackson, Thomas L. *Hoshin Kanri for the Lean Enterprise: Developing Competitive Capabilities and Managing Profit*, New York: Productivity Press, 2006.

Jacobs, Robert W. *Real Time Strategic Change*, San Francisco: Berret-Koehler Publishers, 1994.

Kanter, Rosabeth Moss and Barry A. Stein. *Life in Organizations: Workplaces as People Experience Them*, New York: Basic Books, 1978. Lessons from Toyota's Long Drive, Harvard Business Review, July-August, 2007, pp. 74–83.

Kucner, Robert. *A Socio-Technical Study of Lean Manufacturing Deployment in the Remanufacturing Context*. PhD dissertation, University of Michigan, Ann Arbor, November, 2007.

Levering, Robert. *A Great Place to Work*, New York: Random House Inc., 1988.

Liker, Jeffrey K. *The Toyota Way: Fourteen Management Principles from the World's Greatest Manufacturer*, New York: McGraw-Hill, 2004.

Liker, Jeffrey and David P. Meier. *The Toyota Way Fieldbook*, New York: McGraw-Hill, 2006. *Toyota Talent: Developing People the Toyota Way*, New York: McGraw-Hill, 2007.

Liker, J.K., M. Fruin, and P. Adler. (eds.), Remade *in America: Transplanting and Transforming Japanese Production Systems*, New York: Oxford University Press, 1999.

Locke, Edwin A. and Gary P. Latham, *Goal Setting: A Motivational Technique that Works*, Upper Saddle River, NJ: Prentice Hall, 1984.

Menon, Tanya, Jessica Sim, Jeanne Ho-Ying Fu, Chi-yue Chiu, and Ying-yi Hong. "Blazing the Trail versus Trailing the Group: Culture and Perceptions of the Leader's Position." *University of Chicago Working Paper*, 2007.

Morgan, James and Jeffrey Liker. *The Toyota Product Development System: Integrating People, Process, and Technology*, New York: Productivity Press, 2006.

Morrison, Mike. *The Other Side of the Business Card*, New York: McGraw-Hill, 2007.

Nisbett, Richard E, *The Geography of Thought: How Asians and Westerners Think Differently...and Why*, New York: Free Press, 2003.

Ohno, Taiichi. *Workplace Management*, Mukilteo, WA: Gemba Press, 2007.

Pasmore, William A. *Designing Effective Organizations: The Sociotechnical Systems Perspective*, New York: John Wiley and Sons, 1988.

Pascale, Richard, *Managing On the Edge*, New York: Simon & Schuster/ Touchstone, 1991.

Quinn, Robert E. *Deep Change: Discovering the Leader Within*, San Francisco: Jossey Bass, 1996,

Reingold, Edwin. *Toyota: People, Ideas, and the Challenge of the New*. London: Penguin Books, 1999.

Rock, David and Jeffrey Schwartz. "The Neuroscience of Leadership," *Strategy and Business*, Booz Allen Hamilton, Issue 43, May 30, 2006.

Rother, Mike and John Shook. *Learning to See*, Cambridge, MA: Lean Enterprise Institute, 1998.

Schein, Edgar. "Coming to a new awareness of organizational culture," *Sloan Management Review*, Winter 1984, Vol. 25, No. 2, pp. 3–16.

Schein, Edgar, H. *The Corporate Culture Survival Guide*, San Francisco: Jossey-Bass, 1999.

Schein, Edgar H. and Joan V. Gallos (Editors). *Organization Development*, San Francisco: Jossey-Bass, 2006.

Solomon, Jerrold, M. *Who's Counting?* Fort Wayne, IN: WCM Associates, 2003.

Sommer, Robert. *The Mind's Eye: Imagery in Everyday Life*, New York: Delta Books, 1978.

Staw, Barry M., Bobby J. Calder, Randall K. Hess, Lance E. Sandelands (1980). "Intrinsic Motivation and norms about payment," *Journal of Personality* 48(1), 1–14.

Stenzel, Joe (Editor). *Lean Accounting*, Hoboken, NJ: John Wiley, 2007.

Taylor, James C. and David F. Felten, *Performance by Design: Designing Sociotechnical Systems in North America*, Upper Saddle River, NJ: Prentice Hall, 1993.

Tichy, Noel M. and Mary Anne Devanna. *Transformational Leader*, second edition, New York: John Wiley, 1997.

Tietje, Brian C. (2002) When Do Rewards Have Enhancement Effects? An Availability Valence Approach. *Journal of Consumer Psychology*. 12:4, 363–373.

Toyoda, Eiji. *Toyota: Fifty Years in Motion*, first edition, New York: Kodansha America, 1987.

*The Toyota Way 2001*, Toyota Motor Corporation, Japan, Internal Company Document.

Ulrich, David, *Human Resource Champions*, Boston, MA: Harvard Business School Press, 1997.

Weick, Karl, E. and Sutcliffe, Kathleen M. *Managing the Unexpected*, University of Michigan Business School Management Series, San Francisco: John Wiley, 2001.

Whiting, Basil J., *The Quest Program, Toyota, and School in Scott County Kentucky*. Paper prepared for the Manufacturing Institute, Brooklyn, New York, 2002.

Womack, James P., Daniel T. Jones, and Daniel Roos, *The Machine That Changed the World*. New York: Rawson Associates, 1990.

Womack, James and Daniel Jones, *Lean Solutions: How Companies and Customers can Create Value and Wealth Together*, New York: Free Press, 2005.

Womack, James and Daniel Jones. *Lean Thinking: Banish Waste and Create Wealth in Yar Organization*, New York: Simon and Schuster, 1996.

# Index